Genocide

D1002385

Blackwell Readers in Anthropology

As anthropology moves beyond the limits of so-called area studies, there is an increasing need for texts that do the work of synthesizing the literature while challenging more traditional or subdisciplinary approaches to anthropology. This is the object of this exciting new series, *Blackwell Readers in Anthropology*.

Each volume in the series offers seminal readings on a chosen theme and provides the finest, most thought-provoking recent works in the given thematic area. Many of these volumes bring together for the first time a body of literature on a certain topic. The series thus both presents definitive collections and investigates the very ways in which anthropological inquiry has evolved and is evolving.

1 *Anthropology of Globalization: A Reader*
   Edited by Jonathan Xavier Inda and Renato Rosaldo

2 *The Anthropology of Media: A Reader*
   Edited by Kelly Askew and Richard R. Wilk

3 *Genocide: An Anthropological Reader*
   Edited by Alexander Laban Hinton

In preparation

Violence in War and Peace: A Reader
edited by Nancy Scheper-Hughes and Philippe Bourgois

Food: Producing and Consuming Cultures
edited by James L. Watson and Melissa Caldwell

The Anthropology of Space and Place: A Reader
edited by Setha Low and Denise Lawrence-Zuniga

Genocide:
An Anthropological Reader

Edited by

Alexander Laban Hinton

BLACKWELL
Publishers

Copyright © Blackwell Publishers Ltd 2002; editorial matter and organization copyright © Alexander Laban Hinton 2002

First published 2002

2 4 6 8 10 9 7 5 3 1

Blackwell Publishers Inc.
350 Main Street
Malden, Massachusetts 02148
USA

Blackwell Publishers Ltd
108 Cowley Road
Oxford OX4 1JF
UK

All rights reserved. Except for the quotation of short passages for the purposes of criticism and review, no part of this publication may be reproduced, stored in a retrieval system, or transmitted, in any form or by any means, electronic, mechanical, photocopying, recording, or otherwise, without the prior permission of the publisher.

Except in the United States of America, this book is sold subject to the condition that it shall not, by way of trade or otherwise, be lent, resold, hired out, or otherwise circulated without the publisher's prior consent in any form of binding or cover other than that in which it is published and without a similar condition including this condition being imposed on the subsequent purchaser.

Library of Congress Cataloging-in-Publication Data has been applied for.

ISBN 0-631-22354-1 (hardback); 0-631-22355-X (paperback)

British Library Cataloguing in Publication Data

A CIP catalogue record for this book is available from the British Library.

Typeset in 10 on 12 pt Sabon
by Kolam Information Services Pvt. Ltd., Pondicherry, India.
Printed in Great Britain by MPG Books Ltd, Bodmin, Cornwall

This book is printed on acid-free paper.

Contents

Acknowledgments   vii

Introduction: Genocide and Anthropology   1
  Alexander Laban Hinton

Part I   Conceptual Foundations   **25**

1 Genocide   27
   Raphaël Lemkin

2 Text of the UN Genocide Convention   43

3 Genocide: Its Political Use in the Twentieth Century   48
   Leo Kuper

4 Genocide: A Sociological Perspective   74
   Helen Fein

5 Eichmann in Jerusalem: A Report on the Banality of Evil   91
   Hannah Arendt

6 Modernity and the Holocaust   110
   Zygmunt Bauman

Part II   Genocide, History, and Modernity   **135**

7 Victims of Progress   137
   John H. Bodley

8 Culture of Terror – Space of Death: Roger Casement's Putumayo
   Report and the Explanation of Torture   164
   Michael Taussig

 9   National Socialist Germany   192
     Eric R. Wolf

Part III   Manufacturing Difference and "Purification"   **209**

10   "Ethnic Cleansing": A Metaphor for Our Time?   211
     Akbar S. Ahmed

11   Imagined Communities and Real Victims: Self-Determination
     and Ethnic Cleansing in Yugoslavia   231
     Robert M. Hayden

12   A Head for an Eye: Revenge in the Cambodian Genocide   254
     Alexander Laban Hinton

13   Dead Certainty: Ethnic Violence in the Era of Globalization   286
     Arjun Appadurai

Part IV   Coping and Understanding   **305**

14   Fear as a Way of Life   307
     Linda Green

15   The Myth of Global Ethnic Conflict   334
     John R. Bowen

16   Speechless Emissaries: Refugees, Humanitarianism, and
     Dehistoricization   344
     Liisa H. Malkki

Appendix: Websites on Genocide   368

Index   370

Acknowledgments

First, I would like to thank Jane Huber: this book would not have been possible without her encouragement and editorial vision. Her assistant, Sarah Coleman, has been of great help in bringing the book into production, as has Fiona Sewell. Conerly Casey, Steve Jacobs, Helen Fein, and several anonymous reviewers provided excellent suggestions about the content, structure, and organization of the volume. Abdur-Razzaaq Yazin helped compile the list of websites. And finally, I would like to thank Nicole Cooley for her support, encouragement, and help in making this book a reality.

The editor and publishers gratefully acknowledge the following for permission to reproduce copyright material:

Akbar S. Ahmed, "'Ethnic Cleansing': A Metaphor for Our Time?" *Ethnic and Racial Studies* 18, 1 (1995): 1–25. Reprinted by permission of Taylor and Francis Ltd, http://www.tandf.co.uk/journals.

Arjun Appadurai, "Dead Certainty: Ethnic Violence in the Era of Globalization." *Public Culture* 10, 2 (Winter 1998):225–47. Copyright 1998, Duke University Press. All rights reserved. Reprinted with permission.

Hannah Arendt, selection reprinted from *Eichmann in Jerusalem: A Report on the Banality of Evil* by Hannah Arendt, copyright © 1963, 1964 by Hannah Arendt. Used by permission of Viking Penguin, a division of Penguin Putnam Inc.

Zygmunt Bauman, selection reprinted from *Modernity and the Holocaust*. Copyright © 1989 by Zygmunt Bauman. Used by permission of the publisher, Cornell University Press.

John Bodley, selection from *Victims of Progress* (Mountain View, CA: Mayfield Publishing Company, 1999) reprinted by permission of McGraw-Hill Group of Companies Inc.

John R. Bowen, "The Myth of Global Ethnic Conflict." *Journal of Democracy* 7, 4 (1996):3–14. © The Johns Hopkins University Press and National Endowment for Democracy. Reprinted with permission of The Johns Hopkins University Press.

Helen Fein, selection reprinted from *Genocide: A Sociological Perspective* (London: Sage Publications Ltd., 1993).

Linda Green, "Fear as a Way of Life." *Cultural Anthropology* 9, 2 (1994):227–56, reproduced by permission of the American Anthropological Association from *Cultural Anthropology* 9(2). Not for sale or further reproduction.

Robert M. Hayden, "Imagined Communities and Real Victims: Self-Determination and Ethnic Cleansing in Yugoslavia." *American Ethnologist* 23, 4 (1996):783–801, reproduced by permission of the American Anthropological Association from *American Ethnologist* 23(4). Not for sale or further reproduction.

Alexander Laban Hinton, "A Head for an Eye: Revenge in the Cambodian Genocide." *American Ethnologist* 25, 3 (1998):352–77, reproduced by permission of the American Anthropological Association from *American Ethnologist* 25(3). Not for sale or further reproduction.

Leo Kuper, selection reprinted from *Genocide: Its Political Use in the Twentieth Century* (New Haven, CT: Yale University Press, 1981), copyright Penguin Books Ltd., London.

Raphaël Lemkin, selection from *Axis Rule in Occupied Europe* (Washington, DC: Carnegie Endowment for International Peace, 1944) reprinted by permission of the publisher.

Liisa H. Malkki, "Speechless Emissaries: Refugees, Humanitarianism, and Dehistoricization." *Cultural Anthropology* 11, 3 (1996):377–404, reproduced by permission of the American Anthropological Association from *Cultural Anthropology* 11(3). Not for sale or further reproduction.

Michael Taussig, "Culture of Terror – Space of Death: Roger Casement's Putumayo Report and the Explanation of Torture." *Comparative Studies in Society and History* 26, 3 (1984):467–97. Cambridge University Press © Society for the Comparative Study of Society and History.

Text of the UN Convention on Genocide (extract), 1948.

Cesar Vallejo, "The Black Riders," translated by Robert Bly and James Wright. Copyright Narvada and Vallejo (New York: Georges Borchardt Inc.).

Eric R. Wolf, excerpt from "National Socialist Germany" reprinted from *Envisioning Power: Ideologies of Dominance and Crisis* (Berkeley: University of California Press, 1999). Copyright © 1999 The Regents of the University of California. The University of California Press, Berkeley.

The publishers apologize for any errors or omissions in the above list and would be grateful to be notified of any corrections that should be incorporated in the next edition or reprint of this book.

Introduction

Genocide and Anthropology

Alexander Laban Hinton

> There are blows in life so violent – I can't answer!
> Blows as if from the hatred of God; as if before them,
> the deep waters of everything lived through
> were backed up in the soul ... I can't answer!
>
> Not many; but they exist ... They open dark ravines
> in the most ferocious face and in the most bull-like back.
> Perhaps they are the horses of that heathen Attila,
> Or the black riders sent to us by Death.
>   Cesar Vallejo, "The Black Riders"

Genocide is an act that has plagued human beings for centuries: the intentional destruction of a group because of who they are. The death toll almost defies belief. During the twentieth century alone, sixty million people were annihilated by genocidal regimes, the most notorious of which was Nazi Germany. Tens of millions more perished in earlier times, many of whom were characterized as "backward" or "savage" indigenous peoples and destroyed in the name of "progress."

Genocide is also an event that is difficult to understand, analyze, or write about: how can we comprehend or represent the most horrible of deeds?[1] Some have argued that analytical explanation, particularly by those who did not live through genocidal terror, is ultimately a futile exercise, one that inevitably falls short in its task of elucidation and may even mitigate the moral offense of the perpetrators. For many, prose and poetry, like the above poem by Cesar Vallejo, comes closest to capturing the essence of mass murder. Others prefer silence to dispassionate analysis.

A different moral imperative drives many scholars of genocide for, if we do not attempt an explanation, how can we prevent its recurrence in the future? While attempting to remain sensitive to the suffering of the victims and the difficulty of explaining the horrors they endured, many of these scholars, myself included, believe that genocide remains a human behavior, albeit an extreme one, that can and must be explained to whatever extent is possible.

Finally, genocide is a term that confounds scholars, generating contentious debate over its very definition: what, exactly, should be called "genocide," a word that evokes immediate moral outrage? The word has been applied to a wide range of events, including slavery, abortion, and the AIDS epidemic (see Fein 1990; Porter 1982). Terminological rigor is crucial, however, both for analytical clarity and to avoid diluting the meaning of the term. Moreover, the act of genocide has direct legal ramifications: it is a crime under international law.

I have grappled with all of these issues in my own research on the Cambodian genocide (1975–9). In April 1975, after a brutal civil war in which perhaps 600,000 people died, the Khmer Rouge, a group of Maoist-inspired communist rebels led by Pol Pot, seized power. They immediately set out to completely revamp Cambodian society, eliminating Buddhism and market exchange, undermining traditional patterns of familial solidarity, curtailing freedom of choice, movement, and speech, and rusticating the urban population. Everyone was required to work long hours on meager rations and to transform themselves into proper revolutionaries. Almost two million of Cambodia's eight million inhabitants perished in the process from disease, overwork, and starvation or were executed outright: why? How can almost a quarter of a population perish in less than four years? What goes on in the minds of perpetrators when they kill another human being? What is the psychological toll on the victims and survivors?

My research has been driven by such questions. When attempting to answer them, I have sometimes stumbled upon the limits of analytic explanation. For example, how can one convey the suffering of Mum, a woman who began to weep as she described to me how the Khmer Rouge executed her husband and the families of all of her siblings because they had been high-ranking military officers? At such moments I return to Vallejo's words. Nevertheless, I have found that analysis can help us to understand much about genocide. Thus, while it is impossible to convey fully Mum's experience, we can understand many of the reasons why the Khmer Rouge wanted to kill high-ranking soldiers, police, government officials, and civilians associated with the previous regime (see Hinton 1998a, 1998b, 2000, forthcoming).

As an anthropologist, I have also been perplexed by the relative lack of previous research on genocide within the discipline. Anthropologists have been most vocal in defending indigenous peoples against the onslaught of modernity (e.g., Arens 1976; Bischoping and Fingerhut 1996; Bodley 1999; Diamond 1974; Hitchcock and Twedt 1997; Maybury-Lewis 1997; Taussig 1987), but enormous gaps remain. I have yet to find an anthropological article written on the Armenian genocide and, with a few exceptions, anthropologists remained silent about the Holocaust until the mid-1980s – over forty years after the fact.[2] The recent publication dates of the essays included in this volume reflect this bias.

Why have anthropologists failed to engage with the topic of genocide? As Helen Fein notes in her chapter, the anthropological neglect of this topic was shared by other social sciences, which seemed to have pushed genocide into the realm of speciality studies. Within anthropology, there may have been a hesitancy to tackle this issue because it threatened the concept of cultural relativity; how does one suspend moral outrage in the wake of mass murder? Or, perhaps anthropologists shied away from politically volatile issues in the aftermath of their participation in World War II and the Vietnam War effort. The discipline also seems to have been predisposed to focus on small-scale societies while neglecting the large-scale political processes – including violence – that impacted upon them.

Whatever the reasons, anthropologists began to more actively study war and political violence in the 1980s (Ferguson 1989; Nagengast 1994), a trend that eventually contributed to a small body of work on genocide – particularly in the aftermath of Bosnia and Rwanda. As Part I of this book on "Conceptual Foundations" implicitly suggests, anthropologists have a great deal to contribute to the study of genocide. Within genocide studies, much work has focused on more macro-level processes, exploring how genocide is linked to historical, political, economic, and structural factors (see Kuper and Fein, this volume).[3] Similarly, journalists such as Philip Gourevitch (1998) and Misha Glenny (1996) have published powerful accounts of the origins and experience of genocide. Almost none of these studies, however, has examined the local and sociocultural dimensions of genocide, areas of anthropological expertise. It is precisely because anthropologists can link macro-level analysis to the local-level understandings which help give genocide pattern, impetus, and meaning that they stand to make a unique and crucial contribution to our understanding of genocide. This volume of previously published work, along with another book of original essays (Hinton 2002), is intended to lay the ground-work for this "anthropology of genocide."[4]

Genocide: Conceptual Foundations

In the present Convention, genocide means any of the following acts committed with intent to destroy, in whole or in part, a national, ethnical, racial or religious group, as such:
  (a) Killing members of the group;
  (b) Causing serious bodily or mental harm to members of the group;
  (c) Deliberately inflicting on the group conditions of life calculated to bring about its physical destruction in whole or in part;
  (d) Imposing measures intended to prevent births within the group;
  (e) Forcibly transferring children of the group to another group.
                          Article II, 1948 United Nations Genocide Convention

Before exploring some of the insights an anthropology of genocide can provide, I want to briefly examine the concept of genocide itself. The first four selections in Part I, the multidisciplinary "Conceptual Foundations" section, are explicitly concerned with the definition and meaning of the term. These pieces, along with excerpts from two books, Hannah Arendt's *Eichmann in Jersualem* and Zygmunt Bauman's *Modernity and the Holocaust*, are seminal works in the interdisciplinary field of genocide studies. All are texts from various disciplines that anthropologists and other scholars grappling with the issue of genocide should consider.

The word "genocide" did not exist before the twentieth century; Raphaël Lemkin, a Polish jurist, coined the term to account for the atrocities Nazi Germany was committing. As Lemkin notes in the excerpted chapter from his ground-breaking book, *Axis Rule in Occupied Europe* (1944), at the 1933 International Conference for the Unification of Penal Law he unsuccessfully argued for the creation of two new international laws – "crimes of barbarity" and "crimes of vandalism" – that would criminalize the destruction of national, religious, or racial groups. A decade later, in the wake of the horrors being perpetrated in Nazi Germany, Lemkin was referring to the intentional destruction of such groups as "genocide," a term that combined the Greek root *genos* (race, tribe) with the Latin root *cide* (from *caedere*, to kill). In his selection in this volume, Lemkin methodically outlines a wide range of "genocidal techniques" used by the Nazis to attack the foundations of various "national entities." When compared with the next selection in this volume, the text of the 1948 United Nations Genocide Convention, one is struck by the extent to which Lemkin's original conception of genocide was modified in just a few years.

In the excerpt from his book, *Genocide: Its Political Use in the Twentieth Century* (1981), a seminal text that in some ways marks the emergence of the nascent field of genocide studies, Leo Kuper describes these transformations (see also Fein, this volume). Although the term "genocide" was sometimes invoked in the Nuremberg trials, Nazi war criminals were convicted under three main categories of international law: crimes against peace, war crimes, and crimes against humanity. Meanwhile, Lemkin was lobbying at the United Nations for the criminalization of genocide, a law that, while overlapping somewhat with war crimes and crimes against humanity, would move beyond them by protecting social collectivities during times of peace. On December 11, 1946, the United Nations General Assembly passed a resolution calling for legislation that would outlaw genocide, which it defined as the "denial of the right of existence of entire human groups...when racial, religious, political, and other groups have been destroyed, entirely or in part," and encouraged its adoption as law.

When various UN committees began to discuss the wording of the UN Convention, however, a number of controversies ensued. Kuper notes five main issues that structured the debate. First, committee members disagreed over which groups should be protected. Led by the Soviet bloc, which may well have feared being indicted for its domestic treatment of political and class "enemies," several representatives argued that the inclusion of more "mutable" group identities, such as political affiliation, would weaken the Convention because of the difficulty of defining membership. As a result, only "national, ethnical, racial or religious" groups were protected in the final version of the Genocide Convention. Second, problems arose over the issue of intent. For, if genocide involves the "intent to destroy" a group "as such," then it becomes possible for perpetrators to dispute their culpability for the "inadvertent" destruction of domestic groups, particularly indigenous peoples. Thus, when Paraguay was accused of being complicit in the destruction of the Aché Indians in 1974, the government tried to refute the charge through a simple denial of intent (see Arens 1976).

Third, the representatives argued about the types of actions that should be characterized as "genocide." Lemkin had originally proposed a very broad range of genocidal "techniques," including the destruction of a group's cultural way of life. Countries with a history of domestic and international colonization were particularly worried about being indicted on this charge, however, so "cultural genocide" was ultimately dropped from the Convention. (Drawing on another term proposed by Lemkin, scholars now often refer to cultural genocide as "ethnocide.") Fourth, committee members had to confront the problem of numbers. How can genocide be quantified? How many people have to be annihilated before massacre becomes genocide? The final version of the UN Convention did not provide answers to these questions, vaguely referring to the intent to destroy a group "in whole or in part."

Finally, there is the problem of enforcement. While few countries have a problem indicting a genocidal regime that has fallen from power, most become very resistant to passing legislation that could compromise their sovereignty. As opposed to establishing an international tribunal with unrestricted powers of enforcement, the UN Convention ultimately left prosecution to the states themselves (see Article VI), creating a paradoxical situation in which regnant genocidal regimes would effectively be responsible for trying themselves. Nevertheless, it took the United States Congress almost forty years to overcome its fear of indictment and to ratify the Convention, which became international law in 1951 (see LeBlanc 1991). At a conference in Rome in July 1998, a UN Statute for the establishment of an international criminal court was passed by a vote of 120 to 7; the United States, fearing the indictment of US troops in foreign operations, joined Iran, Iraq, China, Libya, Algeria, and Sudan in opposing the Statute. Only two weeks before he left office in January 2001, President Clinton finally signed the treaty, though Senate confirmation remains in doubt.

Helen Fein's selection in this volume, from *Genocide: A Sociological Perspective* (1990), describes the evolution of the concept of genocide, laments the lack of academic research on the topic, outlines some of the key issues in the field of genocide studies, and proposes a new definition of genocide that a number of scholars now use. Specifically, Fein defines genocide as a "sustained purposeful action by a perpetrator to physically destroy a collectivity directly or indirectly, through interdiction of the biological and social reproduction of group members, sustained regardless of the surrender or lack of threat offered by the victim." This definition resolves at least some of the problems with the UN Convention through its inclusiveness (i.e., accounting for the destruction of political and socioeconomic groups) and the distinction between genocide and other forms of political violence (e.g., terrorism, war crimes, episodic massacres). Fein proposes a number of criteria for distinguishing genocide and suggests new directions for research on genocide in the social sciences.

From an anthropological perspective, the UN Convention definition is highly problematic because it privileges certain social categories – race, ethnicity, religion, and nationality – over others. While the marking of social difference is a human universal, the categories into which we parse the world are culturally constructed. Thus, as we move from place to place, we find people being classified in a myriad of ways, ranging from totemistic groups and castes to categories based on sexual orientation and alternative genders. Surely there is a need to take account of such emic social categories as opposed to simply assuming that the categories highly salient in "modern" societies are universal? The International Criminal Tribunal for Rwanda ran into just such a problem when it found that the terms "Hutu" and "Tutsi" could not easily be defined as a racial, ethnic, religious, or national group, the categories listed in the UN Convention; it ultimately concluded that emic distinctions could serve as the basis for prosecution (Magnarella 2002). Even the idea of race, which so many people mistakenly reify as a biological given, is a social myth, created in the context of modernity to classify and to legitimate inequities perpetrated against newly discovered "others" (Gates 1986; Smedley 1999; Williams 1985). Accordingly, most anthropologists would probably favor a Fein-like definition that may encompass far more of the world's categorical diversity.

Of course, this line of thinking could be extended to the concept of genocide itself, which also arose in a particular social and historical context and reflects Western liberal democratic ideals.[5] After all, the term did not exist prior to the 1930s and did not have a corresponding conceptual analog in many societies. Moreover, the international law against genocide protects "individuals" against the violation of their "human rights," while paradoxically guarding the sovereignty of the nation-state. Like the notion of race, concepts of the "individual," "human rights," the "nation-state," and "genocide" are all social constructs linked to the advent of modernity. While few anthropologists would argue that we should do away with the idea of genocide, many would argue for a critical pause before this concept is applied to atrocities committed in other times and places. What, exactly, did it mean to destroy certain groups in ancient Assyria versus a modern, non-European context like Pol Pot's Cambodia? It is precisely through the understanding of such local categories – an anthropological area of expertise – that we may both better comprehend and work to prevent genocide.

Two other selections have been included in Part I. The first, excerpts from Hannah Arendt's book *Eichmann in Jerusalem*, initially published in 1963, raises a number of moral dilemmas about genocide. Arendt argues that Adolf Eichmann, the Nazi officer who coordinated the deportation of Jews to death camps, epitomized the "banality of evil." As opposed to being a sadistic demon, Eichmann seemed all too normal, a thoughtless "cog" in a totalitarian bureaucracy that annihilated people. Eichmann obeyed German law and carried out the orders his superiors gave him, even though they facilitated the death of millions of Jews. Is such a person guilty? And, if so, on what basis? Arendt ultimately answers this question in the affirmative, though not before raising fundamental questions about moral philosophy, international law, totalitarianism, bureaucracy, and modernity itself – and making claims that generated enormous controversy.[6]

In the excerpt from his book, *Modernity and the Holocaust* (1991), Zygmunt Bauman also considers the banality of evil, arguing that, far from being an aberrant throwback to a "premodern" state of "savagery" and "barbarism," the Holocaust was very much the product of modernity – one of its necessary, though not sufficient, conditions. The Holocaust constituted a tragic coalescence of several aspects of modernity. With the emergence of Enlightenment ideals of equality and the uniform citizen, race became a new way of differentiating human beings. Science was enlisted in the effort to create a new hierarchy of the human and not fully human, on top of which the Aryan race stood predominant. Bauman distinguishes such racism (the thoroughly modern construction of a racial social order that may be modified and "improved" through social engineering) from two types of prejudice: "heterophobia" (general fear and anxiety about the unfamiliar) and "contestant enmity" (more specific group hostility toward threatening "others").

Several other dimensions of modernity facilitated the Nazis' racist ambitions. With the rise of the nation-state, power and the means of force are increasingly centralized under state control. Science and technology make this power all the more lethal. To optimize "efficiency," work tasks are increasingly specialized and divided, culminating in impersonal bureaucracies that substitute technical proficiency for moral responsibility. As the division of labor is specialized, each bureaucrat becomes another step removed from the task that is ultimately performed. Distantiation, in turn, facilitates dehumanization, as the human beings whose lives are affected by the task lose their distinctiveness, becoming objects often referred to in euphemistic language. In Nazi Germany, the result was a bureaucrat like Eichmann, who efficiently carried out his tasks, unconcerned about the dehumanized individuals he thereby helped annihilate. While bureaucracy is not inherently genocidal, Bauman argues, it has the potential to facilitate lethal projects of social engineering, particularly when other moral safeguards break down. This is precisely what happened in Nazi Germany, as religious leaders, politicians, and intellectuals stood by – or even applauded or helped out – while Hitler's government annihilated Jews and other "contaminating" groups. Bauman recognizes that many Nazis were brutal anti-Semites. Anti-Semitism alone, however, cannot account for the modern character of the Holocaust.

Genocide, History, and Modernity

Several anthropologists have considered the relationship between genocide, history, and (post)modernity. Like "genocide," the term "modernity" is difficult to define, as illustrated by the number of prominent scholars who have attempted to analyze the character of modern society. Regardless of the differences, most would probably agree that modernity is linked to a set of interrelated processes (see Hall, Held, Hubert, and Thompson 1995): economic (the rise of capitalism and monetarized exchange), political (the emergence of the nation-state and secular forms of government), social (the decline of "traditional" hierarchies and allegiances and the rise of new class, race, and gender-based distinctions), and cultural (the privileging of a new set of secular ideas, many based on the Enlightenment's faith in progress, science, and reason). Moreover, the very idea of "the modern" now carries the positive sense of something favorable, desirable, and improved (Williams 1985).

From an anthropological perspective, the association of modernity with improvement is problematic. This association has served as the basis of much ethnocentrism, as the linkage between the modern and "the West" implies the inferiority of the "traditional" others who are categorically opposed to it. In fact, as the excerpt from John Bodley's (1999) *Victims of Progress* illustrates, this supposed inferiority has been used to legitimate genocide. Specifically, Bodley argues that the abuse and annihilation of indigenous peoples have been justified by one of the key metanarratives of modernity – the idea of "progress." On the one hand, "progress" has been equated with Western technology, market exchange, and industrial "development." These capitalist economies, however, are premised on a "culture of consumption" that promotes ever-expanding consumption and market growth. To increase their market base and pool of natural resources, governments have all too often sought to appropriate the lands of indigenous peoples, who usually have very different cultural assumptions and patterns of subsistence and, Bodley argues, frequently want to be left alone. On the other hand, the physical and cultural destruction of these indigenous peoples has been legitimated in the name of "progress." Government officials, scholars, and development agencies often ethnocentrically assert that they have a moral imperative to "civilize" these child-like "savages," who would desire the wealth and material goods that "civilization" offers if they weren't living in a state of ignorance. In some cases, the resulting death of indigenous peoples has been explained in terms of social Darwinism. Disastrously, somewhere between twenty-five to fifty million indigenous peoples have perished in the name of "progress" during this genocidal process.

As Bodley's chapter points out, many people view modernity as an inevitable process of "development" through which "traditional" peoples are "civilized" and gain the benefits of "progress." Anthropologists and other scholars, however, have emphasized that modernity does not result in a teleological outcome; it is a process that generates a variety of local forms, even within "the West." "Traditional others" are not passive recipients of modernity but active meaning-making agents who, while operating within a set of structural constraints, nevertheless localize the global flow of ideas, technologies, and material goods associated with the modern world. To understand modernity in general, and how modernity is related to genocide in particular, scholars need to explore the complex interplay of culture and history within specific local contexts. The next two selections in this volume highlight this point.

If Bodley's chapter illustrates the ways in which modernity has devastated indigenous peoples throughout the world, Michael Taussig's (1984) essay, "Culture of Terror – Space of Death," explores how these genocidal processes are articulated and transformed within a given time and place. Specifically, Taussig focuses on Roger Casement's report about the horrible abuses that were being perpetrated by rubber traders against Indians living along the Putumayo river in Colombia at the turn of the twentieth century. Taussig argues that this "space of death" was pervaded by enormous fear and uncertainty, which was heightened by a disjointed mixing of Western and local images. It is precisely within such sites of what Taussig calls "epistemic murk" that terror takes on cultural forms, as both perpetrator and victim, colonizer and colonized, attempt to make sense of their encounter with this terrifying and mysterious "other" onto whom their fantasies are projected. For the rubber traders on the Putumayo, Taussig argues, Indians, whom they associated with the wild, savagery, ignorance, and cannibalism, were transformed into the very images they were supposed to signify through acts of terror, brutality, and violence: rites of degradation confirming the inhuman status of the Indians; the burning or inverted crucifixion of the "infidels"; the rape or sexual enslavement of the "lascivious" group's women; the confinement of these inhabitants of "the wild" in cages and stockades; and the murder and dismemberment of "cannibalistic" savages. Through their depictions of such acts, even people like Casement ultimately affirmed the very cultural images that were patterning the violence.

In the selection from his book, *Envisioning Power: Ideologies of Dominance and Crisis* (1999), Eric Wolf explores the interrelationship of power and ideology in Nazi Germany. For Wolf, an understanding of ideology is not possible without a historical analysis, as new ideas are continually being forged out of preexisting cultural materials. During periods of crisis and upheaval, this process is often accentuated, resulting in extreme ideological formations – characteristic of many revitalization movements – that underwrite structural power, or "the power manifest in relationship that not only operates within settings and domains but also organizes and orchestrates the settings themselves" (Wolf 1999:5).[7] Like the Kwakiutl Indians of the Northwest Pacific Coast of North America and the Aztecs of pre-Hispanic Mexico (whom Wolf discusses in earlier chapters of his book), National Socialist Germany forged an ideology that legitimated the rule of the elite and the restructuring of society. In the wake of Germany's defeat in World War I and the socio-economic upheaval that followed, the Nazis forged their ideology of racial purity out of a number of culturally resonant propositions, including the ideas of the German *volk* community, status and hierarchy, anti-Semitism, male honor, social Darwinism, and scientific notions of race. This ideology rationalized Nazi power, anti-Semitic policy, fascist political domination, and, ultimately, the creation of new social contexts in which mass murder could take place.

Manufacturing Difference and "Purification"

To help make sense of and respond quickly to a diverse set of environmental inputs, the human mind has evolved to parse the complex world in which we live into categories (Allport 1979; Bruner 1957; Lévi-Strauss 1967; Maybury-Lewis and Alamagor 1989). This environment includes other human beings, whom we are strongly predisposed to sort, label, and typologize (Hirschfeld 1996). If cognitive psychologists have explored how such mental processing works, anthropologists have demonstrated that this capacity to distinguish difference has generated a vast array of forms across time and place, ranging from clans to races. Such culturally constructed groupings constitute a crucial part of human identity, as they provide a sense of meaning, solidarity, and belonging.

Group identities, however, are also premised on the existence of an "other" from which a "we" is distinguished, often in terms of an ethnocentric set of binary oppositions (for example, modern tropes of the "civilized" colonizer versus the "savage" colonized). The existence of these "others" provides a sort of moral glue that binds the members of a given social group together. Moreover, "others" may serve as objects of projection onto whom negative feelings and ideas may be transferred, thereby inflating one's own sense of self-worth and moral superiority. Mary Douglas (1966) developed an important synthesis of such ideas, linking bodily symbolism to social structure. Just as dirt is "matter out of place," she argued, so too are marginal beings portrayed as a chaotic and dangerous source of contamination that threatens the purity of the social order; group solidarity and cohesion, in turn, are affirmed through symbolic and physical acts of eliminating these contaminants. (Although Douglas did not apply her ideas to genocide, the relevance and importance of her work to the topic are highlighted by the fact that several of the authors in Part III directly draw upon her ideas.)

In genocide, the process of group differentiation and stigmatization is taken to the extreme, usually because of direct or indirect state policy. Here we find another link to modernity, as the homogenizing tendencies of the nation-state lead to an attempt to define citizens and non-citizens. An essentialist equation of people and place is frequently made, sometimes through the type of association between race, language, and culture that Franz Boas (1982) attacked at the turn of the twentieth century. As the claims of the dominant group are naturalized in this manner, it is able to assert the "right" to forcibly remove or eliminate its "out-of-place" victims, sometimes through lethal projects of social engineering.

Anthropologists have a great deal to say about this aspect of the genocidal process. Because of their expertise on the local dimensions of social structure, anthropologists may both point out and critique the ways in which genocidal regimes "manufacture difference" by constructing essentialized categories of identity and belonging. More broadly, anthropologists may illustrate how genocidal regimes motivate their minions to kill by forging their ideologies of hate out of highly salient forms of cultural knowledge (e.g., Hinton forthcoming; Taylor 1999), including those linked to emotionally resonant notions of purity and contamination. The essays in Part III touch on these issues in various ways as they explore how genocidal regimes manufacture difference into us/them oppositions of the good and the bad, the pure and the impure.

For example, in his essay, "'Ethnic Cleansing': A Metaphor for our Time?," Akbar Ahmed (1995) seeks to understand why ethnic cleansing, or the attempt to "purify" a given locale by expelling or eliminating a marked social group, has become so prevalent in recent years. While Ahmed provides a multicausal and wide-ranging answer to this question, he sees ethnic cleansing as intimately linked to late modernity, an era characterized by the undermining of the master tropes of modernity, the weakening of the nation-state, transnational flows of images and people, and a revival of the "traditional." In the midst of the uncertainty, confusion, and anxiety often associated with these processes, many people become increasingly invested in communities and group identities, which afford them greater meaning and self-affirmation. Problems arise when, frequently in the midst of socioeconomic and political crises, these identities are essentialized and scapegoating begins. In late modernity, mass media may play a crucial role in this process by reifying group identity and fomenting what Ahmed calls a "minority complex." As social problems mount, blame is cast upon the minority, who, in the extreme, becomes a "dirty" enemy that must be eliminated. Ahmed also critiques anthropologists for their failure to respond to episodes of ethnic cleansing and genocide, arguing that anthropological insights about the construction of ethnicity and other group identities are of direct relevance to our understanding of mass atrocities. Ahmed's essay concludes with suggestions about how we might prevent ethnic cleansing, such as by encouraging group understanding, undertaking educational initiatives, and increasing the ability of organizations like the UN to respond to developing crises.

Robert Hayden's (1996) essay, "Imagined Communities and Real Victims: Self-Determination and Ethnic Cleansing in Yugoslavia," illustrates many of Ahmed's themes through an examination of ethnic cleansing in the former Yugoslavia. Arguing against primordialist explanations that explain such violence in terms of "age-old hatreds," Hayden notes that, during the 1980s, the former Yugoslavia was characterized by increasing levels of ethnonationalist heterogeneity and interaction. Why, then, was ethnic cleansing taking place there just a few years later? To answer this question, Hayden draws on Douglas' theory of purity and danger, asserting that the identity of given ethnonationalist groups was reimagined so as to render them an impurity that had to be eliminated from the body politic. In particular, Hayden demonstrates how the constitutions of the successor republics in the former Yugoslavia "denaturalized" and justified the exclusion of minority groups by linking citizenship to essentialized cultural traits of the dominant group. This "bureaucratic ethnic cleansing" both provided a legal basis for and embodied a larger ideology of hate which, inflamed by state media, claimed that the purity of the new ethnic nation could only be insured by the forcible removal of this contaminating (minority) "human matter" from places where it did not belong. Ethnic cleansing, or the "forced unmixing" (by law, expulsion, or annihilation) of ethnonationalist groups who had previously coexisted, interacted, and intermarried in the former Yugoslavia, was the result.

Arjun Appadurai's (1998) essay, "Dead Certainty: Ethnic Violence in the Era of Globalization," draws together many of the ideas raised in earlier readings in Part III in attempting to understand the horrible forms of bodily violence that former ethnic neighbors sometimes perpetrate upon another. Like Ahmed, Appadurai maintains that ethnic conflict is linked to a sense of uncertainty and doubt in the wake of globalization in the late modern world. Like Hayden, Appadurai applies Douglas' structural argument about the anxiety caused by category mixture to violent situations in which notions of belonging are being reimagined to exclude "impure" others. Like Taussig, Appadurai maintains that the "spaces of death" in which violence takes place often embody a cultural patterning. Specifically, Appadurai notes that, as global flows of people, ideas, and information have accelerated, people may experience enormous uncertainty about who they are and what they believe. During ethnic conflict, this uncertainty is often brought to the fore, as people are informed by the media and sociopolitical leaders that their former neighbors are now ethnic enemies. Appadurai suggests that the body becomes a theater in which such categorical uncertainty is, at least momentarily, overcome, when the bodies of former social intimates are transformed into the ethnic or political tokens for which they are supposed to stand. Grotesque acts of bodily violence are perpetrated during these "death-cycle rituals," in which self and (enemy) other are marked, classified, and differentiated through mutilation, dismemberment, and death.

My own contribution to this volume (1998), "A Head for an Eye: Revenge in the Cambodian Genocide," explores how genocidal regimes attempt to motivate their followers to annihilate such impure groups by manipulating preexisting forms of knowledge. Because perpetrators are not simply automatons who blindly carry out the ideological dictates of the state, genocidal regimes almost always blend the old with the new so that their lethal ideologies will be effective and make sense to people. Thus, genocidal regimes usually co-opt preexisting cultural knowledge, dressing it up in new ideological guises that maintain familiar and compelling resonances while legitimating new structures of domination and violence against victim groups. The Khmer Rouge model of disproportionate revenge provides an illustration of this point, as the Khmer Rouge revamped preexisting knowledge about disproportionate revenge in accordance with their Marxist-Leninist views of class resentment and contradiction to sanction the killing of "class enemies." Drawing upon peasant anger about intensive US bombing, economic destabilization, and the disrespectful and exploitative way the rich treated the poor, Khmer Rouge ideology gave this sentiment a focus (class struggle) and a target (the "enemy" living in the cities). This new Khmer Rouge model, which encouraged poor peasants to seek vengeance against the capitalist and reactionary classes that had traditionally oppressed them, was publicly instituted in Khmer Rouge speeches, radio broadcasts, political training, songs, slogans, and policy. Many perpetrators found this ideological model highly motivating and sought to annihilate their "impure" class enemies.

Coping and Understanding

Within genocide studies, the majority of research has focused on understanding the genocidal process and seeking ways to prevent future genocides. With the exception of the Holocaust, much less attention has been focused on the aftermaths of genocide, both on how it affects perpetrators, victims, and their descendents and on the ways in which genocide is represented, portrayed, and explained in the media and the academy. While scholars make approximations of death tolls, the more indirect effects of genocide are almost incalculable, encompassing material devastation (e.g., the destruction of homes, property, and infrastructure; poverty, malnutrition, and starvation; economic collapse; minefields), human suffering (e.g., bodily injury; bereavement and intense grief; trauma; chronic fear; mental health problems; living with perpetrators; continued discrimination and structural violence), and social turmoil (e.g., dislocated populations; the loss or disappearance of family, friends, and relatives; the destruction of social institutions and networks; lingering hatreds). These effects are almost always mediated by the international response, including media portrayals, foreign aid, academic analyses, international stigma, criminal tribunals, transnational relief agencies, and a foreign military presence. As the essays in Part IV suggest, anthropologists, many of whom have lived with or worked in societies devastated by genocide, have a great deal to say about the aftermaths of genocide (see also Das, Kleinman, Lock, et al. 2001; Ebihara 1993; Green 1999; Hinton 2002; Kleinman, Das, and Lock 1997; Malkki 1995; Manz 1988; Warren 1993).

Linda Green's (1994) essay, "Fear as a Way of Life," explores the effects that fear has had in Guatemalan society in the wake of genocide. While conducting fieldwork with the people of Xe'caj in the late 1980s, Green was struck by the chronic sense of fear and unease that pervaded and structured their lives. Fear had become a routinized part of social life in a myriad of ways. On the one hand, the villagers lived under constant threat from and surveillance by a nearby military outpost, civil patrols, and unknown neighbors who worked as the "ears" of the government. On the other hand, their fear was generated by more indirect factors, such as disappearing bodies, rumor, innuendo, ambiguous forms of speech, and pervasive mistrust. In this climate of fear, no one was ever completely sure that they were safe.

The people of Xe'caj responded in several ways. Silence, secrecy, and ambiguity provided a protective shield though, ironically, they also served to heighten the sense of fear and mistrust. Green claims that the body also became both a symbol of and a means for expressing their fear and trauma. Many of the Mayan widows with whom Green worked experienced a range of somatic symptoms, including headaches, gastritis, ulcers, weakness, diarrhea, irritability, and sleeplessness. As opposed to diagnosing these symptoms as culturally bound syndromes associated with post-traumatic stress, Green argues that they must be understood in terms of the historical and social context in which they arose. For many of these Mayan women, somatic complaints served as a way of connecting with others, remembering painful events, expressing trauma and a sense of social fragmentation, and protesting the chronic fear, terror, and violence they have had to endure.

In his essay, "The Myth of Global Ethnic Conflict," John Bowen (1996) inveighs against a prevalent notion that such conflicts are the inevitable outcome of suppressed ancient hatreds, barely contained by the nation-state and always waiting to erupt. Drawing on a wide range of counter-examples, including the genocidal violence that took place in Rwanda and the former Yugoslavia in the 1990s, Bowen argues that these "primordialist" explanations are premised upon three erroneous assumptions. First, far from being ancient and unchanging, ethnic identities are historically constructed, modern categories that change over time and are subject to manipulation by ethnonationalist ideologues. Second, primordialist explanations often assume that ethnic groups are prone to violence. Bowen notes that there is nothing inevitable about such conflicts; they usually involve a long period of preparation during which ethnonationalist leaders and state media relentlessly promote fear, hatred, and resentment of the ethnic other. The Rwandan conflict proceeded along these lines, as, over the course of several years, the ruling Hutu elite built up and trained the militias that were to do much of the killing and relentlessly broadcast its ideology of hate. When the genocide began, it did not irrationally "erupt" but proceeded in a fairly organized manner with direction from above. Finally, Bowen argues that, as opposed to constantly threatening sociopolitical stability, ethnic diversity does not increase the likelihood of political violence in any straightforward way. Instead, the probability of ethnic conflict is more directly related to economic conditions, government policy and leadership, and access to power. Rather than increasing our understanding of ethnic conflict, then, primordialist explanations oversimplify complex local realities and obviate intervention in such "inevitable," "ancient," and "irrational" struggles.

If Bowen points out some of the erroneous assumptions that underlie primordialist explanations of genocide and other forms of political violence, Liisa Malkki's (1996) essay, "Speechless Emissaries: Refugees, Humanitarianism, and Dehistoricization," contends that problematic assumptions are also often made about "refugees." Specifically, Malkki contrasts local understandings of what it means to be a refugee with those of relief agencies, international organizations, and the media. Drawing on her fieldwork in Tanzania with Hutu refugees who fled the 1972 Burundi genocide, Malkki argues that, for such displaced persons, refugee status may be a crucial, positive aspect of identity. For these Hutus, being a refugee confers a moral identity bound up with certain myths of history that construct the Tutsis as cunning invaders who overthrew, oppressed, and killed the original Hutu and Twa inhabitants of the land. While in exile, the hardship of refugee life would purify and prepare these Hutus for a triumphant return to their homeland.

Refugee camp administrators in Tanzania, in contrast, tend to view refugees as "exemplary victims" who were in need of care because of their wounds and compromised judgment. Local history and politics, which are central to the identity of

Hutu refugees themselves, are left out of this view of the refugee as "universal humani-tarian subject." This trope of the refugee as humanitarian subject is often taken to an even further extreme by members of the international community. For these journalists, scholars, diplomats, and international organizations, refugees become exemplars of the universal sufferer, often depicted as anonymous and silent members of a "sea of humanity." After discussing how these images were manifest in the 1994 genocide in Rwanda, Malkki concludes by arguing for a "historicizing humanism" that acknow-ledges both the suffering and the history of such displaced peoples.

Toward an Anthropology of Genocide

In his seminal work on the origins of genocide, Leo Kuper (1981) emphasized the importance of viewing genocide as a process and not as a uniform, teleological phenomenon. Like modernity, genocide is generated by a variety of factors and has diverse outcomes. One way to think about this process is through metaphors of priming and heat, what I have elsewhere called "genocidal priming" (Hinton 1997, 2002). To "prime" something is to "make [it] ready" for operation, as in preparing a gun to fire "by inserting a charge of gunpowder or a primer" or "pouring water into a pump or gasoline into a carburetor" (Morris 1976:1040). We might refer to each of the steps that lead to a "discharge" – such as adding gunpowder and cocking the trigger – as a "prime."

Genocidal priming, then, refers to the process by which various primes coalesce, making genocide more or less likely, though by no means an inevitable outcome.[8] We might use a metaphor of heat to describe the extent of genocidal priming. Those situations in which a number of primes are operative in an intense form can be referred to as "hot"; in other "warm" or "cool" cases, the primes will be fewer and less extreme. Moreover, the degree of heat is never static, changing as domestic and international events unfold. Even in an extremely "hot" situation, genocide is by no means preordained. Such violence almost always involves some sort of "genocidal activation" – or a series of direct and indirect, more or less organized pushes from above – that begins to trigger the "charge" that has been primed. Sometimes this process of activation is precipitous, as in Rwanda or Indonesia; in other situations, such as Nazi Germany, Cambodia, and the former Yugoslavia, it is more gradual. Thus, in Rwanda, after a long process of priming, the activation process was quickly set in motion after President Habyarimana's plane was shot down; well-organized and trained Hutu extremists, often getting their orders to kill over the radio, rapidly began to annihilate political moderates and Tutsis.

Discerning these primes and assessing the "heat" of a situation, then, is clearly of crucial importance both to understanding the origins of and preventing genocide. What are these primes? While each genocide has a distinct etiology, similarities exist in the process of genocidal priming. Kuper, for example, argues that most genocides are characterized by at least three key primes: deep structural divisions and an identifiable victim group; a legitimating ideology of hate; and a breakdown in moral restraints. Other scholars, building upon Kuper's work, have identified other primes, such as socioeconomic upheaval, discriminatory political changes, and an apathetic response from the international community (see Charny 1999;

Fein 1990, 1992; Kuper 1985; Melson 1992; Smith 1987, 1999a). In particular, Barbara Harff and Ted Gurr (1998; see also Harff 1998) have identified a number of "accelerators" that may rapidly increase the "heat" in a situation, often initiating the type of escalating spiral of action and reaction that Gregory Bateson (1958, 1972) labeled "schizomogenesis."

In my own work on Cambodia, the notion of priming has proven to be a useful way to think about the events that set the stage for genocide (see Hinton, this volume). The Khmer Rouge came to power after a period of extreme *socioeconomic upheaval*: the economy broke down in the wake of the Vietnam War; the United States intensively bombed parts of the Cambodian countryside, killing thousands, destroying homes, and inciting many youths to join the anti-government movement; foreign troops moved at will through strategic areas; Prince Sihanouk was over-thrown in a coup headed by pro-US elements; and the country was rocked by a civil war in which up to 600,000 people died.

Upon taking power, the Khmer Rouge initiated a number of *structural changes* that radically altered Cambodian society. The DK regime evacuated the cities, disbanded the old government structure, banned Buddhism, undermined familial solidarity and attachment, created cooperatives in which economic production and consumption were collectivized, and abolished money, courts, market exchange, and formal education. Traditional hierarchies were inverted, as the young and the poor were elevated in status over the old and the wealthy. And individuals were reclassi-fied into new categories, including the oppositions between "new people" (those who had supported or lived in government-controlled zones during the civil war) and "old people" (those who had lived in Khmer Rouge zones). In addition to establish-ing the basis for a new communist society, these structural changes had the more lethal effect of *undermining traditional prosocial norms and moral restraints* and institutionalizing *structural divisions* between the rich and the poor, the urbanites and the peasants, and counter-revolutionaries and revolutionaries. The latter were privileged over the former, whose destruction was legitimated by DK policy.

These lethal divisions were intensified by *effective ideological manipulation* that glorified violence and loyalty to the Party leadership. Everyone was either an "enemy" or a "comrade-friend." Khmer Rouge ideology compared life in the new society to an army at war. "Battles" had to be fought on economic "fronts" and against internal "microbes" that had "burrowed from within" and threatened to subvert the revolution. Such enemies, often accused of being agents of the CIA, capitalists, or Vietnamese spies, were severely dehumanized. When orders arrived to root them out, the first community to fall under suspicion was the outgroup at the bottom of society – the "new people." As the purges began, many Khmer Rouge cadre and soldiers also came to be regarded as "traitors" who were accused of failing to carry out their economic objectives, sabotaging the war effort against Vietnam, or planning to overthrow the Party Center. Regardless of whether his or her victim was a friend, a "new person," a former DK official, or even a family member, the ideal new communist citizen would be able to "cut off his or her heart" from the enemy who was "not real Khmer."

The Cambodian case illustrates how the process of priming may unfold, as a series of primes – in this case, socioeconomic upheaval, structural change, intensified structural divisions, diminished moral inhibitions, and an ideology of hate –

increased the "heat" and genocidal potential of the situation. Of course, events could have been different. Other regimes have come to power under similar circumstances and not committed genocidal atrocities.[9] Pol Pot and his associates "activated" the genocidal violence by "pushing" their ideology of hate and promoting lethal policies in specific, deadly ways.

If anthropologists are to make a significant contribution to our comprehension of genocide, then, we must explore this process of genocidal priming and activation, examining how it unfolds in both genocidal and non-genocidal situations. Concepts like "primes" and "accelerators," however, are macro-level explanatory ideas that must be rooted to the complex local realities in which genocide takes place. Anthropologists can provide precisely this type of experience-near understanding. For, what do concepts like "structural division," "socioeconomic upheaval," and "ideologies of hate" mean to perpetrators, victims, and bystanders? In my own work on Cambodia, I have had to wrestle with this tension between emic and etic analysis. Thus, while the Khmer Rouge espoused an extreme ideology of hate, their political discourses blended the old and the new in ways that were both conducive and gave a cultural patterning to the violence (Hinton 1997, 2000, this volume). Macro-level analysis misses this key dimension of explanation when it ignores how the genocidal process is given shape, impetus, and meaning by local knowledge.

Anthropologists therefore have the potential to shed considerable light on genocide by exploring how the dynamics of mass violence are influenced by local understandings and sociocultural dynamics (e.g., cultural change, ritualized behavior, symbolism, revitalization movements, schismogenesis, the construction of identity, thick description, the localization of transnational flows of knowledge, intergroup boundary formation and social relations, conflict resolution, the interplay of structure/agency and power/knowledge, the cultural patterning of violence, and so forth). The essays in this volume, along with an incipient anthropological literature on genocide, illustrate some of the crucial and distinct ways in which anthropological insights can illuminate the genocidal process and its aftermath, ranging from the impact of modernity to the construction of difference to local strategies for coping with trauma and suffering. By drawing together a number of these seminal texts, this volume helps to lay a foundation for and point the way toward an "anthropology of genocide," which is urgently needed as groups of people continue to be annihilated throughout the world.

NOTES

I would like to thank Jane Huber and, especially, Nicole Cooley for their helpful comments and suggestions on this essay.

1   On the difficulty of representing violence and genocide, see Chandler (1999); Daniel (1996); Friedlander (1992); Scarry (1985).
2   Since the mid-1980s, anthropologists have begun to produce some research on the atrocities committed during the Holocaust (e.g., Arnold 1990, 1992; Ballinger 2000; Connor 1989; Conte and Essner 1995; Dumont 1986; Dundes 1984; R. Feldman 2000; Gajek 1990; Hinton 1998d; Jell-Bahlsen 1985; Lewin 1993; Lindholm 1990; Linke 1997, 1999; Schafft

1998, 1999; Stein 1993; Wolf 1999) and, more recently, in Bosnia (e.g., Bringa 1993, 1995; Denich 1994; Eller 1999; A. Feldman 1994; Halpern and Kideckel 2000; Hayden 1999, 2000). Even less material has been written on the genocides that have occurred in non-European countries like Biafra (Diamond 1970, 1974), Burundi (e.g., Malkki 1995), Cambodia (e.g., Ebihara 1990, 1993; Hinton 1996, 1998a, 1998b, 1998c, 2000, forthcoming; Ledgerwood 2001; Marston 1994; Stanton 1993), Guatemala (e.g., Green 1999; Manz 1988; Nelson 1999; Warren 1998), and Rwanda (e.g., Eller 1999; Magnarella 2000; Mamdami 2001; Newbury 1995; Taylor 1999). See also chapters in recent edited volumes on political violence, such as Das, Kleinman, Lock, Ramphele, and Reynolds (2001); Das, Kleinman, Ramphele, and Reynolds (2000); Ferguson (in press); Ferguson and Whitehead (1992); Kleinman, Das, and Lock (1997); Nordstrom and Martin (1992); Nordstrom and Robben (1995); Robben and Suárez-Orozco (2000); Scheper-Hughes and Sargent (1998); Schmidt and Schroder (2001); Sluka (2000); Warren (1993). On the anthropological silence on the topic of genocide, see De Waal (1994); Fein (1990); Kuper (1981); Lewin (1992); Shiloh (1975).

3   For a review of scholarship in the field of genocide studies, see Charny (1988, 1991, 1994, 1999); Fein (1990); Krell and Sherman (1997); Kuper (1981, 1985). See also the journals *Holocaust and Genocide Studies* and the *Journal of Genocide Research* and a number of edited collections, such as Andreopoulos (1994); Brugnola, Fein, and Spirer (1999); Chalk and Jonassohn (1990); Charny (1984); Chirot and Seligmann (2001); Chorbajian and Shirinian (1999); Davies and Gurr (1998); Fein (1992); Freedman-Apsel and Fein (1992); Jongman (1996); Porter (1982); Riemer (2000); Rosenbaum (1996); Smith (1999b); Strozier and Flynn (1996); Totten, Parsons, and Charny (1997); Wallimann and Dobkowski (2000).

4   Because both of these volumes are intended to help establish this foundation for an anthropology of genocide, they share a common focus, cover some of the same cases, and at times have conceptual overlap. Nevertheless, the two books are meant to complement one another: they are structured in different ways, and, with one exception, include different authors with divergent theoretical and ethnographic orientations. This volume consists of previously published articles, begins with a "Conceptual Foundations" section of seminal, non-anthropological selections on genocide and includes a detailed bibliography of anthropological work on genocide and a list of websites on the topic. The other set of original essays illustrates the "cutting edge" of current anthropological research on the topic of genocide. As these contrasts suggest, I have structured the two volumes so that they will fit together well for use in courses on genocide and political violence.

5   See Asad's (1997) essay on Article 5 of the Universal Declaration of Human Rights (on torture and cruelty) for an analog of how such an analysis of genocide might proceed.

6   E.g., Gershom Scholem's (1990) response in "On Eichmann" (see also Bar-On 1990).

7   Wolf (1999:5) distinguishes structural power from three other types of power: potency or capability, coercive force, and organizational power.

8   Let me stress that, through the use of metaphors of priming and heat, I do not want to convey the image of genocide as a primordial conflict waiting to explode. In fact, I want to do exactly the opposite and emphasize that genocide is a *process* that emerges from a variety of factors, or "primes," and that this always involves impetus and organization from above, what I call "genocidal activation." For another use of metaphors of "heat" and "cold" to describe ethnonationalist violence in a manner that argues against primordialist explanations, see Appadurai (1996:164ff.).

9   On "hot" situations that have not developed into genocide, see Kuper (1981). See also Scott (1998) on how a specific cluster of primes – simplified administrative schemes, a high-modernist ideology, authoritarian power, and an incapacitated society – has led to social catastrophes, including genocide (e.g., the Stalinist campaign against the Kulaks). All of these elements were present in the Cambodian genocide.

REFERENCES

Allport, Gordon W. (1979). *The Nature of Prejudice*. 25th anniversary ed. Reading, MA: Addison-Wesley.

Andreopoulos, George J. (ed.) (1994). *Genocide: Conceptual and Historical Issues*. Philadelphia: University of Pennsylvania Press.

Appadurai, Arjun (1996). *Modernity at Large: Cultural Dimensions of Globalization*. Minneapolis: University of Minnesota Press.

Arendt, Hannah (1977). *Eichmann in Jersualem: A Report on the Banality of Evil*. New York: Penguin.

Arens, Richard (ed.) (1976). *Genocide in Paraguay*. Philadelphia: Temple University Press.

Arnold, Bettina (1990). "The Past as Propaganda: Totalitarian Archaeology in Nazi Germany." *Antiquity* 64:464–78.

Arnold, Bettina (1992). "The Past as Propaganda." *Archaeology* (July/August): 30–7.

Asad, Talal (1997). "On Torture, or Cruel, Inhuman, and Degrading Treatment." In Arthur Kleinman, Veena Das, and Margaret Lock (eds.), *Social Suffering*. Berkeley: University of California Press, pp. 285–308.

Ballinger, Pamela (2000). "Who Defines and Remembers Genocide after the Cold War? Contested Memories of Partisan Massacre in Venezia Giulia in 1943–1945." *Journal of Genocide Research* 2(1):11–30.

Bar-On, A. Zvi (1990). "Measuring Responsibility." In Roger S. Gottlieb (ed.), *Thinking the Unthinkable: Meanings of the Holocaust*. Mahwah, NJ: Paulist, pp. 298–314.

Bateson, Gregory (1958). *Naven*. Stanford, CA: Stanford University Press.

Bateson, Gregory (1972). *Steps to an Ecology of Mind*. New York: Ballantine.

Bauman, Zygmunt (1991). *Modernity and the Holocaust*. Ithaca, NY: Cornell University Press.

Bischoping, Katherine and Fingerhut, Natalie (1996). "Border Lines: Indigenous Peoples in Genocide Studies." *Canadian Review of Sociology and Anthropology* 33(4):481–506.

Boas, Franz (1982). *Race, Language, and Culture*. Chicago: University of Chicago Press.

Bodley, John H. (1999). *Victims of Progress*. Mountain View, CA: Mayfield.

Bringa, Tone (1993). "National Categories, National Identification and Identity Formation in 'Multinational' Bosnia." *Anthropology of East Europe Review* 11(1–2):27–34.

Bringa, Tone (1995). *Being Muslim the Bosnian Way*. Princeton, NJ: Princeton University Press.

Brugnola, Orlanda, Fein, Helen, and Spirer, Louise (eds.) (1999). *Ever Again? Evaluating the United Nations Genocide Convention on its 50th Anniversary and Proposals to Activate the Convention*. New York: Institute for the Study of Genocide.

Bruner, Jerome S. (1957). "On Perceptual Readiness." *Psychological Review* 64:123–51.

Chalk, Frank and Jonassohn, Kurt (eds.) (1990). *The History and Sociology of Genocide: Analyses and Case Studies*. New Haven, CT: Yale University Press.

Chandler, David (1999). *Voices from S-21: Terror and History in Pol Pot's Secret Prison*. Berkeley: University of California Press.

Charny, Israel W. (ed.) (1984). *Toward the Understanding and Prevention of Genocide*. Boulder, CO: Westview.

Charny, Israel W. (ed.) (1988). *Genocide: A Critical Bibliographic Review*. New York: Facts on File.

Charny, Israel W. (ed.) (1991). *Genocide: A Critical Bibliographic Review*. Vol. 2. New York: Facts on File.

Charny, Israel W. (ed.) (1994). *Genocide: A Critical Bibliographic Review*. Vol. 3: *The Widening Circle of Genocide*. New Brunswick, NJ: Transaction.

Charny, Israel W. (ed.) (1999). *The Encyclopedia of Genocide*. Santa Barbara, CA: ABC-CLIO.

Chirot, Daniel, and Seligman, Martin E. P. (eds.) (2001). *Ethnopolitical Warfare: Causes, Consequences, and Possible Solutions*. Washington, D C : American Psychological Association.

Chorbajian, Levon and Shirinian, George (eds.) (1999). *Studies in Comparative Genocide*. New York: St. Martin's Press.

Connor, John W. (1989). "From Ghost Dance to Death Camps: Nazi Germany as a Crisis Cult." *Ethos* 17(3):259–88.

Conte, Édouard and Essner, Cornelia (1995). *La Quête de la Race: Une Anthropologie du Nazisme*. Paris: Hachette.

Daniel, E. Valentine (1996). *Charred Lullabies: Chapters in an Anthropography of Violence*. Princeton, NJ: Princeton University Press.

Das, Veena, Kleinman, Arthur, Lock, Margaret, Ramphele, Mamphela, and Reynolds, Pamela (eds.) (2001). *Remaking a World: Violence, Social Suffering, and Recovery*. Berkeley: University of California Press.

Das, Veena, Kleinman, Arthur, Ramphele, Mamphela, and Reynolds, Pamela (eds.) (2000). *Violence and Subjectivity*. Berkeley: University of California Press.

Davies, John L. and Gurr, Ted Robert (eds.) (1998). *Preventive Measures: Building Risk Assessment and Crisis Early Warning Systems*. New York: Rowman and Littlefield.

Denich, Bette (1994). "Dismembering Yugoslavia: Nationalist Ideologies and the Symbolic Revival of Genocide." *American Ethnologist* 21 (2): 367–90.

De Waal, Alex (1994). "Genocide in Rwanda." *Anthropology Today* 10(3):1–2.

Diamond, Stanley (1970). "Reflections on the African Revolution: The Point of the Biafran Case." *Journal of Asian and African Studies* 5(1–2):16–27.

Diamond, Stanley (1974). *In Search of the Primitive: A Critique of Civilization*. New Brunswick, NJ: Transaction.

Douglas, Mary (1966). *Purity and Danger: An Analysis of the Concepts of Pollution and Taboo*. New York: Routledge.

Dumont, Louis (1986). *Essays on Individualism: Modern Ideology in Anthropological Perspective*. Chicago: University of Chicago Press.

Dundes, Alan (1984). *Life is Like a Chicken Coop Ladder: A Portrait of German Culture through Folklore*. Ithaca, NY: Cornell University Press.

Ebihara, May Mayko (1990). "Revolution and Reformulation in Kampuchean Village Culture." In David A. Ablin and Marlowe Hood (eds.), *The Cambodian Agony*. Armonk, NY: M. E. Sharpe, pp. 16–61.

Ebihara, May Mayko (1993). "A Cambodian Village Under the Khmer Rouge, 1975–1979." In Ben Kiernan (ed.), *Genocide and Democracy in Cambodia: The Khmer Rouge, the United Nations and the International Community*. New Haven, CT: Yale University Southeast Asia Studies, pp. 51–63.

Eller, Jack David (1999). *From Culture to Ethnicity to Conflict: An Anthropological Perspective on International Ethnic Conflict*. Ann Arbor: University of Michigan Press.

Fein, Helen (1984). "Scenarios of Genocide: Models of Genocide and Critical Responses." In Israel W. Charny (ed.), *Toward the Understanding and Prevention of Genocide: Proceedings of the International Conference on the Holocaust and Genocide*. Boulder, CO: Westview, pp. 3–31.

Fein, Helen (1990). "Genocide: A Sociological Perspective." *Current Sociology* 38(1):v–126.

Fein, Helen (ed.) (1992). *Genocide Watch*. New Haven, CT: Yale University Press.

Feldman, Allen (1994). "From Desert Storm to Rodney King via ex-Yugoslavia: On Cultural Anaesthesia." *American Ethnologist* 21(2):404–18.

Feldman, Regina M. (2000). "Encountering the Trauma of the Holocaust: Dialogue and Its Discontents in the Broszat–Friedlander Exchanges of Letters." *Ethos* 28(4):551–74.

Ferguson, R. Brian (ed.) (1989). "Anthropology and War: Theory, Politics, Ethics." In D. Pitt and P. Turner (eds.), *The Anthropology of War and Peace*. South Hadley, MA: Bergin and Garvey, pp. 141–59.

Ferguson, R. Brian (ed.) (in press). *The State Under Siege: Political Disintegration in the Post-Cold War Era*. New York: Gordon and Breach.

Ferguson, R. Brian and Whitehead, Neil L. (eds.) (1992). *War in the Tribal Zone: Expanding States and Indigenous Warfare*. Sante Fe: School of American Research Press.

Freedman-Apsel, Joyce and Fein, Helen (eds.) (1992). *Teaching about Genocide: A Guidebook for College and University Teachers. Critical Essays, Syllabi and Assignments*. New York: Institute for the Study of Genocide.

Friedlander, Saul (ed.) (1992). *Probing the Limits of Representation: Nazism and the "Final Solution."* Cambridge, MA: Harvard University Press.

Gajek, Esther (1990). "Christmas Under the Third Reich." *Anthropology Today* 6:3–9.

Gates, Henry Louis, Jr. (ed.) (1986). *"Race," Writing, and Difference*. Chicago: University of Chicago Press.

Glenny, Misha (1996). *The Fall of Yugoslavia: The Third Balkan War*. New York: Penguin.

Green, Linda (1999). *Fear as a Way of Life: Mayan Widows in Rural Guatemala*. New York: Columbia University Press.

Goldhagen, Daniel Jonah (1996). *Hitler's Willing Executioners: Ordinary Germans and the Holocaust*. New York: Alfred A. Knopf.

Gourevitch, Philip (1998). *We Wish to Inform You that Tomorrow We Will be Killed with Our Families: Stories from Rwanda*. New York: Farrar Straus and Giroux.

Hall, Stuart (1995). "Introduction." In Stuart Hall, David Held, Don Hubert, and Kenneth Thompson (eds.), *Modernity: An Introduction to Modern Societies*. Cambridge: Polity, pp. 1–18.

Hall, Stuart, Held, David, Hubert, Don, and Thompson, Kenneth (eds.) (1995). *Modernity: An Introduction to Modern Societies*. Cambridge: Polity.

Halpern, Joel M. and Kideckel, David A. (eds.) (2000). *Neighbors at War: Anthropological Perspectives on Yugoslav Ethnicity, Culture, and History*. University Park, PA: Penn State University Press.

Harff, Barbara (1998). "Early Warning of Humanitarian Crisis: Sequential Models and the Role of Accelerators." In John L. Davies and Ted Robert Gurr (eds.), *Preventive Measures: Building Risk Assessment and Crisis Early Warning Systems*. New York: Rowman and Littlefield, pp. 70–8.

Harff, Barbara and Gurr, Ted (1998). "Systematic Early Warning of Humanitarian Emergencies." *Journal of Peace Research* 35(5):551–79.

Hayden, Robert M. (1999). *Blueprints of a House Divided: The Constitutional Logic of the Yugoslav Conflicts*. Ann Arbor: University of Michigan Press.

Hayden, Robert M. (2000). "Rape and Rape Avoidance in Ethno-Nationalist Conflicts: Sexual Violence in Liminalized States." *American Anthropologist* 102(1):27–41.

Held, David (1995). "The Development of the Modern State." In Stuart Hall, David Held, Don Hubert, and Kenneth Thompson (eds.), *Modernity: An Introduction to Modern Societies*. Cambridge: Polity, pp. 56–89.

Hinton, Alexander Laban (1996). "Agents of Death: Explaining the Cambodian Genocide in Terms of Psychosocial Dissonance." *American Anthropologist* 98(4):818–31.

Hinton, Alexander Laban (1997). "Cambodia's Shadow: An Examination of the Cultural Origins of Genocide." Ph.D. dissertation, Emory University, Department of Anthropology. Ann Arbor, MI: University Microfilms International.

Hinton, Alexander Laban (1998a). "Why Did You Kill? The Dark Side of Face and Honor in the Cambodian Genocide." *Journal of Asian Studies* 57(1):93–122.

Hinton, Alexander Laban (1998b). "A Head for an Eye: Revenge in the Cambodian Genocide." *American Ethnologist* 25(3):352–77.

Hinton, Alexander Laban (1998c). "Genocidal Bricolage: A Reading of Human Liver-Eating in Cambodia." Yale University Genocide Studies Program Working Paper (GS 06): 16–38.

Hinton, Alexander Laban (1998d). "Why Did the Nazis Kill? Anthropology, Genocide, and the Goldhagen Controversy." *Anthropology Today* 14(3):9–15.

Hinton, Alexander Laban (2000). "Under the Shade of Pol Pot's Umbrella: Mandala, Myth, and Politics in the Cambodian Genocide." In Thomas Singer (ed.), *The Vision Thing: Myth, Politics and Psyche in the World*. New York: Routledge, pp. 170–204.

Hinton, Alexander Laban (ed.) (2002). *Annihilating Difference: The Anthropology of Genocide*. Berkeley: University of California Press.

Hinton, Alexander Laban (forthcoming). *Cambodia's Shadow: Cultural Dimensions of Genocide*.

Hirschfeld, Lawrence A. (1996). *Race in the Making: Cognition, Culture, and the Child's Construction of Human Kinds*. Cambridge, MA: MIT Press.

Hitchcock, Robert K. and Twedt, Tara M. (1997). "Physical and Cultural Genocide of Various Indigenous Peoples." In Samuel Totten, William S. Parsons, and Israel W. Charny (eds.), *Century of Genocide: Eyewitness Accounts and Critical Views*. New York: Garland, pp. 372–408.

Jacobs, Steven L. (1999). "The Papers of Raphaël Lemkin: A First Look." *Journal of Genocide Research* 1(1):105–14.

Jell-Bahlsen, Sabine (1985). "Ethnology and Fascism in Germany." *Dialectical Anthropology* 9(3):313–35.

Jongman, Albert J. (ed.) (1996). *Contemporary Genocides: Causes, Cases, Consequences*. Leiden: PIOOM.

Kleinman, Arthur, Das, Veena, and Lock, Margaret (eds.) (1997). *Social Suffering*. Berkeley: University of California Press.

Koenigsberg, Richard A. (1975). *Hitler's Ideology: A Study in Psychoanalytic Sociology*. New York: The Library of Social Science.

Krell, Robert and Sherman, Marc I. (eds.) (1997). *Genocide: A Critical Bibliographic Review*. Vol. 4: *Medical and Psychological Effects of Concentration Camps on Holocaust Survivors*. New Brunswick, NJ: Transaction.

Kuper, Leo (1981). *Genocide: Its Political Use in the Twentieth Century*. New Haven, CT: Yale University Press.

Kuper, Leo (1985). *The Prevention of Genocide*. New Haven, CT: Yale University Press.

Kuper, Leo (1994). "Theoretical Issues Relating to Genocide: Uses and Abuses." In George J. Andreopoulos (ed.), *Genocide: Conceptual and Historical Dimensions*. Philadelphia: University of Pennsylvania Press, pp. 31–46.

LeBlanc, Lawrence J. (1991). *The United States and the Genocide Convention*. Durham, NC: Duke University Press.

Ledgerwood, Judy (ed.) (2001). *Cambodia Emerges from the Past: Eight Essays*. DeKalb, IL: Northern Illinois University.

Lemkin, Raphaël (1944). *Axis Rule in Occupied Europe*. Washington, DC: Carnegie Endowment for International Peace.

Lemkin, Raphaël (1947). "Genocide as a Crime under International Law." *American Journal of International Law* 41:145–51.

Lévi-Strauss, Claude (1967). *Structural Anthropology*, trans. Claire Jacobson and Brooke Grundfest Schoepf. New York: Anchor.

Lewin, Carroll McC. (1992). "The Holocaust: Anthropological Possibilities and the Dilemma of Representation." *American Anthropologist* 94:161–6.

Lewin, Carroll McC. (1993). "Negotiated Selves in the Holocaust." *Ethos* 21:295–318.

Lindholm, Charles (1990). *Charisma*. Oxford: Blackwell.

Linke, Uli (1997). "Gendered Difference, Violent Imagination: Blood, Race, Nation." *American Anthropologist* 99(3):559–73.

Linke, Uli (1999). *Blood and Nation: The European Aesthetics of Race*. Philadelphia: University of Pennsylvania Press.

Magrarella, Paul J. (2000). *Justice in Africa : Rwanda's Genocide, its Courts, and the UN Criminal Tribunal*. Aldershot: Ashgate Publishing.

Magnarella, Paul J. (2002). "Recent Developments in the International Law of Genocide: An Anthropological Perspective on the International Criminal Tribunal for Rwanda." In Alexander Laban Hinton (ed.), *Annihilating Difference: The Anthropology of Genocide*. Berkeley: University of California Press.

Malkki, Liisa (1995). *Purity and Exile: Violence, Memory, and National Cosmology among Hutu Refugees in Tanzania*. Princeton, NJ: Princeton University Press.

Mamdami, Mahmood (2001). *When Victims Become Killers : Colonialism, Nativism and the Genocide in Rwanda*. Princeton, NJ: Princeton University Press.

Manz, Beatriz (1988). *Refugees of a Hidden War: The Aftermath of Counterinsurgency in Guatemala*. Albany: State University of New York.

Marston, John (1994). "Metaphors of the Khmer Rouge." In May M. Ebihara, Carol A. Mortland, and Judy Ledgerwood (eds.), *Cambodian Culture since 1975: Homeland and Exile*. Ithaca, NY: Cornell University Press, pp. 105–18.

Maybury-Lewis, David (1997). *Indigenous People, Ethnic Groups, and the State*. Boston: Allyn and Bacon.

Maybury-Lewis, David and Almagor, Uri (eds.) (1989). *The Attraction of Opposites: Thought and Society in the Dualistic Mode*. Ann Arbor: University of Michigan Press.

Melson, Robert F. (1992). *Revolution and Genocide: On the Origins of the Armenian Genocide and the Holocaust*. Chicago: University of Chicago Press.

Messing, Simon D. (1976). "On Anthropology and Nazi Genocide." *Current Anthropology* 17(2):326–7.

Morris, William (ed.) (1976). *American Heritage Dictionary of the English Language*. Boston: Houghton Mifflin.

Nagengast, Carole (1994). "Violence, Terror, and the Crisis of the State." *Annual Review of Anthropology* 23: 109–36.

Nelson, Diane M. (1999). *A Finger in the Wound: Body Politics in Quincentennial Guatemala*. Berkeley: University of California Press.

Newbury, Catherine (1995). "Background to Genocide: Rwanda." *Issue: A Journal of Opinion* 23(2):12–17.

Nordstrom, Carolyn and Martin, JoAnn (eds.) (1992). *The Paths to Domination, Resistance, and Terror*. Berkeley: University of California Press.

Nordstrom, Carolyn and Robben, Antonius C. G. M. (eds.) (1995). *Fieldwork Under Fire: Contemporary Studies of Violence and Survival*. Berkeley: University of California Press.

Porter, Jack Nusan (ed.) (1982). *Genocide and Human Rights: A Global Anthology*. Washington, DC: University Press of America.

Riches, David (ed.) (1986). *The Anthropology of Violence*. New York: Oxford University Press.

Riemer, Neal (ed.) (2000). *Protection Against Genocide: Mission Impossible?* Westport, CT: Praeger.

Robben, Antonius C. G. M. and Suárez-Orozco, Marcelo M. (eds.) (2000). *Cultures Under Siege: Collective Violence and Trauma*. New York: Cambridge University Press.

Rosenbaum, Alan S. (ed.) (1996). *Is the Holocaust Unique? Perspectives on Comparative Genocide*. Boulder, CO: Westview.

Scarry, Elaine (1985). *The Body in Pain: The Making and Unmaking of the World*. New York: Oxford University Press.

Schafft, Gretchen (1998). "Civic Denial and the Memory of War." *Journal of the American Academy of Psychoanalysis* 26(2):255–72.

Schafft, Gretchen (1999). "Professional Denial." *Anthropology Newsletter* 40(1):56, 54.

Scheper-Hughes, Nancy and Sargent, Carolyn (eds.) (1998). *Small Wars: The Cultural Politics of Childhood*. Berkeley: University of California Press.

Scherrer, Christian P. (1999). "Towards a Theory of Modern Genocide. Comparative Genocide Research: Definitions, Criteria, Typologies, Cases, Key Elements, Patterns and Voids." *Journal of Anthropological Research* 1(1):13–23.

Schmidt, Bettina and Schroder, Ingo (eds.) (2001). *Anthropology of Violence and Conflict*. New York: Routledge.

Scholem, Gershom (1990). "On Eichmann." In Roger S. Gottlieb (ed.), *Thinking the Unthinkable: Meanings of the Holocaust*. Mahwah, NJ: Paulist, pp. 291–7.

Scott, James C. (1998). *Seeing Like a State: How Certain Schemes to Improve the Human Condition Have Failed*. New Haven, CT: Yale University Press.

Shiloh, Ailon (1975). "Psychological Anthropology: A Case Study in Cultural Blindness." *Current Anthropology* 16(4):618–20.

Sluka, Jeffrey A. (2000). *Death Squad: The Anthropology of State Terror*. Philadelphia: University of Pennsylvania Press.

Smedley, Audrey (1999). *Race in North America: Origins and Evolution of a Worldview*. 2nd ed. Boulder, CO: Westview.

Smith, Roger W. (1987). "Human Destructiveness and Politics: The Twentieth Century as an Age of Genocide." In Isidor Wallimann and Michael N. Dobkowski (eds.), *Genocide and the Modern Age: Etiology and Case Studies of Mass Death*. New York: Greenwood Press, pp. 21–39.

Smith, Roger W. (1999a). "State Power and Genocidal Intent: On the Uses of Genocidal in the Twentieth Century." In Levon Chorbajian and George Shirinian (eds.), *Studies in Comparative Genocide*. New York: St. Martin's Press, pp. 3–14.

Smith, Roger W. (ed.) (1999b). *Genocide: Essays Toward Understanding, Early-Warning, and Prevention*. Williamsburg, VA: Association of Genocide Scholars.

Stanton, Gregory H. (1993). "The Cambodian Genocide and International Law." In Ben Kiernan (ed.), *Genocide and Democracy in Cambodia: The Khmer Rouge, the United Nations and the International Community*. New Haven, CT: Yale University Southeast Asia Studies, pp. 141–61.

Stein, Howard F. (1993). "The Holocaust, the Self, and the Question of Wholeness: A Response to Lewin." *Ethos* 21(4):485–512.

Strozier, Charles B. and Flynn, Michael (eds.) (1996). *Genocide, War, and Human Survival*. Lanham, MD: Rowman and Littlefield.

Taussig, Michael (1987). *Shamanism, Colonialism, and the Wild Man: A Study in Terror and Healing*. Chicago: University of Chicago Press.

Taylor, Christopher C. (1999). *Sacrifice as Terror: The Rwandan Genocide of 1994*. Oxford: Berg.

Totten, Samuel, Parsons, William S., and Charny, Israel (eds.) (1997). *Century of Genocide: Eyewitness Accounts and Critical Views*. New York: Garland.

Wallimann, Isidor and Dobkowski, Michael N. (eds.) (2000). *Genocide and the Modern Age: Etiology and Case Studies of Mass Death*. Syracuse, NY: Syracuse University Press.

Warren, Kay B. (ed.) (1993). *The Violence Within: Cultural and Political Opposition in Divided Nations*. Boulder, CO: Westview.

Warren, Kay B. (ed.) (1998). *Indigenous Movements and their Critics: Pan-American Activism in Guatemala*. Princeton, NJ: Princeton University Press.

Williams, Raymond (1985). *Marxism and Literature*. New York: Oxford University Press.

Wolf, Eric R. (1999). *Envisioning Power: Ideologies of Dominance and Crisis*. Berkeley: University of California Press.

Part I

Conceptual Foundations

1

Genocide

Raphaël Lemkin

Genocide – A New Term and New Conception for Destruction of Nations

New conceptions require new terms. By "genocide" we mean the destruction of a nation or of an ethnic group. This new word, coined by the author to denote an old practice in its modern development, is made from the ancient Greek word *genos* (race, tribe) and the Latin *cide* (killing), thus corresponding in its formation to such words as tyrannicide, homocide [*sic*], infanticide, etc.[1] Generally speaking, genocide does not necessarily mean the immediate destruction of a nation, except when accomplished by mass killings of all members of a nation. It is intended rather to signify a coordinated plan of different actions aiming at the destruction of essential foundations of the life of national groups, with the aim of annihilating the groups themselves. The objectives of such a plan would be disintegration of the political and social institutions, of culture, language, national feelings, religion, and the economic existence of national groups, and the destruction of the personal security, liberty, health, dignity, and even the lives of the individuals belonging to such groups. Genocide is directed against the national group as an entity, and the actions involved are directed against individuals, not in their individual capacity, but as members of the national group.

The following illustration will suffice. The confiscation of property of nationals of an occupied area on the ground that they have left the country may be considered simply as a deprivation of their individual property rights. However, if the confiscations are ordered against individuals solely because they are Poles, Jews, or Czechs, then the same confiscations tend in effect to weaken the national entities of which those persons are members.

Genocide has two phases: one, destruction of the national pattern of the oppressed group; the other, the imposition of the national pattern of the oppressor. This imposition, in turn, may be made upon the oppressed population which is allowed to remain, or upon the territory alone, after removal of the population and the colonization of the area by the oppressor's own nationals. Denationalization was the word used in the past to describe the destruction of a national pattern.[2] The author believes, however, that this word is inadequate because: (1) it does not connote the destruction of the biological structure; (2) in connoting the destruction of one national pattern, it does not connote the imposition of the national pattern of the oppressor; and (3) denationalization is used by some authors to mean only deprivation of citizenship.[3]

Many authors, instead of using a generic term, use currently terms connoting only some functional aspect of the main generic notion of genocide. Thus, the terms "Germanization," "Magyarization," "Italianization," for example, are used to connote the imposition by one stronger nation (Germany, Hungary, Italy) of its national pattern upon a national group controlled by it. The author believes that these terms are also inadequate because they do not convey the common elements of one generic notion and they treat mainly the cultural, economic, and social aspects of genocide, leaving out the biological aspect, such as causing the physical decline and even destruction of the population involved. If one uses the term "Germanization" of the Poles, for example, in this connotation, it means that the Poles, as human beings, are preserved and that only the national pattern of the Germans is imposed upon them. Such a term is much too restricted to apply to a process in which the population is attacked, in a physical sense, and is removed and supplanted by populations of the oppressor nations.

Genocide is the antithesis of the Rousseau-Portalis Doctrine, which may be regarded as implicit in the Hague Regulations. This doctrine holds that war is directed against sovereigns and armies, not against subjects and civilians. In its modern application in civilized society, the doctrine means that war is conducted against states and armed forces and not against populations. It required a long period of evolution in civilized society to mark the way from wars of extermination,[4] which occurred in ancient times and in the Middle Ages, to the conception of wars as being essentially limited to activities against armies and states. In the present war, however, genocide is widely practiced by the German occupant. Germany could not accept the Rousseau-Portalis Doctrine: first, because Germany is waging a total war; and secondly, because, according to the doctrine of National Socialism, the nation, not the state, is the predominant factor.[5] In this German conception the nation provides the biological element for the state. Consequently, in enforcing the New Order, the Germans prepared, waged, and continued a war not merely against states and their armies[6] but against peoples. For the German occupying authorities war thus appears to offer the most appropriate occasion for carrying out their policy of genocide. Their reasoning seems to be the following:

The enemy nation within the control of Germany must be destroyed, disintegrated, or weakened in different degrees for decades to come. Thus the German people in the post-war period will be in a position to deal with other European peoples from the vantage point of biological superiority. Because the imposition of this policy of genocide is more destructive for a people than injuries suffered in actual fighting,[7] the German people will be stronger than the subjugated peoples after the war even if the German army is defeated. In this respect genocide is a new technique of occupation aimed at winning the peace even though the war itself is lost.

For this purpose the occupant has elaborated a system designed to destroy nations according to a previously prepared plan. Even before the war Hitler envisaged genocide as a means of changing the biological interrelations in Europe in favor of Germany.[8] Hitler's conception of genocide is based not upon cultural but upon biological patterns. He believes that "*Germanization* can only be carried out with the *soil* and never with *men*."[9]

When Germany occupied the various European countries, Hitler considered their administration so important that he ordered the Reich Commissioners and governors to be responsible directly to him. The plan of genocide had to be adapted to political considerations in different countries. It could not be implemented in full force in all the conquered states, and hence the plan varies as to subject, modalities, and degree of intensity in each occupied country. Some groups – such as the Jews – are to be destroyed completely.[10] A distinction is made between peoples considered to be related by blood to the German people (such as Dutchmen, Norwegians, Flemings, Luxemburgers), and peoples not thus related by blood (such as the Poles, Slovenes, Serbs). The populations of the first group are deemed worthy of being Germanized. With respect to the Poles particularly, Hitler expressed the view that it is their soil alone which *can and should be profitably Germanized*.[11]

Techniques of Genocide in Various Fields

The techniques of genocide, which the German occupant has developed in the various occupied countries, represent a concentrated and coordinated attack upon all elements of nationhood. Accordingly, genocide is being carried out in the following fields.

Political

In the incorporated areas, such as western Poland, Eupen, Malmédy and Moresnet, Luxemburg, and Alsace-Lorraine, local institutions of self-government were destroyed and a German pattern of administration imposed. Every reminder of former national character was obliterated. Even commercial signs and inscriptions on buildings, roads, and streets, as well as names of communities and of localities, were changed to a German form.[12] Nationals of Luxemburg having foreign or non-German first names are required to assume in lieu thereof the corresponding German first names; or, if that is impossible, they must select German first names. As to their family names, if they were of German origin and their names have been changed to a non-German form, they must be changed again to the original German. Persons who have not complied with these requirements within the prescribed period are liable to a penalty, and in addition German names may be imposed on them.[13] Analogous provisions as to changing of names were made for Lorraine.[14]

Special Commissioners for the Strengthening of Germanism are attached to the administration, and their task consists in coordinating all actions promoting Germanism in a given area. An especially active rôle in this respect is played by inhabitants of German origin who were living in the occupied countries before the occupation. After having accomplished their task as members of the so-called fifth column, they formed the nucleus of Germanism. A register of Germans (*Volksliste*)[15] was established and special cards entitled them to special privileges and favors, particularly in the fields of rationing, employment, supervising enterprises of local inhabitants, and so on. In order to disrupt the national unity of the local population, it was declared that non-Germans, married to Germans, may upon their application be put on the *Volksliste*.

In order further to disrupt national unity, Nazi party organizations were established, such as the Nasjonal Samling Party in Norway and the Mussert Party in the Netherlands, and their members from the local population were given political privileges. Other political parties were dissolved.[16] These Nazi parties in occupied countries were also given special protection by courts.

In line with this policy of imposing the German national pattern, particularly in the incorporated territories, the occupant has organized a system of colonization of these areas. In western Poland, especially, this has been done on a large scale. The Polish population have been removed from their homes in order to make place for German settlers who were brought in from the Baltic States, the central and eastern districts of Poland, Bessarabia, and from the Reich itself. The properties and homes of the Poles are being allocated to German settlers; and to induce them to reside in these areas the settlers receive many privileges, especially in the way of tax exemptions.

Social

The destruction of the national pattern in the social field has been accomplished in part by the abolition of local law and local courts and the imposition of German law and courts, and also by Germanization of the judicial language and of the bar. The social structure of a nation being vital to its national development, the occupant also endeavors to bring about such changes as may weaken the national spiritual resources. The focal point of this attack has been the intelligentsia, because this group largely provides national leadership and organizes resistance against Nazification. This is especially true in Poland and Slovenia (Slovene part of Yugoslavia), where the intelligentsia and the clergy were in great part removed from the rest of the population and deported for forced labor in Germany. The tendency of the occupant is to retain in Poland only the laboring and peasant class, while in the western occupied countries the industrialist class is also allowed to remain, since it can aid in integrating the local industries with the German war economy.

Cultural

In the incorporated areas the local population is forbidden to use its own language in schools and in printing. According to the decree of August 6, 1940, the language of instruction in all Luxemburg schools was made exclusively German. The French language was not permitted to be taught in primary schools; only in secondary schools could courses in that language continue to be given. German teachers were introduced into the schools and they were compelled to teach according to the principles of National Socialism.[17]

In Lorraine general compulsory education to assure the upbringing of youth in the spirit of National Socialism begins at the age of six.[18] It continues for eight years, or to the completion of the grammar school (*Volksschule*), and then for three more years, or to the completion of a vocational school. Moreover, in the Polish areas Polish youths were excluded from the benefit of liberal arts studies and were channeled predominantly into the trade schools. The occupant apparently believes that the study of the liberal arts may develop independent national Polish thinking, and therefore he tends to prepare Polish youths for the rôle of skilled labor, to be employed in German industries.

In order to prevent the expression of the national spirit through artistic media, a rigid control of all cultural activities has been introduced. All persons engaged in painting, drawing, sculpture, music, literature, and the theater are required to obtain a license for the continuation of their activities. Control in these fields is exercised through German authorities. In Luxemburg this control is exercised through the Public Relations Section of the Reich Propaganda Office and embraces music, painting, theater, architecture, literature, press, radio, and cinema. Every one of these activities is controlled through a special chamber and all these chambers are controlled by one chamber, which is called the Reich Chamber of Culture (*Reich-skulturkammer*).[19] The local chambers of culture are presided over by the propaganda chief of the National Socialist Party in the given area. Not only have national creative activities in the cultural and artistic field been rendered impossible by regimentation, but the population has also been deprived of inspiration from the existing cultural and artistic values. Thus, especially in Poland, were national monuments destroyed and libraries, archives, museums, and galleries of art carried away.[20] In 1939 the Germans burned the great library of the Jewish Theological Seminary at Lublin, Poland. This was reported by the Germans as follows:

For us it was a matter of special pride to destroy the Talmudic Academy which was known as the greatest in Poland.... We threw out of the building the great Talmudic library, and carted it to market. There we set fire to the books. The fire lasted for twenty hours. The Jews of Lublin were assembled around and cried bitterly. Their cries almost silenced us. Then we summoned the military band and the joyful shouts of the soldiers silenced the sound of the Jewish cries.[21]

Economic

The destruction of the foundations of the economic existence of a national group necessarily brings about a crippling of its development, even a retrogression. The lowering of the standard of living creates difficulties in fulfilling cultural-spiritual requirements. Furthermore, a daily fight literally for bread and for physical survival may handicap thinking in both general and national terms.

It was the purpose of the occupant to create such conditions as these among the peoples of the occupied countries, especially those peoples embraced in the first plans of genocide elaborated by him – the Poles, the Slovenes, and the Jews.

The Jews were immediately deprived of the elemental means of existence. As to the Poles in incorporated Poland, the purpose of the occupant was to shift the economic resources from the Polish national group to the German national group. Thus the Polish national group had to be impoverished and the German enriched. This was achieved primarily by confiscation of Polish property under the authority of the Reich Commissioner for the Strengthening of Germanism. But the process was likewise furthered by the policy of regimenting trade and handicrafts, since licenses for such activities were issued to Germans, and only exceptionally to Poles. In this way, the Poles were expelled from trade, and the Germans entered that field.

As the occupant took over the banks a special policy for handling bank deposits was established in order to strengthen the German element. One of the most widely patronized Polish banks, called the Post Office Savings Bank (PKO), possessed, on the day of the occupation, deposits of millions of Polish citizens. The deposits, however, were repaid by the occupant only to the German depositors upon production by them of a certificate of their German origin.[22] Thus the German element in Poland was immediately made financially stronger than the Polish. In Slovenia the Germans have liquidated the financial cooperatives and agricultural associations, which had for decades proved to be a most efficient instrumentality in raising the standard of living and in promoting national and social progress.

In other countries, especially in Alsace-Lorraine and Luxemburg, genocide in the economic field was carried out in a different manner. As the Luxemburgers are considered to be of related blood, opportunity is given them to recognize the Germanic elements in themselves, and to work for the strengthening of Germanism. If they do not take advantage of this "opportunity," their properties are taken from them and given to others who are eager to promote Germanism.

Participation in economic life is thus made dependent upon one's being German or being devoted to the cause of Germanism. Consequently, promoting a national ideology other than German is made difficult and dangerous.

Biological

In the occupied countries of "people of non-related blood," a policy of depopulation is pursued. Foremost among the methods employed for this purpose is the adoption of measures calculated to decrease the birthrate of the national groups of non-related blood, while at the same time steps are taken to encourage the birthrate of the *Volksdeutsche* living in these countries. Thus in incorporated Poland marriages between Poles are forbidden without the special permission of the Governor (*Reichsstatthalter*) of the district; and the latter, as a matter of principle, does not permit marriages between Poles.[23]

The birthrate of the undesired group is being further decreased as a result of the separation of males from females[24] by deporting them for forced labor elsewhere. Moreover, the undernourishment of the parents, because of discrimination in rationing, brings about not only a lowering of the birthrate, but a lowering of the survival capacity of children born of underfed parents.

As mentioned above, the occupant is endeavoring to encourage the birthrate of the Germans. Different methods are adopted to that end. Special subsidies are provided in Poland for German families having at least three minor children.[25] Because the Dutch and Norwegians are considered of related blood, the bearing, by Dutch and Norwegian women, of illegitimate children begotten by German military men is encouraged by subsidy.[26]

Other measures adopted are along the same lines. Thus the Reich Commissioner has vested in himself the right to act as a guardian or parent to a minor Dutch girl if she intends to marry a German.[27] The special care for legitimation of children in Luxemburg, as revealed in the order concerning changes in family law of March 22, 1941, is dictated by the desire to encourage extramarital procreation with Germans.

Physical

The physical debilitation and even annihilation of national groups in occupied countries is carried out mainly in the following ways.

1 *Racial Discrimination in Feeding.* Rationing of food is organized according to racial principles throughout the occupied countries. "The German people come before all other peoples for food," declared Reich Minister Göring on October 4, 1942.[28] In accordance with this program, the German population is getting 93 percent of its pre-war diet, while those in the occupied territories receive much less: in Warsaw, for example, the Poles receive 66 percent of the pre-war rations and the Jews only 20 percent.[29] The following shows the difference in the percentage of meat rations received by the Germans and the population of the occupied countries: Germans, 100 percent; Czechs, 86 percent; Dutch, 71 percent; Poles (Incorporated Poland), 71 percent; Lithuanians, 57 percent; French, 51 percent; Belgians, 40 percent; Serbs, 36 percent; Poles (General Government), 36 percent; Slovenes, 29 percent; Jews, 0 percent.[30]

The percentage of pre-war food received under present rations (in calories per consumer unit) is the following:[31] Germans, 93 percent; Czechs, 83 percent; Poles (Incorporated Poland), 78 percent; Dutch, 70 percent; Belgians, 66 percent; Poles (General Government), 66 percent; Norwegians, 54 percent; Jews, 20 percent.

As to the composition of food, the percentages of required basic nutrients received under present rations (per consumer unit) are as follows:[32]

Consumer Unit	*Carbohydrates* %	*Proteins* %	*Fats* %
Germans	100	97	77
Czechs	90	92	65
Dutch	84	95	65
Belgians.	79	73	29
Poles (Incorporated Poland)	76	85	49
Poles (General Government)	77	62	18
Norwegians.	69	65	32
French.	58	71	40
Greeks	38	38	1.14
Jews	27	20	0.32

The result of racial feeding is a decline in health of the nations involved and an increase in the deathrate. In Warsaw, anemia rose 113 percent among Poles and 435 among Jews.[33] The deathrate per thousand in 1941 amounted in the Netherlands to 10 percent; in Belgium to 14.5 percent; in Bohemia and Moravia to 13.4.[34] The Polish mortality in Warsaw in 1941 amounted in July to 1,316;[35] in August to 1,729;[36] and in September to 2,160.[37]

2 *Endangering of Health.* The undesired national groups, particularly in Poland, are deprived of elemental necessities for preserving health and life. This latter method consists, for example, of requisitioning warm clothing and blankets in the winter and withholding firewood and medicine. During the winter of 1940–1, only a single room in a house could be heated in the Warsaw ghetto, and children had to take turns in warming themselves there. No fuel at all has been received since then by the Jews in the ghetto.[38]

Moreover, the Jews in the ghetto are crowded together under conditions of housing inimical to health, and in being denied the use of public parks they are even deprived of the right to fresh air. Such measures, especially pernicious to the health of children, have caused the development of various diseases. The transfer, in unheated cattle trucks and freight cars, of hundreds of thousands of Poles from Incorporated Poland to the Government General, which took place in the midst of a severe winter, resulted in a decimation of the expelled Poles.

3 *Mass Killings.* The technique of mass killings is employed mainly against Poles, Russians, and Jews, as well as against leading personalities from among the non-collaborationist groups in all the occupied countries. In Poland, Bohemia-Moravia, and Slovenia, the intellectuals are being "liquidated" because they have always been considered as the main bearers of national ideals and at the time of occupation they were especially suspected of being the organizers of resistance. The Jews for the most part are liquidated within the ghettos,[39] in special trains in which they are transported to a so-called "unknown" destination. The number of Jews who have been killed by organized murder in all the occupied countries, according to the Institute of Jewish Affairs of the American Jewish Congress in New York, amounts to 1,702,500.[40]

Religious

In Luxemburg, where the population is predominantly Catholic and religion plays an important rôle in national life, especially in the field of education, the occupant has tried to disrupt these national and religious influences. Children over fourteen years of age were permitted by legislation to renounce their religious affiliations,[41] for the occupant was eager to enroll such children exclusively in pro-Nazi youth organizations. Moreover, in order to protect such children from public criticism, another law was issued at the same time imposing penalties ranging up to 15,000 Reichsmarks for any publication of names or any general announcement as to resignations from religious congregations.[42] Likewise in Poland, through the systematic pillage and destruction of church property and persecution of the clergy, the German occupying authorities have sought to destroy the religious leadership of the Polish nation.

Moral

In order to weaken the spiritual resistance of the national group, the occupant attempts to create an atmosphere of moral debasement within this group. According to this plan, the mental energy of the group should be concentrated upon base instincts and should be diverted from moral and national thinking. It is important for the realization of such a plan that the desire for cheap individual pleasure be substituted for the desire for collective feelings and ideals based upon a higher morality. Therefore, the occupant made an effort in Poland to impose upon the Poles pornographic publications and movies. The consumption of alcohol was encouraged, for while food prices have soared, the Germans have kept down the price of alcohol, and the peasants are compelled by the authorities to take spirits in payment for agricultural produce. The curfew law, enforced very strictly against Poles, is relaxed if they can show the authorities a ticket to one of the gambling houses which the Germans have allowed to come into existence.[43]

Recommendations for the Future

Prohibition of genocide in war and peace

The above-described techniques of genocide represent an elaborate, almost scientific, system developed to an extent never before achieved by any nation.[44] Hence the significance of genocide and the need to review international law in the light of the German practices of the present war. These practices have surpassed in their unscrupulous character any procedures or methods imagined a few decades ago by the framers of the Hague Regulations. Nobody at that time could conceive that an occupant would resort to the destruction of nations by barbarous practices reminiscent of the darkest pages of history. Hence, among other items covered by the Hague Regulations, there are only technical rules dealing with some (but by no means all) of the essential rights of individuals; and these rules do not take into consideration the interrelationship of such rights with the whole problem of nations subjected to virtual imprisonment. The Hague Regulations deal also with the sovereignty of a state, but they are silent regarding the preservation of the integrity of a people. However, the evolution of international law, particularly since the date of the Hague Regulations, has brought about a considerable interest in national groups as distinguished from states and individuals. National and religious groups were put under a special protection by the Treaty of Versailles and by specific minority treaties, when it became obvious that national minorities were compelled to live within the boundaries of states ruled by governments representing a majority of the population. The constitutions which were framed after 1918 also contain special provisions for the protection of the rights of national groups. Moreover, penal codes which were promulgated at that time provide for the protection of such groups, especially of their honor and reputation.

This trend is quite natural, when we conceive that nations are essential elements of the world community. The world represents only so much culture and intellectual vigor as are created by its component national groups.[45] Essentially the idea of a nation signifies constructive cooperation and original contributions, based upon genuine traditions, genuine culture, and a well-developed national psychology. The destruction of a nation, therefore, results in the loss of its future contributions to the world. Moreover, such destruction offends our feelings of morality and justice in much the same way as does the criminal killing of a human being: the crime in the one case as in the other is murder, though on a vastly greater scale. Among the basic features which have marked progress in civilization are the respect for and appreciation of the national characteristics and qualities contributed to world culture by the different nations – characteristics and qualities which, as illustrated in the contributions made by nations weak in defense and poor in economic resources, are not to be measured in terms of national power and wealth.

As far back as 1933, the author of the present work submitted to the Fifth International Conference for the Unification of Penal Law, held in Madrid in October of that year in cooperation with the Fifth Committee of the League of Nations, a report accompanied by draft articles to the effect that actions aiming at the destruction and oppression of populations (what would amount to the actual conception of genocide) should be penalized. The author formulated two new international law crimes to be introduced into the penal legislation of the thirty-seven participating countries, namely, the crime of *barbarity*, conceived as oppressive and destructive actions directed against individuals as members of a national, religious, or racial group, and the crime of *vandalism*, conceived as malicious destruction of works of art and culture because they represent the specific creations of the genius of such groups. Moreover, according to this draft these new crimes were to be internationalized to the extent that the offender should be punished when apprehended, either in his own country, if that was the situs of the crime, or in any other signatory country, if apprehended there.[46]

This principle of universal repression for genocide practices advocated by the author at the above-mentioned conference, had it been accepted by the conference and embodied in the form of an international convention duly signed and ratified by the countries there represented in 1933, would have made it possible, as early as that date, to indict persons who had been found guilty of such criminal acts whenever they appeared on the territory of one of the signatory countries. Moreover, such a project, had it been adopted at that time by the participating countries, would prove useful now by providing an effective instrument for the punishment of war criminals of the present world conflict. It must be emphasized again that the proposals of the author at the Madrid Conference embraced criminal actions which, according to the view of the author, would cover in great part the fields in which crimes have been committed in this war by the members of the Axis Powers. Furthermore, the adoption of the principle of universal repression as adapted to genocide by countries which belong now to the group of non-belligerents or neutrals, respectively, would likewise bind these latter countries to punish the war criminals engaged in genocide or to extradite them to the countries in which these crimes were committed. If the punishment of genocide practices had formed a part of international law in such countries since 1933, there would be no necessity now to issue admonitions to neutral countries not to give refuge to war criminals.[47]

It will be advisable in the light of these observations to consider the place of genocide in the present and future international law. Genocide is, as we have noted, a composite of different acts of persecution or destruction. Many of those acts, when they constitute an infringement upon honor and rights, when they are a transgression against life, private property and religion, or science and art, or even when they encroach unduly in the fields of taxation and personal services, are prohibited by Articles 46, 48, 52, and 56 of the Hague Regulations. Several of them, such as those which cause humiliations, debilitation by undernourishment, and danger to health, are in violation of the laws of humanity as specified in the preamble to the Hague Regulations. But other acts falling within the purview of genocide, such as, for example, subsidizing children begotten by members of the armed forces of the occupant and born of women nationals of the occupied area, as well as various ingenious measures for weakening or destroying political, social, and cultural elements in national groups, are not expressly prohibited by the Hague Regulations. The entire problem of genocide needs to be dealt with as a whole; it is too important to be left for piecemeal discussion and solution in the future. Many hope that there will be no more wars, but we dare not rely on mere hopes for protection against genocidal practices by ruthless conquerors. Therefore, without ceasing in our endeavors to make this the last war, we must see to it that the Hague Regulations are so amended as expressly to prohibit genocide in any war which may occur in the future. *De lege ferenda*, the definition of genocide in the Hague Regulations thus amended should consist of two essential parts: in the first should be included every action infringing upon the life, liberty, health, corporal integrity, economic existence, and the honor of the inhabitants when committed because they belong to a national, religious, or racial group; and in the second, every policy aiming at the destruction or the aggrandizement of one of such groups to the prejudice or detriment of another.

Moreover, we should not overlook the fact that genocide is a problem not only of war but also of peace. It is an especially important problem for Europe, where differentiation in nationhood is so marked that despite the principle of political and territorial self-determination, certain national groups may be obliged to live as minorities within the boundaries of other states. If these groups should not be adequately protected, such lack of protection would result in international disturbances, especially in the form of disorganized emigration of the persecuted, who would look for refuge elsewhere.[48] That being the case, all countries must be concerned about such a problem, not only because of humanitarian, but also because of practical, reasons affecting the interest of every country. The system of legal protection of minorities adopted in the past, which was based mainly on international treaties and the constitutions of the respective countries, proved to be inadequate because not every European country had a sufficient judicial machinery for the enforcement of its constitution. It may be said, in fact, that the European countries had a more efficient machinery for enforcing civil and criminal law than for enforcing constitutional law. Genocide being of such great importance, its repression must be based not only on international and constitutional law but also on the criminal law of the various countries. The procedure to be adopted in the future with respect to this matter should be as follows.

An international multilateral treaty should provide for the introduction, not only in the constitution but also in the criminal code of each country, of provisions protecting minority groups from oppression because of their nationhood, religion, or race. Each criminal code should have provisions inflicting penalties for genocide practices. In order to prevent the invocation of the plea of superior orders, the liability of persons who *order* genocide practices, as well as of persons who *execute* such orders, should be provided expressly by the criminal codes of the respective countries. Because of the special implications of genocide in international relations, the principle of universal repression should be adopted for the crime of genocide. According to this principle, the culprit should be liable to trial not only in the country in which he committed the crime, but also, in the event of his escape therefrom, in any other country in which he might have taken refuge.[49] In this respect, genocide offenders should be subject to the principle of universal repression in the same way as other offenders guilty of the so-called *delicta juris gentium* (such as, for example, white slavery and trade in children, piracy, trade in narcotics and in obscene publications, and counterfeiting of money).[50] Indeed, genocide should be added to the list of *delicta juris gentium*.[51]

International control of occupation practices

Genocide as described above presents one of the most complete and glaring illustrations of the violation of international law and the laws of humanity. In its several manifestations genocide also represents a violation of specific regulations of the Hague Convention such as those regarding the protection of property, life, and honor. It is therefore essential that genocide procedures be not only prohibited by law but prevented in practice during military occupation.

In another important field, that of the treatment of prisoners of war, international controls have been established in order to ascertain whether prisoners are treated in accordance with the rules of international law (see Articles 86 to 88 of the Convention concerning the Treatment of Prisoners of War, of July 27, 1929).[52] But the fate of nations in prison, of helpless women and children, has apparently not seemed to be so important as to call for supervision of the occupational authorities. Whereas concerning prisoners of war the public is able to obtain exact information, the lack of direct-witness reports on the situation of groups of population under occupation gravely hampers measures for their assistance and rescue from what may be inhumane and intolerable conditions. Information and reports which slip out from behind the frontiers of occupied countries are very often labeled as untrustworthy atrocity stories because they are so gruesome that people simply refuse to believe them. Therefore, the Regulations of the Hague Convention should be modified to include an international controlling agency vested with specific powers, such as visiting the occupied countries and making inquiries as to the manner in which the occupant treats nations in prison. In the situation as it exists at present there is no means of providing for alleviation of the treatment of populations under occupation until the actual moment of liberation. It is then too late for remedies, for after liberation such populations can at best obtain only reparation of damages but never restoration of those values which have been destroyed and which cannot be restored, such as human life, treasures of art, and historical archives.

NOTES

1 Another term could be used for the same idea, namely, *ethnocide*, consisting of the Greek word "ethnos" – nation – and the Latin word "cide."

2 See *Violation of the Laws and Customs of War: Reports of Majority and Dissenting Reports of American and Japanese Members of the Commission of Responsibilities, Conference of Paris, 1919*, Carnegie Endowment for International Peace, Division of International Law, Pamphlet No. 32 (Oxford: Clarendon Press, 1919), p. 39.

3 See Garner, op. cit., Vol. I, p. 77.

4 As classical examples of wars of extermination in which nations and groups of the population were completely or almost completely destroyed, the following may be cited: the destruction of Carthage in 146 BC; the destruction of Jerusalem by Titus in 72 AD; the religious wars of Islam and the Crusades; the massacres of the Albigenses and the Waldenses; and the siege of Magdeburg in the Thirty Years' War. Special wholesale massacres occurred in the wars waged by Genghis Khan and by Tamerlane.

5 "Since the State in itself is for us only a form, while what is essential is its content, the nation, the people, it is clear that everything else must subordinate itself to its sovereign interests." (Adolf Hitler, *Mein Kampf* [New York: Reynal & Hitchcock, 1939], p. 842.)

6 See Alfred Rosenberg, *Der Mythus des 20. Jahrhunderts* (Munich: Hoheneichenverlag, 1935), pp. 1–2: "History and the mission of the future no longer mean the struggle of class against class, the struggle of Church dogma against dogma, but the clash between blood and blood, race and race, people and people."

7 The German genocide philosophy was conceived and put into action before the Germans received even a foretaste of the considerable dimensions of Allied aerial bombings of German territory.

8 See Hitler's statement to Rauschning, from *The Voice of Destruction*, by Hermann Rauschning (New York, 1940), p. 138, by courtesy of G. P. Putnam's Sons: "...The French complained after the war that there were twenty million Germans too many. We accept the criticism. We favor the planned control of population movements. But our friends will have to excuse us if we subtract the twenty millions elsewhere. After all these centuries of whining about the protection of the poor and lowly, it is about time we decided to protect the strong against the inferior. It will be one of the chief tasks of German statesmanship for all time to prevent, by every means in our power, the further increase of the Slav races. Natural instincts bid all living beings not merely conquer their enemies, but also destroy them. In former days, it was the victor's prerogative to destroy entire tribes, entire peoples. By doing this gradually and without bloodshed, we demonstrate our humanity. We should remember, too, that we are merely doing unto others as they would have done to us."

9 *Mein Kampf*, p. 588.

10 *Mein Kampf*, p. 931: "...the National Socialist movement has its mightiest tasks to fulfill:... it must condemn to general wrath the evil enemy of humanity [Jews] as the true creator of all suffering."

11 Ibid., p. 590, n. "...The Polish policy in the sense of a Germanization of the East, demanded by so many, rooted unfortunately almost always in the same wrong conclusion. Here too one believed that one could bring about a Germanization of the Polish element by a purely linguistic integration into the German nationality. Here too the result would have been an unfortunate one: people of an alien race, expressing its alien thoughts in the German language, compromising the height and the dignity of our own nationality by its own inferiority." As to the depopulation policy in occupied Yugoslavia, see, in general, Louis Adamic, *My Native Land* (New York: Harper & Brothers, 1943).

12 For Luxemburg, see order of August 6, 1940.

13 See order concerning the change of first and family names in Luxemburg, of January 31, 1941.

14 *Verordnungsblatt*, 1940, p. 60.

15 As to Poland, see order of October 29, 1941.

16 As to Norway, see order of September 25, 1940.

17 "It is the task of the director to orient and conduct the school systematically according to National Socialist principles." See announcement for execution of the order concerning the elementary school system, February 14, 1941, promulgated in Lorraine by the Chief of Civil Administration.

18 *Verordnungsblatt*, 1941, p. 100.

19 As to organization of the Reich Chamber of Culture, see law of November 1, 1933, *Reichsgesetzblatt*, 1, p. 979.

20 See note of the Polish Minister of Foreign Affairs of the Polish Government-in-Exile to the Allied and neutral powers of May 3, 1941, in *Polish White Book*: Republic of Poland, Ministry of Foreign Affairs, *German Occupation of Poland – Extract of Note Addressed to the Allied and Neutral Powers* (New York: The Greystone Press [1942]), pp. 36–9.

21 *Frankfurter Zeitung*, Wochen-Ausgabe, March 28, 1941.

22 See ordinance promulgated by the German Trustee of the Polish Savings Bank published in *Thorner Freiheit* of December 11, 1940.

23 See Report of Primate of Poznań to Pius XII, *The Black Book of Poland* (New York: G. P. Putnam's Sons, 1942), p. 383.

24 That the separation of males from females was preconceived by Hitler as an element of genocide is obvious from his statement: "'*We are obliged to depopulate*,' he went on emphatically, 'as part of our mission of preserving the German population. We shall have to develop a technique of depopulation. If you ask me what I mean by depopulation, I mean the removal of entire racial units. And that is what I intend to carry out – that, roughly, is my task. Nature is cruel, therefore we, too, may be cruel. If I can send the flower of the German nation into the hell of war without the smallest pity for the spilling of precious German blood, then surely I have the right to remove millions of an inferior race that breeds like vermin! And by "remove" I don't necessarily mean destroy; I shall simply take systematic measures to dam their great natural fertility. For example, I shall keep their men and women separated for years. Do you remember the falling birthrate of the world war? Why should we not do quite consciously and through a number of years what was at that time merely the inevitable consequence of the long war? There are many ways, systematical and comparatively painless, or at any rate bloodless, of causing undesirable races to die out.'" (Rauschning, op. cit., pp. 137–8, by courtesy of G. P. Putnam's Sons.)

25 See order concerning the granting of child subsidies to Germans in the Government General, of March 10, 1942.

26 See order of July 28, 1942, concerning the subsidizing of children of members of the German armed forces in occupied territories, *Reichsgesetzblatt*, 1942, 1, p. 488: "To maintain and promote a racially valuable German heritage, children begotten by members of the German armed forces in the occupied Norwegian and Dutch territories and born of Norwegian or Dutch women will upon the application of the mother be granted a special subsidy and benefit through the offices of the Reich Commissioners for the occupied Norwegian and Dutch territories."

27 See order of February 28, 1941.

28 See *New York Times*, October 5, 1942, p. 4, col. 6.

29 The figures quoted in this and the following two paragraphs have been taken, with the permission of the Institute of Jewish Affairs, from its publication entitled *Starvation over*

Europe (Made in Germany); A Documented Record, 1943 (New York, 1943), pp. 37, 47, 52.

30 Ibid., p. 37.

31 Ibid., p. 47.

32 Ibid., p. 52. For further details, see League of Nations, *World Economic Survey* (Geneva, 1942), pp. 90–1.

33 See *Hitler's Ten-Year War on the Jews* (Institute of Jewish Affairs of the American Jewish Congress, World Jewish Congress, New York, 1943), p. 144.

34 League of Nations, *Monthly Bulletin of Statistics* (Geneva, 1942), Nos. 4, 5, 6.

35 *Nowy Kurjer Warszawski* (Warsaw), August 29, 1941.

36 *Die Nation* (Bern), August 13, 1942.

37 *Poland Fights* (New York), May 16, 1942.

38 *Hitler's Ten-Year War on the Jews*, p. 144.

39 See the Joint Declaration by members of the United Nations, issued simultaneously in Washington and in London, on December 17, 1942: "The attention of the Belgian, Czechoslovak, Greek, Jugoslav, Luxembourg, Netherlands, Norwegian, Polish, Soviet, United Kingdom and United States Governments and also of the French National Committee has been drawn to numerous reports from Europe that the German authorities, not content with denying to persons of Jewish race in all the territories over which their barbarous rule has been extended, the most elementary human rights, are now carrying into effect Hitler's oft-repeated intention to exterminate the Jewish people in Europe.

"From all the occupied countries Jews are being transported in conditions of appalling horror and brutality to Eastern Europe. In Poland, which has been made the principal Nazi slaughterhouse, the ghettos established by the German invader are being systematically emptied of all Jews except a few highly skilled workers required for war industries. None of those taken away are ever heard of again. The able-bodied are slowly worked to death in labor camps. The infirm are left to die of exposure and starvation or are deliberately massacred in mass executions. The number of victims of these bloody cruelties is reckoned in many hundreds of thousands of entirely innocent men, women and children.

"The above-mentioned governments and the French National Committee condemn in the strongest possible terms this bestial policy of cold-blooded extermination. They declare that such events can only strengthen the resolve of all freedom-loving peoples to overthrow the barbarous Hitlerite tyranny. They reaffirm their solemn resolution to insure that those responsible for these crimes shall not escape retribution, and to press on with the necessary practical measures to this end." (*The United Nations Review*, Vol. III [1943], No. I, p. 1.)

40 *Hitler's Ten-Year War on the Jews*, p. 307.

41 See order of December 9, 1940.

42 Ibid.

43 Under Polish law, 1919–39, gambling houses were prohibited; nor did they exist on Polish soil when it was under Russian, German, and Austrian rule before 1914. See *The Black Book of Poland*, pp. 513, 514.

44 "No conqueror has ever chosen more diabolical methods for gaining the mastery of the soul and body of a people." (*Manchester Guardian*, February 28, 1941.)

"We know that there is no war in all our history where such ruthless and deliberate steps have been taken for the disintegration of civilian life and the suffering and the death of civilian populations." (Hugh R. Jackson, Special Assistant to the Director of Foreign Relief and Rehabilitation Operations, US Department of State, in an address before the

National Conference of Social Work, New York, March 12, 1943; printed in Department of State, *Bulletin*, Vol. VIII, No. 194 [March 13, 1943], p. 219.)

45 The idea of a nation should not, however, be confused with the idea of nationalism. To do so would be to make the same mistake as confusing the idea of individual liberty with that of egoism.

46 See Raphaël Lemkin, "Terrorisme," *Actes de la Ve Conférence Internationale pour l' Unification du Droit Pénal* (Paris, 1935), pp. 48–56; see also Lemkin, "Akte der Barbarei und des Vandalismus als *delicta iuris gentium*," *Internationales Anwaltsblatt* (Vienna, November, 1933).

47 See statement of President Roosevelt, *White House Press Release*, July 30, 1943, Department of State, *Bulletin*, Vol. IX, No. 214 (July 31, 1943), p. 62.

48 Adequate protection of minority groups does not of course mean that protective measures should be so stringent as to prevent those who so desire from leaving such groups in order to join majority groups. In other words, minority protection should not constitute a barrier to the gradual process of assimilation and integration which may result from such voluntary transfer of individuals.

49 Of course such an offender could never be tried twice for the same act.

50 Research in International Law (Under the Auspices of the Faculty of Harvard Law School), "Part II. Jurisdiction with Respect to Crime" (Edwin D. Dickinson, Reporter), *American Journal of International Law, Supp.*, Vol. 29 (1935), pp. 573–85.

51 Since not all countries agree to the principle of universal repression (as for example the United States of America), the future treaty on genocide might well provide a facultative clause for the countries which do not adhere to this principle.

52 League of Nations, *Treaty Series*, Vol. 118, p. 343.

REFERENCES

Adamic, Louis (1943). *My Native Land*. New York: Harper and Brothers.

Garner, James W. (1920). *International Law and the World War*. Vol. II. New York: Longmans, Green and Co.

Lemkin, Raphaël (1933). "Akte der Barbarei und des Vandalismus als *delicta iuris gentium*." *Internationales Anwaltsblatt* (Vienna, November).

Lemkin, Raphaël (1935). "Terrorisme. Rapport et projet de textes." *Actes de la Ve Conférence Internationale pour l'Unification du Droit Pénal*. Paris: Editions A. Pedone, p. 48.

2

Text of the UN Genocide Convention

The Contracting Parties

Having considered the declaration made by the General Assembly of the United Nations in its resolution 96 (1) dated 11 December 1946 that genocide is a crime under international law, contrary to the spirit and aims of the United Nations and condemned by the civilized world;

Recognizing that at all periods of history genocide has inflicted great losses on humanity; and

Being convinced that, in order to liberate mankind from such an odious scourge, international cooperation is required;

Hereby agree as hereinafter provided

Article I

The Contracting Parties confirm that genocide whether committed in time of peace or in time of war, is a crime under international law which they undertake to prevent and to punish.

Article II

In the present Convention, genocide means any of the following acts committed with intent to destroy, in whole or in part, a national, ethnical, racial or religious group, as such:

(a) Killing members of the group;
(b) Causing serious bodily or mental harm to members of the group;
(c) Deliberately inflicting on the group conditions of life calculated to bring about its physical destruction in whole or in part;
(d) Imposing measures intended to prevent births within the group;
(e) Forcibly transferring children of the group to another group.

Article III

The following acts shall be punishable:

(a) Genocide;
(b) Conspiracy to commit genocide;
(c) Direct and public incitement to commit genocide;
(d) Attempt to commit genocide;
(e) Complicity in genocide.

Article IV

Persons committing genocide or any of the other acts enumerated in article III shall be punished, whether they are constitutionally responsible rulers, public officials or private individuals.

Article V

The Contracting Parties undertake to enact, in accordance with their respective Constitutions, the necessary legislation to give effect to the provisions of the present Convention and, in particular, to provide effective penalties for persons guilty of genocide or any of the other acts enumerated in article III.

Article VI

Persons charged with genocide or any of the other acts enumerated in article III shall be tried by a competent tribunal of the State in the territory of which the act was committed, or by such international penal tribunal as may have jurisdiction with respect to those Contracting Parties which shall have accepted its jurisdiction.

Article VII

Genocide and other acts enumerated in article III shall not be considered as political crimes for the purpose of extradition.

The Contracting Parties pledge themselves in such cases to grant extradition in accordance with their laws and treaties in force.

Article VIII

Any Contracting Party may call upon the competent organs of the United Nations to take such action under the Charter of the United Nations as they consider appropriate for the prevention and suppression of acts of genocide or any of the other acts enumerated in article III.

Article IX

Disputes between the Contracting Parties relating to the interpretation, application or fulfillment of the present Convention, including those relating to the responsibility of a State for genocide or any of the other acts enumerated in article III, shall be submitted to the International Court of Justice at the request of any of the parties to the dispute.

Article X

The present Convention, of which the Chinese, English, French, Russian, and Spanish texts are equally authentic, shall bear the date of 9 December 1948.

Article XI

The present Convention shall be open until 31 December 1949 for signature on behalf of any Member of the United Nations and of any non-member State to which an invitation to sign has been addressed by the General Assembly.

The present Convention shall be ratified, and the instruments of ratification shall be deposited with the Secretary-General of the United Nations.

After January 1950, the present Convention may be acceded to on behalf of any Member of the United Nations and of any non-member State which has received an invitation as aforesaid.

Instruments of accession shall be deposited with the Secretary-General of the United Nations.

Article XII

Any Contracting Party may at any time by notification addressed to the Secretary-General of the United Nations, extend the application of the present Convention to all or any of the territory for the conduct of whose foreign relations that Contracting Party is responsible.

Article XIII

On the day when the first twenty instruments of ratification or accession have been deposited, the Secretary-General shall draw up a *procès-verbal* and transmit a copy of it to each Member of the United Nations and to each of the non-member States contemplated in article XI.

The present Convention shall come into force on the ninetieth day following the date of deposit of the twentieth instrument of ratification or accession.

Any ratification or accession effected subsequent to the latter date shall become effective on the ninetieth day following the deposit of the instrument of ratification or accession.

Article XIV

The present Convention shall remain in effect for a period of ten years as from the date of its coming into force.

It shall thereafter remain in force for successive periods of five years for such Contracting Parties as have not denounced it at least six months before the expiration of the current period.

Denunciation shall be effected by a written notification addressed to the Secretary-General of the United Nations.

Article XV

If, as a result of denunciations, the number of Parties to the present Convention should become less than sixteen, the Convention shall cease to be in force as from the date on which the last of these denunciations shall become effective.

Article XVI

A request for the revision of the present Convention may be made at any time by any Contracting Party by means of a notification in writing addressed to the Secretary-General.

The General Assembly shall decide upon the steps, if any, to be taken in respect of such request.

Article XVII

The Secretary-General of the United Nations shall notify all Members of the United Nations and the non-member States contemplated in article XI of the following:

(a) Signatures, ratifications, and accessions received in accordance with article XI;
(b) Notifications received in accordance with article XII;
(c) The date upon which the present Convention comes into force in accordance with article XIII;
(d) Denunciations received in accordance with article XIV;
(e) The abrogation of the Convention in accordance with article XV;
(f) Notifications received in accordance with article XVI.

Article XVIII

The original of the present Convention shall be deposited in the archives of the United Nations.

A certified copy of the Convention shall be transmitted to all Members of the United Nations and to the non-member States contemplated in article XI.

Article XIX

The present Convention shall be registered by the Secretary-General of the United Nations on the date of its coming into force.

3

Genocide: Its Political Use in the Twentieth Century

Leo Kuper

"An Odious Scourge"

The word is new, the crime ancient. The preamble to the Convention on Genocide, approved by the General Assembly of the United Nations in December 1948, describes genocide as an odious scourge which has inflicted great losses on humanity in all periods of history.

One recalls the more horrifying genocidal massacres, such as the terror of Assyrian warfare in the eighth and seventh centuries BC, when many cities were razed to the ground and whole populations carried off or brutally exterminated, until the Assyrian empire itself became the victim of its own wars of annihilation; or the destruction of Troy and its defenders, and the carrying off into slavery of the women (as described in the legendary accounts and the Greek tragedies which have come down to us); or the Roman obliteration of Carthage, men, women, and children, the site of the devastated city sown with salt, symbolic of desolation.

But the razing of cities and the slaughter of peoples were not isolated episodes in ancient times. One has only to refer to accounts of the many genocidal conflicts in the Bible and in the chronicles of Greek and Roman historians. However, when Hannah Arendt[1] writes that massacres of whole peoples were the order of the day in antiquity, she cannot have meant that this was the rule or the norm in warfare or conquest. Many circumstances affected the final outcome. Though it was common enough practice to destroy besieged cities and to slaughter their inhabitants, or their male defenders while taking the women and children into slavery, a city which surrendered might be spared this genocidal fate, and in exceptional cases, mercy might even be extended to a city taken by assault.[2]

The names of Genghis Khan and of Timur Lenk have become synonyms for the genocides of a later period. Of Genghis Khan, the Scourge of God, Lamb writes that when he marched with his horde, it was over degrees of latitude and longitude instead of miles; cities in his path were often obliterated, and rivers diverted from their courses; deserts were peopled with the fleeing and dying, and when he had passed, wolves and ravens often were the sole living things in once populous lands.[3]

As to Timur Lenk (Tamerlane), for the vast majority of those to whom the name means anything at all,

it commemorates a militarist who perpetrated as many horrors in the span of twenty-four years as the last five Assyrian kings perpetrated in a hundred and twenty. We think of the monster who razed Isfarā'in to the ground in A.D. 1381; built 2,000 prisoners into a living mound and then bricked them over at Sabzawār in 1383; piled 5,000 heads into minarets at Zirih in the same year; cast his Lūrī prisoners alive over precipices in 1386; massacred 70,000 people and piled the heads of the slain into minarets at Isfahan in 1387; massacred 100,000 prisoners at Delhi in 1398; buried alive 4,000 Christian soldiers of the garrison of Sivas after their capitulation in 1400; and built twenty towers of skulls in Syria in 1400 and 1401.[4]

Again, these were not isolated actors and events in the history of genocide; the war practices of "civilized" peoples in the Middle Ages were often marked by genocidal massacres.[5]

Meanwhile, the wars of religion had already started. They were of course a feature of ancient history, and they continue into our own times. They are merely one form in which the tyranny of an idea becomes charged with genocidal potential. Probably religious ideas do not often act in purity, being generally compounded with other motivations – struggles for power and for possessions, or destructive fury unleashed by threatening events. The religious differences however may indeed be the driving force in genocidal conflict, or they may define the lines along which other conflicts erupt. There may be religious authority for genocide, and even when genocide runs counter to the theology, the warrant for genocide may be found in religious praxis, with religious zeal supplying the fuel for genocide.

The Crusades against the Muslim "infidel" and for the recovery of the holy places almost all started with pogroms against Jews. The first armies of Crusaders did no special harm to the Jews, they plundered Christians and Jews alike; but the hordes that followed "began the holy work of plundering and murdering with the Jews."[6] And the course of the Crusades was marked by the slaughter of Jewish communities. Thus, when the crusading army had finally taken Jerusalem by storm in the year 1099 and had massacred the Muslims, they drove the Jews into a synagogue, set fire to it and burnt all within its walls.[7] At times, Jews were able to offer effective resistance, or they were protected by rulers and by churchmen, or became converts to Christianity; at other times, rather than fall into the hands of the crusaders, whose piety sanctified murder and pillage, they took refuge in mass suicide.

It was not only the Crusades which unleashed these attacks. The Inquisition engaged massively in holy murder. Indeed, whatever the religious conflict, it served as license for the slaughter of Jews. In the suppression of the Christian Albigensian sect in southern France, Jews in that region inevitably suffered with the members of the sect. When the city of Béziers was stormed in AD 1209, the crusading army, organized at the instigation of the Pope and the monk Arnold of Cîteaux, spared "neither dignity, nor sex nor age, nearly 20,000 human beings have perished by the sword . . . After the massacre the town was plundered and burnt, and the revenge of God seemed to rage upon it in a wonderful manner."[8] Since even orthodox Catholics were not spared ("Strike down; God will recognize His own"), there was little reason for indulgence to Jews. In the fifteenth century, Jews were massacred in the suppression of the Hussite sect; and the Crusaders (the German imperial army) threatened, on their return from victory over the Hussites, to wipe the Jewish people from the face of the earth.[9]

Quite apart from religious conflicts, or religious occasions such as Easter, almost any catastrophe might set off massacres of Jews. Thus they were charged with responsibility for the Black Death which ravaged Europe in the fourteenth century, and large numbers of Jewish communities were annihilated, notwithstanding opposition from the Pope, some European rulers, and city councils.[10] It is startling to find within Christian practice in the period of the Crusades, the Inquisition, and the religious wars, all the elements in the major genocide of our day, that of the Nazis against the Jews. There were the laws corresponding to the Nuremberg laws, there were the distinguishing badges, the theory of a Jewish conspiracy, appointed centers of annihilation corresponding to Auschwitz, and some systematic organization, with the Dominican friars for example providing the professional expertise and the bureaucratic cadres in the Inquisition.

The massacre of Jews, however, was quite peripheral to the main religious conflicts between Christians and Muslims, and between Catholics and Protestants. Many genocidal massacres marked the course of these conflicts, which culminated in the persecution of the Huguenots in France and in the Thirty Years' War in Germany. The Massacre of Saint Bartholomew in 1572 and the great exodus from France following the revocation of the Edict of Nantes, stand out in the France following the revocation of the Edict of Nantes, stand out in the tragic history of the Huguenots. The Thirty Years' War in the seventeenth century has always seemed the symbol of the extreme devastation wrought by the unbridled passions of religious conflict. It is generally regarded as dividing "the period of religious wars from that of national wars, the ideological wars from the wars of mere aggression. But the demarcation is as artificial as such arbitrary divisions commonly are. Aggression, dynastic ambition and fanaticism are all alike present in the hazy background behind the reality of the war, and the last of the wars of religion merged insensibly into the pseudo-national wars of the future."[11] In any event, the ideological wars, including religious wars, are very characteristic of the contemporary world.

In our own era, there are the genocidal conflicts linked to the march of colonization and to the process of decolonization. The tyranny of faith persists as a source of genocidal conflict, but more often in the form of political ideology rather than religious belief. Advanced technology facilitates the obliteration of whole communities in the course of international warfare. But the major arena for contemporary genocidal conflict and massacre is to be found within the sovereign state: it is particularly a phenomenon of the plural society.

In much contemporary writing on colonization, especially radical writing, there is a tendency to equate colonization with genocide. This is a conception expressed by Sartre[12] in his indictment of the USA on a charge of genocide in Vietnam. He writes that since the blatant aggression of colonial conquests kindles the hatred of the civilian population, and since the civilians are potentially rebels and soldiers, the colonial troops maintain their authority by perpetual massacres. These are aimed at the destruction "of part of an ethnic, national, or religious group," so as to terrorize the remainder and wrench apart the indigenous society; they are thus genocidal in characters. Sartre introduces the qualification that in situations where there is an infra-structural contradiction arising from the dependence of the colonizers on the labor of the colonized, there are restraints on the extent of the physical destruction of local populations. He introduces no such qualification in his description of colonization as by its very nature an act of cultural genocide: colonization, he argues, cannot take place without systematically liquidating all the characteristics of the native society.

This is a quite unbalanced perspective. If Dakar, the capital of Senegal, suggests a French provincial town, the visitor is under no illusion as he moves round Dakar and into the interior that he is moving among French provincials. If he visits Uganda, he cannot really believe that he is in the English countryside and meeting with the rather curious English locals: nor does Calcutta remind him of Liverpool or Manchester or indeed of any English city whatsoever. He finds himself, in previously colonized countries, in the presence of vigorous indigenous cultures. Culture change, borrowing of items of culture, transformation of institutions – these do not constitute cultural genocide. If one is thinking of the intention to commit cultural genocide, then the term should be reserved for a deliberate policy to eliminate a culture: there are indeed many examples of this intent in the history of colonization, but it is certainly not a universal feature of colonization. If however one is thinking of the actual extinction of a culture, then this is a less common phenomenon, and I would suppose that it is only effected by the physical extinction of the bearers of the culture or their absorption into another group.

So, too, it is overstated to equate colonization with physical genocide. The issue of decolonization could not arise in countries where there had been extensive genocide, and much of colonization has proceeded without genocidal conflict. But certainly the course of colonization has been marked all too often by genocide. In the colonization of North and South America, the West Indies, Australia, and Tasmania, many native peoples were wiped out, sometimes as a result of wars and massacres, or of disease and ecological change, at other times by deliberate policies of extermination.

Moreover, where a somewhat enduring relationship between colonizer and colonized is established, the situation may still be conducive to genocidal massacre. The relationship may be deeply charged with conflict from its inception in an extremely brutal conquest, as in the French conquest of Algeria, with its massacres and other atrocities, and its deliberate destruction of homes and orchards – the ravaging of a land and its people. The struggle to impose and maintain political control is generally accompanied by appropriation of land and other productive resources, giving rise to systematic political and economic exploitation, supported by justifying ideologies. This may have the effect of separating colonizer and colonized into almost distinct species, thereby encouraging extremes of violence. Revolts, or even riots, were often suppressed with great destruction of life and property, or by admonitory massacres. The slaughter of the Herero by the German rulers of South West Africa in 1904 was among the most exterminatory and horrifying of the reprisals for rebellion.

If the religious war is not a major contemporary phenomenon, religious differences have nevertheless been the basis of division in a number of twentieth-century genocides and genocidal conflicts. There were religious differences in the Turkish genocide against Armenians during the First World War and in the genocidal pogroms in the Ukraine at the end of the war. These genocides were followed in the Second World War by the German genocide against Jews. At the end of the Second World War, the partition of India resulted in a genocidal conflict, as an estimated ten million Hindus, Sikhs, and Muslims changed lands, approximately one million never reaching their promised land alive. While a boundary force, largely infected with communal fever, stayed for the most part in barracks, cleaning weapons and boots, "trainloads of Sikh refugees moving east were slaughtered by Muslims in Pakistan and Muslims headed west were butchered by Sikhs and Hindus in India."[13] In 1975 and 1976, there was the genocidal conflict in Lebanon, a conflict powered by many different social forces, but appreciably mobilizing Christians and Muslims in enemy camps.[14] And can one doubt the possibility in the Middle East of a genocidal conflict, colored by religious difference, with an international component chillingly reminiscent of the Nazi era.

However, the role of religious ideas as warrant for, or stimulus to, genocide, has now been taken over by totalitarian political ideologies, of absolute commitment to the remaking of society in conformity with radical specifications, and a rooting out of dissent, as extreme as in the Inquisition. The major examples of the genocidal potentialities of these ideologies in our day are provided by the Nazi regime with its conception of a brave new world of racially tolerated and ordered societies under German hegemony; the Soviet regime, under Stalin, with the Gulag Archipelago receiving, as a sort of "rubbish bin of history," the successive blood sacrifices of the communist utopia; and the recent Pol Pot regime in Cambodia, freely and righteously exterminating in total dedication to a starkly elemental blueprint for living.

In international warfare, technological change facilitates genocidal massacre, as in the bombing of Hiroshima and Nagasaki. An American marine serving in the Vietnam War comments that battlefield "ethics seemed to be a matter of distance and technology. You could never go wrong if you killed people at long range with sophisticated weapons."[15] And the long-range, sophisticated weapons encourage a sort of egalitarian approach to slaughter, drawing no distinction between combatants and non-combatants, the able-bodied and the infirm, the old and the young. While the sheer destructiveness of nuclear warfare imposes restraint on the great powers in the use of this ultimate weapon, no such restraint seems to operate against the use of the more conventional weapons of their advanced technological armoury. If the great powers do not themselves directly engage in the internal conflicts of smaller nations, as the Americans did in Vietnam, they do not hesitate to supply the contending parties with the sophisticated arms for mutual annihilation.

Many of the genocidal conflicts referred to in these pages are internal to the sovereign state. They are particularly a phenomenon of the plural or divided society, in which division persists between peoples of different race or ethnic group or religion, who have been brought together in the same political unit. Colonization, in its arbitrary delineation of metropolitan domains, has been a great creator of plural societies, and there have been many genocides in the process of decolonization or as an early aftermath of decolonization. The struggles for power between Hutu and Tutsi in Rwanda and in Burundi, and between mainland Africans and Arabs in Zanzibar, became genocidal. Partition, as in India, and repression of secessionary movements, as in Bangladesh, and some would say as in Nigeria, have taken a genocidal form.

It is a massive toll of genocidal conflict, if one adds to the civil wars of decolonization, the destruction of scapegoat groups, and the ideological, ethnic, and religious massacres. And it is a particularly threatening scourage of our day and age, facilitated by international concern for the protection of the sovereign rights of the state, by international intervention in the arming of contending sections, and by United Nations *de facto* condonation, which serves as a screen for genocide.

The Genocide Convention

It was a complete delusion to suppose that the adoption of a convention of the type proposed, even if generally adhered to, would give people a greater sense of security or would diminish existing dangers of persecution on racial, religious or national grounds. (Sir Hartley Shawcross, representative of the United Kingdom, in the debate on the Genocide Convention [United Nations General Assembly, Legal Committee, *Summary Records and Annexes*, Session 3, Part 1, Sept.–Dec. 1948, 17])

The Convention on Genocide, approved by the General Assembly of the United Nations on 9 December 1948, defines the crime of genocide as follows:

In the present Convention, genocide means any of the following acts committed with intent to destroy, in whole or in part, a national, ethnical, racial or religious group, as such:

(a) Killing members of the group;
(b) Causing serious bodily or mental harm to members of the group;
(c) Deliberately inflicting on the group conditions of life calculated to bring about its physical destruction in whole or in part;
(d) Imposing measures intended to prevent births within the group;
(e) Forcibly transferring children of the group to another group.

Prior to the Convention, the right of humanitarian intervention on behalf of populations persecuted in a manner shocking to mankind had long been considered part of the law of nations. Giving judgment in one of the Nuremberg trials of Nazi war criminals, the court referred to many precedents for such international intervention.[16] In 1827, England, France, and Russia had intervened to end the atrocities in the Greco-Turkish war. In 1840, the President of the United States, through his Secretary of State, intervened with the Sultan of Turkey on behalf of the persecuted Jews of Damascus and Rhodes. The French intervened to check religious atrocities in Lebanon in 1861. There were protests by various nations to the governments of Russia and Romania with respect to pogroms and atrocities against Jews, and to the government of Turkey on behalf of the persecuted Christian minorities. In 1902, the American Secretary of State addressed to Romania a remonstrance "in the name of humanity" against Jewish persecutions, stating that his government could not be a tacit party to such international wrongs, and in his message to Congress in 1904, the

President of the United States declared, with reference to the Kishniev pogrom in Russia and the "systematic and long-extended cruel oppression of the Armenians," that "there are occasional crimes committed on a vast scale and of such peculiar horror as to make us doubt whether it is not our manifest duty to endeavour at least to show our disapproval of the deed and our sympathy with those who have suffered by it."

To these, we should add the declaration of 24 May 1915 by the governments of France, Great Britain, and Russia, denouncing the massacres of the Armenian population "as crimes against humanity and civilization for which all members of the Turkish government will be held responsible together with its agents implicated in the massacres." And on similar lines, the Commission of Fifteen Members of the Preliminary Peace Conference in its report of 29 March 1919 referred to the liability to criminal prosecution of all those "guilty of offenses against the laws and customs of war or the laws of humanity."[17]

It was the devastation of peoples by the Nazis which provided the impetus for the formal recognition of genocide as a crime in international law, thus laying the basis for intervention by judicial process. Many declarations bear testimony to the sense of outrage as nations experienced or witnessed the atrocities of genocidal warfare. There was the declaration of St. James's Palace in January 1942 by representatives in London of nine European countries overrun by the Nazis. This was made following the German occupation of large areas of Russia and expressed determination to secure the punishment not only of war criminals, but of all those guilty of a violence against civilian populations, having nothing in common with acts of war or political crimes, as understood in civilized countries. The horror was still nameless. In December 1942, a declaration by allied governments expressed the resolve to punish those responsible for the "bestial policy of cold-blooded extermination" against the Jews. Then there were the declarations by Churchill following the slaughter of hostages (the martyrs of Châteaubriant); by Molotov in response to the declaration of St. James's Palace; by Roosevelt after the annihilation of the villages of Lidice and Ležáky in a collective reprisal for the assassination of the protector of Bohemia-Moravia; and finally, the Declaration of Moscow in October 1943, in which England, Russia, and the USA issued a warning that those responsible for, or participants in, the atrocities, massacres, or executions would be sent back for judgment and punishment to the countries in which they had committed their abominations.[18]

The Moscow Declaration was the basis for the Four-Power Agreement of 8 August 1945 between the governments of England, France, Russia, and the USA. It established the Charter for the International Military Tribunal which tried the major war criminals at Nuremberg. Article 6 of the Charter specifies three types of crime falling under the jurisdiction of the tribunal:

(a) Crimes against peace: namely, planning, preparation, initiation or waging of a war of aggression, or a war in violation of international treaties, agreements or assurances, or participation in a common plan or conspiracy for the accomplishment of any of the foregoing.

(b) War Crimes: namely, violations of the laws or customs of war. Such violations shall include, but not be limited to, murder, ill-treatment or deportation to slave labour or for any other purpose of civilian population of or in occupied territory, murder or ill-treatment of prisoners of war or persons on the seas, killing of hostages, plunder of public or private property, wanton destruction of cities, towns or villages, or devastation not justified by military necessity.

(c) Crimes against humanity: namely, murder, extermination, enslavement, deportation and other inhumane acts committed against any civilian population, before or during the war, or persecutions on political, racial or religious grounds of execution of or in connection with any crime within the jurisdiction of the Tribunal, whether or not in violation of the domestic law of the country where perpetrated.

The crimes against peace and the crimes against humanity were then embryonic categories of international law:[19] war crimes were already established as offenses under international law. Genocide would constitute a crime against humanity, though it could also take the form of a war crime, there being much overlapping between the two categories.

The term genocide was now coming into use. It was coined by the jurist, Raphaël Lemkin, whose remarkable achievement it was to initiate a one-man crusade for a genocide convention.[20] As early as 1933, he had submitted to the International Conference for Unification of Criminal Law a proposal to declare the destruction of racial, religious, or social collectivities a crime (of barbarity) under the law of nations.[21] In his very detailed study of Axis Rule in Occupied Europe, published in 1944, he repeated this proposal in somewhat different form. In chapter IX, devoted to genocide, he wrote that "by 'genocide' we mean the destruction of a nation or of an ethnic group. This new word, coined by the author to denote an old practice in its modern development, is made from the ancient Greek word *genos* (race, tribe) and the Latin *cide* (killing), thus corresponding in its formation to such words as tyrannicide, hom[i]cide, infanticide, etc." He explained that generally speaking, genocide does not necessarily mean the immediate destruction of a nation, except when accomplished by mass killings of all members of a nation, but is intended rather to signify a coordinated plan of different actions aiming at the destruction of essential foundations of the life of national groups, with the aim of annihilating the groups themselves.

The term appears in the indictment of the major German war criminals at Nuremberg in 1945, and I think that this must be the first formal recognition of the crime of *genocide*. The defendants were charged with having "conducted deliberate and systematic genocide, viz., the extermination of racial and national groups, against the civilian populations of certain occupied territories in order to destroy particular races and classes of people and national, racial or religious groups, particularly Jews, Poles and Gypsies, and others." But though the Nuremberg Tribunal dealt at great length in its judgment with the substance of the charge of genocide, it did not use this term, nor make any reference to the conception of genocide.[22] In a later trial of one of the Nazi war criminals by the Supreme National Tribunal of Poland, held in August and September 1946, the Prosecutor charged the accused with the crime of genocide (claiming it to be a *crimen laesae humanitatis*) and the Court found that the wholesale extermination of Jews and also of Poles had all the characteristics of genocide in the biological meaning of the term, and embraced in addition the destruction of the cultural life of those nations.[23]

About this time, however, the problem of the prevention and punishment of genocide was already becoming an issue for the United Nations as a result of the lobbying of Raphaël Lemkin, and on 11 December 1946 the General Assembly passed the following resolution (96–I):

Genocide is a denial of the right of existence of entire human groups, as homicide is the denial of the right to live of individual human beings; such denial of the right of existence shocks the conscience of mankind, results in great losses to humanity in the form of cultural and other contributions represented by these groups, and is contrary to moral law and to the spirit and aims of the United Nations. Many instances of such crimes of genocide have occurred, when racial, religious, political and other groups have been destroyed, entirely or in part. The punishment of the crime of genocide is a matter of international concern.

The General Assembly Therefore, Affirms that genocide is a crime under international law which the civilized world condemns, and for the commission of which principals and accomplices – whether private individuals, public officials or statesmen, and whether the crime is committed on religious, racial, political or any other grounds – are punishable.

The resolution continues with an invitation to member states to enact the necessary legislation for the prevention and punishment of genocide, a recommendation for international cooperation in attaining these ends, and a request to the Economic and Social Council of the United Nations to undertake the necessary studies with a view to drawing up a draft convention.

It is important to note that the crime of genocide in this resolution is wholly independent of crimes against peace or of war crimes. A severe limitation in the Nuremberg Charter, as interpreted by the International Military Tribunal, was the linking of crimes against humanity with aggressive war or conventional war crimes. Seemingly a great advance had been made by the resolution of the United Nations General Assembly. The way was now cleared for the protection of racial, religious, political, and other groups against genocidal assaults, not only by foreign governments but also by their own governments, and not only in times of war but also in times of peace.

It is very depressing to read the reports of the debates in the Economic and Social Council, in its Ad Hoc Committee, and in the Sixth (Legal) Committee, as the proposals moved from the first draft of the Secretariat, through the second draft prepared by the Ad Hoc Committee, to the final version adopted by the General Assembly on 9 December 1948. One can see, in the controversies about the wording of the Convention, many of the forces which have rendered it so ineffective. Yet this may be too pessimistic a view. As compared with the failure of the United Nations for very many years even to agree on a definition of aggression for the purpose of defining the crime of aggressive war, it was an appreciable achievement to arrive quite speedily at a definition of genocide and at an agreement on some measures for its prevention and punishment.

In the deliberations of the committees, there were major controversies regarding the groups to be protected, the question of intent, the inclusion of cultural genocide, the problem of enforcement and punishment, the extent of destruction which would constitute genocide, and the essential nature of the crime. Almost every conceivable argument was advanced, and critically tested. The representatives of many nations had considerable experience of genocide on which to draw, and even where there had been no direct exposure in the Second World War, as in the case of Peru, there were historic memories of genocide to inform comment and perspective.

The Nazis had freely exterminated their political opponents within Germany, notably the communists and social democrats. Quite naturally then, in response to the immediate experience of the Second World War, the United Nations resolution of December 1946 referred to the many instances of genocide in which racial, religious, political, and other groups were destroyed, and declared genocide to be a crime under international law whether committed on religious, racial, political, or any other grounds. The resolution was passed unanimously. However, in the deliberations on the framing of the Convention to give effect to this resolution, the Russian representatives launched a vigorous attack in the different committees, starting with the Ad Hoc Committee in spring 1948, against the inclusion of political groups among the groups to be protected. They were supported strongly by the Polish representatives, and also by representatives of other nations.

The Russian representatives argued that the inclusion of political groups was not in conformity "with the scientific definition of genocide and would, in practice, distort the perspective in which the crime should be viewed and impair the efficacy of the Convention," giving "the notion an extension of meaning contrary to the fundamental conception of genocide as recognized by science." "It was during the Nürnberg trials that the term 'genocide' was used for the first time, in particular in the bill of indictment and the reasons adduced for the sentence, where it was defined as follows: extermination of racial and religious groups in the occupied territories."[24] They contended that while the Nazis had exterminated members of political groups, this was because they formed the intellectual elements of populations to be subjugated: the principal objective, however, was the wholesale destruction of the civilian populations which were to be conquered and colonized in pursuance of the Nazi plan for German domination over the world. This was the historical point of departure in the conception of genocide as a crime against racial and national groups, though to be sure this did not make the crimes committed against other groups any the less odious.[25] Some representatives had mentioned historic crimes which might be classed as genocide. In the Russian view, these examples were interesting but had no modern application. Genocide was essentially bound up with fascist and Nazi ideologies, and other similar racial theories spreading national and racial hatred, and aiming at the domination of the so-called "superior" races and the extermination of the so-called "inferior" races.[26]

The etymology of the term, the Russian representative argued, favored this thesis, as did the juridical aspect. The criterion for defining the groups subject to genocide must have an objective character, which excludes the subjective qualities of individuals. "On the basis of that fundamental concept, the groups could easily be distinguished: they were the racial and national groups which constituted distinct, clearly determinable communities." As to the willingness of the delegation of the Soviet Union to include religious groups in parentheses after racial and national groups, this was for the reason that in all known cases of genocide perpetrated on grounds of religion, it had always been evident that nationality or race were concomitant reasons. Placing religious groups in parentheses after racial or national groups would stress the fact that the persecution was always directed against national groups, even when it took the form of religious strife.[27]

Supporting arguments advanced by representatives of different nations sought to establish the distinctive character of membership in a political organization. The Iranian representative argued that if a distinction were recognized "between those groups, membership of which was inevitable, such as racial, religious or national groups, whose distinctive features were permanent, and those, membership of which was voluntary, such as political groups, whose distinctive features were not permanent, it must be admitted that the destruction of the first type appeared most heinous in the light of the conscience of humanity, since it was directed against human beings whom chance alone had grouped together. Although it was true that people could change their nationality as their religion, such changes did not in fact happen very often; national and religious groups therefore belonged to the category of groups, membership of which was inevitable."[28] The Polish representative argued that "the inclusion of provisions relating to political groups, which because of their mutability and lack of distinguishing characteristics did not lend themselves to definition, would weaken and blur the whole Convention."[29]

These arguments as to the transient and unstable nature of political groups constituting an obstacle to their inclusion in the Genocide Convention, were advanced repeatedly. In so doing, representatives disclaimed any intention of denying protection to political groups, but contended that this protection was, or should be, given by national legislation, and that at the international level, the appropriate instruments were those being prepared by the Human Rights Commission.[30] Fears were expressed that inclusion of political groups in the Convention would expose nations to external intervention in their domestic concerns, and "might endanger the future of the Convention because many states would be unwilling to ratify it, fearing the possibility of being called before an international tribunal to answer charges made against them, even if those charges were without foundation. Subversive elements might make use of the Convention to weaken the attempts of their own Government to suppress them."[31] The appeal to expediency, that "the fear of impairing their power to take defensive action against domestic disorders might prevent many states from signing the Convention,"[32] was however explicitly rejected by the Soviet representative as a supporting argument, in favor of a decision based on principle.

The counter-arguments attacked the conception of genocide as linked only to fascism-nazism, and hence to the destruction of racial and national groups, but not of political groups. The French representative argued that the relationship between the crimes of nazism-fascism and genocide was not an established historical fact[33] (implying presumably that genocide was not a necessary part of Nazi-fascist doctrine). The report of the Ad Hoc Committee pointed out that there was genocide before nazism-fascism, and that "as regards the future, it was possible that crimes of genocide would be based on other motives. It would be dangerous to create the idea that genocide should only be punished if it were a product of fascism-nazism, and that the Convention was concerned only with that historical accident."[34]

In a much later session, the French representative commented that " . . . whereas in the past crimes of genocide had been committed on racial or religious grounds, it was clear that in the future they would be committed mainly on political grounds,"[35] and this view received strong support from other representatives.[36] As for the proposed Russian amendment to indicate that religious persecution was always associated with racial and national persecution, the Yugoslav representative objected on the ground of his country's recent experience of genocide for religious motives, as a result of which it had passed laws for the prevention and suppression of religious genocide as such.[37]

Two objections were advanced to the etymological argument, the first on the ground that "there was no absolute concept of genocide... Member States themselves must decide whether they intended to exclude them or not," and furthermore, "the etymology of the word 'genocide' could not determine its definitive meaning, for words evolved and changed in meaning even in legislative texts. Thus, there were no decisive reasons against including the political group in the Convention."[38] A second line of argument sought to define genocide as "the physical destruction of a group which was held together by a common origin or a common ideology... The definition might even be broadened still further to include economic groups. There was nothing to prevent that; the word 'genocide' meant the destruction of a group without implying any distinction between the various groups."[39] The United States delegation did in fact introduce an amendment to extend protection to economic groups, but did not press the issue.

A plethora of attacks was directed against the argument that political groups were too unstable and lacking in identifiability for protection under the Convention. The Nazis had of course found no difficulty in identifying the German communists and social democrats whom they destroyed. If they were identifiable and stable enough to be exterminated, they were identifiable and stable enough to be included among the groups accorded protection against genocide. The United States representative added, among further examples of the identifiability of political groups, the decision of the Allied Control Council to proclaim the abolition of the Nazi Party, and the USSR constitution which recognized the organization of the Communist Party as authorized to nominate candidates for the elections, thus proving that the Communist Party was a coherent and perfectly identifiable group.[40]

An important argument against the exclusion of political groups was that "those who committed the crime of genocide might use the pretext of the political opinions of a racial or religious group to persecute and destroy it, without becoming liable to international sanctions."[41] The representative from Haiti developed the argument further: "...since it was established that genocide always implied the participation or complicity of Governments, that crime would never be suppressed: the Government which was responsible would always be able to allege that the extermination of any group had been dictated by political considerations, such as the necessity for quelling an insurrection or maintaining public order."[42] (These were indeed the grounds on which the government of Burundi defended its recent genocidal massacres of Hutu.)

Granted that political groups should be protected, the Convention on Genocide was the proper instrument for their protection. "The point at issue was not to protect freedom of opinion (that question came within the scope of the protection of human rights) nor was it to prevent States from maintaining internal order in the political field. The issue was to protect political groups against violence, followed by destruction." The proposed protection "applied only to the most horrible form of the crime against a group, that of its physical destruction. It seemed that all States could guarantee that limited measure of protection to political groups."[43]

Political groups survived for many sessions and seemed securely ensconced in the Convention, but on 29 November 1948, the issue was reopened in the Legal Committee on a motion by the delegations of Iran, Egypt, and Uruguay. A compromise seems to have been reached behind the scenes. The United States delegation, though still committed to the principle of extending protection to political groups, was conciliatory. It feared non-ratification of the Convention, and rejection of the proposal for an international tribunal, if political groups were included.[44] On a vote, political groups were expunged. The Convention, as adopted by the United Nations on 9 December 1948, limits genocide to the destruction of national, ethnical, racial, or religious groups.[45]

It would be cynical to suggest that many nations were unwilling to renounce the right to commit political genocide against their own nationals. One must acknowledge that there was cause for anxiety that the inclusion of political groups in the Convention would expose nations to external interference in their internal affairs: this, after all, was the purpose of the Convention, to prevent and punish genocide. The United States was not among the eighty-four nations which ratified the Convention by 31 December 1978. In recent hearings before the Senate Foreign Relations Committee, reference was made to earlier objections, *inter alia*, that the American constitution prevented ratification because genocide was a domestic matter, and though the Committee dismissed the arguments, the United States has still not ratified the Convention.[46] If a relatively stable country such as the USA, which took a leading role in the Nuremberg trials and the Genocide Convention, has reservations about ratification of the Convention, one can understand the reaction against extending protection to political groups in other countries, particularly those in which the political process is very violent (as argued by the Venezuelan delegate).[47] I think though that one may fairly say that the delegates, after all, represented governments in power, and that many of these governments wished to retain an unrestricted freedom to suppress political opposition.

The scope of genocide under the Convention is defined not only by the number of "protected groups," but also by the range of actions qualified as genocide. Raphaël Lemkin, in his detailed study of *Axis Rule in Occupied Europe*,[48] listed the fields in which genocide was being carried out as the political, social, cultural, economic, biological, physical, religious, and moral. Three of these categories appear in the first draft of the Convention by the Secretariat – "physical" genocide (acts causing the death of members of protected groups or injuring their health or physical integrity), "biological" genocide (restriction of births), and "cultural" genocide (destruction of the specific character of the persecuted "group" by forced transfer of children, forced exile, prohibition of the use of the national language, destruction of books, documents, monuments, and objects of historical, artistic, or religious value).[49]

The draft of the Ad Hoc Committee retained these categories with many changes, the "biological" in a much weakened form, and the "cultural" defined as:

any deliberate act committed with the intent to destroy the language, religion, or culture of a national, racial or religious group on grounds of the national or racial origin or religious belief of its members such as:

1. Prohibiting the use of the language of the group in daily intercourse or in schools, or the printing and circulation of publications in the language of the group;

2. Destroying or preventing the use of libraries, museums, schools, historical monuments, places of worship or other cultural institutions and objects of the group.

The inclusion of cultural genocide became an issue of controversy. In this controversy,[50] the roles of the national delegations were somewhat reversed. The Soviet Bloc pressed for inclusion of cultural genocide in the Convention, the Western European democracies opposed. The issue was not whether groups should be protected against attempts to destroy their culture. There were many expressions of horror at cultural genocide, with the Nazi experience still vivid in the perspectives of the delegates. The issue was rather whether the protection of culture should be extended through the Convention on Genocide or in conventions on human rights and rights of minorities. This conflict of views was not sharply ideological, but presumably the representatives of the colonial powers would have been somewhat on the defensive, sensitive to criticism of their policies in non-self-governing territories.

In the result, cultural genocide was excluded from the Convention, though vestiges remain. The Convention makes special reference to the forcible transfer of children from one group to another, and the word ethnical has been added to the list of groups covered by the Convention. This would have the effect of extending protection to groups with distinctive culture or language.[51]

Though cultural genocide has disappeared as a crime under the Convention, it is commonly treated as such in much contemporary writing where it is described as ethnocide. This might be defined as the commission of specified acts "with intent to extinguish, utterly or in substantial part, a culture. Among such ethnocidal acts are the deprivations of opportunity to use a language, practice a religion, create art in customary ways, maintain basic social institutions, preserve memories and traditions, work in cooperation toward social goals."[52]

The initial draft of the Convention by the Secretariat described genocide as constituted by deliberate acts directed against specified groups, with the purpose of destroying the group *in whole or in part*. The phrase *in whole or in part* is omitted from the draft by the Ad Hoc Committee, but reappears in the final text adopted by the General Assembly of the United Nations. Its interpretation is a matter of some difficulty, and there were conflicting views in the discussions of the Legal Committee. What numbers or proportion or sections would constitute a *part* within the definition? From a humanist point of view, it is quite repugnant to weigh the number of deaths which would accord significance in terms of the Convention: death and suffering and ignominy are hardly matters for mathematical calculation. From a legal point of view, which interested the members of the Legal Committee, could one argue that the murder of an individual should be considered genocide if it took place "with a connecting aim," that is to say, if it were directed against persons of the same race, or nationality, or ethnic, or religious group?[53]

I will assume that the charge of genocide would not be preferred unless there were a "substantial" or an "appreciable" number of victims. I would have no difficulty in applying the term to the slaughter of a stratum of the educated of a racial or ethnic group, a common enough occurrence, provided there are "appreciable" numbers. In other cases, as for example the obliteration of a village or villages by the French in

Algeria after the riots in Sétif in 1945, or the slaughter of fifty French hostages, the martyrs of Châteaubriant, or the destruction of Lidice and Ležáky as reprisals for the assassination of German officials in the Second World War, I will use the term "genocidal massacre." I need hardly emphasize the arbitrary nature of this procedure in dealing with a wide range of actions, from the total obliteration of a small village (the "genocidal massacre") to the systematic extermination of millions of Jews by the Nazis.

The crime of genocide under the Convention is not committed simply by the destruction, in whole or in part, of a racial, national, ethnic, or religious group. There must be the intention to destroy. The Convention defines genocide as constituted by specified acts "committed with intent to destroy, in whole or in part, a national, ethnical, racial or religious group, as such." The "inadvertent" wiping out of a group is not genocide.

The draft of the Ad Hoc Committee had offered a more complex formulation of intent in its definition of genocide as "any of the following *deliberate* acts committed with the *intent* to destroy a national, racial, religious or political group, *on grounds of the national or racial origin, religious belief, or political opinion of its members.*" This stimulated a complex debate, which was to be expected, given the varied conceptions of law and of the nature of crime among these representatives of different national legal systems. Often the discussions seemed to be governed by purist preoccupations with legal niceties, or the logic of rigorous analysis, rather than by concern with the substantive issues.

The inclusion of intent in the definition of genocide introduces a subjective element, which would often prove difficult to establish. An attempt to substitute an objective measure proved unsuccessful, and in the result "intent" was retained, the word "deliberate" being deleted as redundant. There still remained the question of further intent, or of motive, represented by the phrase "on grounds of national or racial origin" etc. This limited the grounds which would be necessary to constitute genocide, so that the destruction of a group for profit or because of personal rivalry between tribes could not be charged as genocide. To these examples given in the debate, one might add that presumably the destruction of a group in order to create a brave new world would also not fall within the concept of genocide. The Soviet delegation, consistent with its earlier stand for the exclusion of political groups from the list of protected groups, wished to delete from the enumerated grounds the words "or political opinion of its members." The effect of this would have been equally bizarre – the United Nations declaring that the destruction of an ethnic group because of its political beliefs (say Hutu in Burundi) would not be considered genocide. Understandably, the United Kingdom representative argued that the phrase under discussion was completely useless (the concept of intent having already been expressed at the beginning of the article), and that its inclusion was indeed dangerous, "for its limitative nature would enable those who committed a crime of genocide to claim that they had not committed that crime 'on grounds of' one of the motives listed in the article." The United Kingdom delegation proposed its deletion.[54] In this impasse, the committee adopted a compromise solution proposed by the Venezuelan representative, namely, the substitution of the word "as such" for the enumeration of grounds. This introduces an ambiguity,[55] the resolution of which would presumably rest with the court called upon to try a charge of genocide.

In contemporary extra-judicial discussions of allegations of genocide, the question of intent has become a controversial issue, providing a ready basis for denial of guilt. "Thus in March 1974, the International League for the Rights of Man, joined by the Inter-American Association for Democracy and Freedom, charged the government of Paraguay with complicity in genocide against the Guayaki Indians. In a protest to the United Nations Secretary General, the organizations alleged the following violations, leading to the wholesale disappearance of the Guayaki (Aché) ethnic group, namely:

(1) enslavement, torture, and killing of the Guayaki Indians in reservations in eastern Paraguay;
(2) withholding of food and medicine from them resulting in their death by starvation and disease;
(3) massacre of their members outside the reservations by hunters and slave traders with the toleration and even encouragement of members of the government and with the aid of the armed forces;
(4) splitting up of families and selling into slavery of children, in particular girls for prostitution; and
(5) denial and destruction of Guayaki cultural traditions, including use of their language, traditional music, and religious practices.

This was followed by an attack in the United States Senate, supported by intellectuals and churchmen in Paraguay. To these protestations, the Defense Minister replied quite simply that there was no intention to destroy the Guayaki. "Although there are victims and victimizer, there is not the third element necessary to establish the crime of genocide – that is 'intent.' Therefore, as there is no 'intent,' one cannot speak of 'genocide.'"[56]

A similar issue arose in relation to charges of genocide against the Indians in the Amazon river region of Brazil, to which the Permanent Representative of Brazil replied that

... the crimes committed against the Brazilian indigenous population cannot be characterized as genocide, since the criminal parties involved never eliminated the Indians as an ethnic or cultural group. Hence there was lacking the special malice or motivation necessary to characterize the occurrence of genocide. The crimes in question were committed for exclusively economic reasons, the perpetrators having acted solely to take possession of the lands of their victims.[57]

"Intent" was also an issue in the debate on the nature of the involvement of the USA in Vietnam. In the latter stages of the war, there was "an increasing disposition by critics of American involvement to consider the indiscriminateness and magnitude of destruction on the peoples of Vietnam, Laos and Cambodia as 'genocidal.'"[58] If one draws a legal distinction between the act and the intention, and if one ignores or discounts the circumstances of the American involvement in Vietnam, then it is possible to make the argument that the level and nature of the destruction rained on Vietnam by the USA was suggestive of genocide. Sartre, in his address to the non-governmental International War Crimes Tribunal, spoke of the alternatives offered the people of South Vietnam – "villages burned, the populace subjected to massive bombing, livestock shot, vegetation destroyed by defoliants, crops ruined by toxic aerosols, and everywhere indiscriminate shooting, murder, rape and looting. This is genocide in the strictest sense: massive extermination. The other option: what is *it*? What are the Vietnamese people supposed to do to escape this horrible death? Join the armed forces of Saigon or be enclosed in strategic or today's 'New Life' hamlets, two names for the same concentration camps." We might add to this list the establishment of free-fire zones, the search and destroy missions, the obliteration bombing, the use of high-technology weapons in counter-insurgency, and the devastation model of pacification.

The problem of establishing intent is more complex. On this issue Sartre was hesitant. He did not assert that there was proof that the United States did in fact envision genocide, but simply that nothing prevented the United States from envisaging it, that the genocidal intent was implicit in the facts, and that those who fight the war of the greatest power on earth against a poor peasant people "are *living out* the only possible relationship between an overindustrialized country and an underdeveloped country, that is to say, a genocidal relationship implemented through racism – the only relationship, short of picking up and pulling out."[59] Sartre's argument was weakened by extravagant generalization, but the case is made persuasively by others in more measured legal terms. One can see in these and other controversies how difficult it may be to establish intent in a court of law: governments hardly declare and document genocidal plans in the manner of the Nazis. At a different level, too, that of the forum of public opinion, the requirement of "intent" provides an easy means for evading responsibility. Its omission from a definition of genocide as quite simply the destruction of a human group might have been some contribution to the suppression and punishment of this crime.

The declared purpose of the Convention, in terms of the original resolution of the General Assembly of the United Nations, was to prevent and punish the crime of genocide. Its effectiveness depends in some measure on the procedures devised, and the institutions established, for these purposes. The nature of the provision to be made for enforcement became one of the most controversial issues in the debates, which saw a steady whittling away of the initial proposals.

The first draft, that of the Secretariat, incorporated the principle of universal enforcement, and made provision for both national and international jurisdiction. The principle of universal enforcement had been applied in the suppression of the international crime of piracy on the high seas; the state, whose authorities had arrested the pirates, was competent to exercise jurisdiction, whatever the nationality of the pirates, and wherever on the high seas the crime had been committed. On similar lines, the Secretariat's draft included in the preamble a pledge by the contracting parties to prevent and repress acts of genocide *wherever they may occur*, and in Article VII a further pledge to punish any offender under the Convention within any territory under their jurisdiction, irrespective of the nationality of the offender or of the place where the offense was committed. The principle of universal validity was also incorporated in the provision that the contracting parties might call on the competent organs of the United Nations to take measures for the suppression or prevention of genocide in any part of the world, in which case the parties would do everything in their power to give full effect to the intervention of the United Nations. In the final text, however, the principle of universal repression was eliminated, save to the extent that the United Nations may take action within the scope of its general competence. This was to be expected, for otherwise the representative of one of the great powers, on a visit say to Uganda under Amin, might find himself arraigned on a charge of genocide before the courts of that country. I do not doubt that if pirates had been properly represented at the international convention on piracy, they too would have voted against the principle of universal repression.

In addition to the pledge to punish offenders in areas under their jurisdiction, the Secretariat's draft also imposed on the parties the obligation to provide in their municipal (national) laws for acts of genocide and their punishment, and to commit all persons "guilty" of genocide for trial by an international court, when (1) they are themselves unwilling to try such offenders or to grant extradition to another country, (2) if the acts of genocide were committed by individuals acting as organs of the State or with the support or toleration of the State. It was particularly the provision in regard to an international penal court which aroused a storm of protest.

The establishment of international criminal jurisdiction was attacked as an infringement of national sovereignty, which might stand in the way of the acceptance of the Convention. It implied the existence of an international criminal tribunal, which the Convention however did not establish. States were therefore being asked to accept the creation, at a future date, of an international tribunal, the period of existence and competence of which were left entirely vague. Moreover, since the Convention envisaged that members of governments might be authors of the crime, there was the danger that the attempt to punish offenders through an international tribunal might jeopardize peace.[60]

The arguments in support of an international tribunal emphasized especially the role of governments in genocide. The French delegation had proposed an amendment in the definition of the crime to include the phrase "it is committed, encouraged or tolerated by the rulers of a State." The French representative argued that genocide was bound up with the action, or the culpable abstention from action, of the State.

The theoreticians of nazism and fascism, who had taught the doctrine of the superiority of certain races, could not have committed their crimes if they had not had the support of their rulers; similarly, pogroms had occurred frequently only in countries where no severe legal measures were taken against the perpetrators. Thus the experience of history showed the way; it was inconceivable that human groups should be exterminated while the government remained indifferent; it was inadmissible that the central authority should be powerless to put a stop to mass assassination when homicide was the first of punishable crimes. When the crime of genocide was committed, it was committed either directly by the Governments themselves or at their behest; alternatively, they remained indifferent and failed to use the power which every Government should have in order to ensure public order. Thus, whether as perpetrator, or as accomplice, the Government's responsibility was in all cases implicated.

Hence the task of suppression of the crime could not be left to the governments themselves. It was necessary for international society to intervene; otherwise one would arrive at the absurd position of the future criminal being entrusted with ensuring his own punishment.[61]

There was criticism of the conception of genocide as exclusively a crime of governments. The representative of Pakistan argued that such organizations as fascist or terrorist organizations might commit genocide, not connected in any way with the government in power, as had been the case in Germany under the Weimar Republic, where the government had been unable to take effective action. So too in India, terrorist organizations had been able to massacre hundreds of thousands of people with impunity, for the simple reason that the government was powerless to prevent and suppress these acts of terrorism. The Yugoslav representative thought that, in theory, the French amendment was justified, since in most cases genocide was committed, encouraged, or tolerated by governments, but that in practice it was generally very difficult to establish government responsibility, as for example in Czechoslovakia in 1945, Poland in 1946, and Yugoslavia in 1948, when genocidal bands were introduced into these countries.[62]

In the result, the Legal Committee decided by a narrowly divided vote to eliminate the provision for an international penal tribunal. Later, however, the issue was reopened, after acceptance of a draft resolution that the International Law Commission be requested to study the desirability and possibility of establishing an independent international criminal court for the punishment of persons guilty of genocide, or a criminal chamber of the International Court of Justice. The deletion of political groups from the list of groups protected by the Convention had removed some of the objections to the establishment of an international tribunal, and it became feasible to reintroduce provision for international jurisdiction, though in an optional and conditional form.[63] The final clause in the Genocide Convention (Article VI) now provides for trial by a competent tribunal of the State in the territory of which the act was committed, "or by such international penal tribunal as may have jurisdiction with respect to those Contracting Parties which shall have accepted its jurisdiction."

Further developments have not been encouraging. On the same day as the adoption of the Genocide Convention, the General Assembly invited the International Law Commission to "study the desirability and possibility of establishing an international judicial organ for the trial of persons charged with genocide or other crimes over which jurisdiction will be conferred upon that organ by international conventions." This resulted in a Revised Draft Statute. Meanwhile, by an earlier resolution, the International Law Commission had been instructed to prepare a Draft Code of Offenses against the Peace and Security of Mankind. This draft code, published in 1954, includes among the offenses the crime of genocide. It reads, sadly, like a manual for contemporary international practice. In the General Assembly, discussion of the Revised Draft Statute for an international tribunal "was made contingent upon satisfactory drafting of the Code of Offences against the Peace and Security of Mankind, which in turn was made contingent upon a satisfactory definition of 'aggression,' which problem was assigned to a Special Committee in 1954 and to a further Committee of 35 States in 1967, which has met repeatedly since that time..."[64] A definition of aggression was finally arrived at in 1974, but the project for an international penal tribunal to try charges of genocide still remains in disheartening abeyance.

There were many other controversies in the debate on the Genocide Convention, not central to my argument, and I have omitted them from this discussion. I shall follow the definition of genocide given in the Convention. This is not to say that I agree with this definition. On the contrary, I believe a major omission to be in the exclusion of political groups from the list of groups protected. In the contemporary world, political differences are at the very least as significant a basis for massacre and annihilation as racial, national, ethnic, or religious differences. Then too, the genocides against racial, national, ethnic, or religious groups are generally a consequence of, or intimately related to, political conflict. However, I do not think it helpful to create new definitions of genocide, when there is an internationally recognized definition and a Genocide Convention which might become the basis for some effective action, however limited the underlying conception. But since it would vitiate the analysis to exclude political groups, I shall refer freely, in the following discussion, to liquidating or exterminatory actions against them[....]

Theories of Genocide

The paucity of theoretical speculation about genocide may be due to the fact that it is seen as an extreme manifestation of a broader phenomenon – of violence, of destructiveness, of aggression. This would also explain why the more focused theories tend to deal with specific cases or types of genocide. However, there are some general theoretical observations which we can derive from the preceding discussion.

Though animals do engage in intra-species killing, genocide is essentially a human crime. But this does not mean that it is rooted in human nature. There are convincing arguments to the contrary. Conflict of a potentially genocidal character is not the normal pattern of interaction between social groups. Even in our contemporary world, ravaged as it is by genocidal conflicts, most societies develop and relate to each other without interruption by group annihilating destruction. Some analysts would add the further argument that in the so-called "simple" hunting-gathering societies, warfare was "characteristically unbloody,"[65] but this may be controversial. In any event, the source of genocide is to be found in the social conditions of man's existence. This is central to Fromm's thesis. But the social factors also have some significance in Lorenz's approach,[66] as in his discussion of the discovery of weapons as disturbing the equilibrium between the ability and the inhibition to kill; or the effect on human aggression of the deviation of the ecological and sociological conditions created by culture from those to which human instinctive behavior is phylogenetically adapted; or the genesis of militant enthusiasm in the interaction between an instinctive behavioral pattern and culturally ritualized social norms and rites; or in such suggestions for avoiding aggression as the promotion of personal acquaintance and, if possible, friendship between individual members of different nations, thereby activating the inhibition against killing.

Turning then to these social conditions, since genocide is a crime against a collectivity, it implies an identifiable group as victim. The more specifically focused theories we have been discussing deal with hunting and gathering peoples; hostage groups; the colonized; other nations; the racial and ethnic sections of a society. Maximum identifiability is present where there are marked racial differences: but cultural differences may be equally divisive. In cases where the groups appear to an outside observer to share the same culture, the members of the society may themselves be highly sensitive to minutiae of cultural differences, which in the course of the genocidal conflict cry out for murder. Where there is a high level of segregation, there is no need to rely on personal identifying features. The IRA terrorist who throws a bomb into a public house in Belfast, Northern Ireland, will know from its location that his victims will be Protestant: he can fire indiscriminately on pedestrians in particular localities with reasonable certainty as to their Protestant identity. In situations where there are no obviously identifying physical differences, identifiability can be assured by systems of registration or such other devices as the compulsory wearing of badges. Even political groups recruited from the same population may be readily differentiated from each other as victimizers and victims, and are so differentiated in many societies. The fact that identification on racial, ethnic, religious, or political grounds may not be precise is, of course, no obstacle to genocidal assault.

The plural society [...] is by definition characterized by the presence of identifiable groups. I use the term, in a tradition which derives from Furnivall, to describe societies with persistent cleavages between racial, ethnic, or religious groups. They are a major arena for genocidal conflict. Partly as a result of colonization, which has left numerous states in the Third World with a diversity of peoples between whom a stable accommodation has not yet been achieved, there are many contemporary plural societies with a relatively high potential for genocidal conflict. At the same time, ease of contact and communication between different nations most effectively translates the internal pluralism into international relations and international conflicts. With nuclear armament acting as a deterrent to war between the great powers, they transfer their warring to struggles for domination over smaller nations, whose conflicts with each other and whose domestic conflicts between different sections provide a point of entry and a field of deployment of conventional, but increasingly sophisticated and devastating, weapons. The destructive potentialities of the plural society are thereby greatly magnified.

There must have been periods in the history of human societies when groups committed genocide without benefit of ideologies to incite or justify commission of the crime. In the genocides of our own era, they seem to be invariably present. They are an aspect of many of the theories we have been discussing. Thus in the comments on genocide against hunters and gatherers, we quoted a reference to the Aché people as "rabid rats" in the eyes of their persecutors. This is a common phenomenon, the equating of hunting and gathering peoples with animals, and the hunting them down in the same way as animals. There are similar processes of dehumanization in the ideologies against "hostage" or "stranger" groups, taking the extreme form of demonization in the theory of the Jewish world conspiracy, and rendering the groups readily available as scapegoats and as sacrifices. The elaboration of denigrating and justifying ideologies was an intrinsic part of the colonizing process, and these ideologies are often described as significant factors in the genocidal attacks against colonial peoples.[67] They are present also in the struggles for power between different groups in the process or aftermath of decolonization. And nazism was quite specific in its ideological ordering of peoples on a genocidal scale.

In the debate on the Genocide Convention, one of the delegates argued for the inclusion of political groups among the protected groups, on the ground that "strife between nations had now been superseded by strife between ideologies. Men no longer destroyed for reasons of national, racial or religious hatred, but in the name of ideas and the faith to which they gave birth." There can be no doubt that political ideologies, not revolving round race, ethnicity, or religion, may be a significant element in many highly destructive conflicts, dehumanizing the opposition, and promoting self-righteous conceptions of expendable human groups.

Since genocide is a crime against a collectivity, policies which have the effect of collectivizing the members of the society into polarized sections increase the potentiality for genocide. Thus, in the attempt to deny guerrillas a popular base, there may be a vast relocation of the indigenous people into ill-equipped settlements, with punitive action in the form of collective punishment against whole communities, and a progressive identification of ordinary civilians with the enemy. The use of highly destructive weapons, deployed at long range, against guerrilla forces which disappear into the local population, as in Vietnam, also fails to discriminate between combatants and non-combatants. These processes, and reciprocity in violence, resulting in increasing polarization, may escalate the conflict to a genocidal level. There may however be no struggle, no reciprocity in violence, but a deliberate decision to annihilate a group, and the overwhelming power to carry out the annihilation, as in the German genocide against Jews.

The argument advanced in the debates on the Genocide Convention, that genocide is essentially a crime of governments, has validity, though I would emphasize that it is not exclusively a crime of governments. This involvement of governments directs attention to the role of ruling strata, of elites, in organizing or unleashing genocide or acting in complicity with other groups in the commission of genocide. The strategies and goals of elites may thus be a crucial factor in genocide, whether the genocide takes the form of a direct attack on contending elites and the groups from which they draw support, as in the Tutsi genocide against Hutu in Burundi, or whether it consolidates power indirectly, as in the scapegoat genocidal massacres.

Governments engage in large-scale genocidal massacres not only against racial, ethnic, and religious groups. The liquidation of political groups is a specialty of governments, though not their exclusive prerogative. The line between these forms of annihilation is quite arbitrary, more particularly since political motives usually enter into the genocides against racial, ethnic, or religious groups. It is only in order to follow the definition in the Genocide Convention that I treat the crimes against political groups as a related atrocity. However, there are significant differences which do warrant some separate treatment. The liquidation of political groups may, but does not generally, take the form of root and branch extermination, expressed in the slaughter of men, women, and children.

The involvement of governments and elites in many genocides is a reminder that human actors make choices and decisions, and carry out actions which constitute, or lead to, genocide. Genocide is not an inevitable consequence of certain social conditions within a society. There may be extreme pluralism in a society, with highly antagonistic, polarizing ideologies, division expressed in religion, segregation, employment, social networks, and political party affiliation, a long history of reciprocal violence, and periods of highly escalated conflict. Yet the struggle may stop short of genocide. Northern Ireland is an example of such a society. Notwithstanding the periodic conflagrations in the nineteenth and twentieth centuries, there have been no large-scale genocidal massacres during this period, which also takes in a civil war. I will describe societies of this type as non-genocidal societies, in the sense that there

are effective restraints against genocide, even though many social factors are conducive to the commission of the crime. The study of these societies should offer insight
into inhibitions against genocide even under conditions of the sharpest conflict and
the most acute stress.

NOTES

1   Arendt (1969:288).
2   See the discussion by T. A. Walker (1899) of the evolution of international law among the
    Israelites, the Greeks, and the Romans.
3   Lamb (1927:1).
4   Toynbee (1947:347).
5   See Walker (1899:123–37).
6   Graetz (1894:Vol. III, 298–9).
7   Ibid., 308.
8   Account given by the monk Arnold to the Pope (Graetz 1894:Vol. III, 502).
9   Graetz (1894:Vol. IV, 225).
10 See ibid., 100ff., and Sachar (1967:ch. 15): "similar accusations were made, with similar
    results, at innumerable local plagues down to the mid-sixteenth century" (Cohn
    1967:261).
11 Wedgwood (1939:525).
12 Sartre (1968:37–42).
13 Wolpert (1977:348).
14 See Desjardins (1976:55–6), who discusses the complexity of group alignments in the
    civil war, not reducible to a simple conflict between Muslims and Christians.
15 Caputo (1977:229–30).
16 Trial of Joseph Altstötter and Others, *Law Reports of Trials of War Criminals* (1948:Vol.
    VI, 46–7).
17 Goldenberg (1971:4–5). American members of the Commission issued a dissenting
    report on the grounds that a judicial tribunal deals only with existing law, leaving to
    another forum infractions of moral law and actions contrary to the laws and principles of
    humanity, and that standards of humanity were relative to time, place, and circumstance.
    The ratified treaties make no reference to the laws of humanity, and the Treaty of
    Lausanne was accompanied by a "Declaration of Amnesty." See discussion by Schwelb
    (1946:181–3).
18 Donnedieu de Vabres (1947:81–9) and Schwelb (1946:183–8).
19 See Goldenberg (1971:2).
20 See Hohenberg (1968:86–7).
21 Lemkin (1947:146).
22 *Law Reports of Trials of War Criminals* (1948:Vol. VII, 8).
23 Ibid., 1–10. For a discussion of early trials for genocide, see United Nations, *Study of the
    Question of the Prevention and Punishment of the Crime of Genocide*, E/CN. 4/Sub. 2/
    416, dated 4 July 1978, 6–7. This includes a comprehensive study of the Convention, and
    the controversies in the debates.
24 UN *Economic and Social Council, Official Records*, Session 7, 26 August 1948, 721; UN
    Report of the Ad Hoc Committee on Genocide, 5 April–10 May 1948; and UN *Legal
    Committee, Summary Records, and Annexes*, Session 3, Part 1, 14 October 1948, 104.
25 UN *Legal Committee*, cited above, 104–5.

26 UN *ECOSOC*, Session 7, 26 August 1948, 721–2.
27 UN *Legal Committee*, Session 3, Part 1, 14 October 1948, 105.
28 Ibid., 99
29 UN *ECOSOC*, Session 7, 26 August 1948, 712.
30 UN *Legal Committee*, Session 3, Part 1, 15 October 1948. See also the comment by the Yugoslav representative, UN *Legal Committee*, Session 3, Part 1, 30 September 1948, 10.
31 Ibid., 7 October 1948, 58.
32 UN *ECOSOC*, Session 7, 26 August 1948, 705.
33 Ibid., 26 August 1948, 723.
34 UN *Report of the Ad Hoc Committee on Genocide* (1948:3).
35 UN *ECOSOC*, Session 7, 26 August 1948, 723.
36 See UN *Legal Committee*, Session 3, Part 1, 14 October 1948: Bolivia, 99; Haiti, 103; Cuba, 108.
37 Ibid., 15 October 1948, 117.
38 Ibid., 14 October 1948, 107; 15 October 1948, 114.
39 Ibid., 14 October 1948, 98–9.
40 Ibid., 102. See also the comments of the representative of the United Kingdom on 7 October 1948, 60.
41 Ibid., 14 October 1948, 100.
42 Ibid., 15 October 1948, 113.
43 Ibid., 14 October 1948, 99, and 15 October 1948, 114.
44 Ibid., 29 November 1948, 662.
45 See Article II.
46 On this issue, see *United States Department of State Bulletin*, 62 (16 March 1970); Goldberg and Gardner (1972); *The Fact Finder*, Vol. 31, no. 15 (16 June 1973); and *Hearings before the Committee on Foreign Relations, United States Senate, Ninety-fifth Congress*, First Session, 24 and 26 May 1977.
47 UN *Legal Committee*, Session 3, 7 October 1948, 58.
48 Lemkin (1944:82–9).
49 See Robinson (1960:19), and annexed drafts of the Convention.
50 See the arguments, *pro* and *con*, in UN *Legal Committee*, Session 3, Part 1, 193–7, 201, 205; UN *ECOSOC*, Session 7, 707, 718, 719, 723, 725.
51 See the explanation offered by the Swedish representative who proposed the amendment (UN *Legal Committee*, 13 October 1948, 97–8).
52 Beardsley (1976:86).
53 See UN *Legal Committee*, 7 October 1948, 62 and 13 October 1948, 90–3. See also Robinson (1960: 63) and Drost (1959: 84–5).
54 UN *Legal Committee*, 15 October 1948, 118–21.
55 Ibid., 16 October 1948, 123, 131–6.
56 Lewis (1976: 62–3).
57 United Nations, HR Communication No 478, 29 September 1969.
58 Falk (1974: 123–4).
59 See Sartre (1968:39–42). See also the careful analysis of Sartre's argument from a legal point of view, with an examination of possible approaches to the proof of intent, in Bedau (1974). Note too that United States action in Vietnam has given currency to the concept of *ecocide*, as the intentional destruction of the physical environment needed to sustain human health and life in a given geographical region (see Bedau 1974: 44).
60 UN *ECOSOC*, 26 August 1948, 704–5, 713–14.
61 UN *Legal Committee*, 19 October 1948, 146–7.
62 UN *Legal Committee*, 20 and 21 October 1948, 153–4, 167. See also the argument by the British representative, 1 October 1948, 17–18.

63 See the analysis by Robinson (1960:80–2) and the United Nations' *Study of the Question of the Prevention and Punishment of the Crime of Genocide*, 47–86.
64 Goldenberg (1971: 23 and 18–26).
65 See the references cited in Fromm (1975: 159, 170–6).
66 Lorenz (1977: chs. 13 and 14).
67 See my discussion of the role of ideologies in *Race, Class and Power* (1974: Part One).

REFERENCES

Arendt, Hannah (1969). *Eichmann in Jerusalem*. New York: Viking Press.
Beardsley, Monroe C. (1976). "Reflections on Genocide and Ethnocide." In Richard Arens (ed.), *Genocide in Paraguay*. Philadelphia: Temple University Press, pp. 85–101.
Bedau, Hugo Adam (1974). "Genocide in Vietnam?" In Virginia Held, Sidney Morgenbesser, and Thomas Nagel (eds.), *Philosophy, Morality and International Affairs*. New York: Oxford University Press, pp. 5–46.
Caputo, Philip (1977). *A Rumor of War*. New York: Holt, Rinehart, and Winston.
Cohn, Norman (1967). *Warrant for Genocide*. New York: Harper and Row.
Desjardins, Thierry (1976). *Le Martyre du Liban*. Paris: Plon.
Donnedieu de Vabres (1947). *Le Procès de Nuremberg*. Paris: Editions Domat Montchrestien.
Drost, Pieter (1959). *Genocide* (Vol. II) and *The Crime of State* (Vol. II). Leyden: A. W. Sythoff. *Fact Finder, The* (1973). Vol. 31, no. 15 (16 June).
Falk, Richard A. "Ecocide, Genocide and the Nuremberg Tradition." In Virginia Held, Sidney Morgenbesser, and Thomas Nagel (eds.), *Philosophy, Morality and International Affairs*. New York: Oxford University Press, pp. 123–37.
Fromm, Erich (1975). *The Anatomy of Human Destructiveness*. Greenwich, CT: Fawcett Publications.
Goldberg, Arthur J. and Gardner, Richard N. (1972). "Time to Act on the Genocide Convention." *American Bar Association Journal* 58 (February): 141–5.
Goldenberg, Sydney L. (1971). "Crimes Against Humanity: 1945–1970." *Western Ontario Law Review* 10: 1–55.
Graetz, H. (1894). *History of the Jews*. 6 vols. Philadelphia: The Jewish Publication Society of America.
Hohenberg, John (1968). "The Crusade that Changed the U.N." *Saturday Review* (9 November).
Kuper, Leo (1974). *Race, Class and Power*. London: Duckworth.
Lamb, Harold (1927). *Genghis Khan*. New York: Pinnacle Books.
Law Reports of Trials of War Criminals (1948). Vols. VI, VII, XIX. London: United Nations War Crimes Commission, HMSO.
Lemkin, Raphaël (1944). *Axis Rule in Occupied Europe*. Washington: Carnegie Endowment for International Peace.
Lemkin, Raphaël (1947). "Genocide as a Crime under International Law." *American Journal of International Law* 41: 145–71.
Lewis, Norman (1976). "The Camp at Cecilio Baez." In Richard Arens (ed.), *Genocide in Paraguay*. Philadelphia: Temple University Press, pp. 58–68.
Lorenz, Konrad (1977). *On Aggression*. New York: Harcourt, Brace, and World.
Robinson, N. (1960). *The Genocide Convention*. New York: Institute of Jewish Affairs.
Sachar, Abram Leon (1967). *A History of the Jews*. New York: Knopf.
Sartre, Jean-Paul (1968). "On Genocide." *Ramparts* (February): 37–42.

Schwelb, Egon (1946). "Crimes Against Humanity." *British Yearbook of International Law* 23: 178–226.

Toynbee, Arnold J. (1947). *A Study of History.* London: Oxford University Press.

United Nations

(1) Reports of the proceedings and resolutions of the General Assembly, the Fourth Committee of the General Assembly, the Legal Committee, the Economic and Social Council, the Ad Hoc Committee on Genocide, the Commission on Human Rights, and the Sub-Commission on Prevention of Discrimination and Protection of Minorities.

(2) *Special Reports. Ad Hoc Working Group of Experts on Southern Africa.* E/CN. 4/950 dd. 27 October 1967. E/CN. 4/984/Add. 18 dd. 28 February 1969. E/CN. 4/1075, dd. 15 February 1972 (*Study concerning the question of apartheid from the point of view of international penal law*). A/32/226, dd. 10 October 1977 (*Deaths of detainees and police brutality in South Africa since the Soweto massacres in June 1976*). E/CN. 4/1311, dd. 26 January 1979 (*Violations of Human Rights in Southern Africa*).

(3) *Sub-Commission on the Prevention of Discrimination and Protection of Minorities.* E/CN. 4/Sub. 2/416, dd. 4 July 1978 (*Study of the Question of the Prevention and Punishment of the Crime of Genocide*).

(4) *United Nations Action in the Field of Human Rights.* New York: 1974.

United States

Congress

International Protection of Human Rights. Hearing before the Sub-Committee on International Organizations and Movements of the Committee on Foreign Affairs – House of Representatives, Ninety-Third Congress, First Session. August to December 1973. Washington: US Government Printing Office, 1974.

Department of State

Report on Human Rights Practices in Countries Receiving U.S. Aid. Washington: US Government Printing Office, 1979. "President Nixon Urges Senate Advice and Consent to Ratification of the Treaty on Genocide" *Bulletin* 62 (16 March 1970), 350–3.

Senate Committee on Foreign Relations

Hearings of May 24, 26, 1977 on the International Convention on the Prevention and Punishment of the Crime of Genocide, Washington: US Government Printing Office, 1977 (95th Congress, 1st Session).

Genocide Convention. Hearings Before a Sub-Committee of The Committee on Foreign Relations. US Senate, 81st Congress, 1st Session, April–May 1970. Washington: US Government Printing Office, 1970.

Walker, T. A. (1899). *A History of the Law of Nations.* Cambridge: Cambridge University Press.

Wedgwood, C. V. (1939). *The Thirty Years War.* New Haven, CT: Yale University Press.

Wolpert, Stanley (1977). *A New History of India.* New York: Oxford University Press.

4

Genocide: A Sociological Perspective

Helen Fein

Sociological Recognition of Genocide

There is much more talk of genocide in public discourse than attention to actual genocides. Possibly, the public consciousness that genocide still occurs and is an international crime has been effaced by the diffusion and banalization of the cry of genocide in political rhetoric just as the allegorical boy who cried wolf too often diminished attention to the wolf at the door. Porter observed that

genocide has been applied to all of the following: "race-mixing" (integration of blacks and non-blacks): drug distribution; methadone programs; the practice of birth control and abortions among Third World people; sterilization and "Missippi appendectomies" (tubal ligations and hysterectomies); medical treatment of Catholics; and the closing of synagogues in the Soviet Union. (1982: 9–10)

The trend to exploit genocide as metaphor and slogan continues. Charges of genocide occur regularly in the speeches of anti-abortion and anti-nuclear activists as well as partisans of both sides in the Israeli–Palestinian conflict. Minor examples of misuse I have collected include genocide as a result of suburbanization and of dieting. (All of these are omitted from the bibliography to avoid cluttering it up with citations that do not bear further investigation.)

Despite the prominence of international trials for genocide and war crimes and the Eichmann trial, the implications of the "final solution of the Jewish Question" by Nazi Germany were largely ignored and denied by writers and philosophers with the notable exception of Hannah Arendt (Kazin 1970: 5–6; Rosenberg [1987]: 31–2; Westbrook 1983). Similarly, it was largely overlooked or suppressed by social scientists until the 1970s. To study its recognition by sociologists, I reviewed introductory sociology texts spanning three decades 1947–77 (Fein 1979a). This showed that a minority of texts in all decades defined and recognized genocide; those in the middle decade (1957–67) were least likely to mention genocide while those published last (1968–77) were almost twice as likely to recognize genocide as those in the decade after World War II (47 percent:25 percent). Surveying anthropology, Shiloh found that none of the best-known anthropology texts or leading works in psychological anthropology recognized the Nazi genocide or genocide in general (1975).

The beginning of professional social-scientific interest in genocide was in the 1970s; virtually all the authors surveyed here first began working in this area in the seventies or the eighties. Reviews of library holdings at prominent libraries and of publications in print also show this; the 1970s marked the intellectual take-off stage. New books on genocide have more than doubled in the 1980s. Comparative research on genocide is still, however, almost wholly generated by scholars educated in the USA and writing in English – in the US, Canada, and Israel.

This interest in genocide and its boundaries can be ascribed to several factors, including specific generating conditions emerging in American social movements and political life: foremost among these was the increased legitimation given to ethnicity and collective probing of groups' roots and experiences in response to the emergence of the Black Power movement and the 1967 Seven-Day Israeli war. There were some universalists who decried the recognition of Jews as a political class who had previously denied or glossed over genocide who now focused on other groups as victims. Other scholars – most often from the collectivity of the victims – were more willing than before to question why and how specific groups became victims (Fein 1979a:183–4). This led to the emergence of more sophisticated questions in Holocaust research – no longer focusing solely on the perpetrators and victims – and new and more professional research on the Armenian genocide. And there was the increasing evidence that genocide was hardly just a historical question.

Between 1960 and 1979 there were probably at least a dozen genocides and genocidal massacres – cases include the Kurds in Iraq, southerners in the Sudan, Tutsi in Rwanda, Hutus in Burundi, Chinese and "communists" (see discussion of definition) in Indonesia, Hindus and other Bengalis in East Pakistan, the Aché in Paraguay, many peoples in Uganda, the people of East Timor after the Indonesian invasion in 1975, many peoples in Kampuchea. In a few cases, these events stirred public opinion and led to great campaigns in the West (as did allegations of genocide during the Nigerian civil war) but in most cases, these acts were virtually unnoted in the Western press and not remarked upon in world forums.

Nor were they remarked upon by sociology. Horowitz observes that "Many sociologists exhibit a studied embarrassment about these issues, a feeling that intellectual issues posed in such a manner are melodramatic and unfit for scientific discourse" (1982:3).

The emergence of interest in the Holocaust in the 1970s and the widespread perception of its uniqueness may both have aroused concern about genocide and diminished observation of less planned, less total, and less rationalized cases of extermination. But psychological and disciplinary barriers and status claims also may deter potential researchers. These questions are hard to study, harder to study well, leading one (if a responsible researcher) to improve skills in adjacent disciplines (such as historiography) and extending time demands beyond neat packaged and predictable schedules based on survey-research or other easily amenable source of data.

Further, positivism and professional status claims – indeed, even the claim to dispassionate understanding – sometimes provoke a backlash from genocide survivors. Most emotionally and intellectually sophisticated researchers in this area understand that empathy and passion – indeed, a passion to understand – are compatible and complementary to more dispassionate models of logic and method but this disjuncture is not always understood or respected by some members of their audience. But fear of affronting survivors can be exaggerated as a deterrent: the primary deterrent is our own inhibitors and lack of boldness.

DEFINING GENOCIDE AS A SOCIOLOGICAL CONCEPT

For the last decade, social scientists considering genocide have devised varying definitions and typologies, often reflecting consensus on evaluation of specific cases but dissensus on the borderlines of genocide. Controversy continues not only because genocide is hard to differentiate categorically but because most definers have normative or prescriptive agendas; we are activated by what we feel genocide should encompass – often not wishing to exclude any victims.

Debates recur about the identity of the target group, the scope of acts deemed genocidal, the identity of the perpetrator, the distinction among types of genocide, and whether or how to distinguish intent. This problem has been complicated lately by the convergence of interests linking researchers of genocide and state terror; the latter concentrate more on explanations of state behavior than of the choice of the victim group. Although this may prove to be a much-needed intellectual opening, it can also confound explanations when diverse objectives and behaviors are aggregated.

Because genocide itself occurs in the context of diverse social relations, it is useful to clarify how the term evolved in order to return to the underlying assumptions behind the concept; then I shall suggest a more generic concept, appropriate for sociological usage, paralleling the terms of the UNGC [UN Genocide Convention].

Lemkin's Conception and the UNGC Definition

Lemkin's conception (1944:79) emerged from an attempt to explain and indict German population policy. Later study has shown that Lemkin overidentified commonalities and implied a coherent and common objective in different countries. In fact, Hitler's objectives varied and were not always premeditated (Rich 1973/74). However, Lemkin recognized that Hitler had different population policies and aims in the occupied east and the west: "Germanization" or coerced denationalization and assimilation was not the same as "genocide." According to Lemkin (1944),

genocide does not necessarily mean the immediate destruction of a nation, except when accomplished by mass killings of all members of a nation. It is intended rather to signify a coordinated plan of different actions aiming at the destruction of essential foundations of the life of national groups, with the aim of annihilating the groups themselves. (79)...

Hitler's conception of genocide is based not upon cultural but only biological patterns... Some groups – such as the Jews – are to be destroyed completely. A distinction is made between peoples considered to be related by blood to the German people (such as Dutchmen, Norwegians, Flemings, Luxembourgers), and peoples not thus related by blood (such as the Poles, Slovenes, Serbs). The populations of the first group are deemed worthy of being Germanized. With respect to the Poles particularly, Hitler expressed the view that it is their soil alone which *can and should be profitably Germanized* (81–2)....

In the occupied countries of "people of non-related blood," a policy of depopulation is pursued. Foremost among the methods employed for the purpose is the adoption of measures calculated to decrease the birthrate of the national groups of non-related blood, while at the same time steps are taken to encourage the birthrate of the *Volksdeutsche* living in these countries (86). The physical debilitation and even annihilation of national groups in occupied countries is carried out mainly in the following ways:

1. *Racial discrimination in Feeding*...
2. *Endangering of Health*...
3. *Mass Killings*...(87–8)

First, we note, the object of genocide was always the defeated national group except for the Jews, conceived by the Nazis as a race or anti-race – non-human, super-human, and menacing. Political groups and classes within the nation who were killed and incarcerated by the German occupiers were conceived as members of a national group. Second, Lemkin conceived of genocide as a set of coordinated tactics or means. *Cultural genocide* was not a term used by Lemkin: cultural discrimination may be a tactic to assimilate or to destroy a group. The objective of genocide was both the social disintegration and the biological destruction of the group. Third, Lemkin recognized grades of genocide: some groups were to be immediately and wholly annihilated (the Jews); others (especially the Poles) were to be slowly destroyed by other means to decimate their numbers and decapitate their leadership. The victims might be observed by contemporaries as destroyed in whole or in part. Members of other occupied nations would be allowed to survive as individuals but their national institutions, culture, and group organization would be destroyed and they would become Germanized. Such coerced assimilation without killing or the interruption of procreation and parenting was not cited by Lemkin as genocide. The deliberate destruction of the culture of a distinct group without physical annihilation of its members is most often termed *ethnocide* now.

The United Nations committees that framed the UNGC both further specified the protected groups and delimited the connotations of genocide to (1) biological destruction and serious injury (see Art. II, a, b, and c) and (2) indirect sociobiological destruction by restricting the biological reproduction of group members and breaking the linkage between reproduction and socialization (d and e).

Article II: "In the present Convention, genocide means any of the following acts committed with intent to destroy, in whole or in part, a national, ethnical, racial or religious group as such: (a) Killing members of the group; (b) Causing serious bodily or mental harm to members of the group; (c) Deliberately inflicting on the group conditions of life calculated to bring about its physical destruction in whole or in part; (d) Imposing measures intended to prevent births within the group; (e) Forcibly transferring children of the group to another group."

Three problems are repeatedly noted by critics of the Convention: (1) the gaps in groups covered; (2) the ambiguity of *intent to destroy a group "as such"*; and (3) the inability of non-state parties to invoke the Convention and the failure to set up an independent enforcement body. Since the first two problems bear on the definition (an essential for research), I will concentrate on this criticism. Furthermore, I will argue that the second problem – the question of intent – can be resolved by discriminating intent from motive; intent is purposeful action.

The Convention has been repeatedly criticized for omission of political groups and social classes as target groups; a recent report commissioned by the UN Human Rights Commission recommended its extension to political and sexual groups (Whitaker 1985: 16–19). Drost, an early critic, made these incisive objections:

Man lives not alone but in groups. He belongs to a group either by birth or from choice . . . By leaving political and other groups beyond the purported protection the authors of the Convention also left a wide and dangerous loophole for any government to escape the human duties under the Convention by putting genocide into practice under the cover of executive measures against political or other groups for reasons of security, public order or any other reason of state . . . A convention on genocide cannot effectively contribute to the protection of certain, described minorities when it is limited to particular defined groups . . . It serves no purpose to restrict international legal protection to some groups firstly because the protected members always belong at the same time to other, unprotected groups . . . (1959: Vol. 2, 122–3)

LeBlanc, on the other hand, believes the exclusion of political groups was wise because of the "difficulty inherent in selecting criteria for determining what constitutes a political group," their instability over time, the right of the state to protect itself, and the potential misuses of genocide – labeling of antagonists in war and political conflict (1988: 292–4). He refers to a proposal by Jordan Paust for a new draft convention criminalizing the "Crime of Politicide."

The first draft of the UNGC in the UN Ad Hoc Committee on Genocide extended protection to political groups, groups which were never considered by Lemkin as subjects of genocide. Such inclusion was opposed not only by Soviet bloc states but by other states, an often-overlooked point (LeBlanc 1988: 273–6). That draft also criminalized "cultural genocide" (intentional acts destroying language, religion, and culture) – a proviso opposed by Western states – although Lemkin had never distinguished cultural genocide.

This instigated vigorous debate on the roots and rationale of genocides. Some states expressed fears that the inclusion of political groups would impede the ratification of the Convention because states might anticipate that suppression of subversive elements and disorders could instigate external intervention – states might be called to account. Finally, committee members arrived at an accommodation, deleting both cultural genocide and political groups (Kuper 1981: 24–9). The US accepted the deletion of political groups in exchange for a clause allowing the establishment of an international criminal tribunal (LeBlanc 1988: 277–8). The exclusion of political groups was one of the charges against the UNGC which critics used to prevent its ratification by the US Senate for forty years.

The unpublished work of Lemkin shows that he was fully cognizant that the nature of groups which might be targets changed as forms of social organization and historical situations changed. His examples of genocide or genocidal situations include: Albigensians, American Indians, Assyrians in Iraq, Belgian Congo, Christians in Japan, French in Sicily (ca. 1282), Hereros, Huguenots, Incas, Mongols, the Soviet Union/Ukraine, Tasmania. Apparently, Lemkin did not consider political groups as targets. In a description of an abstract for a book he intended to write, "Introduction to the Study of Genocide," he observed: "The philosophy of the Genocide Convention is based on the formula of the human cosmos. This cosmos consists of four basic groups: national, racial, religious and ethnic. The groups are protected not only by reasons of human compassion but also to prevent draining the spiritual resources of mankind."[1]

Some Sociological Definitions and Issues

Many social scientists have accepted the UNGC definition of genocide explicitly or implicitly (Fein 1979b; Kuper 1981; Porter 1982:12; Harff and Gurr 1987) or a broadened version thereof, including political and social groups (Horowitz 1982: 17–18; Chalk and Jonassohn 1990; Tal 1979). Charny proposes what he calls "a *humanistic* definition ...: the *wanton* murder of human beings on the basis of any identity whatsoever that they share" (1988:4). Legters, who says he generally favors a strict construction of genocide excluding political groups, argues for the inclusion of social classes as class is the unit of social organization in socialist societies (1984:65).

Those who accept the UNGC definition usually acknowledge that mass killings of political groups show similarities in their causes, organization, and motives: some authors refer to these as "genocidal massacres" (Kuper 1981), "ideological massacres" (Fein 1984) or "politicides" (Harff and Gurr 1987).

Virtually everyone acknowledges that genocide is primarily a crime of state. Chalk and Jonassohn refer to the "state or other authority" as perpetrators, encompassing settlers acting in the name of the nation-state (1990:23). Although there is little disagreement over this, heuristically it seems preferable to me to omit variable terms as criteria in a definition: marginal situations in which genocide or genocidal massacres not authorized by the state occur include colonization, civil wars, and the transfer of powers during decolonization. Actors who may have committed genocide without state authorization include soldiers, settlers, and missionaries.

Dadrian (1975), attempting to offer a general explanation encompassing the Armenian genocide, was the first sociologist known to propose a definition – actually an explanation sketch – of genocide. He states:

Genocide is the successful attempt by a dominant group, vested with formal authority and with preponderant access to the overall resources of power, to reduce by coercion or lethal violence the number of a minority group whose ultimate extermination is held desirable and useful and whose respective vulnerability is a major factor contributing to the decision for genocide. (1974:123)

Here explanation has usurped definition; furthermore, it is not clear what is to be observed and classed as genocide except that the perpetrator is a representative of

the dominant group and the victims are a minority group. This elementary distinction was later outmoded by the Khmer Rouge genocide in Kampuchea. I shall later
return to Dadrian's contributions.

Chalk and Jonassohn, beginning to teach a course on the history and sociology of
genocide in the 1980s – some may have seen earlier editions of their (1990) book –
advanced a singular and straightforward definition which is essentially similar to
one they have employed since 1984:

Genocide is a form of one-sided mass killing in which a state or other authority intends to
destroy a group, as that group and membership in it are defined by the perpetrators. (1990:23)

There are several problems with this definition.

1   The limitation of the perpetrator to "a state or other authority." Chalk argues
that if settler murders go unpunished, it is because states do not try to stop them or
prosecute them; hence the state is responsible for condoning them (1988:7). It seems
to me this confuses the question of who is the perpetrator (in definition) with who –
what organization or persons – is responsible for prevention and prosecution.

2   The specification of "one-sided mass killing" implies a numeric threshold or
ratio of victims which may obscure recognition of the earlier stages of genocide.
Their emphasis on mass killing also omits other forms of intentional biological
destruction (see earlier discussion of Lemkin). "One-sided" killing is also problematic; it is unclear whether or when this includes mass killings of groups which may
have an armed party or subgroup either defending themselves or attacking a party or
elite of the dominant group.

3   The definition of the group is open-ended, implying that an endless number of
groups can be constructed, including groups constructed from the paranoid imagination of despots – "wreckers" in Stalin's time. This is in accord with the assumptions
of labeling theory (although the authors do not explicitly draw on this) which posits
that the construction (and destruction) of enemies depends on their labeling by the
powerful. Chalk and Jonassohn explain that their definition follows "W. I. Thomas'
famous dictum that if people define a situation as real it is real in its consequences"
(1990:25). But, like all dicta, this has to be examined to determine how, when, and
why it applies.

The definition of Chalk and Jonassohn has served their goal of casting a wide net,
exploring a range of situations in which people are victimized by definition or at
random – "witches" (the witch-hunt is considered a precursor of genocide), the
Knights Templar, the victims of Shaka's and Stalin's terror. It points the way toward
an emerging theory of terror – murder, torture, and intimidation – and genocide. But
to get there, we need to distinguish both processes. Indeed, Chalk and Jonassohn
reflected in an earlier paper on the different functions served by torture and genocide: torture is a means to control people whom state agents expect to remain as
members of the state; genocide is a means to eliminate a group or people from the
state (1983:13–14). The study of terror should include the explanation of victims
created by definition – conspiracies of witches and wreckers. When and why do
states manufacture victims by labeling them with fictive identities and accusing them
of nonexistent crimes? The labeling perspective is most suggestive for studies of
manufactured deviance for social control.

However, the victims of genocide are generally members of real groups, whether conceived of as collectivities, races, or classes, who acknowledge their existence, although there may be administrative designation of their membership as German authorities designated Jews for "the Final Solution," including some people of Jewish lineage who no longer considered themselves Jews (and did not register voluntarily with the Jewish community) or were members of other religious communities (converts and their children). Had there not been an actual Jewish community with its own institutions, German authorities could not have defined and enumerated Jews, for there was no objective indicator of their alleged criteria of Jewishness – race – which divided "Jews" and "Aryans" categorically.

Harff and Gurr (1987) distinguish genocides (using an abbreviated version of the UNGC) from "politicides" – massacres of political groups in opposition, including groups in rebellion. Thus, Harff and Gurr's universe of politicide includes many cases Chalk and Jonassohn label as genocide; however, other cases included in the Harff and Gurr universe of politicides are excluded from Chalk and Jonassohn's universe of genocide because they include bilateral killing. [...]

A Sociological Definition Proposed

I believe that the UNGC definition of genocide can be reconciled with an expanded – but bounded – sociological definition if we focus on how the core concepts are related. From the root of *genus* we may infer that the protected groups were conceived (by Lemkin and the UN framers) as basic kinds, classes, or subfamilies of humanity, persisting units of society. What is distinctive sociologically is that such groups are usually ascriptive – based on birth rather than by choice – and often inspire enduring particularistic loyalties. They are sources of identity and value; they are the seed-bed of social movements, voluntary associations, congregations, and families; in brief, they are *collectivities*.

Further, these collectivities endure as their members tend to reproduce their own kind (to the extent ingroup marriage is the norm). But collectivities need not be self-reproducing to be cohesive over a given span in time.

The UNGC implies a universalistic norm: each group has a right to exist and develop its own culture, assuming neither their aim or methods are criminal; all collectivities should be protected from such crimes against humanity. One can also argue that political, sexual, and class-denominated status groups or collectivities, just like ethnic and religious collectivities, are basic continuing elements of the community. (Whitaker 1985 made a similar argument for extension of the UNGC.)

There is no categorical line, in fact, between the enduring character of ascribed (heritable) identities and elected or achieved identities: both may be constructed or passed on generationally. Being an Italian working-class Communist Party member may be just as heritable a characteristic as being an Italian church-going Roman Catholic. Indeed, church and party could be regarded as counter-congregations or counter-cultures. Both affiliations may be outcomes of election or ascription, conscience or inheritance.

A new sociological definition should include the following elements: (a) it should clearly denote the object and processes under study and discriminate the latter from related processes; (b) it should stipulate constructs which can be transformed operationally to indicate real-world observable events; and (c) the specification of groups covered should be consistent with our sociological knowledge of both the persistence and construction of group identities in society, the variations in class, ethnic/racial, gender, class/political consciousness and the multiplicity and interaction of peoples' identities and statuses in daily life. Further, (d) it should conform to the implicit universalistic norm and a sense of justice, embracing the right of all nonviolent groups to coexist.

Briefly put,

Genocide is sustained purposeful action by a perpetrator to physically destroy a collectivity directly or indirectly, through interdiction of the biological and social reproduction of group members, sustained regardless of the surrender or lack of threat offered by the victim.

To expand on this sociological definition, one can also show how it encompasses the legal definition {terms of the UNGC are noted in these brackets}.

Genocide is sustained purposeful action [thus excluding single massacres, pogroms, accidental deaths] **by a perpetrator** (assuming an actor organized over a period) **to physically destroy a collectivity** {"acts committed with intent to destroy, in whole or in part a national/ethnical/racial or religious group": Art. 2} **directly** (through mass or selective murders and calculable physical destruction – e.g., imposed starvation and poisoning of food, water, and air – {see Art. 2, a–c}) **or through interdiction of the biological and social reproduction of group members** (preventing births {Art. 2, d} and {"forcibly transferring children of the group to another group": Art. 2, e}, systematically breaking the linkage between reproduction and socialization of children in the family or group of origin).

This definition would cover the sustained destruction of non-violent political groups and social classes as parts of a national (or ethnic/religious/racial) group but does not cover the killing of members of military and paramilitary organizations – the SA, the Aryan Nations, and armed guerrillas.

Documenting *genocide* or **genocide** demands (at the very least) identifying a perpetrator(s), the target group attacked as a collectivity, assessing its numbers and victims, and recognizing a pattern of repeated actions from which we infer the intent of purposeful action to eliminate them. Such inference is easiest to draw when we can cite both preexistent plans or statements of intent and the military or bureaucratic organization of a death machine; seldom do we have both kinds of evidence.

Despite the increased level of violence of modern warfare, we can still distinguish war crimes from genocide and crimes against humanity if we specify the criteria further: the following paradigm aims to clarify this and other questions.

A Paradigm for Detecting and Tracing Genocide

I have culled the elements of a paradigm to detect genocide and to document its course from my own studies and others. Propositions 1–5 state necessary and sufficient conditions for a finding of genocide; these are followed by questions noting the variable characteristics of the criterion specified. Questions 6–14 examine variable reinforcing conditions, contexts, responses, and effects.

1   *There was a sustained attack or continuity of attacks by the perpetrator to physically destroy group members:* (a) Did a series of actions or a single action of the perpetrator leading to the death of members of group X occur? (b) What tactics were used to maximize the number of victims? Tactics include preceding round-ups, isolation, and concentration of victims and orders to report. (c) What means, besides direct killing, were used to destroy the victims or to interdict the biological and social reproduction of the group? Actions may include poisoning air or water, imposed starvation, or disease; forcible prevention of birth; involuntary transfer of children. (d) What was the duration, sequence of actions, and number of victims? Trace the time span, repetition of similar or related actions, and the number of victims.

2   *The perpetrator was a collective or organized actor or commander of organized actors:* Genocide is distinguished from homicide empirically by the fact it is never an act of a single individual – thus we want to know: (a) Were the perpetrators joined as an armed force, paramilitary force or informal band? (b) Was there a continuity of leadership or membership of perpetrators or similar bases of recruitment for such forces? (c) Were these forces authorized or organized by the state to exist? (d) To whom were those forces responsible – an agency of the state, army, or party? (e) Were they organized and garbed to display or to deny government responsibility?

3   *Victims were selected because they were members of a collectivity:* (a) Were victims selected irrespective of any charge against them individually? (b) Were they chosen on the basis of a state administrative designation of their group identity, their own criteria of identity, or by physical, linguistic, or other signs or stigmata of identity? (c) Were they chosen on the basis of status within the collectivity, e.g., priests, religious leaders, or educated class? (d) What was the basis of the collectivity, e.g., religion, race, ethnicity, tribal or linguistic status? (e) Were they pre-selected before killing? Evidence of pre-selection includes their prior legal definition; stripping of citizenship, civil rights, state posts, licenses and benefits, and legal group recognition; segregation and marking; rounding-up and ghettoization or concentration.

4   *The victims were defenseless or were killed regardless of whether they surrendered or resisted*: (a) Is part of the victims' group armed and organized to physically resist the perpetrators' group? (b) Is their level of armament sufficient and is their stated intent to wage war against the perpetrators? Or is it to defend themselves from being seized? (c) Is there evidence (if the victims were armed) that they were purposefully killed after surrender and that unarmed members of the group were systematically killed?

5   *The destruction of group members was undertaken with intent to kill and murder was sanctioned by the perpetrator:* (a) Can deaths of group members be explained as accidental outcomes? (b) Is there evidence of repetition of destruction by design or as a foreseeable outcome? (c) Is there direct evidence of orders or authorization for the destruction of the victims? (d) At what level did the authorization occur? (e) Is there prima facie evidence that the pattern of acts and personnel

involved show that authorities had to plan, organize, or overlook a pattern of destruction? (f) Is there any negative evidence of sanctions against agents responsible for such acts?

6   *Consistency of sanctions for killing group members:* (a) Are there any rules promulgated by the perpetrator to punish or to exonerate individual murder, torture, and rape of members of the victim group? (b) Are there institutional mechanisms to implement such rules? (c) Are there examples of sanctions enforced against murder of members of the victim group or for failure to protect them from attacks by members of the perpetrator group? Are there sanctions for refusing to participate in killing the victims or for reporting commission of killings?

7   *Ideologies and beliefs legitimating genocide:* (a) Is there evidence of an ideology, myth, or an articulated social goal which enjoins or justifies the destruction of the victim? Besides the above, observe religious traditions of contempt and collective defamation, stereotypes, and derogatory metaphor indicating the victim is inferior, subhuman (animals, insects, germs, viruses) or superhuman (Satanic, omnipotent), or other signs that the victims were pre-defined as alien, outside the universe of obligation of the perpetrator, subhuman or dehumanized, or the enemy – i.e., the victim needs to be eliminated in order that we may live (Them or Us). (b) If destructive acts were acknowledged by the perpetrator, how were they labeled and justified? (c) Did the acknowledgement, labeling, and justification change before different audiences?

8   *Contexts of genocide:* Contexts include specific perpetrator–victim interactions and critical conditions of state and society. In the former case, one asks what kinds of relations characterized the perpetrator and victim before genocide. In the latter, one asks in what historical and political context did these acts occur? Contexts include post-revolutionary states, diminishing states losing control of territory after defeat, expanding states and empires colonizing other continents or an undeveloped interior, war between and within states, and eras of consolidation of centralized state power. Social-psychological contexts include social and personal disorganization and cultural crises of identity and meaning.

9   *Bystanders' responses:* What kinds of responses did bystanders, other states, regional and international organizations, make to the perpetrators and victims?

10   *Victims' responses:* How did the victims understand and respond to the situation?

11   *Interactions:* What effect did the bystanders' responses have on the victims and the perpetrators?

12   *Effects on victims:* What was the impact of the genocide on the victims at the time and later? Specify destruction of individuals and the community, personal and social disorganization, post-traumatic stress, and enduring personal and trans-generational consequences.

13   *Effects on the perpetrators:* (a) What was the impact of the genocide on the perpetrators? (b) Could these effects be foreseen or calculated? (c) Were they? (d) Did they acknowledge or deny the genocide? (e) Did they offer restitution or agree to such to the victims later? (f) What effect did their acknowledgment or denial have on their state and society?

14   *Effects on the world system:* How did the recognition or lack of recognition and sanctions against genocide affect the actions of other states and peoples?

Typologies of Genocide and Case-finding

Despite some disagreement of scholars labeling types (see table 4.1) and disparate criteria for subtypes, there seems much agreement between earlier scholars (lines 1–5) on which cases fit into the specific types.

[...] General explanations are difficult because of the diversity of situations and motives for genocide yet the quest for general explanations persists. Yet extensively differentiated types can obfuscate research by diverting analyses into arguments over classification rather than explanation.

The disagreement observed in table 4.1 is primarily between Harff and Gurr (1987, 1988) and others. This can be partly attributed to their inclusion of *politicides* which include victims who are members of groups which have rebelled against the state. [...]

There is no intrinsic reason why we can not simply specify the criteria which discriminate particular types; e.g., the presence of ideology, of organized threat by a party representing the victim, and the inclusion of the victim in the polity.

Table 4.1 Typologies of genocide compared, 1975–90

Types Examples in ( )	I (Holocaust; Armenian gen.)	II (East Pak. 1971, Burundi 1972)	III (Paraguay, Brazil 1970–)	IV	Other
1 Dadrian (1975)	Optimal	Retributive	Utilitarian	Latent	Cultural
2 Kuper (1981)	Against hostage or scapegoat groups	Following decoloniz. of a two-tier system of domination	Against indigenous peoples	Genocidal massacres (Hiroshima; Dresden; Vietnam) **************	
3 Fein (1984)	Ideological	Retributive	Developmental	Despotic	
4 Smith (1987)	Ideological	Retributive Monopolistic	Utilitarian	Institutional	
5 Chalk and Jonassohn (1990)	To implement a belief, ideology or theory	To eliminate a real or potential threat	To acquire economic wealth	To spread terror among real or potential enemies	

* *

	Genocides:		Politicides:
6 Harff and Gurr (1988)	Xenophobic (Aché Indians, Paraguay; Ibos, Nigeria)	Hegemonial (Soviet nationalities)	Retributive Repressive Revolutionary Repressive/ hegemonial
7 Harff and Gurr (1987)	G: "genocide, victims defined communally" (includes examples in classes above)	PG: "politicides against politically-active communal groups" (Burundi, East Pakistan, E. Timor)	GP: "episodes with mixed communal and political victims" (Uganda, Equat. Guinea, Kampuchea)

*******Represents discontinuity between theorists above and below line.

Table 4.2 Defining preconditions and likely victims of different types of genocide

PRECONDITION	Ideological	Retributive	TYPE Developmental	Despotic
Ideology	+	−	−	−
Threat to domination of perpetrator by part or whole of victims' collectivity	−	+	−	−
Dictatorship (likely precondition)	+	−	−	+
Conflict with indigenous people	−	−	+	−
Victims' socioeconomic status				
Working class	−	−	−	−
Middle class	+	−	−	−
Educated class	+	+	−	+
Middleman-minority; "strangers"	+	−	−	+
Hunting and gathering people	−	−	+	−

Table 4.2 shows the necessary conditions for each type of genocide (using labels from my typology, table 4.1, line 3) in the top half and the most likely class of victims in each type in the bottom half; the reader will note the specific victims are discriminated by their group identity rather than their class identity but groups, often being the basis of stratification, can also be observed as parts of different classes with unequal life chances. [...]

A Sociological Research Agenda

Genocide studies could be approached to enrich sociology, probing theses about modernity, development, bureaucracy, and social organization, as well as to better understand genocide. Such studies may become part of a developing interdisciplinary field of human rights or of state repression and terror – both conceptualizations are emerging in political science – or the sociology of ethnic/race relations: or both. They are also related to studies of altruism and helping behavior (e.g., Staub 1989).

In order to both integrate theory and research and to produce new insights, rather than regressing to empty and airy generalizations, we must make our assumptions explicit, codify criteria of genocide and case-finding, take into account both the specificity of particular types and cases of genocide in designing studies, and use a range of skills and methods from different disciplines. Some steps to this end include: clear definition, use of a paradigm for detecting and classing events as genocides or genocidal massacres (as was proposed earlier), and an agenda of questions for research. We need better questions rather than improved ideal-types which sometimes serve as a substitute for what has to be explained. Both to advance basic research and to offer us clues to deterrence, I propose a strategy of comparisons in the following research agenda:

1   Compare the uses of genocide and other strategies of elimination (ethnocide and expulsion) or of inclusion in settler societies in the Americas, Africa, Australia, and New Zealand developed by Old World colonists; consider what accounts for the different results.

2   Evaluate factors which facilitate and deter genocide – group composition, political structure, political culture – by comparative research on contemporary multi-ethnic societies with a high proportion of "minorities at risk" and with a tradition of collective violence, to explain how and when the state sets limits. Compare the use of genocide and genocidal massacre in divided societies with similar compositions but different state formations, elites or guiding ideologies: e.g., India and Pakistan; Indonesia, Malaysia, and Singapore; Honduras and Guatemala.

3   Compare the use of genocide (and other strategies of changing population to fit the definition of the state-people) and the definition of enemies in postrevolutionary and other totalitarian states; when do states define the enemies they need to create a fictive solidarity? Reconsider historical cases – e.g., the Vendée (Secher [1968]).

4   Consider the effect of collective behavior and the dynamic of political processes leading to destruction. How and when do genocidal massacres occur without planning as polities become more polarized? How do collective terrorism, ethnically based parties and movements and forms of governance (Westminster-type parliamentary democracy, decentralized democracies, one-party states, etc.) promote this process? What is the role of third parties in these processes?

5   Assess the incidence, coincidence, and relationship between genocide, interstate war, civil strife, and transitions of state power: decolonization, partition, revolution, coups.

In order to deter genocide, this agenda should include other questions for policy research such as the following.

6   Consider the impact of different means of social change – violent and nonviolent – and strategic adaptations thereof that are needed to destratify societies with high genocidal potential.

7   Systematically assess the extent of genocidal massacre and life-threatening conditions deliberately imposed on indigenous peoples in states today and evaluate the web of causality and responsibility.

8   Monitor and evaluate the level of violation of life-integrity in states which are gross violators of human rights today or have been: all types of state killings, torture, denial of any process, arbitrary imprisonment and deprivation of freedom of movement, forced labor and slavery.

9   Survey social inhibitions against genocide and gross human rights violations within high-risk states by attitude surveys of tolerance toward minorities at risk, belief in democratic norms, hostility toward minorities or outrage against violations of their rights collectively.

10   Consider the impact of international linkages – through patron/client relations, arms transfer, aid, trade and political support – on sustaining or deterring genocidal states as a preliminary to testing strategies to affect or expose such linkages.

11   Probe the effect of international charges of massacre and genocide on states which might have used or were expected to employ genocide against a defeated minority antagonistic to the ruling state elite, e.g., Nigeria and Zimbabwe. Also consider the impact of prompt exposure and international protest against group persecution and killings in cases where killings were stopped: the Baha'i in Iran, suspect ethnic groups or political enemies in Surinam and Kenya in the 1980s.

12   Assess the cause and effect of the failure of states to prosecute genocide, to enforce the Genocide Convention, and to use past perpetrators of genocide (currently the Khmer Rouge) as political agents.

13   Consider the use of all kinds of power – normative, economic, and physical – to change this and the responsibility of world powers, regional powers, and international organizations. Consider the uses of sanctions against the bystanders as well as the perpetrators of genocide. Evaluate what we know from studies of mediation, conciliation, and arbitration: when can such models be drawn on successfully to deter genocide?

Several kinds of research and researchers thus are needed: historical studies to put genocide in the perspective of time, civilization, and the development of the nation-state; macroscopic studies of societies in the same phase of development or presented with (and inflicting on others) the same problems at one time; comparative case-studies of matched cases where similar preconditions indicated that states had the potential for genocide; case-studies of genocides suspected but deterred and other cases where violence was arrested; empirical surveys of the level of collective violence in many states longitudinally; comparative political studies of how states "manage" ethnic conflict and coexistence more or less non-violently; policy studies that might point to means to deter genocide.

This is a heavy agenda – one which merits scholarly and personal investment of resources, I believe. As many have noted, this is a time of possibilities. Perhaps the recent evidence of global demands in authoritarian and totalitarian states for democracy indicates there is also the possibility to counter the "banality of evil" (Arendt 1963) in our time. But democratization itself may lead to freer expressions of intergroup hostility: collective violence, riots, and genocide have already occurred in the USSR, Romania, Bulgaria, and Yugoslavia. In order to deter both collective violence and genocide, the forces leading to destruction need to be better understood. Those leading in the other direction not only need to be understood but must be better nurtured and organized.

NOTE

1   I am grateful to Rabbi Steven L. Jacobs (Birmingham, AL) who is currently editing the Lemkin papers for (1) an inventory of Lemkin's unpublished papers (1942–59) prepared by Kathleen McIntyre for the American Jewish Archives, Cincinnati, Ohio; (2) an inven-

tory of the New York Public Library collection of Lemkin correspondence and writings. The citation is from the NYPL collection, box 2.

REFERENCES

Arendt, Hannah (1963). *Eichmann in Jerusalem: A Report on the Banality of Evil*. New York: Viking Press.

Chalk, Frank (1988). *Definitions of Genocide and Their Implications for Prediction and Prevention*. Montreal: Montreal Institute for Genocide Studies.

Chalk, Frank and Jonassohn, Kurt (1983). "Culture, Persecution, Perpetrator Intent, and Their Effects on the Human Rights Agenda." Paper presented at the 17th World Congress of Philosophy, Montreal, August 21–7.

Chalk, Frank and Jonassohn, Kurt (1988). "The History and Sociology of Genocidal Killings." In I.W. Charny (ed.), *Genocide: A Critical Bibliographic Review*. New York: Facts on File, pp. 39–58.

Chalk, Frank and Jonassohn, Kurt (eds.) (1990). *The History and Sociology of Genocide: Analyses and Case Studies*. New Haven, CT: Yale University Press.

Charny, Israel W. (ed.) (1988). *Genocide: A Critical Bibliographic Review*. New York: Facts on File.

Dadrian, Vahakn (1974). "The Structural Functional Components of Genocide: A Victimological Approach to the Armenian Case." In I. Drapkin and E. Viano (eds.), *Victimology*. Lexington, MA: Heath, pp. 123–35.

Dadrian, Vahakn (1975). "A Typology of Genocide." *International Review of Modern Sociology* 5:201–12.

Drost, Pieter N. (1959). *The Crime of State*. 2 vols. Leyden: A. W. Sythoff.

Fein, Helen (1979a). "Is Sociology Aware of Genocide? Recognition of Genocide in Introductory Sociology Texts in the US, 1947–1977." *Humanity and Society* (August): 177–93.

Fein, Helen (1979b). *Accounting for Genocide: National Responses and Jewish Victimization During the Holocaust*. New York: Free Press.

Fein, Helen (1984). "Scenarios of Genocide: Models of Genocide and Critical Responses." In Israel W. Charny (ed.), *Toward the Understanding and Prevention of Genocide: Proceedings of the International Conference on the Holocaust and Genocide*. Boulder, CO: Westview, pp. 3–31.

Harff, Barbara and Gurr, Ted (1987). "Genocides and Politicides since 1945: Evidence and Anticipation." *Internet on the Holocaust and Genocide* 13:1–7.

Harff, Barbara and Gurr, Ted (1988). "Toward Empirical Theory of Genocides and Politicides: Identification and Measurement of Cases since 1945." *International Studies Quarterly* 37(3):359–71.

Horowitz, Irving Louis (1982). *Taking Lives: Genocide and State Power*. 3rd ed. (augmented). New Brunswick, NJ: Transaction.

Kazin, Alfred (1970). "Living with the Knowledge of the Holocaust, 1945–1970." *Midstream* 116(6):3–8.

Kuper, Leo (1981). *Genocide: Its Political Use in the Twentieth Century*. New Haven, CT: Yale University Press.

LeBlanc, Lawrence J. (1988). "The United Nations Genocide Convention and Political Groups: Should the United States Propose an Amendment?" *Yale Journal of International Law* 13(2):268–94.

Lemkin, Raphaël (1944). *Axis Rule in Occupied Europe*. Washington, DC: Carnegie Endowment for International Peace.

Legters, Lyman H. (1984). "The Soviet Gulag: Is it Genocide?" In Israel W. Charny (ed.), *Toward the Understanding and Prevention of Genocide: Proceedings of the International Conference on the Holocaust and Genocide*. Boulder, CO: Westview, pp. 60–6.

Porter, Jack Nusan (1982). "Introduction." In Jack Nusan Porter (ed.), *Genocide and Human Rights: A Global Anthology*. Washington, DC: University Press of America, pp. 2–33.

Rich, Norman (1973/74). *Hitler's War Aims*. 2 vols. New York: Norton.

Secher, Reynald (1968). *Le Génocide franco-français: La Vendée*. Paris: Presses Universitaires de France.

Shiloh, Ailon (1975). "Psychological Anthropology: A Case Study in Cultural Blindness." *Current Anthropology* 16(4):618–20.

Smith, Roger W. (1987). "Human Destructiveness and Politics: The Twentieth Century as an Age of Genocide." In Isidor Wallimann and Michael N. Dobkowski (eds.), *Genocide and the Modern Age: Etiology and Case Studies of Mass Death*. New York: Greenwood Press, pp. 21–39.

Staub, Ervin (1989). *The Roots of Evil: The Psychological and Cultural Origins of Genocide and Other Forms of Group Violence*. Cambridge: Cambridge University Press.

Tal, Uriel (1979). "On the Study of the Holocaust and Genocide." *Yad Vashem Studies* 13:7–52.

Westbrook, Robert B. (1983). "The Responsibility of Peoples: Dwight Macdonald and the Holocaust." *Holocaust Studies Annual* 1:35–68.

Whitaker, Ben (1985). *Revised and Updated Report on the Question of the Prevention and Punishment of the Crime of Genocide*. New York: United Nations.

5

Eichmann in Jerusalem: A Report on the Banality of Evil

Hannah Arendt

The Accused

Otto Adolf, son of Karl Adolf Eichmann and Maria née Schefferling, caught in a suburb of Buenos Aires on the evening of May 11, 1960, flown to Israel nine days later, brought to trial in the District Court in Jerusalem on April 11, 1961, stood accused on fifteen counts: "together with others" he had committed crimes against the Jewish people, crimes against humanity, and war crimes during the whole period of the Nazi regime and especially during the period of the Second World War. The Nazis and Nazi Collaborators (Punishment) Law of 1950, under which he was tried, provides that "a person who has committed one of these ... offenses ... is liable to the death penalty." To each count Eichmann pleaded: "Not guilty in the sense of the indictment."

In what sense then did he think he was guilty? In the long cross-examination of the accused, according to him "the longest ever known," neither the defense nor the prosecution nor, finally, any of the three judges ever bothered to ask him this obvious question. His lawyer, Robert Servatius of Cologne, hired by Eichmann and paid by the Israeli government (following the precedent set at the Nuremberg Trials, where all attorneys for the defense were paid by the Tribunal of the victorious powers), answered the question in a press interview: "Eichmann feels guilty before God, not before the law," but this answer remained without confirmation from the accused himself. The defense would apparently have preferred him to plead not guilty on the grounds that under the then existing Nazi legal system he had not done anything wrong, that what he was accused of were not crimes but "acts of state," over which no other state has jurisdiction (*par in parem imperium non habet*), that it had been his duty to obey and that, in Servatius' words, he had committed acts "for which you are decorated if you win and go to the gallows if you lose." (Thus Goebbels had

declared in 1943: "We will go down in history as the greatest statesmen of all times
or as their greatest criminals.") Outside Israel (at a meeting of the Catholic Academy
in Bavaria, devoted to what the *Rheinischer Merkur* called "the ticklish problem" of
the "possibilities and limits in the coping with historical and political guilt through
criminal proceedings"), Servatius went a step farther, and declared that "the only
legitimate criminal problem of the Eichmann trial lies in pronouncing judgment
against his Israeli captors, which so far has not been done" – a statement, incidentally, that is somewhat difficult to reconcile with his repeated and widely publicized
utterances in Israel, in which he called the conduct of the trial "a great spiritual
achievement," comparing it favorably with the Nuremberg Trials.

Eichmann's own attitude was different. First of all, the indictment for murder was
wrong: "With the killing of Jews I had nothing to do. I never killed a Jew, or a non-
Jew, for that matter – I never killed any human being. I never gave an order to kill
either a Jew or a non-Jew; I just did not do it," or, as he was later to qualify this
statement, "It so happened . . . that I had not once to do it" – for he left no doubt that
he would have killed his own father if he had received an order to that effect. Hence
he repeated over and over (what he had already stated in the so-called Sassen
documents, the interview that he had given in 1955 in Argentina to the Dutch
journalist Sassen, a former SS man who was also a fugitive from justice, and that,
after Eichmann's capture, had been published in part by *Life* in this country and by
Der Stern in Germany) that he could be accused only of "aiding and abetting" the
annihilation of the Jews, which he declared in Jerusalem to have been "one of the
greatest crimes in the history of Humanity." The defense paid no attention to
Eichmann's own theory, but the prosecution wasted much time in an unsuccessful
effort to prove that Eichmann had once, at least, killed with his own hands (a Jewish
boy in Hungary), and it spent even more time, and more successfully, on a note that
Franz Rademacher, the Jewish expert in the German Foreign Office, had scribbled
on one of the documents dealing with Yugoslavia during a telephone conversation,
which read: "Eichmann proposes shooting." This turned out to be the only "order to
kill," if that is what it was, for which there existed even a shred of evidence.

The evidence was more questionable than it appeared to be during the trial, at
which the judges accepted the prosecutor's version against Eichmann's categorical
denial – a denial that was very ineffective, since he had forgotten the "brief incident
[a mere eight thousand people] which was not so striking," as Servatius put it. The
incident took place in the autumn of 1941, six months after Germany had occupied
the Serbian part of Yugoslavia. The Army had been plagued by partisan warfare ever
since, and it was the military authorities who decided to solve two problems at a
stroke by shooting a hundred Jews and Gypsies as hostages for every dead German
soldier. To be sure, neither Jews nor Gypsies were partisans, but, in the words of the
responsible civilian officer in the military government, a certain Staatsrat Harald
Turner, "the Jews we had in the camps [anyhow]; after all, they too are Serb
nationals, and besides, they have to disappear" (quoted by Raul Hilberg in *The
Destruction of the European Jews*, 1961). The camps had been set up by General
Franz Böhme, military governor of the region, and they housed Jewish males only.
Neither General Böhme nor Staatsrat Turner waited for Eichmann's approval before
starting to shoot Jews and Gypsies by the thousand. The trouble began when Böhme,
without consulting the appropriate police and SS authorities, decided to *deport* all

his Jews, probably in order to show that no special troops, operating under a different command, were required to make Serbia *judenrein*. Eichmann was informed, since it was a matter of deportation, and he refused approval because the move would interfere with other plans; but it was not Eichmann but Martin Luther, of the Foreign Office, who reminded General Böhme that "In other territories [meaning Russia] other military commanders have taken care of considerably greater numbers of Jews without even mentioning it." In any event, if Eichmann actually did "propose shooting," he told the military only that they should go on doing what they had done all along, and that the question of hostages was entirely in their own competence. Obviously, this was an Army affair, since only males were involved. The implementation of the Final Solution in Serbia started about six months later, when women and children were rounded up and disposed of in mobile gas vans. During cross-examination, Eichmann, as usual, chose the most complicated and least likely explanation: Rademacher had needed the support of the Head Office for Reich Security, Eichmann's outfit, for his own stand on the matter in the Foreign Office, and therefore had forged the document. (Rademacher himself explained the incident much more reasonably at his own trial, before a West German court in 1952: "The Army was responsible for order in Serbia and had to kill rebellious Jews by shooting." This sounded more plausible but was a lie, for we know – from Nazi sources – that the Jews were not "rebellious.") If it was difficult to interpret a remark made over the phone as an order, it was more difficult to believe that Eichmann had been in a position to give orders to the generals of the Army.

Would he then have pleaded guilty if he had been indicted as an accessory to murder? Perhaps, but he would have made important qualifications. What he had done was a crime only in retrospect, and he had always been a law-abiding citizen, because Hitler's orders, which he had certainly executed to the best of his ability, had possessed "the force of law" in the Third Reich. (The defense could have quoted in support of Eichmann's thesis the testimony of one of the best-known experts on constitutional law in the Third Reich, Theodor Maunz, currently Minister of Education and Culture in Bavaria, who stated in 1943 [in *Gestalt und Recht der Polizei*]: "The command of the Führer... is the absolute center of the present legal order.") Those who today told Eichmann that he could have acted differently simply did not know, or had forgotten, how things had been. He did not want to be one of those who now pretended that "they had always been against it," whereas in fact they had been very eager to do what they were told to do. However, times change, and he, like Professor Maunz, had "arrived at different insights." What he had done he had done, he did not want to deny it; rather, he proposed "to hang myself in public as a warning example for all anti-Semites on this earth." By this he did not mean to say that he regretted anything: "Repentance is for little children." (*Sic!*)

Even under considerable pressure from his lawyer, he did not change this position. In a discussion of Himmler's offer in 1944 to exchange a million Jews for ten thousand trucks, and his own role in this plan, Eichmann was asked: "Mr. Witness, in the negotiations with your superiors, did you express any pity for the Jews and did you say there was room to help them?" And he replied: "I am here under oath and must speak the truth. Not out of mercy did I launch this transaction" – which would have been fine, except that it was not Eichmann who "launched" it. But he then continued, quite truthfully: "My reasons I explained this morning," and they were as follows: Himmler had sent his own man to Budapest to deal with matters of Jewish emigration. (Which, incidentally, had become a flourishing business: for enormous amounts of money, Jews could buy their way out. Eichmann, however, did not mention this.) It was the fact that "here matters of emigration were dealt with by a man who did not belong to the Police Force" that made him indignant, "because I had to help and to implement deportation, and matters of emigration, on which I considered myself an expert, were assigned to a man who was new to the unit.... I was fed up.... I decided that I had to do something to take matters of emigration into my own hands."

Throughout the trial, Eichmann tried to clarify, mostly without success, this second point in his plea of "not guilty in the sense of the indictment." The indictment implied not only that he had acted on purpose, which he did not deny, but out of base motives and in full knowledge of the criminal nature of his deeds. As for the base motives, he was perfectly sure that he was not what he called an *innerer Schweinehund*, a dirty bastard in the depths of his heart; and as for his conscience, he remembered perfectly well that he would have had a bad conscience only if he had not done what he had been ordered to do – to ship millions of men, women, and children to their death with great zeal and the most meticulous care. This, admittedly, was hard to take. Half a dozen psychiatrists had certified him as "normal" – "More normal, at any rate, than I am after having examined him," one of them was said to have exclaimed, while another had found that his whole psychological outlook, his attitude toward his wife and children, mother and father, brothers, sisters, and friends, was "not only normal but most desirable" – and finally the minister who had paid regular visits to him in prison after the Supreme Court had finished hearing his appeal reassured everybody by declaring Eichmann to be "a man with very positive ideas." Behind the comedy of the soul experts lay the hard fact that his was obviously no case of moral let alone legal insanity. (Mr. Hausner's recent revelations in the *Saturday Evening Post* of things he "could not bring out at the trial" have contradicted the information given informally in Jerusalem. Eichmann, we are now told, had been alleged by the psychiatrists to be "a man obsessed with a dangerous and insatiable urge to kill," "a perverted, sadistic personality." In which case he would have belonged in an insane asylum.) Worse, his was obviously also no case of insane hatred of Jews, of fanatical anti-Semitism or indoctrination of any kind. He "personally" never had anything whatever against Jews; on the contrary, he had plenty of "private reasons" for not being a Jew-hater. To be sure, there were fanatic anti-Semites among his closest friends, for instance László Endre, State Secretary in Charge of Political (Jewish) Affairs in Hungary, who was hanged in Budapest in 1946; but this, according to Eichmann, was more or less in the spirit of "some of my best friends are anti-Semites."

Alas, nobody believed him. The prosecutor did not believe him, because that was not his job. Counsel for the defense paid no attention because he, unlike Eichmann, was, to all appearances, not interested in questions of conscience. And the judges did not believe him, because they were too good, and perhaps also too conscious of the very foundations of their profession, to admit that an average, "normal" person, neither feeble-minded nor indoctrinated nor cynical, could be perfectly incapable of telling right from wrong. They preferred to conclude from occasional lies that he was a liar – and missed the greatest moral and even legal challenge of the whole case.

Their case rested on the assumption that the defendant, like all "normal persons," must have been aware of the criminal nature of his acts, and Eichmann was indeed normal insofar as he was "no exception within the Nazi regime." However, under the conditions of the Third Reich only "exceptions" could be expected to react "normally." This simple truth of the matter created a dilemma for the judges which they could neither resolve nor escape.[...]

Deportations from the Reich – Germany, Austria, and the Protectorate

Between the Wannsee Conference in January, 1942, when Eichmann felt like Pontius Pilate and washed his hands in innocence, and Himmler's orders in the summer and fall of 1944, when behind Hitler's back the Final Solution was abandoned as though the massacres had been nothing but a regrettable mistake, Eichmann was troubled by no questions of conscience. His thoughts were entirely taken up with the staggering job of organization and administration in the midst not only of a world war but, more important for him, of innumerable intrigues and fights over spheres of authority among the various State and Party offices that were busy "solving the Jewish question." His chief competitors were the Higher SS and Police Leaders, who were under the direct command of Himmler, had easy access to him, and always outranked Eichmann. There was also the Foreign Office, which, under its new Undersecretary of State, Dr. Martin Luther, a protégé of Ribbentrop, had become very active in Jewish affairs. (Luther tried to oust Ribbentrop, in an elaborate intrigue in 1943, failed, and was put into a concentration camp; under his successor, Legationsrat Eberhard von Thadden, a witness for the defense at the trial in Jerusalem, became *Referent* in Jewish affairs.) It occasionally issued deportation orders to be carried out by its representatives abroad, who for reasons of prestige preferred to work through the Higher SS and Police Leaders. There were, furthermore, the Army commanders in the Eastern occupied territories, who liked to solve problems "on the spot," which meant shooting; the military men in Western countries were, on the other hand, always reluctant to cooperate and to lend their troops for the rounding up and seizure of Jews. Finally, there were the Gauleiters, the regional leaders, each of whom wanted to be the first to declare his territory *judenrein*, and who occasionally started deportation procedures on their own.

Eichmann had to coordinate all these "efforts," to bring some order out of what he described as "complete chaos," in which "everyone issued his own orders" and "did as he pleased." And indeed he succeeded, though never completely, in acquiring a key position in the whole process, because his office organized the means of transportation. According to Dr. Rudolf Mildner, Gestapo head in Upper Silesia (where Auschwitz was located) and later chief of the Security Police in Denmark, who testified for the prosecution at Nuremberg, orders for deportations were given by Himmler in writing to Kaltenbrunner, head of the RSHA, who notified Müller, head of the Gestapo, or Section IV of RSHA, who in turn transmitted the orders orally to his referent in IV-B-4 – that is, to Eichmann. Himmler also issued orders to the local Higher SS and Police Leaders and informed Kaltenbrunner accordingly. Questions of what should be done with the Jewish deportees, how many should be exterminated and how many spared for hard labor, were also decided by Himmler, and his orders concerning these matters went to Pohl's WVHA, which communicated them to Richard Glücks, inspector of the concentration and extermination camps, who in turn passed them along to the commanders of the camps. The prosecution ignored these documents from the Nuremberg Trials, since they contradicted its theory of the extraordinary power held by Eichmann; the defense mentioned Mildner's affidavits, but not to much purpose. Eichmann himself, after "consulting Poliakoff and Reitlinger," produced seventeen multi-colored charts, which contributed little to a better understanding of the intricate bureaucratic machinery of the Third Reich, although his general description – "everything was always in a state of continuous flux, a steady stream" – sounded plausible to the student of totalitarianism, who knows that the monolithic quality of this form of government is a myth. He still remembered vaguely how his men, his advisers on Jewish matters in all occupied and semi-independent countries, had reported back to him "what action was at all practicable," how he had then prepared "reports which were later either approved or rejected," and how Müller then had issued his directives; "in practice this could mean that a proposal that came in from Paris or The Hague went out a fortnight later to Paris or The Hague in the form of a directive approved by the RSHA" Eichmann's position was that of the most important conveyor belt in the whole operation, because it was always up to him and his men how many Jews could or should be transported from any given area, and it was through his office that the ultimate destination of the shipment was cleared, though that destination was not determined by him. But the difficulty in synchronizing departures and arrivals, the endless worry over wrangling enough rolling stock from the railroad authorities and the Ministry of Transport, over fixing timetables and directing trains to centers with sufficient "absorptive capacity," over having enough Jews on hand at the proper time so that no trains would be "wasted," over enlisting the help of the authorities in occupied or allied countries to carry out arrests, over following the rules and directives with respect to the various categories of Jews, which were laid down separately for each country and constantly changing – all this became a routine whose details he had forgotten long before he was brought to Jerusalem.

What for Hitler, the sole, lonely plotter of the Final Solution (never had a conspiracy, if such it was, needed fewer conspirators and more executors), was among the war's main objectives, with its implementation given top priority, regardless of economic and military considerations, and what for Eichmann was a job, with its daily routine, its ups and downs, was for the Jews quite literally the end of the world. [...]

Judgment, Appeal, and Execution

On June 29, 1961, ten weeks after the opening of the trial on April 11, the prosecution rested its case, and Dr. Servatius opened the case for the defense; on August 14, after a hundred and fourteen sessions, the main proceedings came to an end. The court then adjourned for four months, and reassembled on December 11 to pronounce judgment. For two days, divided into five sessions, the three judges read the two hundred and forty-four sections of the judgment. Dropping the prosecution's charge of "conspiracy," which would have made him a "chief war criminal," automatically responsible for everything which had to do with the Final Solution, they convicted Eichmann on all fifteen counts of the indictment, although he was acquitted on some particulars. "Together with others," he had committed crimes "against the Jewish people," that is, crimes against Jews *with intent to destroy the people*, on four counts: (1) by "causing the killing of millions of Jews"; (2) by placing "millions of Jews under conditions which were likely to lead to their physical destruction"; (3) by "causing serious bodily and mental harm" to them; and (4) by "directing that births be banned and pregnancies interrupted among Jewish women" in Theresienstadt. But they acquitted him of any such charges bearing on the period prior to August, 1941, when he was informed of the Führer's order; in his earlier activities, in Berlin, Vienna, and Prague, he had no intention "to destroy the Jewish people." These were the first four counts of the indictment. Counts 5 through 12 dealt with "crimes against humanity" – a strange concept in the Israeli law, inasmuch as it included both genocide if practiced against non-Jewish peoples (such as the Gypsies or the Poles) and all other crimes, including murder, committed against either Jews or non-Jews, provided that these crimes were not committed with intent to destroy the people as a whole. Hence, everything Eichmann had done prior to the Führer's order and all his acts against non-Jews were lumped together as crimes against humanity, to which were added, once again, all his later crimes against Jews, since these were ordinary crimes as well. The result was that Count 5 convicted him of the same crimes enumerated in Counts 1 and 2, and that Count 6 convicted him of having "persecuted Jews on racial, religious, and political grounds"; Count 7 dealt with "the plunder of property...linked with the murder ...of these Jews," and Count 8 summed up all these deeds again as "war crimes," since most of them had been committed during the war. Counts 9 through 12 dealt with crimes against non-Jews: Count 9 convicted him of the "expulsion of... hundreds of thousands of Poles from their homes," Count 10 of "the expulsion of fourteen thousand Slovenes" from Yugoslavia, Count 11 of the deportation of "scores of thousands of Gypsies" to Auschwitz. But the judgment held that "it has not been proved before us that the accused knew that the Gypsies were being transported to destruction" – which meant that no genocide charge except the "crime against the Jewish people" was brought. This was difficult to understand, for, apart from the fact that the extermination of Gypsies was common knowledge, Eichmann had admitted during the police examination that he knew of it: he had remembered vaguely that this had been an order from Himmler, that no "directives" had existed for Gypsies as they existed for Jews, and that there had been no "research" done on the "Gypsy problem" – "origins, customs, habits, organization...folklore ...economy." His department had been commissioned to undertake the "evacuation" of thirty thousand Gypsies from Reich territory, and he could not remember the details very well, because there had been no intervention from any side; but that Gypsies, like Jews, were shipped off to be exterminated he had never doubted. He was guilty of their extermination in exactly the same way he was guilty of the extermination of the Jews. Count 12 concerned the deportation of ninety-three children from Lidice, the Czech village whose inhabitants had been massacred after the assassination of Heydrich; he was, however, rightly acquitted of the murder of these children. The last three counts charged him with membership in three of the four organizations that the Nuremberg Trials had classified as "criminal" – the SS; the Security Service, or SD; and the Secret

State Police, or Gestapo. (The fourth such organization, the leadership corps of the National Socialist Party, was not mentioned, because Eichmann obviously had not been one of the Party leaders.) His membership in them prior to May, 1940, fell under the statute of limitations (twenty years) for minor offenses. (The Law of 1950 under which Eichmann was tried specifies that there is no statute of limitation for major offenses, and that the argument *res judicata* shall not avail – a person can be tried in Israel "even if he has already been tried abroad, whether before an international tribunal or a tribunal of a foreign state, for the same offense.") All crimes enumerated under Counts 1 through 12 carried the death penalty.

Eichmann, it will be remembered, had steadfastly insisted that he was guilty only of "aiding and abetting" in the commission of the crimes with which he was charged, that he himself had never committed an overt act. The judgment, to one's great relief, in a way recognized that the prosecution had not succeeded in proving him wrong on this point. For it was an important point; it touched upon the very essence of this crime, which was no ordinary crime, and the very nature of this criminal, who was no common criminal; by implication, it also took cognizance of the weird fact that in the death camps it was usually the inmates and the victims who had actually wielded "the fatal instrument with [their] own hands." What the judgment had to say on this point was more than correct, it was the truth: "Expressing his activities in terms of Section 23 of our Criminal Code Ordinance, we should say that they were mainly those of a person soliciting by giving counsel or advice to others and of one who enabled or aided others in [the criminal] act." But "in such an enormous and complicated crime as the one we are now considering, wherein many people participated, on various levels and in various modes of activity – the planners, the organizers, and those executing the deeds, according to their various ranks – there is not much point in using the ordinary concepts of counseling and soliciting to commit a crime. For these crimes were committed en masse, not only in regard to the number of victims, but also in regard to the numbers of those who perpetrated the crime, and the extent to which any one of the many criminals was close to or remote from the actual killer of the victim means nothing, as far as the measure of his responsibility is concerned. On the contrary, in general *the degree of responsibility increases as we draw further away from the man who uses the fatal instrument with his own hands* [my italics]."

What followed the reading of the judgment was routine. Once more, the prosecution rose to make a rather lengthy speech demanding the death penalty, which, in the absence of mitigating circumstances, was mandatory, and Dr. Servatius replied even more briefly than before: the accused had carried out "acts of state," what had happened to him might happen in future to anyone, the whole civilized world faced this problem, Eichmann was "a scapegoat," whom the present German government had abandoned to the court in Jerusalem, contrary to international law, in order to clear itself of responsibility. The competence of the court, never recognized by Dr. Servatius, could be construed only as trying the accused "in a representative capacity, as representing the legal powers vested in [a German court]" – as, indeed, one German state prosecutor had formulated the task of Jerusalem. Dr. Servatius had argued earlier that the court must acquit the defendant because, according to the Argentine statute of limitations, he had ceased to be liable to criminal proceedings against him on May 7, 1960, "a very short time before the abduction"; he now argued, in the same vein, that no death penalty could be pronounced because capital punishment had been abolished unconditionally in Germany.

Then came Eichmann's last statement: His hopes for justice were disappointed; the court had not believed him, though he had always done his best to tell the truth. The court did not understand him: he had never been a Jew-hater, and he had never willed the murder of human beings. His guilt came from his obedience, and obedience is praised as a virtue. His virtue had been abused by the Nazi leaders. But he was not one of the ruling clique, he was a victim, and only the leaders deserved punishment. (He did not go quite as far as many of the other low-ranking war criminals, who complained bitterly that they had been told never to worry about "responsibilities," and that they were now unable to call those responsible to account because these had "escaped and deserted" them – by committing suicide, or by having been hanged.) "I am not the monster I am made out to be," Eichmann said. "I am the victim of a fallacy." He did not use the word "scapegoat," but he confirmed what Servatius had said: it was his "profound conviction that [he] must suffer for the acts of others." After two more days, on Friday, December 15, 1961, at nine o'clock in the morning, the death sentence was pronounced. [...]

Adolf Eichmann went to the gallows with great dignity. He had asked for a bottle of red wine and had drunk half of it. He refused the help of the Protestant minister, the Reverend William Hull, who offered to read the Bible with him: he had only two more hours to live, and therefore no "time to waste." He walked the fifty yards from his cell to the execution chamber calm and erect, with his hands bound behind him. When the guards tied his ankles and knees, he asked them to loosen the bonds so that he could stand straight. "I don't need that," he said when the black hood was offered him. He was in complete command of himself, nay, he was more: he was completely himself. Nothing could have demonstrated this more convincingly than the grotesque silliness of his last words. He began by stating emphatically that he was a *Gottgläubiger*, to express in common Nazi fashion that he was no Christian and did not believe in life after death. He then proceeded: "After a short while, gentlemen, *we shall all meet again*. Such is the fate of all men. Long live Germany, long live Argentina, long live Austria. *I shall not forget them*." In the face of death, he had found the cliché used in funeral oratory. Under the gallows, his memory played him the last trick; he was "elated" and he forgot that this was his own funeral.

It was as though in those last minutes he was summing up the lesson that this long course in human wickedness had taught us – the lesson of the fearsome, word-and-thought-defying *banality of evil*.[...]

Postscript

[...] Even before its publication, this book became both the center of a controversy and the object of an organized campaign. It is only natural that the campaign, conducted with all the well-known means of image-making and opinion-manipulation, got much more attention than the controversy, so that the latter was somehow swallowed up by and drowned in the artificial noise of the former. This became especially clear when a strange mixture of the two, in almost identical phraseology –

as though the pieces written against the book (and more frequently against its author) came "out of a mimeographing machine" (Mary McCarthy) – was carried from America to England and then to Europe, where the book was not yet even available. And this was possible because the clamor centered on the "image" of a book which was never written, and touched upon subjects that often had not only not been mentioned by me but had never occurred to me before.

The debate – if that is what it was – was by no means devoid of interest. Manipulations of opinion, insofar as they are inspired by well-defined interests, have limited goals; their effect, however, if they happen to touch upon an issue of authentic concern, is no longer subject to their control and may easily produce consequences they never foresaw or intended. It now appeared that the era of the Hitler regime, with its gigantic, unprecedented crimes, constituted an "unmastered past" not only for the German people or for the Jews all over the world, but for the rest of the world, which had not forgotten this great catastrophe in the heart of Europe either, and had also been unable to come to terms with it. Moreover – and this was perhaps even less expected – general moral questions, with all their intricacies and modern complexities, which I would never have suspected would haunt men's minds today and weigh heavily on their hearts, stood suddenly in the foreground of public concern.

The controversy began by calling attention to the conduct of the Jewish people during the years of the Final Solution, thus following up the question, first raised by the Israeli prosecutor, of whether the Jews could or should have defended themselves. I had dismissed that question as silly and cruel, since it testified to a fatal ignorance of the conditions at the time. It has now been discussed to exhaustion, and the most amazing conclusions have been drawn. The well-known historico-sociological construct of a "ghetto mentality" (which in Israel has taken its place in history textbooks and in this country has been espoused chiefly by the psychologist Bruno Bettelheim – against the furious protest of official American Judaism) has been repeatedly dragged in to explain behavior which was not at all confined to the Jewish people and which therefore cannot be explained by specifically Jewish factors. The suggestions proliferated until someone who evidently found the whole discussion too dull had the brilliant idea of evoking Freudian theories and attributing to the whole Jewish people a "death wish" – unconscious, of course. This was the unexpected conclusion certain reviewers chose to draw from the "image" of a book, created by certain interest groups, in which I allegedly had claimed that the Jews had murdered themselves. And why had I told such a monstrously implausible lie? Out of "self-hatred," of course.

Since the role of the Jewish leadership had come up at the trial, and since I had reported and commented on it, it was inevitable that it too should be discussed. This, in my opinion, is a serious question, but the debate has contributed little to its clarification. As can be seen from the recent trial in Israel at which a certain Hirsch Birnblat, a former chief of the Jewish police in a Polish town and now a conductor at the Israeli Opera, first was sentenced by a district court to five years' imprisonment, and then was exonerated by the Supreme Court in Jerusalem, whose unanimous opinion indirectly exonerated the Jewish Councils in general, the Jewish Establishment is bitterly divided on this issue. In the debate, however, the most vocal participants were those who either identified the Jewish people with its leadership

– in striking contrast to the clear distinction made in almost all the reports of survivors, which may be summed up in the words of a former inmate of Theresienstadt: "The Jewish people as a whole behaved magnificently. Only the leadership failed" – or justified the Jewish functionaries by citing all the commendable services they had rendered before the war, and above all before the era of the Final Solution, as though there were no difference between helping Jews to emigrate and helping the Nazis to deport them.

While these issues had indeed some connection with this book, although they were inflated out of all proportion, there were others which had no relation to it whatsoever. There was, for instance, a hot discussion of the German resistance movement from the beginning of the Hitler regime on, which I naturally did not discuss, since the question of Eichmann's conscience, and that of the situation around him, relates only to the period of the war and the Final Solution. But there were more fantastic items. Quite a number of people began to debate the question of whether the victims of persecution may not always be "uglier" than their murderers; or whether anyone who was not present is entitled "to sit in judgment" over the past; or whether the defendant or the victim holds the center of the stage in a trial. On the latter point, some went so far as to assert not only that I was wrong in being interested in what kind of person Eichmann was, but that he should not have been allowed to speak at all – that is, presumably, that the trial should have been conducted without any defense.

As is frequently the case in discussions that are conducted with a great show of emotion, the down-to-earth interests of certain groups, whose excitement is entirely concerned with factual matters and who therefore try to distort the facts, become quickly and inextricably involved with the untrammeled inspirations of intellectuals who, on the contrary, are not in the least interested in facts but treat them merely as a springboard for "ideas." But even in these sham battles, there could often be detected a certain seriousness, a degree of authentic concern, and this even in the contributions by people who boasted that they had not read the book and promised that they never would read it.

Compared with these debates, which wandered so far afield, the book itself dealt with a sadly limited subject. The report of a trial can discuss only the matters which were treated in the course of the trial, or which in the interests of justice should have been treated. If the general situation of a country in which the trial takes place happens to be important to the conduct of the trial, it too must be taken into account. This book, then, does not deal with the history of the greatest disaster that ever befell the Jewish people, nor is it an account of totalitarianism, or a history of the German people in the time of the Third Reich, nor is it, finally and least of all, a theoretical treatise on the nature of evil. The focus of every trial is upon the person of the defendant, a man of flesh and blood with an individual history, with an always unique set of qualities, peculiarities, behavior patterns, and circumstances. All the things that go beyond that, such as the history of the Jewish people in the dispersion, and of anti-Semitism, or the conduct of the German people and other peoples, or the ideologies of the time and the governmental apparatus of the Third Reich, affect the trial only insofar as they form the background and the conditions under which the defendant committed his acts. All the things that the defendant did not come into contact with, or that did not influence him, must be omitted from the proceedings of the trial and consequently from the report on it.

It may be argued that all the general questions we involuntarily raise as soon as we begin to speak of these matters – why did it have to be the Germans? why did it have to be the Jews? what is the nature of totalitarian rule? – are far more important than the question of the kind of crime for which a man is being tried, and the nature of the defendant upon whom justice must be pronounced; more important, too, than the question of how well our present system of justice is capable of dealing with this special type of crime and criminal it has had repeatedly to cope with since the Second World War. It can be held that the issue is no longer a particular human being, a single distinct individual in the dock, but rather the German people in general, or anti-Semitism in all its forms, or the whole of modern history, or the nature of man and original sin – so that ultimately the entire human race sits invisibly beside the defendant in the dock. All this has often been argued, and especially by those who will not rest until they have discovered an "Eichmann in every one of us." If the defendant is taken as a symbol and the trial as a pretext to bring up matters which are apparently more interesting than the guilt or innocence of one person, then consistency demands that we bow to the assertion made by Eichmann and his lawyer: that he was brought to book because a scapegoat was needed, not only for the German Federal Republic, but also for the events as a whole and for what made them possible – that is, for anti-Semitism and totalitarian government as well as for the human race and original sin.

I need scarcely say that I would never have gone to Jerusalem if I had shared these views. I held and hold the opinion that this trial had to take place in the interests of justice and nothing else. I also think the judges were quite right when they stressed in their verdict that "the State of Israel was established and recognized as the State of the Jews," and therefore had jurisdiction over a crime committed against the Jewish people; and in view of the current confusion in legal circles about the meaning and usefulness of punishment, I was glad that the judgment quoted Grotius, who, for his part, citing an older author, explained that punishment is necessary "to defend the honor or the authority of him who was hurt by the offence so that the failure to punish may not cause his degradation."

There is of course no doubt that the defendant and the nature of his acts as well as the trial itself raise problems of a general nature which go far beyond the matters considered in Jerusalem. I have attempted to go into some of these problems in the Epilogue, which ceases to be simple reporting. I would not have been surprised if people had found my treatment inadequate, and I would have welcomed a discussion of the general significance of the entire body of facts, which could have been all the more meaningful the more directly it referred to the concrete events. I also can well imagine that an authentic controversy might have arisen over the subtitle of the book; for when I speak of the banality of evil, I do so only on the strictly factual level, pointing to a phenomenon which stared one in the face at the trial. Eichmann was not Iago and not Macbeth, and nothing would have been farther from his mind than to determine with Richard III "to prove a villain." Except for an extraordinary diligence in looking out for his personal advancement, he had no motives at all. And this diligence in itself was in no way criminal; he certainly would never have murdered his superior in order to inherit his post. He *merely*, to put the matter colloquially, *never realized what he was doing*. It was precisely this lack of imagination which enabled him to sit for months on end facing a German Jew who was conducting the police interrogation, pouring out his heart to the man and explaining again and again how it was that he reached only the rank of lieutenant colonel in the SS and that it had not been his fault that he was not promoted. In principle he knew quite well what it was all about, and in his final statement to the court he spoke of the "revaluation of values prescribed by the [Nazi] government." He was not stupid. It was sheer thoughtlessness – something by no means identical with stupidity – that predisposed him to become one of the greatest criminals of that period. And if this is "banal" and even funny, if with the best will in the world one cannot extract any diabolical or demonic profundity from Eichmann, that is still far from calling it commonplace. It surely cannot be so common that a man facing death, and, moreover, standing beneath the gallows, should be able to think of nothing but what he has heard at funerals all his life, and that these "lofty words" should completely becloud the reality of his own death. That such remoteness from reality and such thoughtlessness can wreak more havoc than all the evil instincts taken together which, perhaps, are inherent in man – that was, in fact, the lesson one could learn in Jerusalem. But it was a lesson, neither an explanation of the phenomenon nor a theory about it.

Seemingly more complicated, but in reality far simpler than examining the strange interdependence of thoughtlessness and evil, is the question of what kind of crime is actually involved here – a crime, moreover, which all agree is unprecedented. For the concept of genocide, introduced explicitly to cover a crime unknown before, although applicable up to a point is not fully adequate, for the simple reason that massacres of whole peoples are not unprecedented. They were the order of the day in antiquity, and the centuries of colonization and imperialism provide plenty of examples of more or less successful attempts of that sort. The expression "administrative massacres" seems better to fill the bill. The term arose in connection with British imperialism; the English deliberately rejected such procedures as a means of maintaining their rule over India. The phrase has the virtue of dispelling the prejudice that such monstrous acts can be committed only against a foreign nation or a different race. There is the well-known fact that Hitler began his mass murders by granting "mercy deaths" to the "incurably ill," and that he intended to wind up his extermination program by doing away with "genetically damaged" Germans (heart and lung patients). But quite aside from that, it is apparent that this sort of killing can be directed against any given group, that is, that the principle of selection is dependent only upon circumstantial factors. It is quite conceivable that in the automated economy of a not-too-distant future men may be tempted to exterminate all those whose intelligence quotient is below a certain level.

In Jerusalem this matter was inadequately discussed because it is actually very difficult to grasp juridically. We heard the protestations of the defense that Eichmann was after all only a "tiny cog" in the machinery of the Final Solution, and of the prosecution, which believed it had discovered in Eichmann the actual motor. I myself attributed no more importance to both theories than did the Jerusalem court, since the whole cog theory is legally pointless and therefore it does not matter at all what order of magnitude is assigned to the "cog" named Eichmann. In its judgment the court naturally conceded that such a crime could be committed only by a giant bureaucracy using the resources of government. But insofar as it remains a crime – and that, of course, is the premise for a trial – all the cogs in the machinery, no matter how insignificant, are in court forthwith transformed back into perpetrators, that is to say, into human beings. If the defendant excuses himself on the ground that he acted not as a man but as a mere functionary whose functions could just as easily have been carried out by anyone else, it is as if a criminal pointed to the statistics on crime – which set forth that so-and-so many crimes per day are committed in such-and-such a place – and declared that he only did what was statistically expected, that it was mere accident that he did it and not somebody else, since after all somebody had to do it.

Of course it is important to the political and social sciences that the essence of totalitarian government, and perhaps the nature of every bureaucracy, is to make functionaries and mere cogs in the administrative machinery out of men, and thus to dehumanize them. And one can debate long and profitably on the rule of Nobody, which is what the political form known as bureaucracy truly is. Only one must realize clearly that the administration of justice can consider these factors only to the extent that they are circumstances of the crime – just as, in a case of theft, the economic plight of the thief is taken into account without excusing the theft, let alone wiping it off the slate. True, we have become very much accustomed by modern psychology and sociology, not to speak of modern bureaucracy, to explaining away the responsibility of the doer for his deed in terms of this or that kind of determinism. Whether such seemingly deeper explanations of human actions are right or wrong is debatable. But what is not debatable is that no judicial procedure would be possible on the basis of them, and that the administration of justice, measured by such theories, is an extremely unmodern, not to say outmoded, institution. When Hitler said that a day would come in Germany when it would be considered a "disgrace" to be a jurist, he was speaking with utter consistency of his dream of a perfect bureaucracy.

As far as I can see, jurisprudence has at its disposal for treating this whole battery of questions only two categories, both of which, to my mind, are quite inadequate to deal with the matter. These are the concepts of "acts of state" and of acts "on superior orders." At any rate, these are the only categories in terms of which such matters are discussed in this kind of trial, usually on the motion of the defendant. The theory of the act of state is based on the argument that one sovereign state may not sit in judgment upon another, *par in parem non habet jurisdictionem*. Practically speaking, this argument had already been disposed of at Nuremberg; it stood no chance from the start, since, if it were accepted, even Hitler, the only one who was really responsible in the full sense, could not have been brought to account – a state of affairs which would have violated the most elementary sense of justice. However, an argument that stands no chance on the practical plane has not necessarily been demolished on the theoretical one. The usual evasions – that Germany at the time of the Third Reich was dominated by a gang of criminals to whom sovereignty and parity cannot very well be ascribed – were hardly useful. For on the one hand everyone knows that the analogy with a gang of criminals is applicable only to such a limited extent that it is not really applicable at all, and on the other hand these crimes undeniably took place within a "legal" order. That, indeed, was their outstanding characteristic.

Perhaps we can approach somewhat closer to the matter if we realize that back of the concept of act of state stands the theory of *raison d'état*. According to that theory, the actions of the state, which is responsible for the life of the country and thus also for the laws obtaining in it, are not subject to the same rules as the acts of the citizens of the country. Just as the rule of law, although devised to eliminate violence and the war of all against all, always stands in need of the instruments of violence in order to assure its own existence, so a government may find itself compelled to commit actions that are generally regarded as crimes in order to assure its own survival and the survival of lawfulness. Wars are frequently justified on these grounds, but criminal acts of state do not occur only in the field of international relations, and the history of civilized nations knows many examples of them – from Napoleon's assassination of the Duc d'Enghien, to the murder of the Socialist leader Matteotti, for which Mussolini himself was presumably responsible.

Raison d'état appeals – rightly or wrongly, as the case may be – to *necessity*, and the state crimes committed in its name (which are fully criminal in terms of the dominant legal system of the country where they occur) are considered emergency measures, concessions made to the stringencies of *Realpolitik*, in order to preserve power and thus assure the continuance of the existing legal order as a whole. In a normal political and legal system, such crimes occur as an exception to the rule and are not subject to legal penalty (are *gerichtsfrei*, as German legal theory expresses it) because the existence of the state itself is at stake, and no outside political entity has the right to deny a state its existence or prescribe how it is to preserve it. However – as we may have learned from the history of Jewish policy in the Third Reich – in a state founded upon criminal principles, the situation is reversed. Then a non-criminal act (such as, for example, Himmler's order in the late summer of 1944 to halt the deportation of Jews) becomes a concession to necessity imposed by reality, in this case the impending defeat. Here the question arises: what is the nature of the sovereignty of such an entity? Has it not violated the parity (*par in parem non habet jurisdictionem*) which international law accords it? Does the "*par in parem*" signify no more than the paraphernalia of sovereignty? Or does it also imply a substantive equality or likeness? Can we apply the same principle that is applied to a governmental apparatus in which crime and violence are exceptions and borderline cases to a political order in which crime is legal and the rule?

Just how inadequate juristic concepts really are to deal with the criminal facts which were the subject matter of all these trials appears perhaps even more strikingly in the concept of acts performed on superior orders. The Jerusalem court countered the argument advanced by the defense with lengthy quotations from the penal and military lawbooks of civilized countries, particularly of Germany; for under Hitler the pertinent articles had by no means been repealed. All of them agree on one point: manifestly criminal orders must not be obeyed. The court, moreover, referred to a case that came up in Israel several years ago: soldiers were brought to trial for having massacred the civilian inhabitants of an Arab village on the border shortly before the beginning of the Sinai campaign. The villagers had been found outside their houses during a military curfew of which, it appeared, they were unaware. Unfortunately, on closer examination the comparison appears to be defective on two accounts. First of all, we must again consider that the relationship of exception and rule, which is of prime importance for recognizing the criminality of an order executed by a subordinate, was reversed in the case of Eichmann's actions. Thus, on the basis of this argument one could actually defend Eichmann's failure to obey certain of Himmler's orders, or his obeying them with hesitancy: they were manifest exceptions to the prevailing rule. The judgment found this to be especially incriminating to the defendant, which was certainly very understandable but not very consistent. This can easily be seen from the pertinent findings of Israeli military courts, which were cited in support by the judges. They ran as follows: the order to be disobeyed must be "manifestly unlawful"; unlawfulness "should fly like a black flag above [it], as a warning reading, 'Prohibited.'" In other words, the order, to be recognized by the soldier as "manifestly unlawful," must violate by its unusualness the canons of the legal system to which he is accustomed. And Israeli jurisprudence in these matters coincides completely with that of other countries. No doubt in formulating these articles the legislators were thinking of cases in which an officer who suddenly goes mad, say, commands his subordinates to kill another officer. In any normal trial of such a case, it would at once become clear that the soldier was not being asked to consult the voice of conscience, or a "feeling of lawfulness that lies deep within every human conscience, also of those who are not conversant with books of law... provided the eye is not blind and the heart is not stony and corrupt." Rather, the soldier would be expected to be able to distinguish between a rule and a striking exception to the rule. The German military code, at any rate, explicitly states that conscience is not enough. Paragraph 48 reads: "Punishability of an action or omission is not excluded on the ground that the person considered his behavior required by his conscience or the prescripts of his religion." A striking feature of the Israeli court's line of argument is that the concept of a sense of justice grounded in the depths of every man is presented solely as a substitute for familiarity with the law. Its plausibility rests on the assumption that the law expresses only what every man's conscience would tell him anyhow.

If we are to apply this whole reasoning to the Eichmann case in a meaningful way, we are forced to conclude that Eichmann acted fully within the framework of the kind of judgment required of him: he acted in accordance with the rule, examined the order issued to him for its "manifest" legality, namely regularity; he did not have to fall back upon his "conscience," since he was not one of those who were unfamiliar with the laws of his country. The exact opposite was the case.

The second account on which the argument based on comparison proved to be defective concerns the practice of the courts of admitting the plea of "superior orders" as important extenuating circumstances, and this practice was mentioned explicitly by the judgment. The judgment cited the case I have mentioned above, that of the massacre of the Arab inhabitants at Kfar Kassem, as proof that Israeli jurisdiction does not clear a defendant of responsibility for the "superior orders" he received. And it is true, the Israeli soldiers were indicted for murder, but "superior orders" constituted so weighty an argument for mitigating circumstances that they were sentenced to relatively short prison terms. To be sure, this case concerned an isolated act, not – as in Eichmann's case – an activity extending over years, in which crime followed crime. Still, it was undeniable that he had always acted upon "superior orders," and if the provisions of ordinary Israeli law had been applied to him, it would have been difficult indeed to impose the maximum penalty upon him. The truth of the matter is that Israeli law, in theory and practice, like the jurisdiction of other countries cannot but admit that the fact of "superior orders," even when their unlawfulness is "manifest," can severely disturb the normal working of a man's conscience.

This is only one example among many to demonstrate the inadequacy of the prevailing legal system and of current juridical concepts to deal with the facts of administrative massacres organized by the state apparatus. If we look more closely into the matter we will observe without much difficulty that the judges in all these trials really passed judgment solely on the basis of the monstrous deeds. In other words, they judged freely, as it were, and did not really lean on the standards and legal precedents with which they more or less convincingly sought to justify their decisions. That was already evident in Nuremberg, where the judges on the one hand declared that the "crime against peace" was the gravest of all the crimes they had to deal with, since it included all the other crimes, but on the other hand actually imposed the death penalty only on those defendants who had participated in the new crime of administrative massacre – supposedly a less grave offense than conspiracy against peace. It would indeed be tempting to pursue these and similar inconsistencies in a field so obsessed with consistency as jurisprudence. But of course that cannot be done here.

There remains, however, one fundamental problem, which was implicitly present in all these postwar trials and which must be mentioned here because it touches upon one of the central moral questions of all time, namely upon the nature and function of human judgment. What we have demanded in these trials, where the defendants had committed "legal" crimes, is that human beings be capable of telling right from wrong even when all they have to guide them is their own judgment, which, moreover, happens to be completely at odds with what they must regard as the unanimous opinion of all those around them. And this question is all the more serious as we know that the few who were "arrogant" enough to trust only their own judgment were by no means identical with those persons who continued to abide by old values, or who were guided by a religious belief. Since the whole of respectable society had in one way or another succumbed to Hitler, the moral maxims which determine social behavior and the religious commandments – "Thou shalt not kill!" – which guide conscience had virtually vanished. Those few who were still able to tell right from wrong went really only by their own judgments, and they did so freely; there were no rules to be abided by, under which the particular cases with which they were confronted could be subsumed. They had to decide each instance as it arose, because no rules existed for the unprecedented.

How troubled men of our time are by this question of judgment (or, as is often said, by people who dare "sit in judgment") has emerged in the controversy over the present book, as well as the in many respects similar controversy over Hochhuth's *The Deputy*. What has come to light is neither nihilism nor cynicism, as one might have expected, but a quite extraordinary confusion over elementary questions of morality – as if an instinct in such matters were truly the last thing to be taken for granted in our time. The many curious notes that have been struck in the course of these disputes seem particularly revealing. Thus, some American literati have professed their naive belief that temptation and coercion are really the same thing, that no one can be asked to resist temptation. (If someone puts a pistol to your heart and orders you to shoot your best friend, then you simply *must* shoot him. Or, as it was argued – some years ago in connection with the quiz program scandal in which a university teacher had hoaxed the public – when so much money is at stake, who could possibly resist?) The argument that we cannot judge if we were not present

and involved ourselves seems to convince everyone everywhere, although it seems
obvious that if it were true, neither the administration of justice nor the writing of
history would ever be possible. In contrast to these confusions, the reproach of self-
righteousness raised against those who do judge is age-old; but that does not make it
any the more valid. Even the judge who condemns a murderer can still say when he
goes home: "And there, but for the grace of God, go I." All German Jews unanimously have condemned the wave of coordination which passed over the German
people in 1933 and from one day to the next turned the Jews into pariahs. Is it
conceivable that none of them ever asked himself how many of his own group would
have done just the same if only they had been allowed to? But is their condemnation
today any the less correct for that reason?

The reflection that you yourself might have done wrong under the same circumstances may kindle a spirit of forgiveness, but those who today refer to Christian
charity seem strangely confused on this issue too. Thus we can read in the postwar
statement of the *Evangelische Kirche in Deutschland*, the Protestant church, as
follows: "We aver that before the God of Mercy we share in the guilt for the outrage
committed against the Jews by our own people through omission and silence."[1] It
seems to me that a Christian is guilty before the God of *Mercy* if he repays evil with
evil, hence that the churches would have sinned against mercy if millions of Jews had
been killed as punishment for some evil they committed. But if the churches shared
in the guilt for an outrage pure and simple, as they themselves attest, then the matter
must still be considered to fall within the purview of the God of *Justice*.

This slip of the tongue, as it were, is no accident. Justice, but not mercy, is a matter
of judgment, and about nothing does public opinion everywhere seem to be in
happier agreement than that no one has the right to judge somebody else. What
public opinion permits us to judge and even to condemn are trends, or whole groups
of people – the larger the better – in short, something so general that distinctions can
no longer be made, names no longer be named. Needless to add, this taboo applies
doubly when the deeds or words of famous people or men in high position are being
questioned. This is currently expressed in high-flown assertions that it is "superficial" to insist on details and to mention individuals, whereas it is the sign of
sophistication to speak in generalities according to which all cats are gray and we
are all equally guilty. Thus the charge Hochhuth has raised against a single Pope –
one man, easily identifiable, with a name of his own – was immediately countered
with an indictment of all Christianity. The charge against Christianity in general,
with its two thousand years of history, cannot be proved, and if it could be proved, it
would be horrible. No one seems to mind this so long as no *person* is involved, and it
is quite safe to go one step further and to maintain: "Undoubtedly there is reason for
grave accusations, but the defendant is *mankind* as a whole." (Thus Robert Weltsch
in *Summa Iniuria*, quoted above, italics added.)

Another such escape from the area of ascertainable facts and personal responsibility are the countless theories, based on non-specific, abstract, hypothetical assumptions – from the *Zeitgeist* down to the Oedipus complex – which are so general
that they explain and justify every event and every deed: no alternative to what
actually happened is even considered and no person could have acted differently
from the way he did act. Among the constructs that "explain" everything by
obscuring all details, we find such notions as a "ghetto mentality" among European

Jews; or the collective guilt of the German people, derived from an ad hoc interpretation of their history; or the equally absurd assertion of a kind of collective innocence of the Jewish people. All these clichés have in common that they make judgment superfluous and that to utter them is devoid of all risk. And although we can understand the reluctance of those immediately affected by the disaster – Germans and Jews – to examine too closely the conduct of groups and persons that seemed to be or should have been unimpaired by the totality of the moral collapse – that is, the conduct of the Christian churches, the Jewish leadership, the men of the anti-Hitler conspiracy of July 20, 1944 – this understandable disinclination is insufficient to explain the reluctance evident everywhere to make judgments in terms of individual moral responsibility.

Many people today would agree that there is no such thing as collective guilt or, for that matter, collective innocence, and that if there were, no one person could ever be guilty or innocent. This, of course, is not to deny that there is such a thing as *political* responsibility which, however, exists quite apart from what the individual member of the group has done and therefore can neither be judged in moral terms nor be brought before a criminal court. Every government assumes political responsibility for the deeds and misdeeds of its predecessor and every nation for the deeds and misdeeds of the past. When Napoleon, seizing power in France after the Revolution, said: I shall assume the responsibility for everything France ever did from Saint Louis to the Committee of Public Safety, he was only stating somewhat emphatically one of the basic facts of all political life. It means hardly more, generally speaking, than that every generation, by virtue of being born into a historical continuum, is burdened by the sins of the fathers as it is blessed with the deeds of the ancestors. But this kind of responsibility is not what we are talking about here; it is not personal, and only in a metaphorical sense can one say he *feels* guilty for what not he but his father or his people have done. (Morally speaking, it is hardly less wrong to feel guilty without having done something specific than it is to feel free of all guilt if one is actually guilty of something.) It is quite conceivable that certain political responsibilities among nations might some day be adjudicated in an international court; what is inconceivable is that such a court would be a criminal tribunal which pronounces on the guilt or innocence of individuals.

And the question of individual guilt or innocence, the act of meting out justice to both the defendant and the victim, are the only things at stake in a criminal court. The Eichmann trial was no exception, even though the court here was confronted with a crime it could not find in the lawbooks and with a criminal whose like was unknown in any court, at least prior to the Nuremberg Trials. The present report deals with nothing but the extent to which the court in Jerusalem succeeded in fulfilling the demands of justice.

NOTE

1   Quoted from the minister Aurel v. Jüchen in an anthology of critical reviews of Hochhuth's play – *Summa Iniuria*, Rowohl Verlag, p. 195.

6

Modernity and the Holocaust

Zygmunt Bauman

The Meaning of the Civilizing Process

The etiological myth deeply entrenched in the self-consciousness of our Western society is the morally elevating story of humanity emerging from pre-social barbarity. This myth lent stimulus and popularity to, and in turn was given a learned and sophisticated support by, quite a few influential sociological theories and historical narratives; the link most recently illustrated by the burst of prominence and overnight success of Elias' presentation of the "civilizing process." Contrary opinions of contemporary social theorists (see, for instance, the thorough analyses of multifarious civilizing processes: historical and comparative by Michael Mann, synthetic and theoretical by Anthony Giddens), which emphasize the growth of military violence and untrammelled use of coercion as the most crucial attributes of the emergence and entrenchment of great civilizations, have a long way to go before they succeed in displacing the etiological myth from public consciousness, or even from the diffuse folklore of the profession. By and large, lay opinion resents all challenge to the myth. Its resistance is backed, moreover, by a broad coalition of respectable learned opinions which contains such powerful authorities as the "Whig view" of history as the victorious struggle between reason and superstition; Weber's vision of rationalization as a movement toward achieving more for less effort; psychoanalytical promise to debunk, prise off, and tame the animal in man; Marx's grand prophecy of life and history coming under full control of the human species once it is freed from the presently debilitating parochialities; Elias' portrayal of recent history as that of eliminating violence from daily life; and, above all, the chorus of experts who assure us that human problems are matters of wrong policies, and that right policies mean elimination of problems. Behind the alliance stands fast the modern "gardening" state, viewing the society it rules as an object of designing, cultivating, and weed-poisoning.

In view of this myth, long ago ossified into the common sense of our era, the Holocaust can only be understood as the failure of civilization (i.e., of human purposive, reason-guided activity) to contain the morbid natural predilections of whatever has been left of nature in man. Obviously, the Hobbesian world has not been fully chained, the Hobbesian problem has not been fully resolved. In other words, we do not have as yet enough civilization. The unfinished civilizing process is yet to be brought to its conclusion. If the lesson of mass murder does teach us anything it is that the prevention of similar hiccups of barbarism evidently requires still more civilizing efforts. There is nothing in this lesson to cast doubt on the future effectiveness of such efforts and their ultimate results. We certainly move in the right direction; perhaps we do not move fast enough.

As its full picture emerges from historical research, so does an alternative, and possibly more credible, interpretation of the Holocaust as an event which disclosed the weakness and fragility of human nature (of the abhorrence of murder, disinclination to violence, fear of guilty conscience and of responsibility for immoral behavior) when confronted with the matter-of-fact efficiency of the most cherished among the products of civilization; its technology, its rational criteria of choice, its tendency to subordinate thought and action to the pragmatics of economy and effectiveness. The Hobbesian world of the Holocaust did not surface from its too-shallow grave, resurrected by the tumult of irrational emotions. It arrived (in a formidable shape Hobbes would certainly disown) in a factory-produced vehicle, wielding weapons only the most advanced science could supply, and following an itinerary designed by scientifically managed organization. Modern civilization was not the Holocaust's *sufficient* condition; it was, however, most certainly its *necessary* condition. Without it, the Holocaust would be unthinkable. It was the rational world of modern civilization that made the Holocaust thinkable. "The Nazi mass murder of the European Jewry was not only the technological achievement of an industrial society, but also the organizational achievement of a bureaucratic society."[1] Just consider what was needed to make the Holocaust unique among the many mass murders which marked the historical advance of the human species.

The civil service infused the other hierarchies with its sure-footed planning and bureaucratic thoroughness. From the army the machinery of destruction acquired its military precision, discipline, and callousness. Industry's influence was felt in the great emphasis upon accounting, penny-saving, and salvage, as well as in factory-like efficiency of the killing centres. Finally, the party contributed to the entire apparatus an "idealism," a sense of "mission," and a notion of history-making...

It was indeed the organized society in one of special roles. Though engaged in mass murder on a gigantic scale, this vast bureaucratic apparatus showed concern for correct bureaucratic procedure, for the niceties of precise definition, for the minutiae of bureaucratic regulation, and the compliance with the law.[2]

The department in the SS headquarters in charge of the destruction of European Jews was officially designated as the Section of Administration and Economy. This was only partly a lie; only in part can it be explained by reference to the notorious "speech rules," designed to mislead both chance observers and the less resolute among the perpetrators. To a degree much too high for comfort, the designation faithfully reflected the organizational meaning of activity. Except for the moral repulsiveness of its goal (or, to be precise, the gigantic scale of the moral odium), the activity did not differ in any formal sense (the only sense that can be expressed in

the language of bureaucracy) from all other organized activities designed, moni-
tored, and supervised by "ordinary" administrative and economic sections. Like all
other activities amenable to bureaucratic rationalization, it fits well the sober
description of modern administration offered by Max Weber:

Precision, speed, unambiguity, knowledge of the files, continuity, discretion, unity, strict
subordination, reduction of friction and of material and personal costs – these are raised to
the optimum point in the strictly bureaucratic administration... Bureaucratization offers
above all the optimum possibility for carrying through the principle of specializing administrative functions according to purely objective considerations... The "objective" discharge of
business primarily means a discharge of business according to *calculable rules* and "without
regard for persons."[3]

There is nothing in this description that warrants questioning the bureaucratic
definition of the Holocaust as either a simple travesty of truth or a manifestation
of a particularly monstrous form of cynicism.

And yet the Holocaust is so crucial to our understanding of the modern bureaucratic mode of rationalization not only, and not primarily, because it reminds us
(as if we need such a reminder) just how formal and ethically blind is the bureaucratic pursuit of efficiency. Its significance is not fully expressed either once we
realize to what extent mass murder on an unprecedented scale depended on the
availability of well-developed and firmly entrenched skills and habits of meticulous
and precise division of labor, of maintaining a smooth flow of command and information, or of impersonal, well-synchronized coordination of autonomous yet complementary actions; on those skills and habits, in short, which best grow and
thrive in the atmosphere of the office. The light shed by the Holocaust on our
knowledge of bureaucratic rationality is at its most dazzling once we realize the
extent to which *the very idea of the* Endlösung *was an outcome of the bureaucratic
culture*. [...]

This is not to suggest that the incidence of the Holocaust was *determined* by
modern bureaucracy or the culture of instrumental rationality it epitomizes; much
less still, that modern bureaucracy *must* result in Holocaust-style phenomena. I do
suggest, however, that the rules of instrumental rationality are singularly incapable
of preventing such phenomena; that there is nothing in those rules which disqualifies
the Holocaust-style methods of "social-engineering" as improper or, indeed, the
actions they served as irrational. I suggest, further, that the bureaucratic culture
which prompts us to view society as an object of administration, as a collection of so
many "problems" to be solved, as "nature" to be "controlled," "mastered," and
"improved" or "remade," as a legitimate target for "social engineering," and in
general a garden to be designed and kept in the planned shape by force (the
gardening posture divides vegetation into "cultured plants" to be taken care of,
and weeds to be exterminated), was the very atmosphere in which the idea of the
Holocaust could be conceived, slowly yet consistently developed, and brought to its
conclusion. And I also suggest that it was the spirit of instrumental rationality, and
its modern, bureaucratic form of institutionalization, which had made the Holocaust-style solutions not only possible, but eminently "reasonable" – and increased
the probability of their choice. This increase in probability is more than fortuitously

related to the ability of modern bureaucracy to coordinate the action of a great number of moral individuals in the pursuit of any, also immoral, ends. [...]

The Modernity of Racism

[...] Modernity brought the leveling of differences – at least of their outward appearances, of the very stuff of which symbolic distances between segregated groups are made. With such differences missing, it was not enough to muse philosophically over the wisdom of reality as it was – something Christian doctrine had done before when it wished to make sense out of the factual Jewish separation. Differences had to be created now, or retained against the awesome eroding power of social and legal equality and cross-cultural exchange.

The inherited religious explanation of the boundary – the rejection of Christ by the Jews – was singularly unfit for the new task. Such an explanation inevitably entailed the possibility of exit from the segregated field. As long as the boundary remained clearly drawn and well marked, that explanation served a good purpose. It provided the needed element of flexibility which tied the fate of men to their assumed freedom to earn salvation or commit a sin, to accept or to reject the Divine grace; and it achieved it all without in the slightest detracting from the solidity of the boundary itself. The same element of flexibility, however, would prove disastrous once the practices of segregation had become too half-hearted and lackadaisical to sustain the "naturalness" of the boundary – making it instead a hostage to human self-determination. The modern world-view, after all, proclaimed the unlimited potential of education and self-perfection. Everything was possible, with due effort and good will. Man was at birth a *tabula rasa*, an empty cabinet, later to be covered and filled, in the course of the civilizing process, with contents supplied by the leveling-up pressure of shared cultural ideas. Paradoxically, referring the differences between the Jews and their Christian hosts solely to the distinction of creed and connected rituals, appeared well geared to the modern vision of human nature. Alongside the renunciation of other prejudices, the abandonment of Judaist superstitions, and the conversion to a superior faith, seemed to be proper and sufficient vehicles of self-improvement; a drive only to be expected, and on a massive scale, on the road to the final victory of reason over ignorance.

What truly threatened the solidity of old boundaries was not, of course, the ideological formula of modernity (though it did not strengthen it either), but the refusal of the secularized modern state to legislate differentiated social practices. This was all right as long as the Jews (Drumont's "Mr Cohen") themselves refused to follow the state in its drive toward uniformity, and stuck to their own discriminating practices. Real confusion was caused by those ever-more-numerous Jews, who did take up the offer and accomplish the conversion, either in its bequeathed, religious form, or in its modern form of cultural assimilation. In France, Germany, in the German-dominated part of Austro-Hungary, the likelihood that all Jews would sooner or later be "socialized," or would "self-socialize," into non-Jews, and hence would become culturally indistinguishable and socially invisible, was quite real. In the absence of old customary and legally supported practices of segregation, such absence of visible marks of difference could only be tantamount to wiping out the boundary itself.

Under conditions of modernity, segregation required a modern method of bound-ary-building. A method able to withstand and neutralize the leveling impact of allegedly infinite powers of educatory and civilizing forces; a method capable of designating a "no-go" area for pedagogy and self-improvement, of drawing an unencroachable limit to the potential of cultivation (a method applied eagerly, though with mixed success, to all groups intended to be kept permanently in a subordinate position – like the working classes or women). If it was to be salvaged from the assault of modern equality, *the distinctiveness of the Jews had to be re-articulated and laid on new foundations, stronger than human powers of culture and self-determination.* In Hannah Arendt's terse phrase, Judaism has to be replaced with Jewishness: "Jews had been able to escape from Judaism into conversion; from Jewishness there was no escape."[4]

Unlike Judaism, Jewishness had to be, emphatically, stronger than human will and human creative potential. It had to be located at the level of natural law (the kind of law that ought to be discovered, and then taken account of and exploited for human benefit, but which cannot be wished away, tampered with, or neglected – at least, not without terrible consequences). It is of such a law that Drumont's anecdote was meant to remind his readers: "'Do you want to see how blood speaks?' a French duke once asked his friends. He had married a Rothschild from Frankfurt in spite of his mother's tears. He called his little son, pulled a golden louis from his pocket and showed it to him. The child's eyes lit up. 'You see,' continued the duke, 'the semitic instinct reveals itself straight away.'" Some time later Charles Maurras would insist that "what one is determines one's attitude from the beginning. The illusion of choice, of reason, can only lead to personal *déracinement* and political disaster." To neglect such a law may only be done at one's own, and common, peril – or so we learn from Maurice Barrès: "Caught up in mere words a child is cut off from all reality: Kantian doctrine uproots him from the soil of his ancestors. A surplus of diplomas creates what we may call, after Bismarck, a 'proletariat of graduates'. This is our indictment of the universities; what happens to their product, the 'intellectual,' is that he becomes an enemy of society."[5] The product of conversion – be it religious or cultural – is not the change, but *loss* of quality. On the other side of conversion lurks a void, not another identity. The convert loses his identity without acquiring anything instead. Man *is* before he *acts*; nothing he does may change what he is. This is, roughly, the philosophical essence of racism.

MODERNITY, RACISM, EXTERMINATION

There is an apparent paradox in the history of racism, and Nazi racism in particular.

In the by far most spectacular and the best-known case in this history, racism was instrumental in the mobilization of anti-modernist sentiments and anxieties, and was apparently effective primarily because of this connection. Adolf Stöcker, Die-trich Eckart, Alfred Rosenberg, Gregor Strasser, Joseph Goebbels, and virtually any other prophet, theorist, and ideologue of National Socialism used the phantom of the Jewish race as a lynch-pin binding the fears of the past and prospective victims of modernization, which they articulated, and the ideal *volkisch* society of the future which they proposed to create in order to forestall further advances of modernity. In their appeals to the deep-seated horror of the social upheaval that modernity augured, they identified modernity as the rule of economic and monetary values, and charged Jewish racial characteristics with responsibility for such a relentless assault on the *volkisch* mode of life and standards of human worth. Elimination of the Jews was hence presented as a synonym of the rejection of modern order. This fact suggests an essentially pre-modern character of racism; its natural affinity, so to speak, with anti-modern emotions and its selective fitness as a vehicle for such emotions.

On the other hand, however, as a conception of the world, and even more importantly as an effective instrument of political practice, racism is unthinkable without the advancement of modern science, modern technology, and modern forms of state power. As such, racism is strictly a modern product. Modernity made racism possible. It also created a demand for racism; an era that declared achievement to be the only measure of human worth needed a theory of ascription to redeem boundary-drawing and boundary-guarding concerns under new conditions which made boundary-crossing easier than ever before. Racism, in short, is a thoroughly modern weapon used in the conduct of pre-modern, or at least not exclusively modern, struggles.

From Heterophobia to Racism

Most commonly (though wrongly), racism is understood as a variety of inter-group resentment or prejudice. Sometimes racism is set apart from other sentiments or beliefs of the wider class by its emotional intensity; at other times, it is set apart by reference to hereditary, biological, and extra-cultural attributes which, unlike the non-racist variants of group animosity, it normally contains. In some cases writers about racism point out the scientific pretensions that other, non-racist yet similarly negative, stereotypes of foreign groups do not usually possess. Whatever the feature chosen, however, the habit of analyzing and interpreting racism in the framework of a larger category of prejudice is seldom breached.

As racism gains in saliency among contemporary forms of inter-group resentment, and alone among them manifests a pronounced affinity with the scientific spirit of the age, a reverse interpretive tendency becomes ever more prominent; a tendency to extend the notion of racism so as to embrace all varieties of resentment. All kinds of group prejudice are then interpreted as so many expressions of innate, natural racist predispositions. One can probably afford not to be too excited by such an exchange of places and view it, philosophically, as just a question of the definitions, which can, after all, be chosen or rejected at will. On a closer scrutiny, however, complacency appears ill-advised. Indeed, if all inter-group dislike and animosity are forms of racism, and if the tendency to keep strangers at a distance and resent their proximity has been amply documented by historical and ethnological research as a well-nigh universal and perpetual attribute of human groupings, then there is nothing essentially and radically novel about the racism that has acquired such a prominence in our time; just a rehearsal of the old scenario, though admittedly staged with somewhat updated dialogues. In particular, the intimate link of racism with other aspects of modern life is either denied outright or left out of focus.

In his recent impressively erudite study of prejudice,[6] Pierre-André Taguieff writes synonimically of racism and heterophobia (resentment of the different). [...] I suggest, on the contrary, that *it is precisely the nature, function, and the mode of operation of racism that sharply differ from heterophobia* – that diffuse (and sentimental rather than practical) unease, discomfort, or anxiety that people normally experience whenever they are confronted with such "human ingredients" of their situation as they do not fully understand, cannot communicate with easily, and cannot expect to behave in a routine, familiar way. Heterophobia seems to be a focused manifestation of a still wider phenomenon of anxiety aroused by the feeling that one has no control over the situation, and that thus one can neither influence its development, nor foresee the consequences of one's action. Heterophobia may appear as either a realistic or an irrealistic objectification of such anxiety – but it is likely that the anxiety in question always seeks an object on which to anchor, and that consequently heterophobia is a fairly common phenomenon at all times and more common still in an age of modernity, when occasions for the "no control" experience become more frequent, and their interpretation in terms of the obtrusive interference by an alien human group becomes more plausible.

I suggest as well that, so described, *heterophobia ought to be analytically distinguished from contestant enmity*, a more specific antagonism generated by the human practices of identity-seeking and boundary-drawing. In the latter case, sentiments of antipathy and resentment seem more like emotional appendages to the activity of separation; separation itself demands an activity, an effort, a sustained action. The alien of the first case, however, is not merely a too-close-for-comfort, yet clearly separate category of people easy to spot and keep at a required distance, but a collection of people whose "collectiveness" is not obvious or generally recognized; its collectiveness may be even contested and is often concealed or denied by the members of the alien category. The alien in this case threatens to penetrate the native group and fuse with it – if preventive measures are not set out and vigilantly observed. The alien, therefore, threatens the unity and the identity of the alien group, not so much by confounding its control over a territory or its freedom to act in the familiar way, but by blurring the boundary of the territory itself and effacing the difference between the familiar (right) and the alien (wrong) way of life. This is the "enemy in our midst" case – one that triggers a vehement boundary-drawing bustle, which in its turn generates a thick fall-out of antagonism and hatred to those found or suspected guilty of double loyalty and sitting astride the barricade.

Racism differs from both heterophobia and contestant enmity. The difference lies neither in the intensity of sentiments nor in the type of argument used to rationalize it. *Racism stands apart by a practice of which it is a part and which it rationalizes: a practice that combines strategies of architecture and gardening with that of medicine – in the service of the construction of an artificial social order, through cutting out the elements of the present reality that neither fit the visualized perfect reality, nor can be changed so that they do.* In a world that boasts the unprecedented ability to improve human conditions by reorganizing human affairs on a rational basis, racism manifests the conviction that a certain category of human beings cannot be incorporated into the rational order, whatever the effort. In a world notable for the continuous rolling back of the limits to scientific, technological, and cultural manipulation, racism proclaims that certain blemishes of a certain category of people cannot be removed or rectified – that they remain beyond the boundaries of reforming practices, and will do so for ever. In a world proclaiming the formidable capacity of training and cultural conversion, racism sets apart a certain category of people that cannot be reached (and thus cannot be effectively cultivated) by argument or any other training tools, and hence must remain perpetually alien. To summarize: in the modern world distinguished by its ambition to self-control and self-administration racism declares a certain category of people endemically and hopelessly resistant to control and immune to all efforts at amelioration. To use the medical metaphor; one can train and shape "healthy" parts of the body, but not cancerous growth. The latter can be "improved" only by being destroyed.

The consequence is that *racism is inevitably associated with the strategy of estrangement*. If conditions allow, racism demands that the offending category ought to be removed beyond the territory occupied by the group it offends. If such conditions are absent, racism requires that the offending category is physically exterminated. Expulsion and destruction are two mutually exchangeable methods of estrangement.

Of the Jews, Alfred Rosenberg wrote: "Zunz calls Judaism the whim of [the Jewish] soul. Now the Jew cannot break loose from this 'whim' even if he is baptized ten times over, and the necessary result of this influence will always be the same: lifelessness, anti-Christianity and materialism."[7] What is true about religious influence applies to all the other cultural interventions. Jews are beyond repair. Only a physical distance, or a break of communication, or fencing them off, or annihilation, may render them harmless.

Racism as a Form of Social Engineering

Racism comes into its own only in the context of a design of the perfect society and intention to implement the design through planned and consistent effort. In the case of the Holocaust, the design was the thousand-year *Reich* – the kingdom of the liberated German Spirit. It was that kingdom which had no room for anything but the German Spirit. It had no room for the Jews, as the Jews could not be spiritually converted and embrace the *Geist* of the German *Volk*. This spiritual inability was articulated as the attribute of heredity or blood – substances which at that time at least embodied the other side of culture, the territory that culture could not dream of cultivating, a wilderness that would be never turned into the object of gardening. (The prospects of genetic engineering were not as yet seriously entertained.)

The Nazi revolution was an exercise in social engineering on a grandiose scale. "Racial stock" was the key link in the chain of engineering measures. In the collection of official plaidoyers of Nazi policy, published in English on Ribbentrop's initiative for the purposes of international propaganda and for this reason expressed in a carefully tempered and cautious language, Dr. Arthur Gütt, the Head of the National Hygiene Department in the Ministry of Interior, described as the major task of the Nazi rule "an active policy consistently aiming at the preservation of racial health," and explained the strategy such policy had necessarily to involve: "If we facilitate the propagation of healthy stock by systematic selection and by elimination of the unhealthy elements, we shall be able to improve the physical standards not, perhaps, of the present generation, but of those who will succeed us." Gütt had no doubt that the selection-cum-elimination such a policy envisaged "go along the lines universally adopted in conformity with the researches of Koch, Lister, Pasteur, and other celebrated scientists"[8] and thus constituted a logical extension – indeed, a culmination – of the advancement of modern science.

Dr. Walter Gross, the Head of the Bureau for Enlightenment on Population Policy and Racial Welfare, spelled out the practicalities of the racial policy: reversing the current trend of "declining birth-rate among the fitter inhabitants and unrestrained propagation among the hereditary unfit, the mentally deficient, imbeciles and hereditary criminals, etc."[9] As he writes for an international audience unlikely to applaud the determination of the Nazis, unencumbered as they were by things so irrational as public opinion or political pluralism, to see the accomplishment of modern science and technology to their logical end, Gross does not venture beyond the necessity to sterilize the hereditary unfit.

The reality of racial policy was, however, much more gruesome. Contrary to Gütt's suggestion, the Nazi leaders saw no reason to restrict their concerns to "those who will succeed us." As the resources allowed, they set about to improve the *present* generation. The royal road to this goal led through the forceful removal of *unwertes Leben*. Every vehicle would do to secure progress along this road. Depending on circumstances, references were made to "elimination," "ridding," "evacuation," or "reduction" (read "extermination"). Following Hitler's command of 1 September 1939, centers had been created in Brandenburg, Hadamar, Sonnenstein, and Eichberg, which hid under a double lie: they called themselves, in hushed conversations between the initiated, "euthanasia institutes," while for the wider consumption they used still more deceitful and misleading names of a Charitable Foundation for "Institutional Care" or the "Transport of the Sick" – or even the bland "T4" code (from 4 Tiergartenstrasse, Berlin, where the coordinating office of the whole killing operation was located).[10] When the command had to be rescinded on 28 August 1941 as the result of an outcry raised by a number of prominent luminaries of the Church, the principle of "actively managing the population trends" was in no way abandoned. Its focus, together with the gassing technologies that the euthanasia campaign had helped to develop, was merely shifted to a different target: the Jews. And to different places, like Sobibór or Chelmno.

Unwertes Leben remained the target all along. For the Nazi designers of the perfect society, the project they pursued and were determined to implement through social engineering split human life into worthy and unworthy; the first to be lovingly cultivated and given *Lebensraum*, the other to be "distanced," or – if the distancing proved unfeasible – exterminated. Those simply alien were not the objects of strictly racial policy: to them, old and tested strategies traditionally associated with contestant enmity could be applied: the aliens ought to be kept beyond closely guarded borders. Those bodily and mentally handicapped made a more difficult case and called for a new, original policy: they could not be evicted or fenced off as they did not rightfully belong to any of the "other races," but they were unworthy to enter the thousand-year *Reich* either. The Jews offered an essentially similar case. They were not a race like the others; they were an anti-race, a race to undermine and poison all other races, to sap not just the identity of any race in particular, but the racial order itself. (Remember the Jews as the "non-national nation," the incurable enemy of the nation-based order as such.) With approval and relish, Rosenberg quoted Weiniger's self-deprecatory verdict on the Jews as "an invisible cohesive web of slime fungus (plasmodium), existing since time immemorial and spread over the entire earth."[11] Thus the separation of the Jews could only be a half-measure, a station on the road to the ultimate goal. The matter could not possibly end with the cleansing of Germany of the Jews. Even residing far from the German borders, the Jews would continue to erode and disintegrate the natural logic of the universe. Having ordered his troops to fight for the supremacy of the *German* race, Hitler believed that the war he kindled was waged in the name of *all races*, a service rendered to racially organized humankind.

In this conception of social engineering as a scientifically founded work aimed at the institution of a new, and better, order (a work which necessarily entails the containment, or preferably elimination, of any disruptive factors), racism was indeed resonant with the world-view and practice of modernity. And this, at least, in two vital respects.

First, with the Enlightenment came the enthronement of the new deity, that of Nature, together with the legitimation of science as its only orthodox cult, and of scientists as its prophets and priests. Everything, in principle, had been opened to objective inquiry; everything could, in principle, be known – reliably and truly. Truth, goodness, and beauty, that which is and that which ought to be, had all become legitimate objects of systematic, precise observation. In turn, they could legitimize themselves only through objective knowledge which would result from such observation. [...]

Second – from the Enlightenment on, the modern world was distinguished by its activist, engineering attitude toward nature and toward itself. Science was not to be conducted for its own sake; it was seen as, first and foremost, an instrument of awesome power allowing its holder to improve on reality, to reshape it according to human plans and designs, and to assist it in its drive to self-perfection. Gardening and medicine supplied the archetypes of constructive stance, while normality, health, or sanitation offered the archmetaphors for human tasks and strategies in the management of human affairs. Human existence and cohabitation became objects of planning and administration; like garden vegetation or a living organism they could not be left to their own devices, lest they should be infested by weeds or overwhelmed by cancerous tissues. Gardening and medicine are functionally distinct forms of the same activity of *separating and setting apart useful elements destined to live and thrive, from harmful and morbid ones, which ought to be exterminated.*

Hitler's language and rhetoric were fraught with images of disease, infection, infestation, putrefaction, pestilence. He compared Christianity and bolshevism to syphilis or plague; he spoke of Jews as bacilli, decomposing germs, or vermin. "The discovery of the Jewish virus," he told Himmler in 1942, "is one of the greatest revolutions that have taken place in the world. The battle in which we are engaged today is of the same sort as the battle waged, during the last century, by Pasteur and Koch. How many diseases have their origin in the Jewish virus...We shall regain our health only by eliminating the Jew."[12] In October of the same year, Hitler proclaimed: "By exterminating the pest, we shall do humanity a service."[13] The executors of Hitler's will spoke of the extermination of Jews as *Gesundung* (healing) of Europe, *Selbsttreinigung* (self-cleansing), *Judensäuberung* (cleansing-of-Jews). In an article in *Das Reich*, published on 5 November 1941, Goebbels hailed the introduction of the Star of David badge as a measure of "hygienic prophylactic." The isolation of the Jews from a racially pure community was "an elementary rule of racial, national, and social hygiene." There were, Goebbels argued, good people and bad people, as much as there are good and bad animals. "The fact that the Jew still lives among us is no proof that he also belongs with us, just as a flea does not become a domestic animal because it lives in the house."[14] The Jewish question, in the words of the Foreign Office Press Chief, was "eine Frage der politischen Hygiene."[15] [...]

To sum up: well before they built the gas chambers, the Nazis, on Hitler's orders, attempted to exterminate their own mentally insane or bodily impaired compatriots through "mercy killing" (falsely nicknamed "euthanasia"), and to breed a superior race through the organized fertilization of racially superior women by racially superior men (eugenics). Like these attempts, the murder of Jews was an exercise in the rational management of society. And a systematic attempt to deploy in its service the stance, the philosophy, and the precepts of applied science. [...]

The Uniqueness and Normality of the Holocaust

[...] Murderous motives in general, and motives for mass murder in particular, have been many and varied. They range from pure, cold-blooded calculation of competitive gain, to equally pure, disinterested hatred or heterophobia. Most communal strifes and genocidal campaigns against aborigines lie comfortably within this range. If accompanied by an ideology, the latter does not go much further than a simple "us or them" vision of the world, and a precept "There is no room for both of us," or "The only good injun is a dead injun." The adversary is expected to follow mirror-image principles only if allowed to. Most genocidal ideologies rest on a devious symmetry of assumed intentions and actions.

Truly modern genocide is different. *Modern genocide is genocide with a purpose.* Getting rid of the adversary is not an end in itself. It is a means to an end: a necessity that stems from the ultimate objective, a step that one has to take if one wants ever to reach the end of the road. *The end itself is a grand vision of a better, and radically different, society.* Modern genocide is an element of social engineering, meant to bring about a social order conforming to the design of the perfect society.

To the initiators and the managers of modern genocide, society is a subject of planning and conscious design. One can and should do more about the society than change one or several of its many details, improve it here or there, cure some of its troublesome ailments. One can and should set oneself goals more ambitious and radical: one can and should remake the society, force it to conform to an overall, scientifically conceived plan. One can create a society that is objectively better than the one "merely existing" – that is, existing without conscious intervention. Invariably, there is an aesthetic dimension to the design: the ideal world about to be built conforms to the standards of superior beauty. Once built, it will be richly satisfying, like a perfect work of art; it will be a world which, in Alberti's immortal words, no adding, diminishing, or altering could improve.

This is a gardener's vision, projected upon a world-size screen. The thoughts, feelings, dreams, and drives of the designers of the perfect world are familiar to every gardener worth his name, though perhaps on a somewhat smaller scale. Some gardeners hate the weeds that spoil their design – that ugliness in the midst of beauty, litter in the midst of serene order. Some others are quite unemotional about them: just a problem to be solved, an extra job to be done. Not that it makes a difference to the weeds; both gardeners exterminate them. If asked or given a chance to pause and ponder, both would agree; weeds must die not so much because of what they are, as because of what the beautiful, orderly garden ought to be.

Modern culture is a garden culture. It defines itself as the design for an ideal life and a perfect arrangement of human conditions. It constructs its own identity out of distrust of nature. In fact, it defines itself and nature, and the distinction between them, through its endemic distrust of spontaneity and its longing for a better, and necessarily artificial, order. Apart from the overall plan, the artificial *order* of the garden needs tools and raw materials. It also needs defense – against the unrelenting danger of what is, obviously, a disorder. The order, first conceived of as a design, determines what is a tool, what is a raw material, what is useless, what is irrelevant, what is harmful, what is a weed or a pest. It classifies all elements of the universe by their relation to itself. This relation is the only meaning it grants them and tolerates – and the only justification of the gardener's actions, as differentiated as the relations themselves. From the point of view of the design all actions are instrumental, while all the objects of action are either facilities or hindrances.

Modern genocide, like modern culture in general, is a gardener's job. It is just one of the many chores that people who treat society as a garden need to undertake. If garden design defines its weeds, there are weeds wherever there is a garden. And weeds are to be exterminated. Weeding out is a creative, not a destructive activity. It does not differ in kind from other activities which combine in the construction and sustenance of the perfect garden. All visions of society-as-garden define parts of the social habitat as human weeds. Like all other weeds, they must be segregated, contained, prevented from spreading, removed, and kept outside the society boundaries; if all these means prove insufficient, they must be killed.

Stalin's and Hitler's victims were not killed in order to capture and colonize the territory they occupied. Often they were killed in a dull, mechanical fashion with no human emotions – hatred included – to enliven it. They were killed because they did not fit, for one reason or another, the scheme of a perfect society. Their killing was not the work of destruction, but creation. They were eliminated, so that an objectively better human world – more efficient, more moral, more beautiful – could be established. A Communist world. Or a racially pure, Aryan world. In both cases, a harmonious world, conflict-free, docile in the hands of their rulers, orderly, controlled. People tainted with ineradicable blight of their past or origin could not be fitted into such an unblemished, healthy and shining world. Like weeds, their nature could not be changed. They could not be improved or reeducated. They had to be eliminated for reasons of genetic or ideational heredity – of a natural mechanism, resilient and immune to cultural processing.

The two most notorious and extreme cases of modern genocide did not betray the spirit of modernity. They did not deviously depart from the main track of the civilizing process. They were the most consistent, uninhibited expressions of that spirit. They attempted to reach the most ambitious aims of the civilizing process most other processes stop short of, not necessarily for the lack of good will. They showed what the rationalizing, designing, controlling dreams and efforts of modern civilization are able to accomplish if not mitigated, curbed, or counteracted.

These dreams and efforts have been with us for a long time. They spawned the vast and powerful arsenal of technology and managerial skills. They gave birth to institutions which serve the sole purpose of instrumentalizing human behavior to such an extent that any aim may be pursued with efficiency and vigor, with or without ideological dedication or moral approval on the part of the pursuers. They legitimize the rulers' monopoly on ends and the confinement of the ruled to the role of means. They define most actions as means, and means as subordination – to the ultimate end, to those who set it, to supreme will, to supra-individual knowledge.

Emphatically, this does not mean that we all live daily according to Auschwitz principles. From the fact that the Holocaust is modern, it does not follow that modernity is a Holocaust. The Holocaust is a byproduct of the modern drive to a fully designed, fully controlled world, once the drive is getting out of control and running wild. Most of the time, modernity is prevented from doing so. Its ambitions clash with the pluralism of the human world; they stop short of their fulfillment for the lack of an absolute power absolute enough and a monopolistic agency monopolistic enough to be able to disregard, shrug off, or overwhelm all autonomous, and thus countervailing and mitigating, forces.

Peculiarity of Modern Genocide

When the modernist dream is embraced by an absolute power able to monopolize modern vehicles of rational action, and when that power attains freedom from effective social control, genocide follows. A modern genocide – like the Holocaust. The short circuit (one almost wishes to say: a chance encounter) between an ideologically obsessed power elite and the tremendous facilities of rational, systemic action developed by modern society, may happen relatively seldom. Once it does happen, however, certain aspects of modernity are revealed which under different circumstances are less visible and hence may be easily "theorized away."

Modern Holocaust is unique in a double sense. *It is unique among other historic cases of genocide because it is modern. And it stands unique against the quotidianity of modern society because it brings together some ordinary factors of modernity which normally are kept apart.* In this second sense of its uniqueness, only the combination of factors is unusual and rare, not the factors that are combined. Separately, each factor is common and normal. And the knowledge of saltpeter, sulfur, or charcoal is not complete unless one knows and remembers that, if mixed, they turn into gunpowder.

The simultaneous uniqueness and normality of the Holocaust has found excellent expression in the summary of Sarah Gordon's findings:

systematic extermination, as opposed to sporadic pogroms, could be carried out only by extremely powerful government, and probably could have succeeded only under the cover of wartime conditions. It was only the advent of Hitler and his radical anti-Semitic followers and their subsequent centralization of power that made the extermination of European Jewry possible...

[T]he process of organized exclusion and murder required cooperation by huge sections of the military and bureaucracy, as well as acquiescence among the German people, whether or not they approved of Nazi persecution and extermination.[16]

Gordon names several factors which had to come together to produce the Holocaust; radical (and [...] modern: racist and exterminatory) anti-semitism of the Nazi type; transformation of that anti-Semitism into the practical policy of a powerful, centralized state; that state being in command of a huge, efficient bureaucratic apparatus; "state of emergency" – an extraordinary, wartime condition, which allowed that government and the bureaucracy it controlled to get away with things which could, possibly, face more serious obstacles in time of peace; and the non-interference, the passive acceptance of those things by the population at large. Two among those factors (one can argue that the two can be reduced to one: with Nazis in power, war was virtually inevitable) could be seen as coincidental – not necessary attributes of a modern society, though always its possibility. The remaining factors, however, are fully "normal." They are constantly present in every modern society, and their presence has been made both possible and inescapable by those processes which are properly associated with the rise and entrenchment of modern civilization.

In the preceding chapter I have tried to unravel the connection between radical, exterminatory anti-Semitism and the sociopolitical and cultural transformations usually referred to as the development of modern society. In the last chapter of the book I shall attempt to analyze those social mechanisms, also set in motion under contemporary conditions, that silence or neutralize moral inhibitions and, more generally, make people refrain from resistance against evil. Here I intend to focus on one only, yet arguably the most crucial among the constituent factors of the Holocaust: the typically modern, technological-bureaucratic patterns of action and the mentality they institutionalize, generate, sustain, and reproduce.

There are two antithetical ways in which one can approach the explanation of the Holocaust. One can consider the horrors of mass murder as evidence of the fragility of civilization, or one can see them as evidence of its awesome potential. One can argue that, with criminals in control, civilized rules of behavior may be suspended, and thus the eternal beast always hiding just beneath the skin of the socially drilled being may break free. Alternatively, one can argue that, once armed with the sophisticated technical and conceptual products of modern civilization, men can do things their nature would otherwise prevent them from doing. To put it differently; one can, following the Hobbesian tradition, conclude that the inhuman pre-social state has not yet been fully eradicated, all civilizing efforts notwithstanding. Or one can, on the contrary, insist that the civilizing process has succeeded in substituting artificial and flexible patterns of human conduct for natural drives, and hence made possible a scale of inhumanity and destruction which had remained inconceivable as long as natural predispositions guided human action. I propose to opt for the second approach, and substantiate it in the following discussion.

The fact that most people (including many a social theorist) instinctively choose the first, rather than the second, approach, is a testimony to the remarkable success of the etiological myth which, in one variant or another, Western civilization has deployed over the years to legitimize its spatial hegemony by projecting it as temporal superiority. Western civilization has articulated its struggle for domination in terms of the holy battle of humanity against barbarism, reason against ignorance, objectivity against prejudice, progress against degeneration, truth against superstition, science against magic, rationality against passion. It has interpreted the history of its ascendance as the gradual yet relentless substitution of human mastery over nature for the mastery of nature over man. It has presented its own accomplishment as, first and foremost, a decisive advance in human freedom of action, creative potential, and security. It has identified freedom and security with its own type of social order; Western, modern society is defined as *civilized* society, and a civilized society in turn is understood as a state from which most of the natural ugliness and morbidity, as well as most of the immanent human propensity to cruelty and violence, have been eliminated or at least suppressed. The popular image of civilized society is, more than anything else, that of the absence of violence; of a gentle, polite, soft society.

Perhaps the most salient symbolic expression of this master-image of civilization is the sanctity of the human body: the care which is taken not to invade that most private of spaces, to avoid bodily contact, to abide by the culturally prescribed bodily distance; and the trained disgust and repulsion we feel whenever we see or hear of that sacred space being trespassed on. Modern civilization can afford the fiction of the sanctity and autonomy of the human body thanks to the efficient mechanisms of self-control it has developed, and on the whole successfully reproduced in the process of individual education. Once effective, the reproduced mechanisms of self-control dispose of the need of subsequent external interference with the body. On the other hand, privacy of the body underlines personal responsibility for its behavior, and thus adds powerful sanctions to the bodily drill. (In recent years the severity of sanctions, keenly exploited by the consumer market, have finally produced the tendency to interiorize demand for the drill; development of individual self-control tends to be itself self-controlled, and pursued in a DIY fashion.) Cultural prohibition against coming into too close a contact with another body serves therefore as an effective safeguard against diffuse, contingent influences which may, if allowed, counteract the centrally administered pattern of social order. Non-violence of the daily and diffuse human intercourse is an indispensable condition, and a constant output, of the centralization of coercion.

All in all, the overall non-violent character of modern civilization is an illusion. More exactly, it is an integral part of its self-apology and self-apotheosis; in short, of its legitimizing myth. It is not true that our civilization exterminates violence due to the inhuman, degrading, or immoral character of the latter. If modernity.

is indeed antithetical to the wild passions of barbarism, it is not at all antithetical to efficient, dispassionate destruction, slaughter, and torture . . . As the quality of thinking grows more rational, the quantity of destruction increases. In our time, for example, terrorism and torture are no longer instruments of passions; they have become instruments of political rationality.[17]

What in fact has happened in the course of the civilizing process, is the redeployment of violence, and the redistribution of access to violence. Like so many other things which we have been trained to abhor and detest, violence has been taken out of sight, rather than forced out of existence. It has become invisible, that is, from the vantage point of narrowly circumscribed and privatized personal experience. It has been enclosed instead in segregated and isolated territories, on the whole inaccessible to ordinary members of society; or evicted to the "twilight areas," off-limits for a large majority (and the majority which counts) of society's members; or exported to distant places which on the whole are irrelevant for the life-business of civilized humans (one can always cancel holiday bookings).

The ultimate consequence of all this is the concentration of violence. Once centralized and free from competition, means of coercion would be capable of reaching unheard of results even if not technically perfected. Their concentration, however, triggers and boosts the escalation of technical improvements, and thus the effects of concentration are further magnified. As Anthony Giddens repeatedly emphasized (see, above all, his *Contemporary Critique of Historical Materialism* (1981), and *The Constitution of Society* (1984)), the removal of violence from the daily life of civilized societies has always been intimately associated with a thoroughgoing militarization of inter-societal exchange and inner-societal production of order; standing armies and police forces brought together technically superior weapons and superior technology of bureaucratic management. For the last two centuries, the number of people who have suffered violent death as the result of such militarization has been steadily growing to reach a volume unheard of before.

The Holocaust absorbed an enormous volume of means of coercion. Having harnessed them in the service of a single purpose, it also added stimulus to their further specialization and technical perfection. More, however, than the sheer quantity of tools of destruction, and even their technical quality, what mattered was the way in which they were deployed. Their formidable effectiveness relied mostly on the subjection of their use to purely bureaucratic, technical considerations (which made their use all but totally immune to the countervailing pressures, such as they might have been submitted to if the means of violence were controlled by dispersed and uncoordinated agents and deployed in a diffuse way). Violence has been turned into a technique. Like all techniques, it is free from emotions and purely rational. "It is, in fact, entirely reasonable, if 'reason' means instrumental reason, to apply American military force, B-52's, napalm, and all the rest to 'communist-dominated' Viet-Nam (clearly an 'undesirable object'), as the 'operator' to transform it into a 'desirable object.'"[18]

Effects of the Hierarchical and Functional Divisions of Labor

Use of violence is most efficient and cost-effective when the means are subjected to solely instrumental-rational criteria, and thus dissociated from moral evaluation of the ends. [...] [S]uch dissociation is an operation all bureaucracies are good at. One may even say that it provides the essence of bureaucratic structure and process, and with it the secret of that tremendous growth of mobilizing and coordinating potential, and of the rationality and efficiency of action, which modern civilization has

achieved thanks to the development of bureaucratic administration. The dissociation is by and large an outcome of two parallel processes, which are both central to
the bureaucratic model of action. The first is the *meticulous functional division of
labor* (as additional to, and distinct in its consequences from, linear graduation of
power and subordination); the second is the *substitution of technical for a moral
responsibility.*

All division of labor (also such division as results from the mere hierarchy of
command) creates a distance between most of the contributors to the final outcome
of collective activity, and the outcome itself. Before the last links in the bureaucratic
chain of power (the direct executors) confront their task, most of the preparatory
operations which brought about that confrontation have been already performed by
persons who had no personal experience, and sometimes not the knowledge either,
of the task in question. Unlike in a pre-modern unit of work, in which all steps of the
hierarchy share in the same occupational skills, and the practical knowledge of
working operations actually grows toward the top of the ladder (the master knows
the same as his journeyman or apprentice, only more and better), persons occupying
successive rungs of modern bureaucracy differ sharply in the kind of expertise and
professional training their jobs require. They may be able to put themselves imagina-
tively into their subordinates' position; this may even help in maintaining "good
human relations" inside the office – but it is not the condition of proper performance
of the task, nor of the effectiveness of the bureaucracy as a whole. In fact, most
bureaucracies do not treat seriously the romantic recipe that requires every bureaucrat, and particularly those who occupy the top, to "start from the bottom" so that
on the way to the summit they should acquire, and memorize, the experience of the
entire slope. Mindful of the multiplicity of skills which the managerial jobs of
various magnitudes demand, most bureaucracies practice instead separate avenues
of recruitment for different levels of the hierarchy. Perhaps it is true that each soldier
carries a marshal's baton in his knapsack, but few marshals, and few colonels or
captains for that matter, keep soldiers' bayonets in their briefcases.

What such practical and mental distance from the final product means is that most
functionaries of the bureaucratic hierarchy may give commands without full knowledge of their effects. In many cases they would find it difficult to visualize those
effects. Usually, they only have an abstract, detached awareness of them; the kind of
knowledge which is best expressed in statistics, which measure the results without
passing any judgment, and certainly not moral ones. In their files and their minds the
results are at best diagrammatically represented as curves or sectors of a circle;
ideally, they would appear as a column of numbers. Graphically or numerically
represented, the final outcomes of their commands are devoid of substance. The
graphs measure the *progress* of work, they say nothing about the nature of the
operation or its objects. The graphs make tasks of widely different character mutually exchangeable; only the quantifiable success or failure matter, and seen from that
point of view, the tasks do not differ.

All these effects of distance created by the hierarchical division of labor are
radically magnified once the division becomes functional. Now it is not just the
lack of direct, personal experience of the actual execution of the task to which
successive commands contribute their share, but also the lack of similarity between
the task at hand and the task of the office as a whole (one is not a miniature version,

or an icon, of the other), which distances the contributor from the job performed by the bureaucracy of which he is a part. The psychological impact of such distantiation is profound and far-reaching. It is one thing to give a command to load bombs on the plane, but quite different to take care of regular steel supply in a bomb factory. In the first case, the command-giver may have no vivid, visual impression of the devastation the bomb is about to cause. In the second case, however, the supply manager does not, if he chooses to, have to think about the use to which bombs are put at all. Even an abstract, purely notional knowledge of the final outcome is redundant, and certainly irrelevant as far as the success of his own part of the operation goes. In a functional division of labor, everything one does is in principle *multifinal*; that is, it can be combined and integrated into more than one meaning-determining totality. By itself, the function is devoid of meaning, and the meaning which will be eventually bestowed on it is in no way preempted by the actions of its perpetrators. It will be "the others" (in most cases anonymous and out of reach) who will some time, somewhere, decide that meaning. "Would workers in the chemical plants that produced napalm accept responsibility for burned babies?" ask Kren and Rappoport. "Would such workers even be aware that others might reasonably think they were responsible?"[19] Of course they wouldn't. And there is no bureaucratic reason why they should. The splitting of the baby-burning process in minute functional tasks and then separating the tasks from each other have made such awareness irrelevant – and exceedingly difficult to achieve. Remember as well that it is chemical plants that produce napalm, not any of their individual workers...

The second process responsible for distantiation is closely related to the first. The substitution of technical for moral responsibility would not be conceivable without the meticulous functional dissection and separation of tasks. At least it would not be conceivable to the same extent. The substitution takes place, to a degree, already within the purely linear graduation of control. Each person within the hierarchy of command is accountable to his immediate superior, and thus is naturally interested in his opinion and his approval of the work. However much this approval matters to him, he is still, though only theoretically, aware of what the ultimate outcome of his work is bound to be. And so there is at least an abstract chance of one awareness being measured against the other; benevolence of superiors being confronted with repulsiveness of the effects. And whenever comparison is feasible, so is the choice. Within a purely linear division of command, technical responsibility remains, at least in theory, vulnerable. It may still be called to justify itself in moral terms and to compete with moral conscience. A functionary may, for instance, decide that by giving a particular command his superior overstepped his terms of reference, as he moved from the domain of purely technical interest to that charged with ethical significance (shooting soldiers is OK; shooting babies is a different matter); and that the duty to obey an authoritative command does not extend so far as to justify what the functionary considers as morally unacceptable deeds. All these theoretical possibilities disappear, however, or are considerably weakened, once the linear hierarchy of command is supplemented, or replaced, by functional division and separation of tasks. The triumph of technical responsibility is then complete, unconditional, and for all practical purposes, unassailable.

Technical responsibility differs from moral responsibility in that it forgets that the action is a means to something other than itself. As outer connections of action are effectively removed from the field of vision, the bureaucrat's own act becomes an end in itself. It can be judged only by its intrinsic criteria of propriety and success. Hand-in-hand with the vaunted relative autonomy of the official conditioned by his functional specialization comes his remoteness from the overall effects of divided yet coordinated labor of the organization as a whole. Once isolated from their distant consequences, most functionally specialized acts either pass moral test easily, or are morally indifferent. When unencumbered by moral worries, the act can be judged on unambiguously rational grounds. What matters then is whether the act has been performed according to the best available technological knowhow, and whether its output has been cost-effective. Criteria are clear-cut and easy to operate.

For our topic, two effects of such context of bureaucratic action are most important. First is the fact that the skills, expert knowledge, inventiveness, and dedication of actors, complete with their personal motives that prompted them to deploy these qualities in full, can be fully mobilized and put to the service of the overall bureaucratic purpose even if (or perhaps because) the actors retain relative functional autonomy toward this purpose and even if this purpose does not agree with the actors' own moral philosophy. To put it bluntly, *the result is the irrelevance of moral standards for the technical success of the bureaucratic operation.* The instinct of workmanship, which according to Thorstein Veblen is present in every actor, focuses fully on proper performance of the job in hand. The practical devotion to the task may be further enhanced by the actor's craven character and severity of his superiors, or by the actor's interest in promotion, the actor's ambition or disinterested curiosity, or by many other personal circumstances, motives, or character features – but, on the whole, workmanship will suffice even in their absence. By and large, the actors want to excel; whatever they do, they want to do well. Once, thanks to the complex functional differentiation within bureaucracy, they have been distantiated from the ultimate outcomes of the operation to which they contribute, their moral concerns can concentrate fully on the good performance of the job at hand. Morality boils down to the commandment to be a good, efficient, and diligent expert and worker.

Dehumanization of Bureaucratic Objects

Another, equally important, effect of bureaucratic context of action is *dehumanization of the objects of bureaucratic operation*; the possibility to express these objects in purely technical, ethically neutral terms.

We associate dehumanization with horrifying pictures of the inmates of concentration camps – humiliated by reducing their action to the most basic level of primitive survival, by preventing them from deploying cultural (both bodily and behavioral) symbols of human dignity, by depriving them even of recognizably human likeness. As Peter Marsh put it, "Standing by the fence of Auschwitz, looking at these emaciated skeletons with shrunken skin and hollowed eyes – who could believe that these were really people?"[20] These pictures, however, represent only an extreme manifestation of a tendency which may be discovered in all bureaucracies, however benign and innocuous the tasks in which they are currently engaged. I suggest that the discussion of the dehumanizing tendency, rather than being focused on its most sensational and vile, but fortunately uncommon, manifestations, ought to concentrate on the more universal, and for this reason potentially more dangerous, manifestations.

Dehumanization starts at the point when, thanks to the distantiation, the objects at which the bureaucratic operation is aimed can, and are, reduced to a set of quantitative measures. For railway managers, the only meaningful articulation of their object is in terms of tons per kilometer. They do not deal with humans, sheep, or barbed wire; they only deal with the cargo, and this means an entity consisting entirely of measurements and devoid of quality. For most bureaucrats, even such a category as cargo would mean too strict a quality-bound restriction. They deal only with the financial effects of their actions. Their object is money. Money is the sole object that appears on both input and output ends, and *pecunia*, as the ancients shrewdly observed, definitely *non olet*. As they grow, bureaucratic companies seldom allow themselves to be confined to one qualitatively distinct area of activity. They spread sideways, guided in their movements by a sort of *lucrotropism* – a sort of gravitational pulling force of the highest returns on their capital. As we remember, the whole operation of the Holocaust was managed by the Economic Administration Section of the *Reichsicherheithauptamt*. We know that this one assignment, exceptionally, was not intended as a stratagem or a camouflage.

Reduced, like all other objects of bureaucratic management, to pure, quality-free measurements, human objects lose their distinctiveness. They are already dehumanized – in the sense that the language in which things that happen to them (or are done to them) are narrated, safeguards its referents from ethical evaluation. In fact, this language is unfit for normative-moral statements. It is only humans that may be objects of ethical propositions. (True, moral statements do extend sometimes to other, non-human living beings; but they may do so only by expanding from their original anthropomorphic foothold.) Humans lose this capacity once they are reduced to ciphers.

Dehumanization is inextricably related to the most essential, rationalizing tendency of modern bureaucracy. As all bureaucracies affect in some measure some human objects, the adverse impact of dehumanization is much more common than the habit to identify it almost totally with its genocidal effects would suggest. Soldiers are told to shoot *targets*, which *fall* when they are *hit*. Employees of big companies are encouraged to destroy *competition*. Officers of welfare agencies operate *discretionary awards* at one time, *personal credits* at another. Their objects are *supplementary benefit recipients*. It is difficult to perceive and remember the humans behind all such technical terms. The point is that as far as the bureaucratic goals go, they are better not perceived and not remembered.

Once effectively dehumanized, and hence canceled as potential subjects of moral demands, human objects of bureaucratic task-performance are viewed with ethical indifference, which soon turns into disapprobation and censure when their resistance, or lack of cooperation, slows down the smooth flow of bureaucratic routine. Dehumanized objects cannot possibly possess a "cause," much less a "just" one; they have no "interests" to be considered, indeed no claim to subjectivity. Human objects become therefore a "nuisance factor." Their obstreperousness further strengthens the self-esteem and the bonds of comradeship that unite the functionaries. The latter see themselves now as companions in a difficult struggle, calling for courage, self-sacrifice, and selfless dedication to the cause. It is not the objects of bureaucratic action, but its subjects who suffer and deserve compassion and moral praise. They may justly derive pride and assurance of their own dignity from crushing the recalcitrance of their victims – much as they are proud of overriding any other obstacle. Dehumanization of the objects and positive moral self-evaluation reinforce each other. The functionaries may faithfully serve any goal while their moral conscience remains unimpaired.

The overall conclusion is that the bureaucratic mode of action, as it has been developed in the course of the modernizing process, contains all the technical elements which proved necessary in the execution of genocidal tasks. This mode can be put to the service of a genocidal objective without major revision of its structure, mechanisms, and behavioral norms.

Moreover, contrary to widespread opinion, bureaucracy is not merely a tool, which can be used with equal facility at one time for cruel and morally contemptible, at another for deeply humane purposes. Even if it does move in any direction in which it is pushed, bureaucracy is more like a loaded dice. It has a logic and a momentum of its own. It renders some solutions more, and other solutions less, probable. Given an initial push (being confronted with a purpose), it will – like the brooms of the sorcerer's apprentice – easily move beyond all thresholds at which many of those who gave it the push would have stopped, were they still in control of the process they triggered. Bureaucracy is programmed to seek the optimal solution. It is programmed to measure the optimum in such terms as would not distinguish between one human object and another, or between human and inhuman objects. What matters is the efficiency and lowering of costs of their processing.

The Role of Bureaucracy in the Holocaust

It so happened in Germany half a century ago that bureaucracy was given the task of making Germany *judenrein* – clean of Jews. Bureaucracy started from what bureaucracies start with: the formulation of a precise definition of the object, then registering those who fitted the definition and opening a file for each. It proceeded to segregate those in the files from the rest of the population, to which the received brief did not apply. Finally, it moved to evicting the segregated category from the land of the Aryans which was to be cleansed – by nudging it to emigrate first, and deporting it to non-German territories once such territories found themselves under German control. By that time bureaucracy developed wonderful cleansing skills, not to be wasted and left to rust. *Bureaucracy which acquitted itself so well of the task of cleansing Germany made more ambitious tasks feasible, and their choice well-nigh natural.* With such a superb cleaning facility, why stop at the *Heimat* of the Aryans? Why refrain from cleaning the whole of their empire? True, as the empire was now ecumenical, it had no "outside" left where the dumping ground for the Jewish litter could be disposed of. Only one direction of deportation remained; upward, in smoke.

For many years now historians of the Holocaust have been split into the "intentionalist" and the "functionalist" camps. The first insist that killing the Jews was from the start Hitler's firm decision, waiting only for opportune conditions to emerge. The second credit Hitler with only a general idea of "finding a solution" to the "Jewish problem": clear only as far as the vision of "clean Germany" goes, but vague and muddled as to the practical steps to be taken to bring that vision closer. Historical scholarship ever more convincingly supports the functionalist view. Whatever the ultimate outcome of the debate, however, there is hardly any doubt that the space extending between the idea and its execution was filled wall-to-wall with bureaucratic action. Neither is there any doubt that however vivid was Hitler's imagination, it would have accomplished little if it had not been taken over, and translated into routine process of problem-solving, by a huge and rational bureaucratic apparatus. Finally, and perhaps most importantly, the bureaucratic mode of action left its indelible impression on the Holocaust process. Its fingerprints are all over the Holocaust history, for everyone to see. True, bureaucracy did not hatch the fear of racial contamination and the obsession with racial hygiene. For that it needed visionaries, as bureaucracy picks up where visionaries stop. But bureaucracy made the Holocaust. And it made it in its own image.

Hilberg has suggested that the moment the first German official had written the first rule of Jewish exclusion, the fate of the European Jews was sealed. There is a most profound and terrifying truth in this comment. What bureaucracy needed was the definition of its task. Rational and efficient as it was, it could be trusted to see the task to its end.

Bureaucracy contributed to the perpetuation of the Holocaust not only through its inherent capacities and skills, but also through its immanent ailments. The tendency of all bureaucracies to lose sight of the original goal and to concentrate on the means instead – the means which turn into the ends – has been widely noted, analyzed, and described. The Nazi bureaucracy did not escape its impact. Once set in motion, the machinery of murder developed its own impetus: the more it excelled in cleansing the territories it controlled of the Jews, the more actively it sought new lands where it could exercise its newly acquired skills. With the approaching military defeat of Germany, the original purpose of the *Endlösung* was becoming increasingly unreal. What kept the murdering machine going then was solely its own routine and impetus. The skills of mass murder had to be used simply because they were there. The experts created the objects for their own expertise. We remember the experts of Jewish Desks in Berlin introducing every new petty restriction on German Jews who had long before all but disappeared from German soil; we remember the SS commanders who forbade the *Wehrmacht* generals from keeping alive the Jewish craftsmen they badly needed for military operations. But nowhere was the morbid tendency of substituting the means for the ends more visible than in the uncanny and macabre episode of the murder of Romanian and Hungarian Jews, perpetrated with the Eastern Front just a few miles away, and at an enormous cost to the war effort: priceless rail carriages and engines, troops and administrative resources were diverted from military tasks in order to cleanse distant parts of Europe for the German habitat which was never to be.

Bureaucracy is intrinsically *capable* of genocidal action. To *engage* in such an action, it needs an encounter with another invention of modernity: a bold design of a better, more reasonable and rational social order – say a racially uniform, or a classless society – and above all the capacity of drawing such designs and determination to make them efficacious. Genocide follows when two common and abundant inventions of modern times meet. It is only their meeting which has been, thus far, uncommon and rare. [...]

Periods of deep social dislocations are times when this most remarkable feature of modernity comes into its own. Indeed, at no other time does society seem to be so formless – "unfinished," indefinite, and pliable – literally waiting for a vision and a skillful and resourceful designer to give it a form. At no other time does society seem so devoid of forces and tendencies of its own, and hence incapable of resisting the hand of the gardener, and ready to be squeezed into any form he chooses. *The combination of malleability and helplessness constitutes an attraction which few self-confident adventurous visionaries could resist. It also constitutes a situation in which they cannot be resisted.*

The carriers of the grand design at the helm of modern state bureaucracy, emancipated from the constraints of non-political (economic, social, cultural) powers; this is the recipe for genocide. Genocide arrives as an integral part of the process through which the grand design is implemented. *The design gives it the legitimation; state bureaucracy gives it the vehicle; and the paralysis of society gives it the "road clear" sign.*

NOTES

1 Christopher R. Browning, "The German Bureaucracy and the Holocaust," In Alex Grobman and Daniel Landes (eds.), *Genocide: Critical Issues of the Holocaust* (Los Angeles: The Simon Wiesenthal Center), p. 148.

2 Leo Kuper, *Genocide: Its Political Use in the Twentieth Century* (New Haven, CT: Yale University Press, 1981), p. 121.

3 H. H. Gerth and C. Wright Mills (eds.), *From Max Weber* (London: Routledge and Kegan Paul, 1970), pp. 214, 215. In her comprehensive survey and partisan evaluation of the treatment of the Holocaust by the historians (*The Holocaust and the Historians* (Cambridge, MA: Harvard University Press, 1981)), Lucy S. Dawidowicz objects against equating the Holocaust with other cases of mass murder, like the wiping out of Hiroshima and Nagasaki: "The purpose of the bombing was to demonstrate America's superior military power"; the bombing "was not motivated by a wish to wipe out the Japanese people" (pp. 17–18). Having made this evidently true observation, Dawidowicz nevertheless misses an important point: the killing of the two hundred thousand Japanese was conceived (and executed) as a searched-for effective means to implement the set goal; it was, indeed, a product of rational problem-solving mentality.

4 Hannah Arendt, *Origins of Totalitarianism* (London: Allen and Unwin, 1962), p. 87.

5 J. S. McClelland (ed.), *The French Right* (London: Jonathan Cape, 1970), pp. 88, 32, 178.

6 Cf. Pierre-André Taguieff, *La Force du préjugé: Essai sur le racisme et ses doubles* (Paris: La Découverte, 1988).

7 Alfred Rosenberg, *Selected Writings* (London: Jonathan Cape, 1970), p. 196.

8 Arthur Gütt, "Population Policy." In *Germany Speaks* (London: Thornton Butterworth, 1938), pp. 35, 52.

9 Walter Gross, "National Socialist Racial Thought," In *Germany Speaks*, p. 68.

10 Cf. Gerald Fleming, *Hitler and the Final Solution* (Oxford: Oxford University Press, 1986), pp. 23–5.

11   Alfred Rosenberg (ed.), *Dietrich Eckart: Ein Vermächtnis* (Munich: Eher, 1928). Quoted after George L. Mosse, *Nazi Culture: A Documentary History* (New York: Schocken Books, 1981), p. 77.

12   H. R. Trevor-Roper, *Hitler's Table Talk* (London, 1953), p. 332.

13   Norman Cohn, *Warrant for Genocide* (London: Eyre and Spottiswoode, 1967), p. 87. There is ample evidence that the language used by Hitler whenever he discussed the "Jewish question" was not chosen merely for its rhetoric or propagandistic value. Hitler's attitude toward Jews was visceral rather than cerebral. He indeed experienced the "Jewish question" as a matter akin to hygiene – a behavioral code he felt strongly about and with which he was obsessed. One will probably understand how much Hitler's disgust for the Jews emanated from, and chimed in with, his genuinely puritan sensitivity to all matters of health and hygiene when one ponders the response he gave in 1922 to the question asked by his friend Josef Hell: what would he do with the Jews once he had full discretionary powers? Promising to hang all Munich Jews on the gallows especially erected along the Marienplatz, Hitler did not forget to stress that the hanged Jews would remain hanging "until they stink; they will hang there as long as the principles of hygiene permit" (quoted after Fleming, *Hitler and the Final Solution*, p. 17). Let us add that these words were spluttered in a fit of rage, in a "state of paroxysm," with Hitler apparently not in control of himself; even then – or perhaps particularly on that occasion – the cult of hygiene and health obsession revealed the tightness of the grip in which it held Hitler's mind.

14   Marlis G. Steinert, *Hitler's War and the Germans: Public Mood and Attitude during the Second World War*, trans. Thomas E. J. de Witt (Athens, OH: Ohio University Press, 1977), p. 137.

15   Raoul Hilberg, *The Destruction of The European Jews* (New York: Holmes and Meiar, 1983), Vol. III, p. 1023.

16   Sarah Gordon, *Hitler, Germans, and the "Jewish Question"* (Princeton: Princeton University Press, 1984), pp. 48–9.

17   George A. Kren and Leon Rappoport, *The Holocaust and the Crisis of Human Behaviour* (New York: Holmes and Meier, 1980), p. 140.

18   Joseph Weizenbaum, *Computer Power and Human Reason: From Judgment to Calculation* (San Francisco: W. H. Freeman, 1976), p. 252.

19   Kren and Rappoport, *The Holocaust and the Crisis*, p. 141.

20   Peter Marsh, *Aggro: The Illusion of Violence* (London: J. M. Dent and Sons, 1978), p. 120.

Part II

Genocide, History, and Modernity

7

Victims of Progress

John H. Bodley

INDIGENOUS PEOPLES AND CULTURE SCALE

Perhaps anthropology's most striking and relevant generalization about small-scale cultures is that they are totally different from both our own global-scale culture and the large-scale ancient civilizations that preceded us.... The secret of tribal success is almost certainly related to the absolute small scale of their populations and the relative simplicity of their technology, but the real key lies in the structure of the culture itself. In fact, small-scale cultures represent an almost total contrast to the adaptive strategy and basic cultural design to our own unproven cultural experiment.

Bodley (1996: 10–11)

Indigenous peoples have been engaged in a political struggle to defend themselves and their resources against encroaching states for at least the past 6,000 years, since states first appeared. States and indigenous peoples have contrasting and often opposing ways of life, and they will have difficulty being neighbors under the best of circumstances. Historically, indigenous peoples steadily yielded ground against advancing states, but until the beginning of the industrial revolution – barely 200 years ago – they still effectively controlled much of the world. Conquest through colonization by industrial nations destroyed millions of indigenous peoples and countless cultural groups. Most surviving indigenous groups lost their political independence and now have only a precarious control over their resources. As of 1997, an estimated 220 million indigenous peoples were scattered over the world, usually in remote areas that are prime targets for resource development by outside interests.

Until recently, scholars in academic disciplines such as anthropology and history observed the destruction of indigenous peoples and sometimes contributed to it with their theories of evolutionary progress. Anthropologists served more directly as agents of colonial governments and worried about their data disappearing. Humanitarian anthropologists, politicians, and missionaries predicted the demise of indigenous peoples and attempted to alleviate the suffering of those people with ethnocentric programs of limited protectionism and civilizing "uplift," which effectively denied any possibility that indigenous people might maintain their independence. The crucial point is that even those who were sympathetic with the "plight" of indigenous peoples were not yet willing to either challenge the legitimacy of colonialism or recognize cultural autonomy as a basic human right. However, indigenous peoples did not disappear. They are still defending themselves, and they appeal to the international community for support. New possibilities are emerging as indigenous peoples continue to organize themselves politically and as the concept of human rights expands to include the cultural, political, and territorial rights of indigenous peoples.

Culture Scale, Culture Process, and Indigenous Peoples

Indigenous peoples are unique in the contemporary world because they share a small-scale way of life that is organizationally and technologically less complex than that of urban-based societies organized by political centralization, market exchanges, and industrial production. The concept of culture scale highlights the uniqueness of indigenous peoples and their cultures. At the same time, it avoids ethnocentric labels that suggest evolutionary stages. The concept also avoids the romantic notion of the so-called noble savage. Small-scale cultures with reduced complexity have enormous human advantages, especially because people living in smaller, lower-density populations may be able to enjoy greater democracy, freedom, equality, and security than people living in large, dense populations, where they usually are divided sharply by differential access to vital resources, wealth, and power. In small-scale cultures, where all households have assured access to food and shelter and the rewarding experiences offered by their culture, there is less cultural incentive to accumulate wealth. Likewise, there is little incentive to expand the population and its consumption of resources.

Indigenous peoples share a unique cultural pattern that was the product of millennia of cultural development, culminating in the emergence of fully modern humans at least 50,000 years ago. The most basic features of this culture – maximum social equality and domestic self-sufficiency – exhibited remarkable stability, and small-scale human groups proliferated across the globe and adapted to virtually all biotic communities. Because this small-scale cultural pattern seems to have coevolved with the human species and is concerned primarily with satisfying basic human needs for nutrition and security, it is appropriate to call the process *sapienization*. In other words, small-scale cultures are concerned primarily with the biological production and maintenanace of human beings and with the cultural production and maintenance of human societies and cultures. The sapienization process is shared by all humans and involves at least five cultural aspects that people use to meet their human needs. These are:

- Symbolization (producing abstract concepts)
- Materialization (giving physical form to concepts)
- Verbalization (producing human speech)
- Socialization (producing permanent human societies)
- Enculturation (reproducing culture)

We may call small-scale societies and cultures produced by sapienization *tribal* to emphasize the absence of political centralization. This term works well when applied to small-scale cultures that exist in a world of small-scale cultures but changes when we consider such groups in states. The term *tribal* is perhaps best restricted to small-scale cultures that retain significant political and economic autonomy. In the modern world, the term *tribal* is even more problematic because [...] "tribes" often were created by colonial governments as political units, with "chiefs" appointed for administrative purposes. In some areas, *tribe* is used as a self-designation by indigenous peoples, although others may reject it as derogatory or divisive.

The term *indigenous peoples* is also somewhat problematic. Since the early 1970s, the widely accepted formal definition of *indigenous* is "original inhabitants of a region who do not have a significant role in the government." This is, of course, a political definition and says nothing about the culture, even though it connotes "tribal" or "formerly tribal." When I use the term indigenous peoples, I mean a group of people who identify themselves with a specific, small-scale, cultural heritage. However, I acknowledge many distinctions based on historical realities. As an ideal type, small-scale culture is best represented by mobile foragers operating in a world of foragers. Although the cultural traits that I identify as the defining features of small-scale culture are certainly fundamental, the essential stability of small-scale culture was threatened and many sorts of changes were introduced by the following processes and events:

1 15,000 BP: sedentarization and the emergence of village life
2 12,000 BP: domestication and the emergence of farming and herding
3 6,000 BP: politicization and the emergence of politically organized, large-scale cultures
4 500 BP: commercialization and the emergence of commercially organized, global-scale cultures

These processes have unfolded over the past 15,000 years and have surely changed the context within which small-scale cultures operate. For example, among full-time mobile foragers such as Australian Aborigines, control of ritual knowledge and residence in a camp group probably regulated the use of resources more than ownership of territory, whereas knowledge of wild plant resources was no doubt widely shared. By contrast, sedentary villagers and food producers may be concerned more with regulating the use of resources through formal descent structures. Huge cultural differences developed with the emergence of large-and global-scale cultures.[...]

PROGRESS AND INDIGENOUS PEOPLES

> The Industrial Revolution disrupts and transforms all preceding cultures in West and
> East alike, and at the same time throws their resources into a common pool.
>
> Graham (1971:193)

Indigenous peoples are being drastically affected by the global-scale culture, and
their cultural patterns and in many cases the peoples themselves are disappearing as
the scale of culture expands. For many years, economic development experts did not
acknowledge that increased cultural scale, related to economic growth, could actually reduce human well-being by transforming the cultural systems that support
people. The historical experience of indigenous people illuminates a growth process
that is beginning to negatively affect even non-indigenous local communities
throughout the world. [I seek] to dispel some of the widely held ethnocentric miscon-
ceptions concerning the disappearance of indigenous cultures and focus attention on
the basic causes. These causes reveal serious problems within the global culture
itself. Understanding them is the first step toward accommodating cultural diversity.

Progress: The Commercial Explosion

In the mid-eighteenth century, the commercialization process and the related technological developments associated with the industrial revolution launched the developing Western nations on an explosive growth in population and consumption
called "progress," which led to an unprecedented assault on the world's indigenous
peoples and their resources. Within the 250 years since then the world has been
totally transformed, many self-sufficient small-scale cultures have disappeared, and
dramatic resource shortages and environmental disasters have materialized. Now
that many researchers are struggling to explain why the global-scale culture seems to
be floundering in its own success, anthropologists are beginning to realize that the
first and most ominous victims of industrial progress were the several million
indigenous people who still controlled over half the globe in 1820 and who shared
a relatively stable, satisfying, and proven cultural adaptation. It is highly significant
and somewhat unsettling to realize that the cultural systems of these first victims of
progress present a striking contrast to the characteristics of the global-scale culture
(see Bodley 1985).

The commercialization process was nothing less than an *explosion* because of the
unparalleled scope and the catastrophic nature of the transformations that it initiated. Phenomenal increases in both population and per capita consumption rates
were the two most critical correlates of commercialization because they quickly led
to overwhelming pressure on natural resources.

The acceleration in world population growth rates and their relationship to
industrial progress have been well documented. Immediately prior to the industrial
revolution, for example, the doubling time of the world's population was approximately 250 years. However, after industrialization was under way, the European
population of 1850 doubled in just over eighty years, and the European populations

of the United States, Canada, Australia, and Argentina tripled between 1851 and 1900 (Woodruff 1966). The doubling time of the world's population reached its lowest point of about thirty-three years (an annual growth rate of over 2 percent) during the period 1965–73. By 1986, the global rate of population growth had declined only slightly to 1.8 percent a year. In contrast, clear anthropological evidence shows that small-scale populations grow slowly and use their natural resources conservatively. The relative stability of such populations is due only partly to higher mortality rates; it is also attributed to social, economic, and religious controls on fertility, the significance of which is still not fully understood. Although small-scale populations have the capacity for growth, and may expand rapidly into empty lands, they are politically and economically designed to operate most effectively at low densities and low absolute size.

The Culture of Consumption

The increased rates of resource consumption accompanying commercialization have been even more critical than mere population increase. Above all else, commercial civilization is a culture of *consumption*, and in this respect it differs most strikingly from small-scale cultures. Commercial economies are founded on the principle that consumption must be ever expanded, and complex systems of mass marketing and advertising have been developed for that specific purpose. Social stratification in commercial societies is based primarily on inequalities in material wealth and is both supported and reflected by differential access to resources. Commercial ideological systems stress belief in continual economic growth and progress and characteristically measure "standard of living" in terms of levels of material consumption.

Small-scale cultures contrast strikingly in all of these aspects. Their economies are geared to the satisfaction of basic subsistence needs, which are assumed to be fixed, and a variety of cultural mechanisms serve to limit material acquisitiveness and to redistribute wealth. Wealth itself is rarely the basis of social stratification, and there is generally free access to natural resources for all. These contrasts are the basis for the in compatibility between small-scale and global-scale cultures and are the traits that are the sources of particular problems when indigenous peoples are conquered by commercial societies.

The most obvious consequences of the consumption patterns of small-scale cultures are that these cultures tend to be highly stable, make light demands on their environments, and can easily support themselves within their own boundaries. The opposite situation prevails for the culture of consumption. Almost overnight, the commercially organized nations ate up their own local resources and outgrew their boundaries. This was dramatically apparent in England, where local resources comfortably supported small-scale cultures for thousands of years, but after 100 years of commercial progress the area was unable to meet its basic needs for grain, wood, fibers, and hides. Between 1851 and 1900, Europe was forced to export thirty-five million people because it could no longer support them (Woodruff 1966). In the United States, where commercial progress has gone the furthest, since 1970 Americans have been consuming per capita some fifteen times more energy than neolithic agriculturalists and seven times the world average in non-renewable resources. They are also importing vast tonnages of food, fuels, and other resources to support themselves.

Indeed, few if any commercial nations can now supply from within their own boundaries the resources needed to support further growth or even to maintain current consumption levels. It should not be surprising, then, that the "underdeveloped" resources controlled by the world's self-sufficient tribal peoples were quickly appropriated by outsiders to support their own commercial progress.

Resource Appropriation and Acculturation

In case after case, government programs for the progress of indigenous peoples directly or indirectly force culture change, and these programs in turn are linked invariably to the extraction of indigenous peoples' resources to benefit the national economy. From the strength of this relationship between "progress" and the exploitation of resources, we might even infer that indigenous peoples would not be asked to surrender their resources and independence if industrial societies learned to control their own culture of consumption. This point must be made explicit, because considerable confusion exists in the enormous culture change literature regarding the basic question of why small-scale cultures seem inevitably to be acculturated or modernized by commercial civilization. Until recently, the consensus, at least among economic development writers, was the ethnocentric view that contact with superior global-scale culture causes indigenous peoples to voluntarily reject their own cultures in order to obtain a better life. Other writers, however, seemed curiously mystified by the entire process. An example of this latter position can be seen in Julian Steward's summary of a monumental study of change in traditional cultures in eleven countries. Steward (1967:20–1) concluded that, although many startling parallels could be identified, the causal factors involved in the modernization process were still "not well conceptualized."

This inability to conceptualize the causes of the transformation process in simple, non-ethnocentric terms – or indeed the inability to conceptualize the causes at all – may be due to the fact that the analysts were members of the culture of consumption that today is the dominant world culture type. The most powerful cultures have always assumed a natural right to exploit the world's resources wherever they find them, regardless of the prior claims of indigenous populations. Arguing for efficiency and survival of the fittest, early colonialists elevated this "right" to the level of an ethical and legal principle that could be invoked to justify the elimination of any cultures that were not making "effective" use of their resources.

Members of the expanding culture rationalized as "natural" evolutionary processes that eliminated groups considered to be either culturally or racially inferior. They thought this "selection" process was so natural and "inevitable" that nothing could prevent it. For example, in 1915 Paul Popenoe told the scientists assembled in Washington, DC, for the 19th International Congress of Americanists that the mass destruction of native Americans following the European invasion was "a process of racial purification of weak stocks." The Indian was "killed off by natural selection." Popenoe declared: "The native succumbed to the process of evolution, and no conceivable kindnesses from their conquerors could have prevented this elimination" (1915:620). Certainly, disease was a major factor in New World depopulation, but it was accompanied by conquest and colonization, which were political processes for which people were responsible. Treating ethnocide and genocide as scientific law is to mask their underlying political causes.

These old attitudes of social Darwinism are embedded in our ideological system and are common in the early professional literature on culture change. In fact, one development writer declared: "Perhaps entire societies will lack survival value and vanish before the onslaught of industrialization" (Goulet 1971:266). This viewpoint also appears in modern theories of cultural evolution, where it is expressed as the "Law of Cultural Dominance":

That cultural system which more effectively exploits the energy resources of a given environment will tend to spread in that environment at the expense of less effective systems. (Kaplan 1960:75)

Apart from the obvious ethical implications involved here, upon close inspection all of these theories expounding the greater adaptability, efficiency, and survival value of the dominant industrial culture proved to be misleading. Of course, as a culture of consumption, the global-scale culture is uniquely capable of consuming resources at tremendous rates, but this does not make it a more *effective* culture than low-energy small-scale cultures, if stability or long-run ecological success is taken as the criterion for "effectiveness." Likewise, the assumption that a given environment is not being exploited effectively by a small-scale culture may merely reflect the unwillingness of national political authorities to allow local groups to manage their own resources for their own interests. We should expect, then, that members of the culture of consumption would probably consider another culture's resources to be underexploited and to use this as a justification for appropriating them.

"Optimum" land use for hill tribes

The experience of the Chittagong Hills peoples of East Pakistan (Bangladesh since 1972) provides an excellent example of the process by which commercialization leads to a shortage of resources at the national level and ultimately results in the political conquest and dispossession of indigenous peoples who have preserved their resources more effectively. Along with other parts of the world – thanks to the intervention of commercial nations – East Pakistan had such a severe population explosion that by 1965 population densities reached an average of 470 people per square kilometer and the soil resources of the country were being pushed to the limits. As the crunch on resources worsened, the government made dramatic efforts to emulate the economic development route of the developed nations and soon directed special attention to the still largely self-sufficient Chittagong Hills areas, which had managed to remain outside of the cash economy and had avoided major disruptions due to commercial intrusion. The French anthropologist Claude Lévi-Strauss (1951), who visited the area in 1950, found the hill tribes flourishing and observed that the Chittagong Hills "form a kind of anthropological sanctuary." Although the twelve ethnic groups making up the hill tribes were not totally isolated, they had enjoyed considerable political autonomy, especially under British control. However, the areas were beginning to show population growth and subsequent pressure on their own resources due to shortening swidden cycles. But with only thirty-five people per square kilometer, they remained an island of low population density and "underdeveloped" resources in what had suddenly become an impoverished and overpopulated country.

External exploitation of resources in the interests of the national economy initially focused on the forests of the Chittagong Hills. Twenty-two percent of the district was declared a forest "reserve," a "Forest Industries Development Corporation" was organized by the provincial government, and in 1953 lumber and paper mills were in operation to facilitate the modern commerical utilization of the region's bamboo and tropical hardwoods. In 1962, the largest river in the area was dammed to supply hydroelectric power to help feed the rising energy demands of East Pakistan's urban affluent. In the process, however, 673 square kilometers of the best agricultural land were converted into a lake, further aggravating the land scarcity that was already developing because of earlier disruptions of the population–resources balance and requiring the resettlement and "rehabilitation" of many hill people.

Still dissatisfied with the level of resource exploitation in the Chittagong Hills, in 1964 the Pakistani government enlisted an eleven-member international team of geologists, soil scientists, biologists, foresters, economists, and agricultural engineers to devise a master plan for the integrated development of the area based on what they considered to be optimum land-use possibilities. The team worked for two years with helicopters, aerial photographs, and computers. They concluded that regardless of how well the traditional economic system of shifting cultivation and subsistence production may have been attuned to its environment in the past, today it "can no longer be tolerated" (Webb 1966:3232). The research team decided that the hill tribes should allow their land to be used primarily for the production of forest products for the benefit of the national economy because it was not well suited for large-scale cash cropping. The report left no alternative to the Chittagong Hills peoples, as a member of the research team observes:

More of the Hill tribesmen will have to become wage earners in the forest or other developing industries, and purchase their food from farmers practicing permanent agriculture on an intensive basis on the limited better land classes. It is realized that a whole system of culture and an age-old way of life cannot be changed overnight, but change it must, and quickly. The time is opportune. The maps and the basic data have been collected for an integrated development toward optimum land use. (Webb 1966:3232)

The government policy of "optimum" land use brought immediate disaster for the hill tribes (Mey 1983; Nietschmann 1985; Zaman 1985). The USAID-funded Kaptai Dam inundated 253 square miles of the hill tribes' land, including much of the best cultivable land, and displaced 100,000 people. At the same time, the government allowed large-scale entry by Bengali settlers, who practiced plow agriculture and began to further displace the hill tribe people. In 1977, the Bangladeshi military initiated a genocidal extermination policy against the hill tribes. By 1982, some 400,000 Bengali settlers held hill tribe lands and were supported by 30,000 government troops. Two years later international organizations reported that 185,000 hill people had been killed. The Snati Bahini, a guerrilla organization formed to defend the interests of the hill people, proved unable to prevent the slaughter (IWGIA [International Work Group for Indigenous Affairs] Newsletter 1984, 37:15–17). By 1996, assaults against the hill tribes were continuing, and some 45,000 hill people were living in refugee camps in India, according to Survival International.

The Role of Ethnocentrism

Although resource exploitation is clearly the basic cause of the destruction of small-scale populations and their cultures, it is important to identify the underlying ethnocentric attitudes that are often used to justify exploitative policies. *Ethnocentrism*, the belief in the superiority of one's own culture, is vital to the integrity of any culture, but it can threaten the well-being of other peoples when it becomes the basis for forcing irrelevant standards upon another culture. Anthropologists may justifiably take credit for exposing the ethnocentrism of nineteenth-century writers who described indigenous peoples as badly in need of improvement, but they often overlook the ethnocentrism that occurs in the modern professional literature on economic development. Ironically, ethnocentrism threatens small-scale cultures even today through its support of culturally insensitive government policies.

Ethnocentrism and ethnocide

Anthropologists have been quick to stress the presumed deficiencies of tribal cultures as a justification for externally imposed change or a rejection of proposals that tribals be granted political autonomy. For example, in 1940 British anthropologist Lord Fitzroy Raglan, who later became president of the Royal Anthropological Institute, declared that tribal beliefs in magic were a chief cause of "folly and unhappiness" and the "worst evils of the day." He argued that as long as tribals persist in such beliefs the rest of the world cannot be considered civilized. In his view, existing tribes constituted "plague spots" that threatened to reinfect civilized areas, and the rapid imposition of civilization was the only solution. He declared:

We should bring to them our justice, our education, and our science. Few will deny that these are better than anything which savages have got. (Raglan 1940:62)

American anthropologist Arthur Hippler (1979) echoed Raglan's remarks. In a debate with Gerald Weiss over the merits of tribal autonomy, Hippler argued that national religions are superior to the "terrors of shamanism." He found "our own culture" more exciting, interesting, and varied, and better at promoting human potential than are "backward" tribal cultures, and he assumed that all tribals would inevitably be drawn to it. Hippler suggested that only internal oppression from tribal elders prevents tribals from improving their culture. Not surprisingly, Hippler specifically opposed autonomy proposals for the defense of tribal groups because autonomy would keep people "backward" against their will. Furthermore, he argued that "culture" is an abstraction, not something that can be defended or "saved" from extinction. Thus, ethnocide, the destruction of a cultural or an ethnic group, could not occur. In his response, Weiss (1988) exposed the ethnocentrism of Hippler's position point by point.

Crude customs and traditions

Ethnocentrism by culture-change professionals, as illustrated in the following example from India, has often been a powerful support for coercive government policies directed against tribal peoples. A group of Indian scholars and administrators presented an unsympathetic view of tribal culture in a series of papers and speeches at a seminar on new policy directions for the hill tribes of North East India, which was held in Calcutta in 1966 (Mittra and Das Gupta 1967). Some participants in the seminar complained that prior British administrators had committed the fundamental error of placing tribal culture above the "basic need for human progress" (Moasosang 1967:51), because for a time they had attempted to prevent the economic exploitation of the region by non-tribal peoples. Throughout the seminar, participants attacked the entire range of traditional culture on ethnocentric grounds. They called the tribal economic system backward, wasteful, and in need of "scientific permanent farming" (Nag 1967:90); an Indian professor complained of "crude customs and traditions" and characterized the tribal Garo peoples as being steeped in "primitive ignorance," "tradition-bound," and "static." Participants called for more thorough research to determine whether Garo society could be lifted out of its "morass of backwardness, traditionalism, and pseudo-modernism" (Kar 1967:80–90).

In one paper curiously entitled "An Outlook for a Better Understanding of Tribal People" (Thiek 1967:103–9), an enlightened tribal member characterized his tribal kin as backward, lacking in culture, and living in darkness. Not only were these people described as cultureless, but according to an educated official they also lacked language:

You see, unfortunately here they do not have a language, what they speak is an illiterate dialect, lacking grammar and orthography. (Chatterjee 1967:20)

A few years earlier, an Indian sociologist supported the conclusion that tribal languages are "merely corruptions of good speech and unworthy of survival." He wanted to see these people adopt the "more highly evolved" Indo-Aryan languages, because he considered the tribal peoples to be nothing more than backward Hindus (Ghurye 1963:187–90).

Technological ethnocentrism

Development writers with tractors and chemicals to sell have expressed more ethnocentrism in their treatment of traditional economic systems than for any other aspect of small-scale culture. These writers automatically assume that small-scale economies must be unproductive and technologically inadequate and therefore consistently disregard the abundant evidence to the contrary. It has long been fashionable to attack the supposed inefficiency of shifting cultivation and pastoral nomadism and the precariousness of subsistence economies in general. But it could be argued that it is industrial subsistence techniques that are inefficient and precarious. Mono-crop agriculture, with its hybrid grains and dependence on chemical fertilizers, pesticides, and costly machinery, is extremely expensive in terms of energy demands and is highly unstable because of its susceptibility to disease, insects, and the depletion of critical minerals and fuels. The complexity of the food distribution system in global-scale commerical society also makes it vulnerable to collapse because of the breakdowns in the long chain from producer to consumer. In contrast, small-scale systems are highly productive in terms of energy flow and are much stabler ecologically. They also have efficient and reliable food distribution systems.

Cultural reformers almost unanimously agree that all people share our desire for what we define as material wealth, prosperity, and progress and that others have different cultures only because they have not yet been exposed to the superior technological alternatives offered by the global-scale culture. Supporters of this view seem to minimize the difficulties of creating new wants in a culture and at the same time make the following questionable and ethnocentric assumptions:

1   The materialistic values of commercial cultures are cultural universals.
2   Small-scale cultures are unable to satisfy the material needs of their peoples.
3   Commerical goods are, in fact, always superior to their handcrafted counterparts.

Unquestionably, small-scale cultures represent a rejection of the materialistic values of the global culture. Yet, individuals can be made to reject their traditional values if outside interests create the necessary conditions for this rejection. Far more is involved here than a mere demonstration of the superiority of commercialization.

The ethnocentrism of the second assumption is obvious. Clearly, small-scale cultures could not have survived for half a million years if they did not do a reasonable job of satisfying basic human needs.

The third assumption – the superiority of commercial goods and techniques – deserves special comment because abundant evidence indicates that many of the material accouterments of the global culture may not be worth their real costs, regardless of how appealing they may seem initially. To cite a specific example, it could be argued that the bow is superior to a gun in some cultural and environmental contexts, because it is far more versatile and more efficient to manufacture and maintain. A single bow can be used for both fishing and hunting a variety of animals. Furthermore, bow users are not dependent on an unpredictable external economy, because bows can be constructed of local materials and do not require expensive ammunition. At the same time, use of the bow places some limits on game harvesting and demands a closer relationship between humans and animals, which may have great adaptive significance. Hames (1979) has shown that Amazon Indians who have adopted shotguns have dramatically increased their hunting yields, but these gains do not entirely offset the extra labor that must go into raising the money to support the new technology. Furthermore, the increased hunting efficiency also means that vulnerable species are more likely to be depleted.

Many of the ethnocentric interpretations of small-scale cultures are understandable when we realize that development writers often mistakenly attribute to them the conditions of starvation, ill health, and poverty, which actually may be related to industrialization or commercialization. Self-sufficient small-scale cultures cannot be considered underdeveloped. "Poverty" is an irrelevant concept in small-scale societies, and poverty conditions do not result from subsistence economies *per se*.

Tribal wards of the state

In the past, writers on international law and colonial experts often called on the *wardship principle* in an effort to justify harsh government programs of culture change directed against tribal peoples. This so-called legal principle reflects the grossest ethnocentrism in that it considers tribal peoples to be incompetent or childlike. It defines the relationship between tribal peoples and the state as that of a benevolent parent-guardian and a ward who must be protected from his or her own degrading culture and gradually reformed or corrected. According to the wardship principle, the state is under a moral obligation to make all tribal peoples share in the benefits of civilization – that is, in health, happiness, and prosperity as defined primarily in terms of consumption.

This legal inferiority of tribal peoples has contributed significantly to the speed with which their acculturation or "reform" can occur and has worked marvelously to satisfy both the conscience and the economic needs of modern states.

Placing tribal peoples in the legal category of incompetent or childlike reflects a tendency to view tribal culture as abnormal or sick. This obviously ethnocentric theme runs throughout the colonial literature, in which the civilization process is often described as *mental* correction, but this same theme has continued to appear in the modern literature: some economic development writers have lumped tribal peoples indiscriminately with underdeveloped peoples, referred explicitly to economic underdevelopment as a "sickness," spoken of the "medicine of social change," and compared change agents to brain surgeons (Arensberg and Niehoff 1964:4–6). It appears that the attitudes of some modern cultural reformers were unaffected by the discovery of ethnocentrism.

A sacred trust of civilization

As we have seen, the modern civilizing mission undertaken by governments against tribal peoples was supported by a variety of ethnocentric assumptions, some of which were recognized as principles of international law. Not surprisingly, therefore, prestigious international organizations such as the United Nations also threw their support behind official attempts to bring civilization to all peoples – whether or not they desired it.

During the second half of the nineteenth century, the colonizing commercial nations began to justify their scramble for foreign territories as a fulfillment of a sacred duty to spread their form of civilization to the world. When the major imperialist powers met in 1884–5 at Berlin to set guidelines for the partitioning of Africa, they pledged support for the civilizing crusade and promised to assist missionaries and all institutions "calculated to educate the natives and to teach them to understand and appreciate the benefits of civilization" (General Act of the 1884–5 Berlin Africa Conference). This position was reiterated and took on a more militant tone in Article 2 of the Brussels Act of 1892, which called on the colonial powers to raise African tribal peoples to civilization and to "bring about the extinction of barbarous customs." This constituted an internationally approved mandate for ethnocide in the interests of progress.

Whereas such attitudes are perhaps to be expected from colonial nations at the height of their power, they seem inappropriate when expressed by world organizations dedicated to peace and self-determination of peoples. Nevertheless, the 1919 League of Nations Covenant in Article 22 gave "advanced nations" responsibility for "peoples not yet able to stand by themselves under the strenuous conditions of the modern world," thereby placing many tribal peoples officially under tutelage as a "sacred trust of civilization." In fact, this sacred trust proved to be a profitable colonial booty for the trust powers because it gave them the internationally recognized right to exploit the resources of thousands of square kilometers of formerly non-state territory while making only token allowance for the wishes of the native peoples involved. Under the 1945 United Nations Charter, many of these same tribal peoples were identified as "peoples who have not yet attained a full measure of self-government," and their continued advancement was to be promoted by their guardians "by constructive measures of development" (Articles 73 and 76, UN Charter). Here again, responsibility for deciding what constitutes tribal peoples' welfare was effectively taken from them and was legally placed in the hands of outside interests. The carefully worded and seemingly non-derogatory phrases "peoples not yet able to stand by themselves" and "non-self-governing" are glaringly ethnocentric and derogatory because these peoples had governed themselves for thousands of years without the support of politically organized state governments. Of course, they were unable to defend themselves against the incursions of militant, resource-hungry states. But many modern nations exist only at the discretion of more powerful nations, and the UN Charter would not advocate making all militarily weak nations surrender their political autonomy to their stronger neighbors.

Civilization's Unwilling Conscripts

It now seems appropriate to ask the obvious question: how do autonomous tribal peoples themselves feel about becoming participants in the progress of commercial civilization? Because of the power at their disposal, commercial cultures have become so aggressively ethnocentric that they have difficulty even imagining that another lifestyle – particularly one based on fundamentally different premises – could possibly have value and personal satisfaction for the peoples following it. Happily arrogant in their own supposed cultural superiority, many people of commercial cultures assume that those in other cultures may realize their obsolescence and inferiority and may eagerly desire progress toward the better life. This belief persists in the face of abundant evidence that independent tribal peoples are not anxious to scrap their cultures and would rather pursue their own form of the good life undisturbed. Peoples who have already chosen their major cultural patterns and who have spent generations tailoring them to local conditions are probably not even concerned that another culture might be superior to theirs. Indeed, it can perhaps be assumed that people in any autonomous, self-reliant culture would prefer to be left alone. Left to their own devices, tribal peoples are unlikely to volunteer for civilization or acculturation. Instead:

Acculturation has always been a matter of conquest . . . refugees from the foundering groups may adopt the standards of the more potent society in order to survive as individuals. But these are conscripts of civilization, not volunteers. (Diamond 1960:vi)

Free and informed choice

The question of choice is a critical point because many development authorities have stressed that tribal peoples should be allowed to choose progress. This view was obvious at a 1936 conference of administrators, educators, and social scientists concerning education in Pacific colonial dependencies, where it was stated that choices regarding cultural directions "must lie with the indigenous people themselves" (cited in Keesing 1941:84). Anthropologists at a more recent international conference in Tokyo took the same position when they called for "just and scientifically enlightened programs of acculturation which allow the peoples concerned a free and informed basis for choice" (Eighth International Congress of Anthropological and Ethnological Sciences, Resolution on Forced Acculturation, 1968, cited in Sturtevant 1970:160). Apparently, no one noticed the obvious contradiction between a scientific culture change program and free choice, or even the possible conflict between *free* and *informed*. The official position of the Australian government on free choice for the Aborigine in 1970 indicates the absurdities to which such thinking can lead:

The Commonwealth and State governments have adopted a common policy of assimilation which seeks that all persons of Aboriginal descent will choose to attain a similar manner and standard of living to that of other Australians and live as members of a single Australian community. (Australia, Commonwealth Bureau of Census and Statistics 1970:967)

Those who so glibly demand choice for tribal peoples do not seem to realize the problems of directly instituting such a choice, and at the same time they refuse to acknowledge the numerous indicators that tribal peoples have already chosen their own cultures instead of the progress of civilization. In fact, the question of choice itself is probably ethnocentric and irrelevant to the peoples concerned. Do we choose civilization? is not a question that tribal peoples would ask, because they in effect have already answered it. They might consider the concept of choosing a way of life to be as irrelevant in their own cultural context as asking a person if he or she would choose to be a tree.

It is also difficult to ask whether tribal peoples desire civilization or economic development because affirmative responses will undoubtedly be from individuals already alienated from their own cultures by culture modification programs, and their views may not be representative of their still autonomous tribal kin.

Other problems are inherent in the concept of free and informed choice. Even when free to choose, tribal peoples would not generally be in a position to know what they were choosing and would certainly not be given a clear picture of the possible outcomes of their choice, because the present members of industrial cultures do not know what their own futures will be. Even if tribal peoples could be given a full and unbiased picture of what they were choosing, obtaining that information could destroy their freedom to choose, because participation in such an "educational" program might destroy their self-reliance and effectively deny them their right to choose their own tribal culture. An obvious contradiction exists in calling for culture change in order to allow people to choose or not to choose culture change. The authorities at the 1936 conference referred to earlier were caught in just such Alice-in-Wonderland double talk when they recommended the promotion of formal education programs (which would disrupt native culture) so that the people could freely decide whether they wanted their cultures disrupted:

It is the responsibility of the governing people, through schools and other means, to make available to the native an adequate understanding of non-native systems of life so that these can be ranged alongside his own in order that his choices may be made. (Cited in Keesing 1941:84)

Such a program of education might sound like a sort of "cultural smorgasbord," but in fact there is only one correct choice allowed – tribal peoples must choose progress.

One further problem overlooked in the "free choice" approach is that of the appropriateness of industrial progress or of any foreign cultural system in a given cultural and environmental context – even if freely chosen. Should Eskimos be encouraged to become nomadic camel herders or to develop a taste for bananas? Does the American "car complex" belong on a Micronesian coral atoll of four square kilometers? What will be the long-term effects of a shift from a self-reliant subsistence economy to a cash economy based on the sale of a single product on the uncertain world market? There are inescapable limits to what can constitute a successful human adaptation in a given cultural and environmental setting.

We ask to be left alone

At this point we will again ask the question posed earlier regarding whether tribal people freely choose progress. This question has actually been answered many times by independent tribal peoples who, in confrontations with industrial civilization, have (1) ignored it, (2) avoided it, or (3) responded with defiant arrogance. Any one of these responses could be interpreted as a rejection of further involvement with progress.

Many of the Australian Aborigines reportedly chose the first response in their early contacts with members of Western civilization. According to Captain Cook's account of his first landing on the Australian mainland, Aborigines on the beach ignored both his ship and his men until they became obnoxious. Elkin (1951) confirmed that this complete lack of interest in white people's habits, material possessions, and beliefs was characteristic of Aborigines in a variety of contact settings. In many cases, tribal peoples have shown little interest in initial contacts with civilized visitors because they simply assumed that the visitors would soon leave and they would again be free to pursue their own way of life undisturbed.

Among contemporary tribal peoples who still retain their cultural autonomy, rejection of outside interference is a general phenomenon that cannot be ignored. The Pygmies of the Congo represent a classic case of determined resistance to the incursions of civilization. Turnbull (1963), who studied the Pygmies intensively in their forest environment, was impressed that these people, in spite of being in contact with outsiders for a long time, had successfully rejected foreign cultural domination for hundreds of years. Attempts by Belgian colonial authorities to settle them on plantations ended in complete failure, basically because the Pygmies were unwilling to sacrifice their way of life for one patterned for them by outsiders whose values were irrelevant to their environment and culture. According to Turnbull, the Pygmies deliberated over the changes proposed by the government and opted to remain within their traditional territory and pursue their own way of life. Their decision was clear:

So for the Pygmies, in a sense, there is no problem. They have seen enough of the outside world to feel able to make their choice, and their choice is to preserve the sanctity of their own world up to the very end. Being what they are, they will doubtless play a masterful game of hide-and-seek, but they will not easily sacrifice their integrity. (Turnbull 1963)

Anthropologist Luigi Cavalli-Sforza (1986), who coordinated a series of long-term multidisciplinary field studies of Pygmies throughout Africa beginning in 1966, confirmed Turnbull's basic conclusion about the Pygmy rejection of directed change. He attributes the remarkable 2,000-year persistence of Pygmies as a distinct people to the attractiveness of their way of life and the effectiveness of their enculturation practices. But like Turnbull, he also cites the importance of the forest itself and the Pygmies' successful symbiosis with their village-farmer neighbors. The most critical threat to Pygmies is now deforestation and disruption of their exchange relationships caused by the invasion of new colonists and the development of large-scale coffee plantations (Bailey 1982; Hart and Hart 1984; Peacock 1984). As the forest shrinks, there simply will be no place for Pygmies as forest peoples. Bailey warns: "Unless sufficient areas of forest are set aside, a unique subsistence culture based on hunting and gathering forest resources will be lost in the Ituri [rain forest] and throughout central Africa forever" (1982:25).

Avoiding progress: Those who run away

Direct avoidance of progress represents what is a widespread, long-established pattern of cultural survival whose implications should not be ignored by those who promote change.

Throughout South America and many other parts of the world, many non-hostile tribal peoples have made their attitudes toward progress clear by choosing to follow the Pygmies' game of hide-and-seek and actively avoiding all contact with outsiders. In the Philippines, a term meaning "those who run away" has been applied to tribal peoples who have chosen to flee in order to preserve their cultures from government influence (Keesing and Keesing 1934:87).

Many little-known tribal peoples scattered in isolated areas around the world have, in fact, managed to retain their cultural integrity and autonomy until recently by quietly retreating farther and farther into more isolated refuge areas. As the exploitative frontier has gradually engulfed these stubborn tribes, the outside world periodically has been surprised by the discovery of small pockets of unknown "Stone Age" peoples who have clung tenaciously to their cultures up to the last possible moment. The extent and significance of this phenomenon have seldom been recognized by the public at large and certainly not by professional agents of culture change. In South America throughout the twentieth century, many different groups, including the Xeta, the Kreen-a-kore in Brazil, various Panoan speakers such as the Amarakaeri and Amahuaka in headwater areas of the Peruvian Amazon, and the Akuriyo of Surinam, have been found using stone tools and deliberately avoiding contact with outsiders. These determined people are generally peaceful, except when harassed too severely. To avoid contact they prefer to desert their homes and gardens and thrust arrows point-up in their paths, rather than resort to violence. All that even the most persistent civilized visitors usually find – if they do manage to locate the natives' well-hidden villages – are empty houses and perhaps smoldering cooking fires. If a village is disturbed too often, the people abandon the site and relocate in a more isolated place. When, after continuous encroachment, their resource base shrinks to the point that it will no longer support their population and there is no place to which they can retreat, or when violent attacks by civilized raiders and introduced illnesses reduce their numbers to the point that they are no longer a viable society, then they must surrender to progress. Most of the groups that we know about have stopped hiding. The most successful groups would have remained completely hidden, and it seems likely that a few remain in that category.

How successfully some of these groups have managed to avoid contact can be seen in the case of the Akuriyo Indians of Surinam. These foraging people were first seen by outsiders in 1937, when a Dutch expedition discovered them while surveying the Surinam–Brazil border. After this brief encounter the Akuriyo remained out of sight for nearly thirty years until American missionaries began to find traces of their camps. The missionaries were determined to make contact with them in order to win them for Christianity, but it was three years before they finally succeeded with the assistance of ten missionized Indians, shortwave radios, and airplanes. They tracked the Akuriyo along their concealed trails through a succession of hastily abandoned camps until they caught up with a few women and children and an old man who, with obvious displeasure, asked the first man who greeted them, "Are you a tiger that you smelled me out?" This small group had been left behind by others who had gone in search of arrow canes to defend themselves against the intruders. The Indians allowed the missionary party to remain with them only one night. Refusing to reveal either their tribal or their personal identities, they fed and traded with the intruders and then insisted that they leave. The mission Indians sang hymns and tried to tell them about God, but the Akuriyo were unimpressed. According to the missionaries:

The old chief commented that God must really be good. He said he knew nothing about Him, and that he had to leave now to get arrow cane. (Schoen 1969)

Obviously these people were expressing their desire to be left alone in the most dignified and elegant terms. But the missionaries proceeded to make plans for placing Christianized Indian workers among them and requested "for the sake of this tribe" that the Surinam government grant their mission exclusive permission to supervise further contacts with the Akuriyo. Within a short time, contact was reestablished, and the mission was able to encourage about fifty Akuriyo to settle in mission villages. Tragically, in barely two years 25 percent of the group had died and only about a dozen people still remained in the forest (Kloos 1977).

Whereas the Akuriyo are an example of a group avoiding contact in a remote area, many other examples can be cited of small tribes that have survived successfully on the fringes of civilized areas. One of the most outstanding of such cases was the discovery in 1970 that unknown bands of Indians were secretly living within the boundaries of the Iguazú Falls national park in Argentina (Bartolomé 1972).

Some observers argue that these cases do not represent real rejections of civilization and progress because these people were given no choice by their hostile neighbors, who refused to share the benefits of civilization, and so they were forced to pretend that they didn't desire these benefits. Critics point out that such people often eagerly steal or trade for steel tools. This argument misses the real point and represents a misunderstanding of the nature of culture change. Stability and ethnocentrism are fundamental characteristics of all cultures that have established a satisfactory relationship with their environment. Some degree of change, such as adopting steel tools, may well occur to enhance an ongoing adaptation and to prevent greater change from occurring.

Cultural Pride Versus Progress

The pride and defiance of numerous tribal peoples in the face of forced culture change are unmistakable and have often been commented upon by outsiders. The ability of these cultures to withstand external intrusion is related to their degree of ethnocentrism, or to the extent to which tribal individuals feel self-reliant and confident that their own culture is best for them. The hallmark of such ethnocentrism is the stubborn unwillingness to feel inferior even in the presence of overwhelming enemy force.

A case of calm but defiant self-assurance of this sort is offered by a warrior-chief of the undefeated Xavante (Shavante) of central Brazil, who had personally participated in the 1941 slaying of seven men of a "pacification" mission sent by the Brazilian government to end the Xavante's bitter fifty-year resistance to civilization. As further evidence of their disdain for intruders, the Xavante shot arrows into an Air Force plane and burned the gifts it dropped (*Life* 1945, 18:70–2). After one Xavante community finally accepted the government's peace offers in 1953, the Air Force flew the chief to Rio de Janeiro in order to impress him with the superiority of the Brazilian state and the futility of further resistance. To everyone's amazement, he observed Rio, even from the air, with absolute calm. He was then led into the center of a soccer field to be surrounded by thousands of applauding fans, and it was pointed out to him how powerful the Brazilian state was and how unwise it was for the Xavante to be at war with it. The chief remained unmoved and responded simply: "This is the white man's land, mine is Xavante land" (Fabre 1963:34–5). The Xavante have been militant in defense of their lands since "pacification" and have forcibly expelled settlers and occupied government offices to force the authorities to fulfill their promise of legal protections (Maybury-Lewis 1983). A Xavante leader, Mario Juruna, carried the struggle further into the political arena by winning election to Brazil's House of Representatives in 1982. Juruna has campaigned effectively for the land rights of Brazilian Indians at both the national and the international level.

The Principle of Stabilization

According to theories of cultural evolution, adaptation, and integration, resistance to change is understandable as a natural cultural process. If the technological, social, and ideological systems of a culture gradually specialize to fit the requirements of successful adaptation to a specific environment, other cultural arrangements become increasingly difficult, if not impossible, to accommodate without setting in motion major disruptive changes that have unforeseen consequences. Resistance to change – whether it be direct avoidance of new cultural patterns, overt ethnocentrism, or open hostility to foreigners – may thus be seen as a significant means of adaptation because it operates as a "cultural isolating mechanism" (Meggers 1971:166) to protect successfully established cultures from the disruptive effects of foreign cultural elements. The resulting "stability" refers to a relative lack of change in the major cultural patterns and does not imply complete changelessness in all the nuances of culture because minor changes probably occur constantly in all cultures. Stability is such a fundamental characteristic of cultures that it has been formulated as a general principle: "A culture at rest tends to remain at rest" (Harding 1960:54). A corollary of this so-called principle of stabilization states:

When acted upon by external forces a culture will, if necessary, undergo specific changes only to the extent of and with the effect of *preserving* unchanged its fundamental structure and character. (Harding 1960:54)

As change agents are well aware, resistance to change is based not only on the natural resistance or inertia of already established cultural patterns, but also on the realization by the people concerned of the risks of experimenting with unproven cultural patterns. Either the rewards of adopting new ways must appear to be worth the risks, or some form of coercion must be applied. However, change agents convinced of their own cultural superiority tend to overlook the fact that native fears about the dangers of untested innovations may be justified. Peoples that reject such unproven cultural complexes as miracle grains, pesticides, and chemical fertilizers may prove in the long run to be wiser and better adapted to their natural environments.

For peoples in relatively stable, self-reliant cultures, resistance to change is a positive value. It is only in commercial cultures that such emphasis is placed on change for its own sake and that, among those who make a profession of promoting change, cultural stability is given a negative connotation and is identified as backwardness and stagnation. [...]

THE UNCONTROLLED FRONTIER

Atrocities of the Putumayo

World demand for rubber began to rise in the 1870s after the development of vulcanization, and particularly after 1900, when the automotive industry began to become important. As a result, the price of rubber soared, and the Amazon regions of Brazil and Peru, which were the primary sources of natural rubber, became major new frontier areas as thousands of outsiders arrived to share in the wealth. This initiated a period of frantic economic activity called the rubber boom, which continued until about 1915, when East Indian plantation rubber captured the world market. Regular labor was scarce in the Amazon, but because tribal Indians were numerous in many of the rubber zones, they quickly became the backbone of the new extractive industry. The Indians were especially useful because they could be induced to work for cheap trade goods. They were largely self-sufficient and knew the rubber forests perfectly. Best of all, however, the prevailing attitudes of the local government and military officials were highly favorable toward allowing relatively uncontrolled economic exploitation of the Indians, who were considered to be savages in need of civilization.

Given this setting, serious abuses were almost certain to occur. In fact, what followed was the ruthless exploitation and incredibly violent destruction of thousands of people, which must have fully equaled the cruelest periods of the Spanish conquest. The need for Indian laborers in the rubber zones became so great that merely luring them to work with trade goods was not enough, and undisguised slaving activities became institutionalized. Slave raids, popularly known as *correrías*, were commonly reported occurrences even outside the rubber zones and involved armed gangs assaulting isolated Indian settlements, killing the resisting men, and capturing the women and children to be sold as slaves. Not surprisingly, these activities were widely approved as economically advantageous and necessary civilizing measures, as the following commentary by a contemporary Peruvian writer indicates:

It is not strange, then, that there exists the cruel procedure known as *correrías*, which consists of surprising the habitations of some tribe and taking the members of it prisoner. These prisoners are taken to far territories and are dedicated to work.... This catechization has the advantage that the individual soon obtains precise concepts of the importance that his personal work has in the commerce of civilized people.... In our century, the procedure is cruel and wounds all the fibers of our sensibility; *but one must recognize the powerful and rapid help that it lends to civilization.* (Palacios i Mendiburu 1892:289–90; my translation, emphasis supplied)

Under the direction of large corporations such as the British-owned Peruvian Amazon Company, Ltd., a highly profitable system of rubber production was formulated in which a number of regional company officials controlled managers who organized the scattered tribal populations into local sections and directed the actual rubber-gathering activities. Section managers kept records of their Indian laborers and assigned them specific rubber quotas, which had to be carried to the regional administrators at regular intervals. Many of these lower-level company officials, or rubber barons, wielded enormous power and lived lavishly in great houses surrounded by Indian servants and concubines and armed bodyguards. In the Putumayo district of Peru, where some 12,000 Indians were reported to be working in 1905 (Fuentes 1908), it was common knowledge that rubber barons regularly used direct physical violence to increase production. Indians who failed to meet their assigned quotas or who attempted to escape were flogged and tortured or simply shot. Even though these actions occurred openly and were widely reported, the government refused to take any action against known offenders.

Finally, in 1907 an outraged Peruvian as a private citizen presented the local court and newspapers with a carefully documented formal denunciation of unspeakable atrocities committed against the Putumayo Indians. The denunciation, which named twenty prominent individuals as responsible, detailed specific crimes of rape, slavery, torture by flogging and mutilation, and mass murder by shooting, poisoning, starvation, and burning – all of which reportedly resulted in the deaths of thousands of Indians. These reports shocked the nation, and the president of Peru called on local officials to make investigations. Because of the involvement of a British company, the matter was even debated in the British Parliament and Sir Roger Casement was sent to investigate. A local Peruvian judge, Carlos Valcarcel, also conducted his own investigation; soon the testimony of eyewitnesses and the discovery of mass burials and other physical evidence left no doubt that crimes of immense proportion had occurred (Valcarcel 1915). The scale of the atrocities is made evident by comparing the estimated 50,000 pre-1886 Indian population of the Putumayo district with the estimated population of only 10,000 by about 1910 (Casement in Hardenburg 1912: 336–7; Steward 1948). The precise figure will never be known, but it is certain that thousands of Indians died.

The attitude of the local government officials toward these crimes was continued denial and inaction. The judge who had pursued the case was suspended, and the most prominent of the accused company officials was praised for his talent and capital with which he had brought economic progress to the department (Fuentes 1908:113). In this case, the frontier was being left deliberately uncontrolled. [. . .]

Demographic Impact of the Frontier

Wherever the European has trod, death seems to pursue the aboriginal.
Charles Darwin, cited in Merivale 1861:541

Severe depopulation of tribal peoples is a characteristic future of the frontier process and has been reported by observers from all parts of the world during the past 150 years. As early as 1837, the members of the Select Committee on Aborigines found tribal populations to be declining at alarming rates in areas invaded by British colonists. They noted that the Indians of Newfoundland had been exterminated by 1823 and that the Canadian Cree had declined from 10,000 to 200 since 1800. They also found "fearful" depopulation in the Pacific where reportedly the Tasmanians would soon be extinct, and they found that the Australian Aborigines were vanishing from the earth.

In retrospect, it is clear that what the Select Committee was reporting on at that time was only the beginning of a catastrophic decline in tribal populations that continued in most areas of the world for another 100 years. Table 7.1 indicates the scale of some of this depopulation. According to these figures, tribal populations in lowland South America (east of the Andes and exclusive of the Caribbean) and North America (north of Mexico) were reduced by 95 percent, or by nearly 15 million, by 1930. It is noteworthy that in these areas much of this reduction has occurred *since* 1800 and can be only partly attributed to the Spanish and Portuguese conquests, which decimated large populations in the Orinoco, the lower Amazon, and eastern Brazil and Bolivia prior to 1800. Certainly in North America, with the exception of some portions of the Southwest and California, and the eastern seaboard, most of the depopulation occurred after 1800. In Polynesia, Micronesia, and Australia, the population has been reduced by approximately 80 percent, or more than 1.25 million, since 1800. If allowances are made for further depopulation in areas not included in table 7.1, such as Siberia, southern Asia, island Southeast Asia, southern Africa, and Melanesia, and if Morel's estimate for the Congo is accepted, it might be estimated that during the 150 years between 1780 and 1930 world tribal populations were reduced by at least thirty million as a result of the spread of global-scale cultures. A more realistic estimate would place the figure at perhaps fifty million. Such an incredible loss has no parallel in modern times and

Table 7.1 World survey of tribal depopulation

	Precontact population	Population lowpoint	Depopulation
North America (US and Canada)	7,000,000[a]	390,000[b]	6,610,000
Lowland South America	8,500,000[c]	450,000[d]	8,050,000
Oceania			
Polynesia[e]	1,100,000	180,000	920,000
Micronesia[f]	200,000	83,000	117,000
Melanesia			
Fiji[f,g]	300,000	85,000	215,000
New Caledonia[h]	100,000	27,000	73,000
Australia[i]	300,000	60,500	239,500
Africa			
Congo[j]			8,000,000
	Estimated total depopulation		24,224,500

[a,b]Thornton (1987:30,32). [c]Denevan (1976: 291).   [d]Dobyns (1966: 415).
[e,f] Keesing (1941).   [g,h]Roberts (1969).
[i]Rowley (1970:384). More recent estimates place the precontact population at as high as a million, but such a figure is not yet widely accepted.
[j]Morel in Louis and Stengers (1968: 123). (Suret-Canale 1971: 36–7 gives a more liberal estimate of twelve million for the depopulation of the French Congo alone between 1900 and 1921.)

must have been a major factor in the "acculturation" of tribal peoples. This was genocide on a grand scale and was widely recognized as such at the time [...].

The "population reduction" as discussed here is not strictly a record of "deaths," because in theory a population could experience increased mortality and show no population decline if fertility rates also increased. There could be many more deaths than those indicated by the "reduction" figures. However, in the case of many tribal groups it is likely that frontier disturbances caused a decline in fertility.

These population losses have greater meaning when their impact on specific tribal groups is examined, because countless groups were never able to recover from such massive depopulation and simply became extinct whereas those that did survive were seriously weakened. The speed with which many groups were engulfed by the frontier was a critical factor in the ultimate outcome. The Tasmanians, for example, were reduced by almost 98 percent, from a population of 5,000 to 111, within thirty years. In western Victoria, the aboriginal population of perhaps 4,000 was reduced to 213 after less than forty years of settlement, and within fifty years anthropologists could find no one who could reliably describe their traditional culture (Corris 1968). In California, 75 percent of an estimated 85,000 Yokut and Wintun Indians were swept away by epidemic diseases in 1830–3 (Cook 1955).

In more recent times there have been reports of rapid rates of decline for many South American tribal groups. In Tierra del Fuego, for example, nomadic Indians such as the Ona and Yahgan, who may have numbered more than 8,000 as recently as 1870, were effectively extinct by 1950. In Brazil alone, an estimated 87 of 230 groups known to be in existence in 1900 were extinct by 1957 (Ribeiro 1957), and many other surviving groups experienced drastic declines following white contacts. Among the most dramatic cases recorded for Brazil are the Caraja, estimated to number 100,000 in 1845, 10,000 in 1908, and 1,510 in 1939 (Lipkind 1948:180). The Araguaia Kayapo, who numbered 8,000 in 1903, were reduced to 27 by 1929 (Dobyns 1966). More recently, the Kreen-a-kore were reduced from 300 to 35 in 1979, just six years after agreeing to establish permanent contact with the national society (Davis 1977:69–73; Latin America Political Report 1979, 13[3]:19). Depopulation of this magnitude clearly constitutes a major source of stress for any culture, particularly when it occurs in the context of conquest and economic exploitation.

The causes of tribal depopulation have been well understood, at least since the Select Committee's 1837 Report designated frontier violence, disease, alcohol, firearms, and demoralization as the principal causes. Ultimately, all of these causes can be reduced to the political decisions of national governments to encourage the invasion of tribal territories. However, there have been some ethnocentric attempts to attribute depopulation to inherent tribal decadence and racial inferiority and to suggest that civilization merely accelerated a decline that was already occurring. This view has been supported by some missionaries and government inquiries and by not a few scholars, such as the historian Stephen Henry Roberts, who spoke vaguely of a "general racial decline, an indefinable *malaise* of the stock itself" (Roberts 1969:59). This explanation is no longer regarded seriously by anthropologists and was vigorously rejected years ago by the British anthropologists W. H. Rivers (1922) and George Pitt-Rivers (1927), who showed how culture contact was responsible for the depopulation of the Pacific.

The only problem remaining for more recent writers to debate has been the difficulty of assessing *which* contact factors are the most critical. Some place special emphasis on the role of disease; others stress the importance of physical violence. Certainly both of these factors were important, but they should not detract attention from other indirect factors, because complex interrelationships and feedback mechanisms are operating among all of the variables leading to depopulation. For example, dispossession often forced enemy groups into intense competition for greatly reduced resources, and the availability of firearms made the resulting conflicts far more destructive than previous conflicts. These increased conflicts, combined with other new disturbances in economic and social patterns (such as those related to debt peonage), often placed new stresses on tribal societies and weakened them to the point that they willingly accepted outside control and welfare. Even depopulation itself is a form of stress that can lead to further depopulation by threatening the subsistence base. Rivers (1922) speculated that the sudden total transformation experienced by many tribes caused a form of shock that made people stop producing or desiring children, whereas in some cases they simply died because life was no longer worth living. Although this explanation is now in disrepute, it seems difficult to disprove.

Increased mortality alone does not account for the complete disappearance of so many tribal peoples: other cultural variables are involved. Ironically, the special adaptive mechanisms of tribal cultures designed to prevent *overpopulation*, such as abortion, infanticide, and the ideal of a small family, may have actually contributed to *depopulation* and even extinction when frontier conditions drastically elevated mortality rates. There is little reliable data on this point because the importance of these population-regulating devices has only recently been recognized, but anthropologists have cited these factors to explain the depopulation of the Tapirape in Brazil (Wagley 1951) and the Yap islanders in Micronesia (Schneider 1955).

REFERENCES

Arensberg, Conrad M. and Niehoff, Arthur H. (1964). *Introducing Social Change: A Manual for Americans Overseas*. Chicago: Aldine.

Australia, Commonwealth Bureau of Census and Statistics (1970). *Official Yearbook of the Commonwealth of Australia*, no. 56. Canberra.

Bailey, Robert (1982). "Development in the Ituri Forest of Zaire." *Cultural Survival Quarterly* 6(2): 23–5.

Bartolomé, Miguel Alberto (1972). "The Situation of the Indians in the Argentine: The Chaco Area and Misiones Province." In W. Dostal (ed.), *The Situation of the Indian in South America*. Geneva: World Council of Churches, pp. 218–51.

Bodley, John H. (1985). *Anthropology and Contemporary Human Problems*. 2nd ed. Palo Alto, CA, and London: Mayfield.

Bodley, John H. (1996). *Anthropology and Contemporary Human Problems*. 3rd ed. Mountain View, CA: Mayfield.

Cavalli-Sforza, Luigi Luca (ed.) (1986). *African Pygmies*. New York: Academic Press.

Chatterjee, Suhas (1967). "Language and Literacy in the North-Eastern Regions." In Rathin Mittra and Barun Das Gupta (eds.), *A Common Perspective for North-East India*. Calcutta: Pannalal Das Gupta, pp. 19–23.

Cook, Sherburne F. (1955). "The Epidemic of 1830–1833 in California and Oregon." *University of California Publications in American Archaeology and Ethnology* 43: 303–26.

Corris, Peter (1968). *Aborigines and Europeans in Western Victoria*. Occasional Papers in Aboriginal Studies no. 12, Ethnohistory Series no. 1. Canberra: Australian Institute of Aboriginal Studies.

Davis, Shelton H. (1977). *Victims of the Miracle: Development and the Indians of Brazil*. Cambridge: Cambridge University Press.

Denevan, William M. (1976). "Epilogue." In William M. Denevan (ed.), *The Native Population of the Americas in 1492*. Madison: University of Wisconsin Press, pp. 289–92.

Diamond, Stanley (1960). "Introduction: The Uses of the Primitive." In Stanley Diamond (ed.), *Primitive Views of the World*. New York: Columbia University Press, pp. v–xxix.

Dobyns, Henry F. (1966). "Estimating Aboriginal American Population: An Appraisal of Techniques with a New Hemispheric Estimate." *Current Anthropology* 7(4): 395–449.

Elkin, A. P. (1951). "Reaction and Interaction: A Food Gathering People and European Settlement in Australia." *American Anthropologist* 53: 164–86.

Fabre, D. G. (1963). *Más Allá del Rio das Mortes*. Buenos Aires: Ediciones Selectas.

Fuentes, Hildebrando (1908). *Loreto – Apuntes Geográficos, Históricos, Estadísticos, Politicos y Sociales*. Vol. II. Lima: Imprenta de la Revista.

Ghurye, G. S. (1963). *The Scheduled Tribes*. 3rd ed. Bombay: G. R. Bhatkal.

Goulet, Denis (1971). *The Cruel Choice: A New Concept in the Theory of Development*. New York: Atheneum.

Graham, A. C. (1971). "China, Europe and the Origins of the Modern Science." *Asia Major* 16 (parts 1–2): 178–196.

Hames, Raymond B. (1979). "A Comparison of the Efficiencies of the Shotgun and the Bow in Neotropical Forest Hunting." *Human Ecology* 7(3): 219–52.

Hardenburg, Walter E. (1912). *The Putumayo, the Devil's Paradise: Travels in the Peruvian Amazon Region and an Account of the Atrocities Committed upon the Indians Therein*. London: T. F. Unwin.

Harding, Thomas G. (1960). "Adaptation and Stability." In Marshall Sahlins and Elman Service (eds.), *Evolution and Culture*. Ann Arbor: University of Michigan Press, pp. 45–68.

Hart, John A. and Hart, Terese B. (1984). "The Mbuti of Zaire." *Cultural Survival Quarterly* 8(3): 18–20.

Hippler, Arthur E. (1979). "Comment on 'Development in the Non-Western World.'" *American Anthropologist* 81: 348–9.

Kaplan, David (19609). "The Law of Cultural Dominance." In Marshall D. Sahlins and Elman R. Service (eds.), *Evolution and Culture*. Ann Arbor: University of Michigan Press, pp. 69–92.

Kar, Parimal Chandra (1967). "A Point of View on the Garos in Transition." In Rathin Mittra and Barun Das Gupta (eds.), *A Common Perspective for North-East India*. Calcutta: Pannalal Das Gupta, pp. 91–102.

Keesing, Felix M. (1941). *The South Seas in the Modern World*. Institute of Pacific Relations International Research Series. New York: John Day.

Keesing, Felix M. and Keesing Marie (1934). *Taming Philippine Headhunters: A Study of Government and of Cultural Change in Northern Luzon*. London: George Allen and Unwin.

Kloos, Peter (1977). *The Akuriyo of Surinam: A Case of Emergence from Isolation*. IWGIA Document no. 27. Copenhagen: IWGIA.

Lévi-Strauss, Claude (1951). "Social Science in Pakistan." *International Social Science Bulletin* 3(4): 825–31.

Lipkind, William (1948). "The Carajá." In Julian Steward (ed.), *Handbook of South American Indians*. Vol. III. Bureau of American Ethnology Bulletin 143. Washington, DC: Smithsonian Institution, pp. 179–91.

Louis, Roger and Stengers, Jean (1968). *E. P. Morel's History of the Congo Reform Movement*. Oxford: Clarendon Press.

Maybury-Lewis, David (1983). "The Shavante Struggle for their Lands." *Cultural Survival Quarterly* 7(1): 54–5.

Meggers, Betty J. (1971). *Amazonia: Man and Culture in a Counterfeit Paradise*. Chicago: Aldine.

Merivale, Herman (1861). *Lectures on Colonization and Colonies*. London: Green, Longman and Roberts.

Mey, Wolfgang E. (1983). "Dammed for Progress: About the Perversity of State and Nation-Building in Bangladesh – The Chittagong Hill Tracts Case." Paper presented at symposium, "The Fourth World: Relations between Minority Peoples and Nation-States." 11th International Congress of Anthropological and Ethnological Sciences, Vancouver, Canada.

Mittra, Rathin and Das Gupta, Barun (1967). *A Common Perspective for North-East India*. Calcutta: Pannalal Das Gupta.

Moasosang, P. (1967). "The Naga-Search for Self-Identity." In Rathin Mittra and Barun Das Gupta (eds.), *A Common Perspective for North-East India*. Calcutta: Pannalal Das Gupta, pp. 51–7.

Nag, Amit Kumar (1967). "The Society in Transition in the Mizo District." In Rathin Mittra and Barun Das Gupta (eds.), *A Common Perspective for North-East India*. Calcutta: Pannalal Das Gupta, pp. 80–90.

Nietschmann, Bernard (1985). "Indonesia, Bangladesh: Disguised Invasion of Indigenous Nations." *Fourth World Journal* 1(2): 89–126.

Palacios i Mendiburu, S. (1892). "Conferencia sobre la colonizacion de Loreto." *Boletin de la Sociedad Geografica de Lima* 2: 267–312.

Peacock, Nadene (1984). "The Mbuti of Northeast Zaire." *Cultural Survival Quarterly* 8(2): 15–17.

Pitt-Rivers, George H. (1927). *The Clash of Culture and the Contact of Races*. London: George Routledge and Sons.

Popenoe, Paul (1915). "One Phase of Man's Modern Evolution." *International Congress of Americanists* 19: 617–20.

Raglan, Lord Fitzroy R. S. (1940). "The Future of the Savage Races." *Man* 40:62.

Ribeiro, Darcy (1957). *Culturas e Linguas Indigenas do Brasil*. Separata de Educacão e Cieñcias Socais no. 6. Rio de Janeiro: Centro Brasileiro de Pesquisas Educacionais.

Rivers, W. H. R. (1922). *Essays on the Depopulation of Melanesia*. Cambridge: Cambridge University Press.

Roberts, Stephen Henry (1969). *Population Problems of the Pacific*. New York: AMS Press. (Reprint of 1927 edition)

Rowley, Charles D. (1970). *The Destruction of Aboriginal Society*. Vol. 1: *Aboriginal Policy and Practice*. Canberra: Australian National University Press.

Schneider, David (1955). "Abortion and Depopulation on a Pacific Island: Yap." In B. D. Paul (ed.), *Health, Culture, and Community*. New York: Russel Sage, pp. 211–35.

Schoen, Ivan L. (1969). "Contact with the Stone Age." *Natural History* 78(1): 10–18, 66–7.

Steward, Julian H. (1948). "The Witotoan Tribes." In Julian H. Steward (ed.), *Handbook of South American Indians*. Vol. III. Bureau of American Ethnology Bulletin 143. Washington, DC: Smithsonian Institution, pp. 749–62.

Steward, Julian H. (ed.) (1967). *Contemporary Change in Traditional Societies*. Urbana: University of Illinois Press.

Sturtevant, William C. (1970). "Resolution on Forced Acculturation." *Current Anthropology* 11(2): 160.

Suret-Canale, Jean (1971). *French Colonialism in Tropical Africa, 1900–1945*. New York: Pica Press.

Thiek, Hrilrokhum (1967). "An Outlook for a Better Understanding of the Tribal People." In Rathin Mittra and Barun Das Gupta (eds.), *A Common Perspective for North-East India*. Calcutta: Pannalal Das Gupta, pp. 103–9.

Thornton, Russell (1987). *American Indian Holocaust and Survival: A Population History since 1492*. Norman and London: University of Oklahoma Press.

Turnbull, Colin M. (1963). "The Lesson of the Pygmies." *Scientific American* 208(1): 28–37.

Valcarcel, Carlos A. (1915). *El Proceso del Putumayo y sus Secretos Inauditos*. Lima: H. La Rosa.

Wagley, C. (1951). "Cultural Influences on Population." *Revista do Museu Paulista* 5: 95–104.

Webb, W. E. (1966). "Land Capacity Classification and Land Use in the Chittagong Hill Tracts of East Pakistan." *Proceedings of the Sixth World Forestry Congress* 3: 3229–32.

Weiss, Gerald (1988). "The Tragedy of Ethnocide: A Reply to Hippler." In John H. Bodley (ed.), *Tribal Peoples and Development Issues: A Global Overview*. Mountain View, CA: Mayfield, pp. 124–33.

Woodruff, William (1966). *Impact of Western Man*. London: Macmillan.

Zaman, M. Q. (1985). "Tribal Survival in the Chittagong Hill Tracts of Bangladesh." *Man in India* 65(1): 58–74.

8

Culture of Terror – Space of Death: Roger Casement's Putumayo Report and the Explanation of Torture

Michael Taussig

This essay is about torture and the culture of terror, which for most of us, including myself, are known only through the words of others. Thus my concern is with the mediation of the culture of terror through narration – and with the problems of writing effectively against terror.

Jacobo Timerman ends his recent book, *Prisoner without a Name, Cell without a Number*, with the imprint of the gaze of hope in the space of death.

Have any of you looked into the eyes of another person, on the floor of a cell, who knows that he's about to die though no one has told him so? He knows that he's about to die but clings to his biological desire to live, as a single hope, since no one has told him he's to be executed.

I have many such gazes imprinted upon me . . .

Those gazes which I encountered in the clandestine prisons of Argentina and which I've retained one by one, were the culminating point, the purest moment of my tragedy.

They are here with me today. And although I might wish to do so, I could not and would not know how to share them with you.[1]

The space of death is crucial to the creation of meaning and consciousness, nowhere more so than in societies where torture is endemic and where the culture of terror flourishes. We may think of the space of death as a threshold, yet it is a wide space whose breadth offers positions of advance as well as of extinction. Sometimes a person goes through it and returns to us to tell the tale, like Timerman, who entered it, he says, because he believed the battle against military dictatorship had to be fought.[2]

Timerman fought with words, with his newspaper *La Opinion*, in and against the silence imposed by the arbiters of discourse who beat out a new reality in the prison cells where the torturers and the tortured came together. "We victims and victim-izers, we're part of the same humanity, colleagues in the same endeavor to prove the existence of ideologies, feelings, heroic deeds, religions, obsessions. And the rest of humanity, what are they engaged in?"[3]

The construction of colonial reality that occurred in the New World has been and will remain a topic of immense curiosity and study – the New World where the Indian and the African became subject to an initially far smaller number of Christians. Whatever conclusions we draw as to how that hegemony was so speedily effected, we would be most unwise to overlook or underestimate the role of terror. And by this I mean us to think through terror, which as well as being a physiological state is also a social fact and a cultural construction whose baroque dimensions allow it to serve as the mediator *par excellence* of colonial hegemony. The space of death is one of the crucial spaces where Indian, African, and white gave birth to the New World.

This space of death has a long and rich culture. It is where the social imagination has populated its metamorphosing images of evil and the underworld: in the Western tradition, Homer, Virgil, the Bible, Dante, Bosch, the Inquisition, Baudelaire, Rimbaud, *Heart of Darkness*; in Northwest Amazonian tradition, zones of visions, communication between terrestrial and supernatural beings, putrefaction, death, rebirth, and genesis, perhaps in the rivers and land of maternal milk bathed eternally in subtle green light of coca leaves.[4] With European conquest and colonization, these spaces of death blend as a common pool of key signifiers or caption points binding the culture of the conqueror with that of the conquered. The space of death is preeminently a space of transformation: through the experience of death, life; through fear, loss of self and conformity to a new reality; or through evil, good. Lost in the dark woods, then journeying through the underworld with his guide, Dante achieves paradise only after he has mounted Satan's back. Timerman can be a guide for us, analagous to the ways Putumayo shamans I know are guides to those lost in the space of death.

An old Ingano Indian from the Putumayo once told me of this space:

With the fever I was aware of everything. But after eight days I became unconscious. I knew not where I was. Like a madman I wandered, consumed by fever. They had to cover me up where I fell, mouth down. Thus after eight days I was aware of nothing. I was unconscious. Of what people were saying, I remembered nothing. Of the pain of the fever, I remembered nothing; only the space of death – walking in the space of death. Thus, after the noises that spoke. I remained unconscious. Now the world remained behind. Now the world was removed. Well, then I understood. Now the pains were speaking. I knew that I would live no longer. Now I was dead. My sight had gone. Of the world I knew nothing, nor the sound of my ears. Of speech, nothing. Silence. And one knows the space of death, there . . . And this is death – the space that I saw. I was in its center, standing. Then I went to the heights. From the heights a star-point seemed my due. I was standing. Then I came down. There I was searching for the five continents of the world, to remain, to find me a place in the five continents of the world – in the space in which I was wandering. But I was not able.

We might ask: What place in the five continents of the world will the wanderer in the space of death find himself? And by extension: Where will a whole society find itself? The old man fears the evil of sorcery, the struggle for his soul. Between himself, the sorcerer, and the curing shaman, the five continents are sought and fought for. Yet here there is laughter too, puncturing the fear of the mystery, reminding us of Walter Benjamin's comment on the way in which romanticism may perniciously misunderstand the nature of intoxication. "Any serious exploration of occult, surrealistic, phantasmagoric gifts and phenomena," he writes,

> presupposes a dialectical intertwinement to which a romantic turn of mind is impervious. For histrionic or fanatical stress on the mysterious side of the mysterious takes us no further; we penetrate the mystery only to the degree that we recognize it in the everyday world, by virtue of a dialectical optic that perceives the everyday as impenetrable, the impenetrable as everyday.[5]

From Timerman's chronicle and texts like Miguel Angel Asturias's *El señor presidente* it is abundantly clear that cultures of terror are based on and nourished by silence and myth in which the fanatical stress on the mysterious side of the mysterious flourishes by means of rumor and fantasy woven in a dense web of magical realism. It is also clear that the victimizer needs the victim for the purpose of making truth, objectifying the victimizer's fantasies in the discourse of the other. To be sure, the torturer's desire is also prosaic: to acquire information, to act in concert with large-scale economic strategies elaborated by the masters and exigencies of production. Yet equally if not more important is the need to control massive populations through the cultural elaboration of fear.

That is why silence is imposed, why Timerman, the publisher, was so important, why he knew when to be silent and close off reality in the torture chamber. "Such silence," he tells us,

> begins in the channels of communication. Certain political leaders, institutions, and priests attempt to denounce what is happening, but are unable to establish contact with the population. The silence begins with a strong odor. People sniff the suicides, but it eludes them. Then silence finds another ally: solitude. People fear suicides as they fear madmen. And the person who wants to fight senses his solitude and is frightened.[6]

Hence, there is the need for us to fight that solitude, fear, and silence, to examine these conditions of truth-making and culture-making, to follow Michel Foucault in "seeing historically how effects of truth are produced within discourses which are in themselves neither true nor false."[7] At the same time we not only have to see, we also have to see anew through the creation of counterdiscourses.

If effects of truth are power, then the question is raised not only concerning the power to speak and write, but as to what form shall that counterdiscourse take. This issue of form has lately been of much concern to those involved in writing histories and ethnographies. But faced with the endemicity of torture, terror, and the growth of armies, we in the New World are today assailed with a new urgency. There is the effort to understand terror, in order to make *others* understand. Yet the reality at stake here makes a mockery of understanding and derides rationality, as when the young boy Jacobo Timerman asks his mother, "Why do they hate us?" And she replies, "Because they do not understand." And after his ordeal, the old Timerman writes of the need for a hated object and the simultaneous fear of that object – the almost magical inevitability of hatred. "No," he concludes, "there can be no doubt my mother was the one who was mistaken. It is not the anti-Semites who must be made to understand. It is we Jews."[8]

Hated and feared, objects to be despised, yet also of awe, the reified essence of evil in the very being of their bodies, these figures of the Jew, the black, the Indian, and woman herself, are clearly objects of cultural construction, the leaden keel of evil and of mystery stabilizing the ship and course that is Western history. With the cold war we add the communist. With the time bomb ticking inside the nuclear family, we add the feminists and the gays. The military and the New Right, like the conquerors of old, discover the evil they have imputed to these aliens, and mimic the savagery they have imputed.

What sort of understanding – what sort of speech, writing, and construction of meaning by any mode – can deal with and subvert that?

On one thing Timerman is clear. To counterpose the eroticization and romanticization of violence by the same means or by forms equally mystical is a dead end. Yet to offer one or all of the standard rational explanations of the culture of terror is similarly pointless. For behind the search for profits, the need to control labor, the need to assuage frustration, and so on, lie intricately construed long-standing cultural logics of meaning – structures of feeling – whose basis lies in a symbolic world and not in one of rationalism. Ultimately there are two features; the crudest of empirical facts such as the electrodes and the mutilated human body, and the experience of going through torture. In his text Timerman does create a powerful counterdiscourse, precisely because, like torture itself, it moves us through that space of death where reality is up for grabs, to confront the hallucination of the military. His text of madness and evil establishes a revolutionary and, to my mind, sound poetics because it finds its counterweight and sanity in what I take to be the most difficult of political positions marked out by a contradictory space between socialism and anarchism. He is to Victor Serge as V. S. Naipaul is to Arthur Koestler and Joseph Conrad.

Conrad's way of dealing with the terror of the rubber boom in the Congo was *Heart of Darkness*. There were three realities there, comments Frederick Karl: King Leopold's, made out of intricate disguises and deceptions; Roger Casement's studied realism; and Conrad's, which, to quote Karl, "fell midway between the other two, as he attempted to penetrate the veil and yet was anxious to retain its hallucinatory quality."[9]

This formularization is sharp and important: *to penetrate the veil while retaining its hallucinatory quality*. It evokes Paul Ricoeur's two hermeneutics in his major discussion of Freud: that of suspicion (or reduction) and that of revelation.[10] As to the political effect of *Heart of Darkness*, while Ian Watt regards it as the enduring and most powerful literary indictment of imperialism,[11] I am not so sure that its strikingly literary quality and hallucinatory filminess do not finally blind and stun the reader into a trance, drowning in a sea-storm of imagery. The danger here lies with aestheticizing horror, and while Conrad manages to stop short of doing that, we must realize that just to the side lurks the seductive poetics of fascism and the imaginative source of terror and torture embedded deep within us all. The political and artistic problem is to engage with that, to maintain that hallucinatory quality, while effectively turning it against itself. That would be the true catharsis, the great counterdiscourse whose poetics we must ponder in the political terrain now urgently exposed today; the form wherein all that appeals and seduces in the iconography and sensuality of the underworld becomes its own force for self-subversion. Foucault's concept of discourse eludes this aspiration and concept of dialectically engaged subversion. But it is with this poetics that we must develop the cultural politics appropriate to our times.

Casement offers a useful and startling contrast to Conrad, all the more vivid because of the ways their paths crossed in the Congo in 1890, because of the features common to their political backgrounds as exiles or quasi-exiles from imperialized European societies, Poland and Ireland, and because of an indefinable if only superficial similarity in their temperaments and love of literature. Yet it was Casement who resorted to militant action on behalf of his native land, organizing gun running from Germany to the rebels at Dublin for Easter Sunday 1916, and was hung for treason, while Conrad resolutely stuck to his task as an artist, bathed in nostalgia and guilt for Poland, lending his name but otherwise refusing to assist Casement in the Congo Reform Society, claiming he was but a "wretched novelist." The key text for our purposes is Conrad's letter to his beloved friend and socialist, the aristocrat don Roberto, otherwise known as R. B. Cunninghame Graham (whom Jorge Borges regards together with that other great English romantic, W. H. Hudson, as providing the most accurate sketches and literary works of nineteenth-century Pampa society). In this letter, dated 26 December 1903, Conrad salutes don Roberto on the excellence of his book on the great Spanish conquistador, Hernando de Soto, and especially for the sympathetic insight into the souls of the *conquistadores* – the glamor, the pathos, and romance of those times – which functions as an anodyne inducing one to forget the modern *conquistadores* such as Leopold and the lack of romance and vision in nineteenth- and early twentieth-century bourgeois imperialism. Conrad then goes on to inform don Roberto about "a man called Casement" and his plans for a Congo reform society to stop the terror associated with the rubber industry there, the same terror which inspired Conrad's novella. Conrad likens Casement to a *conquistador*, and indulges in a hopelessly romanticized image of him – curtly corrected by Brian Inglis, one of Casement's biographers, seventy years later.[12] What is so galling and instructive about this sort of indulgence, which stems from and informs Conrad's theory of poetics as formulated in the introduction to *The Nigger of the Narcissus*, is that at the time of Casement's trial for treason and vilification as a homosexual in 1916, Conrad displayed a permutation of the romanticism which had led him almost to deify the Casement he first met in the Congo in 1890. Writing to John Quinn, Conrad re-images his first acquaintance with Casement, now pigeonholing him not as in the *Congo Diary* as a man who "thinks, speaks well, [is] most intelligent and very sympathetic," but as a labor recruiter. He goes on to disparage Casement as a romantic opportunist and adds:

He was a good companion, but already in Africa I judged that he was a man, properly speaking, of no mind at all. I don't mean stupid. I mean he was all emotion. By emotional force (Congo report, Putumayo – etc) he made his way, and sheer emotionalism has undone him. A creature of sheer temperament – a truly tragic personality: all but the greatness of which he had not a trace. Only vanity. But in the Congo it was not visible yet.[13]

Yet it remains a fact that Casement's reports on the Congo and the Putumayo did much to stop the pervasive brutality there and, in Edmund Morel's opinion, "innoculated the diplomacy of this country [Britain] with a moral toxin" such that "historians will cherish these occasions as the only two in which British diplomacy rose above the commonplace."[14]

In addition to the coincidences of imperialist history, what brings Casement and Conrad together is the problem they jointly create concerning the rhetorical power and political effect of social realism and mythic realism. Between the emotional consul-general who wrote effectively on the side of the colonized as a realist and a rationalist, and the great artist who did not, lie many of the crucial problems concerning the domination of culture and cultures of domination.

The Putumayo Report

At this point it is instructive to analyze briefly Casement's Putumayo report, which was submitted to Sir Edward Grey, head of the British Foreign Service, and published by the House of Commons on 13 July 1913 when Casement was forty-nine years old.

At the outset it should be noted that Casement's attachment to the cause of Irish home rule and his anger at British imperialism made his almost life-long work as a British consul extremely fraught with contradiction; in addition, he felt his experiences in Africa and South America increased his understanding the effects of the colonialism in Ireland, which in turn stimulated his ethnographic and political sensibilities regarding conditions south of the equator. He claimed, for example, that it was his knowledge of Irish history which allowed him to understand the Congo atrocities, whereas the Foreign Office could not because the empirical evidence made no sense to them. In a letter to his close friend Alice Green he noted:

I knew the Foreign Office would not understand the thing, for I realized that I was looking at this tragedy with the eyes of another race of people once hunted themselves, whose hearts were based on affection as the root principle of contact with their fellow men, and whose estimate of life was not something eternally to be appraised at its market price.[15]

In the article he wrote for the respected *Contemporary Review* in 1912, he argued that the Putumayo Indians were more highly developed, morally speaking, than their white oppressors. The Indian lacked a competitive streak; he was "a socialist by temperament, habit, and possibly, age-long memory of Inca and pre-Inca precept." In conclusion, Casement asked, "Is it too late to hope that by means of the same humane and brotherly agency, something of the goodwill and kindness of Christian life may be imparted to the remote, friendless, and lost children of the forest?"[16] He later referred to the peasants of Connemara in Ireland as "white Indians."[17]

The essence of his 136-page Putumayo report, based on seven weeks of travel in 1910 through the rubber-gathering areas of the jungles of the Caraparaná and Igaraparaná affluents of the middle reaches of the Putumayo river, and on some six months in the Amazon basin, lay in its detail of the terror and tortures together with Casement's explanation of causes and his estimate of the toll in human life. Putumayo rubber would be unprofitable were it not for the forced labor of local Indians, principally those called Huitotos. For the twelve years from 1900, the Putumayo output of some 4,000 tons of rubber cost thousands of Indians their lives. Deaths from torture, disease, and possibly flight had decreased the population of the area by around 30,000 during that time.[18]

The British government felt obliged to send Casement as its consular representative to the Putumayo because of the public outcry aroused in 1909 by a series of articles in the London magazine, *Truth*; the series depicted the brutality of the rubber company, which since 1907 had been a consortium of Peruvian and British interests in the region. Entitled "The Devil's Paradise: A British Owned Congo," these articles were the work of a young "engineer" and adventurer from the United States named Walter Hardenburg, who had with a companion entered the remote corner of the Amazon basin from the Colombian Andes in 1907 and had been taken prisoner by the Peruvian Rubber Company founded by Julio César Arana in 1903. Hardenburg's chronicle is to an important extent an elaboration on a text basic to the Putumayo saga, an article published in the Iquitos newspaper *La Sanción* shortly before its publication was suspended by the Peruvian government and Arana.

Asserting that the rubber trees are in rapid decline and will be exhausted in four years' time because of the rapacity of the production system, the article continues by declaring that the peaceful Indians work night and day collecting rubber without the slightest remuneration. They are given nothing to eat or wear. Their crops, together with the women and children, are taken for the pleasure of the whites. They are inhumanly flogged until their bones are visible. Given no medical treatment, they are left to die after torture, eaten by the company's dogs. They are castrated, and their ears, fingers, arms, and legs are cut off. They are also tortured by means of fire, water, and crucifixion tied head-down. The whites cut them to pieces with machetes and dash out the brains of small children by hurling them against trees and walls. The elderly are killed when they can no longer work. To amuse themselves, company officials practice shooting, using Indians as targets, and on special occassions such as Easter Saturday – Saturday of Glory – shoot them down in groups or, in preference, douse them in kerosene and set them on fire to enjoy their agony.[19]

In a letter written to Hardenburg by an employee of the company we read how a "commission" was sent out by a rubber-station manager to exterminate a group of Indians for not bringing in sufficient rubber. The commission returned in four days with fingers, ears, and several heads of Indians to prove the orders had been carried out.[20] On another occasion, the manager called in hundreds of Indians to assemble at the station:

He grasped his carbine and machete and began the slaughter of these defenseless Indians, leaving the ground covered with over 150 corpses, among them men, women, and children. Bathed in blood and appealing for mercy, the survivors were heaped with the dead and burned to death, while the manager shouted, "I want to exterminate all the Indians who do not obey my orders about the rubber that I require them to bring in."

"When they get drunk," adds the correspondent, "the upper-level employees of the company toast with champagne the man who can boast of the greatest number of murders."[21]

The drama perhaps most central to the Putumayo terror, quoted from an Iquitos newspaper article in 1908, and affirmed as fact by both Casement and Hardenburg, concerns the weighing-in of rubber brought by the Indians from the forest:

The Indian is so humble that as soon as he sees that the needle of the scale does not mark the ten kilos, he himself stretches out his hands and throws himself on the ground to receive the punishment. Then the chief [of the rubber station] or a subordinate advances, bends down, takes the Indian by the hair, strikes him, raises his head, drops it face downwards on the ground, and after the face is beaten and kicked and covered with blood, the Indian is scourged. This is when they are treated best, for often they cut them to pieces with machetes.[22]

In the rubber station of Matanzas, continues the writer, "I have seen Indians tied to a tree, their feet about half a yard above the ground. Fuel is then placed below, and they are burnt alive. This is done to pass the time."

Casement's report to the House of Commons is staid and sober, somewhat like a lawyer arguing a case and in marked contrast to his diary covering the same experience. He piles fact on brutal fact, suggests an over-all analysis, and makes his recommendations. His material comes from three sources: what he personally witnessed; testimony of 30 Barbados blacks who, with 166 others, were contracted by the company during 1903–4 to serve as overseers, and whose statements occupy 85 published foolscap pages; and, interspersed with Casement's direct observations, numerous stories from local residents and company employees.

Early on in the report, in a vivid throwaway line, he evokes the banality of the cruelty. "The employees at all the stations passed the time when not hunting Indians, either lying in their hammocks or in gambling."[23] The unreal atmosphere of ordinariness, of the ordinariness of the extraordinary, can be startling. "At some of the stations the principal flogger was the station cook – two such men were directly named to me, and I ate the food they prepared, while many of their victims carried my baggage from station to station, and showed often terrible scars on their limbs inflicted at the hands of these men."[24]

From the evidence of scarring, Casement found that the "great majority" (perhaps up to 90 percent) of the more than 1,600 Indians he saw had been badly beaten.[25] Some of the worst affected were small boys, and deaths due to flogging were frequent, either under the lash, or more frequently, a few days later when the wounds became maggot infested.[26] Floggings occurred when an Indian brought in insufficient rubber and were most sadistic for those who dared to flee. Flogging was mixed with other tortures such as near drowning, "designed," as Casement points out, "to just stop short of taking life while inspiring the acute mental fear and inflicting much of the physical agony of death."[27] Casement was informed by a man who had himself often flogged Indians that he had seen mothers flogged because their little sons had not brought in enough rubber. While the boy stood terrified and crying at the sight, his mother would be beaten "just a few strokes" to make him a better worker.[28]

Deliberate starvation was resorted to repeatedly, sometimes to frighten, more often to kill. Men and women were kept in the stocks until they died of hunger. One Barbadian related how he had seen Indians in this situation "scraping up the dirt with their fingers and eating it." Another declared he had seen them eating the maggots in their wounds.[29]

The stocks were sometimes placed on the upper verandah or residential part of the main dwelling house of the rubber stations, in direct view of the manager and his employees. Children, men, and women might be confined in them for months, and some of the Barbados men said they had seen women raped while in the stocks.[30]

Much of the surveillance and punishment was carried out by the corps of Indian guards known as the *muchachos*. Members of this armed corps had been trained by the company from an early age, and were used to control *salvajes* other than those to whom they were kin. Casement thought them to be generally every bit as evil as their white masters.[31] When Barbados men were present, they were frequently assigned the task of flogging, but, Casement emphasizes, "no monopoly of flogging was enjoyed by any employee as a right. The chief of the section frequently himself took the lash, which, in turn, might be wielded by every member of the civilized or 'rational staff.'"[32]

"Such men," reports Casement, "had lost all sight or sense of rubber-gathering – they were simply beasts of prey who lived upon the Indians and delighted in shedding their blood." Moreover, the station managers from the areas where Casement got his most precise information were in debt (despite their handsome rates of commission), running their operations at a loss to the company which in some sections ran to many thousands of pounds sterling.[33]

It is necessary at this point to note that although the Indians received the brunt of the terror, whites and blacks were also targets. Whether as competitors for Indian rubber gatherers, like the independent Colombian rubber traders who first conquered the Putumayo and were then dislodged by Arana's company in 1908, or as employees of the company, extremely few escaped the ever-present threat of degradation and torture. Asked by Casement if he did not know it to be wrong to torture Indians, one of the Barbados men replied that he was unable to refuse orders, "that a man might be a man down in Iquitos, but 'you couldn't be a man up there.'"[34] In addition, most of the company's white and black employees were themselves trapped in a debt-peonage system, but one quite different from the one the company used in controlling its Indians.

From the testimony of the Barbados men it is clear that dissension, hatred, and mistrust ran riot among all members of the company – to the degree that one has to consider seriously the hypothesis that only in their group ritualization of torturing Indians could such anomie and mistrust be held in check, thus guaranteeing to the company the solidarity required to sustain it as an effective social unit.

To read Casement's secondhand and Hardenburg's eyewitness accounts of the company attacks against independent white Colombian traders is to become further aware of the ritualistic features which assured the violence of the Putumayo rubber boom of its success as a culture of terror.

Casement's Analysis

Casement's main line of analysis lies with his argument that it was not rubber but labor that was scarce in the Putumayo, and that this scarcity was the basic cause of the use of terror. Putumayo rubber was of the lowest quality, the remoteness of its source made its transport expensive relative to rubber from other zones, and wages for free labor were very high. Hence, he reasons, the company resorted to the use of forced labor under a debt-peonage system, and used torture to maintain labor discipline.

The problem with this argument, which assumes the purported rationality of business and the capital-logic of commodities (such as labor), is that it encounters certain contradictions and, while not exactly wrong, strikes me as giving insufficient weight to two fundamental considerations. The first consideration concerns the forms of labor and economic organization that local history and Indian society made available, or potentially available, to world capitalism in the jungles of the Putumayo. The second, put crudely, is that terror and torture do not derive only from market pressure (which we can regard here as a trigger) but also from the process of cultural construction of evil as well. "Market pressure" assumes the paradigm of scarcity essential to capitalist economism and capitalist socioeconomic theory. Leaving aside the question of how accurate a depiction of capitalist society results from this paradigm, it is highly dubious that it reveals much of the reality of the Putumayo rubber boom where the problem facing capitalist enterprise was precisely that there were no capitalist social institutions and no market for abstract labor into which capital could be fed and multiplied. Indeed, one could go further to develop an argument which begins with the premise that it was just this lack of commoditized social relationships, in interaction with commodity forces emanating from the world rubber market, that accounts for the production of torture and terror. We can say that the culture of terror was functional to the needs of the labor system, but that tells us little about the most significant contradictions to emerge from Casement's report, namely, that the slaughter of this precious labor was on a scale vast beyond belief, and that, as Casement himself states, not only were the station managers costing the company large sums of money but that "such men had lost all sight or sense of rubber-gathering – they were simply beasts of prey who lived upon the Indians and delighted in shedding their blood." To claim the rationality of business for this is to claim and sustain an illusory rationality, obscuring our understanding of the way business can transform the use of terror from the means into an end in itself.

The consideration of local history and economic organization requires far fuller treatment than can be attempted here. But it should be noted in passing that "scarcity" of labor cannot refer to a scarcity of Indians, of whom there seems to have been an abundance, but rather to the fact that the Indians would not work in the regular and dependable manner necessary to a large-scale capitalist enterprise. Casement downplayed this phenomenon, now often referred to as "the backward sloping supply curve of labor," and did so even though in the Congo he had himself complained that the problem was that the natives would not work;[35] he felt sure that if paid with more goods, the Indians would work to the level required by the company without force. Many people with far longer experience in the Putumayo denied this naive assertion and pointed out, with logic as impeccable as Casement's, that the scarcity of labor and the ease with which the Indians could live off the forest obliged employers elsewhere in the Putumayo to treat them with consideration.[36] In either case, however, with or without use of coercion, the labor productivity obtained fell far short of what employers desired.

The contradictions mount further on close examination of the debt-peonage system, which Casement regards as slavery. It was a pretext, he says, that the Indian in such a relation was in debt, for the Indian was bound by physical force to work for the company and could not escape.[37] One then must ask why the company persisted in this pretense, especially given the means of coercion at its disposal.

Accounts of advances paid in goods (such as machetes, cloth, shotguns) were supposedly kept for each rubber gatherer; the advances were roughly equal to fivepence per pound weight of rubber, which was fetching three shillings tenpence on the London market in 1910. (In West Africa, natives were paid an equivalent of between two shillings and two shillings sixpence per pound of "Ibi Red niggers" rubber, equal in quality to the Putumayan.)[38] A station manager told Casement that the Indians never asked the price or value of rubber. Sometimes a single coin was given, and Casement met numbers of Indian women wearing necklaces made of coins.[39] Joaquin Rocha writes that the Indians of the Tres Esquinas rubber station valued money not as a means of exchange but as a precious object; they would beat coins into smooth and shining triangular shapes to use as nose rings or ear pendants.[40] Yet, it would be naive to suppose that the Indians lacked interest or understanding of the terms of trade and of what the whites got for rubber in the outside world. "You buy these with the rubber we produce," said an Indian chief as one entranced, looking through Casement's binoculars.[41] Casement was told that the station managers would fix the quantity of rubber due from each individual according to the goods that had been advanced, and in this connection Father Gridilla relates an episode of interest from when he traveled up the Caraparaná in 1912.

It was at a time when thousands of Indians came to the rubber station of La Occidente to deliver rubber. First there was a great dance lasting five days – the sort of event Joaquin Rocha a decade earlier likened to a harvest festival. Then the rubber was handed over and goods were advanced, Father Gridilla commenting "the savages don't know money, their needs are very limited, and they ask only for shotguns, ammunition, axes, machetes, mirrors, and occasionally hammocks." An Indian he described as a corpulent and ugly savage declined to accept anything and, on being pressed, replied, "I don't want anything. I've got everything." The whites insisted again and again that he must ask for something. Finally he retorted, "I want a black dog!" "And where am I going to find a black dog or even a white one if there aren't any in all of Putumayo?" responded the station manager. "You ask me for rubber," replied the savage, "and I bring rubber. If I ask for a black dog you have to give me one!"[42]

Relying on stories told him, Hardenburg wrote that the Indians received their advances with great pleasure, because if they did not, they were flogged to death.[43]

Pretext as it was, the debt which ensured peonage was nonetheless real, and as a pretense its magical realism was as essential to the labor organization of the Putumayo rubber boom as is the "commodity fiction" Karl Polanyi describes for a mature capitalist economy.[44] To analyze the construction of these fictional realities we need now to turn to some of their more obviously mythic features, enclosed as they are in the synergistic relation of savagery and business, cannibalism and capitalism. Interrogated by the British Parliamentary Select Committee on Putumayo in 1913, Julio César Arana, the driving force of the rubber company, was asked to clarify what he meant when he stated that the Indians had resisted the establishment of civilization in their districts, that they had been resisting for many years, and had practiced cannibalism. "What I mean by that," he replied, "is that they did not admit of exchange, or anybody to do business with them – Whites, for example."[45]

Jungle and Savagery

There is a problem that I have only hinted at in all of the accounts of the atrocities of the Putumayo rubber boom. While the immensity of the cruelty is beyond question, most of the evidence comes through stories. The meticulous historian would seize upon this fact as a challenge to winnow out truth from exaggeration or understatement. But the more basic implication, it seems to me, is that *the narratives are in themselves evidence of the process whereby a culture of terror was created and sustained.*

Two interlacing motifs stand out: the horrors of the jungle, and the horrors of savagery. All the facts are bent through the prism formed by these motifs, which, in keeping with Conrad's theory of art, mediate effective truth not so much through the dissemination of information as through the appeal of temperaments through sensory impressions. Here the European and colonist image of the primeval jungle with its vines and rubber trees and domination of man's domination stands forth as the colonially apt metaphor of the great space of terror and deep cruelties. (Europe – late nineteenth century, penetrating the ancient forests of the tropics.) Carlos Fuentes asserts that Latin American literature is woven between the poles formed by nature and the dictator, in which the destructiveness of the former serves to reflect even more destructive social relations. A Colombian author, José Eustacio Rivera writes in the 1920s as a debt-entrapped peon in the Putumayo:

I have been a *cauchero* [rubber gatherer] and I will always be a *cauchero*. I live in the slimy mire in the solitude of the forests with my gang of malarial men, piercing the bark of trees whose blood runs white, like that of gods. . . . I have been and always will be a *cauchero*. And what my hand inflicts on the trees, it can also inflict on men.[46]

In *Heart of Darkness*, the narrator, Marlow, sits back, like a Buddha, introducing his yarn, prefiguring the late nineteenth-century colonial exploitation of the Congo by evoking a soldier of imperial Rome, moving through the marshes of the Thames.

Land in a swamp, march through the woods, and in some inland post feel the savagery, the utter savagery, had closed around him, – all that mysterious life of the wilderness that stirs in the forest, in the jungles, in the hearts of wild men. There's no initiation either into such mysteries. He has to live in the midst of the incomprehensible, which is also detestable. And it has a fascination, too, that goes to work upon him. The fascination of the abomination – you know, imagine the growing regrets, the longing to escape, the powerless disgust, the surrender, the hate.

The Capuchin father, Gaspar de Pinell, who made a legendary *excursión apostólica* to the Huitotos and other savage tribes in the Putumayo forests in the late 1920s, records how his white guide, a man of much experience, sickened and sought cure from a Huitoto shaman (whom the padre calls a witch) rather than from the pharmacy of the whites. He died shortly thereafter, providing Father Pinell with the moral dilemma of the colonist: "This shows," he wrote, "that it is more likely that the civilized man will become a savage on mixing with Indians, than the Indians are likely to become civilized through the actions of the civilized."[47] And with a torrent of phenomenological virtuosity, his colleague, Father Francisco de Vilanova, addresses the same vexing problem, only here it is the Putumayo jungle which constitutes the great figure of savagery. In a book describing Capuchin endeavors among the Huitotos from the 1920s on, we read:

It is almost something unbelievable to those who do not know the jungle. It is an irrational fact that enslaves those who go there. It is a whirlwind of savage passions that dominates the civilized person who has too much confidence in himself. It is a degeneration of the spirit in a drunkenness of improbable but real circumstances. The rational and civilized man loses respect for himself and his domestic place. He throws his heritage into the mire from where who knows when it will be retrieved. One's heart fills with morbidity and the sentiment of savagery. It becomes insensible to the most pure and great things of humanity. Even cultivated spirits, finely formed and well educated, have succumbed.[48]

But of course it is not the jungle but the sentiments men project into it that is decisive in filling their hearts with savagery. And what the jungle can accomplish, so much more can its native inhabitants, the wild Indians, like those tortured into gathering rubber. It must not be overlooked that the colonially constructed image of the wild Indian here at stake was a powerfully ambiguous image, a seesawing, bifocalized, and hazy composite of the animal and the human. In their human or human-like form, the wild Indians could all the better reflect back to the colonists the vast and baroque projections of human wildness that the colonists needed to establish their reality as civilized (not to mention business-like) people. And it was only because the wild Indians were human that they were able to serve as labor – and as subjects of torture. For it is not the victim as animal that gratifies the torturer, but the fact that the victim is human, thus enabling the torturer to become the savage.

How Savage were the Huitotos?

The savagery of the wild Indians occupied a key role in the propaganda of the rubber company. Hardenburg writes that the Huitotos "are hospitable to a marked degree," and that while the Church improves their morals, in the company's domain, priests have been carefully excluded. "Indeed," he continues, "in order to frighten people and thus prevent them from entering the region, the company has circulated the most blood curdling reports of the ferocity and cannibalism of these helpless Indians, whom travellers such as myself have found to be timid, peaceful, mild, industrious and humble."[49] Father Pinell has published a document from Peru describing a film commissioned by Arana's company in 1917. Shown in the cinemas of Lima, it portrayed the civilizing effect of the company on "these savage regions that as recently as 25 years ago were peopled entirely by cannibals. Owing to the energy of this tireless struggler [Arana] they have been converted into useful elements of labor."[50]

Propaganda usually flowers only where the soil has been long and well prepared, and it seems to me that Arana's was no exception since the mythology of savagery dates from times long before his. Yet, the passions unleashed by the rubber boom invigorated this mythology with a seductive power. Before probing further into the ways the rubber company acquired the savagery it imputed to the Indians, it is necessary to pause and examine the colonists' mythology and folklore concerning the Upper Amazon forest people.

Time and again Casement tells us that the Huitotos and all Upper Amazon Indians were gentle and docile. He downplays their cannibalism, says that they were thoughtless rather than cruel, and regards their docility as a *natural* and remarkable characteristic. This helps him to explain the ease with which they were conquered and forced to gather rubber.

An Indian would promise anything for a gun, or for some of the other tempting things offered as inducements to him to work rubber. Many Indians submitted to the alluring offer only to find that once in the "conquistadores'" books they had lost all liberty, and were reduced to unending demands for more rubber and varied tasks. A cacique or "capitán" might be bought over to dispose of the labor of his clan, and as the cacique's influence was very great and the natural docility of the Indian a remarkable characteristic of Upper Amazon tribes, the work of conquering a primitive people and reducing them to a continual strain of rubber-finding was less difficult than might at first be supposed.[51]

Yet, on the other hand, such docility makes the violence of the whites even harder to understand.

Many points can be contested in Casement's rendering here, such as his assertion of the degree of chiefly power and the deceptive simplicity he evokes with regard to the issue of toughness and tenderness in a society so foreign to his own. It should also not be forgotten that the story he wanted to tell was one of innocent and gentle child-like Indians brutalized by the rubber company, and this controlling image gives his report considerable rhetorical power. In addition there was his tendency to equate the sufferings of the Irish with those of the Indians and see in both of their preimperialist histories a culture more humane than that of their civilizing overlords. (Conrad never indulged in that kind of transference.) Still another factor blended with the foregoing, and that was the innate tenderness of Casement's character and his ability to draw that quality out of others, as testified by numerous people. It is this aspect of his homosexuality, and not sexual lust, which should be dwelt on here, as shown, for example, in this note in his Putumayo diary:

... floggings and putting in guns and floggings with machetes across the back .... I bathed in the river, delightful, and Andokes [Indians] came down and caught butterflies for Barnes and I. Then a captain [Indian chief] embraced us laying his head down against our breasts. I never saw so touching a thing, poor soul, he felt we were their friends.[52]

Alfred Simson, an Englishman who traveled the Putumayo and Napo rivers in the 1880s and spent far more time there than Casement, conveys a picture quite different from Casement's. An example is his description of the Zaparos, who, like the Huitotos, were considered by the whites to be wild Indians. Noting that they raided other groups and abducted their children for sale to white traders, Simson goes on to state:

When unprovoked they are, like really wild Indians, very shy and retiring, but are perfectly fearless, and will suffer no one, either whites or others, to employ force with them. They can only be managed by tact, good treatment, and sometimes simple reasoning: otherwise resenting ill-treatment or an attempt to resort to blows, [they react] with the worst of violence . . . . At all times they are changeable and unreliable, betraying under different circumstances, and often apparently under the same, in common with so many of their class, all the most opposite traits of character, excepting perhaps servility – a true characteristic of the old world – and stinginess, which I have never observed in them. The absence of servility is typical of all the independent Indians of Ecuador.[53]

And he observes that "they also gain great enjoyment from the destruction of life. They are always ready to kill animals or people, and they delight in it."[54]

Simson was employed on the first steam launch to ascend the Putumayo, that of Rafael Reyes, later a president of Colombia. Hence he witnessed the opening of the region to modern commerce, and was in a special position to observe the institutionalization of ideologies concerning race and class. Not only does he present a contrary and more complex estimate of Indian toughness than does Casement: he also provides the clue and ethnographic motif necessary to understand why such contrary images coexist and flourish, how Indian images of wildness come halfway, as it were, to meet and merge with white colonial images of savagery, and, finally, how such imagery functions in the creation of terror.

It is first necessary to observe that the inhabitants of the Putumayo were, according to Joaquin Rocha at the turn of the century, divided into two great classes of social types: whites and savage Indians. The category, whites (also referred to as "rationals," Christians, and "civilized"), included not only people phenotypically white, but also mestizos, negros, mulattos, Zambos, and Indians "of those groups incorporated into civilization since the time of the Spanish conquest."[55] Simson takes us further into this classification, and although his remarks here pertain to the *montaña* region at the headwaters of the rivers, they seem to me generally applicable to the middle reaches of the Putumayo as well, and are certainly relevant to the understanding of colonist culture.

Simson notes that what he calls the "pure Indians of the forest" are divided, by whites and Spanish-speaking Indians, into two classes; Indians (*Indios*) and heathens (*infieles*). The *Indios* are Quichua-speaking, salt-eating, semi-Christians, while the heathens, also known as *aucas*, speak distinct languages, eat salt rarely, and know nothing of baptism or of the Catholic Church.[56] In passing it should be observed that today, if not in times long past, the term *auca* also connotes cannibals who roam the forest naked, are without marriage rules, and practice incest.

Simson also states that the term *auca* as commonly understood bears "the full meaning it did anciently in Peru under the Incas. It includes the sense of infidel, traitor, barbarian, and is often applied in a malignant sense." In Peru it was used, he says, "to designate those who rebelled against their king and incarnation of their deity, the Inca."[57] Whether or not this assertion is historically accurate (as it certainly seems to be) is somewhat beside the point, for its importance lies in its character as a myth informing everyday life at the time of the rubber boom.

Simson's second major point about *aucas* concerns their animal-like qualities, so pronounced, he says, that they partake of the occult and spiritual. With reference to the Zaparos, for example, he writes that their perceptions of eye and ear are perfectly marvelous, and surpass those of the non-*auca* Indians considerably. Their knowledge of the forest is so perfect that they often travel at night in unknown parts. They are great fighters, and can detect sounds and footmarks where white men perceive nothing. On the trail of an animal, they suddenly swerve, then change again as if following the scent of their prey. Their motions are cat-like and they move unscathed through the entangled underwood and thorns. To communicate with each other, they generally imitate the whistle of the toucan or partridge – and all this is in marked contrast to non-*aucas* or civilized Indians, "who stand in fear and respect of them, but despise or affect to despise them as infidels behind their backs."[58]

I should add that the highland Indian shaman with whom I work in the Colombian Andes which overlook the Putumayo jungles regards the jungle shamans below as *aucas*, as animal/spirit hybrids possessing great magic. He singles out the Huitotos as a spiritual force with whom he makes a mystical pact in incantations and songs, with or without hallucinogens, to assure the success of his own magical battles with evil.

It is crucial to grasp the dialectic of sentiments involved here by the appellation *auca*, a dialectic enshrouded in magic and composed of both fear and contempt – identical to the mysticism, hatred, and awe projected onto the Zionist socialist Timerman in the torture chambers of the military. In the case of the *aucas*, this projection is inseparable from the imputation of their resistance to sacred imperial authority and the further imputation of magical power possessed by lowland forest dwellers as a class and by their oracles, seers, and healers – their shamans – in particular. Moreover, this indigenous, and what may well be a pre-Colombian, construction blends with the medieval European mythology of the Wild Man brought to the Andes and the Amazon by the Spaniards and Portuguese. Today, in the upper reaches of the Putumayo with which I am acquainted, the mythology of *auca* and Wild Man underlies the resort to Indian shamans by white and black colonists who seek cure from sorcery and hard times, while these very same colonists despise Indians as savages.[59] In the rubber boom, with its desperate need for Indian labor, the same mythology nourished incalculable cruelty and paranoia on the part of the whites. It is to this mythic endowment inherited by world capitalism in the jungles of the Putumayo that we need to pay attention if we are to understand the irrational "excesses" of the terror and torture depicted by Casement.

Fear of Indian Rebellion

Casement mentions the possibility that, in addition to their drive for profit, the whites' fear of Indian rebellion impelled them toward viciousness. But in keeping with his stress on Indian docility, he gives four reasons why Indian rebellion was unlikely. Indian communities were disunited long before the advent of the rubber boom, while the whites were armed and well organized. The Indians were poorly armed and their blowpipes, bows, and lances had been confiscated. Most important in his opinion was the fact that the elders had been systematically murdered by the company for the crime of giving "bad advice."[60]

Rocha, who was in the area some seven years before Casement, thought differently. He claims that the whites feared the consequences of the Indians' hatred and that this fear was central to their policies and thought. "Life for the Whites in the land of the Huitotos," he declares, "hangs by a thread." Small uprisings were common, and he provides an account of one of these.

In 1903 the Colombian Emilio Gutiérrez navigated up the Caquetá from Brazil searching for Indians to use to establish a rubber station. Reaching the area whose conquest he desired, he sent the bulk of his men back to carry in merchandise, and he and three others remained. While asleep, Gutiérrez and the companions were killed by wild Indians. Hearing the news, other whites prepared to retaliate when news reached them that thirty of Gutiérrez's civilized Indian work force had also been killed, all at the same time yet in different parts of the jungle. Indians working for whites were set in pursuit of the rebels; some were caught and killed outright, some were taken as prisoners for the whites, and the majority escaped. A few were captured and eaten by the Indian mercenaries – so the tale goes.[61]

In 1910 Casement heard the same episode from a Peruvian, who introduced his story by saying that the methods used by Colombian conquerors were very bad. In this version, the rebel Indians decapitated Gutiérrez together with an unstated number of other whites and exposed their skulls on the walls of their "drum house," keeping the limbless bodies in water for as long as possible to show them off to other Indians. Casement's informant said he had found the bodies of twelve others tied to stakes, assuring Casement that the reason they had not been eaten was that Indians "had a repugnance to eating white men, whom they hated too much." Terrible reprisals subsequently fell upon the Indians, notes Casement.[62]

Considered separately, and especially in relation to Rocha's version, this account of Casement's establishes the point that the white fear of Indian rebellion was not unjustified, but that, in addition, such rebellion was perceived in a mythic and colonially paranoid vision in which the image of dismemberment and cannibalism glowed vividly.

Fear of Cannibalism

Cannibalism acquired great ideological potency for the colonists from the beginning of the European conquest of the New World. The figure of the cannibal was elaborated and used for many sorts of ends, responding as it did to some of the most powerful symbolic forces known to humankind. It could be used to justify enslavement and as such was apparently important in the early economy of Brazil,[63] thereby affecting even the headwaters of the Amazon such as the Putumayo where cannibalism was kept luridly alive in the imagination of the whites down to the era of the rubber boom.

Rocha provides many examples. He signals his arrival at Huitoto territory writing of "this singular land of the cannibals, the land of the Huitotos conquered by a dozen valiant Colombians repeating the heroism of their Spanish ancestors."[64] The rubber traders, he emphatically asserts, have tried to stamp out cannibalism with severe punishments. Yet cannibalism is an addiction. The Huitotos think they can deceive the whites about this, but "they succumb to the satisfaction of their beastly appetites."[65] The most notorious of the modern *conquistadores*, the Colombian Crisóstomo Hernandez (a Colombian highlands mulatto who had fled the police and sought refuge in the jungle), had, so Rocha was told, killed all the children, women, and men of an Indian long house because they practiced cannibalism – a surprising story given the need for labor, yet typical of white folk tales in the Putumayo.[66]

Don Crisóstomo was the hero of another legendary story as well, one which makes the point that although Indian customs could conflict with those of whites, as, for example, in their "misunderstandings" over the value of money and of work, there were nevertheless ritual features of Indian culture which whites could harness to the needs of the rubber company. The practice of sometimes delivering rubber in conjunction with a great dance as a prelude to a sort of gift-giving exchange, as reported by Gridilla and Rocha, has been mentioned. Even more interesting is the rite the whites called *chupe del tabaco*, or tobacco-sucking, by adult Indian men during most if not all ritual occasions, a rite which perhaps fascinated the whites even more than it did the Indians.

Seated in a circle, usually at night, with the women and children set back in their hammocks but within earshot, the men took turns to place a finger in a thick concoction of cooked tobacco juice and then sucked it. Hardenburg reports that this ceremony was indispensable to any fiesta or to solemnize any agreement or contract. These were times when the men in general and the chief in particular held forth with great oratory lasting perhaps the entire night. "This is the Huitoto's solemn oath," writes Hardenburg, "and is never said to be broken. Whenever the whites wish to enter into any important agreement with the Indians, they always insist upon this ceremony being performed."[67] Casement says the same, yet goes on to quote from a French explorer, Eugenio Robuchon, under whose name it was written that this rite was one "in which the Indians recall their lost liberty and their actual sufferings, and formulate terrible vows of vengeance against the whites."[68]

Rocha was told that Crisóstomo Hernandez was a marvelously skilled orator, taking his place as a *capitán* or *capitán general* among the circle of Indian men. Gathering with a large assembly of chiefs around the tobacco pot, don Crisóstomo would orate in Huitoto language and style from eight in the evening till four in the morning, with such power of seduction that the chiefs unanimously adopted his proposals. This, says Rocha, was before he reigned through terror and military might; his dominion came to rest on force of arms, yet it was through oratory that he initiated his conquest, "because for the Huitotos, he was their king and god."[69]

The story which most impressed Rocha was the one about the Huitoto rite of judicial murder, or capital punishment. One can easily imagine the chords of exotic terror it provoked among the colonists and employees of the rubber company listening to it in the chit-chat of a jungle night.

All the individuals of the nation that has captured the prisoner retire to an area of the bush to which women are absolutely prohibited, except for one who acts a special role. Children are rigorously excluded also. In the center, a pot of cooked tobacco juice is placed for the pleasure of the men, and in a corner seated on a little bench and firmly bound is the captive.

Clasping each other's arms, the savages form a long line, and to the sound of drum beats advance dancing very close to the victim. They retreat and advance many times, with individuals separating to drink from the pot of tobacco. Then the drum stops for the dancing cannibals, and so that the unfortunate victim can see how much he is going to lose by dying, the most beautiful girl of the tribe enters, regally attired with the most varied and brilliant feathers of the birds of these woods. The drum starts again, and the beautiful girl dances alone in front of and almost touching him. She twists and advances, showering him with passionate looks and gestures of love, turning around and repeating this three or four times. She then leaves, terminating the second act of this solemn occasion. The third follows with the same men's dance as before, except that each time the line of dancers approaches the prisoner, one of the men detaches himself and declaims something like this: "Remember when your people killed Jatijiko, man of our nation whom you couldn't take prisoner because he knew how to die before allowing himself to be dragged in front of your people? We are going to take vengeance of his death in you, you coward, that doesn't know how to die in battle like he did." Or else: "Remember when you and your people surprised my sister Jifisino bathing, captured her and while alive made a party of her flesh and tormented her until her last breath? Do you remember? Now you god-cursed man we are going to devour you alive and you won't die until all traces of your bloody flesh have disappeared from around our mouths."

Following this is the fourth and last act of the terrifying tragedy. One by one the dancers come forward and with his knife each one cuts a slice of meat off the prisoner, which they eat half roasted to the sound of his death rattle. When he eventually dies, they finish cutting him up and continue roasting and cooking his flesh, eating him to the last little bit.[70]

Narrative Mediation: Epistemic Murk

It seems to me that stories like these were the groundwork indispensable to the formation and flowering of the colonial imagination during the Putumayo rubber boom. "Their imagination was diseased," wrote the Peruvian judge Rómulo Paredes in 1911, referring to the rubber-station managers, "and they saw everywhere attacks by Indians, conspiracies, uprisings, treachery etc.; and in order to save themselves from these fancied perils . . . they killed, and killed without compassion."[71] Far from being trivial daydreams indulged in after work was over, these stories and the imagination they sustained were a potent political force without which the work of conquest and of supervising rubber gathering could not have been accomplished. What is essential to understand is the way in which these stories functioned to create, through magical realism, a culture of terror dominating both whites and Indians.

The importance of this fabulous work extends beyond the epic and grotesque quality of its content. The truly crucial feature lies in creating an uncertain reality out of fiction, a nightmarish reality in which the unstable interplay of truth and illusion becomes a social force of horrendous and phantasmic dimensions. To an important extent all societies live by fictions taken as reality. What distinguishes cultures of terror is that the epistemological, ontological, and otherwise purely philosophical problem of reality-and-illusion, certainty-and-doubt, becomes infinitely more than a "merely" philosophical problem. It becomes a high-powered tool for domination and a principal medium of political practice. And in the Putumayo rubber boom this medium of epistemic and ontological murk was most keenly figured and objectified as the space of death.

In his report, Paredes tells us that the rubber-station managers lived obsessed with death. They saw danger everywhere and thought solely of the fact that they were surrounded by vipers, tigers, and cannibals. It is these ideas of death, he writes, which constantly struck their imaginations, making them terrified and capable of any act. Like children who read the *Arabian Nights*, he goes on to say, they had nightmares of witches, evil spirits, death, treason, and blood. The only way they could live in such a terrifying world, he observes, was by themselves inspiring terror.[72]

Sociological and Mythic Mediation: The *Muchachos*

If it was the telling of tales which mediated inspiration of the terror, then it behooves us to inquire a little into the sociological agency which mediated this mediation, namely, the corps of Indian guards trained by the company and known as the *muchachos*. For in Rómulo Paredes' words, they were "constantly devising executions and continually revealing meetings of Indians 'licking tobacco' – which meant an oath to kill white men – imaginary uprisings which never existed, and other similar crimes."[73]

Mediating as civilized or rational Indians between the savages of the forest and the whites of the rubber camps, the *muchachos* personified all the critical distinctions in the class and caste system of rubber production. Cut off from their own kind, whom they persecuted and betrayed and in whom they inspired envy and hatred, and now classified as civilized yet dependent on whites for food, arms, and goods, the *muchachos* wrought to perfection all that was horrifying in the colonial mythology of savagery – because they occupied the perfect sociological and mythic space to do so. Not only did they create fictions stoking the fires of white paranoia, they embodied the brutality which the whites feared, created, and tried to harness to their own ends. In a very literal sense, the *muchachos* traded their identity as savages for their new social status as civilized Indians and guards. As Paredes notes, they placed at the disposal of the whites "their special instincts, such as sense of direction, scent, their sobriety, and their knowledge of the forest."[74] Just as they bought rubber from the wild Indians of the forest, so the whites also bought the *auca*-like savage instincts of the Indian *muchachos*.

Yet, unlike rubber, these savage instincts were manufactured largely in the imaginations of the whites. All the *muchachos* had to do in order to receive their rewards was to objectify and through words reflect back to the whites the phantoms that populated colonist culture. Given the centuries of colonial mythology concerning the *auca* and the Wild Man, and given the implosion of this mythology in the contradictory social being of the *muchachos*, the task was an easy one. The *muchachos*' stories were, in fact, stories within a much older story encompassing the *muchachos* as objects of a colonialist discourse rather than as its authors.

The trading system of debt-peonage established by the Putumayo rubber boom was thus more than a trade in white goods for rubber gathered by the Indians. It was also a trade in terrifying mythologies and fictional realities, pivoted on the mediation of the *muchachos*, whose storytelling bartered betrayal of Indian realities for the confirmation of colonial fantasies.

The Colonial Mirror

I began this essay stating that my concern was with the mediation of the culture of terror through narration, and with the problems of writing against terror. In part my concern stemmed from my problems in evaluating and interpreting the "facts" constituted in the various accounts of the Putumayo atrocities. This problem of interpretation grew ever larger, eventually bursting into the realization that that problem is precisely what is central to the culture of terror – not only making effective talking and writing against terror extremely difficult, but, even more to the point, making the terrible reality of the death squads, disappearances, and torture all the more effectively crippling of people's capacity to resist.

While much attention is given to "ideology" in the social sciences, virtually none as far as I know is given to the fact that people delineate their world, including its large as well as its micro-scale politics, in stories and story-like creations and very rarely, if ever, in ideologies (as customarily defined). Surely it is in the coils of rumor, gossip, story, and chit-chat where ideology and ideas become emotionally powerful and enter into active social circulation and meaningful existence. So it was with the Putumayo terror, from the accounts of which it seems clear that the colonists and rubber company employees not only feared but also themselves created through narration fearful and confusing images of savagery – images which bound colonial society together through the epistemic murk of the space of death. The systems of torture they devised to secure rubber mirrored the horror of the savagery they so feared, condemned – and fictionalized. Moreover, when we consider the task of creating counterrepresentations and counterdiscourses, we must take stock of the way that most if not all the narratives reproduced by Hardenburg and Casement, referring to and critical of the atrocities, were similarly fictionalized, drawing upon the same historically molded source that men succumbed to when torturing Indians.

Torture and terror in the Putumayo were motivated by the need for cheap labor. But labor *per se* – labor as a commodity – did not exist in the jungles of the Caraparaná and Igaraparaná affluents of the Putumayo. What existed was not a market for labor but a society and culture of human beings whom the colonists called Indians, irrationals, and savages, with their very specific historical trajectory, form of life, and modes of exchange. In the blundering colonial attempt to dovetail forcibly the capitalist commodity-structure to one or the other of the possibilities for rubber gathering offered by these modes of exchange, torture, as Casement alludes, took on a life of its own: "Just as the appetite comes in the eating so each crime led on to fresh crimes."[75] To this we should add that, step by step, terror and torture became *the* form of life for some fifteen years, an organized culture with its systematized rules, imagery, procedures, and meanings involved in spectacles and rituals that sustained the precarious solidarity of the rubber company employees as well as beating out through the body of the tortured some sort of canonical truth about Civilization and Business.

It was not commodity fetishism but debt fetishism drenched in the fictive reality of the debt-peonage institution, with its enforced "advances" and theater-like farce of business exchanges, that exercised the decisive force in the creation of terror, transforming torture from the status of a means to that of the mode if not, finally, the very aim of production.

From the reports of both Timerman and Casement it is obvious that torture and institutionalized terror is like a ritual art form, and that far from being spontaneous, *sui generis*, and an abandonment of what are often called "the values of civilization," such rites have a deep history deriving power and meaning from those values.

What demands further analysis here is the mimesis between the savagery attributed to the Indians by the colonists and the savagery perpetrated by the colonists in the name of what Julio César Arana called civilization.[76]

This reciprocating yet distorted mimesis has been and continues to be of great importance in the construction of colonial culture – *the colonial mirror* which reflects back onto the colonists the barbarity of their own social relations, but as imputed to the savage or evil figures they wish to colonize. It is highlighted in the Putumayo in the colonist lore as related, for instance, through Joaquin Rocha's lurid tale of Huitoto cannibalism. And what is put into discourse through the artful story telling of the colonists is the same as what they practiced on the bodies of Indians.[77]

Tenaciously embedded in this artful practice is a vast and mystifying Western history and iconography of evil in the imagery of the inferno and the savage – wedded to and inseparable from paradise, utopia, and the good. It is to the subversion of that apocalyptic dialectic that all of us would be advised to bend our counterdiscursive efforts, in a quite different poetics of good-and-evil whose cathartic force lies not with cataclysmic resolution of contradictions but with their disruption.

Post-Enlightenment European culture makes it difficult if not impossible to penetrate the hallucinatory veil of the heart of darkness without either succumbing to its hallucinatory quality or losing that quality. Fascist poetics succeed where liberal rationalism self-destructs. But what might point a way out of this impasse is precisely what is so painfully absent from all the Putumayo accounts, namely, the narrative and narrative mode of the Indians which does desensationalize terror so that the histrionic stress on the mysterious side of the mysterious (to adopt Benjamin's formula) is indeed denied by an optic which perceives the everyday as impenetrable, the impenetrable as everyday. At least this is the poetics of the sorcery and shamanism I know about in the upper reaches of the Putumayo, but that is another history for another time, not only of terror but of healing as well.

NOTES

1 Jacobo Timerman, *Prisoner without a Name, Cell without a Number* (New York: Vintage Books, 1982), p. 164.
2 Timerman, *Prisoner*, p. 28.
3 Ibid., p. 111.
4 Gerardo Reichel-Dolmatoff, *Amazonian Cosmos: The Sexual and Religious Symbolism of the Tukano Indians* (Chicago: University of Chicago Press, 1971).
5 Walter Benjamin, "Surrealism: The Last Snapshot of the European Intelligentsia." In the collection of his essays entitled *Reflections,* trans. Edmund Jephcott, ed. and intro. Peter Demetz. (New York and London: Harcourt Brace Jovanovich, 1978), pp. 189–90.
6 Timerman, *Prisoner*, p. 52.
7 Michel Foucault, "Truth and Power." In *Power/Knowledge*, ed. Colin Gordon (New York: Pantheon, 1980), p. 118.
8 Timerman, *Prisoner*, pp. 62, 66.
9 Frederick R. Karl, *Joseph Conrad: The Three Lives* (New York: Farrar, Straus, and Giroux, 1979), p. 286.

10   Paul Ricoeur, *Freud and Philosophy: An Essay on Interpretation* (New Haven, CT, and London: Yale University Press, 1970).

11   Ian Watt, *Conrad: In the Nineteenth Century* (Berkeley and Los Angeles: University of California Press, 1979), p. 161.

12   Brian Inglis, *Roger Casement* (London: Hodder Paperbacks, 1974), p. 32. The text of Conrad's letter to Cunninghame Graham reads: "I can assure you that he [Casement] is a limpid personality. There is a touch of the conquistador in him too; for I've seen him start off into an unspeakable wilderness swinging a crook-handled stick for all weapons, with two bulldogs, Paddy (white) and Biddy (brindle) at his heels, and a Loanda boy carrying a bundle for all company. A few months afterwards it so happened that I saw him come out again, a little leaner, a little browner, with his stick, dogs and Loanda boy, and quietly serene as though he had been for a stroll in a park." Inglis comments: "Time had embroidered Conrad's recollection. Casement himself described what the construction work entailed, in a letter to his young cousin [and] the countryside through which the railway was being constructed, he told her, consisted of grassy plains covered with scrub – inhospitable, but hardly unspeakable." The Jorge Borges reference is "About the Purple Land." In *Borges: A Reader*, ed. Emir Rodriguez Monegal and A. Reid (New York: Dutton, 1981), pp. 136–9.

13   Karl, *Joseph Conrad*, p. 289n. The full text of Conrad's letter to Cunninghame Graham may be found in C. T. Watts, *Joseph Conrad's Letters to R. B. Cunninghame Graham* (Cambridge: Cambridge University Press, 1969), pp. 148–52. Also see *Joseph Conrad: Congo Diary and Other Uncollected Pieces*, ed. Zdzislaw Najder (Garden City, NY: Doubleday, 1978), p. 7.

14   Inglis, *Roger Casement*, p. 46.

15   Ibid., p. 131.

16   Ibid., p. 214.

17   Ibid., p. 234.

18   Some authorities glean Casement's report and state the figure of 30,000 deaths from 1900 to 1912 as a fact, while others, who had some knowledge of the area and its history, either present different figures (a wide range) or state that it is impossible to give any figure because census-taking was impossibly difficult. Furthermore, how much of the population decrease was due to disease (especially smallpox), and how much to torture or flight, is a very vexed question. Similarly, the number of Huitotos living in the Igaraparaná and Caraparaná region in the late nineteenth century is variously stated as around 50,000 all the way up to a quarter of a million (!), the latter estimate being that of Joaquin Rocha, *Memorandum de un viaje* (Bogotá: Editorial El Mercurio, 1905), p. 138. In any event, the number of Indians in the area seems to have been extremely large by Upper Amazon standards and an important cause for the establishment of rubber trading there. It is worth nothing that Casement in his report was extremely cautious in presenting figures on population and population decrease. He gives details of the problem in his evidence presented to the British Parliamentary Select Committee on Putumayo (*House of Commons Sessional Papers*, 1913, vol. 14, p. 30, #707). Father Gaspar de Pinell, *Un viaje por el Putumayo el Amazonas* (Bogotá: Imprenta Nacional, 1924), pp. 38–9, presents an excellent discussion, as does his *Excursión apostólica por los ríos Putumayo, San Miguel de Sucumbios, Cuyabueno, Caquetá, y Caguán* (Bogotá: Imprenta Nacional, 1929 (also dated 1928)), pp. 227–35.

19   Walter Hardenburg, *The Putumayo: The Devil's Paradise. Travels in the Peruvian Amazon Region and an Account of the Atrocities Committed upon the Indians Therein* (London: T. Fisher Unwin, 1912), p. 214. The first publication of Hardenburg's revelations, in the magazine *Truth* in 1909, began with this article from the Iquitos newspaper,

La Sanción. These articles, and probably the later book, were possibly ghostwritten by Sidney Paternoster, assistant editor of *Truth*.

20 Hardenburg, *Putumayo*, p. 258.

21 Ibid., pp. 260, 259.

22 Ibid., p. 236. Also cited by Casement in his Putumayo report to Sir Edward Grey. There Casement declares that this description was repeated to him "again and again . . . by men who had been employed in this work." Roger Casement, "Correspondence respecting the Treatment of British Colonial Subjects and Native Indians employed in the Collection of Rubber in the Putumayo District," *House of Commons Sessional Papers*, 14 February 1912 to 7 March 1913, vol. 68 (hereafter cited as Casement, *Putumayo Report*), p. 35.

23 Casement, *Putumayo Report*, p. 17.

24 Ibid., p. 34.

25 Ibid., pp. 33, 34.

26 Ibid., p. 37.

27 Ibid., p. 39.

28 Ibid., p. 37.

29 Ibid., p. 39.

30 Ibid., p. 42.

31 Ibid., p. 31. From various estimates it appears that the ratio of armed supervisors to wild Indians gathering rubber was somewhere between 1:16 and 1:50. Of these armed supervisors, the *muchachos* outnumbered the whites by around 2:1. See Howard Wolf and Ralph Wolf, *Rubber: A Story of Glory and Greed* (New York: Covici, Friede, 1936), p. 88; US Consul Charles C. Eberhardt, *Slavery in Peru*, 7 February 1913, report prepared for US House of Representatives, 62d Cong., 3d Sess., 1912, H. Doc. 1366, p. 112; Roger Casement, British Parliamentary Select Committee on Putumayo, *House of Commons Sessional Papers*, 1913, vol. 14, p. xi; Casement, *Putumayo Report*, p. 33.

32 Casement, *Putumayo Report*, p. 33.

33 Ibid., pp. 44–5.

34 Ibid., p. 55.

35 Inglis, *Roger Casement*, p. 29.

36 Rocha, *Memorandum de un viaje*, pp. 123–4, asserts that because the Indians are "naturally loafers" they postpone paying off their advances from the rubber traders, thus compelling the traders to use physical violence. Eberhardt, *Slavery in Peru*, p. 110, writes that "the Indian enters the employ of some rubber gatherer, often willingly, though not infrequently by force, and immediately becomes indebted to him for food etc . . . . However, the scarcity of labor and the ease with which the Indians can usually escape and live on the natural products of the forest oblige the owners to treat them with some consideration. The Indians realize this and their work is not at all satisfactory, judging from our standards. This was particularly noticeable during a recent visit I made to a mill where 'cachassa' or aguadiente is extracted from cane. The men seemed to work when and how they chose, requiring a liberal amount of the liquor each day (of which they are all particularly fond), and if this is not forthcoming or they are treated harshly in any way they run to the forests. The employer has the law on his side, and if he can find the runaway he is at liberty to bring him back; but the time lost and the almost useless task of trying to track the Indian through the dense forests and small streams makes it far more practical that the servant be treated with consideration in the first place."

37 Casement, British Parliamentary Select Committee on Putumayo, *House of Commons Sessional Papers*, 1913, vol. 14, p. 113, #2809.

38   E. D. Morel, British Parliamentary Select Committee on Putumayo, *House of Commons Sessional Papers*, 1913, vol. 14, pp. 553, 556. Also see the evidence of the British accountant, H. Parr, of the Peruvian Amazon Company, in 1909–10, at the La Chorrera station (pp. 336–48).

39   Casement, *Putumayo Report*, p. 50.

40   Rocha, *Memorandum de un viaje*, p. 75.

41   Peter Singleton-Gates and Maurice Girodias, *The Black Diaries* (New York: Grove Press, 1959), p. 261.

42   P. Alberto Gridilla, *Un año en el Putumayo* (Lima: Colección Descalzos, 1943), p. 29. Rocha's description is of a Colombian rubber trading post, and not one of Arana's; Rocha, *Memorandum de un viaje*, pp. 119–20.

43   Hardenburg, *Putumayo*, p. 218.

44   Karl Polanyi, *The Great Transformation* (Boston: Beacon Press, 1957), p. 72. Cf. Michael Taussig, *The Devil and Commodity Fetishism in South America* (Chapel Hill: University of North Carolina Press, 1980).

45   Julio César Arana, Evidence to the British Parliamentary Select Committee on Putumayo, *House of Commons Sessional Papers*, 1913, vol. 14, p. 488, # 12,222.

46   See Carlos Fuentes, *La nueva novela hispanoamericana* (Mexico, DF: Editorial Joaquin Mortiz, 1969), pp. 10–11. José Eustacio Rivera, *La vorágine* (Bogotá: Editorial Pax, 1974), pp. 277, 279.

47   Pinell, *Excursión apostólica*, p. 156.

48   P. Francisco de Vilanova, introduction to P. Francisco de Igualada, *Indios Amazonicas: Colección Misiones Capuchinas*, vol. VI (Barcelona: Imprenta Myria, 1948).

49   Hardenburg, *Putumayo*, p. 163.

50   Pinell, *Excursión apostólica*, p. 196.

51   Casement, *Putumayo Report*, pp. 27–8.

52   Singleton-Gates and Girodias, *Black Diaries*, p. 251.

53   Alfred Simson, *Travels in the Wilds of Ecuador and the Exploration of the Putumayo River* (London: Samson Low, 1886), p. 170.

54   Ibid., pp. 170–1.

55   Rocha, *Memorandum de un viaje*, p. 64.

56   Simson, *Travels*, p. 58. It is worth noting that during the seventeenth or eighteenth century missionaries worked among at least some of the Indian groups Simson designates as *auca*, and thus it is not true that they (to quote Simson), "know nothing of the Catholic Church." See P. José Chantre y Herrera, *Historia de las misiones de la Companía de Jesus en el Marañon español, 1637–1767* (Madrid: Imprenta de A. Avrial, 1901), pp. 283, 321–8, 365–9.

57   Simson, *Travels*, p. 58. This meaning of rebel against the Inca is sustained, referring to the Auracanians of Chile, in John M. Cooper, "The Auracanians," in Vol. II of *The Handbook of South American Indians*, ed. Julian H. Steward (New York: Cooper Square, 1963), p. 690. For the eastern *montaña* of the northern Andes, the term *auca* means pagan as against Christian Indians, according to Steward and Alfred Metraux, "Tribes of the Ecuadorian and Peruvian Montaña," in Vol. III of the *Handbook*, pp. 535–656, esp. p. 629 (Zaparos), p. 637 (Canelos/Napos), p. 653 (Quijos). Unlike Simson, the mere traveler, these anthropologists of the *Handbook* fail dismally to indicate the magical and mythic connotations of the term *auca*.

58   Simson, *Travels*, pp. 166, 168.

59   Michael Taussig, "Folk Healing and the Structure of Conquest." *Journal of Latin American Lore* 6:2 (1980): 217–78.

60   Casement, *Putumayo Report*, p. 45.

61   Rocha, *Memorandum de un viaje*, pp. 125–6.

62 Casement, *Putumayo Report*, p. 30. Father Pinell was told of a large uprising by rubber-working and other Indians along the Igaraparaná in 1917; the use of Peruvian troops was required to put it down. Pinell, *Un viaje*, pp. 39–40.

63 An excellent discussion of this is to be found in David Sweet, "A Rich Realm of Nature Destroyed: The Middle Amazon Valley, 1640–1750" (Ph.D. diss;, University of Wisconsin, 1975), I, pp. 113–14, 116, 120, 126, 130–1, 141, 347.

64 Rocha, *Memorandum de un viaje*, pp. 92–3.

65 Ibid., p. 118.

66 Ibid., pp. 106–7.

67 Hardenburg, *Putumayo*, p. 155. For use of coca in the *chupe del tabaco*, see Joseph F. Woodroffe, *The Upper Reaches of the Amazon* (London: Methuen, 1914), pp. 151–5. With regard to the reliability and sources of Hardenburg's statements, it is perhaps of use to cite some of the evidence he gave to the British Parliamentary Select Committee on Putumayo, *House of Commons Sessional Papers*, 1913, vol. 14. Asked what he saw himself of actual cruelties to the Indians, Hardenburg replied, "Of actual crimes being committed I did not see anything, practically; all I saw was that the Indians in [the rubber station of] El Encanto were nearly naked and very thin and cadaverous-looking; I saw several scores of them, and I saw what they were being fed on" (p. 510, #12848). His information came through accounts from other people: "Infact, I think I might say that most of the people came through others. They would say, 'I know another man who could state this and that,' and they would bring them" (p. 511, #12881). Asked if he questioned these people in detail about their statements, Hardenburg replied, "I cannot say I did much of that" (p. 511, #12882). It was, said Hardenburg, general knowledge that the atrocities were occurring. This "general knowledge" is precisely what I have been at pains to track down, not because I believe that the atrocities were less than described by the several authors upon whom I draw, but because it is this general knowledge in the shape of mythic narratives which acts as a screen and as a network of signifiers without which "the facts" would not exist. More specifically, the function of this screen of signifiers is to heighten dread and hence the controlling function of the culture of terror. Casement's evidence is altogether of another category, being more carefully gathered, cross-checked, etcetera, and as a result of it we can affirm reports, such as Hardenburg's, which are less well substantiated. Nevertheless, Casement's evidence serves not to puncture the mythic character so much as indicate its terrific reality.

68 Casement, *Putumayo Report*, p. 48. Robuchon's text appeared as a book ("Official Edition"), printed in Lima in 1907 and entitled *En el Putumayo y sus afluentes*. It was edited by Carlos Rey de Castro, a lackey of Julio César Arana's and one-time Peruvian consul in Brazil, from Robuchon's papers after his mysterious death in the Putumayo rain forest. Judging from Rey de Castro's book on the Putumayo, *Los pobladores del Putumayo* (Barcelona: Imp. Vda de Luis Tasso, 1917), and his relation to Arana, one can surmise that it would be unwise to read the Robuchon text as though it were really Robuchon's unadulterated work. The chances are that it was edited with a view to presenting a case favorable to Arana. The importance of prehistory, "ethnohistory," and Indian history in the ideological war for world opinion is well brought out by Rey de Castro's bold stroke in his *Los pobladores del Putumayo*, in which he sets out to prove that the Huitotos and adjacent Indian groups are in reality descendant from the *orejones* of Cuzco in the interior of Peru – thus supposedly strengthening the Peruvian claims over the Putumayo rubber zone and its indigenous inhabitants.

69 Rocha, *Memorandum de un viaje*, p. 111.

70 Ibid., pp. 116–17.

71 Rómulo Paredes, "Confidential Report to the Ministry of Foreign Relations, Peru," September 1911, translated in Eberhardt, *Slavery in Peru*, p. 146. Paredes's work is

explained and put into context in a mass of testimony in the book of Carlos A. Valcarcel, *El proceso del Putumayo* (Lima: Imp. Comercial de Horacio La Rosa, 1915).

72 Paredes, "Confidential Report," in Eberhardt, *Slavery in Peru*, p. 158.

73 Ibid., p. 147. I am grateful to Fred Chin and Judy Farquahar of the Department of Anthropology at the University of Chicago for impressing upon me the importance the *muchachos* as a mediating force. Then of course one should not omit the role of the blacks recruited in Barbados, mediating between the whites and the Indians. In much the same way as the British army from the mid-nineteenth century on deployed different colonial and ethnic groups so as to maximize reputations for ferocity and checking one against the other, the British and Peruvian rubber company used its "ethnic soldiers" in the Putumayo.

74 Paredes, "Confidential Report," in Eberhardt, *Slavery in Peru*, p. 147.

75 Casement, *Putumayo Report*, p. 44.

76 See pp. 174–5 above.

77 Illustrations of the way in which this following of the letter of the tale was enacted in the torture of Indians can be found in the rare instances of dialogue that Casement allows his witnesses in the section of his report given over to testimony by men recruited in Barbados, as, for example:

"And you say you saw the Indians burnt?" Consul-General Casement asked Augustus Walcott, born in the Caribbean island of Antigua but twenty three years before.
"Yes."
"Burnt alive?"
"Alive."
"How do you mean? Describe this."
"Only one I see burnt alive."
"Well, tell me about that one?"
"He had not work 'caucho,' he ran away and he kill a 'muchacho,' a boy, and they cut off his two arms and legs by the knee and they burn his body. . . ."
"Are you sure he was still alive – not dead when they threw him on the fire?"
"Yes, he did alive. I'm sure of it – I see him move – open his eyes, he screamed out. . . ."
"Was Aurelio Rodriguez [the rubber-station manager] looking on – all the time?"
"Yes, all the time."
"Giving directions?"
"Yes, Sir."
"He told them to cut off the legs and arms?"
"Yes."

There was something else the Consul-General could not understand and he called Walcott back to explain what he meant by saying, "because he told the Indians that we was Indians too, and eat those –." What he meant, Casement summarized, was that the station manager, Señor Normand, in order "to frighten the Indians told them that the negroes were cannibals, and a fierce tribe of cannibals who eat people, and that if they did not bring in rubber these black men would be sent to kill and eat them" (Casement, *Putumayo Report*, pp. 115, 118).

Another, more complicated, example follows:

"Have you ever seen Aguero kill Indians?" the Consul-General asked Evelyn Bateson, aged twenty five, born in Barbados, and working in the rubber depôt of La Chorrera.
"No, Sir; I haven't seen him kill Indians – but I have seen him send 'muchachos' to kill Indians. He has taken an Indian man and given him to the 'muchachos' to eat, and they

have a dance of it...."

"You saw the man killed?"

"Yes, Sir. They tied him to a stake and they shot him, and they cut off his head after he was shot and his feet and hands, and they carried them about the section – in the yard and they carries them up and down and singing, and they carries them to their house and dances...."

"How do you know they ate them?"

"I heard they eat them. I have not witnessed it, Sir, but I heard the manager Señor Aguero tell that they eat this man."

"The manager said all this?"

"Yes, Sir, he did." (Casement, *Putumayo Report*, p. 103)

This sort of stimulation if not creation of cannibalism by colonial pressure is also recorded in missionaries' letters concerning King Leopold's Congo Free State and the gathering of rubber there. See, for example, the account of Mr. John Harris in the work by Edmund Morel, *King Leopold's Rule in Africa* (New York: Funk and Wagnalls, 1905), pp. 437–41.

9

National Socialist Germany

Eric R. Wolf

Our third case study looks at Germany in its incarnation as the Third, National Socialist (NS) Reich, which was supposed to last a thousand years and ended in destruction and defeat only twelve years after its birth in 1933. When that Reich began, the NS anthem, the "Horst-Wessel Lied," proclaimed that "millions already look full of hope upon the swastika / the day has come for freedom and for bread." When it ended, the German historian Friedrich Meinecke characterized its trajectory from promise to ruin as "The German Catastrophe" (1950).

This inquiry focuses on the ideas that guided this paroxysm of events. The German catastrophe was of course the vortex of other catastrophes: Jewish, French, Gypsy, Polish, and Russian, to name but a few way stations on the descent into hell. What the National Socialists wrought is, without a doubt, a cause of moral outrage, but outrage is not enough. It is vital that we gain an analytic purchase on what transpired, precisely because it embodied a possibility for humankind, and what was once humanly possible can happen again. There is probably no single all-encompassing explanation for the phenomenon, but we can hope to assemble and assess some of the elements for a comprehensive understanding.

I shall argue that German National Socialism is better understood as a movement akin to the cargo cults and ghost dances studied by anthropologists than as a rational deployment of means to pragmatic ends. Its ideology projected the overthrow of the existing order and its forcible replacement by a new regime of "bread and hope." Writing in 1933 on the Hitler Movement "from the perspective of a participant," the German anthropologist Wilhelm E. Mühlmann called it a "chiliastic millenarianism" (1933: 129).[1] More generally, anthropologists have labeled such phenomena as "nativism," "millenarianism," or "chiliasm." Anthony Wallace saw all such movements as efforts at "revitalization," that is, "deliberate, organized attempts by some members of a society to construct a more satisfying culture by rapid acceptance of a pattern of multiple innovations" (1956: 265). Thinking of National Socialism as such an effort is useful because it points us toward questions about the tensions and contradictions produced by antecedent social and political arrangements in the Germanies. At the same time, it was unlike most other efforts at revitalization, in that it aimed to enhance vitality by linking it to apocalyptic visions of racial corruption and sought renewed life for the Germanic few by destruction of the many who were judged to be "subhuman." This ideological vision it pursued with singular tenacity, becoming increasingly lethal, both to its followers and to its victims. It took a world war and the death of millions to halt this homicidal project.

The quantity of material published on NS Germany is enormous and still growing. This is partly due to the fact that we are not yet sure what made the ensemble work, either as a whole or as a sum of its parts. Some believe that it will never be possible to comprehend the realities of the Third Reich; others hold – as I do – that we must make the attempt, even if our efforts prove only partial and inconclusive. It is a way of remembering; it may also help us mark out our directions in the future.

Disagreements on how to understand this virulent Reich abound. There are knowledgeable interpreters who conceptualize "the German catastrophe" as the outcome of a distinctive historical trajectory of German history, the fateful *Sonderweg*, while others see the twelve-year episode as merely a temporary deviation along an otherwise unobstructed autobahn to modernity. Scholars differ further on who supported the NS regime actively, and why, and who only pretended to support it while striving to maintain a measure of distance. Some experts emphasize the "intentions" and actions of Adolf Hitler or his intimate advisors, while others stress the interest politics pursued by particular institutions or the improvised "functional" decision making by lower-level personnel (see Mason 1981). [...]

An extended listing of writings on National Socialism is beyond the scope of this discussion and would, in any case, soon be obsolete, but I want to indicate some waymarks that have been important for this inquiry. I remain partial to the concept of the *Sonderweg*, which stresses the historical peculiarities of development in the Germanies, because I think that local, regional, and national divergences matter everywhere. The trajectory of the Germanies did not duplicate what happened in England or France, Russia or Poland, and there is much to gain from trying to define what made the Germans historically "peculiar."[2] [...]

Seeking Explanation

Attempts to explain this frenzy of brutality and killing have taken a number of forms, many of them understandably addressed to the question of who could be held responsible for initiating and executing the decisions. Posing that kind of question has yielded substantial knowledge about the identity and intentions of individual participants, as well as about means they employed, but such information does not yet address the larger question of what rendered such a genocidal project possible at all. That question requires a grasp of the conditions within which intentions and the choice of means arise and develop. It is necessary to distinguish between general and proximate conditions, always with the aim of visualizing both levels in their mutual connection.

The search for general conditions has often begun by asking how this could have happened at all within "modern civilization." Posing the question that way usually assumes that "modernity" means progress in the rule of reason and the belief that rationality will liberate humankind from ignorance and brutality. There have been critics of this perspective, of course, from the conservative Right, with its traditional distrust of reason, and from the Left, who came to fear the use of rationality in domination (Horkheimer and Adorno 1972). The sociologist Zygmunt Bauman has built on these critiques to ask what in "modernity" specifically might underwrite so massive a genocidal project (1989). He points to such features as the extensive division of labor in society, which separates people working in different domains; the awesome development of technology; the growth of large and impersonal bureaucracies, which can produce cumulative results without ever having to inquire into the reasons for what is being done; and the triumphant growth of science and the rational modes of thought associated with it. All these features were implicated, he argues, in the way the NS regime became established and then erupted into violence on a continental scale. This complex of features "was not the Holocaust's sufficient condition; it was, however, most certainly its necessary condition.... It was the rational world of modern civilization that made the Holocaust thinkable" (Bauman 1989:13).

Other discussions dovetail with Bauman's analysis. Omer Bartov has stressed the human implications of "industrial killing" in World War I, suggesting that "modern war provides the occasion and the tools, the manpower and the organization, the mentality and the imagery necessary for the perpetration of genocide" (1996:50). The wars of colonization and imperialist expansion fought by Europeans against native populations may have had a similar effect. These wars produced ideologies promising to "uplift" the colonized, but also calls to "exterminate the brutes." Germany was a latecomer in the competition for colonies overseas, but it grafted imperialist projects for seizure of *Lebensraum* upon older traditions of conquest and settlement in the Slavic East (Smith 1986: 145–52). These projects came to the fore during World War I and gained a new life through the sanguinary operations of the Freikorps afterward. The invasion of the Soviet Union took up these earlier efforts, reinforced by an ideological vision of triumph of the Germanic master race (*Herrenrasse*) over the "subhuman" Slavs.

If anti-Semitism is posed as a general condition for the Judeocide, it is important to remember that, like all general and proximate conditions, it developed and changed over time. A purely synchronic analysis would risk essentializing the set of relations it proposed as significant. It would therefore be an error to interpret the Judeocide as simply another repetition of the same anti-Semitism that has "always" characterized relations between Jews and non-Jews in Germany as elsewhere.

Bauman has made an interesting effort to show why this approach would fall short (1989: 64–5). He argues that we need to distinguish among various responses to "strangers in our midst": fear and resentment of what is different ("heterophobia"); efforts to draw boundaries between the we-group and those thought to encroach upon it ("contestant enmity"); and the outright removal of people in the offending category (which he labels "racism"). These categories will shade into each other in any particular case, and the term "racism" may be inapt. Yet Bauman's typology has the merit of seeing heterophobia, separation, removal, and annihilation as possible phases in a social process of escalation and thus raises also the question of how to account for the shifting of social gears from one level to the next.

In the Germanies heterophobia of Jews was certainly ancient and widespread, and contestant enmity was managed by segregating Jews as a pariah people within the confines of the ghettos. The rise of explicitly anti-Semitic movements in the 1870s, however, brought on a qualitative change in relations between non-Jews and Jews, because the inimical contest was now deployed in the context of a mass market of political options in which mobilized groups and parties competed for control of the political terrain. In this context anti-Semitism became politically effective only when it forged alliances with other interest groups on different grounds. Thus, in 1907, the "Ariosophist" and editor of a "Library for the Blond-Haired and Male Supremacists" Adolf Lanz (who called himself Jörg Lanz von Liebenfels) declared that being "purely anti-Semitic" was not enough: anti-Semitism had to develop a positive side in the vision of the unified *Volksgemeinschaft* of people and race.

Just as depictions of anti-Semitism have to be tied to the contexts in which it made its appearance and became politically salient, so also one must not assume that it had the same form and degree of intensity throughout a given group. Many Germans drew a distinction between individual Jews and Jews in general, as Himmler well understood when he addressed the SS Group Leaders in 1943: "'The Jewish people are to be exterminated.' ... And then they come along, the eighty million worthy Germans, and each one of them produces his decent Jew. It's clear the others are swine, but this one is a fine Jew" (in Noakes and Pridham 1995: 1199). Even within the NS leadership some were more passionately Judeophobic than others. Only one-quarter of the 581 "early" National Socialists who wrote autobiographies for sociologist Theodore Abel evidenced a virulent anti-Semitism; among the rest the intensity varied greatly, both in absolute terms and relative to other concerns (Abel 1938; Merkl 1975: 499). Rainer Baum may have been close to the mark when he concluded that for many, perhaps most, the Judeocide was "a sideshow, something that you did not bother about while engaged in the big show, securing a place for yourself in the wonderland of the New Order in Europe" (1981: 9).

Where Bauman spoke to the general conditions that might underlie the Judeocide, the social psychologist Herbert Kelman tried to identify the proximate conditions required to remove the customary restraints on open violence against individuals and groups (1973). He proposed three such conditions. The first is the authorization of such violence by legally entitled superior authorities. This condition was put in place through the encouragement of violence by the NS state and the predatory competition it sponsored. The second condition is the development and perfection of a bureaucracy able to deploy violence "by the book." As we have seen, a technology and bureaucracy of violence against Jews and others was increasingly elaborated, especially after 1939. Raul Hilberg lists twenty-seven different institutions and organizations involved in carrying out the process of destruction (1992: 21–4).

Kelman's third condition for the unleashing of violence, once authorized and routinized, is that the victims be *dehumanized*. This condition was met through the exercise of "cold" bureaucratic violence coupled with rabid propaganda. As long as Germans and Jews still lived under conditions of heterophobia or contestant enmity, members of the Volk might conceivably still experience a momentary human identification with their opposite "others." Once such others are defined as disease organisms or agents of universal entropy, the imagery of evil becomes abstract and powerful enough to justify not merely severance but destruction.

The Orchestration of Brutality

No discussion of the Judeocide would be complete without reference to its extraordinary cruelty. As Goldhagen has stressed (1996), accounts of the mass killings of Jews tend to represent most of the perpetrators as either neutral or reluctant operators of an impersonal killing machine that produced dead bodies the way an assembly line produces packaged products. Those who enjoyed showing off their power, and the "scientists" who experimented on live humans, are then explained either as exceptional sadists or as mental Svengalis who could separate the sensitive, domestic part of their selves from their murderous egos through "doubling." What these explanations miss is the extreme degree of routine lethal violence against women, children, and men.

There can be no doubt that some people found Jew-baiting pleasurable and exciting. Certainly the ways in which the regime invited and rewarded acts of institutional violence against political opponents, as well as Jews, changed what Norbert Elias called the balance between self-constraint and constraint by others. Warriors trained to be hard and pitiless took pride in directing their passions – disciplined within – against designated targets. Turning all men into soldiers, as well as demanding that women serve as handmaidens of warrior masculinity, reinforced the repression of pity, lest one appear weak to oneself or to others, while self-esteem could be enhanced by multiplying the suffering of enemies, especially those defined as "subhumans." Since ideology furnished ready-made stereotypes accounting for why things are the way they are – which were rendered immune to critical discussion – the would-be warrior could concentrate on how things were done rather than ask why, and garner recognition for his heroism.

A small-group experiment set up to simulate a prison has shown how quickly ordinary, self-controlled people can turn to destructive and humiliating behavior against stigmatized others (Haney, Banks, and Zimbardo 1973). The sociologist Philip Zimbardo divided a group of male American student volunteers randomly into prisoners, dressed in ridiculous gowns and caps, and prison guards in uniforms and dark glasses. The prisoners were then subjected to humiliating and undignified regulations. In ways quite unforeseen, these conditions gave rise to a cumulative cycle of behaviors, with the prison guards devising ever more degrading acts while the prisoners responded with acts of self-humiliation. The experiment had to be discontinued before it got out of hand, but it suggests that social conditions more than individual motivations drive behavior under such circumstances. Such sequences of behavior went on uninterruptedly as the German regime carried out its program of mass homicide in the conquered lands to the east. In this escalation of human misery NS ideology furnished ready-made formulas to define the problem to be solved and to select ways to solve it. [. . .]

Discussion

In the cases previously described, we saw that Kwakiutl ideology carried forward older cultural understandings to strengthen the chiefship against the challenges of new times, while Tenochca ideology sacralized state making by an upstart elite and provided the rationale for war and political expansion. The National Socialist ideology developed in a different structural context – that of a twentieth-century industralized nation-state in modern Europe, a region characterized by diverse national histories and wide-ranging flows of different ideas. The greater complexity of the NS case material, however, is also due to the abundance of detailed historical information. This information allows us not only to see ideology in its functional connections with particular hierarchical social orders but also to grasp the relationship between ideology and structures of power, as both were made and unmade in one of the most fateful episodes in recent history. The ideology of National Socialism that guided the Third Reich, which was largely systematized in Hitler's *Mein Kampf*, was not a "reflection" of existing social realities. It was a medley of propositions developed during the nineteenth century, and even before, out of diverse social and economic arrangements. This conceptual amalgam was used by the National Socialists to underwrite a project for political domination and expansion that had to be imposed and maintained by force as well as persuasion and that was only partially achieved.

As in the first two cases, I have argued that the nexus between ideas and power must be located in processes that unfold in space and time. The events that surrounded the NS seizure of power were triggered by the German defeat in World War I and by the economic and political dislocations that followed, but the general conditions from which these immediate causes sprang have their origins in a longer course of German history. I emphasized that two sets of circumstances in that history had recurrent consequences. One was the persistence of local particularisms, supported by the fragmentation of the Germanies into multiple political bodies and entities. These polities not only strove to encompass the loyalties of their subjects but they long enforced local bodies of law and distinctive religious affiliations. The multiplication of local arrangements worked against political unification, created obstacles to economic interchange within the Germanies and with the rest of Europe, and curtailed German participation in the transoceanic expansion that founded the empires of other European nations.

The second set of circumstances underlined was the proliferation of social distinctions and their counterparts in status honor. Variable by locality, region, and political entity, these distinctions of ascriptive social honor set off aristocrats and commoners, as well as members of despised occupations "outside the categories of social honor" altogether, and numerous subcategories of each. Such codes also separated Christians and Jews. In all cases, these social ascriptions defined as well the economic and political abilities and disabilities of each category. Produced within the narrow orbits of multiple principalities, the distinctions worked to confine the inhabitants within the limits of these domains, while ordinances governing social disparities multiplied all across the German lands.

These circumstances not only had consequences for the organization of society and polity, but at the same time they gave rise to tendencies to modify or even undo them. Further pressures were generated in response to ideas introduced from outside the Germanies. Most significant were the reactions to France and the French Revolution. The France of the seventeenth and eighteenth centuries impressed people in the Germanies by its political unity around a stellar royal court, located in a capital city. The comportment and ideas elaborated in Paris and centered on its royal establishment became the cynosure of German princes and aristocrats, who copied French political, artistic, and intellectual styles. Many of the effervescent new ideas produced by the French Enlightenment found resonance in the Germanies, and even critiques of the political order often received a sympathetic hearing. Yet when the French Revolution decapitated the aristocracy and its armies crossed into the German lands to implement the program of liberty, equality, and fraternity, the efforts to impose a universal order under French hegemony were a direct challenge to German political parochialism and codes of social honor.

The reaction in the Germanies against this imposition transformed ideas about national identity into anti-French and anti-foreign nationalism. It built on French Enlightenment notions of the moral and collective body of "the people" but offered a vision of shared cultural identity in the German Volk in place of a project of political unification. This vision fortified hopes for a Reich of all the Germans, but it spelled out no practical politics to turn that dream into reality. Politicians assented to reforms "from above," on the Prussian model, but failed in various efforts to install a liberal and democratic federalism, inspired by French or English thought. There were also some attempts to modify the ascribed social hierarchies, but these were altered more directly and more brutally by the forces of capitalist transformation than by changes of policy and law. The resulting pressures produced reactions particularly against Jews, who were increasingly identified with the destabilization of customary hierarchies through their legal emancipation in some regions and their visibility in monetary transactions. As local and regional exponents of liberal and democratic ideas increasingly lost influence, Bismarck was able to consolidate a strongly militaristic and bureaucratic Second Reich under Prussian aegis in 1871. This Reich came to an end with the German defeat in World War I and the abdication in 1918 of the last Hohenzollern emperor in favor of a republic and a new constitution drafted at Weimar.

With the benefit of hindsight, one can see that ideas which would play strategic roles in power struggles after World War I had already emerged in the preceding, contradiction-ridden century. One was the concept of the Germans as a Volk, characterized by a common cultural soul but not yet including all Germans within an encompassing Reich. Another was the conception of society as an ordered hierarchy of distinctions, an idea that was increasingly challenged by the all-too-real social and economic changes flowing from capitalist expansion. These changes produced new social categories and groups and rearranged relations among the classes. They diminished the power and prestige of an aristocracy based on control of titles and lands in favor of moneyed wealth; impoverished many small merchants, artisans, and peasants; and multiplied the proletariat. As shown in the spread of the dueling complex, the titled nobility and the merely rich developed common forms of crypto-aristocratic sociability. At the bottom of the social hierarchy the workers, excluded altogether from the circle of social honor, formed their own class-based organizations with distinctive social and cultural patterns of associational life and forged strong connections with the parties of the Left. At the turn of the century, intellectuals like Möller van der Bruck, Spengler, and Weber spoke for a strategy whereby Germany would integrate the working class through an alliance of industrial and military elites with nationalist labor leaders, who could draw the proletariat away from international socialism.

The development of political anti-Semitism toward the end of the century laid further groundwork for what was to come. Increasingly, anti-Semites formulated distinctions between the Volk and the Jews not on religious or social lines but in terms of raciological science, representing Jews both as *artfremd* – different in body as well as spirit from the "Aryan" host population – and as collectively responsible for all the problems of the Germans since time immemorial. Arguably, this mode of discourse available to all the Germans – divided by regional distinctiveness, political affiliation, and religion – underlined common bonds in the midst of counterfactual economic realities and class relations.

The loss of World War I, and the economic, social, and political convulsions of the weak republic that followed, led to the rise of National Socialism. Upon its seizure of power in 1933, the movement succeeded in dissolving Parliament and dismantling the legal and constitutional guarantees developed by the Weimar Republic. It put an end to political parties, destroyed the autonomous organizations of the working class, and placed labor under the control of the state. By using force to eliminate independent labor politics, the new regime "solved" the problem of labor participation in national governance. The new government also abrogated limits to rearmament and embarked on a program of rearming the nation and preparing it for war. It maintained most government bureaucracies, together with their Prussian traditions, but complemented them with a multiplicity of parallel institutions and organizations specifically tied to the NS party. Ultimate decision-making power was in the hands of the Führer, but the actual implementation of his policies was hammered out through competition and accommodation among power blocs – coalitions of elite groups variously drawn from industry, government, army, and party. At the same time, widening opportunities for employment and political careers enhanced social mobility for many.

As part and parcel of this project of installing NS power, Hitler and his collaborators forged an ideology out of the fragmented ideas that had gained currency before World War I. Like the protagonists of other revitalization movements, they represented National Socialism as a heroic effort to restore a world "turned upside down" to health and vitality. Drawing together many of the kindred themes familiar from the past, Hitler added a novel twist with his particular conception of the *Volksgemeinschaft*.

This community of the Volk would not be confined to the territory of the Second Reich but would embrace Germans everywhere. It would not be the society ruled over by traditional elites advocated by the conservatives but would include plebeians and aristocrats alike and draw on the capacities of all strata. Furthermore, while many understood the Volk-community as a people organized to furnish material and spiritual support, for Hitler it was a project to create a cultural-political entity able to compete and emerge victorious in the relentless struggle for dominance. This view was grounded in a cosmology that saw the world as a scenario of strife in which the strong were rewarded and the weak destroyed. Germany had lost the last war because it had grown weak; to rebuild its strength it was first necessary to make war on weakness. Ultimately that weakness was due to undermining of the hereditary endowment that had ennobled the Aryans in the Golden Age before race mixture. Making war on weakness would require that the *Volksgemeinschaft* not subordinate itself to the state, as envisaged in conservative thought, but employ the state as an instrument – a warrior sword – to restore racial purity, strength, and will.

Making war on Germany's weakness meant first destroying the enemies within – socialists, communists, Jews, and Gypsies. There could, however, be no end to internal war, since Germany had allowed its primordial Aryan substance to be polluted. Hence there was need for a state that would purify the desirable biological strains through eugenics and racial selection. The state would also repair the weakened moral fiber of the people by hardening it in military training patterned on the experience of the Prussian army. Yet these measures of military socialization were only means to create a nation-at-arms, imbued by its Führer and his paladins with the fanatical will to reverse past defeats and start once more on a road to conquest that would lead to the fantasized Aryan Reich.

This ideology thus implied a program of endless control, training, and vigilance to develop the master race that would dominate in the cosmic struggle. In this struggle, the ultimate enemy was represented by the Jew. Where the Aryans were called to be powerful masters, able to command inferior people to construct culture, egalitarian and parasitic Jewry represented their antithesis. It was necessary to defeat these demons: first through the destruction of Jewry everywhere, and second, through victory over Judeo-Bolshevism, the tyranny over Slavdom supposedly instituted by the Revolution of 1917. Once the Jews were gone and the Slavic East freed from their grip, nature would be restored to its proper course, and the Germanic victors would be able to build upon Slavic labor the "Holy Teutonic Reich of the German Nation."

War, however, would never end. If war made possible more abundant life, the defense and expansion of that life would necessitate further war. The struggle would require, generation after generation, the natural selection of new candidates for mastery, possessed of the will to dominate and legitimizing their claims to rulership through waging war. If nature required an endless life-and-death struggle, such a vision left no room for any human goals that might look beyond the struggle and strive to transcend it. Thus, the ideology was in the grip of a vicious circle requiring the obsessive repetition of the death-dealing struggle that had allowed the life-carrying group to prevail in the first place.

This ideology, however, could not be fully realized, because it misrepresented the operational environment in which it was put to work. It may have motivated many Germans to vote for the National Socialists, but never in numbers large enough to win an uncoerced election. The movement did not come to power electorally, only through the manipulations of a conservative clique, and it always required the use of force and violence to maintain its grip on society. It never set up a unitary Führer-state but produced instead a duplication of party organizations and government institutions and dispersed state power among competing and shifting coalitions of power holders. These arrangements served many interest groups in the context of an ever-expanding war effort, but they gave rise to serious tensions that might have erupted even if the war had been won.

The regime was able to rearm and to occupy Austria and Czechoslovakia without opposition, and it proved victorious in lightning strikes against a militarily weak Poland and a defeatist France. Meeting only sporadic resistance, it was largely unhindered in carrying out the Judeocide, but it also paid an economic and military price in assigning energies and resources to this ideological task. It misjudged on wholly ideological grounds the fighting will and capacity of the Western allies, and even more so that of the Soviet Union, against which it opened an all-out war in 1941. On April 30, 1945, Hitler shot himself in his underground headquarters; the next day the despised Soviet soldiers raised their flag over the gutted Reichstag building in Berlin. [...]

CODA

The three cases presented in this book [*Envisioning Power*] revealed societies under increasing stress, facing a multiplicity of tensions posed by ecological, social, political, or psychological crises. In each case the response entailed the development of an ideology that Kroeber would have characterized as an "extreme expression." These ideologies, carried forward by elites, were fashioned out of preexisting cultural materials, but they are not to be understood as disembodied cultural schemata. They addressed the very character of power in society, specifically the power that structured the differentiation, mobilization, and deployment of social labor, and they rooted that power in the nature of the cosmos.

Kwakiutl society confronted the encroachment of a novel political-economic order that put relations of status and precedence under severe strain. The Tenochca wrestled with the great changes brought about by their rapid rise from a mercenary warrior band to control of a regional empire. National Socialist Germany emerged from the shambles of a lost war and the transvaluation of social relations wrought by political change and economic crisis. In the three instances, such challenges played a part in mobilizing groups for action. They also provided contexts and opportunities that propelled some social groups and segments to the fore while weakening and demobilizing others. Each of the cases showed culture being made and unmade (in Richard Fox's terms) as people engaged each other in diverse social, economic, and political arenas. Old ideas were rephrased to fit different circumstances, and new ideas were presented as age-old truths. Culture is constructed in such encounters, but these are staged, prosecuted, and resolved through the exercise of power.

Structural Power and Ideology

Distinctive as these three cases are, they are yet amenable to an analysis that stresses how ideas intertwine with power around the pivotal relationships that govern social labor. In each case, that structural power engendered ideas that set up basic distinctions between the organizers of social labor and those so organized, between those who could direct and initiate action to others and those who had to respond to these directives. The dominant mode of mobilizing social labor set the terms of structural power that allocated people to positions in society; the ideas that came to surround these terms furnished propositions about the differential qualifications or disqualifications of persons and groups and about the rationales underlying them. [...]

The travails of the imagination in the service of power is even more evident in the case of National Socialist Germany. Prelude to that phenomenon was a century in which the Germanies underwent a convulsive transition from local artisanry to industrial capitalism and an abrupt political unification whereby multiple, socially distinctive local and regional entities were brought under the aegis of a militaristic and bureaucratic Prussia. The resulting dissonances incubated utopian aspirations for a spiritually and culturally unified Volk, aspirations that were further exacerbated by defeat in World War I, as well as by the economic and political dislocations under the republic that followed. National Socialist ideology drew many themes from this cumulation of turmoils, such as the concept of the people as the source of ultimate sovereignty, which was borrowed from the armamentarium of the French Revolution, notions of a plebeian and nationalist populism, and ideas that identified the advocates of equality, pacifism, utilitarianism, and internationalism with Germany's enemies within and without.

Although it called itself "socialist," the new regime did not alter the capitalist relations that had guided the country's mobilization of social labor throughout its forward thrust into industrial capitalism after the mid-nineteenth century (see Wolf 1982: 77–9). It abolished Parliament, broke the political and social power of labor organizations, and curtailed the free movement of workers. While maintaining the basic order of capitalist relations in the workings of the economy, the National Socialists subjected it to their "primacy of politics." Decisions regarding labor were now to be negotiated among power blocs, in which representatives of the Führer played strategic roles. At the same time, ideology was unleashed to rearm the national "will" and build an industrial machine for war.

As among the Kwakiutl and Tenochca, the ideology formulated to justify rulership built on a cosmology. It envisioned the world as Nature, a scenario in which human groups, subject to the same forces that operated in animal and plant communities, were ranged against one another in constant struggle. When this vision was combined with the "scientific" view that human types or "races" had distinct natural origins and different inborn potentialities, history could be reconceptualized as a struggle in Nature for predominance of the Aryan race. There was, however, no certainty that victory would always go to the fittest, who could be defeated by misfits through conspiracy and deceit. The ideology thus added another element. Drawing on old German lore as well as notions imported from abroad, it built into its myth-history a terrifying force of entropy and disintegration, identifiable as the Jew.

Victory therefore required a counterforce to destroy this demonic organism: the National Socialist party and movement led by the Führer. This would institute a new Volksgemeinschaft dedicated to "warding off the Jews" and purifying its blood through racial selection. Cleansing itself of any taints of biological and psychological weakness, it would become indomitable in the pursuit of war. National Socialist propaganda fused its ideological rhetoric with displays of warlike emblems and with shows of physical violence in mass rallies, marches, street fights, and beer-hall brawls. Collective violence, with its exhortations to soldierly masculinity and habitus, further knit together participants and prospective recruits. National Socialist ideology and "propaganda of the deed" fueled the cataclysmic project of conquest and destruction that was to follow.

These three cases serve as entry points into a discussion of ideology, but as historical manifestations they remain incommensurate. They do not conform to a common social type; nor do they furnish a sample of a range of ideologies characterized by a common denominator. In each instance, the regnant ideology had its roots in a distinctive prior cultural history. Moreover, the use of ideology in the three societies had profoundly different effects in the operational world. [...]

National Socialist Germany sought to undo and avenge past defeats through concentrated ideological rearmament in the pursuit of war and conquest. Internally, society was to be recast around hierarchically organized bodies of warlike men, and the agents of national weakness were to be extirpated. Wars waged abroad were to underwrite extensive projects of domination and to reduce stipulated populations to helots. In the process, both internal mobilization and external war gained a self-reinforcing genocidal momentum that brutalized and murdered people by the millions and ended only with the collapse of the German war machine.

In the three cases ideology helped orient society to act within the field of its operations, yet it did so in different ways and within different structural contexts. The three ideologies differed in cultural form and logic, and formulated rationales for action within the distinctive circumstances of each. Most significantly, they were variable in their effects. Thus, specification of ideologies in cultural terms can only be a part of our task. We must also know how these cultural forms engage with the material resources and organizational arrangements of the world they try to affect or transform.

The Problem of Cosmology

In all three cases, the power of the controllers of social labor over those made subject to these controls was formulated as cosmological imperatives, which at once required the exercise of power and supported its execution. Power was thus made to depend not merely on "production" (the active interchange of humans with nature) and on "society" (the normatively governed interactions among humans) but also on relationships with imaginary elements and beings projected beyond tangible experience into metaphysical worlds.

This thrust into metaphysics is not easily accommodated by anthropological efforts to explain human doings as practical ways of obtaining practical results. This is so despite the fact that the transactions of people with imaginary beings are both observable and describable, in that people engage in behaviors they then talk about. We have sought not so much to engage the imaginary as to explain it away, reducing "the output of minds" to seemingly more basic substrates.

One way of explaining ideas has been to see them as outcomes of productive activity or social action; another way has been to treat them as epiphenomena of ecological processes. A more elaborate phrasing has been to link systems of ideas used to classify aspects of the world to patterns of social and political organization, either as direct effects of social arrangements or as related to them in a functional fit. Explaining these imaginings as variables in ecological or social systems can indeed elucidate their functions, but it does not speak either to how ecology and society are articulated with imaginary entities or to the characteristics of the imaginings themselves. [...]

The ideologies in the three cases envision and project such imaginary worlds. Each one centers upon key predicates, axiomatic conditions asserted to be true of that world. The Kwakiutl assigned transhuman values to certain kinds of objects and made their distribution and exchange a major theme of their lives. Circulation of these objects was understood to govern the exchanges of vital powers between humans and animals, and among groups of humans. Privileges and agency in circulating the objects were assigned to chiefs and their heirs; these privileges entailed the obligation to enact the "strict law that bids us dance" (Masco 1995: 41). The Tenochca imagined that they owed life to the gods and that war and sacrifice were necessary to requite the debts thus incurred. Tenochca royals and nobility were accorded the functions of carrying on sacred war and of immolating chosen victims to feed the gods and maintain the cyclical rhythms of the world. For the National Socialists, the struggle for survival through war was the *raison d'être* of existence. To fight that war required strength, which demanded that the people foster and conserve the hereditary endowment of their Aryan forebears. Therefore, the Führer, his party cadres, and his soldiers saw themselves as carrying out the law of nature: to harden the nation and to destroy the Jew, the primordial source of its debility. [...]

Culture and Power

We return now to a consideration of culture and of the way power is implicated in cultural ideas. [...]

[W]e need a concept like "culture" because we still lack a convincing way to understand how the human mind can produce such great socially patterned variability in "minding." Psychobiological inquiries have substantially enlarged our understanding of human nervous systems, but they have not yet achieved a consensus on how nervous systems manage perception, cognition, and language, even less on how they permit such a luxuriant variability of responses both on the collective and on the individual level. This capacity to vary thought and behavior is at the root of the human ability to bring forth new cultural forms and to speak of things never spoken of before; it underwrites human self-organization and creativity. Specifically, we are still unable to account psychobiologically either for metaphors and metonyms or for the ability – crucial to culture – to draw together different systems of thought and action by extending and multiplying sign-dependent connotations across different domains.

The concept of culture remains serviceable as we move from thinking about what is generically human to the specific practices and understandings that people devise and deploy to deal with their circumstances. It is precisely the shapeless, all-encompassing quality of the concept that allows us to draw together – synoptically and synthetically – material relations to the world, societal organization, and configurations of ideas. Using "culture," therefore, we can bring together what might otherwise be kept separate. People act materially upon the world and produce changes in it; these changes then affect their ability to act in the future. At the same time, they make and use signs that guide their actions upon the world and upon each other. In the process they deploy labor and understandings and cope with power that both directs that labor and informs those understandings. Then, when action changes both the world and people's relationships to one another, they must reappraise the relations of power and the propositions that their signs have made possible. These activities can be separated out analytically; but in enacting real life people engage and activate bodies and minds as whole persons. If we want to understand how humans seek stability or organize themselves to manage change, we need a concept that allows us to capture patterned social flow in its multiple interdependent dimensions and to assess how idea-dependent power steers these flows over time. "Culture" is such a concept.

Yet to this end, we must both make culture more flexible and open-ended and connect it with power. Efforts to strip culture of the attributes of totality and homogeneity have been under way in anthropology for some decades, as have efforts to make more of its distributive character – namely, the variation of cultural phenomena among genders and generations, status groups and classes – and to understand how this variation is coordinated. Anthropology is also rich in studies that demonstrate what Robert Lowie called "generalizations of limited validity" (1948:53), showing how people organize themselves for different kinds of work, engage in reciprocity and exchange, or employ techniques to call up the spirits; and such studies invite the question of how patterned behavior in one domain bears upon that in another. Once heterogeneity and variation are recognized, along with the awareness that the entities described in those terms are likely to intertwine in wider fields of involvement, the question appropriately becomes who and what holds it together – in Anthony Wallace's terms, how that diversity is organized (1970:23–4). Immediately, then, we must ask who and what is organized, by what kinds of imperatives, on what level. If organization has no central core – no motivating Hegelian spirit, no economy "in the last instance," or Mother Nature in the guise of the environment – how are we to understand the manner in which organizing imperatives are orchestrated?

I believe that we can approach these questions by bringing together a concept of culture with structural power. By calling attention to the nexus that defines and governs the deployment of social labor, the notion of structural power points to how people are drawn into articulation within the social ensemble. That needs to be addressed before further questions can be asked about specific forms of tactical power used by individuals and groups to gain resources or advantages over others. I have also argued that a concept of structural power leads to the issue of how the distinctions that segment a population are rendered manifest. The case material suggests that these distinctions are defined and anchored in specific cosmologies that represent them as attributes of the order of things, in both the temporal and the logical sense. Aspects of cosmology are further extended and elaborated into ideologies that explain and justify the aspirations of particular claimants to power over society.

What makes people receptive to such power-laden ideas? It is sometimes assumed that humans act to maximize the complexity and orderliness of their experience (Wallace 1970:169), but this generalization needs to be treated with caution. The readiness of many people to live with contradictions, as well as the proclivity of most to pay little heed to internal cognitive coherence, suggests that the installation of a vision of cosmic order is more likely to be an imperative for those trying to organize power than the reflection of a general striving for cognitive consistency. This becomes all the more likely when we recall Rappoport's characterization of ultimate sacred propositions as ambiguous, mystifying, and cryptic and when we remember that what is at stake in the establishment of a cosmology is the propagation of "perlocutionary truths" that do not maximize the organization of minds so much as move them in a certain direction.

Cosmologies and ideologies do, however, exhibit an ability to connect questions of power with the existential concerns of everyday life. The ideologies in all three cases focused explicitly on matters of life and death, and they imparted to the holders of structural power a superhuman aura of involvement with them. The wielders of power assumed the guise of extraordinary beings whose intimacy with the sources of vitality enabled them to marshal the forces of growth and destruction that govern society. The issues posed by ideology have had too little attention in anthropology since the advent of functionalism and structuralism. Yet they deal with what a society or culture is *about*. At this millennial transition, the human capacity to envision imaginary worlds seems to be shifting into high gear. For anthropologists and others, greater concern with how ideas and power converge seems eminently warranted.

NOTES

1   On Mühlmann's political course, see Hauschild (1987).
2   This point came clear to me from reading the German refugee anthropologist Paul Kosok's *Modern Germany: A Study of Conflicting Loyalties* (1933); Mack Walker's *German Home Towns* (1971); and Norbert Elias' *Studien über die Deutschen* (1989). Any inquiry into the history of ideas and ideology in Germany must also draw on George L. Mosse's work on the development of political symbolism in Germany (1975, 1981), as well as Fritz Stern's account of the making of Germanic ideology (1974).

REFERENCES

Abel, Theodore (1938). *Why Hitler Came to Power.* Englewood Cliffs, NJ: Prentice Hall.
Bartov, Omer (1996). *Murder in Our Midst: The Holocaust, Industrial Killing, and Representation.* New York and Oxford: Oxford University Press.
Baum, Rainer C. (1981). *The Holocaust and the German Elite: Genocide and National Suicide in Germany, 1871–1945.* Toronto: Rowman and Littlefield.
Bauman, Zygmunt (1989). *Modernity and the Holocaust.* Ithaca, NY: Cornell University Press.
Goldhagen, Daniel J. (1996). *Hitler's Willing Executioners: Ordinary Germans and the Holocaust.* New York: Knopf.
Haney, Craig, Banks, Curtis, and Zimbardo, Philip (1973). "Interpersonal Dynamics in a Simulated Prison." *International Journal of Criminology and Psychology* 1:69–97.

Hauschild, Thomas (1987). "Völkerkunde im Dritten Reich." In Helge Gerndt (ed.), *Volkskunde and Nazionalsozialismus*. Munich: Münchner Vereinigung für Volkskunde, pp. 245–59.

Hilberg, Raul (1992). *Perpetrators, Victims, Bystanders: The Jewish Catastrophe 1933–1945*. New York: HarperCollins.

Horkheimer, Max and Adorno, Theodor W. (1972). *Dialectics of Enlightenment*. New York: Seabury Press.

Kelman, Herbert (1973). "Violence without Moral Restraint." *Journal of Social Issues* 29:29–61.

Lowie, Robert H. (1948). *Social Organization*. New York: Rinehart.

Masco, Joseph (1995). " 'It Is a Strict Law That Bids Us Dance': Cosmologies, Colonialism, Death, and Ritual Authority in the Kwakwaka'wakw Potlatch, 1849 to 1922." *Comparative Studies in Society and History* 37:41–75.

Mason, Tim (1981). "Intention and Explanation: A Current Controversy about the Interpretation of National Socialism." In Gerhard Hirschfeld and Lothar Kettenacker (eds), *Der Führerstaat: Mythos und Realität*. Stuttgart: Klett-Cotta, pp. 21–40.

Merkl, Peter H. (1975). *Political Violence under the Swastika: 581 Early Nazis*. Princeton, NJ: Princeton University Press.

Mosse, George L. (1975). *The Nationalization of the Masses: Political Symbolism and Mass Movements in Germany from the Napoleonic Wars through the Third Reich*. Ithaca, NY: Cornell University Press.

Mosse, George L. (1981). *The Crisis of German Ideology: Intellectual Origins of the Third Reich*. New York: Schocken Books.

Mühlmann, Wilhelm E. (1933). "Die Hitler-Bewegung. Bemerkungen zur Krise der bürgerlichen Kultur." *Soziologus, Zeitschrift für Völkerpsychologie und Soziologie* 9:129–40.

Noakes, J. and Pridham, G. (eds.) (1995). *Nazism, 1919–1945*. Vol. 3: *Foreign Policy, War and Racial Extermination: A Documentary Reader*. Exeter Studies in History, 13. Exeter: University of Exeter Press.

Smith, Woodruff D. (1986). *The Ideological Origins of Nazi Imperialism*. New York and Oxford: Oxford University Press.

Stern, Fritz (1974). *The Politics of Cultural Despair: A Study in the Rise of the Germanic Ideology*. 2nd ed. Berkeley: University of California Press.

Wallace, Anthony F. C. (1956). "Revitalization Movements." *American Anthropologist* 58:264–81.

Wallace, Anthony F. C. (1970). *Culture and Personality*. 2nd ed. New York: Random House.

Wolf, Eric (1982). *Europe and the People Without History*. Berkeley and Los Angeles: University of California Press.

Part III

Manufacturing Difference and "Purification"

10

"Ethnic Cleansing": A Metaphor for Our Time?

Akbar S. Ahmed

Introduction

Academic papers usually begin with a proposition or thesis; I wish to start with an autobiographical confession. My analysis and interest in the subject are not entirely of an academic nature. True, as an anthropologist, I am interested in ethnicity and ethnic boundaries, that is, how people define themselves and are defined by others on the basis of genealogy, language, and customs. But I also approach ethnicity as someone who has had to come to terms with it in respect of my own identity, throughout my life.

From early childhood I was aware of the fact of ethnic differences which could lead to ethnic animosity and ethnic violence. Such differences accounted for my parents choosing to live in Pakistan when it was created in 1947. Large Indian provinces, as big as large European countries, were ethnically cleansed with all the attendant rape, torture, and destruction. About ten million people crossed each other as Hindus and Sikhs headed for India and Muslims for Pakistan; about one million died. Ethnic cleansing, clearly, is not a new phenomenon although it is disguised for us under a new term.

In Pakistan where I grew up and worked, although the vast majority of people belong to one religion, Islam, and Islam condemns discrimination based on ethnic background, it matters a great deal to which ethnic group you belong. In 1971 I was in what was then East Pakistan and which became Bangladesh in that year, and I saw, first-hand, the power of ethnic identity, how it could challenge successfully loyalty to a common religion.

Here, in the UK, I am given yet another identity, one based on color and race: I am seen as black or Asian. Those who do not like Asians call them "Paki," a term which denotes racial abuse. (What they perhaps do not know is that "Paki" derives from the Urdu word pure and it is no bad thing being called pure even by swearing, snarling skinheads). Yet others learning that I am a Muslim have reservations, implying that all those with a traditional religious belief are fanatics or extremists or what the media call fundamentalists. For some Muslims, suspicious and resentful of the Western establishment, I am a Fellow of a Cambridge College and therefore sullied. Multiple identities have thus been imposed on me.

Viewing the turbulence of South Asia I once envied what seemed the secure and fixed identity of being American or European. The passion generated by race and religion, I read in my American and British textbooks, was a characteristic of backward societies, those that were not modern. I now know that Northern Ireland can be as violent in its ethnic and religious hatred as the worst affected place in South Asia. In Wales and Scotland ethnic resentment against the English surfaces easily. In parts of London the color of your skin can make you a target for abuse and assault. There are flash-points in the United States and Germany and France ready to explode into ethnic violence. To be an English-speaking male from the West in some parts of the Middle East is to know fear, to be vulnerable to the horrors of kidnapping. I no longer envied American or European identity.

Clearly I was not alone in my ethnic susceptibilities. It seemed that all of us were confronted with the same questions. What is my ethnic identity? How does the past shape it? How does it affect my life and those who are not like me? Why are the hatred and violence based on ethnic opposition so intense and so widespread? What is its relationship with the collapse of the project of modernity and the beginnings of a post-Cold War, post-Communism, postmodernity period? Is the ethnic cleansing in Bosnia a consequence of these changes and is it restricted to Bosnia alone? Has ethnic cleansing become the cognitive and affective symbol of, or metaphor for, our postmodern age?

In attempting to answer these questions my academic and personal interests in the subject coincide. I need to understand it in all its complexity to make sense of it. I therefore come to the subject with urgency and conviction and I hope with academic rigor.

Beginnings and Endings

In examining the worst excesses of ethnic cleansing we are transfixed by Bosnia which has given the chilling euphemism "ethnic cleansing" to the late twentieth century. It is the suffering of the Bosnians that challenges frontally European self-perception and self-identity, a fact not fully appreciated here in Britain (see Bell-Fialkoff 1993; Meron 1993; Mestrovic 1994; Schopflin 1993; Vulliamy 1994). Where, we may legitimately ask, are the much vaunted European liberal values – humanism, civilization, and the rule of law?

The ethnic killings and hatred are a consequence of the collapse of the Soviet Union, it is argued. There is even some nostalgia for the old certainties. At least there was no mass murder, no ethnic cleansing, people say, forgetting one of the champion ethnic cleansers of history, Stalin. Others argue that the excesses of Bosnia are a reflection of the ethnic violence which took place half a century ago, of an inevitable ethnic denouncement. Some smugly talk of the conflict in the Balkans as typical of that area; they reflect cultural if not outright racial prejudice.

This is reductionism and simplification of complex historical events that are taking place on a global scale. There are many peoples facing persecution in our world – Muslims elsewhere in the Balkans especially in Kosovo, Palestinians, Kurds, Kashmiris, the Chittagong Hill Tribes, the East Timorese are examples.

However much Bosnia hypnotizes us, we need to broaden our frame of reference beyond Bosnia in order to draw universal principles and locate global explanations. We may then understand ethnic cleansing in our time. The explanations we provide are interlinked, some links strong, others tenuous, some fueling the ethnic violence directly, others contributing to it more indirectly. Cumulatively they ensure that no society is immune, black or white, secular or religious, industrial or agricultural. Nevertheless, our exploration of those explanations is tentative and can only suggest further areas of research.

We note the collapse of the idea of Communism but we also need to be aware of another, more significant, collapse taking place, and that is the notion of modernity with its cluster of ideas, derived in the main from the Enlightenment, such as freedom of speech, humanism, rationality, and secularism. To this was added subsequently economic and scientific progress. Sociologists like Max Weber placed these ideas firmly in Europe through explanations of a specifically European brand of Christianity. Because modernity was located in and spread from Europe over the last two centuries it allowed Europe to become the standard-bearer of civilization, indeed of the future. Cultural and racial superiority was implied. During the high noon of empire, authors like Jules Verne and H. G. Wells extolled the virtues of modern ways to and for all the world with the naivety of enthusiastic schoolboys but its European dimension was clearly assumed.

However, modernity had its dark side even in Europe. Bauman, citing Weber (Bauman 1991: 14), blames it, in part at least, for the Holocaust:

The most shattering of lessons deriving from the analysis of the "twisted road to Auschwitz" is that – in the last resort – *the choice of physical extermination as the right means to the task of Entfernung was a product of routine bureaucratic procedures*: means–ends, calculus, budget balancing, universal rule application . . . The "Final Solution" did not clash at any stage with the rational pursuit of efficient, optimal goal-implementation. On the contrary, *it arose out of a genuinely rational concern, and it was generated by bureaucracy true to its form and purpose.* (Ibid., p. 17)

Those who believed in modernity saw other systems, Buddhist, Hindu, or Islamic, for example, as anachronistic. They would be obliterated in due course in the triumphalist march of Western rationalism and progress. Modernity has therefore always been viewed with ambiguity by people in Africa and Asia; it is too closely associated with European colonization and the rejection of religious and traditional ways.

We cannot say with certainty when modernity began to falter – there is no dramatic equivalent to the fall of the Berlin Wall in 1989 which symbolized the collapse of Communism. But the process of collapse had been gathering momentum. It became increasingly apparent since the middle of [the twentieth] century that modernity could not solve all our problems. In the last decade or two the loss of optimism combined with other developments: law and order deteriorated in the cities, unemployment grew, families fell apart, and the use of illegal drugs and alcoholism spread. Bosnia, and all it stands for, was perhaps the last straw.

What follows after modernity is still uncertain. Some like Anthony Giddens (1991) note continuity in modernity and use the phrase high or late modernity. Others call it postmodernity – the social condition formed by information technologies, globalism, fragmentation of lifestyles, hyper-consumerism, the fading of the nation-state and experimentation with tradition (the related concept, postmodernism, is the philosophical critique of grand narratives). Some write of a post-Cold War period or post-Communism, yet others see a time of ethnic and religious revivalism. However, in noting the revivalism we point out the yearning for pre-modernity, a desire to recreate a mythical past and imagined purity. In that sense the revivalism reflects anti-modernity. It is characteristic of the age that its names are not original and reflect a relationship with the past.

What is certain is that the changes after Communism, the Cold War, and the failure of Western modernity have universal implications. The cement binding different peoples in the large blocs and uniting them in the grand narratives has cracked. This is most notable in the former Soviet Union. But in France, in Germany, even in Britain, we can also trace the dramatic rise of racism in the last years to the dark underside of modernity. Political opinion polls reflect the growing strength of the racist. By calling the racists neo-Nazis the media acknowledge the Nazi past. We hear louder and louder the voices of racism in Europe: "Expel the foreigners," "They are noisy and dirty," "They mean disorder and drugs," "They are not like us – cleanse our land of them."

A similar process is also to be noted globally. Hindus and Muslims in South Asia, Muslims and Jews in the Middle East, Russians and non-Russians in Russia – those ambiguous about modernity but frozen for half a century in the Cold War structures – are falling back on an imagined primordial identity, to their own traditions and culture. People define themselves in terms of the ethnic other, usually a group that has lived as neighbors.

Importantly for purposes of our argument no one group is entirely isolated from ethnic passions. If Hindus terrorize the Muslim minority in India during communal rioting, in turn, they are terrorized in Bangladesh and Pakistan by the majority Muslims. In Kashmir Muslims have been killed and tortured by the thousand. Half a million troops are deployed in Kashmir to crush the Muslim uprising. This is a great human tragedy but there is another human tragedy also taking place simultaneously in Kashmir which is not known outside India. Hindus, who have lived in Kashmir for centuries, have fled the land out of fear; Kashmir is thus ethnically cleansed of them. Most Indians only see the plight of the Hindus, most Pakistanis that of the Muslims.

Yet in order to understand ethnicity an objective approach is needed. As an anthropologist I believe my subject has much to say about the nature of ethnic conflict. Yet somewhat to my bafflement anthropology has been conspicuous by its absence in the commentary on the major international events of the last few years like the Gulf war and the conflict in Bosnia.

Yet surely anthropologists need to explain for the general public why in some countries there is relatively little ethnic cleansing (for instance in Fiji in spite of the coups)? Or why it is particularly vicious in a certain period of history? Why some minorities have adjusted relatively well in an alien cultural environment (like the Sikhs in the UK), while others are less successful (consider the anti-Arab prejudice since the 1970s also in the UK)? Finally, what role does ethnicity itself play in ethnic cleansing?

Rediscovering Ethnicity

The understanding of ethnicity is therefore crucial to our task. Yet despite the efforts of Western social scientists the popular imagination and popular media continue to reflect traditional ignorance and prejudice when dealing with ethnicity.

Ideas and arguments about ethnicity are usually based on the assumption that ethnic identity is a characteristic of primordial and tribal societies, that only society in North America and Western Europe represents modernity. Modern society has moved beyond, evolved away from, religion, belief, and custom. In any case there is little nostalgia in the West for religion which is popularly associated with bigotry, superstition, and intolerance. Only backward societies cling to the past. Progress, science, rationality are the key words although they are difficult to quantify; tradition, tribe, and religion represent the outmoded and obsolete past. Not surprisingly Western anthropologists studying African or Asian peoples once routinely classified them as "savage," "primitive," or "tribal" – you only have to glance at the titles of one of the celebrated LSE names, Malinowski, for confirmation.

Those working in or on Communist societies and those of a Marxist persuasion also analyzed ethnicity and religion as remains of the discredited feudal and traditional order. According to their social trajectory ethnic and religious identity, although present, would in time fade away as people became equal citizens in the modern world. Clearly this has not happened for the majority of the world population and the failure of these analysts is spectacular.

Indeed, the problem of defining key concepts such as ethnicity, race, nation, and tribe that has faced social scientists is symptomatic of this malaise (Barth 1969; Helm 1971; Ahmed 1976, 1980; Godelier 1977; Ahmed and Hart 1984). What, for example, is a group of Scots in the Scottish highlands? With its clans, language, and customs is it a tribe, an ethnic group, a race, or a nation? While the classic anthropological text on tribes, *African Political Systems* (Fortes and Evans-Pritchard 1940), restricted the definition to groups like the Bushmen and the Zulu some anthropologists like Max Gluckman (1971) included as "tribal," along with the Bushmen and the Nuba, the Scots, the Irish, and the Welsh. The debate continues.

Walker Connor (1993) contributed to the discussion by combining ethnicity and nationalism and used the term "ethnonationalism." He is right to underline the irrational and emotional well-springs of ethnonationalism – hence the title of his ERS/LSE lecture: *Beyond Reason* – and its capacity to influence group behavior. But the category creates analytic problems. Surely in certain places, as in India, we need to accept the religious rather than the strictly ethnic dimension of large-scale confrontation?

Ethnicity in one place and religion in another are the central concerns of our time. Indeed, in some areas of conflict "ethnic cleansing" is a misnomer. In most cases it is straightforward religious genocide as with the Muslims in Bosnia. So to restrict the term rigidly to ethnicity is incomplete at best and misleading at worst. When we employ the term we shall do so broadly and generally to indicate notions of exclusivity in a group, based around a cluster of symbols such as language, religion, or historical memory, vehemently opposing and in turn opposed by neighbors with similar ideas of identity expressed with corresponding fervor. "Ethnic cleansing" is the sustained suppression by all means possible of an ethnically or religiously different group with the ultimate aim to expel or eliminate it altogether.

Although we are pointing to the widespread nature and intensity of ethnic cleansing we are not suggesting it is characteristic of or exclusive to our age. Elimination, as in Bosnia, and segregation, as in the Occupied Territories of Israel, of the other (hated and weaker) group have been practiced in the past: the *Reconquista* and *Inquisition* in Spain and *Glaubenskrieg* in Germany (reaching a climax with the Nazi Holocaust) are examples of the former; apartheid in South Africa and Indian Reservations in the USA for the latter.

However, the exercise of grappling with the definitions of tribe, ethnic group, race, and so on may be a red herring. What we really need to analyze is why members of a group – ethnic or religious – want to oppose members of another group with such intensity that they are prepared to inflict the most horrific cruelty on them? We are thus really examining the causes for the radicalization of mass culture and the worldwide growth in and acceptance of extremism, fanaticism, and violence as a solution to the ethnic problem. It is on this that we need to focus for purposes of our analysis in the otherwise amorphous and shifting global landscape.

Ethnic hatred has a mimetic quality: the opposed groups mirror the hatred, rhetoric, and fears of each other. It makes everyone an outsider; and it makes everyone a target. Everywhere – in the shopping arcade, at the bus stop, in the cinema, in your living room – you are vulnerable to sudden, random violence. Anger and hatred are easily created.

The hatred is generalized, universal, and maintained at a high level. For those in traditional societies it is engendered by the dangers posed to the core unit of society, the family, whether the extended or nuclear variety. In urbanized and industrialized society this threat is exacerbated as the family is under stress externally and internally: externally from migration, immigration, unemployment; internally from divorce, drugs, alcoholism. All this creates an anger at the world around and a scapegoat is easy to locate.

Members of the neighboring ethnic group are dirty outsiders, fifth-columnists, disloyal, speak a different language and have different customs. They must be cleansed. This argument can be heard not only in the Balkans but in one form or another in other parts of the world where ethnic clashes are taking place. The mindless cruelty takes in everyone – children, the elderly, the sick – as long as they belong to the other side. It is this combination of perceived ethnic threat and personal vulnerability that forces people to fall back on community and group. There is logic here. If formal networks fail, the more informal ones may assist.

With international structures, like the UNO, not to be trusted (as in Bosnia, Palestine, Kashmir) people fall back on their own group. The belief provides a security in an age of confusion and uncertainty, protection against the imagined or real conspiracies of the enemy. It also inures us to the stories of cruelty that we know exist. By adopting an ethnic position people simplify complex ones, and by talking of national honor and glory disguise the cruelty of their compatriots.

As a parenthesis I might point out the implications of this line of argument for Edward Said's *Orientalism* (1978; see also 1993). Said's thesis is based on the idea of the other (for Europe it is, famously, Islam). The other is out there geographically and culturally, dark, backward, and mysterious to be dominated and exploited. In contrast to this external other is the internal other which we are pointing out: it is home-grown, among us, speaking our language and reflecting our customs, and sometimes it is stronger than us. Said's other is only a limited tool of analysis for our post-Orientalism argument.

Ethnic cleansing in one sense has leveled the categories that divided the global community – First World, Second World, Third World or North-South or East-West. In various degrees and in different forms ethnic cleansing is in evidence everywhere, not only in Bosnia but elsewhere from Bonn to Bombay, Cairo to Karachi. Cities like New York and Los Angeles, where entire neighborhoods are based on color and more or less out of bounds for those of the wrong color, are ethnically cleansed; a similar conceptual strategy to that in Bosnia is at work. Ethnic cleansing has made us all "primitives," "savages," "tribals" – *pace* Malinowski.

For their insensitivity during the Holocaust many governments made the puerile excuse that they were not aware of what was taking place in Germany. The gory daily news from Bosnia – or with less frequency but equal to it in the spirit of violating human rights from Israel, Iraq, or India – shown on television or discussed in print has little impact on the governments of the world; they appear to have developed compassion immunity. These stories are reduced to little more than voyeurism.

As with the Holocaust many ask questions of a deep and disturbing nature: "Why does God – if there is a God – tolerate this suffering? Why doesn't God punish the aggressor, the rapist, and the murderer? What happened to the idea that good triumphs over evil?" If there is a divine parabolic lesson in Bosnia it has escaped most people.

For a Muslim events in Bosnia are truly shocking. The holy Quran clearly preaches tolerance and understanding. Indeed, there is an anthropologically illuminating verse which talks of the wonders of the world, the diversity of races, and points to this: "O Human Beings! Behold, We have created you all out of a male and a female and have made you into nations and tribes so that you might come to know one another – not that you may despise each other" (Surah *Al-Hujurat*, Verse 13). It is this spirit of ethnic that is under attack in our world.

Perhaps for us as academics the most distressing aspect of ethnic cleansing is the involvement of those who are educated and considered to be the pillars of modern society: the doctors, lawyers, engineers, and writers. (Not surprisingly, the Jewish mass murderer who killed about fifty and wounded 200 Muslims kneeling at prayer in Hebron in February 1994 was a medical doctor.) We need to be cautious here. Although ethnic loyalty tends to be a tidal wave which sweeps all before it we can cite many courageous people precisely from this class who stand up to and expose their own community (for example, Mestrovic in the Balkans in 1994; the Jewish women in Israel in 1993; Makiya in Iraq in 1993 and Padgaonkar – with too many others to name – in India in 1993. Padgaonkar, chief editor of *The Times of India*, was dubbed the chief editor of *The Times of Pakistan* in Bombay by Hindu communalists when he attempted balanced reporting of the riots after Ayodhya and published the book *When Bombay Burned*; this is the equivalent of the white liberal who earns himself the contemptuous title "nigger lover" from his people for supporting black issues).

Unfortunately these exceptions do not disprove the ethnic rule that members of the other ethnic group are considered aliens or enemies irrespective of their merits. Let us now explore some explanations for ethnic cleansing.

The Economic Argument

Perhaps the most commonly cited man-in-the-street explanation of ethnic cleansing is the global economic crisis. It is directly related to modernity running its course, to the loss of confidence in the future for the world community. There is a general economic crisis in the world – call it recession or by some other jargon. Unemployment figures are high. Even educated people walk the streets looking for jobs. Prospects are poor. The long-term global forecast is pessimistic, keeping in view the continuing population explosion in Africa and Asia. Poverty turns men into beasts. It is in this context that minorities – the Bangladeshis in Tower Hamlets or the Muslims in Bombay – become targets of irrational emotions. Matters are made worse by pointing to those individuals who have prospered. "They are taking all the jobs. They are being given all the housing. They must not be allowed to get away with this pampering."

There is a strong argument to be made correlating economic deprivation and ethnic confrontation. Whether in Gaza or in Kashmir the government has made virtually no economic investment. The neglect is interpreted as ethnic prejudice. However, it is not only the minority that feels neglected. It is striking that each major section of society views its central problems in a similar light, casting itself as victim, and complains of injustice, blaming its misfortunes on the ethnic or religious enemy, members of which are citizens and neighbors.

While the economic argument is valid up to a point it is also limited, for economic statistics or material progress are taken as a yardstick of life itself, an end in themselves. Yet poverty has never been an excuse for violence and intolerance; indeed, material austerity and spiritual development are central planks of most Asian religious thinking. This was made clear by the examples of the great spiritual messengers of history – Moses, the Buddha, Jesus, and the Prophet of Islam. In our century men like Mahatma Gandhi and women like Mother Teresa have advocated the message of austerity and simplicity with success. Human beings clearly cannot live by bread alone.

Globalization and the Mass Media

Globalization and the mass media provide us with another explanation for ethnic cleansing. Let us explore this idea with the caution that, while globalization is a characteristic of postmodernity, it is also a direct consequence and in many significant ways a continuation of modernity. Giddens in his definition of globalization draws our attention to the relationship:

Globalisation means that, in respect of the consequences of at least some disembedding mechanisms, no one can "opt out" of the transformations brought about by modernity: this is so, for example, in respect of the global risks of nuclear war or of ecological catastrophe. (Giddens 1991: 22)

Globalization draws in people all over the world who willingly or reluctantly participate in a global culture (see Nash 1989; Giddens 1990, 1991; Robertson 1991; Beck 1992; Fukuyama 1992; Ahmed 1993e; Huntington 1993; Moynihan 1993; Ahmed and Donnan 1994; Turner 1994; Ahmed and Shore, in press).

Satellite TV, the VCR, communications technology, and developments in transport have made this possible (for an illuminating discussion on ideology and mass communication see Thompson 1990; for the role of the media in disasters and relief see Benthall 1993). McDonald's and Mickey Mouse, "Dallas" and "Dynasty," Coca Cola and Levis, Toyota and Sony as much as ideas of mass democracy and human rights are now the universally recognized signs of this global culture whatever their country of origin. "Globalization," sighs one of the pundits studying it, "is, at least empirically, not in and of itself a 'nice thing,' in spite of certain indications of 'world progress'" (Robertson 1992: 6).

It is still early days for media studies, and the influence of the media on how people behave needs to be explored at greater length by social scientists. There is a tendency to dismiss media studies as an upstart and not take it seriously. This is a mistake because we can learn a great deal about contemporary life through media studies. Besides, it is salutary to recall the derision with which economics, sociology, and anthropology – each in its turn – were greeted by fellow scientists when these subjects attempted to secure a foothold in academe.

Today TV, the VCR, satellite dishes, and newspapers spread information and images more quickly and more widely than ever before in history. The consequences for our argument are enormous. For most of the population on this planet the reductive and hedonist images are a mirage, the hyper-consumerism out of reach. Envy, frustration, and anger result. The need to lame someone, to find scapegoats, is great. Radicalization and violence follow.

We know that state-controlled television in Belgrade played a crucial role in manipulating and articulating Serb identity. It showed pictures of atrocities, often of Serb victims, which confirmed in people's minds the necessity to stand together against a hostile world bent on denying them dignity and statehood. Ethnic passions were aroused and ethnic cleansing appeared justified.

With its tendency to simplify complex issues the media also allow both a false and dangerous argument to circulate, one mounted by the chauvinistic and aggressive middle class, the keepers of the ethnic flame, that there is a "global conspiracy" to keep the nation or race down and prevent it from becoming great and fulfilling its destiny, that the minorities play the role of a fifth-column in this exercise. Across the world this complaint is echoed. Let us examine the situation in India (for the recent high-quality literature on religion and the rise of extremism in India, mainly written by Indians, see Engineer 1984; Akbar 1988; McLeod 1989; Phadnis 1989; Graham 1990; Gopal 1991; Tully 1991; Das 1992; Madan 1992; Ahmed 1993b, 1993d; Basu et al., 1993; Padgaonkar 1993).

The Hindu backlash was almost inevitable and needs to be explained. The vast majority of the population was Hindu but in the postcolonial rhetoric – secularism, national progress, socialism – Hindu identity was in danger of being submerged. Hindus felt justifiably aggrieved. Among India's founding fathers were men of great piety like Mahatma Gandhi and Sardar Patel but it was the first Prime Minister, Jawaharlal Nehru, who influenced independent India the most with his secular, tolerant, and modern ideas. However, in the eyes of the traditional and orthodox, modernity appeared to demean, disempower, and marginalize custom and belief. The Marxist vocabulary of the intellectuals added insult to injury.

By the 1970s with Nehru not long gone from the scene, Hindu revivalism began to gather momentum and Indira Gandhi, always a political animal, abandoned her father's position for an openly communal one. The globalization process and its aggressive cultural manifestation, especially of American origin, further alienated and threatened Indians – Hindus and Muslims – and forced them to hark back (a point perceptively raised by Iyer 1992; also see Amin 1994).

The political and cultural atmosphere in the 1980s was charged. The mildest reservation about or the merest hint of opposition to the Hindu cause by a Muslim would risk swift, noisy, and painful retribution. It would be a feeling familiar to a Muslim Bosnian in Serb-controlled Bosnia with reservations about the battle of Kosovo, a Copt about the capacity of the Egyptian state to protect Christian churches and property, a Palestinian about the fairness of the state of Israel, a Kurd about the humanity of Saddam Hussein's regime, a Jew about the Islamic revolution in Iran, and a Bangladeshi Hindu about Islamic revivalism in Bangladesh.

A glance at the long list of credits of the major and popular television series depicting a mythical Hindu past, *Mahabharat*, *Ramayana*, and *Chanakya* (all shown in Britain), will illustrate the position of the Muslims in India today; the names are almost exclusively Hindu. It is assumed that only Hindus can make or contribute to "religious" films. Notions of purity and exclusiveness are implied and ethnic boundaries clearly drawn. This, too, it can be argued, is a side of ethnic cleansing. (The process works both ways in South Asia: the popular Pakistani series *Dhoop Kinarey* – also shown in Britain – has almost all Muslim names in the credit list.)

This was not always so in Indian films (see Ahmed 1992b). One of the most significant contributions to the idea of a genuinely multicultural and multireligious India was made by the Bombay cinema in the early decades of independence. It may have been an ideal but it inspired millions. One of the most famous Hindu devotional songs from the popular film *Kohinoor* (1960) provides an example. It was sung on screen by Dilip Kumar (Yusuf Khan), written by Shakeel Badayuni, directed by Naushad, and actually sung by Mohammad Rafi, all four Muslims. This was a remarkable comment on Indian tolerance and synthesis. It reflected the spirit of the founding fathers: Mahatma Gandhi, Jawaharlal Nehru, Maulana Azad. It is this spirit which is under threat and which worries many Hindus, who wish to see it preserved. The minorities are simply terrorized by the new mass violence.

Films like *Mahabharat*, *Ramayana* and *Chanakya* did not necessarily aim to have a contemporary political message but were watched by an estimated 600 million people every week and this, in itself a unique media phenomenon, created a highly religious atmosphere in the 1980s. It generated a nationwide glow of pride and identity – a specifically Hindu pride and identity. The images projected an idealized Hindu past, a society in harmony, in flower.

Had the matter ended there – television as entertainment – that would have been admirable and innocuous. But a subtext could be discerned: the ideal picture was shattered by invaders from outside India; Muslims were to blame. The series assisted in setting a chain of events in motion. Some media pundits in the BJP, a party floundering on the verge of extinction, at this point joined the emotions generated by the mass media and a political issue concerning the birthplace of Lord Ram at Ayodhya where a medieval mosque stood. Overnight its fortunes changed – from two seats in parliament to 119 – although the results of the latest State election in north India indicate the support of the BJP may have peaked.

So while Hindus thrilled at the doings of the attractive warrior-hero figure of Lord Ram on television they were angered by the mosque at Ayodhya. A vigorous campaign daubed the legend "Declare with pride your Hinduism" on walls, posters, and hoardings all over India. A not so subtle subliminal message was contained in this slogan: vote for those who identified with Hinduism (like the BJP). The BJP notably, but also the Congress, then recruited the stars from the television series, who were treated almost like gods in India, as their parliamentary candidates. They helped mobilize public opinion in demanding the mosque at Ayodhya be replaced by a temple. Widespread tension all over India resulted in frequent large-scale riots in the name of Lord Ram.

Hindu extremists were now offering Muslims throughout India the standard choices of ethnic cleansing: absorption into Hinduism by accepting Lord Ram and becoming "Hindu Mohammedans," or expulsion (to Pakistan or Saudi Arabia or wherever). The third choice was to prepare for the destruction of life and property. From the *Reconquista* in Spain to the Occupied Territories in Israel subjugated minorities have confronted these dilemmas.

The transformation of what its devout and thoughtful followers see as a philosophic, humane, and universal religious tradition to a bazaar vehicle for ethnic hatred and political confrontation saddens many Hindus. The mosque at Ayodhya was destroyed in December 1992 and an orgy of killing followed all over India in which the paramilitary and security forces were later implicated (the world saw them on television screens idly standing by as the frenzied mob in Ayodhya went about its business). Horror stories circulated of Muslims being burnt alive or raped while video recorders filmed them. In Bombay mobs stopped men and forced them to drop their trousers; those circumcised were identified as Muslim and stabbed. The link between the media and politics, between the religious-cultural assertion of identity of one group and the persecution of another, is suggested.

There were also immediate and serious international repercussions: Hindus were attacked and their temples destroyed in Pakistan and Bangladesh while angry mobs demanded a "holy war" against India in retaliation. In Britain tension was created between the Hindu and Muslim communities and Hindu temples were mysteriously damaged. The span of responses confirms our other argument that to understand ethnic violence we need to keep its global context before us.

Although commentators singled out the BJP as the main culprit behind the ethnic violence this is incorrect and misleading; indeed, elements in the Congress had long compromised on its secular position. Others too – influential opinion-makers like bureaucrats, media commentators, and academics – had been transformed and abandoned their earlier secular neutrality on communal issues. Those who were dismayed by this trend were reduced to powerless spectators.

Let us not make the mistake of the critics of the BJP by simplification of a complex phenomenon. Beneath every case of ethnic cleansing is layer upon layer of history and culture. The movement for a separate Muslim state, the creation of Pakistan (seen by many Hindus in a religious light, as sacrilege, as the division of Mother India itself), the wars between India and Pakistan, the perception of a threatening Islamic revivalism (in neighbors like Pakistan and Bangladesh and also, of course, Iran) and the continuing problems of the Muslim minority in adjusting to the new realities of India all contributed to the ethnic suppuration.

Indeed, as early as the 1930s Gowalkar (1938), one of the most influential Hindu ideologues, had argued that if Hitler could finish off the Jews in Germany then the Hindus ought to be able to do the same to the Muslims in India. Hindu extremists even today continue to use the unsavory language of the Nazis. The tradition of virulent propaganda against Muslims disguised as scholarly research continues (Oak 1990; Elst 1992). Muslims in these books are depicted as whoring and pillaging drunks, breaking Hindu temples and buildings. These stereotypes feed into the mass media and neatly reinforce Hindu chauvinism which is calculated to win the Hindu vote.

The argument will be made that India is, after all, Asia, Third World, backward, a society stuck in the rut of religion and tradition, that the influence on society of television is a sign of such societies. It would be incorrect. Not only in India but throughout the world what we see on our television screens helps to form our ideas. The argument that the sex and violence shown on television influence people awaits long-term statistical findings but on the surface appears plausible. They inure people to cruelty. Children grow into adulthood convinced that the simple solution is to kill or maim or hurt. Not surprisingly, American pilots, on at least one carrier, about to bomb Iraq the following day during the Gulf war, were shown sadistic, porno-graphic films ("Dying to Please Nobody" by Marilyn French in *The Sunday Times*, 10 October 1993). Not surprisingly either, the young killers of little James Bulger here in the UK had grown up on a diet of "video nasties."

In December 1993 half a dozen young men raped for over an hour two young girls barely in their teens who were dragged from a McDonald's in London. About twenty other men stood round and cheered. The inspiration for this is not difficult to guess. Dozens of American films have depicted the same scene. That the gang was predominantly black gave the incident an ethnic dimension (life was also imitating art a few weeks earlier when a black – or to use the politically correct term Afro-American – gunman walked along a New York underground train shooting anyone not of his color).

No Heroes Any More

The mass media are also responsible, because of their aggressive irreverence and unceasing probing, for the lackluster leadership of today. Our age has produced a distinctly mediocre set of leaders. Political scientists need to investigate this phenomenon further so that we become enlightened. Consider the list at random – Clinton in America, Major in the United Kingdom, Kohl in Germany, Yeltsin in Russia, Rao in India, Mubarak in Egypt. Many of us, I am sure, are not even aware of the names of the heads of government in China and Japan.

Charismatic leaders are not always the best leaders and those like Hitler and Stalin were ardent supporters of ethnic cleansing. So what makes some charismatic leaders extraordinary is their ability to stand up to majority opinion when it comes to matters of principle. We have the example of Mahatma Gandhi agreeing to the creation of Pakistan, however much it pained him, if that was what the Muslims wanted, and then starting a fast to death unless Hindus stopped killing Muslims in India. A Hindu fanatic killed him, accusing him of being too sympathetic to the Muslims. There was De Gaulle in France who took the unpopular decision of giving independence to Algeria. For many French it was the ultimate betrayal and De Gaulle's life was constantly under threat. And there was Churchill whose support for the Jews overruled the anti-Semitism at the Foreign Office.

In contrast, Rao in India, a year after promising to reconstruct the mosque in Ayodhya, still vacillates. In France north African immigrants are the subject of the crudest form of racism and the prime minister's office talks openly of smelly and dirty aliens. Charles Pasqua and others have powerfully and mendaciously linked crime and immigration. Pasqua talks of returning immigrants to Africa "by the planeload and the boatload." He has tapped a vast reservoir of votes and added a new and dangerous dimension to both issues.

The Failure of the Nation-State

The failure of the nation-state to provide justice and inspire confidence, and the frustrations that it engenders, is another consequence of the collapse of modernity and of the rise of ethnic identity. Modernity was expressed by the form and idea of the nation-state. "National identity" emerged as a byproduct of the formation of the nation-state, itself impelled by "industrialization" (Gellner 1983; Giddens 1991). But in large parts of the world the nation-state itself is under challenge: in East Europe, in the lands that once constituted the USSR, in the Middle East, in South Asia, and in Africa. Boundaries are being redrawn or rejected. As old states are threatened new ones are demanded or formed.

In their haste to depart, after the international climate changed following World War II, the colonialists took little time or effort when demarcating the new nations. Tribes and villages were sometimes divided between nations (in the case of the Kurds, the tribe was divided between five nations). Half a century of living together should have cemented the new states. This is not so.

One reason is the blatant discrimination that the state practices in favor of the dominant group. It is not being suggested that the state legally supports the subjugation or the elevation of a group. On the contrary, states are based on modern notions of equality and justice and in some cases appear to favor minorities (as in India where the Constitution in this regard compares favorably to the putatively advanced countries like France and Germany). Rather, that even state functionaries are now contaminated with ethnic hatred.

Most dangerously for the health of the state the majority has developed a "minority complex" – whether in Serbia, Israel, Iraq, or India. Through a process of Alice-in-Wonderland logic it has come to believe, and proclaims for all to hear, that its population is in danger of being swamped (the minority breed like rabbits); its economy is in crisis (the minority act as a brake); it is the victim of an international conspiracy (the minority are a fifth-column) and law and order have collapsed (the minority are responsible for the drugs and gun-culture). To be a member of what is seen as the pestilential minority by the majority is almost to be a *persona non grata*, irrespective of the merits of the individual (whether Muslim in India, Hindu in Bangladesh, Palestinian in Israel, or Kurd in Iraq). The minority argue that the nation-state has meant suppression of their identity usually by brute force. Torture and death are common methods. Besides, the majority monopolize economic and political power, they point out. Democracy, they rightly claim, means perpetual subordination and humiliation. Ultimately, they fear, they will be wiped off the face of the earth.

A significant ethnic lesson is drawn from Bosnia. Many are now skeptical about the plausibility of plural or multicultural societies in the future. "If the Serbs can do this to the Muslims who even married Serbs, what hope is there for integration? Is the idea of integration irretrievably lost?" There were no easy answers even by optimists. The only security, it seems, was in reversion to primordial identity, a return to the idea of the tribe, of purity in an impure and menacing world.

An important idea, widely believed, is that international organizations which should have ensured justice, law and order, and the rule of law have failed. The United Nations is the primary example. It has failed the Bosnians, the Palestinians, and the Kashmiris. Resolution after resolution is passed regarding the destiny of these people and blatantly ignored.

For Muslims the world over Bosnia, Palestine, and Kashmir signify the hostility to Islam in our times, of the persecution of Muslim minorities in particular. Muslims are convinced that fellow Muslims are being raped, killed, and uprooted because of their religion. Muslim anger and anguish echo the heart-rending cry of Shakespeare's Jew: "Hath not a Jew eyes? hath not a Jew hands, organs, dimensions, senses, affections, passions?"

The historical past is evoked in each case. For instance, when discussing Bosnia Muslims believe that the West which is capable of stopping the genocide will not do so because it does not want a viable Muslim nation in Europe. The last Muslim kingdom was extinguished in 1492 in Granada, Spain, and Europeans, 500 years later, have not changed. Muslims, both globally and in Bosnia, suggest that European ideas of humanism, freedom, and equality appear to be applicable only to white Europeans with a Christian background (Ahmed 1992c, 1993c; Mestrovic 1994; also *Impact International* and "*Q*" *News* published in London). It is in this context that commentators construct the global confrontation between Islam and the West (Ahmed 1988, 1992a, 1993a, 1993e; Huntington 1993).

Matters are complicated as ethnic groups across international borders are prepared to assist their oppressed kin (India accuses Pakistan of assisting the Kashmiris, Israel the Arabs of aiding the Palestinians, and so on). Once again the majority feel threatened and talk of fifth-columns. Unless free and fair channels of representation are available and unless the majority genuinely consider the needs of the minority, the democracy in these countries will be incomplete and the nation-state will continue to be challenged as the minorities demand their own state.

We also need to point to the nation-state and nuclear proliferation. In the context of our arguments, until a decade or two ago, the nuclear option did not exist outside the Cold War structure. Today it does. India and Pakistan have fought three wars. They are poised for a fourth. Tension is at a peak following the destruction of the Ayodhya mosque and the revolt in Kashmir. This time the war will be nuclear, a total war; it will also be total madness. No one can win.

It is not difficult to conjecture what extremists on either side – Serbs or Bosnians in the Balkans, Jews or Palestinians in the Middle East, Hindus or Muslims in South Asia – would do if allowed to decide whether a bomb should be dropped on their enemy. It would solve all their problems, they will say enthusiastically. Holocaust solutions have always been popular with those who believe in eliminating supposedly inferior races.

Ethnocentric perceptions lull us into believing that nuclear weapons are more unsafe in the hands of the north Korean leaders than in American or British ones. However, any finger, whether yellow or white, on the nuclear button is dangerous although the safeguards are greater in a democracy. The fact is that nuclear proliferation poses a major danger to the world. The question of nuclear weapons needs to be addressed urgently on a global level.

Rape as Policy in Ethnic Cleansing

Rape is one of the most infamous acts on man's long list of infamy, one suggesting deep psychological and emotional disturbance. Because rape is so intimately tied to ideas of honor and disgrace people are reluctant to discuss it. Yet to learn about the true nature of ethnic and religious conflict social scientists need to study rape or sexual intimidation.

We know that in Bosnia rape is used deliberately as an instrument of war, a fact confirmed by innumerable international organizations and media reports. Dogs, men affected by the HIV virus, and gangs taking turns are used to rape women in what have been exposed as rape camps. Small girls are raped in front of their mothers by soldiers taking turns. Rape is known as an ugly face of battle committed by soldiers in the heat of war. But in the manner it is used in the Balkans it is chillingly sinister. Civilians, administrators, students – ordinary people – are all involved as active participants or as spectators.

Bosnia is not alone in this regard. There is also considerable evidence gathered by international human rights organizations and by Indian writers that Indian troops in Kashmir are using the same tactics. There may not be official rape camps as in Bosnia but troops have regularly surrounded villages, expelled the men, and raped their women all night. After the destruction of the Ayodhya mosque the police were clearly implicated in organizing riots in Bombay and Surat against Muslims which involved rape. Iraq and Israel, the former in a crude way, the latter in a more subtle manner, also use sexual tactics to intimidate minorities, we learn from the book *Cruelty and Silence* by an Iraqi expatriate writer (Makiya 1993). Iraqi soldiers force Kurd women from camps taking them to be raped; Israelis lock up Arab women in security cells for the night with threatening men. An organization of brave Israeli women risked the wrath of the authorities and documented the widespread cases of sexual abuse by the Israeli police in *Women for Women Political Prisoners*, published in December 1989 in Jerusalem.

The woman is twice punished: by the brutality of the act and by the horror of her family. Notions of honor, modesty, and motherhood are all violated. Rape strikes families at their most vulnerable point especially in traditional societies where, in certain tribes, illegitimate sexual acts are wiped out by death alone (Ahmed 1980). It is thus deliberately employed by ethnic neighbors who are fully aware of its expression as political power and cultural assertion to humiliate the internal other.

The sociological implications are clear for the purposes of our argument: rape as a final line divides one group from the other; the state, through its forces, becomes the rapist, raping its own citizens, those it is sworn to protect. Bitterness is at a peak. So is the nature of hatred in the response. Blood and revenge follow. A spiral of violence is set in motion. All the key notions of modernity – justice, rule of law, rationalism, civic society – are negated by the criminal nature of ethnic rape. For the victim and her family it is no longer an age of modernity and progress but one of barbarism and darkness.

The Uses of the Past

Finally, to justify the acts of humiliation like rape and as a consequence of the general sense of disillusionment with international and national bodies, the collapse of law and order, and the conviction that the only security lies in one's own people, is the increasingly creative use of historical-religious arguments which, in turn, support ethnic cleansing.

History is employed to buttress ethnic and religious polemics and, more importantly, to reclaim and reconstruct ethnic identity by a whole range of commentators, academics, and politicians (Ahmed 1993b, 1993d). Thus, Kosovo in the Balkans, Jerusalem in the Middle East, or Ayodhya in India are not just neutral historical place names; they are also deeply emotive and affective symbols of identity. They rally the community as they provide it with a visible proof of the perfidious enemy by reviving bitter memories from a distant past. In the mass media such history translates itself into kitsch, sentimentality, and commercialization; it also becomes popular and accessible. In the vacuum caused by the collapse of the grand narratives like Communism the indigenous becomes both relevant and inevitable. Honor, identity, and the media, the past and the future, the rise of what is called fundamentalism or revivalism all relate to the historical reference points.

Historical-religious mythology feeds the ethnic passions of the Russians (like Zhirinovsky) and Serbs (like Arkan) who talk of a Christian crusade, Jews and Muslims in the Middle East and Hindus and Muslims in South Asia who view each other as enemies in a holy war. "God is with us," the faithful pronounce with utter conviction and sincere belief.

It is this zeal which drives men in Bosnia to burn the sign of the cross on to the bodies of innocent Muslims and impale them in crucifixion (Goytisolo 1993; Yusuf 1993). This is not the spirit of Jesus but it is a crude ethnic justification for the murder and mayhem. The first target is the village mosque. The destruction of these buildings is to be condemned on religious as well as architectural grounds, for most of them are centuries old. *The Heart Grown Bitter,* the title of an anthropological account of Greek ethnic war refugees in Cyprus by Peter Loizos (1981), tellingly describes the plight of the ethnically dispossessed.

Most academics who have dismissed such historical mythology as irrelevant to our modern lives do not fully appreciate its power and influence. We are pointing to zealous supporters of ethnic superiority who number in the millions across the world and their governments which have access to nuclear weapons.

Conclusion: Into the Millennium

Prognosis is difficult for the post-Cold War, post-Communism, postmodern age that is forming but it is likely that the next millennium will open with limited but intensely messy ethnic conflicts – with vigorous ethnic cleansing – on-going low-intensity wars in which there are no real winners or losers, no major defeats or victories, no defined battlefields or boundaries. We need to pull back from this nightmare Hobbesian scenario of the future to restore a balance between tradition and modernity, local custom and culture, respect for law and the way of others. Above all, we need more imagination and tolerance in dealing with others.

It can be done. The last year or two have provided us with some dramatic examples of a silver lining to the dark ethnic cloud. Old-standing ethnic enemies shook hands, an act symbolic of the wish to remove the vast psychological and cultural barriers that divided them and their people: Rabin and Arafat in Washington, but also the British and Irish prime ministers over Northern Ireland and the black and white leaders over South Africa. In Germany, in spite of widespread and vicious ethnic violence, Dr Ravindra Gujjula, an Indian, was elected the first Asian mayor in history. In December 1993 the Vatican reconciled with Judaism thus closing the hostility of two millennia. These significant gestures need to be more than media events and to be followed by concrete steps; the ethnic fires still rage on the ground.

Important steps need to be taken to encourage ethnic understanding. The first and most important is to underline the plurality of our world, that although people are divided by birth, language, and religion they belong to the same species. To counter narrow nationalism we need to stress the extent of interdependence in today's world, growing all the time so as to encourage people to think internationally. Organizations like the United Nations, weak and ineffective in the face of ethnic crises, need urgent structural changes and larger budgets. Human rights and minority groups must be protected not only under the law but in the spirit of good neighborliness. The idea of tolerance and understanding needs to be encouraged through the mass media. We have seen the mass media acting as a source of division, let us see its positive side (for example, see Benthall 1993 for its impact on disasters and relief). For a start, it can become aware of the stereotypes it builds up of the other and avoid them.

Education is another way to discourage ethnic hatred. Ill-defined ideas and prejudices in a student's mind easily develop into prejudice for the other. Islam and

Hinduism need to be taught seriously as regular subjects in Britain; Christianity in Sudan and Pakistan, and so on. We need to call for an intensification of inter-faith dialogue. There is so much common ground; spokespersons for the different faiths should point to it and act upon it. We need more Christians and non-Christians in Europe, Jews and Muslims in the Middle East, and Hindus and Muslims in South Asia sitting across tables in serious discussion.

Never before in human history have the global and the local, the high and the low, the past and the present, the sacred and the profane, the serious and the frivolous been so bewilderingly juxtaposed and so instantly available to stimulate, confuse, and anger the individual. Violence is almost inevitable, the ethnic victim often at hand. Globally, the disillusioned children and inheritors of modernity live in what the academics have termed "a risk culture" (Giddens 1991: 3) or "risk society" (title of Beck 1992; also see Giddens 1990; Ahmed 1992a; Ahmed and Donnan 1994; Turner 1994; Ahmed and Shore, in press).

In concluding, we have pointed out the links between globalization, radicalization, sexual intimidation, the mass media, the uses of religious mythology, and ethnic and religious violence in the aftermath of the collapse of modernity. There is clearly cause and effect here. We have noted that victims of ethnic intolerance in one part of the world are themselves aggressors in other parts through the acts of those who share their religion or ethnicity. Every group appears to be susceptible to the ethnic virus. Ethnic cleansing, we have suggested, ranges from the outright barbarity of death and rape camps to the more subtle but also traumatic cultural, political, and economic pressures brought to bear on the minority.

In ethnic cleansing the human race faces a moral collapse leading to the most diabolical acts of cruelty. Yet our world also possesses the capacity and resources to tackle other pressing problems that we face like hunger and disease. Clearly, the global community is at some kind of dramatic crossroad, a cusp, a critical point in history.

Ethnic cleansing is the dark and ugly side of human nature. To contain it and to combat it we need first to understand it. Therefore to examine ethnic cleansing is not to look at the aberrant or the marginal or the temporary – the specialist's area of interest; it is to come face to face with our age, our nature, and our aspirations; it is to confront the human condition.

REFERENCES

Ahmed, Akbar S. (1976). *Millennium and Charisma among Pathans: A Critical Essay in Social Anthropology*. London: Routledge.

Ahmed, Akbar S. (1980). *Pukhtun Economy and Society: Traditional Structure and Economic Development in a Tribal Society*. London: Routledge.

Ahmed, Akbar S. (1988). *Discovering Islam: Making Sense of Muslim History and Society*. London: Routledge.

Ahmed, Akbar S. (1991). "Anthropology 'Comes Out'?" *Anthropology Today* 7, no. 3 (June).

Ahmed, Akbar S. (1992a). *Postmodernism and Islam: Predicament and Promise*. London: Routledge.

Ahmed, Akbar S. (1992b). "Bombay Films: The Cinema as Metaphor for Indian Society and Politics". *Modern Asian Studies* 26 (2): 289–320.

Ahmed, Akbar S. (1992c). "Palestine Revisited." *New Statesman and Society* (November 20).

Ahmed, Akbar S. (1993a). *Living Islam: From Samarkand to Stornoway.* London: BBC Books.

Ahmed, Akbar S. (1993b). "The History-Thieves: Stealing the Muslim Past?" *History Today* 43 (January).

Ahmed, Akbar S. (1993c). "New Metaphor in the 'New World Order.'" *Impact International* (March 12 – April 8): 24–7.

Ahmed, Akbar S. (1993d). "Points of Entry: The Taj Mahal." *History Today* 43 (May).

Ahmed, Akbar S. (1993e). "Media Mongols at the Gates of Baghdad." *New Perspective Quarterly* 10 (Summer).

Ahmed, Akbar S. and Donnan, Hastings (eds.) (1994). *Islam, Globalisation and Postmodernity.* London: Routledge.

Ahmed, Akbar S. and Hart, David (eds.) (1984). *Islam in Tribal Societies: From the Atlas to the Indus.* London: Routledge.

Ahmed, Akbar S. and Shore, Cris (eds.) (in press). *The Future of Anthropology: Its Relevance to the Contemporary World.* London: Athlone.

Akbar, M. J. (1988). *Riot after Riot.* India: Penguin.

Amin, Samir (1994). "India Faces Enormous Danger from Globalization." *Mainstream* 32, no. 9 (January 15), New Delhi.

Barth, F. (1969). "Introduction and Pathan Identity and its Maintenance." In *Ethnic Groups and Boundaries: The Social Organization of Culture Difference.* London: Allen and Unwin.

Basu, Tapan et al. (1993). *Khaki Shorts and Saffron Flags: A Critique of the Hindu Right.* London: Sangam Books.

Bauman, Zygmunt (1991). *Modernity and the Holocaust.* Cambridge: Polity Press.

Beck, Ulrich (1992). *Risk Society: Towards a New Modernity,* trans. Mark Ritter. London: Sage Publications. (Originally published in 1986).

Bell-Fialkoff, Andrew (1993). "A Brief History of Ethnic Cleansing." *Foreign Affairs* (Summer).

Benthall, Jonathan (1993). *Disasters, Relief and the Media.* London: I. B. Tauris and Co.

Connor, Walker (1993). "Beyond Reason: The Nature of the Ethnonational Bond." Annual ERS/LSE Lecture, 1992. *Ethnic and Racial Studies* 16, no. 3 (July).

Das, Veena (ed.) (1992). *Mirrors of Violence: Communities, Riots and Survivors in South Asia.* Delhi: Oxford University Press.

Elst, Koenraad (1992). *Negationism in India: Concealing the Record of Islam.* New Delhi: Voice of India.

Engineer, Asghar Ali (ed.) (1984). *Communal Riots in Post-Independence India.* London: Sangam Books.

Fernandez, C. and Fernandes, Naresh (1993). "A City at War with Itself." In D. Padgaonkar (ed.), *When Bombay Burned.* New Delhi: UBS Publishers and Distributors.

Fortes, M. and Evans-Pritchard, E. E. (1940). *African Political Systems.* Oxford: Oxford University Press.

Fukuyama, Francis (1992). *The End of History and the Last Man.* London: Hamish Hamilton.

Gellner, E. (1983). *Nations and Nationalism.* Oxford: Blackwell.

Giddens, Anthony (1990). *Consequences of Modernity.* Cambridge: Polity Press.

Giddens, Anthony (1991). *Modernity and Self-Identity: Self and Society in the Late Modern Age.* Cambridge: Polity Press.

Gluckman, M. (1971). *Political, Law and Ritual in Tribal Society.* Oxford: Blackwell.

Godelier, M. (1977). *Perspectives in Marxist Anthropology.* Cambridge: Cambridge University Press.

Gopal, Sarvepalli (ed.) (1991). *Anatomy of a Confrontation: Ayodhya and the Rise of Communal Politics in India.* India: Penguin.

Gowalkar, M. S. (1938). *We or Our Nationhood Defined.* India: Nagpur.

Goytisolo, Juan (1993). "Terror Town." *New Statesman and Society* (December 17–31).

Graham, Bruce (1990). *Hindu Nationalism and Indian Politics: The Origins and Development of Bharatiya Jana Sangh.* Cambridge: Cambridge University Press.

Helm, J. (ed.) (1971). *Essays on the Problem of Tribe.* American Ethnological Society, University of Washington Press, USA.

Huntington, Samuel P. (1993). "The Clash of Civilizations?" *Foreign Affairs* (Summer).

Iyer, Krishna (1992). "Review of Ahmed 1992a." In *Economic and Political Weekly* (November 7) Bombay.

Loizos, Peter (1981). *The Heart Grown Bitter: A Chronicle of Cypriot War Refugees.* Cambridge: Cambridge University Press.

McLeod, W. H. (1989). *Who is a Sikh? The Problem of Sikh Identity.* Oxford: Clarendon Press.

Madan, T. N. (ed.) (1992). *Religion in India.* India Readings in Sociology and Social Anthropology. Oxford and Delhi: Oxford University Press. (Originally published in 1991).

Makiya, Kanan (1993). *Cruelty and Silence: War, Tyranny, Uprising, and the Arab World.* London: Jonathan Cape.

Meron, Theodor (1993). "The Case for War Crimes Trials in Yugoslavia." *Foreign Affairs* (Summer).

Mestrovic, Stjepan G. (1994). *The Balkanization of the West: The Confluence of Postmodernism with Postcommunism,* London: Routledge.

Moynihan, Daniel Patrick (1993). *Pandaemonium: Ethnicity in International Politics.* Oxford: Oxford University Press.

Nash, Manning (1989). *The Cauldron of Ethnicity in the Modern World.* Chicago: University of Chicago Press.

Oak, P. N. (1990). *Some Blunders of Indian Historical Research.* New Delhi: Bharati Sahitya Sadan.

Padgaonkar, Dileep (ed.) (1993). *When Bombay Burned.* New Delhi: UBS Publishers and Distributors.

Phadnis, Urmila (1989). *Ethnicity and Nation-Building in South Asia.* New Delhi: Sage Publications.

Robertson, Roland (1991). "The Globalization-Paradigm: Thinking Globally." In D. G. Bromley (ed.), *Religion and Social Order.* Greenwich, CT: JAI Press, pp. 207–24.

Robertson, Roland (1992). *Globalization: Social Theory and Global Culture.* London: Sage Publications.

Said, Edward (1978). *Orientalism.* London: Routledge.

Said, Edward (1993). *Culture and Imperialism.* London: Chatto and Windus.

Schopflin, George (1993). "The Rise and Fall of Yugoslavia." In John McGarry and Brendan O'Leary (eds.), *The Politics of Ethnic Conflict Regulation.* London: Routledge.

Thompson, John B. (1990). *Ideology and Modern Culture.* Cambridge: Polity Press.

Tully, Mark (1991). *No Full Stops in India.* London: Viking.

Turner, B. S. (1994). *Orientalism, Postmodernism and Globalism: Intellectuals in the Modern World,* London: Routledge.

Vulliamy, Ed (1994). *Seasons in Hell: Understanding Bosnia's War.* New York: Simon and Schuster.

Yusuf, Feyyaz (1993). "Christian Radicalism Stirs the Serbs." *"Q" News* (December 10–17).

11

Imagined Communities and Real Victims: Self-Determination and Ethnic Cleansing in Yugoslavia

Robert M. Hayden

You know, I'm a Hegelian: I know that the suffering of individuals is irrelevant to the greater processes of history.

> High official, "Republika Srpska," March 1994

Of course, it would be best to resolve problems with the minorities through negotiation, but we should never rule out military force.

> High official, Committee for Human Rights and Rights of Minorities, parliament of the Republic of Croatia, March 1994

We will not become a nation until being a Serb is more important than living where your ancestors lived.

> Radovan Karadžić, then President of "Republika Srpska," September 13, 1995

The collapse of the former Yugoslavia has been accompanied by violence that has shocked the world, particularly because it is happening in Europe, albeit in the Balkans.[1] The horror and revulsion that anthropologists share with others (e.g., Kideckel 1995) may, however, obscure the logic of the wars of the Yugoslav secessions and succession, especially the fatal incompatibility of the objectified or reified cultures (Handler 1988:14–16; Kapferer 1988:4, 22) at the base of the several nationalist enterprises with the living cultures of the areas that have been the sites of the worst violence.

The geography of the violence is an important consideration because the wars in the former Yugoslavia since 1991 have taken place almost entirely within regions that were among the most "mixed" – those in which the various nations of Yugoslavia were most intermingled. The extraordinary violence that has shattered these places was not the fury of nationalist passions long repressed by communism, as many journalists and politicians would have it. I argue instead that the wars have been about the forced unmixing of peoples whose continuing coexistence was counter to the political ideologies that won the free elections of 1990. Thus extreme nationalism in the former Yugoslavia has not been only a matter of imagining allegedly "primordial" communities, but rather of making existing heterogeneous ones unimaginable. In formal terms, the point has been to implement an essentialist definition of the nation and its state in regions where the intermingled population formed living disproof of its validity: the brutal negation of social reality in order to reconstruct it.

It is this reconstruction that turns the imagination of community into a process that produces real victims. This is not a Cartesian distinction or the manifestation of an analytical attachment to a symbolic-materialist framework. The fortunate members of the imagined community are as material as the unfortunates who have been excluded. Instead, I wish to pursue the power of a system of reified, prescriptive culture to disrupt the patterns of social life – culture in an analytical sense – that would contradict them. The point is certainly structuralist as per Mary Douglas (1966; see also Herzfeld 1993:22), in that "ethnic cleansing" is (to describe blood-shed in a bloodless manner) the removal of specific kinds of human matter from particular places. At the same time "ethnic cleansing" may also be a corollary to an inverted Lévi-Straussian myth of nation, a myth that does not provide a logical model capable of overcoming contradictions in existing social structure but instead proclaims that the existing social structure is contrary to logic and must therefore be destroyed.

As a process of homogenization "ethnic cleansing" can take many forms. Within areas in which the sovereign group is already an overwhelming majority, homogen-ization can be brought about by legal and bureaucratic means, such as denying citizenship to those not of the right group, thus also inducing those members of minorities who can assimilate to do so while evicting those who cannot assimilate or refuse to do so. In more mixed areas, homogenization requires more drastic meas-ures – the physical expulsion, removal, or extermination of the minority population. Although it is only the third of these processes that has come to be known as "ethnic cleansing" since the Yugoslav wars began, it is important to recognize that legal and bureaucratic discrimination is aimed at bringing about the same result: the elimin-ation of the minority.

Conceptually, the violence of ethnic cleansing may be seen as deriving from the clash of a prescriptive model of culture (culture-as-ideology) with what exists on the ground (culture-as-lived) but is not in accordance with the prescription. Phrasing the matter in this way is not to privilege the traditional subject matter of anthropol-ogy but, rather, to accommodate the current importance in "the West" of culture-as-ideology (what Verena Stolcke has termed "cultural fundamentalism" (1995)) as the key term in a rising political rhetoric of exclusion in Western Europe. A similar distinction, accommodating another rhetoric of exclusion and domination, is Ashis Nandy's differentiation of "faith," or "religion as way of life," from "ideology," "religion as . . . identifier of populations" in South Asia (1990:70). "Religious nation-alism" in India (van der Veer 1994) is comparable analytically to the "cultural nationalism" of Europe.[2] In both cases, what is contrasted is the difference between prescriptive views of what "culture" or "religion" *must* be and the ways in which people in particular places actually live. The imperative here is not only normative – what the culture should be – but also supposedly descriptive, thereby reproducing assumptions of the way the world really is, which is why the purported cultural deviation is abnormal.

At a time when many anthropologists routinely challenge any form of empiricism, a contrast between "ideology" and "the way people actually live" may seem naive. Yet surely patterns of social life – the use of one script instead of another, rates of intermarriage, or rates of the utilization of lexical items – are observable and may often not be congruent with prescriptive views of what such patterns should be. It is this lack of congruence between the present reality of life as lived and the objectification of life as it suddenly must be lived that produces the mortal horrors of ethnic cleansing.

Thus the juxtaposition of "reality" and "imagination" in my title has more than a rhetorical bite. The point of this analysis is to show the logic of the translation of category violation into mass violence, to adapt Michael Herzfeld's (1993:33) comment on Peter Loizos' work (1988) on intercommunal killing in Cyprus. Where Loizos was concerned with explaining the violence of certain individuals, however, I wish to consider the logic of the category system on which the ethnic nation-state is based as providing the inducement for mass violence. In this regard my point is similar to that of Herzfeld (1993). While the bureaucratic activities that Herzfeld analyzes include genocide, his emphasis is, however, elsewhere. My purpose is to address directly the mass violence that has so shocked observers, myself included. Further, the phenomenon I examine is not a matter of the production of "indifference," defined as "the rejection of common humanity" or as a "denial of identity" (Herzfeld 1993:1). On the contrary, the processes that I analyze recognize people as humans (albeit, perhaps, as inferior ones) and assign consequences to identities that the subjugated group does, in fact, claim. Serbs in Croatia, for example, may have claimed that identity more frequently after 1990 than they did in the preceding few decades, when many identified themselves as "Yugoslav." The meaning of the identity, however, changed.

Constitutions as Legitimation for Ethnic Cleansing

In this essay I look at the constitutions of the successor republics to the former Yugoslavia as manifesting and institutionalizing nationalist ideologies that aim to construct homogeneous nation-states in heterogeneous territories. I am concerned with the logic of the construction of a particular kind of state, the nation-state, when the word *nation* has connotations that Americans view as "ethnic," not primary in current American usage of the term. When Croatia is constitutionally defined as the "national state of the [ethnic] Croat people" (Constitution of the Republic of Croatia 1990, preamble) or Slovenia as the state of the sovereign Slovene people, "We, the people" has a very different meaning than it does in currently dominant American imagery.

Constitutions are among the most important subjects for the study of the implementation of nationalist ideologies precisely because they are meant to be *constitutive*, providing not only the conceptual framework for the state, but also the institutional means to make the state conform to that model. When the states envisioned by the constitutions exclude many residents from the bodies political and social, as in the successor states to the former Yugoslavia, the seemingly bloodless media of constitutions and laws are socially violent and may often induce bloodshed. My initial goal in this essay is thus to connect the cultural construction of "nation" with the legal constitution of states in the context of the former Yugoslavia and its successor republics. The analysis promises to be useful for other cases of ethnic nationalism, since some of the constitutional and legal phenomena found in the ex-Yugoslavia cases have close parallels elsewhere, particularly in Europe.

The homogenization of a heterogeneous polity may be achieved through forced assimilation or expulsion, as well as through border revision (see Macartney 1934:427–49). While compulsory assimilation may be less overtly violent than what is now called "ethnic cleansing," the two processes are based on the same principles and seem to be merely different strategies to bring about the same end. Resorting to physical violence occurs where cultural geography is most heterogeneous, thus rendering domination by non-violent means difficult (see Hayden 1995a). In this essay I consider "bureaucratic ethnic cleansing" as well as direct violence, recognizing both as consequences of the same logic in different social settings.

Long-Distance Fieldwork: The Ethnography of Ideology

Analyzing constitutions as mechanisms for turning nationalist ideologies into social practice is an enterprise for which traditional models of ethnography seem inapposite. The analysis of nationalist movements must be based on an analysis of texts produced by the proponents and opponents of any particular nationalist vision (see, e.g., Handler 1988:27–9; Verdery 1991:19–20), a move that may push the post-Geertzian metaphor of culture-as-text to its ultimate extreme. Yet these texts cannot be analyzed in isolation from the field of social relations in which they have been produced, read, and interpreted in thought and action (Verdery 1991:20). Fieldwork in the societies that are the referents of specific nationalist discourses seems to be a prerequisite for such a contextual analysis of nationalist texts. Certainly the meaning of a text varies with its audience but, in the study of nationalist ideologies, the range of meanings of texts that the authors and their primary audiences have in mind is ascertainable. To ascertain these meanings, however, requires a deep knowledge of the field of social relations that can only be achieved through protracted participation and observation in the society under study.

Yet the fieldwork required may be of a kind that does not fit into the traditional anthropological mode of "being there." Once the ethnographer has acquired a substantial base of knowledge of the social field in which nationalist texts are produced, it is often possible to monitor developments in this social field from a distance. Texts travel in newspapers, on the radio, and often, these days, on e-mail, so that someone in America may have an electronic version of today's newspapers from India, the former Yugoslavia, or elsewhere via the Internet. In this regard there are e-mail networks centering on Serbs and Serbia, Croats and Croatia, Bosnia,

Macedonia, and Slovenia, thereby making an extraordinary range of materials instantly available to researchers and other participant-observers throughout the world. Thus a knowledgeable reader can stay current on politics and ideological constructions in the former Yugoslavia without spending much time in the former Yugoslav republics.

Long-distance fieldwork of this kind is simply a corollary to the "transnational" conditions that anthropologists have noted in recent years (e.g., Appadurai 1991; Basch et al. 1994). If an Indian-born American anthropologist on a field trip to South India discovers that the temple priest he wishes to see is in Texas (Appadurai 1991:201), it requires no stretching of the concept of fieldwork to suggest that the researcher could go to Texas to question the priest. Nor is this a new situation in anthropology. After all, Lewis Henry Morgan gathered much of his kinship material for *Systems of Consanguinity and Affinity* (1870) by questioning "natives" – Japanese and various American Indians – who happened to be where Morgan was, in Rochester, Albany, or New York.

The possibility of doing long-distance fieldwork, however, may be predicated on first having done substantial field research of the more traditional anthropological variety, involving long-term residence in the society in question and linguistic fluency. Fieldwork from afar certainly benefits enormously from short visits to the location of local concern. This has certainly been the case in the present project. My research on the links between nationalist ideologies and their constitutional expression in what was then Yugoslavia began in 1989 after I had already spent more than three of the preceding eight years working in the country on other projects. Since then, visits of four months in 1991, a few days in 1993, one of three weeks and another of two months in 1994, and ten days in 1995 have enabled me to augment my analysis of texts with focused interviews.

The Multinational Federation and its Demise

Given the meanings of "Balkanization" in English (but see Bakić-Hayden and Hayden 1992; Todorova 1994) and the widespread assumption that the various Yugoslavs have always fought each other, it is necessary to substantiate the assertion that the former Yugoslavia, if not exactly a peaceable kingdom, was a state in which ethnic or nationalist tensions did not always – or even often – dominate daily life. Accordingly, in this section and the following part of this essay I explore the community of Yugoslavia by examining evidence of heterogeneity in the territories of the country and the intermingling, in all senses, of its component peoples.

The Yugoslavia that existed from 1945 until 1991, a multinational state in which no single group comprised a majority, was premised on multiculturalism. Although it was composed of republics in which all but one had a clear majority of the group for which it was named (e.g., Serbs in Serbia, Croats in Croatia), all of these republics also had sizable minority populations. The republic of Bosnia and Hercegovina, the exception, had no majority group: in 1981 its population comprised Muslims (39.5 percent), Serbs (32.0 percent), Croats (18.4 percent), "Yugoslavs" (7.9 percent), and "others and unknown" (2.2 percent). In the 1991 census these proportions were, respectively, 43.7 percent, 31.4 percent, 17.3 percent, 5.5 percent, and 2.1 percent (Petrović 1992:4). At the other end of the spectrum, the most homogeneous republic, Slovenia, had a population that was 90.5 percent Slovene in 1981 and 87.6 percent Slovene in 1991 (Petrović 1992:9).

The political geography of the country reflected these territorial concentrations. The Socialist Federal Republic of Yugoslavia (1945–91/92) was a federation of six republics (Bosnia-Hercegovina, Croatia, Macedonia, Montenegro, Serbia, and Slovenia) and two "autonomous provinces" within the republic of Serbia (Vojvodina and Kosovo). With the exception of Bosnia-Hercegovina, each republic or autonomous province was the area of the greatest territorial concentration of one of the major national groups that comprised Yugoslavia. Thus in 1991, 99.3 percent of the Slovenes in Yugoslavia lived in Slovenia, while 70.6 percent of the Montenegrins lived in Montenegro.

In the free elections held in 1990 after the collapse of the League of Communists, the winning message in each republic was one of classic nationalism: Serbia for Serbs, Croatia for Croats, Slovenia for Slovenes, and Macedonia for Macedonians. In Bosnia-Hercegovina the vote resembled an ethnic census, with Muslim, Serb, and Croat nationalist parties accounting for about 80 percent of the total, in proportions only slightly less than those of each national group in the population of the republic; the most important party standing for a civil state of equal citizens, the Alliance of Reform Forces of Yugoslavia of the federal prime minister, received only 5.6 percent of the vote – less than the 6.0 percent received by the "reformed" communists (see Hayden 1993a). The victorious politicians in Serbia, Slovenia, and Croatia worked independently, and for their own reasons, to disable the federal government, thereby attaining the de facto state sovereignty mentioned earlier (Woodward 1995; see also Jović 1995). Thus each republic except Bosnia-Hercegovina became a true nation-state based on the sovereignty of the majority national group.

The separate nationalist political movements were justified on the grounds of "self-determination." This famous concept, however, had a specific meaning in Yugoslav politics and popular culture, one that had grim implications for any concept of a civil state of equal citizens. A statement in the first line of the 1974 Yugoslav Constitution about "the right of every nation to self-determination, including the right to secession"[3] referred, not to the populations or citizens of republics, but to the nations, *narodi* (singular: *narod*), of Yugoslavia, ethnically defined. While these "nations" were recognized as having their several republics, it was the "nations," not the republics, that were described as having united to form the Yugoslav state; the Yugoslav republics, unlike those of the Soviet Union, did not have a right to secede.

This seemingly arcane distinction between "nation" and "republic" as the bearer of rights was actually of vital political importance. The key to the separate nationalist political movements in Yugoslavia after 1989 was the explicit conflation of the "nation," ethnically defined, and the "state." Although this formulation was hardly new to European history, it did have sinister implications for minorities in states that were suddenly defined as the nation-states of their respective ethnic majorities. By definition, anyone not of the majority ethno-nation could only be a citizen of second class. The key to this distinction lay in the concept of *sovereignty*. As nationalist politicians came to power in the various Yugoslav republics after the elections of 1990, they rewrote their respective republican constitutions to justify the state on the sovereignty of the ethnically defined nation (*narod*) in which others might be citizens but could not expect an equal right to participate in control of the state.

The politics of nationalism in Yugoslavia in the late 1980s and early 1990s thus turned territories populated by concentrations of the various national groups into states in which the members of the majority nation were sovereign (see Denich 1994; Hayden 1992a). The presumption of the politics was that the various Yugoslav peoples could not live together and that therefore their common state had to be divided. The electoral success of this message meant the defeat of the "Yugoslav idea" of a common state of the south Slavic peoples, an ideology that had been devised as a counter and rival to the separate national ideologies of each group (see A. Djilas 1991). To reverse Benedict Anderson's evocative phrase (1983), the disintegration of Yugoslavia into its warring components in 1991–2 marked the failure of the imagination of a Yugoslav community. This failure of the imagination, however, had real and tragic consequences: the Yugoslav community that could not be maintained, and thus has become unimaginable, had actually existed in many parts of the country. Indeed, it is my argument that the spatial patterning of the war and its terrible ferocity are due to the fact that in some regions the various Yugoslav peoples were not only coexisting but also becoming increasingly intermingled. In a political situation premised on the incompatibility of its components, these mixed territories were both anomalous and threatening since they served as living disproof of the nationalist ideologies. For this reason, the mixed regions could not be permitted to survive as such, and their populations, which were mixing voluntarily, had to be separated militarily.

Heterogeneity, Mixed Marriages, and "Yugoslavs"

Despite the maintenance of high levels of territorial concentration of the various national groups in their respective republics, the levels of ethnonational heterogeneity throughout most of Yugoslavia were increasing. In Slovenia, for example, the concentration of the Slovene population increased from 97.7 percent of Slovenes residing in Slovenia in 1981 to 99.3 percent in 1991 (Petrović 1992:15). During this same decade, however, the homogeneity of Slovenia decreased: 90.5 percent of the population were Slovenes in 1981, compared with 87.6 percent in 1991 (Petrović 1992:9). Nor was Slovenia unusual in this regard. From 1953 to 1981 almost all of the territories of Yugoslavia became increasingly heterogeneous (Petrović 1987:48); that is, in almost all republics and provinces, the percentage of the population that was made up by the majority national group declined. The exceptions were the two autonomous provinces in Serbia, Vojvodina and Kosovo. In Vojvodina the Serbian majority increased, in part because of the low birthrate among the next largest group, the Hungarians. In Kosovo the Albanian majority increased, in part because of the high Albanian birthrate and the massive Serbian emigration from the province.[4] Between 1981 and 1991, heterogeneity increased in Montenegro, Macedonia, Slovenia, and Serbia, but decreased in Croatia[5] and Bosnia-Hercegovina (Petrović 1992).

Accompanying the increasing heterogeneity of most of the republics was an increase in the rates of intermarriage between members of the different national groups. Intermarriage is usually thought to indicate increasing assimilation and to increase integration of social groups (e.g., Blau et al. 1982). From the early 1950s through the 1980s, "mixed" marriages increased both in absolute numbers and in proportion to all marriages throughout most of Yugoslavia (*Vreme* 1991), but were particularly common between Serbs and Croats, and between Serbs and Muslims in Bosnia-Hercegovina. Not surprisingly, the highest rates of intermarriage occurred in the places in which the populations were the most intermingled: the large cities, the province of Vojvodina, Bosnia-Hercegovina, and the parts of Croatia that had large numbers of Serbs and Croats.[6]

If we consider the frequency of the claim that Serbs and Croats suffer from age-old hatreds, it is worth scrutinizing their increasingly close coexistence in Croatia after 1945 despite the terrible massacres of Serbs by the fascist "Independent State of Croatia" from 1941 to 1945.[7] According to the 1991 census, 12.2 percent of the population of Croatia were Serbs, primarily residing in Zagreb, but otherwise concentrated in several parts of the republic – specifically Slavonija, Banija, Kordun, and Lika. In Lika the population was almost entirely Serb, and there were few intermarriages. In areas where Serbs and Croats lived together, however, they intermarried in large numbers. For example, in the town of Petrinja in Banija, where the population was almost equally divided between Serbs and Croats, about 25 percent of the marriages were mixed, while in the major towns of Slavonija the percentages of mixed marriages climbed to 35 percent in the town of Pakrac (*Borba* 1991).

Mixed marriages produce children of mixed background. Already by 1981, approximately one-third of the children born in Slavonijan towns such as Osijek were of mixed Serb-Croat background (*Borba* 1991). Bosnia-Hercegovina had the highest percentage of "mixed" children – 15.9 percent overall – also concentrated in the most mixed areas. Even Slovenia, the republic with the highest concentration of its national minority group, had large numbers of "mixed" or "foreign" births: 7.9 percent issuing from mixed marriages, with another 19.0 percent from non-Slovene marriages, leaving only 73.1 percent of children issuing from "purely Slovene" marriages (*Borba* 1991).

Another indicator of heterogeneity can be found in the figures on those who identified themselves in the censuses as "Yugoslavs" instead of as Serbs, Croats, Muslims, or any other national group. Between the 1971 and 1981 censuses the numbers of "Yugoslavs" increased sharply from 1.3 to 5.4 percent of the total population (Burg and Berbaum 1989). The distribution of these ethnic "Yugoslavs" was nevertheless far from consistent throughout Yugoslavia. In 1981 they lived primarily in Belgrade and the Vojvodina in Serbia, in the major industrial centers in Bosnia-Hercegovina, Istria, and some larger centers in Croatia, as well as in the "mixed" regions of Croatia (Petrović 1987:152–3; *Danas* 1991). The age distribution of these Yugoslavs in 1981 indicated that this identity was preferred by younger people, which led some researchers to conclude tentatively (and subject to the rise of precisely the type of nationalist politics that destroyed Yugoslavia in the late 1980s) that Yugoslavia was developing an increasing sense of community and that support for the multinational community was likely to increase, as would self-identification as Yugoslavs (Burg and Berbaum 1989).

Although these statistics do not indicate that national identity vanished, it is clear that national identity was not a primary focus of most people's concerns in the early

1980s. Ethnographers from mixed regions have consistently reported that while national differences were recognized, tensions were low in the 1980s until political events from outside of these regions overtook them (Bringa 1993 [Bosnia]; Jambrešić 1993 [Banija]; Olsen 1993 [Slavonija]).[8]

The rise of mutually hostile nationalisms led to a sharp decline in the percentage of Yugoslavs throughout the country, from 5.4 percent in 1981 to 3.0 percent in 1991 – a 41.3 percent drop. Again, the rates of decline by republic were not even. The percentage of Yugoslavs dropped most dramatically in Croatia, from 8.2 to 2.2 percent (a 72.3 percent drop) but also declined everywhere else: Bosnia-Hercegovina by 26.5 percent, Serbia by 28.1 percent, and Slovenia by 53.4 percent (Petrović 1992). The percentages of Yugoslavs remained highest, however, in the most mixed regions: Bosnia-Hercegovina (5.5 percent) and the mixed areas of Croatia – where Yugoslavs had been most numerous in 1981 (*Danas* 1991).

It should be noted that the decline in the number of self-identified "Yugoslavs" may often have represented a calculated assessment that continuing to identify oneself as such for official purposes was becoming increasingly hazardous. At the time of the census (April 1991) I was told by a number of people that they would prefer to continue to identify themselves as Yugoslavs but were afraid that doing so could cost them their jobs, and perhaps even their property, in the chauvinist political climate then dominant.[9]

Through the early 1980s, then, most parts of Yugoslavia showed an increasing heterogenization of populations, accompanied by increasing numbers of mixed marriages and births of children of mixed parentage, and a rise in the percentage of those who identified themselves as "Yugoslav" rather than as members of any of the ethnonational categories. But the distribution of these factors was not random. Instead, heterogeneity was concentrated in the central part of the territory of Yugoslavia: the republic of Bosnia-Hercegovina, the parts of Croatia bordering Bosnia-Hercegovina and Vojvodina, and Vojvodina itself. In these parts of Yugo-slavia, the idea that the Yugoslav peoples could not live peacefully together was empirical nonsense. It was perhaps because these regions constituted living disproof of the nationalist ideologies that became politically dominant after the late 1980s that, except for Vojvodina, those territories in which the intermingling of the populations was most complete have been the major theaters of the war. This is not to attribute causation to the structural argument; empirical priority must be given to the fact that the nationalists claimed the same "mixed" territories and were willing to fight over them. But the structural argument provides the basis for understanding how the empirical facts of "cleansing" become acceptable, even seemingly desirable.[10]

Constitutionalizing Nationalism

Contrary to the official rhetoric both of winners and of most Western observers, the free elections of 1990 in Yugoslavia did not replace state socialism with democracy. Instead, the transition was from regimes dedicated to advancing the interests of that part of the population defined constitutionally as "the working class and all working people" (see Hayden 1992a) to regimes dedicated to advancing the interests of that part of the population defined as the ethnonational majority. In this sense, the transition was from state socialism to state chauvinism, and socialism's "class enemy" was replaced by the national enemy identified by the particular local chauvinism (Hayden 1992a). Not surprisingly, these national enemies were primarily the members of the largest minority in each polity, along with any members of the majority who might try to support rights for the minority.

Once in power, the victorious nationalists in each republic began to enact systems of *constitutional nationalism*, meaning constitutional and legal systems devised to ensure the dominance of the majority ethnonational group (see Hayden 1992a). Thus, for example, the constitution of Croatia (1990)[11] gives in its preamble a capsule history of the efforts of the Croat "nation" (*narod*) to establish "full state sovereignty." After mentioning the "inalienable . . . right of the Croat nation to self-determination and state sovereignty," the Republic of Croatia is "established as the national state of the Croat nation and the state of the members of other nations and minorities that live within it" (Constitution of the Republic of Croatia 1990, preamble). In all these passages, "Croat nation" (*Hrvatski narod*) has an ethnic connotation and excludes those not ethnically Croat. This exclusionary definition of the bearer of sovereignty is reinforced by the emblems of the state – a flag and coat-of-arms bearing designs associated only with Croats (art. 11) – and the specification that the official language and script of Croatia are "the Croatian language and Latin script" (art. 12), thereby excluding the Serbian dialects and the Cyrillic alphabet customarily used to write them.[12] Similar formulations of constitutional nationalism have arisen in other republics (Hayden 1992a:658–63).

The transition from state socialism to state chauvinism is seen in the formulations of state identity and purpose contained in the various republican constitutions. Whereas the socialist constitutions grounded the state in the dual sovereignty of "the working class and all working people" and "the nations and nationalities" of Yugoslavia, the collapse of socialism left only one sovereign (Samardzic 1990:31). Furthermore, the formation of a state for each of these sovereign "nations" was justified by the right of self-determination. This is seen in the preambles or prefatory parts to the various constitutions (emphasis added in each case):

Proceeding from . . . the inalienable and inextinguishable *right to self-determination and state sovereignty of the Croation nation*, the Republic of Croatia is established as the national state of the Croatian nation and the state of members of other nations and minorities who are its citizens. (Constitution of the Republic of Croatia 1990, preamble)

Resting upon the historical, cultural, spiritual and statehood heritage *of the Macedonian nation* and upon their centuries' long struggle for national and social freedom, as well as for the creation *of their own state* . . . Macedonia is established as the national state of the Macedonian nation. (Constitution of the Republic of Macedonia 1991, preamble)

On the basis of the historical *right of the Montenegrin nation to its own state*, established in centuries of struggle for freedom . . . the Parliament of Montenegro . . . enacts and proclaims the Constitution of the Republic of Montenegro. (Constitution of the Republic of Montenegro 1991, preamble)

Proceeding from the centuries-long struggle *of the Serbian nation* for independence . . . determined to establish a democratic *state of the Serbian nation* . . . the citizens of Serbia enact the Constitution of the republic of Serbia. (Constitution of the Republic of Serbia 1992, preamble)

Proceeding from . . . the basic and lasting *right of the Slovene nation to self-determination* and from the historical fact that *Slovenes* have, over centuries of struggle for national liberation formed their national identity and *established their own statehood*, the Parliament of the Republic of Slovenia enacts the Constitution of the Republic of Slovenia. (Constitution of the Republic of Slovenia 1990, preamble)

Although not internationally recognized, the "Republic of Serbian Krajina," the self-proclaimed Serbian state in Croatia, defined itself in its constitution in much the same terms as the recognized successor states above:[13]

Proceeding from the *right of the Serbian nation to self-determination* . . . and the centuries-long struggle for freedom . . . , determined to *establish a democratic state of the Serbian nation on its own historical and ethnic space*, in which the other citizens are guaranteed the realization of their national rights, a state based on the *sovereignty belonging to the Serbian nation* and other citizens in it . . . the Serbian nation of the Republic of Serbian Krajina . . . enacts the Constitution of the republic of Serbian Krajina. (Constitution of the Republic of Serbian Krajina 1991, preamble)

Similarly, the "Republika Srpska," the Serbian "entity" in Bosnia-Hercegovina, proclaimed:

Proceeding from the inalienable and untransferable natural *right of the Serbian nation to self-determination, self-organization and association*, on the bases of which it freely establishes its own political status and secures its economic, social and cultural development. . . . To proclaim [*the Serbian nation's*] *determination to decide independently its own fate and to proclaim its firm will to establish its own sovereign and democratic state*. . . . The Parliament of the Serbian nation in Bosnia and Hercegovina enacts the Constitution of the Republika Srpska. (Constitution of the Republika Srpska 1992, preamble)

In each of these preambles, the word *nation* (*narod* in all of the languages involved) has an ethnic connotation; *narod* has the same root (*rod*) as the verb *roditi* (to give birth, to be born). When preceded by the ethnic adjective (Croatian, Macedonian, Montenegrin, Serbian, Slovenian), the constructions exclude those not of the specified ethnicity. From the excerpts above, and particularly the phrases emphasized, it is clear that the various formerly Yugoslav republics are considered to be manifestations of the right to self-determination – meaning the right to form one's own state – of the majority, titular nation (*narod*), even when some expression is given to the equality of minorities. Again, a contrast can be made with the Preamble of the US Constitution, which provides simply that "We the People of the United States . . . do ordain and establish this Constitution."[14]

Bosnia-Hercegovina, like the former Yugoslav federation itself, represents the failure of an attempt to define the state in such a way as to recognize the sovereignty of all of its constituent groups without privileging any of them. The last socialist constitution of Bosnia-Hercegovina (1974) defined the republic as

a socialist democratic state and a socialist self-management democratic community of working people and citizens, the nations [*narodi*] of Bosnia and Hercegovina – Muslims, Serbs, Croats, and members of other nations and nationalities living within it, based on the rule and self-management of the working class and all working people and on the sovereignty and equality of the nations of Bosnia and Hercegovina and the members of the other nations and nationalities that live within it. (art. 1)

As socialism collapsed this definition was replaced by a constitutional amendment, so that the definition of the state in Article 1 read:

The Socialist Republic of Bosnia and Hercegovina is a democratic sovereign state of equal citizens, of the nations of Bosnia and Hercegovina – Muslims, Serbs and Croats, and members of other nations and nationalities living within it.[15]

Yet this definition did not satisfy the aspirations of Serbian and Croatian political figures in Bosnia-Hercegovina. In part because of problems of defining the state, no new constitution for Bosnia-Hercegovina was ever passed, and, as Yugoslavia collapsed, the Serb and Croat leaders in Bosnia proclaimed their own self-determining regions within the republic. These regions quickly became quasi-states, closely linked to Serbia and Croatia, respectively, and were independent of the supposedly sovereign government of Bosnia-Hercegovina in Sarajevo (see Shoup 1994). The war that followed effected the partition of Bosnia-Hercegovina into regions that were meant to be, and are fast becoming, ethnically "pure" (see Hayden 1993a). This partition was inevitable once Yugoslavia collapsed because the self-determination of the Yugoslav *nations* (*narodi*), the political program that succeeded in 1990, meant that the Serbs and Croats of Bosnia-Hercegovina would be drawn inevitably toward union with their ethnic confrères.[16] Thus "self-determination" brought on the civil war that destroyed Bosnia-Hercegovina.

The Constitution of the Federation of Bosnia and Hercegovina that was written with the help of American diplomats and signed in Washington, DC, by Croats and Muslims in March 1994, is based on a constitutional nationalism that excludes Serbs from the sovereign peoples of Bosnia-Hercegovina. While the preamble states, "The peoples and citizens of Bosnia and Hercegovina, determined to establish full national equality, democratic relations, and the highest standard of human rights and freedoms, hereby create a Federation," Article 1 then asserts that

Bosniacs and Croats, as constituent peoples (along with others) and citizens of the republic of Bosnia and Hercegovina, in the exercise of their sovereign rights, transform the internal structure of the territories with a majority of Bosniac and Croat population in the Republic of Bosnia and Hercegovina into a Federation.[17]

The term *Bosniac*, an Anglicization of *Bošnjak*, has a purely Muslim referent and is not the same as *Bosnian* (*Bosanac*), and is a term for ethnic Muslims that avoids the specifically religious implications of *Muslimani*. In any event, this constitution excludes Serbs from the structure of the federation, apportioning executive offices to Muslims/Bosniacs and Croats (IV.B.1. arts. 2–5) and ensuring veto power in the legislature to Muslim/Bosniac and Croat delegations but not to others (IV.A.4 art. 18). The exclusion of Serbs became apparent immediately after the constitutional draft was signed in Washington, DC, when a Sarajevo conference of Serbs who were loyal to the idea of a multiethnic Bosnian state asked to be included in negotiations. They were ignored (*New York Times* 1994). The Dayton-Paris peace treaty that in December 1995 brought the Bosnian war to at least a temporary halt manifests constitutional nationalism in much the same way as the Federation constitution of 1994 by giving Muslims and Croats superior rights over all others in their portion of Bosnia, and the same to Serbs in theirs (see Hayden 1995b).

Citizenship: Denaturalization as Bureaucratic Ethnic Cleansing

In popular speech and in the rhetoric of many international documents, the world is composed of nations. At the levels of law and politics, however, it is composed of states. Citizens of a state almost always possess rights that non-citizens do not share, and this was certainly true in the republics of the former Yugoslavia. As these states achieved independence their governments began to write rules to determine who could stay and who could not, who could work and who could not, who could vote and who could not, who would receive medical insurance or other benefits and who would not, and who would be permitted to own real property and who would not. In each case, citizens were entitled to the rights and benefits; non-citizens were – at best – only temporarily entitled to them. Thus the question of citizenship in the successor states to the former Yugoslavia is one of utmost importance to the people living in them, since those who do not attain citizenship will be denied the rights essential for any kind of normal life.

It must be emphasized that for many the question of citizenship was new. As noted earlier, the constitution of Yugoslavia had provided for a single, uniform Yugoslav citizenship and guaranteed the equality of Yugoslav citizens throughout the country. Suddenly, however, the citizenship of many residents in the newly independent states became questionable. New citizenship laws, written to privilege the members of the sovereign majority in each case, have worked to discriminate against residents who were not members of the majority groups. In essence, the new citizenship regimes have simultaneously extended citizenship to non-resident members of the majority ethnonation through easy naturalization while denying citizenship to many residents who are not of the right group. This last process turns residents who had been equal citizens of federal Yugoslavia into foreigners of their own republics, a process we might call *denaturalization*.

Neither of these phenomena is unique to the formerly Yugoslav republics. The easy extension of citizenship to non-resident ethnonational-religious confrères is well known (as in Ireland and Israel), while the denial of citizenship to large numbers of people who until then were thought to have held it was the purpose of the 1981 British Nationality Act (Gilroy 1987). In this last case, however, many of the "denaturalized" potential citizens were not resident in Britain at that time. The combination of the easy naturalization of non-residents with the denaturalization of residents seems uncommon, but is manifested now in the successor states of the former Yugoslavia and the former Soviet Union (see Brubaker 1992, 1993). The power of an imagined ethnic community (Anderson 1983) to break up actually existing communities in these post-communist settings is clear.

With the demise of Yugoslavia, the immediate practical question for many citizens of those erstwhile states was citizenship in one of the successor states. Here, laws and policies have varied. At the most inclusive end, the Slovenian Citizenship Act of 1991 offered citizenship to all citizens of another Yugoslav republic who had resided in Slovenia on the day that the plebiscite on independence was held, and most applicants have been granted citizenship (Mazowiecki 1993a:44). Even so, approximately 50,000 citizens of Yugoslavia who were counted in the 1991 census as residing in Slovenia have become foreigners there since the independence of that republic (*Vreme* 1993:33). Other states have been far less accommodating. Unlike the Slovenian law, the law on Croatian Citizenship of 1991 made no special provision for citizens of other Yugoslav republics but instead rendered them all "foreigners" who were required to seek naturalization. Furthermore, Serbs in Croatia have complained that their requests for citizenship or for naturalization have been denied (see Mazowiecki 1992:22, 1993a:26–8). Although the Croatian authorities have denied discriminating against Serbs, relatively large numbers of requests for citizenship have been rejected (*Vreme* 1993:34). The Law on Croatian Citizenship permits the authorities there to reject a citizenship application even though the applicant has met all the criteria if they "are of the opinion that there are reasons in the interest of the Republic of Croatia for refusing the request for the acquisition . . . of citizenship" (art. 27, sec. 2). The same article provides that these authorities need not state their reasons for rejecting an application (art. 27, sec. 3). Thus, as the Serbs have complained, the opportunity for discrimination certainly exists.[18]

The laws governing citizenship and naturalization are interesting because they are the mechanisms through which the imagination of an ethnonational community is made manifest and actualized. Specifically, these laws provide the grounds for the acquisition of membership in the community, thus revealing the principles thought to define it. Again, the Law on Croatian Citizenship (1991) is interesting.[19] Article 8 of this law stipulates the following:

A foreign citizen who files a petition for acquiring Croatian citizenship may acquire Croatian citizenship by naturalization if he meets the following requirements:

(1) [age requirement: 18]
(2) [omitted]
(3) that before the filing of the petition, he had a registered place of residence for a period of not less than five years uninterrupted on the territory of the Republic of Croatia.
(4) that he is proficient in the Croatian language and Latin script.
(5) that a conclusion can be drawn from his conduct that he adheres to the laws and customs prevailing in the Republic of Croatia and that he accepts Croatian culture.

At first glance Section 3 and 4 of this article do not seem to be overly controversial, but both open wide opportunities for discriminatory application. The residency requirement depends on the interpretation of the qualification "uninterrupted" (*neprekidno*). More interesting is the language qualification. The dialects of what has until now been known as Serbo-Croatian or Croato-Serbian are myriad and intermixed, with some Serbian populations speaking dialects similar to those spoken by most Croats, and some Croat populations speaking dialects similar to those spoken by most Serbs (see Hammel 1993: 7–8). Serbs prefer to use the Cyrillic alphabet, while Croats almost never use it. Thus the language criterion is problematic: is someone who speaks the Belgrade dialect proficient in the "Croatian language"? Who decides, and on what grounds? Would a "Serbian" dialect qualify if the speaker is an ethnic Croat but not otherwise?

Section 5, however, is most revealing. What, exactly, does it mean to "accept Croatian culture," and how does one conduct oneself to show such acceptance? Since the primary distinguishing feature of Croatian culture is Roman Catholicism, must one convert to that faith? If not, what does accepting Croatian culture entail? This provision of the law takes a concept that anthropologists have regarded as descriptive and analytical and makes it prescriptive; yet the concept remains empty of specific content.

It is this prescription of culture that turns it into an object (Kapferer 1988:2; cf. Handler 1988:14). The essentialism involved verges on racism when it entails viewing reified culture as somehow surviving transplantation into another country where the chosen people are a minority.[20] In the Croatian case, these implications become clear in the special rules for emigrants and their descendants (art. 11) and for members of the Croatian nation (*narod*) who do not reside in Croatia (art. 16). In regard to both categories, Croatian citizenship can be acquired even though the applicant does not meet the requirements stated in Article 8, sections 1–4, but these candidates must still meet the requirement of section 5. To an anthropologist the complete separation between language and culture inevitably seems odd; yet it is restated twice and so seems not to have been a slip of the drafter's pen. This provision provides a tool for extending citizenship only to ethnic Croats (e.g., the child of Croat emigrés from Croatia or of ethnic Croats from Serbia) while denying it to others similarly situated (e.g., the child of Serb emigrés from Croatia). Taken together, the naturalization provisions of the Law on Croatian Citizenship may lead to situations in which, for example, a Muslim from Bosnia, long resident in Croatia and a native speaker of a Croatian dialect of what used to be called Serbo-Croatian, is denied citizenship, while an ethnic Croat from the United states, who has never been to Croatia and who doesn't know the language, is granted Croatian citizenship. While the actual number of such cases in Croatia is unknown, it is interesting to note that the Slovenian provisions in regard to naturalization also privilege ethnic Slovenes, and that while 50,000 residents of Slovenia who were citizens of the former Yugoslavia have not acquired Slovenian citizenship, 25,000 ethnic Slovenes from outside of Slovenia have done so (*Vreme* 1993:34).[21] Again the power of the imagined ethnic community to break up communities on the ground is apparent. The new citizenship laws provide the legal means to exclude individuals from citizenship on ethnic grounds – in essence, bureaucratic ethnic cleansing.

Self-Determination, Homogenization, and "Ethnic Cleansing"

The logic of "national self-determination" in Yugoslavia not only legitimates homogenization of the population but has also made that process so logical as to be irresistible. The course of the war has followed this logic of establishing the nation-state by eliminating minorities. What can be done bureaucratically by a majoritarian regime in a state with a numerically overwhelming majority, however, must be accomplished in other ways if the majority is not secure in its rule – specifically, military conquest and the subsequent expulsion of the unwanted population.

The Serbs, who initially took by far the greatest amount of territory, have also committed by far the largest number of human rights violations. Nevertheless, the

1993 Croatian offensives to establish an ethnically pure Herceg-Bosna followed the same course in central Bosnia (Mazowiecki 1993a:8–10; 1994:6) and Mostar (Mazowiecki 1993a). "Population exchanges" have been part of this effort (Mazowiecki 1994:9–10).

The result of the war as of late 1994 was the more or less complete exchange of populations outside of Sarajevo, as shown in table 11.1.

During the spring and summer of 1995, this process of expelling populations increased on the part of all parties. In May a Croatian offensive against the Serb enclave of Western Slavonia led to the expulsion of virtually all Serbs from that part of Croatia. In July Serb forces took two of the Muslim "safe areas" in eastern Bosnia and expelled or killed all residents. In August a Croatian offensive in the Krajina expelled close to 200,000 Serbs from Croatia, the single largest incidence of ethnic cleansing in the wars. Thus, between June 1991 and August 1995, more than 85 percent of the Serb population of Croatia was forced to leave the country (*Vreme* 1995).

As in Croatia, the summer of 1995 brought even greater waves of "ethnic cleansing" by the various forces. In July – as I have just mentioned – the Bosnian Serbs captured two Muslim "safe areas" in eastern Bosnia and expelled or killed the inhabitants. In September the Muslims, with the support of the Croatian army, began an offensive in western Bosnia that drove tens of thousands of Serbs out of west-central Bosnia, just north of a line running from Jajce to Bihac. Before the war began much of this region had been populated almost exclusively by Serbs. The effects of all these military actions on population distribution are summarized in table 11.2.

Despite much-publicized protestations that the international community would never accept the ethnic partition of Bosnia, the Dayton-Paris peace treaty does precisely this by recognizing that Bosnia is composed of two "entities": the Croat-Muslim "federation" and "Republika Srpska," each under its own constitution (Hayden 1995b). Since, as I have shown above, these constitutions define their respective states in ethnic terms, this agreement under international sponsorship legitimates the ethnic partition of Bosnia. But that partition had already been

Table 11.1 United Nations High Commission for Refugees (UNHCR) population estimates

	1991 Census	*November 1994 estimate*
Croat-Muslim federation		
Serbs	205,185	36,000
Muslims and Croats	1,209,804	1,673,000
Serb-held territories		
Serbs	928,857	1,169,000
Muslims and Croats	838,190	73,000
Eastern enclaves		
Serbs	20,000	none
Muslims	80,000	115,000

Source: Balkan War Report 1995:5

Table 11.2 Population estimates for the areas of control in Bosnia and Hercegovina

Region[a]	Muslims	Serbs	Croats	Total population
Bihac region	200,000	5,000	6,000	211,000
Northern Bosnia (Banja Luka region)	7,000–10,000	660,000–730,000	3,000	660,000–730,000
Central Bosnia	850,000–1,000,000	20,000	130,000	850,000–1,000,000
Government-held areas of Sarajevo	230,000	30,000	20,000	280,000
Eastern Bosnia (Serb-held)	5,000[b]	530,000–560,000		535,000–560,000
Croat-held areas (Western Hercegovina and Central Bosnia)	100,000	5,000	550,000	655,000

[a] The information in this table originated from a map issued by the US Government's Bosnian Task Force.
[b] Muslims and Croats
Source: US Government 1995

accomplished on the ground. The multiethnic Bosnia that was once actual, and for that reason prescriptive from the point of view of the international community, no longer exists and thus can no longer be prescriptive.

From Optimism of the Intellect to Pessimism of the Will

The analysis of ethnic cleansing as a manifestation of the incompatibility of the objectified or reified cultures at the base of the several nationalist enterprises with the living cultures of the areas that have been the sites of the worst violence is at once intellectually reassuring and deeply disturbing. It is encouraging intellectually to know that anthropological frameworks of analysis can explain the violence that has destroyed what had been the ethnically mixed regions of the former Yugoslavia. A rationalist might propose that since we know so much about the phenomena involved, perhaps we can prevent their recurrence in another place and time.

Yet another stream of rational thought induces pessimism. The circumstance that induces ethnic cleansing is one of category violation. While it may be that contradictions are not resolved in myth and dream, in the realm of cultural politics the drive to make the world conform to a vision of the way it supposedly should be is powerful. That the vision is flawed empirically is irrelevant. Indeed, once the vision receives general support, its empirical falsity simply adds ferocity to the drive to accomplish it.

A comparative look also gives further pause for thought. What we now call ethnic cleansing has been seen quite often in the twentieth century, above all in Europe, but not only there. A look at some examples shows that the process has often succeeded in creating a new reality. For example, Poland expelled six million Germans in 1945, while three million Jews were eliminated from Poland in the period 1939–46, most being killed or deported in the Holocaust. The result has been the creation of one of the most ethnically pure states in Europe, a condition that is generally seen as to Poland's advantage in attaining post-socialist "democracy." Similarly, the expulsion of more than three million Germans from Czechoslovakia in 1945 has rendered the now independent Czech republic ethnically pure and thus, like Poland, ready for democracy. Hungary, the other leading candidate for the European Union and NATO, became ethnically pure after World War I through its exclusion of those territories where Hungarians and others lived together. Thus Slovakia, Romania, and Serbia have internal ethnic tensions with Hungarians, but Hungary has none in its own territory. In the Yugoslav wars, Croatia's expulsion of its Serbs was viewed by the American Ambassador to Croatia as a positive step in resolving the Yugoslav conflicts (*OMRI Daily Report* 1995). "Ethnic cleansing" in Europe is thus a phenomenon that has proven successful both in recreating social reality and in gaining political acceptance.

Faced with this historical experience and with that of the Yugoslav wars, perhaps I may be excused if I adapt and reverse Gramsci's famous dictum. We can now, as anthropologists, understand very well the processes that lead to ethnic cleansing; but we can also see how unlikely it is that, once started, they can be stopped. Optimism of the intellect here leads to pessimism of the will.

NOTES

1   Attempts to distinguish "the Balkans" from "Europe" have been central to much of the political discourse over the legitimacy or necessity of political acts concerning Yugoslavia's collapse and subsequent wars, both by Yugoslav politicians and by those on the world stage who have had to deal with them (see Bakić-Hayden 1995; Bakić-Hayden and Hayden 1992; Todorova 1994). Considering the extent of the devastation that Europeans have wrought on each other, to say nothing of the rest of the world, in what Günther Grass has called "the century of expulsions" (1992:27) such rhetorical exercises are suspect and are rejected here.

2   While I cannot explore the matter in this article, I suggest that what Gunnar Myrdal (1944) identified as the basis of the "American dilemma" – racism – is paralleled in different idioms elsewhere, such as a "European dilemma" of nationalism, or a South Asian one of "communalism." Note that in all cases, the dilemma is a moral one, caused by the persistent existence of supposedly "natural" distinctions in politics that profess aspirations toward democracy.

3   Constitution of the Socialist Federal Republic of Yugoslavia 1974: "Introductory Part, Basic Principles."

4   Bosnia-Hercegovina showed a rather different trend: the Serbian plurality recorded there in 1961 became a Muslim plurality in 1971, after the recognition of "Muslim" as a nationality in 1967 and the subsequent change in the declaration of nationality by many who had called themselves Serbs in 1961 (see Petrović 1987:47).

5   The increase in the percentage of Croats in Croatia in the 1991 census was apparently the result of a shift by many who had identified themselves as "Yugoslav" in 1981, to "Croat." The number of "Yugoslavs" in Croatia declined by 72 percent between these two censuses: from 8.2 percent of the population in 1981 to 2.2 percent in 1991 (Petrović 1992:7).

6   I am not convinced by the recent argument by Botev and Wagner (1993) that intermarriage did *not* increase in Yugoslavia, an argument that considers aggregate data on the

level of the republic and thus is not sensitive to regional variations. Furthermore, the symbolic value of what they view as small numbers of intermarriages was great. Contrary to their reasoning, Ivan Šiber of the University of Zagreb has documented a sharp decline in intermarriages in Croatia since 1991 and interprets this as a sign of the homogenization of the population (*Feral Tribune* 1994).

7   The extent of these massacres became a topic of hot debate in the late 1980s, with Croatian historians attempting to minimize the numbers (see Boban 1990; for a discussion of this see Boban 1991; Hayden 1992b, 1993b, 1994). Croatian sensitivity on this topic can be seen in a ferocious attack – far in excess of normal standards of propriety in American scholarship – on Hayden's comments on Boban by a second Croat writer (Knežević 1993; reply in Hayden 1993b). A recent, extremely careful analysis of the data on World War II victims in Yugoslavia (Bogosavljević 1995) gives figures far lower than most Serbs imagine but far higher than most Croats will admit.

8   The transformation of the people in a mixed Muslim–Croat village from neighbors of different faiths into enemies of different nationalities is seen in Tone Bringa's stunning ethnographic film, *Bosnia: We Are All Neighbors*, broadcast in America on PBS in May 1994 (Bringa 1994).

9   Some respondents to the census registered a protest against the whole process by listing themselves as Eskimos, Bantus, American Indians, Citroëns, lightbulbs, and refrigerators – among other fanciful categories. The deadly nature of the categories was brought home to participants at a seminar on "Beyond Genocide" at John Jay College in New York in April 1993, when a human rights group from the town of Zenica in Bosnia-Hercegovina used leftover blank copies of the 1991 census forms as the paper for a book of pictures of atrocities committed on the Muslims of Bosnia-Hercegovina.

10 The phrasing of the last two sentences owes much to suggestions by Bette Denich. The reasonableness, in Western philosophical terms, of the competing nationalist claims is explained by Vladimir Gligorov (1995).

11 In this section of the essay and the one that follows it, a great deal of emphasis is given to the analysis of Croatian constitutional and legal materials. Unfortunately, in the political climate surrounding the demise of the former Yugoslavia, the analysis of Croatian materials is frequently perceived by Croats as "anti-Croat," "pro-Serbian," or "disproportionate" if less space is devoted to the analysis of Serbian materials. Since this article deals primarily with constitutional and legal materials, however, it focuses on those documents that best exemplify the points under discussion, which are Croatian. Serbian materials are less revealing, not because Serbs manifest the phenomena at issue any less than do Croats, but rather because the Serbian regime of Slobodan Milošević has put into place constitutional and legal structures that look progressive but that have little bearing on the actions of that authoritarian state (see also Hayden 1992a:660). The criticism is in any event misguided, since it is based on the assumption that Croatian materials should be immune to analysis because of the actions of the Serbs, a proposition that is difficult to defend in regard to academic work.

12 To be sure, this same constitutional article contains a second clause permitting the use, in particular local jurisdictions, of another language and script, "*under conditions established by statute*" (emphasis added). Both limitations, however, are suspect. If local jurisdictional lines are gerrymandered so that no minority is anywhere a local majority, the constitutional provision becomes meaningless. Furthermore, the subjugation of a supposed constitutional right to ordinary legislation vitiates the right. Thus, for example, a statute providing that one could use the "Serbian language in Cyrillic script" to write to the Minister for Religious Affairs, *and only for that purpose*, would be constitutional yet serve to deny, in a practical sense, the supposed "right."

13   The "Republic of Serbian Krajina" was destroyed by Croatian military action in August
     1995 and almost all of its population was expelled from Croatia.
14   The US Constitution as written in 1787 did recognize a difference between "free persons"
     and "all other persons," and excluded "Indians not taxed" (art. 1, sec. 2). Furthermore,
     American citizenship was limited by law to only "white persons" until after the Civil War,
     and even then naturalization was permitted only to "white persons" and "Africans or
     persons of African descent" until 1952 (see Gettys 1934). A more appropriate contrast
     might therefore be the Preamble to the Constitution of India (1950), designed to imple-
     ment a democratic system in a polity fragmented along lines of caste, religion, and
     language, as well as social class:

     We, the people of India, having solemnly resolved to constitute India into a sovereign,
     secular, democratic republic and to secure to all its citizens: Justice . . . Liberty . . . Equality
     . . . Fraternity . . . do hereby adopt, enact and give to ourselves this constitution. (Consti-
     tution of India 1950, preamble)

15   Amendment LX to the Constitution of the Socialist Republic of Bosnia and Hercegovina
     (*Službeni List Socijalističke Republike Bosne i Hercegovine*), 46:499, no. 21, July 31,
     1990.
16   The Vance–Owen plan, which ostensibly was aimed at preserving a single Bosnia-
     Hercegovina, recognized this fact of political life by opposing the division of Bosnia-
     Hercegovina into only three ethnically determined regions, saying that,

     a confederation formed of three such states would be inherently unstable, for at least two
     would surely forge immediate and stronger connections with neighboring states of the
     former Yugoslavia than they would with the other two units of Bosnia and Hercegovina.
     (International Conference on the Former Yugoslavia 1992)

     Nevertheless, the Vance–Owen plan for dividing Bosnia-Hercegovina into ten completely
     autonomous regions was unrealistic, since it amounted to proclaiming a house divided to
     be a condominium despite the demonstrated willingness of many of the residents to raze
     the edifice (see Hayden 1993a).
17   From the Constitution of the Federation of Bosnia and Hercegovina (draft of March 13,
     1994, 5 p.m.), obtained from the Embassy of Croatia, Washington, DC, in English as one
     of three (with Croatian and Bosnian) original languages.
18   As is the case with the constitutional provisions (see note 12 above), Serbia is less
     susceptible to analysis because that state, and the Federal Republic of Yugoslavia that
     contains it, is hardly a legal state at all. In the present instance, there is no new citizenship
     law in Serbia, and I am not aware of any analysis of Serbian practices in this regard. The
     bureaucratic requirements for obtaining citizenship in the new Yugoslavia (*Vreme* 1992)
     and the general pressure on minorities in that country (see Mazowiecki 1992:27–36;
     1993a:32–42), however, indicate that the situation there is likely to be manipulated in
     order to discriminate against non-Serbs.
19   *Zakon o hrvatskom državljanstvu*, *Narodne Novine* 1991 #53:1466–9; amended in
     Narodne Novine 1992, #28:659.
20   Stolcke (1995) distinguishes "cultural fundamentalism" from racism but considers only
     the political rhetoric surrounding immigration, not that linking emigrés with the home-
     land. It is this latter link that must envision culture as an attribute of birth and thus as
     substance rather than as simply a code for conduct.
21   Again it is necessary to state that the situation in regard to the determination of Serbian
     citizenship is no different (Mazowiecki 1993b: 26–7). Because Serbia has been an inter-

national pariah since 1992, probably few are clamoring to acquire its citizenship. Indeed, I have met many Serbs who would like to acquire Croatian, Macedonian, or even Bosnian citizenship for purely pragmatic reasons, such as facilitating travel and emigration. Most have found this impossible to do, however, even when their parents were from those republics.

REFERENCES

Anderson, Benedict (1983). *Imagined Communities: Reflections on the Origin and Spread of Nationalism*. London: Verso.

Appadurai, Arjun (1991). "Global Ethnoscapes: Notes and Queries for a Transnational Anthropology." In Richard Fox (ed.), *Recapturing Anthropology: Working in the Present*. Santa Fe, NM: School of American Research Press, pp. 191–210.

Bakić-Hayden, Milica (1995). "Nesting Orientalisms: The Case of Former Yugoslavia." *Slavic Review* 54:917–31.

Bakić-Hayden, Milica, and Hayden, Robert (1992). "Orientalist Variations on the Theme 'Balkans': Symbolic Geography in Recent Yugoslav Cultural Politics." *Slavic Review* 51:1–15.

Balkan War Report (1995). December 1994–January 1995:5.

Basch, Linda, Schiller, Nina Glick, and Blanc, Cristina Szanton (1994). *Nations Unbound: Transnational Projects, Postcolonial Predicaments and Deterritorialized Nation-States*. Amsterdam: Gordon and Breach.

Blau, Peter, Blum, Terry, and Schwartz, Joseph (1982). "Heterogeneity and Intermarriage." *American Sociological Review* 47:45–61.

Boban, Ljubo (1990). "Jasenovac and the Manipulation of History." *East European Politics and Societies* 4:580–92.

Boban, Ljubo (1991). "Still More Balance on Jasenovac and the Manipulation of History." *East European Politics and Societies* 6:213–17.

Bogosavljević, Srdjan (1995). "Drugi Svetski Rat – Žrtve u Jugoslaviji." *Republika* (Belgrade), June 1–15, 1995: XI–XVI.

Bogosavljević, Srdjan, Goati, Vladimir, Grebo, Zdravko, Hasanbegović, Jasminka, Janjić, Dušan, Jojić, Branislava, and Shoup, Paul (1992). *Bosna i Hercegovina izmedju Rata i Mira*. Belgrade and Sarajevo: Forum za Etničke Odnose.

Borba (1991). September 30:11.

Botev, Nikolai, and Wagner, Richard (1993). "Seeing Past the Barricade: Ethnic Intermarriage in Yugoslavia during the Last Three Decades." *Anthropology of East Europe Review* 11(1–2):27–34.

Bringa, Tone (1993). "National Categories, National Identification and Identity Formation in 'Multinational' Bosnia." *Anthropology of East Europe Review* 11(1–2): 69–76.

Bringa, Tone (1994). *Bosnia: We Are All Neighbors*. London: Granada Television (Disappearing Worlds). Film.

Brubaker, Rogers (1992). "Citizenship Struggles in Soviet Successor States." *International Migration Review* 26: 269–91.

Brubaker, Rogers (1993). "Nationhood and the National Question in the Soviet Union and Post-Soviet Eurasia: An Institutionalist Account." *Theory and Society*.

Burg, Steven, and Berbaum, Michael (1989). "Community, Integration and Stability in Multinational Yugoslavia." *American Political Science Review* 83:535–54.

Danas (1991). August 6:21.

Denich, Bette (1994). "Dismembering Yugoslavia: Nationalist Ideologies and the Symbolic Revival of Genocide." *American Ethnologist* 21:367–90.

Djilas, Aleksa (1991). *The Contested Country*. Cambridge, MA: Harvard University Press.

Douglas, Mary (1966). *Purity and Danger: An Analysis of Concepts of Pollution and Taboo*. London: Routledge.

Feral Tribune (1994). January 11.

Gettys, Luella (1934). *The Law of Citizenship in the United States*. Chicago: University of Chicago Press.

Gilroy, Paul (1987). *There Ain't No Black in the Union Jack*. Chicago: University of Chicago Press.

Gligorov, Vladimir (1995). "What if They Will Not Give Up?" *East European Politics and Societies* 9:499–512.

Grass, Günther (1992). *The Call of the Toad*. New York: Harcourt, Brace, Jovanovich.

Hammel, Eugene A. (1993). "Demography and the Origins of the Yugoslav Civil War." *Anthropology Today* 9(1):4–9.

Handler, Richard (1988). *Nationalism and the Politics of Culture in Quebec*. Madison: University of Wisconsin Press.

Hayden, Robert M. (1992a). "Constitutional Nationalism in the Formerly Yugoslav Republics." *Slavic Review* 51:654–73.

Hayden, Robert M. (1992b). *The Beginning of the End of Federal Yugoslavia: The Slovenia Amendment Crisis of 1989*. University of Pittsburgh Center for Russian and East European Studies, The Carl Beck Papers no. 1001.

Hayden, Robert M. (1993a). *The Partition of Bosnia and Herzegovina, 1990–93*. RFE/RL Research, May 28, 1993:1–14.

Hayden, Robert M. (1993b). "On Unbalanced Criticism." *East European Politics and Societies* 7:577–82.

Hayden, Robert M. (1994). "Recounting the Dead: The Rediscovery and Reinterpretation of Wartime Massacres in Late- and Post-Communist Yugoslavia." In Rubie S. Watson (ed.), *Memory and Opposition under State Socialism*. Santa Fe, NM: School of American Research, pp. 167–84.

Hayden, Robert M. (1995a). "Constitutional Nationalism and the Logic of the Wars in Yugoslavia." Paper presented at conference on "Post-Communism and Ethnic Mobilization." Cornell University, Ithaca, NY: April 21–23.

Hayden, Robert M. (1995b). "The 1995 Agreements on Bosnia and Herzogovina and the Dayton Constitution." *East European Constitutional Review* 4(4):59–68.

Herzfeld, Michael (1993). *The Social Production of Indifference: Exploring the Symbolic Roots of Western Bureaucracy*. Chicago: University of Chicago Press.

International Conference on the Former Yugoslavia (1992). Document STC/2/2. October 27:5.

Jambrešić, Renata (1993). "Banija: An Analysis of Ethnonymic Polarization." In Lada Feldman, Ines Prica, and Reana Senjkovic (eds.), *Fear, Death and Resistance: An Ethnography of War: Croatia 1991–1992*. Zagreb: Institute of Ethnology and Folklore Research, pp. 73–118.

Jović, Borisav (1995). *Poslednji Dani SFRJ*. Belgrade: Politika.

Kapferer, Bruce (1988). *Legends of People, Myths of State*. Washington, DC: Smithsonian Institution Press.

Kideckel, David (1995). "Human Rights in Former Yugoslavia." *Society for the Anthropology of Europe Bulletin* 9(3):1.

Knežević, Anto (1993). "Some Questions about a 'Balanced' Discussion." *East European Politics and Societies* 7:155–66.

Law on Croatian Citizenship (*Zakon o hrvatskom državljanstvu*) (1991). *Narodne Novine* #53:1466–9.

Law on Croatian Citizenship (*Zakon o hrvatskom državljanstvu*) (1992). *Narodne Novine* #28:659.

Loizos, Peter (1988). "Intercommunal Killing in Cyprus." *Man* (n.s.) 23:639–53.

Macartney, Carlile A. (1934). *National States and National Minorities*. London: Oxford University Press.

Mazowiecki, Tadeusz (1992). *Report on the Situation in the Territory of the Former Yugoslavia prepared by Mr. Tadeusz Mazowiecki, Special Rapporteur of the Commission on Human Rights*. United Nations, General Assembly and Security Council, document A/47/666 and S/24809 (annex), November 17.

Mazowiecki, Tadeusz (1993a). *Situation of Human Rights in the Territory of the Former Yugoslavia*. United Nations, Economic and Social Council, document E/CN.4/1993/50, February 10, 1993.

Mazowiecki, Tadeusz (1993b). *Fifth Periodic Report on the Situation of Human Rights in the Territory of the Former Yugoslavia*. United Nations, Economic and Social Council, document E/CN.4/1994/47 November 17.

Mazowiecki, Tadeusz (1994). *Sixth Periodic Report on the Situation of Human Rights in the Territory of the Former Yugoslavia*. UN document E/CN.4/1994/110 February 21.

Morgan, Lewis Henry (1870). *Systems of Consanguinity and Affinity of the Human Family*. Washington, DC: Smithsonian Institution Press.

Myrdal, Gunnar (1944). *An American Dilemma: The Negro Problem and Modern Democracy*. New York: Harper and Brothers.

Nandy, Ashis (1990). "The Politics of Secularism and the Recovery of Religious Tolerance." In Veena Das (ed.), *Mirrors of Violence: Communities, Riots and Survivors in South Asia*. Delhi: Oxford University Press, pp. 69–93.

New York Times (1994). September 1:A–15.

Olsen, Mary Kay G. (1993). "Bridge on the Sava: Ethnicity in Eastern Croatia, 1981–1991." *Anthropology of East Europe Review* 11(1–2):54–62.

OMRI (Open Media Research Institute [formerly Radio Free Europe/Radio Liberty]) *Daily Report* (1995). Weekday news service release via e-mail. August 10, Part 2.

Petrović, Ruža (1987). *Migracije u Jugoslaviji i Etnički Aspekt*. Belgrade: SSO Srbije.

Petrović, Ruža (1992). "The National Composition of Yugoslavia's Population, 1991." *Yugoslav Survey* 1992(1):3–24.

Samardzic, Slobodan (1990). *Jugoslavija pred Iskušenjem Federalizma*. Belgrade: Strućna Knjiga.

Shoup, Paul (1994). "The Bosnian Crisis of 1992." In Sabrina Ramet (ed.), *Beyond Yugoslavia*. Boulder, CO: Westview Press, pp. 155–87.

Stolcke, Verena (1995). "Talking Culture: New Boundaries, New Rhetorics of Exclusion in Europe." *Current Anthropology* 36:1–24.

Todorova, Maria (1994). "The Balkans: From Discovery to Invention." *Slavic Review* 53:453–82.

US Government (1995). "Population Estimates and Areas of Control in Bosnia and Herzegovina, November 8." Map 737639 (ROO895).

van der Veer, Peter (1994). *Religious Nationalism: Hindus and Muslims in India*. Berkeley: University of California Press.

Verdery, Katherine (1991). *Nationalist Ideology under Socialism: Identity and Cultural Politics in Ceausescu's Romania*. Berkeley: University of California Press.

Vreme (1991). March 11:31.

Vreme (1992). August 3:16–17.

Vreme (1993). March 8:33–4.

Vreme (1995). August 28:8–11.

Woodward, Susan (1995). *Balkan Tragedy: Chaos and Dissolution after the Cold War*. Washington, DC: Brookings Institution.

12

A Head for an Eye: Revenge in the Cambodian Genocide

Alexander Laban Hinton

> To outsiders, and often to ourselves, Cambodia looked peaceful enough. The farmers bound to their planting cycles. Fishermen living on their boats.... The wide boulevards and the flowering trees of our national capital, Phnom Penh. All that beauty and serenity was visible to the eye. But inside, hidden from sight the entire time, was *kum. Kum* is a Cambodian word for a particularly Cambodian mentality of revenge – to be precise, a long-standing grudge leading to revenge much more damaging than the original injury. If I hit you with my fist and you wait five years and then shoot me in the back one dark night, that is *kum....* Cambodians know all about *kum.* It is the infection that grows on our national soul.
>
> Haing Ngor, *A Cambodian Odyssey*

In April 1975 the Khmer Rouge overthrew the US-backed Lon Nol regime, thus ending a bloody civil war in which perhaps six hundred thousand Cambodians had died.[1] The Khmer Rouge quickly reorganized Democratic Kampuchea (DK) along strict communist lines that glorified peasant life. The cities were emptied and their inhabitants sent to live and work in the countryside as "new" people (*brâcheachon tmey*) who constituted the bottom social strata below cadre, soldiers, and "old" people (*brâcheachon chas*) who had lived under Khmer Rouge rule during the war.[2] Economic production and consumption were collectivized, Buddhism banned, and the family subordinated to the Party Organization, Ângkar. As a result of starvation, overwork, disease, and outright execution, over one and a half million of Cambodia's eight million inhabitants – more than 20 percent of the population – perished by the time Vietnam invaded the country in January 1979 (Kiernan 1996).

How do such genocides come to take place?[3] While social scientists in other fields have addressed this question, anthropology has remained largely silent on the origins of large-scale genocide (De Waal 1994; Kuper 1981; Lewin 1992; Shiloh 1975). Anthropologists have conducted some research on the atrocities committed during the Holocaust (e.g., Connor 1989; Dumont 1986; Gajek 1990; Jell-Bahlsen 1985; Lewin 1993; Stein 1993) and, more recently, in Bosnia (e.g., Bringa 1993, 1995;

Denich 1994; Hayden 1996). Even less material has been written on the genocides that have occurred in non-European countries like Cambodia and Rwanda (but see Ebihara 1990, 1993; Hinton 1996, 1997; Malkki 1995, 1996; Marston 1985, 1994).

Nevertheless, there are encouraging signs that anthropology stands poised to begin making a significant contribution to the comparative study of genocide. In recent years, the number of anthropological analyses of political violence has greatly proliferated as anthropologists have attempted to explain the origins of conflicts in Sri Lanka (e.g., Daniel 1996; Kapferer 1988; Tambiah 1986, 1992), Ireland (e.g., Aretxaga 1995, 1997; Feldman 1991; Sluka 1989), Argentina (e.g., Robben 1996; Suárez-Orozco 1990), and other locales (Besteman 1996; Coronil and Skurski 1991; Das 1990; Desjarlais and Kleinman 1994; Lan 1985; Nordstrom 1997; Nordstrom and Martin 1992; Nordstrom and Robben 1995; Riches 1986; Tambiah 1989, 1996; Taussig 1987; Warren 1993; see also Nagengast 1994). These scholars have demonstrated the crucial ways in which violence is linked to social and cultural factors.

In this essay, which is based on fifteen months of fieldwork in Cambodia,[4] I provide an example of how such anthropological insights can be applied to large-scale genocide. In particular, I will show how the Cambodian cultural model of disproportionate revenge (*karsângsoek*) contributed to the genocidal violence that occurred during DK. In contrast to a biblical conception of revenge that is premised on the talion principle of "an eye for an eye," the Cambodian model of disproportionate revenge involves disproportionate retaliation against one's enemy, what I call "a head for an eye." In the first section of this essay I summarize *Tum Teav*, a violent epic poem that enacts an extreme version of this cultural model; it concludes with King Rama's (*Reamea*) obliteration of Governor Archoun's (*Ârchoun*) family line seven generations removed. I then describe the Cambodian cultural model of disproportionate revenge in greater detail, noting that it may vary in severity and scale. In the third section I demonstrate how the most lethal forms of this model were directly manipulated in Khmer Rouge ideological discourse about a "class grudge," thus providing a template for much of the group vengeance that took place in DK.

I should note, however, that the cultural model of disproportionate revenge does not guide Cambodian behavior in a deterministic manner. Cultural models may be differentially internalized, vary in their distribution and saliency across contexts, and have disparate degrees of motivational force for people (D'Andrade and Strauss 1992; Shore 1996; Strauss and Quinn 1994).[5] Moreover, when a person acts, he or she often has a variety of available options. Cambodians who are publicly insulted will therefore not automatically seek disproportionate revenge (Hinton 1997). Drawing on an alternative set of Buddhist norms,[6] they may choose "to block/control [their] hearts" (*tuap chett*) or to "disperse [their] anger" (*rumsay komboeng*). Other Cambodian strategies for controlling anger include internalization, the use of culturally constituted defense mechanisms, and low-level or indirect expression. Even if individuals come to hold a grudge for the insult, they choose when, how, and whether to seek revenge.

Such choices, however, are not made in a vacuum. Human behavior is both enabled and constrained by sociocultural structures – including cultural models that are an important part of what scholars have variously termed "habitus"

(Bourdieu 1977, 1990), "practical consciousness" (Giddens 1984), "discourse" (Foucault 1979, 1980), and "hegemony" (Williams 1977). Just as the Kabyle sense of honor consists of internalized generative schemes ("structured structures") that organize ("structuring structures") Kabyle practice (Bourdieu 1977), so too is the cultural model of disproportionate revenge a form of knowledge which most Cambodians have internalized and may be inclined to enact in given circumstances. Such cultural knowledge constitutes a crucial site upon which genocidal regimes can work. Within an appropriate historical and sociocultural context, those who articulate genocidal ideologies often use these highly salient cultural models to motivate individuals to commit violent atrocities (e.g., Goldhagen 1996; Hinton 1997; see also Kapferer 1988). As we shall see, this is exactly what happened during DK, as the exponents of Khmer Rouge ideology invoked the Cambodian cultural model of disproportionate revenge.

The Story of *Tum Teav*

The Cambodian cultural model of disproportionate revenge is clearly embodied in *Tum Teav* (Sânthor Mok 1986), the most famous romantic epic in Cambodia.[7] The story of *Tum Teav*, which bears some similarity to *Romeo and Juliet*, was first composed or put into writing by the nineteenth-century poet Sânthor Mok and is thought to have a partial basis in historical fact. (Because Sânthor Mok's manuscript was in poor shape, a poet named Saom reworked *Tum Teav* in 1915.) *Tum Teav* is taught in schools throughout the country, recounted orally by village elders and parents, and sometimes dramatically enacted on special occasions. Almost all Cambodians are thus familiar with this legend, which has never been translated into English.

Set in the sixteenth century, *Tum Teav* begins when Tum, a handsome young monk, sets out with a fellow monk and friend, Bic, to sell bamboo rice containers for their pagoda. When they arrive at a village in Tbaung Khmum province, the inhabitants coax Tum, who has a lovely voice, into singing religious chants. Teav, a beautiful young girl who is just entering womanhood, hears Tum sing, falls in love with him, and sends Tum a message telling him about her feelings. After Tum returns to his pagoda, he cannot eat or sleep because he misses Teav so much. Tum decides to disrobe against the will of the chief monk, who has foreseen that Tum will soon die if he does this. Tum and Bic return to Tbaung Khmum. Meanwhile, the powerful governor of the province, Archoun, has asked Teav's mother for permission to marry Teav to his son. Teav's mother is jubilant about the prospect of her daughter's marriage into a family of great wealth and honor. Teav, however, refuses to consent to the marriage because she longs for Tum. When Tum arrives in Tbaung Khmum, he goes to Teav's house and professes his love for her. She invites him to stay with her and they sleep together. The next day, Teav's mother returns from an overnight trip to find Tum there. Not knowing that Tum and Teav are lovers, she agrees to let Tum stay at the house.

The king of Cambodia, Rama, hears of Tum's wonderful singing and sends for him to come and sing at the palace. King Rama is so impressed by his singing that he asks Tum to remain at the palace as a court singer. Meanwhile, the king has sent emissaries throughout the land to find him a wife. In Tbaung Khmum, the emissaries see Teav and decide she would be a perfect match for the king. Hoping to curry favor with the king, Archoun agrees to break off his son's engagement to Teav. Teav's mother is even more pleased at this marriage prospect. Teav and Tum continue to long to be together. When Teav arrives at the palace, King Rama calls for Tum to come and sing for his prospective bride. Upon seeing that the bride is Teav, Tum decides to risk death by singing about his love affair with Teav. The king becomes extremely angry, but Teav tells the king that Tum has spoken the truth. King Rama's anger diminishes and he arranges for the two of them to be married.

Upon hearing that her daughter has married the impoverished Tum, Teav's mother becomes very upset. She decides to send a message to Teav saying that she is gravely ill and asking Teav to return home to nurse her back to health. Meanwhile, she goes to see the powerful provincial governor, Archoun, and arranges for Teav to be married to Archoun's son. When Teav discovers her mother's real intentions, she is heartbroken and sends Tum a letter explaining what has transpired. Tum becomes furious and immediately returns to Tbaung Khmum.

Tum and Bic arrive in Tbaung Khmum on the day of the wedding. After working his way through the crowd, Tum calls out for Teav who comes and reaffirms her love for him. Upon seeing Tum, Archoun is filled with rage and orders his guards to kill Tum. They capture Tum and beat him until he falls dead under a Bo tree. Teav runs to the spot, takes out a knife, cuts her throat, and then dies on top of Tum's body. After these events, Bic returns to the palace and tells the king what has happened. King Rama becomes irate that Archoun has killed Tum and disregarded his authority, and orders his army to prepare to go to Tbaung Khmum. When they arrive, Archoun, who is extremely frightened, brings gifts and food to the king in order to assuage his anger. King Rama ignores his supplications and commands that Archoun's family and relatives seven generations removed be buried up to their necks in the ground and then have their heads raked off by an iron plow and harrow. In addition, all the members of Archoun's political faction are to be boiled alive and the residents of the district forbidden to leave the area. After King Rama's subordinates carry out his orders to eliminate Archoun's family line and faction in this way, King Rama returns to his palace.[8] In the next section, I will explain how King Rama's actions embody the Cambodian cultural model of disproportionate revenge.

A Head for an Eye: The Cambodian Cultural Model of Disproportionate Revenge

Since I was little, I have not wanted to argue with anyone. Even if another person does something that makes me mad, I don't want to argue with them. I try to control my heart (*tuap chett*). If I argue with another person, I might stop speaking to them forever after, but I wouldn't want to fight them. But I know in my heart, if I ever did get into a fight with someone, I would beat them until they were no longer alive. I would beat them to death at once. I wouldn't want the person to live because I know he would take revenge upon me on a later day. So I don't want to argue with anyone.

Cambodian male, mid-twenties

There is also "Khmer" – meaning a way to resort immediately to maximum violence, not so much to *resolve* a conflict as to *suppress* its root cause. This aspect of Khmer personality has been touched upon but not yet fully studied.

Serge Thion, *Watching Cambodia*

As Ngor notes in the opening epigraph of this essay, one of the most chronic and volatile sources of violence in Cambodia is a "grudge" (*kum, kumkuon, kum-num, kongkuon*) that leads to the desire for "disproportionate revenge" (*karsâng-soek*). One women's rights worker succinctly described the origins of a grudge to me as follows: "A person will hold a grudge when he or she understands that another person has done something very bad to him or her; he or she will have this one thought kept inside his or her heart." While such a grudge most often arises when another person (or group) makes the individual in question (or that person's group) suffer (e.g., by murdering a family member), lose power (e.g., by deposing that person from office), and/or lose face (e.g., by dishonoring that person by a slight), it almost always involves anger, shame, and the desire to "defeat" (*chneah*) a foe.

Vengeance has a distinct moral basis in Cambodian culture. The root of the word *sângsoek, sâng*, refers to the moral obligation "to return (an object), to pay back (debt), to pay for damage" (Headley 1977:1039). One of the greatest virtues in Cambodia is repaying (*sâng*) the "kindness" (*kun*) of others. Thus, Cambodians are morally obliged to "repay the good deeds" (*sângkun*) that their parents, relatives, teachers, and patrons have done for them. An ingrate who ignores this debt (*romilkun*) is widely detested. Whereas in many Judeo-Christian societies such moral debts are often viewed as analogous to a commercial transaction (Johnson 1993), in Cambodia they frequently create a personalized relationship between the two parties involved. In general, those who receive a good deed will acknowledge their debt through greater respect, loyalty, and attachment to the benefactor, although the intensity and structure of the bond will vary according to the situation and the respective status of each person in the dyad. The increased respect given to the person who does the good deed signals the benefactor's elevation in hierarchical standing *vis-à-vis* the debtor.

By extension, we can see that revenge is the moral inverse of gratitude (see Benedict 1946).[9] Just as people must return a good deed, so too are they morally obliged to repay a bad deed. The word *sângsoek* literally means "to pay back" (*sâng*) "the enemy" (*soek*). Moreover, the injured party's obligation to repay an enemy for whatever the latter has done creates a bond between them. A Cambodian bearing malice is often said to be "tied, linked" (*châng*) to an enemy by anger or a grudge (*châng komhoeng, châng kumnum*). During the post-Khmer Rouge communist period (SOC/PRK), for example, the government sponsored a national holiday on May 20 that was popularly known as the "Day to Remain Tied in Anger" (or, sometimes, the "Day of Hate"). In each district, people would gather at the local DK killing field to listen to government officials and victims speak about the atrocities that had occurred under the Khmer Rouge regime. Villagers often carried knives, axes, clubs, or placards saying things like "Defeat the Pol Pot, Khieu Samphan, Ieng Sary Clique" or "Remember Life under Pol Pot who tried to Destroy the Cambodian Lineage." The holiday no doubt served as an effective device to keep many people "tied in anger" against the Khmer Rouge, who were still engaged in guerrilla warfare against the government.

This type of grudge can result from either a single "happening" (*preuttekar*) or a series of smaller events that gradually add up. On the one hand, a person will often desire revenge when someone else does "something very bad" to that individual. Thus Tum has a grudge against Archoun who is attempting to remarry Teav to his son, and a large proportion of the Cambodian populace continues to bear malice toward the Khmer Rouge who were responsible for their great suffering and the deaths of family members. Similarly, in November of 1994, when the American evangelist Mike Evans arrived in Cambodia promising to cure the blind and heal the crippled, people from all over the country sold their possessions to come to Phnom Penh to attend his healing and proselytizing rallies. While he gave out free Bibles, Evans failed to provide any miracle cures. By the third night, the attendees realized that they had been duped by a foreigner and began to riot. One police officer predicted that if "he stays, he dies" (*Phnom Penh Post* 1994:21). Evans barely escaped Cambodia with his life; he continues to have enemies there who want to pay him back for his bad deed. (After Evans had returned to the United States, he reported to his American congregation that his trip to Cambodia had been a great success.)

Alternatively, a grudge may gradually develop as a person endures a series of small yet memorable "happenings." While usually able to manage their anger so that open disputes do not break out, Cambodians do not always simply forget about a matter. Lim, a research assistant who had formerly been a soldier, once told me, "Cambodians never forget – they remember things forever. After several little anger-provoking happenings, they will begin to hold a grudge." This pattern of silently harboring resentment may be initially modeled for children when they fight. Parents will separate quarreling children and tell them not to argue, but usually do not tell them to apologize to or to make peace with their adversaries. To do so would involve a slight loss of face for both the child and the parents. As one informant explained, "To say 'excuse me' makes them too lowly. It is like saying 'please let me lose.' Sometimes the parents of a kid who loses a fight will become extremely angry." The result is that children often "do not learn how to forget their anger" and will occasionally hold a small grudge and may stop speaking to those with whom they have been fighting for several days, months, or even forever afterward.

Cambodians have a variety of phrases that express the idea of storing away the memory of events that have angered them. They sometimes say that a person takes such anger (or a grudge) and "hides it inside the body" (*leak tuk knong kluen*), "puts (or keeps) it in the head" (*tuk knong khuor kbal*), or "buries (or hides) it in the heart" (*bângkap/leak knong chett*). For example, a young man named Tic, who was from a moderately poor family, was invited to attend a wedding at the home of one of the richest families in Kompong Cham city. When Tic arrived at the receiving line, however, the parents and the bridal couple did not smile or politely greet him. He stated, "I lost face and had a small heart. These rich people were not paying adequate respect to me because I am poor. I got drunk at the wedding and hid my anger so they wouldn't know." While Tic said that he did not have a grudge against the family, he was nevertheless "hiding his anger inside his heart." A series of such minor incidents can make a person resentful and angry, a condition that

Cambodians sometimes call being "seized with painful anger" (*chheu chap*).[10] As we shall see, such a build-up of class resentment proved quite lethal during DK when Khmer Rouge ideology encouraged the poor to take revenge upon the rich for past abuses.

What is common to the above examples of malice is a pattern in which an event or a series of smaller incidents causes a person to suffer or be shamed, which, in turn, leads to anger, resentment, and, ultimately, the desire for revenge. A Cambodian who has a big grudge is sometimes said to want to "eat the flesh and sip the blood" (*si sach hot cheam*) of the enemy. Despite this strong desire to take revenge, however, Cambodians recognize that it is often not propitious to repay a bad deed immediately. A grudge thus contains an element of latent potentiality and is frequently long-lasting. One religious wise man (*achar*) explained, "A grudge is packaged anger that has not yet come out; it remains inside, always hot, but it doesn't leave. It keeps waiting until 'I' (*ânh*) have the opportunity to strike immediately." To maintain an element of surprise or to prevent a powerful adversary from taking the initiative, Cambodians bearing malice will often try to hide their animosity from their foes. Like anger, a grudge is usually kept hidden. During everyday interactions, Cambodians may therefore smile and act politely toward an enemy; when the appropriate occasion arises, however, they will act.

Those who are unable to seek revenge in person may decide to hire a killer or order a subordinate to perform the deed. Several Cambodian journalists have been murdered by assassins weeks or months after having written insulting articles about government officials and businessmen. Alternatively, people sometimes hire sorcerers to cast black magic upon their adversaries (see also Wikan 1990 on the Balinese). After Mike Evans had fled Cambodia, for example, it was reported that some Cambodians harassed and attacked his Christian followers with black magic (Mang 1995:17). Many Cambodians are extremely frightened of black magic, which, they believe, can make a person terminally ill, and will try to protect themselves by wearing such magical objects as a pig's fang, a fragment of an elephant's tusk, a piece of gold, a magical string, an inscribed cloth, a Buddha amulet, or some combination of these.

Why does a Cambodian grudge frequently lead to revenge that, as Ngor notes in the opening epigraph, is "much more damaging than the original injury?" Earlier I pointed out that benefactors gain respect, elevate their status, and create moral debts by performing good deeds. Conversely, the perpetrator of a bad deed shows disrespect toward, lowers the status of, and "defeats" (*chneah*) the recipient who, in turn, has a moral obligation to repay the bad action. Merely to repay this debt with an equivalent act, however, would leave the parties on an equal footing. Because Cambodians are strongly motivated to want to be "higher than" others, they will strive to defeat – and thus rise above – their adversary by doing something even worse to them. As Ngor notes, "If I hit you with my fist and you wait five years and then shoot me in the back one dark night, that is *kum*" (1987:9). Such an action can at least partially "purify one's honor" (*star ketteyos*) and destroy the enemy's reputation. Thus, the head of a Buddhist society explained that Cambodians who hold a grudge "desire to take vengeance in a manner that exceeds the initial offense because they want to win and not to be ashamed before others. When they win, they have honor and others will look at them and not think that they are inferior."

One night, for example, a Kompong Cham policeman named Hong got drunk and began arguing with someone. After the conflict escalated, Hong began firing his AK-47 in the air and yelling loudly. Another policeman, Moly, went to intercede. Hong pointed his gun at Moly and threatened him, "If you come any closer, I'll blow you away." Moly was extremely angry and, when he returned to his station, said, "So, little Hong was trying to be hard with me (*ânh*). Well, I'm strong, too, and I'm going to defeat him." Moly called a relative who was Hong's superior and explained what had happened. Perhaps twenty minutes later, the chief and several policemen arrived on the scene, arrested Hong, and threw him in jail. To frame this example in the terms of my argument, Hong did "something bad" to Moly and made him lose face and appear "inferior" (*an*). Moly's resulting shame and anger quickly developed into a grudge. Moly took revenge that exceeded Hong's original bad deed by having him imprisoned. By doing so, Moly restored his own honor, "defeated" Hong, and demonstrated that he was the superior person.

Lim told me an even more violent story that occurred when he was an officer during the post-Khmer Rouge communist period (SOC) and Vietnamese troops were still on Cambodian soil. After a drunken Vietnamese soldier had threatened to rape a local Cambodian woman, Lim sent one of his soldiers over to the Vietnamese barracks to intercede. Perhaps after an argument had broken out, some of the Vietnamese soldiers shot and killed one of Lim's men. Lim stated, "At that point my heart stopped being afraid and I wanted to kill any Vietnamese that I saw." That night, Lim deployed his troops around the area. Several heavily armed Vietnamese soldiers broke into a house and raped a different woman. When they came out, Lim's troop killed them all. Afterward, they cut the hands and heads off the dead Vietnamese soldiers who had murdered his private and left the dismembered bodies by the side of the road for all to see. Lim explained that he had a grudge against the Vietnamese because he lost face when they killed his soldier and disregarded his authority. By daring to exact revenge against them, Lim restored his honor.

The desire to seek such disproportionate vengeance may be partially rooted in socialization practices related to honor and shame. From a young age, children are taught to seek praise and to avoid losing face. Children are frequently punished by shaming and given warnings that they should not behave in ways that would make them and their families "shamed before others." The resulting acute sensitivity to the opinion of others may be reinforced by parental comments about how they and their family must never lose standing or otherwise be inferior to others. Such lessons take on heightened meaning as children grow older, begin to be evaluated in earnest, and feel anger when slighted. While young adults may internalize various strategies for managing anger, such as those prohibitions taught by Buddhism, they also learn an alternative moral basis for harboring resentment and avenging insults that damage their honor. They may draw this conclusion from real-life observations, the lack of parental pressure to "make up" fights, a vindictive animistic cosmos, moral beliefs about returning (*sâng*) a good or bad deed, the extreme cultural valuation of being "higher than" others, and stories like *Tum Teav* and the *Reamker*, the Cambodian version of the *Ramayana*. One teacher explained that, as a result of such enculturation, Cambodians who feel that they have been greatly wronged or shamed may "hold a grudge and want to defeat their foes to the point of eating their flesh and sipping their blood. The Cambodian character is such that these people will strive on; they cannot lose and stop thinking about the matter."

The second crucial reason why a Cambodian grudge results in disproportionate revenge is the view that a person must "completely defeat the enemy" (*phchanh phchal*) in order to deter further retaliation. The phrase *phchanh phchal* literally means "to defeat, vanquish" in such a manner as "to cause [the opponent] to be afraid and not dare to repeat the same act" (Headley 1977:614; see also Bun 1973:179ff.). Cambodians who bear malice realize that after they have exacted revenge, their victims will in turn desire to repay the bad deed. To prevent the cycle from continuing, it is in the avenger's best interest to make a preemptive strike that will mute this desire by fear or by death.[11] As one informant explained, "*Phchanh phchal* means that you want the enemy to see what you have done and to be scared and respect you . . . to be so afraid that [that person] won't dare to fight back." Those who can successfully *phchanh phchal* thus end up on top and stay there, looking down on their completely defeated (or dead) foes.

When Moly defeated Hong, for instance, he demonstrated his superiority and power in such a way that Hong and others would be afraid to challenge him in the future. Likewise, Lim claimed that after he had dismembered the corpses of the Vietnamese soldiers and left them lying by the side of the road, "the other Vietnamese soldiers were so scared that they didn't dare go far from their barracks or try to take revenge against me." Another example of *phchanh phchal* comes from a contemporary Cambodian movie, *Revenge by Marriage*, in which a young man, Sakun, marries a woman in order to exact revenge upon her brother who had severely beaten Sakun in the past. After the marriage, Sakun takes a second wife and treats the first wife like a servant. Her family, in turn, can do nothing because if they kill him she will be a widow and if she leaves him she will be a divorcée – both situations that can bring great shame to women in Cambodia. Sakun's revenge thus "completely defeats" his enemy, the first wife's brother.

The extreme form of *phchanh phchal* consists of killing one's enemies and possibly their family lines as well. While people may exact revenge in such a manner that their adversary has been completely defeated for the moment, it is possible that the vanquished foe's fortune may later change for the better, allowing an opportunity for revenge. In fact, several Cambodian proverbs warn of the danger that a person who currently shows fear and respect may rise to a powerful position in the future (Fisher-Nguyen 1994). One way to prevent such potential retribution is, as Serge Thion notes in the epigraph that began this section, to suppress its root cause: to kill the enemy in order to preempt the possibility of revenge. Thus the polite, soft-spoken, young Cambodian male cited at the beginning of this section stated that he always tried to control his heart and to avoid getting into a major dispute because he knew that he would have to beat his adversary to death in order to prevent that person from taking revenge on a later day. A further problem arises, however, since it is likely that someone in the deceased foe's family will seek disproportionate revenge for the death. The head of a Cambodian non-governmental organization pointed out, "When a son sees people kill his father, he will be seized with painful anger (*chheu chap*). After he has grown up, he will try to kill all of the people connected to his father's death. He won't just kill one person, he will kill many."

While only possible in situations in which a person has great power, the most extreme Cambodian solution to this predicament is to kill the enemy and "cut off his or her family line" (*phtach pouch, sângsoek suor pouch, prâlay pouch sas*). The origins of this tradition go far back in Cambodian history to times when, after winning a war, a victorious Cambodian king would sometimes attempt to kill the opposing king and his entire family line (Bun 1973). As we shall see, much DK violence can be viewed as a modern example of "cutting off a familial line." Other parallels also exist. During the Sihanouk regime, for example, the families of Sihanouk's political enemies were sometimes harassed, imprisoned, or both (Bun 1973). Similarly, Lim told me that when he was in the army he was once stationed in an area that was renowned for its high prevalence of sorcery. At one point, several soldiers died after their stomachs had swollen up, a sign of black magic. Lim and his troops gathered together the families of all the suspected sorcerers, over fifty people in all, and executed every one of them. Lim explained, "We had a grudge against them after they cast black magic and killed our soldiers, so we took disproportionate revenge. If we had just killed the sorcerers, their children would have been angry and tried to kill us later on. So we cut off the entire family line, just like during the Pol Pot period."

During the recent political upheaval in Cambodia, several incidents of "cutting off the family line" were rumored to have occurred. First, in a desperate attempt to hold onto power in June 1997, Pol Pot was said to have had Son Sen (his former DK Minister of Defense), the latter's wife Yun Yat, and ten of their family members and relatives executed (Barber and Chaumeau 1997:3). Some reports held that, after killing them, Pol Pot's troops ran over their heads with a truck. Second, during the July 1997 coup rumors abounded that Hun Sen's troops had killed the families of some of Prince Ranariddh's loyalists. Ranariddh's top general, Nhek Bun Chhay, alleged, "Hun Sen's forces not only killed the men who are soldiers, but he killed the families of [Ranariddh's Funcinpec Party] soldiers. Whole families, women and children" (Barber 1997:7). His claims, however, have never been substantiated. Finally, between 1993 and 1997, the Khmer Rouge supposedly conducted internal purges in which entire families were annihilated (Levy 1998). Krom Khuon, a former Khmer Rouge soldier, recalled, "Sometimes I would see a car full of soldiers come.... They would take the whole family into the forest in a truck. Then the soldiers would come back without the family" (cited in Levy 1998). Thousands of these victims were said to be buried in a massive killing field called "Gravel Hill."

The tradition of "cutting off a family line" is also clearly enacted in *Tum Teav*. When Tum hears that Teav is to be remarried to Archoun's son, he becomes incensed at Archoun and Teav's mother, both of whom clearly look down on him because he is from a lower-class background. Tum sets out to Tbaung Khmum to restore his honor by avenging the slight and taking back Teav. But the sad truth is that a poor youth like Tum stands little chance of defeating Archoun who is powerful and has many guards. By daring to go to the wedding and to call for Teav, Tum is able to make Archoun lose face before his followers and guests. Archoun, however, quickly retaliates by having Tum killed. In the end, it is left to Tum's patron, King Rama, to take symbolic revenge for Tum. King Rama both literally and figuratively takes "a head for an eye" by ordering that Archoun and his relatives seven generations removed be buried up to the neck in the ground and that their heads be cut off by plow and harrow. By "cutting off the family line," King Rama guarantees that none of Archoun's relatives will seek revenge against him in the future. To ensure further that no members of Archoun's faction will attempt subsequent retaliation, King Rama has them boiled alive. This sequence of events clearly illustrates the Cambodian cultural model of disproportionate revenge – albeit in its most extreme form of "completely destroying" the enemy – and provides a culturally salient root metaphor of "little" people who gain a powerful patron to help them exact revenge on enemies who have done "something bad" to them.

Drawing on the above, we may schematize the Cambodian cultural model of a grudge leading to disproportionate revenge in the following manner:[12]

Cambodian REVENGE (*karsângsoek*): "A Head for an Eye" ("Disproportionate")

Event:	• A does a bad deed to B
Judgment:	• B loses face and/or suffers
	• A is now "higher than" and "looks down upon" B
	• B must return (*sâng*) the bad deed to A (grudge/ *kum*)
	• B should aim for the "complete defeat" of A (*phchanh phchal*)
Complication:	• A tries to prevent B from returning the bad deed
Expectation:	• B should return the bad deed to A (disproportionately)
Moral Inference:	• B has a moral obligation to disproportionately return the bad deed to A
	• A should receive the disproportionate bad deed from B
Status Inference:	• B will be "higher than" A
	• B's honor will be cleansed (*star ketteyos*)
	• A will (hopefully) not attempt further retaliation against B

Extending this framework to *Tum Teav*, we can schematize the events of the narrative as follows, keeping in mind that it is left to King Rama to exact disproportionate revenge for Tum in symbolic fashion:

REVENGE in *Tum Teav*: "A Head for an Eye" ("Disproportionate")

Event:	• Archoun does a bad deed to Tum
Judgment:	• Tum loses face and suffers
	• Archoun is "higher than" and "looks down upon" Tum
	• Tum must return the bad deed to Archoun
	• Tum should aim for the "complete defeat" of Archoun
Complication:	• Archoun tries to prevent Tum from taking revenge

Expectation:	• Tum should return the bad deed to Archoun (disproportionately)
Moral Inference:	• Tum has a moral obligation to disproportionately return the bad deed to Archoun • Archoun should receive the disproportionate bad deed from Tum
Status Inference:	• Tum will be "higher than" Archoun • Tum's honor will be cleansed • Archoun will (hopefully) not attempt further retaliation against Tum

In the next section, I will show how the Cambodian cultural model of disproportionate revenge embedded within the story of *Tum Teav* provided a legitimizing and highly motivating basis for much violence during DK. After describing traditional sources of peasant resentment toward the rich, I will point out how the Khmer Rouge often tried to use ideological discourse to turn these feelings into a class grudge. Like Rama, the Khmer Rouge often attempted to exact revenge in such a manner as to destroy the former supporters of Lon Nol completely.

Disproportionate Revenge in Democratic Kampuchea

To develop ideology, so that there is always the revolutionary attitude and the class (proletarian) attitude in the party.... is to conduct internal ideological indoctrination so that the initial attitude taken is conserved firmly, and the Marxist-Leninist class leaning and devotion to class struggle is retained always to win power by annihilating the enemy regime...and to create class ardor and fury. This ardor and fury must be aroused according to the contradiction of the day whether it be large or small. Thus, ideological force will be converted into a burning material force which will dare to engage in struggle, attack the enemy and win final victory over the enemy even if he is very strong.

Pre-1975 Summary of Annotated Party History (Jackson 1989:262)

To dig up grass, one must also dig up the roots.

Khmer Rouge saying

In early 1967 hundreds of peasants from the Samlaut subdistrict in Battambang province revolted. Fed up with the government's new policy of directly purchasing the rice crop from farmers at prices far below the black market rate, high levels of debt, heavy-handed treatment by local soldiers, corruption, and the reallocation of their land, peasant rebels murdered two soldiers and stole their weapons on the morning of April 2 (Chandler 1991; Kiernan and Boua 1982; Martin 1994). Carrying banners denouncing the government and US imperialism, the peasants destroyed a youth agricultural camp, attacked two government outposts, and killed a local official later that day. During the next few weeks, the revolt quickly expanded. In order to put down this threat to civil order, Sihanouk's government sent additional troops into the area and used increasingly brutal tactics to suppress the "red" rebellion. Peasant villages were razed to the ground. Suspects were beaten, imprisoned, and summarily executed. There were even rumors that the government paid a bounty for the severed heads of rebels (Kiernan and Boua 1982:173). Estimates of the number of the dead ranged from hundreds to thousands.

While the Samlaut rebellion did not overthrow the Sihanouk government, it illustrated the existence of a substantial base of disaffected peasants who could potentially be incited to join the Khmer Rouge movement. In fact, between 1952 and 1970, the proportion of landless peasants rose from 4 to 20 percent of the population (Kiernan 1985; Kiernan and Boua 1982); still others remained heavily in debt or owned only a small amount of land. (Landlordism was highest in the Battambang region where the Samlaut rebellion broke out.) These numbers undoubtedly rose as the civil war progressed and the US carpet bombing of Cambodia increased. The number of disaffected peasants "probably never formed a majority in the Cambodian countryside. But they *were* numerous enough for Pol Pot to build a viable recruitment strategy targeting poor peasants, and particularly their teenage children" (Kiernan 1996:7; see also Vickery 1984).[13] Many of these people harbored a great deal of anger toward the rich and urban dwellers and quickly embraced Khmer Rouge ideology about class struggle.

One major source of resentment was the disrespectful way in which many rich people treated the poor. Like the Japanese (Lebra 1976:128), Cambodians lose face and become extremely upset when others act arrogantly toward them. Such behavior implies that the arrogant person is making the evaluation (*aoy tamlei*) that one is "inferior" and can be "looked down upon" (*moel ngeay*). As demonstrated by Tum's rage toward Archoun and Tic's anger after he was slighted at the rich family's wedding, the memory of such shameful events is usually "buried in the heart" and may induce a strong desire for revenge. This type of resentment is illustrated by a story that Khieu Samphan's younger brother told me occurred while Samphan was living in Phnom Penh as a representative in the National Assembly. (Khieu Samphan was one of Pol Pot's most loyal and closest associates.)

One day, Samphan took his mother and two brothers to buy chicken feed in an outlying rural district. After they arrived, Samphan went off to make his purchase, leaving his family in the car with their dog. Since it was hot, they opened the door a bit to let in some air. When a crowd of children from the village began peering inside the car, the dog broke free and bit a young boy who began to bleed a little. When they heard the child crying, many adult villagers gathered around the car and prevented those inside from leaving the area. "They were really angry. They pointed at us saying, 'You have a car and a dog that you let bite the poor. You must look down on the poor.' Some had clubs and knives, like they wanted to beat us to take revenge for our dog having bitten the child. We were really scared."

When he saw what was happening, Samphan ran over and began speaking with the district chief, who had just arrived on the scene. The district chief asked for Samphan's identification card and, after seeing who was standing before him, informed the crowd that their anger was directed at Khieu Samphan. Because Samphan was popular with the poor at the time, the villagers quickly calmed down and told him not to worry about the matter. Samphan nevertheless insisted on taking the child to a local clinic to have his wound bandaged. When the family was returning home later and Samphan's brother expressed his animosity toward the crowd, Samphan chuckled and told him, "When you see this you should be happy. The people were angry and wanted to beat you because they thought you were a capitalist who... looked down upon them. They hate capitalists and the rich, just like they hate thieves." As we shall see, such feelings, normally kept "buried in the heart," proved to be a fertile ground for Khmer Rouge ideology.

A second grievance the poor had against the rich was a sense of the relatively greater suffering they had been made to endure, frequently as a direct result of exploitation by the rich and powerful. While many Cambodians were indebted to moneylenders who frequently charged an interest rate of more than 10 percent (Delvert 1961; Kiernan and Boua 1982), the poorest of all were often forced to farm for landlords. Even those who owned land were resentful of how little they received for their hard work in comparison to the rich. Albeit in a much more moderate form, such animosity toward the rich persists, partially explaining why the Khmer Rouge continue to enjoy popular support in some rural areas. A peasant told me, "The farmers feel that they work hard but only get a little for their effort. They only have a little money to purchase things. Rich people, in contrast, have it easier and have lots of money. They also make a profit from the farmers to whom they sell and from whom they profit." One can only imagine how angry peasants would become if forced to sell their crops to the government at a price far below the potential value. The Samlaut rebellion illustrated the explosiveness of such feelings.

Finally, the civil war itself was a source of great anger for the poor. After being deposed and allying himself with the Khmer Rouge, Prince Sihanouk appealed to his rural "children" to take arms with him against the traitorous and illegitimate Lon Nol government.[14] Thus, a man named Khel stated that he and many other youths in his village joined the Khmer Rouge because "in general the people loved the king and he was the head of the Khmer Rouge military front." US bombing also greatly increased rural discontent. During the course of the war, American bombers dropped 540,000 tons of explosives on Cambodian soil, resulting in economic destabilization, the deaths of up to one hundred and fifty thousand people, and the displacement of tens of thousands of others (Kiernan 1996; see also Shawcross 1987). Many Cambodians joined the Khmer Rouge out of anger at the destruction of their homes and the deaths of loved ones. Khel explained, "The American B-52s dropped too many bombs. It made the people become seized with painful anger (*chheu chap*) and want to fight against the Lon Nol regime." Another cadre explained that the bombing made it "easy for the Khmer Rouge to win the people over" (Kiernan 1996:23).

Khmer Rouge ideology took the resentment stemming from all these sources and gave it a common focus (class struggle) and target (the urban population). Political education sessions were geared, as the epigraph at the beginning of this section illustrates, to "create class ardor and fury." Recruits were taught basic communist doctrine, which held that the suffering of the poor (*vonnah âtun*) was due to the exploitation (*chih choan*; literally "to ride" and "step on," see Headley 1977:240, 259 and Chandler 1991:242) of the capitalist class (*vonnah neaytun*). Lohr, a former guard at the infamous Tuol Sleng prison and interrogation center in Phnom Penh, explained that the Khmer Rouge "told us that the poor were poor because of the rich and the rich were rich because of the poor. They wanted us to become seized with painful anger about this exploitation, to hate and to fight bravely against the capitalist, feudal, and landlord classes, the rich big people who harmed the poor."

Criticism and self-criticism meetings, propaganda sessions, disciplinary precepts, and revolutionary songs, slogans, and plays were all geared to developing this proper revolutionary "consciousness" (*sâte'aram*) that would be filled with "burning rage toward the enemy" (Carney 1977:51). The very notion of "class struggle" (*tâsou vonnah*) drew on a Cambodian cultural model of warriors who "struggle" or "fight bravely" (*neak tâsou*, see Headley 1977:311) against the enemy. Like Tum, the poor were supposed to be filled with anger and heroically fight back against their arrogant oppressors. Thus, while a person like Khel might have joined the Khmer Rouge because Sihanouk was overthrown, he was quickly indoctrinated into communist ideology: "Their political education consisted of telling us to be seized with painful anger against the oppressor class. They spoke about this all the time." The dispossessed and the young, who were likened, in a Maoist metaphor, to "a blank page on which we can write anything we want" (Picq 1989:60), proved most susceptible to this propaganda. On returning from political indoctrination sessions, many of these recruits were described as dedicated and well-disciplined "fanatics" (Quinn 1976:24).

Khmer Rouge ideologies attempted to focus the "burning rage" of these fanatics upon the urban centers, the bastions of capitalism. This goal was often not difficult to achieve given the initial resentment many of the poor felt toward rich city people who allegedly looked down upon them, enjoyed a much easier life, and supported Lon Nol, who was responsible for the overthrowing of Sihanouk and the carpet bombing of the countryside. Khmer Rouge propaganda employed slogans such as "trees in the country, fruit in the town" (Soth 1980:44) to inflame still further this rural animosity toward the cities. A current government official explained, "They brainwashed people to believe that the Lon Nol regime was a capitalist regime, and that the very poor, who had been oppressed and swindled by the rich, had to fight bravely to defeat Lon Nol." Moreover, the cities were portrayed as corrupt and immoral centers of undue foreign influence. On the one hand, rich city people were reported to spend their time living in luxurious houses, eating well, sipping cognac, and visiting prostitutes (the "cognac and concubine circuit") while the peasants toiled in the countryside producing their "fruit." On the other hand, Phnom Penh was said to be filled with "American lackeys" and to contain a disproportionately large number of ethnic Chinese and Vietnamese (Kiernan 1996:5). City people were not only capitalist exploiters, but also not "real Khmer." They were, rather, a hated enemy who should be "crushed" (*kamtech khmang*) by "class ardor and fury."

By drawing on preexisting resentment and focusing it on the city, Khmer Rouge ideology effectively fostered a rural class grudge (*kumnum vonnah*) against the urban population. The city people had done "something bad" to the poor by making them suffer and lose face. One or more of these "happenings" led the poor to be "seized with painful anger" (*chheu chap*), which they stored inside themselves. The Khmer Rouge inflamed this hidden resentment into a class grudge that motivated many of the poor to want to "eat the flesh and sip the blood" of their enemies. One "new" person explained that the Khmer Rouge "sometimes called this 'igniting class anger.' They made people in the countryside have a grudge against the urbanites by teaching them about class contradiction. When we left the cities, the rural population considered us their enemies." Like Tum, the poor needed a powerful patron to help them exact disproportionate revenge against this hated enemy. The Khmer Rouge Party Organization, or Ângkar, fulfilled this role. DK class revenge can therefore be schematized as follows:

DK CLASS REVENGE: **"A Head for an Eye"** (**"Disproportionate"**)

Event:	• City people do bad deeds to the poor
Judgment:	• The poor lose face and suffer
	• City people are "higher than"/"look down upon" the poor
	• The poor must return (*sâng*) the bad deed to the city people (class grudge, *kumnum vonnah*)
	• The poor should aim for the "complete defeat" of the city people
Complication:	• City people prevent the poor from returning the bad deed
Expectation:	• The poor should return the bad deed to city people (disproportionately)
Moral Inference:	• The poor have a moral obligation to disproportionately return the bad deed to the city people
	• City people should receive the disproportionate bad deed from the poor (Ângkar as powerful patron)
Status Inference:	• The poor will be "higher" than city people
	• The honor of the poor will be cleansed (*star ketteyos*)
	• The city people will (hopefully) not attempt further retaliation against the poor

This class grudge facilitated a great deal of violence during DK. By the end of the war, the "ignited class anger" was burning at full force. In Battambang province, for example, Khmer Rouge appeared "contemptuous and aloof" just after liberation and later reportedly admitted that they had been "fired by 'uncontrollable hatred' for members of the 'old society.' 'We were so angry when we came out of the forest,' one speaker allegedly said, 'that we didn't want to spare even a baby in its cradle'" (Chandler et al. 1976:2, 9). This hatred was quickly directed at the first targets of revenge, the Lon Nol government and military. Leading officials were rounded up and executed, and a concerted attempt was made to identify other potential enemies. Urbanites being evacuated out of the cities were asked to give background information about their former occupations. Many who told the truth were taken away to be killed. Others were sent to be "re-educated" in special camps or through rural peasant life. Up to two hundred thousand people may have been killed during this first wave of DK killing (Thion 1993:166). Like King Rama, the Khmer Rouge sought to "destroy the enemy completely" by annihilating the entire leadership of the Lon Nol regime, a point to which I shall return.

Instead of ending the vengeance after this initial period of violence, the Khmer Rouge attempted to keep the class grudge inflamed. Haing Ngor, who was a "new" person during DK, related how, during a public propaganda dance, costumed cadres would pound their chests with clenched fists and repeatedly shout at the top of their lungs: "'BLOOD AVENGES BLOOD!'...Blood avenges blood. You kill us, we kill you. We 'new' people had been on the other side of the Khmer Rouge in the civil war.... Symbolically, the Khmer Rouge had just announced that they were going to take revenge" (Ngor 1987:140–1). In fact, the color of blood, red, was a prominent theme in Khmer Rouge propaganda and provided a metaphoric call for revenge. The national anthem contained numerous mentions of spilled "blood," which provided a reason for people to maintain their "unrelenting hatred." In a September 27, 1977 speech, Pol Pot explained that a "blood call has been incorporated into our national anthem. Each sentence, each word shows the nature of our people's struggle. This blood has been turned into class and national indignation" (FBIS 1977:H25). Similarly, the Khmer Rouge flag was red and glorified by "The Red Flag" song, often sung in unison before meetings:

> Glittering red blood blankets the earth – blood given up to
> liberate the people: the blood of workers, peasants, and
> intellectuals; blood of young men, Buddhist monks, and girls.
> The blood swirls away, and flows upward, gently, into the
> sky, turning into a red, revolutionary flag.
> Red flag! red flag! flying now! flying now!
> O beloved friends, pursue, strike and hit the enemy.
> Red flag! red flag! flying now! flying now!
> Don't leave a single reactionary imperialist (alive): drive
> them from Kampuchea. Strive and strike, strive and strike,
> and win the victory, win the victory!
>
> (Chandler et al. 1976:14)

Like the national anthem, "The Red Flag" song, with its analogy between blood sacrifice and the color red and its encouragement to "strike and hit the enemy," urged cadres to maintain their class grudge until not "a single reactionary imperialist" was left alive.

Realizing to whom such ideology would have the greatest appeal, the Khmer Rouge placed the extreme poor and the young in local-level positions of power during DK. These individuals had the greatest reason to hate their "class enemies" and to be loyal to their powerful new patron, Ângkar. Khmer Rouge propaganda attempted to keep their memory fresh about how the city people had caused them to suffer and feel humiliated. One radio broadcast reminded the poor, "Our brothers and sisters lived a most miserable life, enduring all manner of hardships.... They never had enough food, never were happy and never had an opportunity to receive [an education]. Our brothers and sisters were looked down upon, regarded as animals" (FBIS 1976:H1). Such propaganda, combined with basic political education about class struggle, was often effective in encouraging low-level cadres to seek revenge against their class enemies. One "old" person recounted how his village leader, Boan, was changed by such Khmer Rouge ideology: "At first Boan was like us. After they had brainwashed him, however, his heart and thoughts changed. He became angry at the people, particularly the rich and soldiers. Boan was an ignorant person and couldn't write much . . . but he loved Ângkar and would report on people who were then killed." Ngor once made a pun to some other "new" people in his work group that such Khmer Rouge cadre were not "communist" (*kommuyonis*) but "revenge people" (*kum-monuss*). "'That's what they are at the lower level,' I said, 'revenge people.' 'All they know is that city people like us used to lord it over them and this is their chance to get back. That's what they are, communist at top and *kum-monuss* at the bottom'" (Ngor 1987:159).

Revenge against the "new" people was further legitimated by a variety of dehumanizing practices. If the poor had disproportionately suffered in comparison to, and been looked down upon by, the rich, the situation was now reversed. While the pattern and scope of conditions varied (Vickery 1984), "new" people tended to receive less food, be treated more harshly, have fewer rights, and be killed more readily than "old" people. Long work hours, starvation rations, a lack of freedom, miserable living conditions, and constant terror quickly robbed them of their humanity.[15] One "new" person described what happened to people in a particularly difficult region of Cambodia: "We were hungry, too tired to wash or clean our clothes, and we lost all sense of hygiene. We didn't care what we ate as long as we could put something in our stomachs. We didn't mind where we had a shit, or who saw us. Disease spread through the village – cholera, malaria, dysentery, diarrhoea and skin infections" (May 1986:165). Such "new" people were "depositees," the lowest level of a new tripartite DK social structure that included "candidates" and "full rights people." Suspect from the start as "class enemies" who were tainted by city life and no longer "pure" Khmer, they constituted the bottom stratum of society, one that was greatly devalued and became the explicit target of persecution.

In many cases, "new" people were regarded as analogous to animals. Like water buffalo, they were sometimes required to pull a plow or cart and might be whipped if they failed to work hard enough (see, for example, Stuart-Fox 1985:60; Szymusiak 1986:147). One "new" person recounted how at meetings cadres often urged people to be like oxen: "Comrade Ox never refused to work. Comrade Ox was obedient. Comrade Ox did not complain. Comrade Ox did not object when his family was killed" (Yathay 1987:171). A soldier told another "new" person that it would be better for her sick mother to die "than [it would be for] a cow. The cows are good. They help us a lot and do not eat rice. They are much better than you pigs" (Moyer 1991:123). Since "new" people were like animals, cadres were justified in harming them. A "new" person who did something wrong could therefore be "discarded" (*veay chal*) without much of a qualm. Several people I interviewed mentioned a chilling Khmer Rouge saying that was invoked in such situations or as a threat: "To keep you is no gain; to destroy you is no loss" (*tuk min chomnenh yok chenh min khat*). One Cambodian-American refugee has even used this slogan as the title of her book about her experiences during DK (Criddle and Mam 1987).

Given such dehumanization and the Khmer Rouge ideology that fostered a sense of class grudge and glorified violence against the enemy, it is not surprising that revenge killings continued to take place long after the first wave of DK executions. Having annihilated most of the Lon Nol government's leadership, the Khmer Rouge began gradually to kill off other "class enemies" such as rich "capitalists," intellectuals, professionals, and lower-ranking soldiers, police, and government employees. Local cadres continued to research people's backgrounds. Upon arriving at a new village, a woman named Yum explained that a cadre "asked my husband what he had done. He lied and told them he had ridden a cyclo bike and guarded a house. The cadre said, 'If so, why are your hands, legs, and face so nice?' They asked him to prove that he was really from the countryside by plowing a rice field and doing other peasant tasks." Because he had grown up performing such labor in a rural village, Yum's husband was able to do successfully what the cadre asked. In the end, however, the Khmer Rouge still found out that her husband had been a soldier. Yum added, "There were people from our village living there who knew my husband's occupation. Whoever hated us told the Khmer Rouge that my husband had been a soldier." After learning about this family of Lon Nol soldiers, the district security office gave orders for them to be executed. Yum began to cry as she recounted how her husband's brother, who worked at the district office, arrived that evening with some guns and provisions and fled with his brothers into the rainy night, never to be seen again.

The family of a young woman named Gen experienced a similar tragedy, which I will recount in detail. When local officials began researching people's backgrounds, her family could not hide the fact that her father, Tak, had been a teacher during the Lon Nol period, since he had taught in the area. Tak eventually went to the local hospital because his stomach had become swollen because of the lack of food. A few days later, Tak was told to gather his things because he was being transferred to the regional hospital. Instead of going there, Tak was taken to an area behind the hospital and killed. Witnesses told Gen that when the killers returned, they were covered in blood.

One of them, Tralok, had been a student of Tak's. Gen explained, "My father was an extremely strict teacher and would frequently hit his students in order to make them want to learn. Tralok was a particularly lazy and disobedient student and was beaten often. These beatings really hurt, so Tralok became angry at and held a grudge against my father." Afterwards, Tralok was overheard bragging that, before killing Tak, he told him (using superior-to-inferior prefixes), "When you (*hâ'aeng*) were my (*ânh*) teacher, you beat me and made me hurt. Now, I will repay your 'good' deeds (*sângkun*) in turn. I will kill and discard you, so that you can no longer be such a mean teacher."

Perhaps two months later, Gen's mother went to the hospital to get an injection to make her feel better. Before administering the shot, the doctor, Khon, supposedly asked, "Are you Tak's wife?" When she responded affirmatively, Khon filled the syringe with a white liquid. Gen's mother died immediately after receiving the shot. Earlier in the day, cadres had been asking where Gen's mother was and then, upon hearing that she had gone to the hospital, went and spoke with Khon. Gen has no doubt they ordered Khon to kill her mother.

Three of Gen's sisters were the next to be killed. The oldest, Srey, had a silk scarf (*krâma*) that had been used in their parents' wedding ceremony. The subdistrict head, Rom, saw the scarf and "suggested" that Srey give it to her, but Srey refused because the scarf had such sentimental value. Gen explained, "When my elder sister didn't give the scarf to her, Rom became very angry with this new person who thought she was better than an old person. Rom held a grudge against my sister and waited for an opportunity to get back at her." A few days later, Srey was plowing a field and swore at one of her oxen. Rom was nearby and claimed that Srey had sworn at her. That evening, one of Rom's minions told Srey that Rom wanted to see her. Gen's other elder sister insisted upon coming along because she was afraid something bad would happen to Srey; they took along their youngest sibling who was just an infant.

Later, after DK, Heng, a person who worked with Rom at the subdistrict office, told Gen that Srey and her sister were tied up and led away to a local killing field by Rom and a group of five or six other people. Rom reportedly said to Srey (using superior-to-inferior prefixes), "So, you were trying to act tough with me and wouldn't give me your scarf. This is what you get." Upon hearing this, Srey, despite having her arms tied, began to kick wildly at her captors, managing to tear some of their clothes. Rom was incensed. Gen recounted what supposedly happened next: "They stripped off her clothes and made her stand there naked in front of the group, some of whom were men. One of them then grabbed my infant sister and smashed her head against a tree stump. Her head burst open with a pop and she died at once." Next, they made Srey watch as her other sister was executed. Rom and the other executioners then began to beat Srey all over the body. "Rom told my sister, 'It's going to be a long time before you are dead.' They punched and kicked her all over until she was finally finished off. She suffered so much. It's so sad." A few days later, Gen and her younger sister made a dramatic escape from the village. Unfortunately, Gen's four younger brothers were still in the area living with an uncle. Rom sent for them and had them work at the local pagoda, which was being used by the Khmer Rouge as a prison. Their job was to carry out the prisoners' excrement. Just before the end of DK, the boys were all executed after being forced to dig their own graves.

The destruction of Gen's entire family illustrates how the Khmer Rouge attempted to take disproportionate revenge in such a manner as to "destroy completely" (*phchanh phchal*) their class enemies. Because the Khmer Rouge were so powerful, they were able to engage in the most extreme form of *phchanh phchal* – killing off the enemy's line. Gen sadly explained, "The Khmer Rouge had a grudge against my family because my father had been a government worker during the previous regime. They were seized with painful anger and wanted to take revenge against 'new' people like us. They wanted to cut off our entire familial line so no one would be left to seek vengeance against them on a later day." Many other Cambodian family lines were similarly destroyed during DK. For example, eight out of nine of Yum's husband's siblings (seven of whom had been in the army) were executed. Every person in four of these siblings' families was killed. In some cases, the Khmer Rouge would simply load families of "new" people into trucks and take them to local execution centers to be exterminated. The Khmer Rouge actually had a saying, cited at the beginning of this section, which encouraged such slaughter: "To dig up grass, one must also dig up the roots" (*chik smav trauv chik teang reus*). Echoing the explanation of many others, a former DK village chief of Gen's village told me that this phrase meant that cadres "were supposed to 'dig up' the entire family of an enemy – husband, wife, kids, sometimes from the grandparents down – so that none remained . . . to kill off the entire line at once so that none of them would be left to seek revenge later, in turn."

Thus the severity of much DK killing can be seen as following the script of the Cambodian model of disproportionate revenge illustrated by the story of *Tum Teav*. Like Tum, many of the poor were angry at the rich and powerful who looked down upon them and made them suffer. The Khmer Rouge used this ideology to inflame this feeling of resentment even further, trying to make its followers completely "seized with painful anger" (*chheu chap*) to the point of wanting to avenge their class grudge. Khieu Samphan's brother explained, "The destruction of the Cambodian people can be [largely] understood in terms of the resentment (*chheu chap*) of the destitute (*neak ât*) who suffered and were looked down upon. . . . Their resentment became a grudge that was repaid (*sâng*) when they had power. . . they repaid [this debt] by killing."

Just as King Rama took revenge for Tum, so too Ângkar provided a means for the poor and the young to wreak vengeance upon these "class enemies," most of whom were, at least during the first phase of DK, "new" people. Moreover, like King Rama, the Khmer Rouge exacted revenge that was disproportionate to the initial offense and "completely destroyed" their enemy. King Rama cut off the heads of Archoun's relatives seven generations removed and boiled his associates to death. The Khmer Rouge first killed off virtually the entire military and governmental leadership of the Lon Nol regime and then set out to eradicate other suspected enemies and, in many cases, part or all of their family lines. By taking "a head for an eye," King Rama and the Khmer Rouge were attempting both to demonstrate their superiority over a foe who had previously done "something bad" to them and to prevent the cycle of vengeance from continuing thereafter.

As is illustrated by the revenge killings that took place at the end of DK, the Khmer Rouge were not totally successful in preventing such retaliation. One woman described how Son, a harsh village head whom she had watched kill two ethnic Vietnamese, was himself killed by an irate mob: "They were angry at him for all he had done. I went and watched as a great number of people beat him and cut off his head." Similarly, one of Rom's associates named Phat fled into the jungle when the Vietnamese invaded Cambodia. After hiding for a few days, Phat tried to sneak into a village to steal some food one night and was shot and wounded. A crowd soon gathered and began to beat Phat. Another woman whose husband had been killed by Phat said, "More and more people kept coming, grandfathers and grandchildren. They really hated her because she had killed so many people. I hit her two times, too. I hated her because she had killed my husband. We wanted revenge." Most Cambodians can relate a similar violent story about the post-DK revenge killing of former Khmer Rouge cadres. As illustrated by Son's murder, many of these stories involve decapitation, perhaps a symbolic act that indexes the avenger's desire to take "a head for an eye" (see, for example, May 1986:241ff.; Ngor 1987:362; Stuart-Fox 1985:152; Szymusiak 1986:209).

Conclusion

Many Cambodians who suffered greatly during DK continue to hold a grudge against the Khmer Rouge. When I asked her how she feels when she sometimes sees Tralok, for example, Gen responded, "I get really hot and angry inside my heart. My heart is still tied in wanting revenge. I want to ask him, 'What did my father do to you to make you kill him? You were beaten because you were lazy.' When I think about him, I get so angry." Such feelings were no doubt what the post-Khmer Rouge communist government (SOC/PRK) was trying to exploit when they held the "Day to Remain Tied in Anger." Because the cultural model of disproportionate revenge remains so entrenched in Cambodian society, it is difficult to prevent such cycles of revenge from occurring.

Nevertheless, potential solutions do exist. As I noted in my introductory remarks, Cambodians have alternatives to taking revenge. Individuals who have been slighted or harmed may choose to invoke Buddhist norms of emotion control and forgiveness. Others may take comfort in the Buddhist notion that the form of future rebirth is determined by actions in the present. Thus some Cambodians, like Gen, say that Pol Pot will be reincarnated as a *bret*, perhaps the most hideous, despicable, and evil spirit in the Cambodian religious cosmology (Ang 1987; Ebihara 1968). On an institutional level, legal and educational practices could be modified. If the rampant corruption within the Cambodian judicial system were reduced, for example, Cambodians bearing malice might feel less desire to exact revenge personally. Moreover, a Nuremberg-like trial of the surviving Khmer Rouge leaders, now made possible by the Cambodian Genocide Program, might satisfy many Cambodians, as a symbolic severing of the collective Khmer Rouge head. Alternatively, during class sessions on texts like *Tum Teav*, teachers could analyze, point out the detrimental results of, and explain the different options to the cultural model of disproportionate revenge. Whatever the means, Cambodians would benefit greatly if the destructiveness that often results from the cultural model of disproportionate revenge were to be prevented.

In conclusion, I have attempted to provide an example of how anthropology can contribute to our understanding of large-scale genocide. In particular, I have demonstrated how the Cambodian cultural model of disproportionate revenge served as a template for part of the genocidal violence that occurred in DK. It is crucial for anthropologists to point out how cultural models come to serve as templates for violence, since such implicit cultural knowledge often provides fodder for genocidal ideologies. As Naomi Quinn and Dorothy Holland have noted, "To be successful, ideologies must appeal to and activate preexisting cultural understandings, which are themselves compelling . . . though ideologues may mold and adapt cultural models to their own devices" (1987:13). Thus Khmer Rouge ideology about class struggle, which played upon the traditional suffering and humiliation of the poor, served to transform the anger and resentment of many of the regime's followers into a class grudge. These cadres and soldiers in turn used the traditional cultural model of disproportionate revenge as a template for committing genocidal atrocities. The result was the death of hundreds of thousands of "enemies" and, often, of their families. Pointing out how cultural knowledge is employed in this lethal manner constitutes one important way in which anthropologists can increase our knowledge about the genocidal events that have occurred in Turkey, Nazi Germany, and Cambodia, and have more recently taken place in Bosnia and Rwanda.

NOTES

1   After leading his country to independence from the French in 1953, Prince Sihanouk dominated the political scene in the Kingdom of Cambodia. International affairs (the Vietnam War and the Cold War) contributed to his downfall in 1970, when a coup took place. General Lon Nol then headed the newly formed Khmer Republic until 1975, when his government was overthrown by the Khmer Rouge, a group of Maoist-inspired communist rebels who gained legitimacy and a great deal of rural support when Sihanouk joined them after the coup. During the next four years, Democratic Kampuchea (DK) was reorganized along strict communist lines that glorified peasant life and the revolution. Khmer Rouge antagonism and military raids into Vietnam eventually led the Vietnamese to invade in January of 1979. The Vietnamese army routed the Khmer Rouge and set up the People's Republic of Kampuchea (PRK), which was opposed by guerrilla forces located on the Thai border. After the Vietnamese army withdrew in 1989, the PRK renamed itself the State of Cambodia (SOC) and initiated a series of reforms to improve the country's image both within and outside the country. This government held power until the 1993 UN-sponsored elections, when the new Royal Government of Cambodia (RGC) was established. Sihanouk was crowned king and the government was jointly run by his son, First Prime Minister Prince Ranariddh, and the ex-leader of SOC, Second Prime Minister Hun Sen. The increasingly contentious relations between the prime ministers led Hun Sen to launch a coup on July 5, 1997. At the time of writing, an internationally brokered agreement has allowed Ranariddh and other opposition candidates to return from exile and participate in national elections scheduled for July 26, 1998.

2   All transliterations are based on Franklin E. Huffman's Franco-Khmer transcription system as reproduced in Heder and Ledgerwood (1996:xvii). I should also note that "new" people included both urbanites and rural refugees who had fled to the cities during the civil war.

3   Article II of the United Nations Genocide Convention defines genocide as "acts committed with intent to destroy, in whole or in part, a national, ethnical, racial or religious group, as such" (see Kuper 1981). Given the conceptual vagueness of this definition, there has been some debate about whether the violence that took place in Cambodia can be accurately classified as genocidal (Kiernan 1993). I believe that it is appropriate to use this term in this case because ethnic groups (Muslim Chams and ethnic Vietnamese, Chinese, and Thai) and religious groups (Buddhists and Christians) were subject to systematic elimination, both through outright execution and through the imposition of extremely harsh living conditions (see also Fein 1993; Hawk 1988, 1990; Kiernan 1986, 1988; Stanton 1993). Moreover, the original Genocide Convention definition excluded political groups and social classes because of pressure from countries like the Soviet Union that feared being indicted. To correct for this bias, many genocide scholars have redefined genocide in a more inclusive manner (e.g., Chalk and Jonassohn 1990; Charny 1994; Fein 1990; Kuper 1981). Thus Fein defines genocide as "sustained purposeful action by a perpetrator to physically destroy a collectivity directly or indirectly, through interdiction of the biological and social reproduction of group members, sustained regardless of the surrender or lack of threat offered by the victim" (1990:24). Under this definition and given the purges, the attack on "new" people, and the execution of members of the Lon Nol military and government, the repression under DK can clearly be classified as genocide. See Andreopoulos (1994) for an examination of the historical and conceptual issues surrounding the use of the term *genocide*.

4   I collected ethnographic data in Kompong Cham and Phnom Penh during 1992 and 1994–5. In addition to gathering data through intensive participant-observation, I also

conducted over 100 tape-recorded interviews on Cambodian ethnopsychology, socialization practices, violence, and the Khmer Rouge genocide (1975–9); spent several months observing and videotaping life in families and primary schools; and collected relevant research data from Cambodian school texts, books on Cambodian character and socialization practices, didactic poems, proverbs, newspapers, videos, and forced confessions, a study guide for interrogators, a cadre notebook, and other documentary material from the Tuol Sleng Museum of Genocidal Crimes archive in Phnom Penh. In order to discern the cultural models that contribute to violence in Cambodia, I used methods of model testing refined by other researchers (e.g., Agar 1986; D'Andrade and Strauss 1992; Holland and Quinn 1987; Shore 1996).

5 It is important to recognize that, by conceptualizing cultural models in this manner, scholars are able to discuss notions of "culture" and "ethos" without falling into the overly reductive stereotyping of "national character" studies. As Strauss and Quinn have noted, cultural models may be both shared and differentially internalized, since they have "centripetal" and "centrifugal" tendencies (1994; see also Shore 1996). On the one hand, cultural models may be durable (learned patterns that are established through experience), historically enduring (while the potential for transformation exists, cultural models inform an individual's publicly enacted behavior and beliefs and therefore tend to be re-created in later generations), thematic (some cultural models are highly salient across a variety of contexts and constitute an important part of what is often called an "ethos" or "worldview"), and shared (because members of a culture are often exposed to and internalize similar schematic patterns). On the other hand, cultural models are never completely identical (because people have distinct life histories and unique experiences that give rise to idiosyncratic models or alter the emotional and motivational valences associated with given cultural models) and may be socially distributed (individuals and social groups often have differential access to knowledge and are exposed to disparate types of experiences that shape their cultural models in distinct ways). Thus, while the Cambodian cultural model of disproportionate revenge is widely shared by and highly salient for many Cambodians, it is not a generic part of their "national character."

6 Cambodia has sometimes been characterized as a "gentle land" full of smiling, kind Buddhists. This stereotype led some Western, Christian observers, forgetful of the many atrocities committed in the name of a religion that stresses "brotherly love," to wonder how these Buddhists could participate in a bloody genocide. There are several responses to such a question. First, Buddhism was banned during DK, thus undermining traditional Buddhist prosocial norms. Second, while Buddhism certainly promotes an ethic of non-violence in many contexts, it can also legitimate the use of force against "enemies" who threaten the social order. Thus Buddhist monks have sometimes supported violent protests in countries like Cambodia (Kiernan and Boua 1982) and Sri Lanka (Kapferer 1988; Tambiah 1992). Third, Buddhism constitutes just one – albeit an important one – of the many sources from which Cambodian cultural models are derived. The Cambodian religious cosmos alone is a complex amalgam of Buddhist, animist, Hindu, and even Chinese conceptions (Ebihara 1968, 1987). Fourth, Cambodian behavior is informed by numerous non-religious cultural models (Hinton 1996, 1997). To stereotype Cambodians as smiling, non-violent Buddhists is thus an erroneous oversimplification that ignores the complexities of Buddhism, the Cambodian religious system, and Cambodian culture in general.

7 Given the lack of ethnographic and historical research on Cambodian revenge, it is difficult to assess the ethnohistorical origins of this cultural model. The sources that do exist, however, suggest that it has had a long history. Thus a Cambodian didactic poem (*chbap bros*) composed between the fourteenth and eighteenth centuries explicitly warns that vindictiveness creates a "hot fury" that leads people "to stop fearing death" as they

"scheme to annihilate [their adversaries]." Likewise, Bun (1973) states that ancient Cambodian kings often sought to take revenge against their foes by destroying them and their family lines. While an analysis of how the Cambodian cultural model of disproportionate revenge has changed over time is beyond the scope of this essay, existing information thus indicates that its general schematic features have persisted for at least several centuries. This schematic constancy is responsible for the similarity among different cases of disproportionate revenge; contextual factors and individual agency create variation in the cultural model's exact use and instantiation.

8   As in other Southeast Asian societies, the Cambodian kinship system is bilateral – people figure descent on both their maternal and paternal sides (Ebihara 1968, 1986; Ledgerwood 1992). While the primary Cambodian social unit is the household, which may be composed of nuclear, stem, or extended family members, or of some combination thereof, a person usually includes other cognatic – or, more rarely, "fictive" – kin within the circle of "relatives" (*bâng b'aun, nheate*). An extended group of such relatives is sometimes called a "clan" (*trâkoul*) or "string" (*Khsae royeah*). Because the people in such networks of relatives often support and help one another, in matters of nepotism and vengeance as in other domains, they constitute a threat to enemies of the leader or of other members of the network. By totally obliterating Archoun's family line and faction, Rama was making sure there would be no one left to avenge Archoun's death.

9   Anthropological interest in revenge dates back at least as far as early evolutionist ideas about the progression of civilization. While a large proportion of earlier research approached vengeance from a structural-functionalist perspective (Black-Michaud 1975; Evans-Pritchard 1969; Otterbein and Otterbein 1965; Peristiany 1966), more recent analyses have also examined sociobiological (Chagnon 1988; Daly and Wilson 1988) and sociocultural factors (Benedict 1946; Boehm 1984; Keiser 1986). Surprisingly, almost nothing has been written on revenge in Cambodia or other Southeast Asian societies (but see parts of Barth 1993 and Mulder 1994).

10 Although *chheu chap* literally means to be "seized with pain or agony," the term takes on the connotation of "being seized with painful or agonizing anger" in certain contexts such as that described above. Accordingly, I will hereafter translate the term as "being seized with painful anger" (see also Ledgerwood 1997:91).

11 Making an analogy with boxing, Bun describes the spirit of *phchanh phchal* as follows:

> If a person knocks down his opponent, he will not stand quietly by the side. Instead, he will run forward and begin kicking his foe in order to add onto the injury, sometimes doing so until the loser is knocked unconscious or perhaps even dies.... He does not consider himself to have won until his opponent has fallen down unconscious or dies.... This is the Cambodian character... [if not completely defeated], the loser, in turn, will not be content to remain defeated and will develop a grudge against his opponent and the matter will go on.... A person might even secretly stab his foe from behind the back. (1973:180–1)

12 The Cambodian model of disproportionate revenge ("a head for an eye") can be contrasted with the biblical tradition of "an eye for an eye." Johnson (1993:41ff.), for example, has illustrated that Judeo-Christian morality is frequently based on the assumption that social interactions are analogous to commercial transactions and involve a metaphorical language of exchange, debt, credit, and balance. Thus people might say, "She was *enriched* by the relationships" or "They *paid me* with gratitude for all my efforts." Actions are conceptualized "as commodities exchanged, and we expect their (metaphorical) values to balance out in the end. If I perform good acts, I build up a form of moral credit. If I harm you, then you deserve a certain restitution or payback that

balances out the harm done" (Johnson 1993:45). By extension, the biblical "eye for an eye" model of revenge can be schematized in the following manner (adapted from Johnson 1993:48):

REVENGE Schema: "An Eye for an Eye" ("Getting Even")

Event:	• A gives *something bad* to B
Judgment:	• A owes *something good* to B (to balance out the bad)
Complication:	• A will not give *something good* to B
Expectation:	• B should take *something good* from A
Moral Inferences:	• A has an obligation to give *something good* to B
	• B has a right to receive *something good* from A
Monetary Inferences:	• B exacts payment from A

13   While Cambodian scholars generally agree that the Khmer Rouge were successfully able to draw recruits from the ranks of the extreme poor and the young, some disagree over how widespread such peasant support was before 1975 (see Frieson 1991; Kiernan 1996; Kiernan and Boua 1982; and Vickery 1984). This debate dovetails with larger academic discussions about how peasant grievances, often of long duration, are mobilized by revolutionary movements within a particular set of sociocultural, economic, political, and historical circumstances (see Moore 1966; Popkin 1979; Scott 1976; Skocpol 1979; Thaxton 1983; Wolf 1969). Interestingly, although analyses of peasant revolutions often mention revenge as a motivating factor, none delineates the precise cultural form it takes in given societies. I would argue that doing so is of crucial importance since revolutionary leaders must adapt their ideological discourse to preexisting cultural models that make sense to their followers. Disparate cultural models of revenge also have different entailments. Thus, within an appropriate set of historical and socioeconomic conditions, the culture-specific form of the Cambodian cultural model of disproportionate revenge facilitated genocide. In other revolutions, indigenous concepts of "revenge" might not do so. Accordingly, scholars must take such cultural factors into account in order to fully explain the origins of genocide.

14   Sihanouk's actions can also be partially explained as the result of a grudge. When he was overthrown, Sihanouk lost a great deal of power and face, particularly given all of the disparagement that the new government cast upon him and his family. In order to pay back Lon Nol and Sirik Matak for their "bad deed" and to restore his own honor, Sihanouk allied himself with the Khmer Rouge, who potentially could provide him with the revenge he desired. One informant explained:

Sihanouk was the one who gave Lon Nol power, but Lon Nol deposed him. Sihanouk was really angry and had a grudge against Lon Nol. . . . The people loved King Sihanouk and fled into the forest to struggle with him. The Khmer Rouge would never have defeated Lon Nol if they hadn't had Sihanouk on their side.

Sihanouk's actions resemble those of other Cambodians who hold such great malice that they are willing to lose everything for the sake of vengeance.

15   Clearly, "old" people also suffered greatly during DK. Echoing the sentiments of many other "old" people with whom I spoke, one Banyan villager told me that Khmer Rouge cadres "treated us like animals. Like a chicken, we didn't have the right to protest. We didn't dare say anything for fear they would kill us. They could discard us like an

animal." Since I am examining class revenge in this essay, my analysis is primarily geared to exploring the way in which the Khmer Rouge used ideological discourse and policy to encourage the impoverished and young cadres and soldiers, whom they put in positions of power, to take revenge against their former oppressors. While many other "old" people may also have enjoyed seeing their former "class enemies" executed, not all the poor hated city people. Some "old" people were friendly toward, and even tried to help, "new" people.

REFERENCES

Agar, Michael H. (1986). *Speaking of Ethnography.* Beverly Hills, CA: Sage.

Andreopoulos, George J. (ed.) (1994). *Genocide: Conceptual and Historical Dimensions.* Philadelphia: University of Pennsylvania Press.

Ang Chouléan (1987). *Les Êtres surnaturels dans la religion populaire Khmère.* Collection Bibliothèque Khmère, Série Travaux et Recherches. Paris: Centre de Documentation et de Recherche sur la Civilisation Khmere.

Aretxaga, Begoña (1995). "Dirty Protest: Symbolic Overdetermination and Gender in Northern Ireland Ethnic Violence". *Ethos* 23:123–48.

Aretxaga, Begoña (1997). *Shattering Silence: Women, Nationalism, and Political Subjectivity in Northern Ireland.* Princeton, NJ: Princeton University Press.

Barber, Jason (1997). "Leaner Bun Chhay Vows to Fight On." *Phnom Penh Post,* August 15:7.

Barber, Jason, and Chaumeau, Christine (1997). "Power Struggle Shatters KR Leadership". *Phnom Penh Post,* June 27:3.

Barth, Fredrik (1993). *Balinese Worlds.* Chicago: University of Chicago Press.

Benedict, Ruth (1946). *The Chrysanthemum and the Sword: Patterns of Japanese Culture.* Boston: Houghton Mifflin.

Besteman, Catherine (1996). "Violent Politics and the Politics of Violence: The Dissolution of the Somali Nation-State." *American Ethnologist* 23:579–96.

Black-Michaud, Jacob (1975). *Cohesive Force: Feud in the Mediterranean and the Middle East.* Oxford: Blackwell.

Boehm, Christopher (1984). *Blood Revenge: The Anthropology of Feuding in Montenegro and Other Tribal Societies.* Lawrence: University of Kansas Press.

Bourdieu, Pierre (1977). *Outline of a Theory of Practice,* trans. Richard Nice. New York: Cambridge University Press.

Bourdieu, Pierre (1990). *The Logic of Practice,* trans. Richard Nice. Stanford, CA: Stanford University Press.

Bringa, Tone (1993). "National Categories, National Identification and Identity Formation in 'Multinational' Bosnia." *Anthropology of East Europe Review* 11 (1–2):27–34.

Bringa, Tone (1995). *Being Muslim the Bosnian Way: Identity and Community in a Central Bosnian Village.* Princeton, NJ: Princeton University Press.

Bun Chân Mol (1973). *Châret Khmaer* (Cambodian character). Phnom Penh: Kehâdtan 79, distributor.

Carney, Timothy (ed.) (1977). *Communist Party Power in Kampuchea (Cambodia): Documents and Discussion.* Ithaca, NY: Cornell University Southeast Asia Program.

Chagnon, Napolean A. (1988). "Life Histories, Blood Revenge, and Warfare in a Tribal Population." *Science* 239:985–92.

Chalk, Frank, and Jonassohn, Kurt (1990). *The History and Sociology of Genocide: Analyses and Case Studies.* New Haven, CT: Yale University Press.

Chandler, David P. (1991). *The Tragedy of Cambodian History: Politics, War, and Revolution since 1945.* New Haven, CT: Yale University Press.

Chandler, David P., Kiernan, Ben and Muy Hong Lim (1976). *The Early Phases of Liberation in Northwestern Cambodia: Conversations with Peang Sophi.* Melbourne: Monash University Centre of Southeast Asian Studies Working Papers.

Charny, Israel W. (1994). "Toward a Generic Definition of Genocide." In George J. Andreopoulos (ed.), *Genocide: Conceptual and Historical Dimensions.* Philadelphia: University of Pennsylvania Press, pp. 64–94.

Connor, John W. (1989). "From Ghost Dance to Death Camps: Nazi Germany as a Crisis Cult." *Ethos* 17:259–88.

Coronil, Fernando, and Skurski, Julie (1991). "Dismembering and Remembering the Nation: The Semantics of Political Violence in Venezuela." *Comparative Studies in Society and History* 33(2):288–337.

Criddle, Joan D., and Teeda Butt Mam (1987). *To Destroy You Is No Loss: The Odyssey of a Cambodian Family.* New York: Anchor Books.

Daly, Martin, and Wilson, Margo (1988). *Homicide.* New York: Aldine De Gruyter.

D'Andrade, Roy and Strauss, Claudia (eds.) (1992). *Human Motives and Cultural Models.* New York: Cambridge University Press.

Daniel, E. Valentine (1996). *Charred Lullabies: Chapters in an Anthropography of Violence.* Princeton, NJ: Princeton University Press.

Das, Veena (ed.) (1990). *Mirrors of Violence: Communities, Riots, and Survivors in South Asia.* Delhi: Oxford University Press.

Delvert, Jean (1961). *Le Paysan Cambodgien.* Paris: Mouton.

Denich, Bette (1994). "Dismembering Yugoslavia: Nationalist Ideologies and the Symbolic Revival of Genocide." *American Ethnologist* 21:367–90.

Desjarlais, Robert and Kleinman, Arthur (1994). "Violence and Demoralization in the New World Order." *Anthropology Today* 10(5):9–12.

De Waal, Alex (1994). "Genocide in Rwanda." *Anthropology Today* 10(3):1–2.

Dumont, Louis (1986). *Essays on Individualism: Modern Ideology in Anthropological Perspective.* Chicago: University of Chicago Press.

Ebihara, May Mayko (1968). "Svay, A Khmer Village in Cambodia." Ph.D. dissertation, Columbia University. Ann Arbor, MI: University Microfilms.

Ebihara, May Mayko (1986). "Kin Terminology and the Idiom of Kinship in Cambodia/Kampuchea." Paper presented at the SSRC/Indochina Studies Program Workshop on "Kinship and Gender in Indochina." University of Northern Illinois, July 26–7.

Ebihara, May Mayko (1987). "Khmer Religion." In Mircea Eliade (ed.), *The Encyclopedia of Religion*, 8. New York: Macmillan, pp. 290–2.

Ebihara, May Mayko (1990). "Revolution and Reformulation in Kampuchean Village Culture." In David A. Ablin and Marlowe Hood (eds.), *The Cambodian Agony.* Armonk, NY: M. E. Sharpe, pp. 16–61.

Ebihara, May Mayko (1993). "A Cambodian Village under the Khmer Rouge, 1975–1979." In Ben Kiernan (ed.), *Genocide and Democracy in Cambodia: The Khmer Rouge, the United Nations, and the International Community.* New Haven, CT: Yale University Southeast Asia Studies, pp. 51–63.

Evans-Pritchard, E. E. (1969). *The Nuer: A Description of the Modes of Livelihood and Political Institutions of a Nilotic People.* New York: Oxford University Press.

FBIS (Foreign Broadcast Information Service) (1976). *Asia and Pacific Report.* Springfield, VA: US Department of Commerce. January 1: H1.

FBIS (1977). *Asia and Pacific Report.* Springfield, VA: US Department of Commerce. October 4: H25.

Fein, Helen (1990). "Genocide: A Sociological Perspective." *Current Sociology* 38(1):1–126.

Fein, Helen (1993). "Revolutionary and Antirevolutionary Genocides: A Comparison of State Murders in Democratic Kampuchea, 1975 to 1979, and in Indonesia, 1965 to 1966." *Comparative Studies in Society and History* 35:796–823.

Feldman, Allen (1991). *Formations of Violence: The Narrative of the Body and Political Terror in Northern Ireland*. Chicago: University of Chicago Press.

Fisher-Nguyen, Karen (1994). "Khmer Proverbs: Images and Rules." In May M. Ebihara, Carol A. Mortland, and Judy Ledgerwood (eds.), *Cambodian Culture since 1975: Homeland and Exile*. Ithaca, NY: Cornell University Press, pp. 91–104.

Foucault, Michel (1979). *Discipline and Punish: The Birth of the Prison*, trans. Alan Sheridan. New York: Vintage.

Foucault, Michel (1980). *The History of Sexuality*. Vol. 1: *An Introduction*, trans. Robert Hurley. New York: Vintage.

Frieson, Kate G. (1991). "The Impact of Revolution on Cambodian Peasants: 1970–1975." Ph.D. dissertation, Monash University, Australia. Ann Arbor, MI: University Microfilms.

Gajek, Esther (1990). "Christmas under the Third Reich." *Anthropology Today* 6(4):3–9.

Giddens, Anthony (1984). *The Constitution of Society: Outline of the Theory of Structuration*. Berkeley: University of California Press.

Goldhagen, Daniel Jonah (1996). *Hitler's Willing Executioners: Ordinary Germans and the Holocaust*. New York: Alfred A. Knopf.

Hawk, David (1988). "The Cambodian Genocide." In Israel Charny (ed.), *Genocide: A Critical Bibliographic Review*. New York: Facts on File, pp. 137–54.

Hawk, David (1990). "International Human Rights Law and Democratic Kampuchea." In David A. Ablin and Marlowe Hood (eds.), *The Cambodian Agony*. Armonk, NY: M. E. Sharpe, pp. 118–45.

Hayden, Robert M. (1996). "Imagined Communities and Real Victims: Self-Determination and Ethnic Cleansing in Yugoslavia." *American Ethnologist* 23:783–801.

Headley, Robert K., Jr., et al. (1977). *Cambodian–English Dictionary*, vols. 1 and 2. Washington, DC: Catholic University of America Press.

Heder, Steve and Ledgerwood, Judy (eds.) (1996). *Propaganda, Politics, and Violence in Cambodia: Democratic Transition under United Nations Peace-Keeping*. Armonk, NY: M. E. Sharpe.

Hinton, Alexander Laban (1996). "Agents of Death: Explaining the Cambodian Genocide in Terms of Psychosocial Dissonance." *American Anthropologist* 98:818–31.

Hinton, Alexander Laban (1997). "Cambodia's Shadow: An Examination of the Cultural Origins of Genocide." Ph.D. dissertation, Emory University. Ann Arbor, MI: University Microfilms.

Holland, Dorothy and Quinn, Naomi (eds.) (1987). *Cultural Models in Language and Thought*. New York: Cambridge University Press.

Jackson, Karl D. (1989). "The Ideology of Revolution." In Karl D. Jackson (ed.), *Cambodia 1975–1978: Rendezvous with Death*. Princeton, NJ: Princeton University Press, pp. 37–78.

Jell-Bahlsen, Sabine (1985). "Ethnology and Fascism in Germany." *Dialectical Anthropology* 9:313–35.

Johnson, Mark (1993). *Moral Imagination: Implications of Cognitive Science for Ethics*. Chicago: University of Chicago Press.

Kapferer, Bruce (1988). *Legends of People, Myths of State: Violence, Intolerance, and Political Culture in Sri Lanka and Australia*. Washington, DC: Smithsonian Institution Press.

Keiser, R. Lincoln (1986). "Death Enmity in Thull: Organized Vengeance and Social Change in a Kohistani Community." *American Ethnologist* 13:489–505.

Kiernan, Ben (1985). *How Pol Pot Came to Power: A History of Communism in Kampuchea, 1930–1975*. London: Verso.

Kiernan, Ben (1986). "Kampuchea's Ethnic Chinese under Pol Pot: A Case of Systematic Social Discrimination." *Journal of Contemporary Asia* 16(1):18.

Kiernan, Ben (1988). "Orphans of Genocide: The Cham Muslims of Kampuchea under Pol Pot." *Bulletin of Concerned Asian Scholars* 20(4):2–33.

Kiernan, Ben (ed.) (1993). *Genocide and Democracy in Cambodia: The Khmer Rouge, the United Nations, and the International Community.* Monograph Series 41. New Haven, CT: Yale University Southeast Asian Studies.

Kiernan, Ben (ed.) (1996). *The Pol Pot Regime: Race, Power, and Genocide in Cambodia under the Khmer Rouge, 1975–79.* New Haven, CT: Yale University Press.

Kiernan, Ben and Boua, Chanthou (eds.) (1982). *Peasants and Politics in Kampuchea, 1942–1981.* Armonk, NY: M. E. Sharpe.

Kuper, Leo (1981). *Genocide: Its Political Use in the Twentieth Century.* New Haven, CT: Yale University Press.

Lan, David (1985). *Guns and Rain: Guerrillas and Spirit Mediums in Zimbabwe.* Berkeley: University of California Press.

Lebra, Takie Sugiyama (1976). *Japanese Patterns of Behavior.* Honolulu: University of Hawaii Press.

Ledgerwood, Judy L. (1992). *Analysis of the Situation of Women in Cambodia: Research on Women in Khmer Society.* Phnom Penh: UNICEF.

Ledgerwood, Judy L. (1997). "The Cambodian Tuol Sleng Museum of Genocidal Crimes: National Narrative." *Museum Anthropology* 21:82–98.

Levy, Marc (1998). "Tales of Cambodia's Latest 'Killing Field.'" *Camnews* 1(634.3):June 8.

Lewin, Carroll McC. (1992). "The Holocaust: Anthropological Possibilities and the Dilemma of Representation." *American Anthropologist* 94:161–6.

Lewin, Carroll McC. (1993). "Negotiated Selves in the Holocaust." *Ethos* 21:295–318.

Malkki, Liisa H. (1995). *Purity and Exile: Violence, Memory, and National Cosmology among Hutu Refugees in Tanzania.* Chicago: University of Chicago Press.

Malkki, Liisa H. (1996). "Speechless Emissaries: Refugees, Humanitarianism, and Dehistoricization." *Cultural Anthropology* 11:377–404.

Mang Channo (1995). "The Stones Being Thrown at Christians." *Phnom Penh Post*, March 10:17.

Marston, John (1985). "Language Reform in Democratic Kampuchea." M.A. thesis, University of Minnesota.

Marston, John (1994). "Metaphors of the Khmer Rouge." In May M. Ebihara, Carol A. Mortland, and Judy Ledgerwood (eds.), *Cambodian Culture since 1975: Homeland and Exile.* Ithaca, NY: Cornell University Press, pp. 105–18.

Martin, Marie Alexandrine (1994). *Cambodia: A Shattered Society,* trans. Mark W. McLeod. Berkeley: University of California Press.

May, Someth (1986). *Cambodian Witness: The Autobiography of Someth May.* New York: Random House.

Moore, Barrington, Jr. (1966). *Social Origins of Dictatorship and Democracy: Lord and Peasant in the Making of the Modern World.* Boston: Beacon.

Moyer, Nancy (1991). *Escape from the Killing Fields: One Girl Who Survived the Cambodian Holocaust.* Grand Rapids, MI: Zondervan.

Mulder, Niels (1994). *Inside Thai Society: An Interpretation of Everyday Life.* Bangkok: Editions Duang Kamol.

Nagengast, Carole (1994). "Violence, Terror, and the Crisis of the State." *Annual Review of Anthropology* 23:109–36.

Ngor, Haing (1987). *A Cambodian Odyssey.* New York: Macmillan.

Nordstrom, Carolyn (1997). *A Different Kind of War Story.* Philadelphia: University of Pennsylvania Press.

Nordstrom, Carolyn and Martin, JoAnn (eds.) (1992). *The Paths to Domination, Resistance, and Terror*. Berkeley: University of California Press.

Nordstrom, Carolyn and Robben, Antonius C. G. M. (eds.) (1995). *Fieldwork under Fire: Contemporary Studies of Violence and Survival*. Berkeley: University of California Press.

Otterbein, Keith F. and Otterbein, Charlotte Swanson (1965). "An Eye for an Eye, A Tooth for a Tooth: A Cross-Cultural Study of Feuding." *American Anthropologist* 67:1470–82.

Peristiany, J. G. (ed.) (1966). *Honour and Shame: The Values of Mediterranean Society*. London: Weidenfeld and Nicolson.

Phnom Penh Post (1994). "They Said It . . . The Movers and Shakers." December 30:21.

Picq, Laurence (1989). *Beyond the Horizon: Five Years with the Khmer Rouge*. New York: St. Martin's Press.

Popkin, Samuel (1979). *The Rational Peasant: The Political Economy of Rural Society in Vietnam*. Berkeley: University of California Press.

Quinn, Kenneth M. (1976). "Political Change in Wartime: The Khmer Krahom Revolution in Southern Cambodia, 1970–1974." *US Naval War College Review* (Spring):3–31.

Quinn, Naomi and Holland, Dorothy (1987). "Culture and Cognition." In Dorothy Holland and Naomi Quinn (eds.), *Cultural Models in Language and Thought*. New York: Cambridge University Press, pp. 3–40.

Riches, David (ed.), (1986). *The Anthropology of Violence*. New York: Blackwell.

Robben, Antonius C. G. M. (1996). "Ethnographic Seduction, Transference, and Resistance in Dialogues about Terror and Violence in Argentina." *Ethos* 24:71–106.

Sânthor Mok (1986). *Tum Teav*. Paris: Centre de Documentation et de Recherche sur la Civilisation Khmère.

Scott, James C. (1976). *The Moral Economy of the Peasant: Rebellion and Subsistence in Southeast Asia*. New Haven, CT: Yale University Press.

Shawcross, William (1987). *Sideshow: Kissinger, Nixon and the Destruction of Cambodia*. New York: Simon and Schuster.

Shiloh, Ailon (1975). "Psychological Anthropology: A Case Study in Culture Blindness?" *Current Anthropology* 16:618–20.

Shore, Bradd (1996). *Culture in Mind: Cognition, Culture, and the Problem of Meaning*. New York: Oxford University Press.

Skocpol, Theda (1979). *States and Social Revolutions: A Comparative Analysis of France, Russia, and China*. New York: Cambridge University Press.

Sluka, Jeffrey A. (1989). *Hearts and Minds, Water and Fish: Support for the IRA and INLA in a Northern Irish Ghetto*. Greenwich, CT: JAI Press.

Soth Polin (1980). "Pol Pot's Diabolical Sweetness." *Index on Censorship* 5:43–5.

Stanton, Gregory H. (1993). "The Khmer Rouge and International Law." In Ben Kiernan (ed.), *Genocide and Democracy in Cambodia: The Khmer Rouge, the United Nations and the International Community*. Monograph Series 41. New Haven, CT: Yale University South East Asia Studies, pp. 141–61.

Stein, Howard F. (1993). "The Holocaust, the Self, and the Question of Wholeness: A Response to Lewin." *Ethos* 21:485–512.

Strauss, Claudia and Quinn Naomi (1994). "A Cognitive/Cultural Anthropology." In Robert Borofsky (ed.), *Assessing Cultural Anthropology*. New York: McGraw-Hill, pp. 297–312.

Stuart-Fox, Martin (1985). *The Murderous Revolution: Life and Death in Pol Pot's Kampuchea Based on the Personal Experiences of Bunheang Ung*. Chippendale, Australia: Alternative Publishing Cooperative.

Suárez-Orozco, Marcelo M. (1990). "Speaking of the Unspeakable: Toward a Psychosocial Understanding of Responses to Terror." *Ethos* 18:353–83.

Szymusiak, Molyda (1986). *The Stones Cry Out: A Cambodian Childhood, 1975–1980,* trans. Linda Coverdale. New York: Hill and Wang.

Tambiah, Stanley Jeyaraja (1986). *Sri Lanka: Ethnic Fratricide and the Dismantling of Democracy.* Chicago: University of Chicago Press.

Tambiah, Stanley Jeyaraja (1989). "Ethnic Conflict in the World Today." *American Ethnologist* 16:335–49.

Tambiah, Stanley Jeyaraja (1992). *Buddhism Betrayed? Religion, Politics, and Violence in Sri Lanka.* Chicago: University of Chicago Press.

Tambiah, Stanley Jeyaraja (1996). *Leveling Crowds: Ethnonationalist Conflicts and Collective Violence in South Asia.* Berkeley: University of California Press.

Taussig, Michael (1987). *Shamanism, Colonialism, and the Wild Man: A Study in Terror and Healing.* Chicago: University of Chicago Press.

Thaxton, Ralph (1983). *China Turned Rightside Up: Revolutionary Legitimacy in the Peasant World.* New Haven, CT: Yale University Press.

Thion, Serge (1993). *Watching Cambodia: Ten Paths to Enter the Cambodian Tangle.* Bangkok: White Lotus.

Vickery, Michael (1984). *Cambodia 1975–1982.* Boston: South End Press.

Warren, Kay B. (ed.) (1993). *The Violence Within: Cultural and Political Opposition in Divided Nations.* Boulder, CO: Westview.

Wikan, Unni (1990). *Managing Turbulent Hearts: A Balinese Formula for Living.* Chicago: University of Chicago Press.

Williams, Raymond (1977). *Marxism and Literature.* Oxford: Oxford University Press.

Wolf, Eric R. (1969). *Peasant Wars of the Twentieth Century.* New York: Harper and Row.

Yathay, Pin (1987). *Stay Alive, My Son.* New York: Simon and Schuster.

13

Dead Certainty: Ethnic Violence in the Era of Globalization

Arjun Appadurai

Under what conditions is group violence between previous social intimates associated with certain forms of *uncertainty* regarding ethnic identity? In sketching an approach to this question, I build on an argument against primordialism developed in a previous work (Appadurai 1996) and lay the foundations for a larger study of ethnic violence currently in progress.

In one widely shared perspective, ethnic violence, as a form of collective violence, is partly a product of propaganda, rumor, prejudice, and memory – all forms of knowledge and all usually associated with heightened conviction, conviction capable of producing inhumane degrees of violence. But there is an alternative approach to ethnic violence, with roots traceable to Durkheim's (1951) work on anomie and Simmel's (1950) ideas about the stranger. This tradition of thinking – which focuses on doubt, uncertainty, and indeterminacy – has surfaced recently in many different ways: it animates the ongoing work of Zygmunt Bauman (1997) on the roles of the stranger, the consumer, the parvenu, and the vagabond as social archetypes of the postmodern world. It appears, too, in the work of Piotr Hoffman (1986, 1989) on doubt, time, and violence. Julia Kristeva's (1991) work on strangers, a philosophical reflection clearly prompted by the renewed fear of xenophobia in France, belongs to this tradition. This line of thought has also been invoked, at least implicitly, in several recent anthropological works on ethnic violence. These works have in common the sound intuition that, given the growing multiplicity, contingency, and apparent fungibility of the identities available to persons in the contemporary world, there is a growing sense of radical social uncertainty about people, situations, events, norms, and even cosmologies.

Some of these works discuss the politics of the body in such a world of uncertainty. In others, there is a recognition that what is new about these uncertainties has something to do with the forces of globalization – weakened states, refugees, economic deregulation, and systematic new forms of pauperization and criminalization. This latter connection is especially suggestively made in Bauman (1997). Yet, to my knowledge, no single work has sought to explore the precise ways in which the ethnic body can be a theater for the engagement of uncertainty under the special circumstances of globalization. This link is an important preoccupation of the essay that follows.

Significant steps to engage these challenges are found in a growing body of work on ethnic violence by anthropologists (Daniel 1996; Das 1990, 1995; Desjarlais and Kleinman 1994; Devisch 1995; Hayden 1996; Herzfeld 1997; Jeganathan 1997; Malkki 1995; Nordstrom 1997; Tambiah 1996). Part of what emerges from this work is a consensus that the ethnic labels and categories involved in contemporary ethnic violence are frequently products of recent state policies and techniques, such as censuses, partitions, and constitutions. Labels such as "Yugoslav", "Sikh," "Kurd," and "Muslim," which *appear* to be the same as long-standing ethnic names and terms, are frequently transformations of existing names and terms to serve substantially new frameworks of identity, entitlement, and spatial sovereignty.

Given the high-level mobilization of such names and terms, three consequences follow. First, given the increasingly porous borders between nation-states in matters of arms, refugees, trade, and mass media,[1] these ethnic names and terms become highly susceptible to transnational perturbation. Second, where local identities and identifications often were far more important than higher-order names and terms, modern state-level forces tend to generate large-scale identities (such as Latino, Scheduled Caste, and Serb), which become significant imagined affiliations for large numbers of persons, many of whom reside across large social, spatial, and political divides. Third, and by extension, the angers, frustrations, and quarrels of small (face-to-face) communities and larger mega-ethnic groupings tend to affect each other directly and explosively, so that certain communities, in Robert Hayden's provocative phrase, become unimaginable (1996:783).

Since the subject of ethnic violence is large and horrifying in its range and variety, this essay confines itself to violence involving neighbors, friends, and kinsmen – persons and groups who have some degree of prior social familiarity. Thus the organized violence of police, armed hoodlums, professional torturers and investigators, and paid ethnic militias is not discussed here, except as it directly informs the problem of violence between socially proximate persons.[2] Also, rather than focus on all forms of violent confrontation, the discussion will concentrate on those associated with appalling physical brutality and indignity – involving mutilation, cannibalism, rape, sexual abuse, and violence against civilian spaces and populations. Put simply, the focus here is on bodily brutality perpetrated by ordinary persons against other persons with whom they may have – or could have – previously lived in relative amity.

This focus allows an examination of limiting conditions and extreme cases for exploring the role of *uncertainty* in extreme ethnic violence. Focusing on bodily violence between actors with routine – and generally benign – prior knowledge of one another is also a way to illuminate threshold or trigger conditions, where managed or endemic social conflict gives way to runaway violence.

Although transregional contacts and transnational processes have antecedents and anticipations over centuries (Abu-Lughod 1993; Wallerstein 1974) in the form of what we refer to as world-systems, there is a widely shared sense that there is something new about these processes and systems in the last few decades. The word *globalization* (both as a socioeconomic formation and as a term of folk ideology in journalism and in the corporate world) marks a set of transitions in the global political economy since the 1970s, in which multinational forms of capitalist organization began to be replaced by transnational (Rouse 1995), flexible (Harvey 1989), and irregular (Lash and Urry 1987, 1994) forms of organization, as labor, finance, technology, and technological capital began to be assembled in ways that treated national boundaries as mere constraints or fictions. In contrast with the multinational corporations of the middle of the century which sought to transcend national boundaries while working within existing national frameworks of law, commerce, and sovereignty, the transnational corporations of the last three decades have increasingly begun to produce recombinant arrangements of labor, capital, and technical expertise which produce new forms of law, management, and distribution. In both phases global capital and national states have sought to exploit each other, but in the most recent decades it is possible to see a secular decline in the sovereignty of national states in respect to the workings of global capital. These changes – with accompanying changes in law, accounting, patenting, and other administrative technologies – have created "new markets for loyalty" (Price 1994) and called existing models of territorial sovereignty into question (Sassen 1996).

It is not difficult to see that the speed and intensity with which both material and ideological elements now circulate across national boundaries have created a new order of uncertainty in social life. Whatever may characterize this new kind of uncertainty, it does not easily fit the dominant, Weberian prophecy about modernity in which earlier, intimate social forms would dissolve, to be replaced by highly regimented bureaucratic-legal orders, governed by the growth of procedure and predictability. The links between these forms of uncertainty – one diacritic of the era of globalization – and the worldwide intensification in ethnocidal violence inform this essay and are explicity addressed in its conclusion.[3]

The forms of such uncertainty are certainly various. One kind of uncertainty is a direct reflection of census concerns – how many persons of this or that sort really exist in a given territory? Or, in the context of rapid migration or refugee movement, how many of "them" are there now among "us"?[4] Another kind of uncertainty is about what some of these mega-identities really mean: what are the normative characteristics of what the constitution defines as a member of an OBC (Other Backward Caste) in India? A further uncertainty is about whether a particular person *really* is what they claim or appear to be or have historically been. Finally, these various forms of uncertainty create intolerable anxiety about the relationship of many individuals to state-provided goods – ranging from housing and health to safety and sanitation – since these entitlements are frequently directly tied to who "you" are, and thus to who "they" are. Each kind of uncertainty gains increasing force whenever there are large-scale movements of persons (for whatever reason), when new rewards or risks attach to large-scale ethnic identities, or when existing networks of social knowledge are eroded by rumor, terror, or social movement. Where one or more of these forms of social uncertainty come into play, violence can create a macabre form of certainty and can become a brutal technique (or folk discovery-procedure) about "them" and, therefore, about "us." This conjecture might make special sense in the era of globalization.

The first step toward such an understanding must be the most obvious and striking feature of such violence, which is its site and target – the body. Even a quick scan of the extensive literature suggests that the human body is the site of the most horrifying acts of ethnic violence. It might seem banal to say that the body is the site of the worst possible infliction of pain, terror, indignity, and suffering, in comparison with property or other resources. Yet it is clear that the violence inflicted on the human body in ethnic contexts is never entirely random or lacking in cultural form. Wherever the testimony is sufficiently graphic (Das 1990; Feldman 1991; Malkki 1995; Sutton 1995), it becomes clear that even the worst acts of degradation – involving feces, urine, body parts; beheading, impaling, gutting, sawing, raping, burning, hanging, and suffocating – have macabre forms of cultural design and violent predictability.

The single most forceful anthropological account of such design is Liisa Malkki's 1995 description of the memories of Hutu refugees in Tanzania in the 1980s of the genocidal violence perpetrated against them principally in the early 1970s in Burundi. This study, which brings together themes of exile, morality, memory, space, and nationalism in its effort to interpret genocidal violence, has many points of convergence with the principal arguments made here. But just two issues raised by Malkki directly concern me: the forms of bodily violence and the relationship of purity to identity.

Built around partially standardized accounts (mythico-histories) by Hutu refugees in Tanzania of the ethnocidal violence they experienced in Burundi since the 1960s, but especially in the bloodbath of 1972 directed against the Hutu majority, Malkki shows how questions of identification and knowledge of the ethnic body lay at the heart of the atrocious violence of this moment. Discussing a detailed response to her question of "how it could be possible to know a person's identity with certainty enough to kill," Malkki shows how earlier colonial efforts to reduce the complex social differences among local ethnic groups to a simple taxonomy of racial-physical signs had come to be further elaborated in the 1970s and 1980s. These "necrographic" maps were the basis for detailed, technical recollections of the ways in which death was administered to victims in specific, humiliating, and drawn-out ways. Malkki (following Feldman 1991) suggests that these maps of bodily difference are themselves delicately poised between acquired knowledge and techniques of detection. These maps "help construct and imagine ethnic difference," and "through violence, bodies of individual persons become metamorphosed into specimens of the ethnic category for which they are supposed to stand" (Malkki 1995:88). A slightly different approach to the relationship between "bodies," "persons," and "identities" appears in this essay.

In the account that Malkki presents of the mythico-historical presentation of how Tutsi killers used shared maps of physical differences to identify Hutu, it is clear that the process is racked with instability and uncertainty (even in survivors' views of the uncertainty faced by their killers), so that multiple physical tests have to be applied. Malkki offers a bold interpretation of the specific ways in which Hutu men and women were killed (often with sharp bamboo sticks, using the grid of vagina, anus, and head; often removing fetuses from pregnant women intact and forcing the mother to eat the fetus). She concludes that these recollected practices, played out on the necrographic maps of the Hutu ethnic body, "seem to have operated through certain routinized symbolic schemes of nightmarish cruelty" (92).

It remains to draw out the link between the mapped body of the ethnic other and the peculiar and specific brutalities associated with ethnic murder. While much of Malkki's analysis strikes me as deeply persuasive, what is vital for the present argument is the link between indeterminacy and brutality in the negotiations over the ethnic body.[5] Although it is difficult to be sure (especially for an analyst who is one step away from Malkki's firsthand exposure to these narratives), there is enough evidence to suggest that we are looking here at a complex variation of Mary Douglas' classic arguments about "purity and danger" (1966) and about the body as a symbolic map of the cosmos (1973). In her classic argument about "matter out of place" (which Malkki also discusses), Douglas made a symbolic-structural link between categorical mixture, the cognitive anxiety it provokes, and the resultant abhorrence of taxonomic hybridity in all sorts of social and moral worlds. In subsequent work on body symbolism, Douglas showed how and why the body works to compress and perform wider cosmological understandings about social categories and classifications. Several recent analysts of ethnic violence have made useful recourse to Douglas' ideas about purity and category-mixture (Hayden 1996; Herzfeld 1992, 1997) in addressing issues of ethnic cleansing in Europe.

The argument here owes a direct debt to Douglas, but some distinctions are worth making. While Douglas takes a cosmology (a system of categorical distinctions) as culturally given, thus leading to taboos against "matter out of place," ethnic violence introduces contingency into this logic, for the situations discussed here are explicitly about cosmologies in flux, categories under stress, and ideas striving for the logic of self-evidence. What is more, the sort of evidence presented by Malkki (and supported by similar accounts from Ireland, India, and Eastern Europe) suggests an inversion of the logic of indeterminacy, category-mixture, and danger identified by Douglas. In Malkki's evidence, for example, the body is both a source and a target of violence. The categorical uncertainty about Hutu and Tutsi is played out not in the security of the "body maps" shared by both sides but by the instability of the signs of bodily difference: not all Tutsis are tall; not all Hutu have red gums; not all noses help identify Tutsi, nor do all modes of walking help identify Hutu.

In a word, real bodies in history betray the very cosmologies they are meant to encode. So the ethnic body, both of victim and of killer, is itself potentially *deceptive*. Far from providing the map for a secure cosmology, a compass from which mixture, indeterminacy, and danger may be discovered, the ethnic body turns out to be itself unstable and deceptive. It is this reversal of Douglas' cosmologic that might best explain macabre patterns of violence directed against the body of the ethnic other. The peculiar formality – the specific preoccupation with particular body parts – is an effort to stabilize the body of the ethnic other; to eliminate the flux introduced by somatic variation, by mixture and intermarriage; and to evict the possibility of further somatic change or slippage. It is difficult to be sure whether such a shift in the role of the body in ethnic violence is a qualitatively new feature either of modernity or of the most recent decades of globalization or simply an intensification of earlier tendencies. I shall return to this interpretive challenge later.

This sort of brutality belongs to the theater of divination, sorcery, and witchcraft. It literally turns a body inside out and finds the proof of its betrayal, its deceptions, its definitive otherness, in a sort of premortem autopsy (see also Feldman 1991: 110–15), which, rather than achieving death because of prior uncertainty, achieves categorical certainty through death and dismemberment. In Peter Geschiere's recent and magisterial analysis of witchcraft in West Africa (1997), with special reference to regional variation in the Cameroon, we are presented with a powerful reminder that witchcraft and sorcery, far from being static cultural forms, are elastic and highly flexible moral discourses for bringing to "account" new forms of wealth, inequality, and power. They both feed and are fed by news of national politics, global flows of commodities, and rumors of illegitimate flows of people and goods. Flourishing in an atmosphere of rumor, deception, and uncertainty, these discourses place large-scale political and economic uncertainties onto maps of kinship and its local discourses of equity and morality. Among the Maka of Cameroon, witchcraft is focused on the frightening figure of the *djambe*, a small creature that occupies the body of the victim and drives the victim to sacrifice his or her kin, to participate in nocturnal anthropophagic banquets, and thus to "introduce treason into the most reliable space in Maka society" (40), the space of kinship and the household. We shall return to the themes of treason, cannibalism, and morality shortly. For the moment, though this is not Geschiere's principal concern, let us note that in the many variations on witchcraft and sorcery studied by anthropologists in sub-Saharan Africa, going back to Evans-Pritchard's classic study (1937) of these matters among the Azande, the sources of witchcraft and sorcery often involve forces and creatures embedded inside the body of the victim/perpetrator, and the establishment of guilt and accountability often involves techniques of bodily investigation, whether of other animals or of humans. Finally, Geschiere is able to show that witchcraft links the world of kinship to the world of ethnicity and politics in Cameroon and is held responsible for the newfound wealth and potential power of large ethnic groups. This extension of an idiom of intimacy gone awry to large-scale suspicion of adversarial ethnic groups is a matter that will be reengaged shortly.

For now, it is sufficient to note that the macabre regularities and predictabilities of ethnocidal violence cannot be taken as simple evidence of "calculation" or as blind reflexes of "culture."[6] Rather, they are brutal forms of bodily discovery – forms of vivisection; emergent techniques for exploring, marking, classifying, and storing the bodies of those who *may* be the "ethnic" enemy. Naturally, these brutal actions do not create any real or sustainable sense of secure knowledge. Rather, they exacerbate the frustration of the perpetrators. Worse, they create the condition for preemptive violence among those who fear being victims. This cycle of actual violence and the expectation of violence finds its fuel in certain spatial conditions of information flow, human traffic, and state intervention.

Anthropology has long known about the ways in which the body is a theater for social performances and productions (Bourdieu 1977; Comaroff 1985; Douglas 1966; Martin 1992; Mauss 1973; van Gennep 1965). Combining Malkki's material on ethnic violence in Burundi with Geschiere's study of witchcraft in Cameroon, against the backdrop of Douglas' pathbreaking work on category confusion, power, and taboo, allows us to see that the killing, torture, and rape associated with ethnocidal violence is not simply a matter of eliminating the ethnic other. It involves the use of the body to establish the parameters of this otherness, taking the body apart, so to speak, to divine the enemy within. In this sense, the fruitful studies of witchcraft logics in Africa might have much wider interpretive salience.

The role of the body as a site of violent closure in situations of categorical uncertainty is closely allied with a theme that has already been touched upon, the theme of deception. The literature on ethnocidal violence is shot through with the related tropes of deception, treachery, betrayal, imposture, and secrecy. Considerable sustenance for this view of the suspicion, uncertainty, and cognitive paranoia about the identity of the ethnic enemy comes from a variety of sources. Benedict Anderson has shown the salience of the Nazi fear about the "secret agency" of Jews in Germany, and the desperate deployment of all sorts of means to smoke out the "real" Jews, many of whom seemed "Aryan" and "German" in every regard (Anderson 1991). The murder of Jews under Hitler constitutes a large area of research and of ongoing debate that exceeds the scope of this essay. But the importance of Nazi ideas of racial purity (Aryan-Germanness) for the extraordinary genocidal violence directed against Jews seems beyond debate.

The idea of Jews as "pretenders" – as ethnic quislings, as a cancer within the German social body – draws our attention to a crucial way in which the Nazi handling of the Jewish body far exceeds the logic of scapegoating, stereotyping, and the like. What it shows is how those needs, under certain conditions, evolve into policies for mass extermination of the ethnic other. This brutally modern fact, which is the peculiarly horrifying feature of the Holocaust (associated with its totality, its bureaucratization, its "banality," its goal of complete ethnonational purification), is certainly complicated by the special history of European anti-Semitism.[7] But in its drive for purity through ethnocide and its "medicalization of anti-semitism" (Proctor 1995: 172) it sets the stage for the ethnic cleansing of, at least, Eastern Europe, Rwanda-Burundi, and Cambodia in the last two decades, the era of globalization. In the case of Nazi racial ideology, the idea of the Jew as secret agent brings together the ambivalence of German Nazis about race, religion, and economy. Jews were the perfect sites for the exploration of Nazi uncertainty about both Christianity and capitalism. Like the Hutu for the Tutsi, the Jews were "the enemies within," always potential threats to German national-racial purity, secret agents of racial corruption, of international capital (and, paradoxically, of communism).

As Malkki shows, the theme of secrecy and trickery pervaded Hutu ideas about the Tutsi elite that governed Rwanda. Here seen from the vantage point of the victims, their oppressors appear as "thieves who stole the country from the indigenous Hutu," as innately skilled in the arts of deception (1995: 68). The Hutu were seen as foreigners who hid their origins, as malign tricksters who were "hiding their true identity" (72).

The trope of deception, fake identity, and betrayal finds further support in the context of the violence perpetrated in North India since the 1980s in struggles between Hindus and Sikhs, articulated eventually in powerful demands for an autonomous Sikh state (Khalistan). In the discourse of Sikh militants in India, Veena Das (1995) has shown the importance of concern with "counterfeit" claims to Sikh identity, even where such claims pertained to identities that were not the most legitimate forms of Sikhness. In a chapter on Sikh militant discourse, Das shows how, in the key years of the early 1980s, a Sikh militant discourse emerged in the Punjab which identified the state with Hinduism and Hindus with a dangerous effeminacy that threatened the community of Sikhs conceived as male. This discourse selectively identified key events in the Sikh past and present so as to play down the crucial tensions between Sikhs and Muslims in favor of the current opposition between Sikhs and Hindus. Das has much to say about history and memory, speech and violence, gender and the state. But her crucial concern is with the ways in which militant discourse both represents and induces the possibility of violence through its graphic mobilization of sexual, personal, and political images and narratives and exhortations. In many ways, Das shows how the public speeches of Sikh militants, such as Sant Bhindranwale, transform the experience of individuals into the shame of the community, and thus all violence committed in the name of the Sikhs is justified as individual action against collective injustice, as a step toward martyrdom. The many rich details of this analysis of Sikh militant discourse cannot be engaged here, but two phenomean concerning identity addressed by Das are relevant.

Especially in the speeches of Bhindranwale, as cited by Das, a running theme is the question of who the Sikhs really are. One vital issue in mobilizing the uncertainty surrounding what it means to be Sikh concerns a breakaway group among the Sikhs, called the Nirankaris. Here is what Das has to say about Sikh militant violence against the Nirankaris in the 1970s and 1980s:

There is a huge mistrust of alternative definitions of the Sikh community. This comes to the fore in the relationship between Sikh militants and communities on the peripheries of Sikhism. One such community is the Nirankaris, who may be considered a sectarian development within Sikhism. Since the followers of this sect worship a living guru, this being contrary to orthodox Sikh teaching, they were declared enemies of the *panth* in 1973 by the priests of the Golden Temple. In April 1978 some of Bhindranwale's followers clashed violently with the Nirankaris on both sides. . . .

Though it acknowledges that they *were* a sect with close connections with the Sikhs, their present forms of worship are considered unacceptable; they are declared "counterfeit Nirankaris." . . . The Nirankaris are declared to be agents of the Hindu government, whose only mission is to destroy Sikhs. (1995: 133–4)

So here is a vivid example of having to bring the killing close to home to clarify who real Sikhs are and what the label *Sikh* really means. Note the ideas of "counterfeit Nirankaris" and of "agents" of the hostile group (Hindus), along with the terrible fury against the "pure" Sikh. We are back here with the theme of purity, first remarked by Douglas (1966), then elaborated by Malkki (1995), Hayden (1996), and Michael Herzfeld (1997) in various directions. In Malkki's account, this ideology of the pure and the counterfeit explains the paradoxical sense among Hutu living in refugee camps in Tanzania that their very exile was the sign of their purity as "Hutu" (and anticipates Bauman's (1997) reflections on purity, strangers, and otherness). While the Nazi case shows the power of the discourse of purity for the powerful majority (often using the idiom of the minority as a "cancer" within the social body), the Sikh case shows the domino effect of violent efforts to cleanse, as they ripple through the victim group, creating further efforts to cleanse gray areas and achieve complete clarity and purity. Of course, clarity and purity are not identical concerns, nor do they call forth similar forms of motive and commitment. While clarity is a matter of cognition, purity is a matter of moral coherence. These dimensions seem to converge in the collective heat of ethnocide, where the logic of cleansing seems both dialectical and self-perpetuating, as one act of "purification" calls forth its counterpart both from and within the ethnic "other." Likewise, purification and clarification appear to be in a dialectical and productive relationship.

The terror of purification and the vivisectionist tendencies that emerge in situations of mass violence also blur the lines between ethnicity and politics. Indeed, just as ethnocide is the limiting form of political violence, so certain forms of political hysteria lead to a quasi-ethnic preoccupation with somatic strategies. This somatic rendition of political identities offers another angle on the issue of masks, counterfeits, and treachery. A powerful example of this dynamic comes from China, where Donald Sutton (1995) interprets the significance of widespread reports of cannibalism in Guangxi Province in China in 1968, toward the tail end of the violent phase of the Cultural Revolution. Again, this complex essay takes up a large range of fascinating issues involving cannibalism in the cultural history of this region, its reactivation under the violent conditions of the Cultural Revolution, the complex relations between regional politics and the politics of Beijing, and so on.

What is striking for our purposes in Sutton's analysis is the issue of violence among persons who live in considerable social proximity to one another. Consider this chilling description of the general forms of events of what Sutton calls "political cannibalism": the forces of law and order, not the rebels, were the killers and eaters. Moreover, the forms of cannibalistic consumption varied within a narrow range. People agreed on the best body parts and insisted on them being cooked; and the selection, killing, and consuming of victims were relatively systematized (1995: 142).

By closely examining what were referred to in Wuxuan as "human flesh banquets" and what were known during this period as "struggles" (ritualized events involving accusation, confession, and physical abuse of suspected class enemies), Sutton is able convincingly to show that, while these episodes involved ostensible political categories of persons, their logic appears fully compatible with the sorts of violence we would usually call ethnic. In analyzing a related case from Mengshan, Sutton shows how the designation of a man as a "landlord" made him such a convincing villain that a neighbor did not warn him of his impending murder by a local group of militia.

Sutton also demonstrates how political labels took on immense somatic force: an urban youth cited in one of his sources says of the former landlords, "I felt that deep in their hearts they still wanted to overthrow everything and kill all of us. In movies, they had awful faces. And in the village when I saw them I feared them and thought they were repulsive to look at. I guess ugliness is a psychological thing" (1995: 161). This remarkable quotation offers a brief glimpse of how political labels (such as "landlord," "class enemy," and "counterrevolutionary") become powerful bearers of affect, and of how, in at least some cases, verbal propaganda and mass-mediated images can literally turn ordinary faces into abominations that must be destroyed.[8] In a final, crucial piece of data from Sutton's essay, a former party leader, when expelled from the party in the early 1980s on the grounds of his earlier cannibalism, says with contempt: "Cannibalism ... ! It was the flesh of a landlord that was eaten, the flesh of a secret agent" (162).

With this example, we are back again with the problem of identification and uncertainty, the transformation of neighbors and friends into monsters, and the idea that social appearances are literally masks (Fitzpatrick 1991, 1995), beneath which truer, deeper, more horrible forms of identity may subsist. "Secret agency" is found in a wide range of sources that deal with ethnic violence, and it is an indicator of the crucial trigger of the sense of betrayal, treachery, and deception that seems to underwrite its most dramatic expressions. This essay about political cannibalism from China casts an eerie light on descriptions from Bosnian concentration camps in which men were made to bite off the genitals of friends or fellow prisoners and similar hints of forced cannibalism in other contexts.

Ethnocidal violence evidently mobilizes some sort of ambient rage about the body as a theater of deception, of betrayal, and of false solidarity. Whenever the charge of categorical treachery is made to appear plausible, secret agents are unmasked, impure ethnicities are exposed, and horribly cancerous identities are imputed to what we may call the inner body, numerous collective forms of vivisection seem possible, with the most ordinary of people as their perpetrators.

In many of these forms of violence, we can see a horrible range of intimacies. It is of course true that the most extreme forms of ethnic violence involve major dramas of power, of degradation, of violation, and of emotional and physical pain. It is also true that some of this is explicable as part of a cycle of memory and countermemory, where one remembered atrocity becomes the basis for another. But something else is present in at least some of these situations – that is, this violence is a horrible effort to expose, penetrate, and occupy the material form – the body – of the ethnic other. This may well be the key to the many ways in which sexuality is implicated in recent global forms of ethnic violence. Eating the liver or heart of the exposed "class enemy" is surely a horrible form of intimacy, and one does not have to make recourse to deeper structural theories about "friendly" cannibalism to see that eating the enemy is one way of securing a macabre intimacy with the enemy who was so recently a friend.[9] Making one prisoner bite off the genitals of another is an even more grotesque way of simultaneously inflicting deep pain, injury, and insult while imposing a brutal sort of intimacy between enemy bodies.

This may be the place to briefly note that rape in such circumstances is not only tied up with special understandings of honor and shame, and a possible effort to abuse the actual organs of sexual (and thus ethnic) reproduction, but is additionally the most violent form of penetration, investigation, and exploration of the body of the enemy. These factors may account for the renewed salience of rape in ethnic violence. Rape, from this point of view, is the counterpart to the examination of males suspected to be Muslim (in places like Bombay) to check whether they are circumcised. Like the wooden stakes driven through the anus of the ethnic enemy and up into his skull (in the case of Hutu-Tutsi ethnocide reported by Malkki) the penis in ethnocidal rape is simultaneously an instrument of degradation, of purification, and of a grotesque form of intimacy with the ethnic other. This is not of course to suggest that the sexual violence directed against men and women – for example, in recent events in Eastern Europe – is the same either in quantity or quality. It is clear that, in the history of warfare generally and of ethnic violence more recently, women bear the largest burden as victims of sexual violence.[10] Still, it may be worth considering that there is something that links the violence of ethnocidal rape with other forms of bodily violation and disposal.

In the end, when all the horrible descriptions are read and all the large-scale political, social, and economic factors are taken into account, the body remains the site of intimacy, and in the many different forms that bodily violence takes in different contexts, there is a common thread of intimacy gone berserk.[11] Looking at the question of uncertainty and vivisection in the context of intimacy returns one to the question of number and abstraction – and thus of globalization – discussed earlier in this essay.

To repeat, one of the key features of the new ethnic categories is their large-scale, officialized quality. In no case of ethnocide of which we have knowledge can it be shown that these categories are innocent of state practices (usually through the census and often involving crucial forms of welfare or potential punishment). The question is, how can forms of identity and identification of such scope – ethnic labels that are abstract containers for the identities of thousands, often millions, of persons – become transformed into instruments of the most brutally intimate forms of violence? One clue to the way in which these large *numerical* abstractions inspire grotesque forms of bodily violence is that these forms of violence – forms that I have called vivisectionist – offer temporary ways to render these abstractions graspable, to make these large numbers sensuous, to make labels that are potentially over-whelming, for a moment, personal.[12]

To put it in a sanitized manner, the most horrible forms of ethnocidal violence are mechanisms *for producing persons* out of what are otherwise diffuse, large-scale labels that have effects but no locations.[13] This is why the worst kinds of ethnic violence appear to call for the word "ritual" or "ritualized" from their analysts. What is involved here is not just the properties of symbolic specificity, sequence, convention, and even tradition in particular forms of violence but something even more deep about rituals of the body: they are always about the production, growth, and maintenance of persons. This "life-cycle" aspect of bodily rituals (remarked by Arnold van Gennep and many distinguished successors in anthropology) finds its most monstrous inversion in what we may call the "death-cycle" rituals of mass ethnocide. These horrible counterperformances retain one deep element in common with their life-enhancing counterparts: they are instruments for making persons out of bodies.[14] It may seem odd to speak of the production of persons out of bodies in an argument that rests on the presumption of prior social intimacy (or its possibility) between agents and victims. But it is precisely in situations where endemic doubts and pressures become intolerable that ordinary people begin to see masks instead of faces. In this perspective, extreme bodily violence may be seen as a degenerate technology for the reproduction of intimacy where it is seen to have been violated by secrecy and treachery.

Through this ritualized mode of concretization we can see how the bodily violence of ethnocide is an instrument for the production of persons in the context of large-scale ethnic identities that have, for whatever reason, turned mutually hostile. It may seem frivolous to suggest that such violence produces persons, in the face of the fact that so much of it is not only degrading and deadly but also literally appears to deconstruct bodies (through various forms of mutilation and butchery). This macabre technique for the production of persons is, of course, special. Nevertheless, in the intimacy and intricacy of preoccupation with body parts and wholes, with penetration and with consumption, with exit and with access, these forms of violence are methods of assuring that some bodies are – without doubt – real persons. The horrible negativity of this technology is that the production of "real" persons out of the bodies of traitors, secret agents, and despised group enemies seems to require their vivisection. Here, too, is the link between intimacy and uncertainty. Where fear about ethnic body snatching and secret agency becomes plausible, then producing "real" ethnic enemies out of the uncertainty posed by thousands of possible secret agents seems to call forth a special order of rage, brutality, and systematicity, all at once. The problem of fake identities seems to demand the brutal creation of real persons through violence. This is the modification I propose to the suggestion of Allen Feldman (1991), echoed by Malkki (1995), that ethnic violence produces abstract tokens of ethnicity out of the bodies of real persons.

Such examples can be multiplied. They testify to one important fact: as large populations occupy complex social spaces and as primary cultural features (clothing, speech styles, residential patterns) are recognized to be poor indicators of ethnicity, there tends to be a steady growth in the search for "inner" or "concealed" signs of a person's "real" identity. The maiming and multilation of ethnicized bodies is a desperate effort to restore the validity of somatic markers of "otherness" in the face of the uncertainties posed by census labels, demographic shifts, and linguistic changes, all of which make ethnic affiliations less somatic and bodily, more social and elective. Mixed marriages, of the sort that have long taken place in many cosmopolitan regions and cities, are the biggest obstacles to simple tests of ethnic "otherness" (Hayden 1996). It is such facts that set the stage for the body as a site for resolving uncertainty through brutal forms of violation, investigation, deconstruction, and disposal.

This proposal – linking categorical uncertainty to the bodily brutalities of ethnocide – builds on other components of a general theory of ethnic violence, many of which are already in place: the classificatory policies of many colonial states; the large involuntary migrations created by such powerful states as Stalin's USSR; the confusions created by policies of affirmative action applied by democratic constitutions to quasi-ethnic classifications, such as the "Scheduled" Castes created by the Indian Constitution; the stimuli of arms, money, and political support involved in diasporic populations, creating what Benedict Anderson (1994) has called "long-distance" nationalism; the velocity of image circulation created by Cable News Network, the World Wide Web, faxes, phones, and other media in exposing populations in one place to the goriest details of violence in another; the major social upheavals since 1989 in Eastern Europe and elsewhere that have created dramatic fears about winners and losers in the new open market, thus creating new forms of scapegoating, as with Jews and Gypsies in Romania (Verdery 1991).

These larger forces – global mass mediation, increased migration, both forced and voluntary, sharp transformations in national economies, severed links between territory, citizenship, and ethnic affiliation – return us to the theme of globalization, within which the argument was earlier framed. It is not hard to see the general ways in which transnational forces impinge on local ethnic instabilities. Hayden's (1996) discussion of national populations, censuses, and constitutions in the former Yugoslavia, and the resultant drive to eliminate the "unimaginable" in new national formations, is one clear demonstration of the steps that lead from global and European politics (and history) to imperial breakup and ethnic meltdown, especially in those zones characterized by the greatest degree of ethnic mixture through intermarriage. But the road from constitutional mandates to bodily brutality cannot wholly be handled at the level of categorical contradiction. The peculiar and ghastly forms of vivisection that have characterized recent ethnocidal violence (both in Eastern Europe and elsewhere) carry a surplus of rage that calls for an additional interpretive frame, in which uncertainty, purity, treachery, and bodily violence can be linked. This surplus or excess makes sense of the hyperrationalities – noted throughout this essay – that accompany what seems to be the hysteria of these events: the quasi-ritual order, the attention to detail, the specificity of bodily violation, the systematicity of the forms of degradation.

Yet globalization does not produce just one road to uncertainty, terror, or violence. In this essay I have identified a logic for the production of "real persons" which links uncertainty, purity, treachery, and vivisection. There are surely other "ethnocidal imaginaries"[15] in which the forces of global capital, the relative power of states, varying histories of race and class and differences in the status of mass mediation, produce different kinds of uncertainty and different scenarios for ethnocide. The examples I have relied on here – the People's Republic of China in the late 1960s, Central Africa in the 1970s, North India in the early 1980s, and Central Europe in the late 1980s and early 1990s – do not have either the same spatial or temporal relationship to the process of globalization. In each case, the degree of openness to global capital, the legitimacy of the state, the internal and external flow of ethnic populations, and the variety of political struggles over group entitlement were clearly not the same. Though the vivisectionist hypothesis put forward here may not thus apply uniformly in these cases, its critical elements – purity, clarity, treachery, and agency – may well provide key ingredients that might be recombined fruitfully to cast some degree of light on them.

In an earlier effort to analyze the link between large-scale identities, the abstraction of large numbers, and the theater of the body, I suggested that global forces are best seen as imploding into localities, deforming their normative climate, recasting their politics, and representing their contingent characters and plots as instances of larger narratives of betrayal and loyalty (Appadurai 1996:149–57). In the present context, the idea of implosion might account for actions at the most local of globalized sites – the ethnicized body, which, in already confused and contradictory circumstances, can become the most natural, the most intimate, and thus the most horrifying site for tracking the somatic signs of the enemy within. In ethnocidal violence, what is sought is just that somatic stabilization that globalization – in a variety of ways – inherently makes impossible. In a twisted version of Popperian norms for verification in science, paranoid conjectures produce dismembered refutations.[16]

The view advanced here of ethnocidal violence between social intimates is not only about uncertainty about the "other." Obviously, these actions indicate a deep and dramatic uncertainty about the ethnic self. They arise in circumstances where the lived experience of large labels becomes unstable, indeterminate, and socially volatile, so that violent action can become one means of satisfying one's sense of one's categorical self. But of course the violent epistemology of bodily violence, the "theater of the body" on which this violence is performed, is never truly cathartic, satisfying, or terminal. It only leads to a deepening of social wounds, an epidemic of shame, a collusion of silence, and a violent need for forgetting. All these effects add fresh underground fuel for new episodes of violence. This is also partly a matter of the preemptive quality of such violence: let me kill you before you kill me. Uncertainty about identification and violence can lead to actions, reactions, complicities, and anticipations that multiply the preexisting uncertainty about labels. Together, these forms of uncertainty call for the worst kind of certainty: dead certainty.

NOTES

1   Virtually all borders, however rigidly policed, are porous to some extent. I am not suggesting that all borders are equally porous or that all groups can cross particular borders at will. The image of a borderless world is far from what I wish to evoke. Rather, I wish to suggest that borders are increasingly sites of contestation between states and various kinds of non-state actors and interests and that it is only in respect to some populations, commodities, and ideologies that states succeed in maintaining tight borders. Further, the movement of ethnic populations across national borders, whether in flight or not, is frequently a factor in intranational ethnic conflict.

2   However, I do not wish to imply that these different forms and registers of violence are analytically or empirically insulated from one another. Indeed, Claudio Lomnitz (personal communication) has suggested various ways in which the vivisectionist violence between intimates and the banalized violence of professional torturers (especially in Latin America) may be linked through the politics of identity and the state, and thus of globalization. I hope to pursue these suggestions in future work on this subject.

3   It is difficult to make plausible quantitative claims about changes in the incidence of ethnic violence over long periods of time. There is some evidence that intrastate conflict (including ethnic violence) is more frequent today than interstate conflict. It appears that there is a secular increase in extreme forms of bodily violence between ethnic groups, even though many societies are remarkable for their striking degree of ethnic harmony and social order generally. There is no doubt that the amplification of our impressions of ethnic violence through the mass media creates the inherent risk of exaggerating the global occurrence of extreme violence.

4   For a suggestive discussion of the widespread uncertainty concerning the identities of persons, social categories, villages, and even about the link between religion and nationhood during the process of partition in 1947, I am indebted to a draft paper by Gyanendra Pandey, "Can a Muslim Be an Indian?" delivered at the University of Chicago in April 1997. A similar kind of uncertainty, produced by late colonial and postcolonial politics, is remarked by Qadri Ismail (1995) with respect to Sri Lankan Muslim self-understandings of identity.

5   This is the appropriate point at which to acknowledge the pathbreaking contribution of Allen Feldman's study of ethnoreligious violence in Ireland (1991). Most subsequent anthropological studies of violence, including several that I cite here, are in his debt. His brilliant examination of the logic of space, torture, fear, and narrative in Northern

Ireland brings a radical Foucauldian perspective to bear on a series of searing ethnographic observations of militarized ethnic terror. The ways in which Feldman's arguments set the stage for my own are many: they include his observations about interrogation as a ceremony of verification (115), torture as a technique for the production of power out of the body of the victim (115), the medicalization involved in interrogation (122–3), and the role of the corpse, or "stiff," to mark the transfer of larger spatial maps onto the map of the enemy body (73). My effort is to shift the focus away from state-sponsored violence to its "ordinary" forms and agents and to elaborate the links between clarification and purification.

6   This may be the place to note the peculiar relationship between spontaneity and calculation in collective ethnic violence. The emphasis in this essay on uncertainty and vivisection may cast new light on this difficult problem. Existing approaches tend to encounter a missing link between the planned (generally politically motivated) forces behind ethnic violence and the undeniable element of spontaneity. The approach taken here suggests that, at least under certain conditions, the vivisectionist response to uncertainty may mimic modern scientific modes of verification just as the planned aspects of ethnic violence may mimic other legitimate modes of politics that stress procedure, technique, and form. There may thus be an inner affinity between spontaneity and calculation in modern ethnic violence which requires further explanation (cf. Tambiah 1996).

7   There is a vast literature about the relationship between German nationalism, Jewish identity, and the dynamics of the Holocaust. Some of this literature, including some work produced by the Frankfurt School, recognizes the relationship between modernity, irrationality, and the fear of international cosmopolitanism represented by Nazi anti-Semitism. It is also apparent that the banalization and mechanization of death in Nazi Germany had much to do with the Jewish body as a site of fear about abstract forms of capital and identity. The recent debates surrounding Daniel Goldhagen's study (1996) of the involvement of ordinary Germans in the extermination of Jews in Nazi Germany have reopened many of these questions. The scope of this literature makes it impossible to take it up intensively here. Suffice it to say that Nazi policies toward Jews raise issues about both purity and clarity in ethnonational projects, which are closely connected to the argument of this essay.

8   The entire issue of dual identities and split subjectivities has been approached in a highly suggestive manner by Slavoj Žižek (1989) in his creative Lacanian revision of Hegel. As part of this reading, Žižek observes the sense in which anxiety about the resemblance between Jews and Germans is a key part of anti-Semitism. He also notes the peculiar ways in which Stalinist terror demanded that its victims, in political trials, for example, confess their "treason" precisely because they are, in some sense, also "good" communists who recognize the needs of the party for purges and exposures. In both cases, the victims endure the suffering of being both "us" and "them" in reference to a totalizing ideology.

    Sheila Fitzpatrick first pointed out to me the salience of the Stalinist trials of "class traitors" to the general logic of my argument. In her own brief essay on autobiographical narratives and political trials in Stalin's Russia (1995), Fitzpatrick shows that the fear of uncertainty about their class histories affected many Soviet citizens at this time, since everyone had some sort of vulnerability: "Then their Soviet masks would be torn off; they would be exposed as double dealers and hypocrites, enemies who must be cast out of Soviet society. In the blink of an eye, as in a fairy tale, Gaffner the kolkhoz pioneer would become Haffner the Mennonite kulak. A clap of thunder and the face looking back from Ulianova's mirror would be that of Buber the wicked witch, enemy of the Soviet people" (1995: 232; see also Fitzpatrick 1991).

9   This sort of brutal intimacy could be viewed as a fatal deformation of the sort of "cultural intimacy" that Herzfeld (1997) defines as that sense of familiarity, proximity, trust, and

inside knowledge that is preserved by local communities in the face of state taxonomies, policies, and stereotypes. Given the delicate line between popular essentialisms and state essentialisms that Herzfeld notes in his larger analysis, it may not be far-fetched to suggest that some sort of intimacy – gone terrifyingly awry, to be sure – is a feature of the vivisectionist quality of much ethnic violence today.

10 Several colleagues have suggested to me that in the United States and in the advanced industrial societies of Western Europe many of the features that I see in global ethnic violence are strikingly present in domestic abuse directed against women. This comparative insight opens up the wider question of the links between ethnic and sexual violence and of the structural relation between these forms of violence in more and less wealthy societies. In the current context, this link is a reminder that large-scale violence in the context of intimacy is not restricted to the non-European or less-developed countries of the world.

11 This point resonates with the provocative analysis of power and obscenity in the postcolony by Achille Mbembe, where he discusses the dynamics of "the intimacy of tyranny" (1992:22). Here the body appears as the site of greed, excess, and phallocentric power among the ruling elites and thus as the object of scatological intimacy in popular discourse. The relation between this sort of political obscenity and the logic of vivisection which I explore here must await another occasion (see also Mbembe and Roitman 1995).

12 Of course, not all forms of abstraction in social life conduce to violence, nor have such potentially violent forms of abstraction as the map, the census, and models of economic development always led to coercion or conflict. Here, as elsewhere, one needs to examine the multiple vectors of modernity and the particular ways in which they converge and diverge in the era of globalization. In this most recent epoch of globalization, these instruments of abstraction combine with other forces, such as migration, mediation, and secession, to create conditions of heightened uncertainty. But that is not an inherent quantitative or structural property of these abstractions.

13 Here and elsewhere in the essay I have preferred the use of *person* over *subject*, although the Hegelian idea of subjectivity, as well as its Foucauldian version in respect to violence and agency, is deeply relevant to my analysis. While the idea of the subject is more immediately and explicitly tied to the dialectics of modernity, there is no easy bridge between it and the category of the person that continues to be central to the anthropology of the body and of ritual. I hope to engage more fully with the discursive implications of these key terms in future work on this topic. For now, I can only suggest that my use of the term *person* is not intended to foreclose the sorts of readings that for some may more comfortably flow from the substitution in such contexts of the idea of the subject.

14 This part of the analysis resonates with many aspects of Feldman's interpretation (1991) of the ceremonial – indeed, sacrificial – overtones of the interrogation and incarceration of political prisoners by state functionaries in Northern Ireland, as well as his account of the transformations of these eschatological procedures by the victims.

15 I am grateful to Dipesh Chakrabarty (personal communication) for this striking phrase and for alerting me to the dangers of moving from global questions to globalizing answers.

16 The issues alluded to in these concluding remarks will be pursued more fully in the larger work of which this essay is a preview. Close attention will be paid to the question of what distinguishes situations that share a large number of features with other situations of globalized stress but do *not* produce ethnocidal violence. Likewise, the complex epidemiology that relates various forms of knowledge (including propaganda, rumor, and memory) to various forms of uncertainty will be explored more fully.

REFERENCES

Abu-Lughod, Janet L. (1993). *The World System in the Thirteenth Century: Dead-End or Precursor?* Washington, DC: American Historical Association.

Anderson, Benedict R. (1991). *Imagined Communities: Reflections on the Origin and Spread of Nationalism.* London: Verso.

Anderson, Benedict R. (1994). "Exodus." *Critical Inquiry* 20(2):314–27.

Appadurai, Arjun (1996). *Modernity at Large: Cultural Dimensions of Globalization.* Minneapolis: University of Minnesota Press.

Bauman, Zygmunt (1997). *Postmodernity and Its Discontents.* Cambridge: Polity Press.

Bourdieu, Pierre (1977). *Outline of a Theory of Practice.* Cambridge: Cambridge University Press.

Comaroff, Jean (1985). *Body of Power, Spirit of Resistance: The Culture and History of a South African People.* Chicago: University of Chicago Press.

Daniel, E. Valentine (1996). *Charred Lullabies: Chapters in an Anthropography of Violence.* Princeton, NJ: Princeton University Press.

Das, Veena (1990). *Mirrors of Violence: Communities, Riots and Survivors in South Asia.* Delhi: Oxford University Press.

Das, Veena (1995). *Critical Events: An Anthropological Perspective on Contemporary India.* Delhi: Oxford University Press.

Desjarlais, Robert and Kleinman, A. (1994). "Violence and Demoralization in the New World Disorder." *Anthropology Today* 10(5):9–12.

Devisch, René (1995). "Frenzy, Violence and Ethical Renewal in Kinshasa." *Public Culture* 7(3):593–629.

Douglas, Mary (1966). *Purity and Danger: An Analysis of Concepts of Pollution and Taboo.* London: Routledge and Kegan Paul.

Douglas, Mary (1973). *Natural Symbols: Explorations in Cosmology.* London: Routledge.

Durkheim, Emile (1951). *Suicide: A Study in Sociology.* Glencoe, IL: Free Press.

Evans-Pritchard, Edward E. (1937). *Witchcraft, Oracles and Magic among the Azande.* Oxford: Clarendon Press.

Feldman, Allen (1991). *Formations of Violence: The Narrative of the Body and Political Terror in Northern Ireland.* Chicago: University of Chicago Press.

Fitzpatrick, Sheila (1991). "The Problem of Class Identity in Nep Society." In Sheila Fitzpatrick, Alexander Rabinowitch, and Richard Stites (eds.), *Russia in the Era of the Nep: Explorations in Soviet Society and Culture.* Bloomington: Indiana University Press, pp. 12–33.

Fitzpatrick, Sheila (1995). "Lives under Fire: Autobiographical Narratives and Their Challenges in Stalin's Russia." In Martine Godet (ed.), *De Russie et d'ailleurs.* Paris: Institut d'Études Slaves, pp. 225–32.

Geschiere, Peter (1997). *The Modernity of Witchcraft: Politics and the Occult in Postcolonial Africa.* Charlottesville: University Press of Virginia.

Goldhagen, Daniel (1996). *Hitler's Willing Executioners: Ordinary Germans and the Holocaust.* New York: Knopf.

Harvey, David (1989). *The Condition of Postmodernity: An Enquiry into the Origins of Cultural Change.* Oxford: Blackwell.

Hayden, Robert (1996). "Imagined Communities and Real Victims: Self-Determination and Ethnic Cleansing in Yugoslavia." *American Ethnologist* 23(4):783–801.

Herzfeld, Michael (1993). *The Social Production of Indifference: Exploring the Symbolic Roots of Western Bureaucracy.* Chicago: University of Chicago Press.

Herzfeld, Michael (1997). *Cultural Intimacy: Social Poetics in the Nation-State*. New York: Routledge.

Hoffman, Piotr (1986). *Doubt, Time, Violence*. Chicago: University of Chicago Press.

Hoffman, Piotr (1989). *Violence in Modern Philosophy*. Chicago: University of Chicago Press.

Ismail, Qadri (1995). "Unmooring Identity: The Antinomies of Elite Muslim Self-Representation in Modern Sri Lanka." In Pradeep Jeganathan and Qadri Ismail (eds), *Unmaking the Nation: The Politics of Identity and History in Modern Sri Lanka*. Colombo, Sri Lanka: Social Scientists' Association, pp. 55–105.

Jeganathan, Pradeep (1997). "After a Riot: Anthropological Locations of Violence in an Urban Sri Lankan Community." Ph.D. dissertation. Department of Anthropology, University of Chicago.

Kristeva, Julia (1991). *Strangers to Ourselves*. New York: Columbia University Press.

Lash, Scott and Urry, John (1987). *The End of Organized Capitalism*. Madison: University of Wisconsin Press.

Lash, Scott and Urry, John (1994). *Economies of Signs and Space*. London: Sage.

Malkki, Liisa H. (1995). *Purity and Exile: Violence, Memory, and National Cosmology among Hutu Refugees in Tanzania*. Chicago: University of Chicago Press.

Martin, Emily (1992). "The End of the Body?" *American Ethnologist* 19(1):121–40.

Mauss, Marcel (1973). "Techniques of the Body." *Economy and Society* 2(1):70–88.

Mbembe, Achille (1992). "The Banality of Power and the Aesthetics of Vulgarity in the Postcolony," trans. Janet Roitman. *Public Culture* 4(2):1–30.

Mbembe, Achille and Roitman, J. (1995). "Figures of the Subject in Times of Crisis." *Public Culture* 7(2):323–52.

Nordstrom, Carolyn (1997). *A Different Kind of War Story*. Philadelphia: University of Pennsylvania Press.

Pandey, Gyanendra (1997). "Can a Muslim Be an Indian?" Unpublished manuscript.

Price, Monroe E. (1994). "The Market for Loyalties: Electronic Media and the Global Competition for Allegiances." *Yale Law Journal* 104(3):667–705.

Proctor, Robert N. (1995). "The Destruction of 'Lives Not Worth Living.'" In Jennifer Terry and Jacqueline Urla (eds.), *Deviant Bodies*. Bloomington: Indiana University Press, pp. 170–96.

Rouse, Roger (1995). "Thinking through Transnationalism: Notes on the Cultural Politics of Class Relations in the Contemporary United States." *Public Culture* 7(2):353–402.

Sassen, Saskia (1996). *Losing Control? Sovereignty in an Age of Globalization*. New York: Columbia University Press.

Simmel, Georg (1950). "The Stranger." In *The Sociology of Georg Simmel*, trans. and ed. Kurt H. Wolff. Glencoe, IL: Free Press, pp. 402–8.

Sutton, Donald S. (1995). "Consuming Counterrevolution: The Ritual and Culture of Cannibalism in Wuxuan, Guangxi, China, May to July 1968." *Comparative Studies in Society and History* 37(1):136–72.

Tambiah, Stanley J. (1996). *Leveling Crowds: Ethnonationalist Conflicts and Collective Violence in South Asia*. Berkeley: University of California Press.

van Gennep, Arnold (1965). *The Rites of Passage*. London: Kegan Paul.

Verdery, Katherine (1991). *National Ideology under Socialism: Identity and Cultural Politics in Ceausescu's Romania*. Berkeley: University of California Press.

Wallerstein, Immanuel (1974). *The Modern World-System*. San Diego: Academic Press.

Žižek, Slavoj (1989). *The Sublime Object of Ideology*. London: Verso.

Part IV

Coping and Understanding

14

Fear as a Way of Life

Linda Green

The tradition of the oppressed teaches us that "the state of emergency" in which we live is not the exception but the rule.

Walter Benjamin

No power so effectively robs the mind of all its powers of acting and reasoning as fear. To make anything terrible, obscurity seems to be necessary.

William Burke

People want the right to survive, to live without fear.

Doña Petrona

Fear is response to danger, but in Guatemala, rather than being solely a subjective personal experience, it has also penetrated the social memory.[1] And rather than an acute reaction it is a chronic condition. The effects of fear are pervasive and insidious in Guatemala. Fear destabilizes social relations by driving a wedge of distrust within families, between neighbors, among friends. Fear divides communities through suspicion and apprehension not only of strangers but of each other.[2] Fear thrives on ambiguities. Denunciations, gossip, innuendos, and rumors of death lists create a climate of suspicion. No one can be sure who is who. The spectacle of torture and death and of massacres and disappearances in the recent past have become more deeply inscribed in individual bodies and the collective imagination through a constant sense of threat. In the altiplano fear has become a way of life. Fear, the arbiter of power – invisible, indeterminate, and silent.

What is the nature of fear and terror that pervades Guatemalan society? How do people understand it and experience it? And what is at stake for people who live in a chronic state of fear? Might survival itself depend on a panoply of responses to a seemingly intractable situation?

In this essay, I examine the invisible violence of fear and intimidation through the quotidian experiences of the people of Xe'caj. In doing so, I try to capture a sense of the insecurity that permeates individual women's lives wracked by worries of physical and emotional survival, of grotesque memories, of ongoing militarization, of chronic fear. The stories I relate below are the individual experiences of the women with whom I worked; yet they are also social and collective accounts by virtue of their omnipresence (Lira and Castillo 1991; Martin-Baro 1990). Although the focus of my work with Mayan women was not explicitly on the topic of violence, an understanding of its usages, its manifestations, and its effects is essential to comprehending the context in which the women of Xe'caj are struggling to survive.

Fear became the metanarrative of my research and experiences among the people of Xe'caj. Fear is the reality in which people live, the hidden state of (individual and social) emergency that is factored into the choices women and men make. Although this "state of emergency" in which Guatemalans have been living for over a decade may be the norm, it is an abnormal state of affairs indeed. Albert Camus wrote that, from an examination of the shifts between the normal and the emergency, between the tragic and the everyday emerges the paradoxes and contradictions that bring into sharp relief how the absurd (in this case, terror) works (1955).

Violence and Anthropology

Given anthropology's empirical bent and the fact that anthropologists are well positioned to speak out on behalf of the "people who provide us with our livelihood" (Taussig 1978:105), it seems curious that so few have chosen to do so. Jeffrey Sluka has suggested that the practice of sociocultural anthropology with its emphasis on a "cross-cultural and comparative perspective, holistic approach, reliance on participant observation, concentration on local level analysis and 'emic' point of view" is particularly well suited to understanding the subjective, experiential, meaningful dimension of social conflict (1992:20). Anthropologists, however, have traditionally approached the study of conflict, war, and human aggression from a distance, ignoring the harsh realities of people's lives. Although some of the dominant theoretical paradigms utilized in anthropological inquiry over the last century – evolutionism, structural functionalism, acculturation studies, and Marxism – have examined societal manifestations of violence, the lived experiences of their research subjects have often been muted. When social conflict and warfare have been problematized it has been often in abstract terms, divorced from the historical realities of the colonial or capitalist encounter. Throughout the twentieth century, most studies by political anthropologists have emphasized taxonomy over process: for example, the classification of simple or indigenous political systems, political leadership, law, domination, and intertribal relations. After World War I, funding from private sources, such as the Rockefeller Foundation, influenced the research agenda of North American and British anthropologists, which was characterized by studies of order and disorder within a functionalist paradigm (Vincent 1990).

In Mesoamerica, Robert Redfield's 1927 investigation of Tepoztlan is exemplary of the ahistorical nature of acculturation studies (Redfield 1930). Redfield stressed harmony and consensus among the Tepoztecos, describing in detail their cultural traits and "life ways" without mention of recent historical events (the Mexican Revolution) or political realities (ongoing local turmoil in Tepoztlan during his own fieldwork). There were exceptions, of course. Alexander Lesser (1933), Monica Hunter (1936), and Hilda Kuper (1947), for example, were producing politically and socially relevant ethnography during the same period. These studies concerned with the impact of colonialization on marginalized people were marginalized, however (Vincent 1990).

With the upsurge of internecine warfare worldwide since World War II, the number of anthropological studies focusing on the subject of conflict and change increased exponentially. With the advent of the Cold War in the 1950s, counterinsurgency warfare became a common response to the dramatic rise in revolutionary movements in many third-world countries.[3] While repression itself was not new, what was distinct were new patterns of repression and new organizational forms for its implementation which emerged in close association with United States security programs. Some anthropologists became involved in studies that were a result of a US military presence (for example, the controversial Cornell University Studies in Culture and Applied Science), while other anthropologists participated in intelligence activities during the Vietnam War. The emergence of two analytical frameworks within anthropology – neoevolutionary theory (Fried 1967; Sahlins and Service 1960; Service 1962) and Marxism (Gough 1968; Hymes 1969) – mirrored the increasing polarization taking place in the United States in the 1960s. Yet, systematic inquiry on the subject of human rights violations remained elusive. Despite an alarming rise in the most blatant forms of transgressions – repression and state terrorism – the topic has not captured the anthropological imagination (Downing and Kushner 1988). Overwhelming empirical evidence demonstrates that state violence has been standard operating procedure in numerous contemporary societies in which anthropologists have conducted fieldwork for the past three decades.[4]

Paul Doughty, in a stinging commentary of anthropology's claim to authority on the subject of Native Americans, has questioned why monographs have not addressed systematically "the most vital issues that deeply affected all Native Americans since European conquest": death, discrimination, displacement, dispossession, racism, rampant disease, hunger, impoverishment, and physical and psychological abuse (1988:43). Nancy Scheper-Hughes is insightful in this regard. She writes in her eloquent ethnography of everyday violence in northeast Brazil that "a critical practice (of social science research) implies not so much a practical as an epistemological struggle" (Scheper-Hughes 1992:172). Perhaps this is what lies at the heart of anthropology's diverted gaze. What is at stake, it seems, are the struggles between the powerful and the powerless, and what is at issue for anthropologists is with whom to cast their lot.

A number of practitioners today who work in "dangerous field situations" have begun to deconstruct the insidious and pervasive effects and mechanisms of violence and terror, underscoring how it operates on the level of lived experience (Feldman 1991; Lancaster 1992; Nordstrom and Martin 1992; Scheper-Hughes 1992; Peteet 1991; Suárez-Orozco 1990, 1992; Taussig 1987, 1992b). Andrew Turton has pointed out that an examination of power must "include the techniques and modalities of both more physically coercive forms of domination and more ideological and discursive forms and relations between the two, in which fear may be a crucial factor" (1986:39–40). Among anthropologists it is Michael Taussig who has so well captured the complexities and nuances of terror, giving terror sentience (1987).

What is consistently compelling about Taussig's work, despite its sometimes recondite tendencies, is his ability to portray terror viscerally, in effect to take a moral stance against power played out in its more grotesque forms. In Guatemala recent works by Carmack (1988), Manz (1988), AVANCSO (1992), Falla (1992), and Wilson (1991) have begun to document and analyze the testimonies of individual and collective experiences during the most recent reign of terror. Ricardo Falla in his haunting 1992 account of the massacres of the Ixcan, Guatemala, between 1975 and 1982, asks the chilling question of why one ought to write about massacres (and terror). His answer is simple yet provocative: intellectuals can act as intermediaries, to lend their voices on behalf of those who have witnessed and lived through the macabre. This is the anthropologist as scribe, faithfully documenting what the people themselves narrate as their own histories, that which they have seen, smelled, touched, felt, interpreted, and thought. Not to do so, as Scheper-Hughes contends, is an "act of indifference," a hostile act. Monographs can become "sites of resistance," "acts of solidarity," or a way to "write against terror," and anthropology itself employed as an agent of social change (Scheper-Hughes 1992:28).

The Nature of Fear

Writing this essay has been problematic. And it has to do with the nature of the topic itself, the difficulty of fixing fear and terror in words.[5] I have chosen to include some of my own experiences of fear during my field research rather than stand apart as an outsider, an observer, for two reasons. First of all, it was and is impossible to stand apart. It soon became apparent that any understanding of the women's lives would include a journey into the state of fear in which terror reigned and that would shape the very nature of my interactions and relationships in Xe'caj. Second, it was from these shared experiences that we forged common grounds of understanding and respect.

Fear is elusive as a concept; yet you know it when it has you in its grips. Fear, like pain, is overwhelmingly present to the person experiencing it, but it may be barely perceptible to anyone else and almost defies objectification.[6] Subjectively, the mundane experience of chronic fear wears down one's sensibility to it. The routinization of fear undermines one's confidence in interpreting the world. My own experiences of fear and those of the women I know are much like what Taussig aptly describes as a state of "stringing out the nervous system one way toward hysteria, the other way numbing and apparent acceptance" (1992b:11).

While thinking and writing about fear and terror, I was inclined to discuss what I was doing with colleagues knowledgeable about *la situacion* in Central America. I would describe to them the eerie calm I felt most days, an unease that lies just below the surface of everyday life. Most of the time it was more a visceral rather than a visual experience, and I tried, with difficulty, to suppress it.

One day I was relating to a friend what it felt like to pretend not to be disturbed by the intermittent threats that were commonplace throughout 1989 and 1990 in Xe'caj. Some weeks the market plaza would be surrounded by five or six tanks while painted-faced soliders with M-16s in hand perched above us, watching. My friend's response made me nervous all over again. He said that he had initially been upset by the ubiquitous military presence in Central America. He too, he assured me, had assumed that the local people felt the same. But lately he had been rethinking his position since he had witnessed a number of young women flirting with soliders, or small groups of local men leaning casually on tanks. Perhaps, we North Americans, he continued, were misrepresenting what was going on, reading our own fears into the meaning it had for Central Americans. I went home wondering if perhaps I was being "hysterical," stringing out the nervous (social) system. Had I been too caught up in terror's talk?[7] Gradually I came to realize that terror's power, its matter-of-factness, is exactly about doubting one's own perceptions of reality. The routinization of terror is what fuels its power. Such routinization allows people to live in a chronic state of fear with a facade of normalcy, while that terror, at the same time, permeates and shreds the social fabric. A sensitive and experienced Guatemalan economist noted that a major problem for social scientists working in Guatemala is that to survive they have to become inured to the violence, training themselves at first not to react, then later not to feel (see) it. They miss the context in which people live, including themselves. Self-censorship becomes second nature – Bentham's panopticon internalized.

How does one become socialized to terror? Does it imply conformity or acquiescence to the status quo, as my friend suggested? While it is true that, with repetitiveness and familiarity, people learn to accommodate themselves to terror and fear, low-intensity panic remains in the shadow of waking consciousness. One cannot live in a constant state of alertness, and so the chaos one feels becomes infused throughout the body. It surfaces frequently in dreams and chronic illness. In the mornings, sometimes my neighbors and friends would speak of their fears during the night, of being unable to sleep, or of being awakened by footsteps or voices, of nightmares of recurring death and violence. After six months of living in Xe'caj, I too started having my own nighttime hysteria, dreams of death, disappearances, and torture. Whisperings, innuendos, and rumors of death lists circulating would put everyone on edge. One day a friend, Nacho, from Xe'caj came to my house, very anxious. He explained, holding back his tears, that he had heard his name was on the newest death list at the military encampment. As Scheper-Hughes has noted "the intolerableness of the [se] situation[s] is increased by [their] ambiguity" (1992:233). A month later two soldiers were killed one Sunday afternoon in a surprise guerrilla attack a kilometer from my house. That evening several women from the village came to visit; emotionally distraught, they worried that *la violencia*, which had been stalking them, had at last returned. Doña Maria noted that violence is like fire; it can flare up suddenly and burn you.

The people in Xe'caj live under constant surveillance. The *destacamento* (military encampment) looms large, situated on a nearby hillside above town; from there everyone's movements come under close scrutiny. The town is laid out spatially in the colonial quadrangle pattern common throughout the altiplano. The town square, as well as all of the roads leading to the surrounding countryside, are visible from above. To an untrained eye, the encampment is not obvious from below. The camouflaged buildings fade into the hillside, but once one has looked down from there, it is impossible to forget that those who live below do so in a fishbowl. *Orejas* (spies, literally "ears"), military commissioners, and civil patrollers provide the backbone of military scrutiny.[8] These local men are often former soldiers who willingly report to the army the "suspicious" activities of their neighbors.[9]

The impact of the civil patrols (or PACs) at the local level has been profound. One of the structural effects of the PACs in Xe'caj has been the subordination of traditional village political authority to the local army commander. When I arrived in Xe'caj, I first went to the mayor to introduce myself. I asked for his permission to work in the township and surrounding villages, but midway through my explanation, he cut me off abruptly. If I hoped to work here, he explained impatiently, then what I really needed was the explicit permission of the *commandante* at the army garrison. The civil patrols guard the entrances and exits to the villages in Xe'caj, he said. Without permission from the army the civil patrols would not allow me to enter the villages. My presence as a stranger and foreigner produced suspicions. "Why do you want to live and work here with us?" "Why do you want to talk to the widows?" "For whom do you work?" the *alcalde* asked. It was the local army officers who told me it was a free country and that I could do as I pleased, provided I had *their* permission.

One of the ways terror becomes diffused is through subtle messages. Much as Carol Cohn describes in her unsettling 1987 account of the use of language by nuclear scientists to sanitize their involvement in nuclear weaponry, in Guatemala language and symbols are utilized to normalize a continual army presence. From time to time army troops would arrive in *aldeas* (villages) obliging the villagers to assemble for a community meeting. The message was more or less the same each time I witnessed these gatherings. The *commandante* would begin by telling the people that the army is their friend, that the soldiers are here to protect them against subversion, against the communists hiding out in the mountains. At the same time he would admonish them that if they did not cooperate Guatemala could become like Nicaragua, El Salvador, or Cuba. *Subtienente* Rodriquez explained to me during one such meeting that the army is fulfilling its role of preserving peace and democracy in Guatemala through military control of the entire country. Ignacio Martin-Baro has characterized social perceptions reduced to rigid and simplistic schemes such as these as "official lies," in which social knowledge is cast in dichotomous terms, black or white, good or bad, friend or enemy, without the nuances and complexities of lived experience (1989).

Guatemalan soldiers at times arrive in the villages accompanied by US National Guard doctors or dentists who hold clinic hours for a few days. This is part of a larger strategy developed under the Kennedy doctrine of Alliance for Progress, in which civic actions are part of counterinsurgency strategies.[10] Yet the mixing of the two, "benevolent help" with military actions, does not negate the essential fact that "violence is intrinsic to its [the military's] nature and logic" (Scheper-Hughes 1992:224). Coercion through its subtle expressions of official lies and routinization of fear and terror are apt mechanisms that the military uses to control citizens, even in the absence of war.

I was with a group of widows and young orphan girls one afternoon watching a TV soap opera. It was in mid-June, a week or so before Army Day. During one of the commercial breaks, a series of images of Kaibiles appeared on the screen dressed for combat with painted faces, clenching their rifles running through the mountains.[11] Each time a new frame appeared, there was an audible gasp in the room. The last image was of soldiers emerging from behind corn stalks while the narrator said, "The army is ready to do whatever is necessary to defend the country." One young girl turned to me and said, "Si pues, siempre estan lista que se matan la gente" [*sic*] (they are always ready to kill the people).

The use of camouflage cloth for clothing and small items sold at the market is a subtle, insidious form of daily life's militarization. Wallets, key chains, belts, caps, and toy helicopters made in Taiwan are disconcerting in this context. As these seemingly mundane objects circulate, they normalize the extent to which civilian and military life have commingled in the altiplano. Young men who have returned to villages from military service often wear army boots, T-shirts that denote the military zone in which they had been stationed, and their dog tags. The boots themselves are significant. The women would say they knew who it was that kidnapped or killed their family members, even if dressed in civilian clothes, because the men were wearing army boots. When my neighbor's cousin on leave from the army came for a visit, the young boys brought him over to my house so they could show his photo album to me with pride. As the young soldier stood shyly in the background, Juanito and Reginaldo pointed enthusiastically to photographs of their cousin. In one, he was leaning on a tank with his automatic rifle in hand, a bandolier of bullets slung over his shoulder, while in another he was throwing a hand grenade. Yet, these same boys told me, many months after I had moved into my house and we had become friends, that when I first arrived they were afraid I might kill them. And Doña Sofia, Reginaldo's mother, was shocked to learn that I did not carry a gun.

In El Salvador, Martin-Baro analyzed the subjective internalization of war and militarization among a group of 203 children in an effort to understand to what extent they have assimilated the efficacy of violence in solving personal and social problems (1989). While generalizations cannot be drawn from such a limited study, what Martin-Baro found to be significant was that the majority of the children interviewed stated that the best way to end the war and attain peace was to eliminate the enemy (whether understood as the Salvadoran army or the FMLN [Farabundo Manti National Liberation Front]) through violent means. This tendency to internalize violence is what Martin-Baro has referred to as the "militarization of the mind" (1990).

The presence of soldiers and ex-soldiers in communities is illustrative of lived contradictions in the altiplano and provides another example of how the routinization of terror functions. The foot soldiers of the army are almost exclusively young rural Mayas, many still boys of fourteen and fifteen years, rounded up on army "sweeps" through rural towns. The "recruiters" arrive in two-ton trucks grabbing all young men in sight, usually on festival or market days when large numbers of people have gathered together in the center of the pueblo. One morning at dawn, I witnessed four such loaded trucks driving out from one of the towns of Xe'caj, soldiers standing in each corner of the truck with rifles pointed outward, the soon-to-be foot soldiers packed in like cattle. Little is known about the training these young soldiers receive, but anecdotal data from some who are willing to talk suggests that the "training" is designed to break down a sense of personal dignity and respect for other human beings. As one young man described it to me, "Soldiers are trained to kill and nothing more" (see also Forester 1992). Another said he learned (in the army) to hate everyone, including himself. The soldiers who pass through the villages on recognizance and take up sentry duty in the pueblos are Mayas, while the vast majority of officers are ladinos, from other regions of the country, and cannot speak the local language. As a second lieutenant explained, army policy directs that the foot soldiers and the commanders of the local garrisons change every three months, to prevent soldiers from getting to know the people. A small but significant number of men in Xe'caj have been in the army. Many young men return home to their natal villages after they are released from military duty. Yet, their reintegration into the community is often difficult and problematic. As one villager noted, "They [the men/boys] leave as Indians, but they don't come back Indian."

During their time of service in the army, some of the soldiers are forced to kill and maim. These young men often go on to become the local military commissioners, heads of the civil patrol, or paid informers for the army. Many are demoralized, frequently drinking and turning violent. Others marry and settle in their villages to resume their lives as best they can.

I met several women whose sons had been in the military when their husbands had been killed by the army. In one disturbing situation, I interviewed a widow who described the particularly gruesome death of her husband at the hands of the army, while behind her on the wall prominently displayed was a photograph of her son in his Kaibil uniform. When I asked about him, she acknowledged his occasional presence in the household and said nothing more. I was at first at a loss to explain the situation and her silence; later I came to understand it as part of the rational inconsistencies that are built into the logic of her fractured life. On a purely objective level, it is dangerous to talk about such things with strangers. Perhaps she felt her son's photograph might provide protection in the future. Although I ran into this situation several times, I never felt free to ask more about it. I would give the women the opportunity to say something, but I felt morally unable to pursue this topic. The women would talk freely, although at great pains, about the brutal past but maintained a stoic silence about the present. Perhaps the women's inability to talk about the fragments of their tragic experiences within the context of larger processes is in itself a survival strategy. How is it that a mother might be able to imagine that her son (the soldier) would perform the same brutish acts as those used against her and her family? To maintain a fragile integrity, must she block the association in much the same way women speak of the past atrocities as individual acts but remain silent about the ongoing process of repression in which they live? The division of families' loyalties becomes instrumental in perpetuating fear and terror.

In commenting on local violence in San Pedro de la Laguna during the 1980s, Benjamin Paul's analysis is revealing of the relationship between disorder and control and how local factionalism has been manipulated and exploited in rural communities contributing to a breakdown in social structure (Paul and Demarest 1988). It should be noted that San Pedro was less affected by direct army repression and guerrilla activity in the 1980s than many other towns; yet local death squads terrorized the population for over four years. Paul notes that:

It may be tempting to blame the outbreak of violence in San Pedro on social divisiveness and settling old scores, but the temptation should be resisted. Religious competition and vigorous political infighting were features of San Pedro life for decades before 1980 without producing violence. The same can be said for interpersonal antagonisms. They arose in the past and were settled by means short of murder. What disrupted the peace in San Pedro was not the presence of differences and divisions but the army's recruitment of agents and spies that had the effect of exploiting these cleavages. (Paul and Demarest 1988: 153–4)

The Structure of Fear

The "culture of fear" that pervades Guatemalan society has roots in the trauma of the Spanish invasion five centuries earlier. Fear and oppression have been the dual and constant features of Guatemalan history since the arrival of Pedro Alvarado and his conquistadores in the early sixteenth century. The words written in the *Annals of the Cakchiquels* almost five hundred years ago are as meaningful today as then:

> Little by little, heavy shadows and black night enveloped
>   Our fathers and grandfathers
>   And us also, oh, my sons...
>   All of us were thus.
>   We were born to die. (Recinos and Goetz 1953)

Terror is the taproot of Guatemala's past and stalks its present. When speaking of *la violencia* of the 1980s, I was struck by how frequently people used the metaphor of conquest to describe it. "Lo mismo cuando se mato a Tecum Uman" (It is the same as when they killed Tecum Uman), Doña Marta said, alluding to the K'iche-Mayan hero who died valiantly in battle against the Spanish, when describing the recent "whirlwind of death." Although references to the Spanish conquest have become more commonplace on the cusp of its quincentenary, in 1988 and early 1989 rural constructions of local experiences in terms of the invasion were striking, haunting, as if a collective memory had been passed generation to generation. Citing Benjamin, Taussig asserts that "it is where history figures in memory, in an image that flashes forth unexpectedly in a moment of crisis, that contending political forces engage in battle" (1984:88). In this way history engaged through memory becomes a social force comprised of "the power of social experience, imagery and mood, in constructing and deconstructing political consciousness and the will to act politically" (1984:88).

Franciscan documents from the sixteenth century describe the disorder resulting from a local judge's order to burn down towns when Indians refused to comply with official decrees. Lovell writes, "Chaos ensued. Roads and trails were strewn with poor Indian women, tied as prisoners, carrying children on their backs, left to fend for themselves" (1992: epilogue, 34). Five hundred years later publications by anthropologists (Carmack 1988: Falla 1983, 1992; Manz 1988) and numerous international human rights groups recount violations of a similar magnitude (America's Watch 1986, 1990; Amnesty International 1981, 1982, 1987).

Fear has been the motor of oppression in Guatemala. As Brecht noted, "Fear rules not only those who are ruled, but the rulers too" (1976: 296–7). The elite, dominant classes are driven by racist fears of "*indios*" and in more recent decades by the "red menace" of communists to perform the most brutish acts to protect the status quo. There are upper-class ladinos in Guatemala City who deny that the massacres in rural areas ever really happened. In one interview, a ladina journalist noted that

one of the reasons why repression did not cause too big a commotion among Guatemalans in the capital was because it was mainly Indians that were affected. All the suffering that took place was not really suffering because it happened to Indians. The Guatemalan upper class believes that Indians cannot really feel, that an Indian woman will not truly suffer if her husband or children are killed because she is not "the same as us." (Hooks 1991: 48)

Although Suárez-Orozco has described the process of denial in Argentina during the years of the "dirty war" as a psychological coping mechanism for the terror (1992), what stands apart in Guatemala is not the denial of the unthinkable, but a dismissiveness of suffering, rooted in racism. For the women and men of Xe'caj, however, fear is a way of life, and injustice the rule.

Like most fledgling anthropologists, I had been nervous about getting my research underway and was well aware, or so I thought, of the "special" circumstances in which I had chosen to work. By the time I began fieldwork in Guatemala in 1988, it was permissible to discuss openly and publicly *"la situacion"* and *"la violencia"* of the past eight or so years, and the plight of widows and orphans was becoming a matter of public record.[12] Yet, the fragile "democratic opening," which had been welcomed by the majority of the population in 1985, buoyed by a sense of hope when Vinicio Cerezo took office (the first elected civilian president in sixteen years), was in grave danger by 1988. An attempted coup d'état in the spring of 1988 (followed by another in May 1989) dashed any hopes for significant social reform. The military remained firmly in charge, although backstage. In short, the military recognized the need for international and national legitimacy through a return to civilian rule in order to address its severe economic and political crises.

In retrospect, political analysts now define the May 1988 and May 1989 coup attempts as "successful" in all but yielding the presidential seat. What little power the military had relinquished during the electoral process in 1985 had reverted back into the hands of the generals. Although, as these coups demonstrated, the army was far from a monolithic institution (Anderson and Simon 1987; Jonas 1991; Mersky 1989),[13] what was becoming clearer was that Cerezo's role was to be directed toward an international audience. He had, in effect, yielded power to the military without vacating the presidential palace. Human rights violations in the capital and in rural areas continued unabated.

International human rights organizations documented the continuation of systematic human rights violations (see America's Watch 1990 and Amnesty International 1987). Once again, the US-based Council on Hemispheric Affairs named Guatemala as the worst human rights violator in Latin America for 1989, 1990, 1991, and 1992. The massacre of twenty-one *campesinos* in El Aguacate, San Andres Itzapa, Chimaltenango, in 1988; the political assassinations of Hector Oqueli from El Salvador, Gilda Flores, a prominent Guatemalan attorney, and the political leader Danilo Barillas; the killings and disappearances of university students and human rights workers; the 1990 murder of the anthropologist Myrna Mack; systematic torture, threats, and intimidation against countless others throughout the period – all these point to the persistent violence and repression used by the state against its citizenry. While the state has denounced the atrocities, it has tried to explain them away as crimes by delinquents. It has vowed to investigate and prosecute fully those responsible, but few have ever been convicted or have served a prison term for human rights violations – despite the fact that frequently there has been substantial evidence indicating the complicity of state security forces. Thus, with a wink and a nod to its citizens, a policy of impunity makes it clear to everyone who retains power and under what conditions. As Martin-Baro noted, "The usefulness of violence is its effectiveness and the crucial point concerning the proliferation of violence in Central America is its impunity under the law" (1990:344).

Despite a hideous record of documented human rights abuses, the United Nations Commission on Human Rights decided in 1992 for the fifth consecutive year to downplay Guatemala's record by placing it in the advisory rather than violations category. Yet inside the country, repression continued unchecked. Repression is used selectively: to threaten, intimidate, disappear, or kill one or two labor leaders, students, or *campesinos* is to paralyze everyone else with fear. Terror is widespread and generalized. If one crosses the arbitrary line, the consequences are well known; the problem is that one cannot be sure where the line is nor when one has crossed it until it is too late.

After several months of searching for a field site, I settled upon Xe'caj. Although it had been the site of much bloodshed and repression during the early 1980s, *la situacion* was reportedly *tranquila* (calm) in 1988. The terror and fear that pervaded daily life were not immediately perceptible to me. Military checkpoints, the army garrison, and civil patrols were clearly visible; yet daily life appeared "normal." The guerrilla war, which reached an apex in the early 1980s, had ended at least in theory if not in practice. Although guerrilla troops moved throughout the area, clashes between them and the army were limited. The war had reached a stalemate. While the army claimed victory, the guerrillas refused to admit defeat. The battlefield was quiescent, yet political repression continued. Scorched-earth tactics, massacres, and large population displacements had halted, but they were replaced by selective repression and the militarization of daily life. Army General Alejandro Gramajo's now infamous inversion of Karl Marie von Clausewitz's "politics as a continuation of war" was clearly accurate. The counterinsurgency war had transformed everyday life in the altiplano into a permanent state of repression. Economic conditions in this climate were unstable, and the majority of people found themselves more deeply entrenched in poverty, hunger, and misery (Smith 1990). By the mid-1980s, violence in Chimaltenango Department was mostly veiled, and a few development projects began to return cautiously after the elections in 1985. According to Smith (1990), in the 1980s Chimaltenango probably received more development aid per capita than anywhere else in the altiplano; yet rather than alleviating the precarious economic situation in which most people live, conditions continued to worsen. The structure of fear operated on several levels on which military and economic arrangements worked synergistically.

Silence and Secrecy

It was the dual lessons of silence and secrecy that were for me the most enlightening and disturbing. Silence about the present situation when talking with strangers is a survival strategy that Mayas have long utilized. Their overstated politeness toward ladino society and seeming obliviousness to the jeers and insults hurled at them – their servility in the face of overt racism – make it seem as though Mayas have accepted their subservient role in Guatemalan society. Mayan apparent obsequiousness has served as a shield to provide distance and has also been a powerful shaper of

Mayan practice. When Elena disclosed to a journalist friend of mine from El Salvador her thoughts about guerrilla incursions today, her family castigated her roundly for speaking, warning her that what she said could be twisted and used against her and the family. This is reminiscent of what Allen Feldman, in writing about Northern Ireland, says about secrecy as "an assertion of identity and symbolic capital pushed to the margins. Subaltern groups construct their own margins as fragile insulators from the center" (1991:11).

When asked about the present situation, the usual response from most people was "pues, tranquila" – but it was a fragile calm. Later as I got to know people, when something visible would break through the facade of order and the forced propaganda speeches, or in my own town when a soldier was killed and another seriously injured in an ambush, people would whisper fears of a return to *la violencia*. In fact, the unspoken but implied second part of the "Pues, tranquila" is "Ahorita, pero mañana saber" (It's calm now, but who knows about tomorrow?). When I asked a local fellow, who is the head of a small (self-sufficient) development project that is organizing locally, if he were bothered by the army, he said he was not. The army comes by every couple of months and searches houses or looks at his records, but he considered this *tranquila*.

Silence can operate as a survival strategy; yet silencing is a powerful mechanism of control enforced through fear. At times when I was talking with a group of women, our attention would be distracted momentarily by a military plane or helicopter flying close and low. Each of us would lift our heads, watching until it passed out of sight yet withholding comment. Sometimes, if we were inside a house, we might all step out onto the patio to look skyward. Silence. Only once was the silence broken. On that day Doña Tomasa asked rhetorically, after the helicopters had passed overhead, why my government sent bombs to kill people. At Christmas Eve mass in 1989, twenty-five soldiers entered the church suddenly, soon after the service had begun. They occupied three middle pews on the mens' side, never taking their hands off their rifles, only to leave abruptly after the sermon. Silence. The silences in these cases do not erase individual memories of terror; they create instead more fear and uncertainty by driving the wedge of paranoia between people. Terror's effects are not only psychological and individual, but social and collective as well. Silence imposed through terror has become the idiom of social consensus in the altiplano, as Suárez-Orozco has noted in the Argentine context (1990).

The complicity of silence is yet another matter. During the worst of the violence in the early 1980s, when several priests were killed and hundreds, perhaps thousands, of lay catechists were murdered, the Catholic Church hierarchy, with the exception of several Guatemalan bishops, remained rigidly silent. Evangelical churches, like the Central American Mission, which lost large numbers of congregants, also remained silent.

Today a number of development projects work in Xe'caj with women and children who have been severely affected by the violence. They do not, however, address the reality in which people live. These projects provide a modicum of economic aid without acknowledging the context of fear and terror that pervades Xe'caj. When a Vision Mundial (World Vision) administrator explained the project's multi-tiered approach to development, he spoke proudly of the group's emphasis on assisting the "whole" person, materially, emotionally, and spiritually. When I asked him how the project was confronting the emotional trauma of war and repression in which the widows live, he admitted obliquely that they were not. To do so, of course, would put the project workers and the women in jeopardy. Yet to not address the situation perpetuates the "official lies."

Thus the contradictory nature of development itself becomes unraveled in this situation of violence and silence. Development programs serve the state by providing stopgap measures to deep-seated economic, social, and cultural problems, rather than addressing fundamental structural causes of poverty and repression. Development programs also perpetuate the hegemonic discourse of a dominant power structure that does not question the goals of capitalist development. At the same time, at the local level these same projects provide some individual relief for people struggling to survive economically.

On Breaking the Silence

Despite the fear and terror engendered by relentless human rights violations and deeply entrenched impunity, hope exists. Since the appointment in 1983 of Archbishop Prospero Penados del Barrio, the Guatemalan Catholic Church has become increasingly outspoken in its advocacy for peace and social justice. The Guatemalan Bishops' Conference, for example, has issued a number of pastoral letters, beginning with the 1988 *Cry for Land*, that have become important sources of social criticism in the country. In 1990 the Archdiocese of Guatemala opened a human rights office to provide legal assistance to victims of human rights abuses and to report violations to national and international institutions.

One of the collective responses to the silence imposed through terror began in 1984, when two dozen people, mostly women, formed the human rights organization called GAM (Grupo de Apoyo Mutuo). Its members are relatives of some of the estimated forty-two thousand people who "disappeared" in Guatemala over the past three decades. Modeling themselves after the Mothers of Plaza de Mayo in Argentina, a small group of courageous women and men decided to break the silence. They went to government offices to demand that the authorities investigate the crimes against their families. They also turned their bodies into "weapons" to speak out against the violence. As they marched in silence every Friday in front of the national palace with placards bearing the photos of those who had disappeared, they ruptured the official silence, bearing testimony with their own bodies about those who have vanished.

In 1990, Roberto Lemus, a judge in the district court of Santa Cruz del Quiche, began accepting petitions from local people to exhume sites in the villages in which people claimed there were clandestine graves. Family members said they knew where their loved ones had been buried after being killed by security forces. While other judges in the area had previously allowed the exhumations, this was the first time that a scientific team had been assembled, in this case under the auspices of the eminent forensic anthropologist, Clyde Snow. The intent of the exhumations was to gather evidence to corroborate verbal testimonies of survivors in order to arrest those responsible. Because of repeated death threats Judge Lemus was forced into political exile in July 1991. Snow has assembled another team, sponsored by the

American Association for the Advancement of Science, that continues the work in Guatemala at the behest of human rights groups. There are estimated to be hundreds, perhaps thousands, of such sites throughout the altiplano. The clandestine cemeteries and mass graves are the *secreto a voces*, or what Taussig has referred to in another context as the "public secrets" (1992c) – what everyone knows about but does not dare to speak of publicly.

In Xe'caj, people would point out such sites to me. On several occasions when I was walking with them in the mountains, women took me to the places where they knew their husbands were buried and said, "Mira, el esta alli" (Look, he is over there). Others claimed that there are at least three mass graves in Xe'caj itself. The act of unearthing the bones of family members allows individuals to acknowledge and reconcile the past openly, to acknowledge at last the culpability for the death of their loves and to lay them to rest. Such unearthing is, at the same time, a most powerful statement against impunity because it reveals the magnitude of the political repression that has taken place. These were not solely individual acts with individual consequences, but are public crimes that have deeply penetrated the social body and contest the legitimacy of the body politic.

Thus, as has been the case in Uruguay, Argentina, Brazil, and El Salvador (Weschler 1990), it is the dual issues of impunity and accountability that stand between peace and social justice in Guatemala. As such, amnesty becomes both a political and an ethical problem, with not only individual but also social dimensions. The Guatemalan human rights ombudsman (and as of June 1993, president) has suggested that "to forgive and forget" is the only way democracy will be achieved in Guatemala. Ramiro de Léon Carpio, in a newspaper interview in 1991, said, "The ideal would be that we uncover the truth, to make it public and to punish those responsible, but I believe that is impossible,... we have to be realistic" (*La Hora* 1991). Certainly the idea of political expediency has a measure of validity to it. The problem, however, turns on "whether that pardon and renunciation are going to be established on a foundation of truth and justice or on lies and continued injustice" (Martin-Baro 1990:7). Hannah Arendt has argued against forgiveness without accountability, because it undermines the formation of democracy by obviating any hope of justice and makes its pursuit pointless (1973). Secondly, while recognizing that forgiveness is an essential element for freedom, Arendt contends that "the alternative to forgiveness, but by no means its opposite, [which she argues, rather, is vengeance] is punishment, and both have in common that they attempt to put an end to something that without interference could go on endlessly" (Arendt 1958:241). The military's self-imposed amnesty, which has become vogue throughout Latin America in recent years, forecloses the very possibility of forgiveness. Without a settling of accounts democratic rule will remain elusive in Guatemala, as has been the case elsewhere in Latin America. Social reparation is a necessary requisite to healing the body politic in Latin America.

Living in a State of Fear

During the first weeks we lived in Xe'caj, Elena (my capable field assistant) and I drove to several villages in the region talking with women, widows, in small groups, asking them if they might be willing to meet with us weekly over the next year or so. At first many people thought we might be representing a development project and therefore distributing material aid. When this proved not to be the case, some women lost interest while others agreed to participate. During the second week we drove out to Ri Bey, a small village that sits in a wide U-shaped valley several thousand meters lower in altitude than Xe'caj and most of the surrounding hamlets. The one-lane dirt road is a series of switchbacks that cut across several ridges, before beginning the long, slow descent into the valley. Fortunately for me, there was little traffic on these back roads. Bus service had been suspended during the height of the violence in the early 1980s and in the early 1990s is virtually non existent, although a few buses do provide transport to villagers on market day. The biggest obstacle to driving is meeting, head-on, logging trucks carrying rounds of oak and cedar for export. With their heavy loads, it is impossible for them to maneuver, and so I would invariably have to back up- or downhill until I found a turnout wide enough for the truck to pass. Yet, the most frightening experience was rounding a curve and suddenly encountering a military patrol.

On this day in February 1989 it was foggy and misty, and a cold wind was blowing. Although the air temperature was in the 50s (degrees Fahrenheit), the chill penetrated to the bone – "el expresso de Alaska," Elena laughed. Heading north we caught glimpses of the dark ridges of the Sierra de Cuchumatanes brooding in the distance. The scenery was breathtaking; every conceivable hue of green was present: pine, cedar, ash, oak, the wide lush leaves of banana trees, and bromeliades, mingled with the brilliant purple bougainvillea in bloom, and the ivory calla lilies lining the roadway. The milpas lay fallow after the harvest in late January, only the dried stalks were left half-standing leaning this way and that. On each side of the road houses were perched on the slopes surrounded by the milpas. In the altiplano several houses made from a mix of cane or corn stalks, adobe, and wood are usually clustered together. The red tile roofs seen further west have all but disappeared from Xe'caj. Most people now use tin roofs (*lamina*), even though they retain more heat in the hot dry season and more cold when it is damp and raining. Chimaltenango Department was one of the hardest hit by the 1976 earthquake in which more than seventy-five thousand people died and one million were left homeless. Many people were crushed under the weight of the tiles, as roofs caved in upon them. Today, half-burned houses stand as testimony to the scorched-earth campaign, while civil patrollers take up their posts nearby with rifles in hand. Although we frequently saw a number of people on foot, most women and children ran to hide when they saw us coming. Months passed before women and children walking on the road would accept a ride with me. And even then, many did so reluctantly, and most would ask Elena in Kaqchikel if it were true that I wanted to steal their children and whether gringos ate children.[14]

On this particular day Elena and I drove as far as we could and then left my pickup at the top of the hill at the point at which the road became impassable. We walked the last four miles down to the village. Along the way we met local men repairing the large ruts in the road, where soil had washed away with heavy September rains. Soil in this area is sandy and unstable. Most of the trees on the ridge above the road have been clear-cut and the erosion is quite pronounced. The men were putting in culverts and filling in the deep crevasses that dissect the road;

their only tools are shovels and pickaxes. The men are paid US$1.50 per day. This is desirable work, however, because it is one of the few opportunities to earn cash close to home rather than going to the coastal plantations.

As we descended into lower elevations, Elena and I mused over the fact that there are only seven widows in Ri Bey, a village of 300 people. In the several other villages where we had visited women, there were thirty to forty widows or about 15 to 20 percent of the current population. Perhaps there had not been much violence in Ri Bey, I suggested. It was one of the notable features of the military campaign known as "scorched-earth" that neighboring villages fared quite differently – one was destroyed and another left untouched, depending on the army's perceived under-standing of guerrilla support. The military's campaign of terror in the altiplano had happened in two phases. Army strategy began with selective repression against community leaders not only to garner information but also to spread fear. The second phase of the counterinsurgency plan consisted of cutting off rural areas from the city. This began with "sweeping operations" that fanned out from the city first westward to Chimaltenango Department, then southward to Quiche, and later further northward and westward. The massacres and brutality seemed to have an internal logic despite the disorder and panic that they provoked. While some villages were left unscathed, others were completely razed. For example, according to an eyewitness of the massacre in the *aldea* of Los Angelas, Ixcan, on March 23, 1982, the soldiers had a list of pueblos and *aldeas* that were to be targeted (Falla 1992). Moreover, in numerous testimonies of survivors, the army more often than not launched its "reprisals" against the guerrillas by brutally killing the population at large.

Elena and I found Petrona, Tomasa, and a third woman, sitting in front of the school at which we had agreed to meet. We greeted the women and sat down in the sun that was just breaking through the clouds. They had brought several bottles of Pepsi for us to share. I asked Doña Petrona, a small, thin woman with an intelligent face, why there are so few widows in Ri Bey, holding my breath waiting for the hoped-for answer – that the violence there had been much less. She replied that it was because so many people were killed, not just men but whole families, old people, children, women. The village was deserted for several years, people fled to the mountains, the pueblo or the city. Many people never returned – dead or displaced, no one knows for sure.

This was the third village we had visited, and each time it was the same. The women, without prompting, one by one took turns recounting their stories of horror. They would tell the events surrounding the deaths or disappearances of their husbands, fathers, sons, and brothers in vivid detail as if it had happened last week or last month rather than six or eight years ago. And the women – Petrona, Tomasa, Ana, Isabel, Juana, Martina, and Marta – continued to tell me their stories over and over during the time I lived among them. But why? At first as a stranger, and then later as a friend, why were these women repeatedly recounting their Kafka-esque tales to me? What was in the telling? What was the relationship between silence and testimony? As Suárez-Orozco has noted, "testimony [is] a ritual of both healing and a condemnation of injustice – the concept of testimony contains both connotations of something subjective and private and something objective, judicial and political" (1992:367). The public spaces that we were compelled to use to thwart surveillance were transformed into a liminal space that was both private and public in the recounting.

In each of the villages in which I met with women, it was always the same in the beginning. We would meet in groups of three or four in front of the village health post, the school, or the church, always in a public space. It was three months or more before anyone invited me into their home or spoke with me privately and individually. Above all else, they had not wanted the gringa to be seen coming to their house. Under the scrutiny of surveillance, the women were afraid of what others in the village might say about them and me. And when I began to visit people's homes, rumors did spread about Elena and me. The rumors themselves seemed innocuous to me, that I was helping the widows or that I was writing a book about women, yet with potentially dangerous repercussions.

During one particularly tense period, my visits caused an uproar. One day when I arrived to visit with Maria and Marta, I found them both very anxious and agitated. When I asked what was going on, they said that the military commissioner was looking for me, that people were saying I was helping the widows and talking against others in the community. "There are deep divisions within the community; people don't trust one another," explained Marta. "Families are divided, and not everyone thinks alike," Maria added.

When I said that I would go look for Don Martin, the military commissioner, they became very upset. "He said that he would take you to the garrison. Please don't go, Linda. We know people who went into the garrison and were never seen again." "But I have done nothing wrong," I said. "I must talk with them, find out what is wrong." I worried that my presence might reflect negatively on the women. So I went, Elena insisting on accompanying me, dismissing my concerns for her well-being by saying, "Si nos matan es el problema de ellos" (If they kill us, it will be their problem). Fortunately for us, the commissioner was not home; so I left a message with his wife.

The next day I decided to go to the *destacamento* alone. The trek to the garrison was a grueling walk uphill, or so it seemed. The last one hundred yards were the most demanding emotionally. Rounding the bend, I saw several soldiers sitting in a small guardhouse with a machine gun perched on the three-foot stanchion, pointed downward and directly at me. The plight of Joseph K in Franz Kafka's *Trial* (1937 [1925]) flashed through my mind, the character accused of a crime for which he must defend himself but about which he could get no information. "I didn't do anything wrong; I must not look guilty," I told myself over and over. I needed to calm myself, as my stomach churned, my nerves frayed. I arrived breathless and terrified. Ultimately, I knew I was guilty because I was against the system of violence and terror that surrounded me. I asked to speak to the *commandante*, who received me outside the gates. This struck me as unusual and increased my agitation, since I had been to the garrison several times before to greet each new *commandante* and to renew my permission papers to continue my work. On other occasions I had been invited into the compound. The *commandante* said he knew nothing about why I was being harassed by the military commissioner and the civil patrol in Be'cal, and he assured me that I could continue with my work and that he personally would look into the situation. A few days later the *commandante* and several soldiers arrived in the *aldea*, called a community-wide meeting and instructed everyone to cooperate with the "gringa" who was doing a study.

Later when the matter had been settled, some of the women explained their concerns to me. They told me stories of how widows from outlying *aldeas*, who had fled to the relative safety of Xe'caj after their husbands had been killed or kidnapped, had been forced to bring food and firewood for the soldiers at the garrison, and then had been raped and humiliated at gunpoint. One brave woman, the story goes, with a baby on her back, went to the garrison demanding to see her husband. The soldiers claimed he was not there, but she knew they were lying because his dog was standing outside the gates, and she insisted the dog never left his side. Either they still had him or had already killed him. She demanded to know and told them to go ahead and kill her and the baby because she had nothing more to lose. Today she is a widow.

It was the hour before dawn on a March day in 1981. Doña Petrona had arisen early to warm tortillas for her husband's breakfast before he left to work in the milpa. He was going to burn and clean it in preparation for planting soon after the first rains in early May. He had been gone only an hour when neighbors came running to tell her that her husband had been shot and he was lying in the road. When Petrona reached him, he was already dead. With the help of neighbors she took the body home to prepare for burial. Petrona considers herself lucky because she says that at least she was able to bury him herself, unlike so many women whose husbands were disappeared. These are among what Robert Hertz called the "unquiet dead," referring to those who have died a violent or "unnatural" death (1960). Hertz argued that funeral rituals are a way of strengthening the social bond. Without a proper burial these souls linger in the liminal space between earth and afterlife, condemned in time between death and the final obsequies. And yet these wandering "unquiet souls," according to Taussig (1984), may act as intermediaries between nature and the living, buffeting as well as enhancing memories through imagery of a violent history.

The young woman sitting next to Petrona is her daughter, Ana, who is also a widow. Ana took Petrona's nod as a sign to begin. In a quiet voice she said that she was seventeen when her husband was killed on the patio of her house while her two children, Petrona, and her sister stood by helpless and in horror. It was August 1981, five months after her father had been killed. Soldiers came before dawn, pulled her husband out of bed, dragged him outside, punched and kicked him until he was unconscious, and then hacked him to death with machetes.

Tomasa was just beginning to recall the night her husband was kidnapped, when a man carrying a load of wood with a thump line stopped on the path about 50 feet away to ask who I was and why I was in the *aldea*. Don Pedro is the military commissioner in the community. I introduced myself and showed him my permission papers from the *commandante* of the local garrison. After looking at my papers, Pedro told me I was free to visit the community but advised me to introduce myself to the head of the civil patrol. Tomasa anxiously resumed her story. Her husband was disappeared by soldiers one night in early 1982. She said that several days later she went to the *municipio* to register his death, and the authorities told her that if he was disappeared he was not considered dead. She did find his mutilated body some weeks later, but she did not return to register his death until several years later. She was told that she now owed a fine of 100 quetzales because of the lateness of her report. Tomasa planned to leave in a few weeks to pick coffee on a piedmont plantation to earn the money because she wants legal title to her small parcel of land and the house.

The Embodiment of Violence

The women have never recovered from their experiences of fear and repression; they continue to live in a chronic state of emotional, physical, and social trauma. As Suárez-Orozco found among Central American refugees living in Los Angeles, people carry their psychological horror with them even into situations of relative safety (1990). Their nightmares stalk them. The women of Xe'caj carry their pains, their sufferings, and their testimonies in their bodies.

Doña Martina cried bitterly the day her young grandson died of respiratory infection, and another lay gravely ill. She said that she tries to forget the past, but when someone dies, the pain in her heart returns and her nerves come on strong. She fled Be'cal in 1981 with her husband because of death threats. He was hunted down and was disappeared in Guatemala City several months later. She returned home to the village to pick up the pieces of her life as best she could. Today she and her four youngest children share a home with her (older) son and daughter-in-law. Somatic messages such as those borne by these women offer insights into individual distress as a result of misery and war and suggest that there might be other interpretations that do not deny the individual body's (dis)ease but at the same time demonstrate the relational qualities of the body to "emotional, social and political sources of illness and healing" (Scheper-Hughes and Lock 1987). In the case of Guatemala, I want to suggest another reading of the widow's somatization of distress and suffering, that is, that some of the discrete illnesses from which the women suffer may also be a moral response, an emotional survival strategy, to the political repression they have experienced and in which they continue to live. And this response is felt both individually and collectively. Certainly the ways in which the widows of Xe'caj experience their personal emotions of suffering may be construed as idiosyncratic and discrete. That these bodily expressions are also cultural renderings of collective social and political trauma, however, is a fact not lost on the women themselves. The invisible violence of fear and terror becomes visible in the sufferings and sicknesses of the body, mind, and spirit of the widows of Xe'caj. Their silenced voices speak poignantly through their bodies of their sadness, loneliness, and desolation, of chronic poverty and doubt. The women suffer from headaches, gastritis, ulcers, weakness, diarrhea, irritability, inability to sleep, weak blood – disorders usually clustered under the syndrome of post-traumatic distress – and of "folk" illnesses such as *nervios* (nerves), *susto* (fright), and *penas* (pain, sorrow, grief). Simply to categorize their sufferings, however, as either manifestations of clinical syndromes or culture-bound constructions of reality is to dehistoricize and dehumanize the lived experiences of the women.

Doña Isabel has had a constant headache since the day they disappeared her husband seven years ago. It never leaves her, she says. Doña Juana has a chronic pain in her heart because of her sadness; she cannot forget witnessing the brutal killing of her husband and son. Doña Martina cannot eat because of her *nervios*. She worries how she will feed her children, how she will earn money to buy what she needs at the market. Don Jose, a village health promoter, describes in vivid detail the many children who were born during the violence who now have multiple health problems and deficiencies due to *susto*, fear, and malnutrition that their mothers suffered.

What was noteworthy in these instances was that the women of Xe'caj pinpointed the onset of their physical problems to the events surrounding the death or disappearance of their husbands, sons, or fathers and commented on the chronicity of their physical, social, and economic problems. Being "sick" in these cases is inherently dangerous, but the danger is quite different from that described by Talcott Parsons in his seminal article on the social consequences of the "sick role" (1972). In this situation, illness related to political violence is a refusal to break ties with the person who was killed or disappeared through the maintenance of illness. The bereavement process has yet to be completed. It is a moral refusal to get well. The women's illnesses become actual physical representations of the widespread violence against the Mayan civilian population for which there has yet to be a resolution. The body stands as political testimony, as a collective protest strategy. While somatization as a political idiom may be a dangerous game to play, as Scheper-Hughes has noted in the Brazilian context (1992), it also opens possibilities. The women have come to represent the horror they have witnessed through their bodies, and as such, pain and suffering expressed through illness become a powerful communicative force. Their voices may be silenced by fear and terror, but the body itself has become the site of social and political memory.

While I am not suggesting that this constitutes a wholly conscious act on the part of all women, there does seem to be a level of awareness in which the women attribute political causality to particular illnesses. And the widespread nature of these complaints forges a commonality and sense of sharing among the women.

A reexamination of *susto* is useful here. *Susto* is a malady, common throughout Mesoamerica, with undifferentiated symptomatology and which appears to have pre-Columbian antecedents. *Susto* is understood by its victims to be the loss of the essential life force due to fright. Often-reported symptoms include depression, weakness, loss of appetite, restlessness, lack of interest in work duties and personal hygiene, disturbing dreams, fatigue, diarrhea, and vomiting. If left untreated, the victim literally (though often slowly) wastes away.

The literature in medical anthropology is replete with interpretations of illness and sickness in terms of cognitive and symbolic models of meaning. Folk illnesses such as *susto*, *nervios*, and *mal de ojo* have commonly been understood as physiological expressions of individual's maladaptation to societal expectations. The nature of the etiology of *susto* in Western terms has left medical anthropologists baffled, although various explanations have been posited, ranging from mental illness (Pages Larraya 1967), to social behavior as a result of stress (Mason 1973; O'Nell and Selby 1968), cultural transgression, inability or unwillingness to fulfill role expectations (Rubel 1964), or assuming the sick role as a form of protest (Uzzell 1974), to purely biological phenomena such as hypoglycemia (Bolton 1981) and malnutrition (Burleigh 1986).

Recently Rubel, O'Nell, and Collado-Ardon have suggested a middle ground to understand *susto* as an interaction between social and biological factors (1991). While these studies are important steps in discerning the complexities of *susto*, I want to suggest an alternative reading. I argue for an interpretation of *susto* that is situational, an embodied understanding of complex social and political relations – one that links the lived experiences of the physical body with the social, cultural, and body politic (Scheper-Hughes and Lock 1987).

In some cases in Xe'caj, the *susto* from which the women and children suffer is directly related to the terror and fear that they have experienced as a result of political violence. Might *susto* in these cases be seen not solely as a social (and passive) resistance to what has transpired, but as social memory embodied? And at the same time might we take them at their word, that they are *asustado* (frightened) and that *el espiritu se fue* (the spirit/soul has left the body)? I suggest that this is an accurate, literal description of what has happened to them.

Doña Marcela's young son Juanito was *asustado* when he was returning home on a mountain path one evening and ran into a platoon of soldiers. Juanito's father had been killed several years earlier by the army. Now Juanito eats very little, his small edematous body is so lethargic that he hardly moves outside the house. Don Lucas' daughter Marta was only eight when the army came to her village. During the past nine years Marta, who is distant and withdrawn, has grown very little. Marta is thin and pale with a distant gaze. She suffers from *susto*, and when strangers come to the house, she experiences *ataques* during which she appears dead and is unable to speak. When Marta does speak, which is infrequent, Don Lucas describes it as "speaking to everyone and no one." He says that she saw terrible things during the violence, that she was witness to many brutal killings in the village. Don Lucas knows that Marta's spirit has left her body due to fright, but he has been unable to help her. These frail, wasting bodies are themselves testimony to what has happened to the Mayan people. *Susto*, as a result of political violence, not only is an individual tragedy but serves as a powerful social and political record of the transgressions against Mayan people.

Like the *pena* in Doña Martina's heart which is both bodily and emotionally felt, the sicknesses that the women of Xe'caj are experiencing are more than metaphors of their suffering; they are expressions of the rupture of the intricate and immediate connections between the body, mind, and spirit and are expressed in social relations between the individual, social, and body politic. The pain and sadness that Martina experiences in her heart is a direct link to the death of her husband and to have pain no longer is to forget his death. And Martina says that she cannot forget because there has not been justice. The heart is the center of the vital forces of the spirit for Mayan people, and as such it is the center of their awareness and consciousness, as it was once believed in Aristotelian philosophy until Western science "proved" the direct connection between the brain and consciousness. The alliances between Martina and her husband that helped to sustain her have been broken, as have been the social bonds of trust and stability in her community. While I am not arguing that the ongoing chronic pains that the women experience are in themselves a form of social resistance, they do serve to connect the women to each other in their hardships and as such become a mechanism for social commentary and political consciousness.

The women speak of their sufferings and illnesses in terms of the violence and oppression that they suffer as Mayas. "I have these *nervios* because I am poor," Doña Martina explains. "I have this headache because they killed my husband and now I am alone, and it will not go away because I am afraid," Doña Isabel says. Western medicine can in some instances alleviate their symptoms, but it cannot heal their problems. The medicinal plants the women gather in the mountains do relieve some of their pains, but they say things must change before they can be well. As they share their suffering, the women's understanding of their predicaments takes on a more social dialogue that offers hope for the future.

NOTES

1   Connerton has defined social memory as "images of the past that commonly legitimate a present social order" (1989:12). In Guatemala fear inculcated into the social memory has engendered a forced acquiescence on the part of many Mayas to the status quo. At the same time a distinctly Mayan (counter-)social memory exists. Indigenous dances (especially the dance of the *conquista*), oral narratives, the relationship with the *antepasados* maintained through the planting of corn, the weaving of cloth, and religious ceremonies are all examples of Mayan social memory.

2   Fear of strangers is not a new phenomenon in Guatemala. Maude Oakes, in her study of Todos Santos, reported that in the late 1940s local people were reticent to talk with the few strangers who came to the community and that she too was treated with suspicion at the beginning of her fieldwork (1951). With some, Oakes never developed a rapport of trust, a common experience for most fieldworkers. Since the last wave of violence, however, community loyalties have been divided and a level of distrust previously unknown has permeated social life. A climate of suspiciousness prevails in many villages. Olivia Carrescia's two ethnographic films made a decade apart (before and after the violence) in Todos Santos document some of the profound changes wrought by systematic state terror (1982, 1989).

3   Counterinsurgency, or "dirty wars," are campaigns of "state-sponsored terror and repression deliberately carried out against suspected civilian populations" (Nordstrom and Martin 1992:261) who have been the base of support for guerrilla struggles. In Guatemala, for example, this far-reaching strategy includes not only the defeat of the armed insurgency and the destruction of its civilian support, but also a program of pacification of the civilian population (Wickham-Crowley 1990). Horror, fear, and spectacle, along with murder and brutality, are some of the weapons of control used against the population. Specifically, in Guatemala these take the form of disappearances, large population displacements, massacres, local civil militias, and model villages that severely restrict population movement (Barry 1986; Jordahl 1987).

4   A partial list of countries in which state terror has proliferated since the 1960s would include Indonesia, Chile, Guatemala, Kampuchea, East Timor, Uganda, Argentina, the Central African Republic, South Africa, El Salvador, the Philippines, Haiti, Burundi, Bangladesh, Cambodia, Brazil, and Uruguay.

5   Michael Taussig's powerful treatise on the nervous system draws the analogy between the anatomical nervous system and the chaos and panic engendered by tenuous social systems (1992a). He notes that, across the fibers of this fragile network, terror passes at times almost unnoticed, and at others is fetishized as a thing unto itself. In this essay Taussig is preoccupied with the "mode of presentation" of terror in social analysis. He concludes that

this puts writing on a completely different plane than hitherto conceived. It calls for an understanding of the representation as contiguous with that being represented and not as suspended about or distant from the represented, ... that knowing is giving oneself over to a phenomenon rather than thinking about it from above. (Taussig 1992a: 10)

6 See Scarry's (1985) discussion on the inexpressibility of physical pain. While Scarry contends that it is only physical pain that can be characterized with no "referential content, it is not of or for anything" (1985:5), I would argue differently. The power of terror of the sort that is endemic in Guatemala and in much of Latin America lies precisely in its subjectification and silence.

7 Taussig notes that terror's talk is about "ordered disorder," a discourse that turns the "expected" relationship between the normal and the abnormal, the exception and the rule on its head, while it absorbs and conceals the violence and chaos of everyday life through a veneer of seeming stability (1992a).

8 Military commissioners are local men, many of whom have been in the army and in the villages they serve as local recruiters and spies for the army (Adams 1970). The program was instituted nationwide in the 1960s and was one of the initial steps in the militarization of rural areas. The civil patrol system was created in 1982 and constituted a rural militia of over one million men by 1985, over half the highland male population over fifteen years of age. The PACs, as they are known, function to augment military strength and intelligence in areas of conflict, and more importantly to provide vigilance and control over the local population. Although the Guatemalan constitution states explicitly that the PACs are voluntary, failure to participate or opposition to their formation marks one as a subversive in conflictive zones in the altiplano (America's Watch 1986; Stoll 1992).

9 The presence of civil patrols in communities has turned petty feuding into a conduit for vigilante justice of which Paul and Demarest (1988) and Montejo (1987) are exemplary descriptions. As Aguayo has pointed out, in Guatemala counterinsurgency does not stop at the killing of real or imagined enemies, but it "obliges the peasant to violate the human rights of the other peasant ... it seeks not only victims but accomplices" (1983:2).

10 When the insurgents first appeared in the eastern part of Guatemala in the 1960s as a result of an unsuccessful military rebellion, a repressive state apparatus was already in place. Between 1966 and 1968 an estimated six to eight thousand peasants were killed in a government campaign against five hundred insurgents. Subsequently, in an attempt to improve the relationship between the military and the rural population and to eliminate local support for the insurgency, a program of military/civil action was introduced into rural areas under the guidance of US advisors. Many of these development projects in road building, health, and education were financed by US AID (United States Agency for International Development) and were located in areas in which social inequalities were particularly acute and support for the popular forces the strongest. In 1982 the Guatemalan army created a civic affairs department (S-5) to promote development. In a 1987 interview Colonel Mario Enrique Morales, then head of the department, stated, "We now understand that we can gain more with civic action than with war. This represents a very profound change in the military mentality, in the Guatemalan Army; and in this we are being original, we are not copying models ... we have done all of this by ourselves, without foreign advice" (AVANCSO 1988:53).

11 Kaibiles are the elite special forces troops of the Guatemalan army, trained in counter-insurgency tactics. An excerpt from an address by General Juan Jose Marroquin to a graduating class of Kaibiles on December 6, 1989, is revealing: "Kaibil officers are trained to forget all humanitarian principles and to become war machines, capable of enduring whatever sacrifices, because from now on, they will be called Masters of War and Messengers of Death" (*La Hora* 1989).

12 CONAVIGUA (the National Coordinating Committee of Guatemalan Widows), an organization of rural Mayan widows, began its work publicly in September 1988. The

stated goal of the organization is "for dignity and unity of women." The women demand an end to the poverty and repression that mark their lives; they want the right of an education for their children, economic assistance, the end of forced recruitment of their sons into the army, the suspension of obligatory civil patrols, respect for human rights, a voice in the national dialogue, and the right to exhume the clandestine graves of their relatives.

PAVYH (the Assistance Program for Widows and Orphans Victims of the Violence) is a special project mandated by the Guatemalan Congress in 1987 with an appropriation of 10 million quetzales (approximately US$3.5 million at 1987 exchange rates), administered through the Ministry of Special Affairs. A pilot program was started in 1988 in Chimaltenango Department; by 1989 the first phase of the project had been completed in all fourteen departments to be covered under the program. The program consisted of three phrases, the first a census, the second a food distribution program, and the third the initiation of small-scale village projects.

13   Mersky identified the two major camps within the ruling coalition as the "traditionalists" and the "modernists" (1989). Jonas identified the "ruling coalition" as the army, the civilian bourgeoisie, and political parties (1991). The power configuration of this coalition is fragile and often unstable, as the events of the May 1993 coup revealed.

14   Rumors of foreigners and strangers eating children are not limited to the women of Xe'caj or other areas of Guatemala. Scheper-Hughes found similar concerns among the people of northeastern Brazil; she also notes the prevalence of Pishtaco myths among Andean Indians who believed that Indian fat, and in particular Indian children's fat, was used to grease the machinery of the sugar mills (1992:236–7). In the 1980s a biological anthropologist working among Andean people found his research stymied because of rumors that the measurement of fat folds was actually a selecting process designed to choose "the fattest for their nefarious purposes" (Scheper-Hughes 1992:236–7).

REFERENCES

Adams, Richard (1970). *Crucifixion by Power. Essays on Guatemalan National Social Structure 1944–1966*. Austin: University of Texas Press.
Aguayo, Sergio (1983). "Los posibilidades de fascismo guatemalteco." *Uno sumo* (March 21): 11.
America's Watch (1986). *Civil Patrols in Guatemala*. America's Watch Report (August). New York: America's Watch.
America's Watch (1990). *Messengers of Death. Human Rights in Guatemala. November 1988–February 1990*. America's Watch Report. New York: America's Watch.
Amnesty International (1981). "Guatemala: A Government Program of Political Murder." *New York Review of Books* (March 19):38–40.
Amnesty International (1982). *Guatemala: Massive Extrajudicial Executions in Rural Areas under the Government of General Efrain Rios Montt*. Briefing given in London, July.
Amnesty International (1987). *Guatemala: The Human Rights Record*. New York: Amnesty International.
Anderson, Kenneth, and Simon, Jean-Marie (1987). "Permanent Counterinsurgency in Guatemala." *Telos* 73:9–45.
Arendt, Hannah (1958). *The Human Condition*. Chicago: University of Chicago Press.
Arendt, Hannah (1973). *The Origins of Totalitarianism*. New York: Harvest.
AVANCSO (1988). *La politica de desarrollo del estado guatemalteco 1986–1987*. Vol. 7. Guatemala City: Inforpress.

AVANCSO (1992). *Donde esta el futuro? Procesos de reintegracion en comunidades de retornados*. Vol. 8. Guatemala City: Inforpress.

Barry, Tom (1986). *Guatemala: The Politics of Counterinsurgency*. Albuquerque, NM: Resource Center.

Bolton, Ralph (1981). "*Susto*, Hostility, and Hypoglycemia." *Ethnology* 20(4):261–76.

Brecht, Bertolt (1976). "The Anxieties of the Regime." In R. Manheim and J. Willet (eds.), *Bertolt Brecht, Poems 1913–1945*. London: Methuen, pp. 296–7.

Burleigh, Elizabeth (1986). "Patterns of Childhood Malnutrition in San Jose Poaquil, Guatemala." Ph.D. dissertation. University of California, Los Angeles, CA.

Camus, Albert (1955). *The Myth of Sisyphus and Other Essays*. New York: Vintage.

Carmack, Robert (ed.) (1988). *Harvest of Violence: The Mayan Indians and the Guatemalan Crisis*. Norman: University of Oklahoma Press.

Carrescia, Olivia (1982). *Todos Santos Cuchumatan: Report from a Guatemalan Village*. New York: First Run/ICARUS Films.

Carrescia, Olivia (1989). *Todos Santos: The Survivors*. New York: First Run/ICARUS Films.

Cohn, Carol (1987). "Sex and Death in the Rational World of Defense Intellectuals." *Signs* 12(4):687–718.

Connerton, Paul (1989). *How Societies Remember*. Cambridge: Cambridge University Press.

Doughty, Paul (1988). "Crossroad for Anthropology: Human Rights in Latin America." In T. E. Downing and G. Kushner (eds), *Human Rights and Anthropology*. Human Rights and Anthropology, 24. Cambridge: Cultural Survival, pp. 43–72.

Downing, Theodore E. and Kushner, Gilbert (eds.) (1988). *Human Rights and Anthropology*. Report 24. Cambridge: Cultural Survival.

Falla, Ricardo (1983). "The Massacre at the Rural Estate of San Francisco, July 1982." *Cultural Survival Quarterly* 7(1):43–5.

Falla, Ricardo (1992). *Masacres de la Selva. Ixcan, Guatemala, 1975–1982*. Guatemala: Universidad de San Carlos de Guatemala.

Feldman, Alan (1991). *Formations of Violence: The Narrative of the Body and Political Terror in Northern Ireland*. Chicago: University of Chicago Press.

Forester, Cindy (1992). "Conscript's Testimony: Inside the Guatemalan Army." *Report on Guatemala* 13(2):6, 14.

Franco, Jean (1986). "Death Camp Confession and Resistance to Violence in Latin America." *Socialism and Democracy* (Spring/Summer):5–17.

Fried, Morton H. (1967). *The Evolution of Political Society: An Essay in Political Anthropology*. New York: Random House.

Gough, Kathleen (1968). "New Proposals for Anthropologists." Social Responsibility Symposium. *Current Anthropology* 9:403–7.

Guatemalan Bishops' Conference (1988). *Cry for Land: Pastoral Letter*. Guatemala City: Guatemala Bishops' Conference.

Hertz, Robert (1960). "Contribution to the Study of the Collective Representation of Death." In *Death and the Right Hand*. London: Cohen and West, pp. 29–88.

Hooks, Margaret (1991). *Guatemalan Women Speak*. London: Catholic Institute for International Relations.

Hora, La (1989). "Graduacíon de escuela polytechnica." *La Hora* (Guatemala City), December 7:17.

Hora, La (1991). "De Léon Carpio propone la tesis de la Amnistiá para el diálogo." Seccíon a. *La Hora* (Guatemala City), December 27:2.

Hunter, Monica (1936). *Reaction to Conquest: Effects of Contact with Europeans on the Pondo of South Africa*. London: Oxford.

Hymes, Dell (ed.) (1969). *Reinventing Anthropology*. New York: Pantheon.

Jonas, Susanne (1991). *The Battle for Guatemala: Rebels, Death Squads and U.S. Power.* Boulder, CO: Westview.

Jordahl, Mikkel (1987). *Counterinsurgency and Development in the Altiplano: The Role of Model Villages and the Poles of Development in the Pacification of Guatemala's Indigenous Highlands.* Washington, DC: Guatemalan Human Rights Commission.

Kafka, Franz (1937). *The Trial.* New York: Alfred Knopf. (Original work published 1925)

Kuper, Hilda Beemer (1947). *An African Aristocracy: Rank among the Swazi of Bechwanaland.* London: Oxford.

Lancaster, Roger A. (1992). *Life Is Hard: Machismo Danger and the Intimacy of Power in Nicaragua.* Berkeley: University of California Press.

Lesser, Alexander (1933). *The Pawnee Ghost Dance Hand Game: A Study of Cultural Change.* Columbia University Contributions to Anthropology, 16. New York: Columbia University Press.

Lira, Elizabeth and Castillo, Maria Isabel (1991). *Psicologia de la Amenaza Politica y del Miedo Santiago.* Santiago: Ediciones Chile America (CESOC).

Lovell, George (1992). *Conquest and Survival in Colonial Guatemala.* Kingston, ON: Queens University Press.

Manz, Beatriz (1988). *Refugees of a Hidden War. The Aftermath of Counterinsurgency in Guatemala.* Albany: State University of New York Press.

Martin-Baro, Ignacio (1989). "La institucionalizacion de la guerra." Paper presented at the 12th International Psychology Conference [XII] Congreso International Psicologia], Buenos Aires, June 25–30.

Martin-Baro, Ignacio (1990). "La violencia en Centroamerica: Una vision psicosocial." *Revista de Psicologia de El Salvador* 9(35):123–46.

Mason, John W. (1973). "Historical View of the Stress Field." *Journal of Stress Research* (June): 22–36.

Mersky, Marcie (1989). "Empresarios y transicion politica en Guatemala." Unpublished manuscript.

Montejo, Victor (1987). *Testimony: Death of a Guatemalan Village.* Willimantic, CT: Curbstone Press.

Nordstrom, Carolyn and Martin, JoAnn (eds.) (1992). *The Paths to Domination, Resistance and Terror.* Berkeley: University of California Press.

Oakes, Maude (1951). *Two Crosses of Todos Santos.* Princeton, NJ: Princeton University Press.

O'Nell, Carl W. and Selby Henry A. (1968). "Sex Differences in the Incidence of Susto in Two Zapotec Pueblos." *Ethnology* 7:95–105.

Pages Larraya, F. (1967). *La Esquizofrenia en Tierra Ayamaras y Quechuas.* Buenos Aires: Ediciones Drusa.

Parsons, Talcott (1972). "Definition of Health and Illness in the Light of American Values and Social Structure." In E. Gartly (ed.), *Patients, Physicians, and Illness.* Glencoe, IL: Free Press, pp. 107–27.

Paul, Benjamin and Demarest, William (1988). "The Operation of a Death Squad in San Pedro La Laguna." In R. Carmack (ed.), *Harvest of Violence.* Norman: University of Oklahoma Press, pp. 119–54.

Peteet, Julie (1991). *Gender in Crisis: Women and the Palestinian Resistance Movement.* New York: Columbia University Press.

Recinos, Adain and Goetz, Delia (trans.) (1953). *Annals of the Cakchiquels.* Norman: University of Oklahoma Press.

Redfield, Robert (1930). *Tepoztlan: A Mexican Village.* Chicago: University of Chicago Press.

Rubel, Arthur (1964). "The Epidemiology of Folk Illness: *Susto* in Hispanic America." *Ethnology* 3:268–83.

Rubel, Arthur J., O'Nell, Carl W. and Collado-Ardon, Rolando (1991). *Susto, A Folk Illness*. Berkeley: University of California Press.

Sahlins, Marshall and Service, Elman (eds.), (1960). *Evolution and Culture*. Ann Arbor: University of Michigan Press.

Scarry, Elaine (1985). *The Body in Pain: The Making and Unmaking of the World*. Oxford: Oxford University Press.

Scheper-Hughes, Nancy (1992). *Death without Weeping: The Violence of Everyday Life in Brazil*. Berkeley: University of California Press.

Scheper-Hughes, Nancy and Lock, Margaret (1987). "The Mindful Body: A Prolegomenon to Future Work in Medical Anthropology". *Medical Anthropology Quarterly* 1(1):6–41.

Service, Elman (1962). *Primitive Social Organization: An Evolutionary Perspective*. New York: Random House.

Sluka, Jeffrey (1992). "The Anthropology of Conflict." In C. Nordstrom and J. Martin (eds.), *The Paths to Domination, Resistance, and Terror*. Berkeley: University of California Press, pp. 190–218.

Smith, Carol A. (1990). "The Militarization of Civil Society in Guatemala: Economic Reorganization as a Continuation of War." *Latin American Perspectives* 67(4):8–41.

Stoll, David (1992). "Between Two Fires: Dual Violence and the Reassertion of Civil Society in Nebaj, Guatemala." Ph.D. dissertation, Department of Anthropology, Stanford University.

Suárez-Orozco, Marcelo (1990). "Speaking of the Unspeakable: Toward a Psycho-Social Understanding of Responses to Terror." *Ethos* 18(3):353–83.

Suárez-Orozco, Marcelo (1992). "Grammar of Terror: Psychological Responses to State Terrorism in the Dirty War and Post Dirty Argentina." In C. Nordstrom and J. Martin (eds.), The Paths to Domination, Resistance, and Terror. Berkeley: University of California Press, pp. 219–59.

Taussig, Michael (1978). "Nutrition, Development, and Foreign Aid." *International Journal of Health Services* 8(11):101–21.

Taussig, Michael (1984). "History as Sorcery." *Representations* 7:87–109.

Taussig, Michael (1987). *Colonialism, Shamanism, and the Wild Man: A Study in Terror and Healing*. Chicago: University of Chicago Press.

Taussig, Michael (1992a). "Why the Nervous System?" In *The Nervous System*. London: Routledge, pp. 1–10.

Taussig, Michael (1992b). "Terror as Usual: Walter Benjamin's Theory of History as a State of Seige." In *The Nervous System*. London: Routledge, pp. 11–36.

Taussig, Michael (1992c). "Public Secrets." Talk given to the Department of Geography. University of California, Berkeley, CA, February 13.

Turton, Andrew (1986). "Patrolling the Middle Ground: Methodological Perspectives on Everyday Peasant Resistance." *Journal of Peasant Studies* 13:36–48.

Uzzell, Douglas (1974). "*Susto* Revisited: Illness as Strategic Role." *American Ethnologist* 1:369–78.

Vincent, Joan (1990). *Anthropology and Politics*. Tucson: University of Arizona Press.

Weschler, Lawrence (1990). *A Miracle, A Universe: Settling Accounts with Torturers*. New York: Penguin Books.

Wickham-Crowley, Timothy (1990). "Terror and Guerrilla Warfare in Latin America." *Journal of Comparative Studies in Society and History* 32(2):201–16.

Wilson, Richard (1991). "Machine Guns and Mountain Spirits: The Cultural Effects of State Repression among the Q'eqchi of Guatemala." *Critique of Anthropology* 11(1):33–61.

15

The Myth of Global Ethnic Conflict

John R. Bowen

Much recent discussion of international affairs has been based on the misleading assumption that the world is fraught with primordial ethnic conflict. According to this notion, ethnic groups lie in wait for one another, nourishing age-old hatreds and restrained only by powerful states. Remove the lid, and the cauldron boils over. Analysts who advance this idea differ in their predictions for the future: some see the fragmentation of the world into small tribal groups; others, a face-off among several vast civilizational coalitions. They all share, however, the idea that the world's current conflicts are fueled by age-old ethnic loyalties and cultural differences.[1]

This notion misrepresents the genesis of conflict and ignores the ability of diverse people to coexist. The very phrase "ethnic conflict" misguides us. It has become a shorthand way to speak about any and all violent confrontations between groups of people living in the same country. Some of these conflicts involve ethnic or cultural identity, but most are about getting more power, land, or other resources. They do not result from ethnic diversity; thinking that they do sends us off in pursuit of the wrong policies, tolerating rulers who incite riots and suppress ethnic differences.

In speaking about local group conflicts we tend to make three assumptions: first, that ethnic identities are ancient and unchanging; second, that these identities motivate people to persecute and kill; and third, that ethnic diversity itself inevitably leads to violence. All three are mistaken.

Contrary to the first assumption, ethnicity is a product of modern politics. Although people have had identities – deriving from religion, birthplace, language, and so on – for as long as humans have had culture, they have begun to see themselves as members of vast ethnic groups, opposed to other such groups, only during the modern period of colonization and state-building.

The view that ethnicity is ancient and unchanging emerges these days in the potent images of the cauldron and the tribe. Out of the violence in Eastern Europe came images of the region as a bubbling cauldron of ethnonationalist sentiments that were sure to boil over unless suppressed by strong states. The cauldron image contrasts with the American "melting pot," suggesting that Western ethnicities may melt, but Eastern ones must be suppressed by the region's unlikable, but perhaps necessary, Titos and Stalins.

Nowhere does this notion seem more apt than in the former Yugoslavia. Surely the Serbs, Croats, and Bosnians are distinct ethnic groups destined to clash throughout history, are they not? Yet it is often forgotten how small the differences are among the currently warring factions in the Balkans. Serbs, Croats, and Bosnians all speak the same language (Italy has greater linguistic diversity) and have lived side by side, most often in peace, for centuries. Although it is common to say that they are separated by religion – Croats being Roman Catholic, Serbs Orthodox Christian, and Bosnians Muslim – in fact each population includes sizable numbers of the other two religions. The three religions have indeed become symbols of group differences, but religious differences have not, by themselves, caused intergroup conflict. Rising rates of intermarriage (as high as 30 percent in Bosnia) would have led to the gradual blurring of contrasts across these lines.

As knowledgeable long-term observers such as Misha Glenny have pointed out, the roots of the current Balkan violence lie not in primordial ethnic and religious differences but rather in modern attempts to rally people around nationalist ideas. "Ethnicity" becomes "nationalism" when it includes aspirations to gain a monopoly of land, resources, and power. But nationalism, too, is a learned and frequently manipulated set of ideas, and not a primordial sentiment. In the nineteenth century, Serb and Croat intellectuals joined other Europeans in championing the rights of peoples to rule themselves in "nation-states": states to be composed of one nationality. For their part, Serbs drew on memories of short-lived Serb national states to claim their right to expand outward to encompass other peoples, just as other countries in Europe (most notably France) had done earlier. That Balkan peoples spoke the same language made these expansionist claims all the more plausible to many Serbs.[2]

At the same time, Croats were developing their own nationalist ideology, with a twist: rather than claiming the right to overrun non-Croats, it promised to exclude them. Nationalism among the Croats naturally was directed against their strong Serb neighbors. When Serbs dominated the state of Yugoslavia that was created after World War I, Croat resentment of Serbs grew. The most militant of Croat nationalists formed an underground organization called Ustashe ("Uprising"), and it was this group, to which the Nazis gave control of Croatia, that carried out the forced conversions, expulsions, and massacres of Serbs during World War II. The later calls to war of the Serb leader Slobodan Milošević worked upon the still fresh memories of these tragedies.

But the events of World War II did not automatically lead to the slaughters of the 1990s; wartime memories could have been overcome had Yugoslavia's new leaders set out to create the social basis for a multiethnic society. But Marshal Tito chose to preserve his rule by forbidding Yugoslavs from forming independent civic groups and developing a sense of shared political values. Political opposition, whether in Croatia, Serbia, or Slovenia, coalesced instead around the only available symbols, the nationalisms of each region. Tito further fanned nationalist flames by giving Serbs and Croats privileges in each other's territories – Serbs held positions of power in Croatia, and Croats in Belgrade. In the countryside these minority presences added to nationalist resentments. Tito's short-term political cleverness – nostalgic-ally remembered by some in the West – in fact set the stage for later slaughter. Resentments and fears generated by modern state warfare and the absence of a civil society – not ethnic differences – made possible the success of the nationalist politicians Milošević and Franjo Tudjman.

The Legacy of Colonialism

But what about Africa? Surely there we find raw ethnic conflict, do we not? Our understandings of African violence have been clouded by visions, not of boiling cauldrons, but of ancient tribal warfare. I recall a National Public Radio reporter interviewing an African UN official about Rwanda. Throughout the discussion the reporter pressed the official to discuss the "ancient tribal hatreds" that were fueling the slaughter. The official ever so politely demurred, repeatedly reminding the reporter that mass conflict began when Belgian colonial rulers gave Tutsis a monop-oly of state power. But, as happens so often, the image of ancient tribalism was too deeply ingrained in the reporter's mind for him to hear the UN official's message.

What the African official had to say was right: ethnic thinking in political life is a product of modern conflicts over power and resources, and not an ancient impedi-ment to political modernity. True, before the modern era some Africans did consider themselves Hutu or Tutsi, Nuer or Zande, but these labels were not the main sources of everyday identity. A woman living in central Africa drew her identity from where she was born, from her lineage and in-laws, and from her wealth. Tribal or ethnic identity was rarely important in everyday life and could change as people moved over vast areas in pursuit of trade or new lands. Conflicts were more often within tribal categories than between them, as people fought over sources of water, farm-land, or grazing rights.

It was the colonial powers, and the independent states succeeding them, which declared that each and every person had an "ethnic identity" that determined his or her place within the colony or the postcolonial system. Even such a seemingly small event as the taking of a census created the idea of a colony-wide ethnic category to which one belonged and had loyalties. (And this was not the case just in Africa: some historians of India attribute the birth of Hindu nationalism to the first British census, when people began to think of themselves as members of Hindu, Muslim, or Sikh populations.) The colonial powers – Belgians, Germans, French, British, and Dutch – also realized that, given their small numbers in their dominions, they could effectively govern and exploit only by seeking out "partners" from among local people, sometimes from minority or Christianized groups. But then the state had to separate its partners from all others, thereby creating firmly bounded "ethnic groups."

In Rwanda and Burundi, German and Belgian colonizers admired the taller people called Tutsis, who formed a small minority in both colonies. The Belgians gave the Tutsis privileged access to education and jobs, and even instituted a minimum height requirement for entrance to college. So that colonial officials could tell who was Tutsi, they required everyone to carry identity cards with tribal labels.

But people cannot be forced into the neat compartments that this requirement suggests. Many Tutsis are tall and many Hutus short, but Hutus and Tutsis had intermarried to such an extent that they were not easily distinguished physically (nor are they today). They spoke the same language and carried out the same religious practices. In most regions of the colonies the categories became economic labels: poor Tutsis became Hutus, and economically successful Hutus became Tutsis. Where the labels "Hutu" and "Tutsi" had not been much used, lineages with lots of cattle were simply labeled Tutsi; poorer lineages, Hutu. Colonial discrimination against Hutus created what had not existed before: a sense of collective Hutu identity, a Hutu cause. In the late 1950s Hutus began to rebel against Tutsi rule (encouraged by Europeans on their way out) and then created an independent and Hutu-dominated state in Rwanda; this state then gave rise to Tutsi resentments and to the creation of a Tutsi rebel army, the Rwandan Patriotic Front.

The logic of rule through ethnic division worked elsewhere, too. The case of Sri Lanka (formerly Ceylon) shows how, even when colonizers did not favor a single group, colonial rule could foster interethnic violence. The Sinhalese and Tamils of Sri Lanka have a common origin and, contrary to stereotypes of dark Tamils and light-skinned Sinhalese, they cannot easily be distinguished by their physical characteristics. The distinction between them is based mainly on the language spoken. Before the twentieth century there was little conflict between them; indeed, they did not think of themselves as two distinct kinds of people. Then came British rule. As they did throughout their empire, the British ruled Ceylon by creating an English-speaking elite, and, here as elsewhere, their favoritism engendered an opposition. In Ceylon this opposition took on racial and religious overtones. The majority of those who had been left out of the elite spoke Sinhalese and were Buddhists, and they began to promote a racist notion of Sinhalese superiority as an "Aryan race." After independence it was this Sinhalese-speaking group that gained control of the new state of Sri Lanka, and began to exclude Tamils from the best schools and jobs, mainly by requiring competence in Sinhalese. Not suprisingly, Tamils resented this discrimination, and some – initially only a few – launched violent protests in the 1970s. These riots led to massive state repression and, by a logic similar to that shaping Tutsi rebellions in Rwanda, to the creation of the Tamil Tigers (the Liberation Tigers of Tamil Eelam) and their demands for an autonomous Tamil region. As the anthropologist Stanley Tambiah has argued, the island's violence is a late-twentieth-century response to colonial and postcolonial policies that relied on a hardened and artificial notion of ethnic boundaries.[3]

In these cases and many others – Sikhs in India, Maronites in Lebanon, Copts in Egypt, Moluccans in the Dutch East Indies, Karens in Burma – colonial and post-colonial states created new social groups and identified them by ethnic, religious, or regional categories. Only in living memory have the people who were sorted into these categories begun to act in concert, as political groups with common interests. Moreover, their shared interests have been those of political autonomy, access to education and jobs, and control of local resources. Far from reflecting ancient ethnic or tribal loyalties, their cohesion and action are products of the modern state's demand that people make themselves heard as powerful groups, or else risk suffering severe disadvantages.

Fear from the Top

A reader might say at this point: fine, ethnic identities are modern and created, but today people surely do target members of other ethnic groups for violence, do they not? The answer is: less than we usually think, and when they do, it is only after a long period of being prepared, pushed, and threatened by leaders who control the army and the airwaves. It is fear and hate generated from the top, and not ethnic differences, that finally push people to commit acts of violence. People may come to fear or resent another group for a variety of reasons, especially when social and economic change seems to favor the other group. And yet such competition and resentment "at the ground level" usually does not lead to intergroup violence without an intervening push from the top.

Let us return to those two most unsettling cases, Rwanda and the Balkans. In Rwanda the continuing slaughter of the past few years stemmed from efforts by the dictator-president Juvenal Habyarimana to wipe out his political opposition, Hutu as well as Tutsi. In 1990–1 Habyarimana began to assemble armed gangs into a militia called Interahamwe. This militia carried out its first massacre of a village in March 1992, and in 1993 began systematically to kill Hutu moderates and Tutsis. Throughout 1993 the country's three major radio stations were broadcasting messages of hate against Tutsis, against the opposition parties, and against specific politicians, setting the stage for what followed. Immediately after the still unexplained plane crash that killed President Habyarimana in April 1994, the presidential guard began killing Hutu opposition leaders, human rights activists, journalists, and others critical of the state, most of them Hutus. Only then, after the first wave of killings, were the militia and soldiers sent out to organize mass killings in the countryside, focusing on Tutsis.

Why did people obey the orders to kill? Incessant radio broadcasts over the previous year had surely prepared them for it; the broadcasts portrayed the Tutsi-led Rwandan Patriotic Front as bloodthirsty killers. During the massacres, radio broadcasts promised the land of the dead to the killers. Town mayors, the militia, the regular army, and the police organized Hutus into killing squads, and killed those Hutus who would not join in. The acting president toured the country to thank those villagers who had taken part in the massacres. Some people settled personal scores under cover of the massacre, and many were carried away with what observers have described as a "killing frenzy." The killings of 1994 were not random mob violence, although they were influenced by mob psychology.[4]

In reading accounts of the Rwanda killings, I was struck by how closely they matched, point by point, the ways Indonesians have described to me their participation in the mass slaughters of 1965–6. In Indonesia the supposed target was "communists," but there, too, it was a desire to settle personal scores, greed, willingness to follow the army's orders, and fear of retaliation that drove people to do things they can even now barely admit to themselves, even though many of them, like many Hutus, were convinced that the killings stopped the takeover of the country by an evil power. In both countries, people were told to kill the children and not to spare pregnant women, lest children grow up to take revenge on their killers. Americans continue to refer to those massacres in Indonesia as an instance of "ethnic violence" and to assume that Chinese residents were major targets, but they were not: the killings by and large pitted Javanese against Javanese, Acehnese against Acehnese, and so forth.

The two massacres have their differences: Rwanda in 1993–4 was a one-party state that had carried out mass indoctrination through absolute control of the mass media; Indonesia in 1965–6 was a politically fragmented state in which certain factions of the armed forces only gradually took control. But in both cases leaders were able to carry out a plan, conceived at the top, to wipe out an opposition group. They succeeded because they persuaded people that they could survive only by killing those who were, or could become, their killers.

The same task of persuasion faced Serb and Croat nationalist politicians, in particular Croatia's Franjo Tudjman and Serbia's Slobodan Milošević, who warned their ethnic brethren elsewhere – Serbs in Croatia, Croats in Bosnia – that their rights were about to be trampled unless they rebelled. Milošević played on the modern Serb nationalist rhetoric of expansion, claiming the right of Serbs everywhere to be united. Tudjman, for his part, used modern Croat rhetoric of exclusionary national-ism to build his following. Once in power in Croatia, he moved quickly to define Serbs as second-class citizens, fired Serbs from the police and military, and placed the red-and-white "checkerboard" of the Nazi-era Ustashe flag in the new Croatian banner.

Both leaders used historical memories for their own purposes, but they also had to erase recent memories of new Yugoslav identities, tentatively forged by men and women who married across ethnic boundaries or who lived in the cosmopolitan cities. The new constitutions recognized only ethnic identity, not civil identity, and people were forced, sometimes at gunpoint, to choose who they "really" were.[5]

Contrary to the "explanations" of the war frequently offered by Western journal-ists, ordinary Serbs do not live in the fourteenth century, fuming over the Battle of Kosovo; nor is the current fighting merely a playing out of some kind of inevitable logic of the past, as some have written. It took hard work by unscrupulous polit-icians to convince ordinary people that the other side consisted not of the friends and neighbors they had known for years but of genocidal people who would kill them if they were not killed first. For Milošević this meant persuading Serbs that Croats were all crypto-Nazi Ustashe; for Tudjman it meant convincing Croats that Serbs were all Chetnik assassins. Both, but particularly Milošević, declared Bosnian Muslims to be the front wave of a new Islamic threat. Each government indirectly helped the other: Milošević's expansionist talk confirmed Croat fears that Serbs intended to control the Balkans; Tudjman's politics revived Serbs' still remembered fears of the Ustashe. Serb media played up these fears, giving extensive coverage in 1990–1 to the exhumation of mass graves from World War II and to stories of Ustashe terror. This "nationalism from the top down," as Warren Zimmerman, the last US ambassador to Yugoslavia, has characterized it, was also a battle of nation-alisms, with each side's actions confirming the other's fears.

If Rwanda and the Balkans do not conform to the images of bubbling cauldrons and ancient tribal hatreds, even less do other ongoing local level conflicts. Most are drives for political autonomy, most spectacularly in the former Soviet Union, where the collapse of Soviet power allowed long-suppressed peoples to reassert their claims to practice their own languages and religions, and to control their own territory and resources – a rejection of foreign rule much like anti-imperial rebellions in the Americas, Europe, Asia, and Africa. Elsewhere various rebellions, each with its own history and motivations, have typically – and erroneously – been lumped together as "ethnic conflict." Resistance in East Timor to Indonesian control is a twenty-year struggle against invasion by a foreign power, not an expression of ethnic or cultural identity. People fighting in the southern Philippines under the banner of a "Moronation" by and large joined up to regain control of their homelands from Manila-appointed politicians. Zapatista rebels in Chiapas demand jobs, political reform, and, above all, land. They do not mention issues of ethnic or cultural identity in their statements – indeed, their leader is from northern Mexico and until recently spoke no Mayan. Other current conflicts are raw struggles for power among rival factions, particularly in several African countries (Liberia, Somalia, Angola) where rival forces often recruit heavily from one region or clan (giving rise to the notion that these are "ethnic conflicts") in order to make use of local leaders and loyalties to control their followers.[6]

Ethnic Diversity and Social Conflict

This brings us to the third mistaken assumption: that ethnic diversity brings with it political instability and the likelihood of violence. To the contrary, greater ethnic diversity is not associated with greater interethnic conflict. Some of the world's most ethnically diverse states, such as Indonesia, Malaysia, and Pakistan, though not without internal conflict and political repression, have suffered little interethnic violence, while countries with very slight differences in language or culture (the former Yugoslavia, Somalia, Rwanda) have had the bloodiest such conflicts. It is the number of ethnic groups and their relationships to power, not diversity *per se*, that strongly affect political stability. As shown in recent studies by political scientist Ted Gurr, and contrary to popular thinking, local conflicts have not sharply increased in frequency or severity during the last ten years. The greatest increase in local conflicts occurred during the Cold War, and resulted from the superpowers' efforts to arm their client states. (The sense that everything exploded after 1989, Gurr argues, comes from the reassertions of national identity in Eastern Europe and the former Soviet Union.)[7]

By and large, the news media focus on countries racked by violence and ignore the many more cases of peaceful relations among different peoples. Take Indonesia, where I have carried out fieldwork since the late 1970s. If people know of Indonesia, it is probably because of its occupation of East Timor and its suppression of political freedoms. But these are not matters of ethnic conflict, of which there is remarkably little in a country composed of more than three hundred peoples, each with its own distinct language and culture. Although throughout the 1950s and 1960s there were rebellions against Jakarta in many parts of the country, these concerned control over local resources, schooling, and religion. An on-again, off-again rebellion where I work, on the northern tip of Sumatra, has been about control over the region's vast oil and gas resources (although the Western press continues to stereotype it as "ethnic conflict").

Cultural diversity does, of course, present challenges to national integration and social peace. Why do some countries succeed at meeting those challenges while others fail? Two sets of reasons seem most important, and they swamp the mere fact of ethnic and cultural diversity.

First there are the "raw materials" for social peace that countries possess at the time of independence. Countries in which one group has been exploiting all others (such as Rwanda and Burundi) start off with scores to settle, while countries with no such clearly dominating group (such as Indonesia) have an initial advantage in building political consensus. So-called centralized polities, with two or three large groups that continually polarize national politics, are less stable than "dispersed" systems, in which each of many smaller groups is forced to seek out allies to achieve its goals. And if the major ethnic groups share a language or religion, or if they have worked together in a revolutionary struggle, they have a bridge already in place that they can use to build political cooperation.[8]

Take, again, the case of Indonesia. In colonial Indonesia (the Dutch East Indies) the Javanese were, as they are today, the most numerous people. But they were concentrated on Java and held positions of power only there. Peoples of Java, Sumatra, and the eastern islands, along with Malays and many in the southern Philippines, had used Malay as a *lingua franca* for centuries, and Malay became the basis for the language of independent Indonesia. Islam also cut across regions and ethnicities, uniting people on Sumatra, Java, and Sulawesi. Dominance was "dispersed," in that prominent figures in literature, religion, and the nationalist movement tended as often as not to be from someplace other than Java, notably Sumatra. Moreover, people from throughout the country had spent five years fighting Dutch efforts to regain control after World War II, and could draw on the shared experience of that common struggle.[9]

One can see the difference each of these features makes by looking next door at culturally similar Malaysia. Malays and Chinese, the largest ethnic groups, shared neither language nor religion, and had no shared memory of struggle to draw on. Malays had held all political power during British rule. On the eve of independence there was a clear fault line running between the Malay and Chinese communities.

The Importance of Political Choices

But these initial conditions do not tell the whole story, and here enters the second set of reasons for social peace or social conflict. States do make choices, particularly about political processes, that ease or exacerbate intergroup tensions. As political scientist Donald Horowitz has pointed out, if we consider only their starting conditions, Malaysia ought to have experienced considerable interethnic violence (for the reasons given above), whereas Sri Lanka, where Tamils and Sinhalese had mingled in the British-trained elite, should have been spared such violence. And yet Malaysia has largely managed to avoid it while Sri Lanka has not. The crucial difference, writes Horowitz, was in the emerging political systems in the two countries. Malaysian politicians constructed a multiethnic political coalition, which fostered ties between Chinese and Malay leaders and forced political candidates to seek the large middle electoral ground. In Sri Lanka, as we saw earlier, Sinhalese-speakers formed a chauvinist nationalist movement, and after early cooperation Tamils and Sinhalese split apart to form ethnically based political parties. Extreme factions appeared on the wings of each party, forcing party leaders to drift in their directions.

But political systems can be changed. Nigeria is a good example. Prior to 1967 it consisted of three regions – North, South, and East – each with its own party supported by ethnic allegiances. The intensity of this three-way division drove the southeast region of Biafra to attempt to break away from Nigeria in 1967, and the trauma of the civil war that followed led politicians to try a new system. They carved the country into nineteen states, the boundaries of which cut through the territories of the three largest ethnic groups (Hausa, Yoruba, and Igbo), encouraging a new federalist politics based on multiethnic coalitions. The new system, for all its other problems, prevented another Biafra. Subsequent leaders, however, continued to add to the number of states for their own political reasons. The current leader, General Sani Abacha, is now adding to an already expanded list of thirty states; this excessive fragmentation has broken up the multiethnic coalitions and encouraged ethnic politics anew. A similar direction has been pursued by Kenya's Daniel arap Moi, who has created an ethnic electoral base that excludes most Kikuyus, increasing the relevance of ethnicity in politics and therefore the level of intergroup tensions.

What the myth of ethnic conflict would say are ever-present tensions are in fact the products of political choices. Negative stereotyping, fear of another group, killing lest one be killed – these are the doings of so-called leaders, and can be undone by them as well. Believing otherwise, and assuming that such conflicts are the natural consequences of human depravity in some quarters of the world, leads to perverse thinking and perverse policy. It makes violence seem characteristic of a people or region, rather than the consequence of specific political acts. Thinking this way excuses inaction, as when US President Bill Clinton, seeking to retreat from the hard-line Balkan policy of candidate Clinton, began to claim that Bosnians and Serbs were killing each other because of their ethnic and religious differences. Because it paints all sides as less rational and less modern (more tribal, more ethnic) than "we" are, it makes it easier to tolerate their suffering. Because it assumes that "those people" would naturally follow their leaders' call to kill, it distracts us from the central and difficult question of just how and why people are sometimes led to commit such horrifying deeds.

NOTES

1   Two of the most widely read proponents of the view I am contesting are Robert Kaplan, in his dispatches for the *Atlantic* and in his *Balkan Ghosts: A Journey Through History* (New York: St. Martin's, 1993), and (writing mainly on large-scale conflict) Samuel P. Huntington, in "The Clash of Civilizations?" *Foreign Affairs* 72 (Summer 1993): 22–49. My concern is less with the particular difficulties of these writers' arguments, about which others have written, than with the general notion, which, as with all myths, survives the death of any one of its versions.

2   See Misha Glenny, *The Fall of Yugoslavia* (New York: Penguin, 1992), for a balanced and ethnographically rich account of the Balkan wars. On recent tendencies in European nationalisms, see especially Rogers Brubaker, *Nationalism Reframed: Nationhood and*

the *National Question in the New Europe* (Cambridge: Cambridge University Press, 1996). Brubaker makes the important point that "nationalism" should be treated as a category of social and political ideology, and not a pre-ideological "thing."

3 S. J. Tambiah, *Sri Lanka: Ethnic Fratricide and the Dismantling of Democracy* (Chicago: University of Chicago Press, 1986). For a different view on the culture of violence in Sri Lanka, see Bruce Kapferer, *Legends of People, Myths of State* (Washington, DC: Smithsonian Institution Press, 1988).

4 Among recent overviews of massacres in Rwanda and Burundi, see Philip Gourevitch, "The Poisoned Country," *New York Review of Books* (June 6, 1996):58–64, and René Lemarchand, *Burundi: Ethnic Conflict and Genocide* (Cambridge: Cambridge University Press, 1995).

5 That there were memories, fears, and hatreds to exploit is important to bear in mind, lest we go to the other extreme and argue that these conflicts are entirely produced from the top, an extreme toward which an overreliance on rational-choice models may lead some analysts. Russell Hardin's otherwise excellent *One for All: The Logic of Group Conflict* (Princeton, NJ: Princeton University Press, 1995) errs, I believe, in attributing nothing but rational, self-aggrandizing motives to those leaders who stir up ethnic passions, ignoring that they, too, can be caught up in these passions. The cold rationality of leaders is itself a variable: probably Milošević fits Hardin's rational-actor model better than Tudjman, and Suharto better than Sukarno. In Each case, it is an empirical question.

6 The same points could be made concerning the religious version of "ancient hatreds," such as Muslim-Hindu relations in India. However peaceful or conflictual "ancient" relations may have been (and on this issue there continues to be a great deal of controversy among historians of South Asia), the often bloody conflicts of the past ten years in India have been fueled by ambitious politicians who have seen boundless electoral opportunity in middle-class Hindu resentment toward (1) lower castes' claims that they deserve employment and education quotas, and (2) the recent prosperity of some middle-class Muslims. See the penetrating political analyses by Susanne Hoeber Rudolph and Lloyd I. Rudolph in the *New Republic* (March 22, 1993 and February 14, 1994), and a historical and ethnographic study by Peter van der Veer, *Religious Nationalism: Hindus and Muslims in India* (Berkeley: University of California Press, 1994).

7 See Ted Gurr, *Ethnic Conflict in World Politics* (Boulder, CO: Westview, 1994).

8 See Donald L. Horowitz, *Ethnic Groups in Conflict* (Berkeley: University of California Press, 1985), pp. 291–364.

9 I would propose "dispersed dominance" (a situation in which each of several groups considers itself to dominate on some social or political dimension) as a second important mechanism for reducing intergroup conflict alongside the well-known "cross-cutting cleavages" (a situation in which one or more important dimensions of diversity cut across others, as religion cuts across ethnicity in many countries). "Dispersed dominance" takes into account social and cultural dimensions, such as literary preeminence or a sense of social worth stemming from putative indigenous status. It is thus broader than, but similar to, political mechanisms such as federalism, when these mechanisms are aimed at (in Donald Horowitz's phrase) "proliferating the points of power." It is the empirical correlate to the normative position articulated by Michael Walzer in *Spheres of Justice* (New York: Basic Books, 1983) that dominance in one sphere (or dimension) ought not to automatically confer dominance in others.

16

Speechless Emissaries: Refugees, Humanitarianism, and Dehistoricization

Liisa H. Malkki

Massive displacements of people due to political violence and the sight – on television and in newspapers – of refugees as a miserable "sea of humanity" have come to seem more and more common. If these displacements, and media representations of them, appear familiar, so too does the range of humanitarian interventions routinely activated by the movement of people. The purpose of this essay is to explore the forms typically taken by humanitarian interventions that focus on refugees as their object of knowledge, assistance, and management, and to trace the effects of these forms of intervention at several different levels.

One of the things that most immediately demands notice is that the forms of these humanitarian interventions appear to be so inevitable – as do the perennial impasses and systematic failures from which such interventions often suffer (Calhoun 1995:xii; Ferguson 1994). The contemporary crises of mass displacement – especially those of Rwanda and Burundi, which I discuss here – offer an almost laboratory-like, tragic clarity of view into the larger question of humanitarian intervention.

My argument grows out of anthropological field research conducted with Hutu refugees from Burundi living in Tanzania (mostly in three very large refugee camps) since the "selective genocide" of 1972 in Burundi.[1] It also addresses the 1994 genocide in Rwanda and its aftermath. The essay moves through a comparison of the social construction and uses of the refugee category in different social and institutional domains.

In the first section I discuss the social significance of the refugee category for the 1972 Hutu refugees themselves – that is, for persons who have long been legally recognized and documented as real, bona fide political refugees with a well-founded fear of persecution. I trace how the Hutu refugees in a particular context (many of whom still live in refugee camps) had come to appropriate the category as a vital, positive dimension of their collective identity in exile, and in what sense refugee status was a *historicizing condition* that helped to produce a particular political subjectivity.

The second section examines how the staff of the international organizations administering the Hutu refugees in Tanzania conceptualized the term *refugee* in the course of their everyday discussions. While the legal claim to refugee status by the Hutu was acknowledged by these administrators, other, more elaborate normative expectations and definitions of "the refugee" lived – unstated but vigorous – in the shadow of the law. The net effect of the administrators' views, I will argue, was to depoliticize the refugee category and to construct in that depoliticized space an ahistorical, universal humanitarian subject (Barthes 1980; Malkki 1995a:12–13ff.).

In the third section the argument moves to a greater level of generality: the examination of the figure of the refugee as an object of concern and knowledge for the "international community," and for a particular variety of humanism. This exploration will suggest that refugee issues are one privileged site for the study of humanitarian interventions through which "the international community" constitutes itself (Calhoun 1995; Ishay 1995; Malkki 1994; Rusciano and Fiske-Rusciano 1990). The central purpose here is to examine some of the specific effects of the contemporary dehistoricizing constitution of the refugee as a singular category of humanity within the international order of things.[2] Much as in the case of the local refugee administrators in Dar-es-Salaam, one important effect of the bureaucratized humanitarian interventions that are set in motion by large population displacements is to leach out the histories and the politics of specific refugees' circumstances. Refugees stop being specific persons and become pure victims in general: universal man, universal woman, universal child, and, taken together, universal family (Barthes 1980).[3] Of course, refugee populations usually consist of people in urgent need who have been victimized in numerous ways. The problem is that the necessary delivery of relief and also long-term assistance is accompanied by a host of other, unannounced social processes and practices that are dehistoricizing. This dehistoricizing universalism creates a context in which it is difficult for people in the refugee category to be approached as historical actors rather than simply as mute victims. It can strip from them the authority to give credible narrative evidence or testimony about their own condition in politically and institutionally consequential forums (compare Balibar 1988:724; 1995).

That humanitarian interventions tend to be constituted as the opposite of political ones has, of course, a long history and complex reasons behind it (Loescher and Monahan 1989; Zolberg et al. 1989). But the purpose here is not to delve into that history; it is to emphasize the extent to which this opposition is taken for granted, and to ask what the effects of this conventionalized, depoliticizing, universalizing practice are. A vital part of the answer must be, as I will try to show, that in universalizing particular displaced people into "refugees" – in abstracting their predicaments from specific political, historical, cultural contexts – humanitarian practices tend to silence refugees.

A great deal of work has been done in recent years (in several disciplines) on the question of "voice" and representation, silencing and "ethnographic authority" (Clifford 1988:21ff.). Some of this work has tended to move in heavily textualized domains where the potential political stakes in having or not having a voice have slipped beyond the immediate field of vision. It is in the horror of current events in

Rwanda and Burundi, and in the massive displacements of people that have resulted (and that could well multiply in the near future), that the question of voice reveals its importance. There, the systematic disqualification of the refugees' own inescapably political and historical assessments of their predicaments and their futures has been (between the summer of 1994 and now, in February 1996) forming into a contestation between life and death.

It is my hope that an examination of the contemporary political tragedies of the Great Lakes region of Africa will help to make the case that familiar forms of humanitarianism and humanism need careful, vigilant study, especially now – that they should no longer be left to lie in their accustomed circuits of international policy science, but rather should be studied by scholars in many fields. The intent here is not to dismiss humanitarian interventions as useless. The alternatives to humanitarianism that come most easily to mind – utter, uninformed indifference or repressive, undemocratic, mercenary logics – are clearly terrible. But precisely because international interventions (humanitarian and otherwise) are increasingly important, we should have better ways of conceptualizing, designing, and challenging them. This is why it is useful to examine the idea of a universal, ahistorical humanity that forms the basis of much of contemporary progressive politics. This liberal, progressive politics, with its vision of a universal humanity, is hard-wired into the history of anthropology. Perhaps anthropology is, therefore, an especially suitable site from which to begin questioning the workings and effects of these vital concepts and practices.[4]

Refugee Status as Lived by Hutu Refugees in Mishamo, Tanzania

The tens of thousands of Hutu refugees who fled the mass killings by the Tutsi-dominated army in Burundi in 1972 have, for the most part, been living in refugee camps ever since.[5] A much smaller group of these 1972 refugees (some 20,000–30,000) settled spontaneously in and around Kigoma township, and have thus had no experience of prolonged residence inside a refugee camp.[6] My fieldwork (1985–6) was divided between Mishamo, a refugee camp with a population of about 35,000 in western Tanzania's Rukwa region, and the town and environs of Kigoma on Lake Tanganyika, next to the historical crossroads of Ujiji. The biographical and social circumstances of the people in these two settings, the "camp refugees" and the "town refugees," were very different in exile, even though their lives in Burundi prior to 1972 appear to have differed much less. The most relevant contrast in the present context is that the social status of being a refugee had a very pronounced salience in the camp refugees' life-worlds, while in town it generally did not. In Mishamo it was indispensable to understand something of the social and political meaning given collectively to refugeeness and to exile by the camp inhabitants. In contrast, for the people I have called the town refugees, refugee status was generally not a collectively heroized or positively valued aspect of one's social person. Insofar as it was considered relevant at all, it was more often a liability than a protective or positive status.

I have examined this contrast at length elsewhere (Malkki 1995a). But even in its simplest outlines, the case suggests that the elaboration of legal refugee status into a social condition or a moral identity does not occur in an automatic or predictable way, and that even people who fled originally from the "same place" can, and often do, come to define the meaning of refugee status differently, depending on the specific lived circumstances of their exile. In what follows I will focus only on the camp refugees' social imagination of refugeeness because it was their definitions that most directly challenged the refugee administrators' visions of the same.

The most unusual and prominent social fact about the camp of Mishamo was that the refugees who had lived within its confines for so many years were still in 1985–6 continually engaged in an urgent, collective process of constructing and reconstructing a true history of their trajectory as "a people." This was an oppositional process, setting itself against state-approved versions of the history of Burundi. The narrative production of this history in exile was sweeping. Beginning with what anthropologists and other students of mythology have called "myths of foundation," the Hutu refugees' narratives outlined the lost features of the "autochthonous," "original" Burundi nation and the primordial social harmony that was believed to have prevailed among the original inhabitants (the Twa and the Hutu). The narratives of the past then located the coming of the Tutsi in time and space: they were remembered as the pastoral "foreigners from the North" (sometimes as "the Hamites" or "the Nilotes") who came in search of new pastures for their cattle "only 400 years ago." There followed the progressive theft of power from the "natives" (Hutu and Twa) by Tutsi ruse and trickery, and the emergence of an extractive, oppressive social hierarchy. The refugees' historical narratives moved on to the colonial era, concentrating mainly on the period of Belgian administration, and defined the end of formal colonial rule as the defeat of the departing Belgians by Tutsi trickery. The culminating chapter in the refugees' historical narratives of the Burundian past amounted to a vast and painful documentation of the mass killings of people belonging to the Hutu category by Burundi's (mainly Tutsi) army – and, eventually, by Tutsi civilians – in 1972. So many years later, the historical and personal memory of the apocalyptic violence and terror of that era still had a sharp and shocking salience in people's everyday lives.

These historical narratives were ubiquitous in the camp, forming – as I have argued elsewhere with the benefit of more detailed evidence (Malkki 1995a) – an overarching historical trajectory that was fundamentally also a national history of the "rightful natives" of Burundi. The camp refugees saw themselves as a nation in exile. And they thought of exile as an era of moral trials and hardships that would enable them to reclaim the "homeland" in Burundi at some moment in the future.

People in Mishamo tended to see their refugee status, then, as a positive, productive status and as a profoundly meaningful historical identity. Far from being a "mere" legal technicality, or a disabling problem to be endured, refugeeness was clung to both as a protective legal status and as a special moral condition – for it was only by together passing through a period as refugees that the Hutu as "a people" could effect their return to their rightful homeland.

Such a positive light on refugee status should not be taken to mean that the people in question did not notice or suffer from the large and small difficulties of being in exile. Indeed, people in Mishamo were quite aware of their very considerable material and social hardships. But there were two important qualifications to this. First, legal refugee status and UN-issued refugee identity documents were seen as offering at least some protection against possibly even greater hardship. Second, and even more significant, many in the refugee camp were of the opinion that embracing instead of escaping hardships was wise as the knowledge of difficulties would teach and empower people, making them worthier and more able to reclaim the home-land. As one man put it in describing the Tanzanian camp administrators who were often seen as exploitative and oppressive: "They begin to educate us as refugees."

Conversations about refugeeness and exile with people in Mishamo began to suggest, over time, that refugeeness was seen as a matter of *becoming*. They often explained that in the initial stages of exile, the Hutu were not yet true refugees, refugees properly speaking. What they had to say strongly suggested that, socially, there was such a thing as a novice refugee. True or mature refugeeness, then, entailed a cumulative process embedded in history and experience. It had to do, if I have understood correctly, with a certain level of self-knowledge, and the camp was a privileged site for the elaboration of such a knowledge.

Another indication that refugeeness had come to be interiorized as an aspect of people's identities in Mishamo was that it was considered to be inherited from one generation to another as long as the Hutu lived in exile. To quote one person, "If I am a refugee here, of course my child is a refugee also – and so is his child, and his child, until we go back to our native country." This vision, of course, fit well into the narratives of history and exile that were so central in the everyday life of the refugee camp, but it was quite different from the legal definition, and also from the ideal trajectory of refugeeness usually constructed by the staffs of the international aid organizations.[7]

Being a refugee also naturally suggested, even demanded, certain kinds of social conduct and moral stances, while precluding others. Thus, for example, many refugees in Mishamo, in the camp, were continually angered by the conduct of those among them who engaged in commerce – those who had become "merchant refugees." (And, in fact, the most prominent Hutu merchant refugees mostly lived outside the camps, among the so-called spontaneously settling refugees in Kigoma and Ujiji, and in other towns.) As one person exclaimed: "We have not come here to make commerce. We are refugees." This sense of outrage was echoed by another man: "[The merchant refugees,] they become rich. They have cabarets, hotels, restaurants . . . *being refugees!*" As we will see momentarily, the camp refugees and their administrators agreed on the point that a rich refugee was a contradiction in terms; but they came to this conclusion from different premises. The camp refugees recognized that wealth would likely root people in the here and now, making them forget that they were in exile, and thus properly rooted elsewhere. In a curious way, wealth and commerce made people "this-wordly" – while the "other world," of course, was the homeland. And refugeeness, ideally, was an integral part of the process of a future return – just as it was inevitably linked to the past. It should be noted, too, that commerce put Hutu in the position of exploiting other Hutu, thus challenging their corporate solidarity.[8]

This brief account of the social construction and moral imagination of refugeeness in Mishamo has, perhaps, been sufficient to show in what sense refugee identity can be shaped by historical and political context. Why the Hutu had to flee, what the history of political struggle had been in Burundi, how the refugees expected to help bring about a new political order in Burundi: all these were issues inextricably tied to the social meaning of exile. It would therefore have been impossible for them to concentrate only on life within the confines of their camp, as if the camp were not itself deeply within history.

The Social Imagination of Refugee Status among Refugee Administrators in Tanzania

Throughout my field research in Tanzania I was offered crucially important assistance by the United Nations High Commissioner for Refugees (UNHCR) and the Tanganyika Christian Refugee Service (TCRS), that is, by the people who – along with officials of the Tanzanian Ministry of Home Affairs – were charged with administering and assisting the Hutu refugees.[9] UNHCR funded the greatest part of the refugee projects, while TCRS was the principal implementing agency. Linked to the umbrella organization of the Lutheran World Federation, TCRS was (and is) an organization with long experience of refugee work in Tanzania and one of the most effective of such groups in carrying out its mandate.[10]

When I had completed one year of field research in rural western Tanzania in late 1986 and returned to Dar-es-Salaam in preparation for my departure from Tanzania, the TCRS director invited me to his home to speak to TCRS staff about my research. To comply was a very modest way of acknowledging my debt to TCRS and the other organizations that had ferried my mail, given me access to their wireless radios, permitted their mechanics to sell me gasoline and fix my car, opened their library to me, submitted to interviews, furnished valuable maps, and rendered so many other similar services.

At the evening gathering on the terrace of the director's home, I gave an account of what I had heard and thought in the course of the short year in western Tanzania, knowing that numerous people in my audience had much longer experience of living in Tanzania than I. I spoke about the fact that the Hutu refugees in Mishamo saw exile in Tanzania first and foremost not as a tragedy, but as a useful, productive period of hardships that would teach and purify them, and thereby help them to grow powerful enough to return to their homeland on their own terms. That the refugees considered they had undergone hardship in Tanzania was evident, and I tried to give an account of this also. I spoke about the antagonisms that had developed in Mishamo Refugee Settlement as a result of the very hierarchical social organization within it, about resentment over practices that were considered extractive of the refugees' agricultural labor power, about the control of movement through Leave Passes, about the scarcity of secondary and higher education for refugee children, and so on. The most important point I was trying to convey was that the experiential reality of the refugee camp was powerfully shaped by the narrative memory of relationships and antagonisms located in the past in Burundi, antagonisms between the Hutu peasant majority there and the minority Tutsi category that at the time predominated in the military and government. That is, the camp was a site of intense historicity, and to be a refugee was a historicizing and politicizing condition. To study this historicity, I said, had become one of my main activities during the fieldwork.

I knew as I spoke that my findings were in some measure incommensurable with the language of project evaluations and "development" discourse in which refugee issues were so often framed (Ferguson 1994). The results of my research were listened to politely but were clearly not received as particularly useful information by the TCRS staff, who were my audience that evening. What I reported was not completely novel to them. Several among them – especially the Tanzanian staff – had previously heard aspects of the grand historical narrative of the Hutu as a people in exile. (In other organizations, too, there were individual staff members who were sometimes quite knowledgeable about the struggles over history in the region.)[11] But this historical knowledge, this narrative evidence, was, to all intents and purposes, irrelevant and unusable by the organization. Moreover, when it did become relevant to daily operations, it was as a potential trouble factor threatening to complicate the administering of the projects.

My presentation in the director's garden provoked a spirited discussion of what a real refugee was, or ought to be – and whether the Hutu who had come to Tanzania in 1972 still fit the picture. One of the guests heard in my presentation evidence that the Hutu refugees were ungrateful recipients of international assistance, and was moved to challenge the refugee status of the Hutu on grounds of material, economic well-being:

Nowhere else in Africa do these people [refugees] receive their own land to cultivate. Not in Sudan, not in Somalia. They say that these people are refugees; they should not have all the same rights as citizens.

Another TCRS employee added, "In fact, their standard of living is *higher* than in the Tanzanian villages!" While both clearly were referring to complex questions regarding the distribution of poverty, there was also an evident moral intent to say that a real or proper refugee should not be well off. Later in the same discussion, the TCRS director himself commented:

I should show you a film the Norwegians made of the Burundi refugees when they first came. One was showing a bullet wound, someone else a cut, torn clothes, dirty.... They had *nothing*.... These people don't *look* like refugees anymore. If you go to Mishamo [refugee camp] as a visitor, you will think these are just ordinary villagers.

It was not uncommon to hear similar comments from other refugee administrators, whether of TCRS or UNHCR. There was a pronounced tendency to try to identify and fix the "real" refugee on extralegal grounds. And one key terrain where this took place was that of the *visual image* of the refugee, making it possible to claim that given people were not real refugees because they did not look (or conduct themselves) like real refugees. This suggests that refugee status was implicitly understood to involve a performative dimension. The symbolic, social significance of the Hutu refugees' early wounds and physical problems for their administrators emerged only gradually, in the course of numerous exchanges with TCRS and UN staff. It appeared that the staff – in an effort to do their jobs properly and to direct assistance where it might be needed most – were in some manner trying to identify *exemplary victims*.

Frantz Fanon has observed that for "the native," "objectivity is always against him" (cited in McClintock 1992:97). For the refugee, much the same might be said.

In his or her case, wounds speak louder than words. Wounds are accepted as objective evidence, as more reliable sources of knowledge than the words of the people on whose bodies those wounds are found. So the ideal construct, the "real refugee," was imagined as a particular kind of person: a victim whose judgment and reason had been compromised by his or her experiences. This was a tragic, and sometimes repulsive, figure who could be deciphered and healed only by professionals, and who was opaque even (or perhaps especially) to himself or herself.

This set of expectations about the communicative efficacy (Tambiah 1985:123–66) of corporeal wounds – and of the presumed unreliability of the refugees' own narrative firsthand accounts of political violence – should be seen in relation to more general social expectations and interventions directed at refugees in Tanzania. What was conspicuously absent from all the documentary accumulation generated in the refugee camps was an official record of what the refugees themselves said about their own histories and their present predicament.

They were frequently regarded as simply unreliable informants. There was also a more general tendency among some (though by no means all) administrators to characterize the refugees as dishonest, prone to exaggeration, even crafty and untrustworthy. So, in a sense, they had to be cared for and understood obliquely, *despite themselves*. Their bodies were made to speak to doctors and other professionals, for the bodies could give a more reliable and relevant accounting than the refugees' "stories." I often heard the Hutu refugees characterized as persons who were always "telling stories."

Writing in the 1930s, Ernst Bloch defined "realism" as "the cult of the immediately ascertainable fact" (cited in Feldman 1994:406). This useful phrase accurately describes how the figure of the refugee comes to be knowable: it is necessary to cut through "the stories" to get to "the bare facts." It is here that physical, non-narrative evidence assumes such astonishing power. It has all the authority of an "immediately ascertainable fact." In contrast, the political and moral history of displacement that most Hutu in Mishamo themselves insisted on constructing was generally rejected by their administrators as too messy, subjective, unmanageable, hysterical – as just "stories." Set against an ostensibly knowable, visible medical history of injuries or illness, a political history snaking its way from Burundi to Tanzania, from the past to the here and now, weaving people into complex loyalties and unseen relations, presented itself as unstable and unknowable – and as ultimately, or, properly, irrelevant to the practical efforts to administer and care for large refugee populations.

In this manner history tended to get leached out of the figure of the refugee, as imagined by their administrators. This active process of dehistoricization was inevitably also a project of depoliticization. For to speak about the past, about the historical trajectory that had led the Hutu as refugees into the western Tanzanian countryside, was to speak about politics. This could not be encouraged by the camp administrators (whether the Ministry of Home Affairs, TCRS, or UNHCR); political activism and refugee status were mutually exclusive here, as in international refugee law more generally.

The conversation at the TCRS director's home illustrates how the everyday language and practices of those very people who worked with the Hutu because of their refugee status continually acted to destabilize the solidity of the legal category, as documented in the refugees' identity papers. This destabilization occurred along several different axes. On the one hand, there was a continual, informal monitoring of signs of decreasing refugeeness. As the visible signs of one's social refugeeness faded, one's worthiness as a recipient of material assistance was likely to decrease. But there was more to it than that. What emerges from this and other accounts is that the refugees were thought to be at their purest when they first arrived, and when their condition was visibly at its worst. So, instead of refugee status imagined as a state of being attained gradually (as the Hutu camp refugees themselves saw it) or as a legal status that one has or has not, the administrators tended to imagine refugee status as a processual condition that was at its purest and most recognizable early in exile, and was thereafter subject to gradual adulteration over time. All this added up, in a subtle way, to the barely noticeable but nevertheless powerful constitution of the real or true refugee – an ideal figure of which any actual refugees were always imperfect instantiations.

Refugees as Objects of Humanitarian Intervention

The case of Tanzania in the mid-1980s facilitates the effort of identifying (even if tentatively) certain key features in the constitution of the archetypal refugee at the more general level of humanitarian policy discourse. I take as a starting point the observation that there has emerged, in the post-World War II era, a substantially standardized way of talking about and handling "refugee problems" among national governments, relief and refugee agencies, and other non-governmental organizations (Malkki 1995b). I would also suggest that these standardizing discursive and representational forms (or, perhaps more precisely, tendencies) have made their way into journalism and all of the media that report on refugees. As a result, it is possible to discern transnational commonalities in both the textual and the visual representation of refugees. Such transnationally mobile representations are often very easily translated and shared across nation-state borders. And because they are shared among the institutions that locate, fund, and administer refugee projects, these representations can reasonably be expected to carry significant consequences. One of the most far-reaching, important consequences of these established representational practices is the systematic, even if unintended, silencing of persons who find themselves in the classificatory space of "refugee." That is, refugees suffer from a peculiar kind of speechlessness in the face of the national and international organizations whose object of care and control they are. Their accounts are disqualified almost a priori, while the languages of refugee relief, policy science, and "development" claim the production of authoritative narratives about the refugees.[12] In what follows I attempt to look a little more closely at the systemic underpinnings of this form of silencing and speechlessness. I approach this phenomenon from several different directions, starting with a brief look at the complex effects of the visual representation of refugees, especially in the media of photography and documentary film.

   The visual representation of refugees appears to have become a singularly translatable and mobile mode of knowledge about them. Indeed, it is not far-fetched to say that a vigorous, transnational, largely philanthropic traffic in images and visual signs of refugeeness has gradually emerged in the last half-century. Pictures of refugees are now a key vehicle in the elaboration of a transnational social imagination of refugeeness. The visual representation of displacement occurs in many arenas: among refugee administrators (as we have seen), in applied and other academic scholarship (Forbes Martin 1992), among journalists (Drakulič 1993; Kismaric 1989), in the publications of humanitarian and international organizations (UNHCR's *Refugees* magazine), in television fund-raising drives, and even in fashion advertising (I once saw a fashion spread in a Finnish women's weekly magazine, *Anna*, entitled "The Refugee Look"). This global visual field of often quite standardized representational practices is surprisingly important in its effects, for it is connected at many points to the de facto inability of particular refugees to represent themselves authoritatively in the inter- and transnational institutional domains where funds and resources circulate.

The first thing to be noted about the mutual relationship between image and narrative, spectacle and self-representation, is that photographs and other visual representations of refugees are far more common than is the reproduction in print of what particular refugees have said. There are more established institutional contexts, uses, and conventions for pictures of refugees than for displaced persons' own narrative accounts of exile. Indeed, some of these visual conventions seem to speed up the evaporation of history and narrativity.[13]

Mass displacements are often captured as a "sea" or "blur of humanity" (e.g., Lamb 1994:H5)[14] or as a "vast and throbbing mass" (e.g., Warrick 1994:E1)[....]

Feldman's recent essay on "cultural anesthesia" explores these kinds of mass images:

Generalities of bodies – dead, wounded, starving, diseased, and homeless – are pressed against the television screen as mass articles. In their pervasive depersonalization, this *anonymous corporeality* functions as an allegory of the elephantine, "archaic," and violent histories of external and internal subalterns. (1994: 407; emphasis added)

This "anonymous corporeality" is a precise characterization of what happens to refugees in the regimes of representation under discussion here. No names, no funny faces, no distinguishing marks, no esoteric details of personal style enter, as a rule, into the frame of pictures of refugees when they are being imagined as a sea of humanity.

Of course, this anonymous corporeality is not necessarily just a feature of mass scenes; it is equally visible in another conventionalized image of refugees: women and children. This sentimentalized, composite figure – at once feminine and maternal, childlike and innocent – is an image that we use to cut across cultural and political difference, when our intent is to address the very heart of our humanity.

Elsewhere I have also suggested that the visual prominence of women and children as embodiments of refugeeness has to do not just with the fact that most refugees are women and children, but with the institutional, international expectation of a certain kind of *helpessness* as a refugee characteristic (Malkki 1995a: 11). In an article entitled "The Refugee Experience: Defining the Parameters of a Field of Study," Barry Stein notes that "refugees are helped because they are helpless; they must display their need and helplessness" (1981:327). This vision of helplessness is vitally linked to the constitution of speechlessness among refugees: helpless victims need protection, need someone to speak for them. In a sense, the imagined sea of humanity assumes a similar helplessness and speechlessness.

The bodies and faces of refugees that flicker onto our television screens and the glossy refugee portraiture in news magazines and wall calendars constitute spectacles that preclude the "involved" narratives and historical or political details that originate among refugees. It becomes difficult to trace a connection between me/us – the consumers of images – and them – the sea of humanity (compare Calhoun 1995: xiii).[15] Or, more precisely, it becomes difficult to trace a connection, a relationship, other than that of a bare, "mere," common underlying humanity: "We are all human, after all." "As a parent, my heart breaks when I see those dazed Rwandan orphans." These are very human and very decent reactions. One cannot help but feel horror and profound sadness, I think, in the face of such images or in the knowledge that such social circumstances do exist. But it is also possible and, indeed, useful to notice that in their overpowering philanthropic universalism, in their insistence on the secondariness and unknowability of *details* of specific histories and specific cultural or political contexts, such forms of representation deny the very particulars that make of people something other than anonymous bodies, merely human beings.

At first it is difficult to see what might be so problematic in seeing the suffering of people with the eyes of "humanitarian concern" and "human compassion." It is surely better than having no compassion or simply looking the other way. But this is not the issue. The issue is that the established practices of humanitarian representation and intervention are not timeless, unchangeable, or in any way absolute. On the contrary, these practices are embedded in long and complicated histories of their own – histories of charity and philanthropy, histories of international law, peacekeeping, and diplomacy, histories of banishment and legal protection, histories of empires and colonial rule, histories of civilizational and emancipatory discourses and missionary work, histories of World Bank and other development initiatives in Africa, and much more. These humanitarian representational practices and the standardized interventions that go with them have the effect, as they currently stand, of producing anonymous corporeality and speechlessness. That is, these practices tend actively to displace, muffle, and pulverize history in the sense that the Hutu refugees in Mishamo understood history. And they tend to hide the political, or political-economic, connections that link television viewers' own history with that of "those poor people over there" (compare Calhoun 1995; Ferguson 1995, in press).

These processes were in grotesque evidence when the most recent large refugee movements from Burundi began to be photographed in the world's newspapers. In the October 25, 1993, issue of the *Los Angeles Times*, on what the paper calls its "Second Front Page," there was a large photograph of women and children laden with bundles. Underneath was a slim caption:

Hutu tribe refugees cross the border near Rwanda after walking more than 37 miles from Burundi. Tribal violence is believed to have flared up between the Tutsi and Hutu after a Burundi military coup overthrew and killed President Melchior Ndadaye on Thursday. On Sunday, 4,000 people marched through the streets of Bujumbura, the capital, calling for the release of the bodies of the president and of others killed in the coup. (*Los Angeles Times* 1993:A3)

The photo was a very large one, but there was no story to go with it.[16] It was as if this grouping of people – women clothed in colorful cotton wraps, children in ragged T-shirts and shorts, walking bare foot out of Burundi – had just become generic refugees and generic Africans in whose societies tribal violence periodically flares up. It was as if this was all the context that might be required. Whoever got close enough to this cluster of people to take that photograph could have asked them to explain (if not in Kirundi, perhaps in French, or certainly through an interpreter) what had happened to them and what they had witnessed. Instead, there was almost no news from Burundi at all – only this large Associated Press photograph.[17] And this small group of speechless emissaries was allowed to go on its way.

This newspaper photograph helps us to see how "the refugee" is commonly constituted as a figure who is thought to "speak" to us in a particular way: word-lessly. Just the refugee's physical presence is "telling" of his or her immediate history of violence. So we tend to assume, at any rate.

But it is not just that photographs displace narrative testimony. When there is testimony about refugees, it mostly does what the photographs do: it silences the refugees. For it tends to be testimony by "refugee experts" and "relief officials" (or even by those ever-ready "well-placed Western diplomatic sources"), not by refugees themselves. How often have we seen the media image of a (usually white) UN official standing in a dusty landscape, perhaps in Africa, surrounded by milling crowds of black people peering into the camera, and benevolently, efficiently, giving a rundown on their numbers, their diseases, their nutritional needs, their crops, and their birth and mortality rates? This mode of what may be called a "clinical humanitarianism" looks for all the world like an exhaustive report on the displaced masses; and the official is surely trying to be informative, as well as to balance honesty and diplomacy. And yet the scene and the expert voice operate precisely to erase knowledge. In constructing a raw humanity and a pure helplessness, this spectacle all but blocks the possibility of persons stepping forward from the milling crowds, asking for the microphone, and addressing the glassy eye of the camera: "Now, if I may, Sir/Madam, there are numerous things that you have not considered, many details about our history and political circumstances that might assist you in helping us." Such details easily appear as mere quibbles, fine points, and posturing in the face of the other, very powerful narrative of emergency relief, humanitarian intervention, and "raw" human needs.

The visual conventions for representing refugees and the language of raw human needs both have the effect of constructing refugees as a bare humanity – even as a merely biological or demographic presence. This mode of humanitarianism acts to trivialize and silence history and politics – a silencing that can legitimately be described as dehumanizing in most contexts. And yet the mechanisms involved here are more complex than that. For one might argue that what these representa-tional practices do is not strictly to dehumanize, but to humanize in a particular mode. A mere, bare, naked, or minimal humanity is set up. This is a vision of humanity that repels elements that fail to fit into the logic of its framework.

The Stakes in the Humanitarian Interventions in Rwanda, Burundi, and Beyond

The vast displacements of people that occurred in the wake of the fighting and the genocide of 1994 in Rwanda are a good example of what is at stake in the constitution of refugees as such passive objects of humanitarian intervention. This short section will specifically address the effects of the disqualification of refugee knowledge in the matter of their repatriation to Rwanda from Zaire.

It would be impossible to give, especially in a single essay, a thorough account of the complicated history that has culminated in the genocidal massacres of over half a million Rwandan citizens, overwhelmingly Tutsi, and the displacement of several million other Rwandan citizens, mostly Hutu, since April 1994. Important work on the genocide and its aftermath in Rwanda, as well as the contemporary political situation in Burundi, has been done by Reyntjens (1994), Prunier (1995), Lemarchand (1994a, 1994b), Newbury and Newbury (1994, 1995), African Rights (1994), Mbonimpa (1993), Pottier (1994), Jefremovas (n.d.), Guichaoua (1995), Destexhe (1994), and others. The bare outlines, however, are as follows.

Whereas in Burundi the minority Tutsi category controls the military and, effectively, the government, in Rwanda it is the Hutu majority that had been in power for all of its postcolonial history until the Rwandan Patriotic Front (RPF) victory of 1994. The Hutu-led 1961 revolution that crumbled the monarchical system in Rwanda was violent; it resulted in the deaths of some 20,000 (mostly Tutsi) people and produced a sizable presence of exiled Tutsi in Uganda (and elsewhere). It is largely from the ranks of these refugees and their descendants in Uganda that the RPF grew. In October 1990 the RPF attacked Rwanda from Uganda. "Following the attack," Amnesty International reports, "some 7,000 people were arrested, most of them Tutsi; virtually all were subjected to severe beatings and some were killed" (1993: 1). Fighting between the RPF and the Rwandan government forces continued intermittently from 1990 to 1993. On April 6, 1994, the presidents of both Burundi and Rwanda were killed in a plane crash for which responsibility is still being debated. This touched off a nightmarish campaign of mass killings in Rwanda, a campaign made the more appalling because it involved planning and premeditation (Lemarchand 1994a: 1; Newbury and Newbury 1995:2; Prunier 1995). In the days following the crash there were "death squads" that systematically eliminated political opponents of the hard-line faction of the Rwandan government (including both Tutsi and moderate Hutu). Then civilian militias were apparently given "a free hand to just kill every Tutsi in sight" (Lemarchand 1994a:10). From Kigali, the killing spread to other regions of Rwanda. Eventually, many Hutu civilians began to kill their Tutsi neighbors (Smith 1994, cited in Lemarchand 1994a:11). In just a few months, hundreds of thousands of people, mostly Tutsi, were massacred. Most estimates of the death toll fall between 500,000 and 800,000. As RPF forces made advances inside Rwanda, Hutu civilian communities took flight into neighboring countries for fear of retaliation. When the Rwandan army finally collapsed, over a million people moved in the space of a few days into Zaire (and also into Tanzania and elsewhere). The highest number reported for the Rwandan refugee population in the region was 2.2 million. These people have since become objects of world attention as the most awe-inspiring refugee population in the memory of the aid organizations and media working there.

The hundreds of thousands of people living and dying in awful conditions in the Rwanda–Zaire borderlands know better than anyone else on the scene what they have done, what has happened to them, why, and what they can hope for if they return to Rwanda. If anyone is an expert on the apocalyptic Rwandan political situation now, it is they. And yet curious things are happening to their voices. Either they are not heard at all and not quoted in earnest as real, reliable sources by the journalists visiting the Zairean camps, or their words are quoted in ways they never intended (as symptoms of hysteria, evidence of brainwashing, and echoes of super-stitious, gullible Africa). They are being rendered speechless in much the same way that the October 1993 refugees from Burundi's killings were.

This silence is the phenomenon to be understood. It is actually quite a riddle when we consider how much time, effort, and resources refugee agencies and other aid organizations, journalists, politicians, UN peacekeepers, the French and US forces, and countless other expert agencies have had to expend in order to learn anything at all about the setting in which many of them have been deliberating over consequen-tial interventions. One of the most consequential of these interventions still centers on the issue of the repatriation of the refugees from Zaire to Rwanda, a question that has been heatedly discussed ever since 1994.

But before considering the specific question of repatriation, it is worthwhile to try to identify the discursive forms and modes of knowledge that displaced local knowledge and understandings during the genocide and in the months after. At least three discursive registers were readily evident from that early media coverage.

The first register of coverage (dating from the period when massive population displacements had already occurred) emphasized the bodily, physical evidence of violence and atrocity in Rwanda. A colleague has commented, cynically but accur-ately, that this was the period of "blood and gore." Photographic evidence of almost unimaginable violence flooded print media and television. Rivers swelling with bodies distended and bleached by death; crying, disoriented toddlers clinging to the bodies of their dying parents; people with limbs cut off or infected panga slashes over their noses: this flood of terrifying images will not be soon forgotten.[18]

One particularly clear illustration of the place of photographic images in this crisis is to be found in a *Life* magazine special feature called "Eyewitness Rwanda" (1994:74–80). A short opening paragraph introduces six pages of full-color photo-graphs, six pages that seem almost like a religious gesture of mourning. The para-graph ends: "What persists are images – a handful of pictures from among the thousands that have raced before our eyes on videotape or stared out from our daily newspapers. They require no elaboration. In their silence, they tell the story of Rwanda, 1994" (1994:74).

The heavily visual documentation of violence was subsequently joined by the second register: accounts of human tragedy, or what are perhaps most accurately called human interest stories. There were especially many accounts of children in terrible circumstances. Again, the relevant historical and political contexts were missing.

The third register consisted of technical and heroic narratives. Here, the inter-national aid effort had got underway among the Hutu refugees, and the papers were suddenly filled with detailed technical profiles of cholera, of the working principles of the water purification plants being flown in, of oral rehydration techniques, of the construction of airfields, and of the makes and capacities of the military transport planes and other heavy equipment involved in the relief operation centered in Goma. All three of these discursive registers share the feature that they do not require any sustained narrative inputs, any testimonial evidence, from the refugees on whose behalf all the activity was, and still is, being carried out. The refugees were relevant principally as the tragic mass of humanity that needed to be helped first and foremost not to die of cholera, dysentery, or other diseases, to be treated and fed. Epidemics had to be contained, clean drinking water had to be provided, orphans needed to be taken care of, the dead had to be buried (McGreal 1994). The relief workers, medical and other, have understandably been overwhelmed by the enormity of the tragedy in Rwanda and of their mandate in the refugee camps. The genocide left over half a million people dead and untold others wounded, orphaned, widowed, or alone; and the cholera epidemic in the camps in Zaire killed 40,000–50,000 people in little more than a month.[19]

In the face of these terrible epidemics and the sheer mass of the refugee presence, most of the international organizations assisting them, the national governments sending in relief supplies, and even the journalists on site who were mostly echoing all of their policy statements concluded early on that the only solution was to get people to go back into Rwanda. (It is difficult to determine how much agreement there really was among the relief workers, but the dominant stance being reported was – and is – one favoring quick repatriation.)[20] The refugees have in many cases been told they would be safer there than in Zaire. Yet they have consistently expressed grave misgivings about returning. "Expert knowledge" has been terribly at odds with the principals' – the refugees' – knowledge of the situation, and it is clear that the latter has been almost automatically disqualified. For what reasons has this disqualification been considered rational or practically necessary? A vital part of the answer to this riddle is bound up with contemporary forms of humanitarianism. The speechlessness of the newest emissaries of suffering – the refugees from Rwanda – becomes intelligible in this light.

This is where the question of voice – the ability to establish narrative authority over one's own circumstances and future, and, also, the ability to claim an audience[21] – begins to show its teeth, then. Evidence suggests that the overwhelming majority of the Hutu refugees have never considered repatriation wise. They continue to fear retaliation from the new RPF-led government and from ordinary people for crimes for which, they know, the Hutu as a categorical collectivity are thought by many to bear responsibility. And they probably fear the specter of returning to the devastation that their surviving Tutsi neighbors have witnessed. The Rwandan Hutu in Zaire are being urged to go "home," but a question of great practical importance has not been seriously addressed: can the places from which these people fled still serve as their homes (Warner 1994)? The physical sites might be there, even intact, but as social environments they are likely to be alien and terrifying to many. In addition to other considerations, people know that many of their houses and fields are likely to have been occupied by Tutsi repatriating from Uganda after decades in exile there. As Raymond Bonner, one of the few well-informed, seriously engaged journalists covering the Great Lakes region now, reported in November 1994:

Since the war ended in July [1994], a dual repatriation problem has engulfed the tiny war-torn country. Tens of thousands of Tutsi have returned to Rwanda, as many as 300,000 by unofficial counts. They are not among the refugees who fled after the massacres erupted in April, but refugees from ethnic violence of 20 and 30 years ago. Their return is creating demographic and political changes that are potentially explosive. (1994:A3)

While officials of the new RPF government have stated publicly that "squatters must get out of houses when former owners return" from Zaire, the government lacks the means to enforce this; and "sometimes the new occupants have the real owner killed or picked up and taken away, often paying a soldier to do the dirty work" (Bonner 1994:A3). One need only accuse the returnee of complicity in the genocide.

Journalists have mostly echoed the position of the United Nations and several other relief agencies: it is necessary and desirable that the refugees should be repatriated. That the refugees have in general refused to return to Rwanda has been widely attributed, by the United Nations and several other humanitarian agencies and by the international press, to their vulnerability to rumormongering and manipulations by the exiled and defeated remnants of the Rwandan armed forces. There is good evidence that the refugee populations in Zaire are being intimidated by political leaders who wish to keep them in exile (compare Newbury and Newbury 1995; Prunier 1995). But to assume that they are all passive puppets moving mindlessly to the manipulations of a handful of callous politicians of the exiled Rwandan government may be unwise. In the early 1994 coverage of the crisis, the refugees were rendered as superstitious and hysterical, while Rwanda was painted for them as a safe and secure horn of plenty. Of the many news reports along these lines, it is sufficient to quote one:

Aid officials say the estimated 1.2 million Rwandan refugees now facing the agony of Zaire's border camps have about two weeks to go home and harvest the bursting fields of corn, beans and other crops that carpet the lush country. . . . Yet the hungry refugees are fed a steady diet of fear and propaganda by former Hutu government officials and their minions, who insist they will be tortured and killed if they return to Rwanda. They claim that the estimated 30,000 refugees who have crossed the border since Sunday are dead, although journalists and other witnesses have seen them walking home safely. . . . So rumors and threats circulate daily from members of the former regime's murderous militias and the Interahamwe, the armed youth wing of the government party. . . . Their *propaganda machine* is in full swing again. Many refugees insist, for example, that the Tutsi caused the cholera epidemic by poisoning the water. And nearly all are convinced they will be mutilated or killed by the new regime if they go home. "We've heard all the refugees [who went back] have no eyes anymore," 28-year-old Primitiy Mukandemzo warned. . . . Frediana Mukamunana, 54, using her finger to slash in the air as she spoke, shouted: "They cut out the heart, the eyes, the intestines! And they put people in cars and burn them!" "They will put us in houses and burn us," whispered 18-year-old Faustin Ntanshuti. . . . Educated Rwandans are just as terrified. "They will kill all the intellectuals," said Alphonse Harerimana, a physician working at the Doctors Without Borders tent hospital for cholera cases. (Drogin 1994:A3, A11; emphasis added)

Such reports pain the refugees' refusal to comply with the repatriation policy as a symptom of their hysterical, superstitious, overdramatic frame of mind. What fails to be mentioned is that violence such as that described above has repeatedly occurred in the region; there are numerous historical precedents for all these forms of atrocity, as any student of the area knows (African Rights 1994; Malkki 1995a; Prunier 1995). That the refugees talk about such terrifying violence is not a psychological fact but a historical one.

In the face of the refugees' resistance, many tactics and arguments have been used to persuade and cajole the refugees since 1994. UN officials on the scene have on several occasions issued statements emphasizing the safety of returnees in spite of the fact that the United Nations has had no adequate staff of mobile observers on site within Rwanda, and no good way of knowing what has become of those who actually returned. The following was reported on July 27, 1994:

Wilkinson of the U.N. refugee agency said not a single returnee is known to have been injured or killed by soldiers of the new regime. "All the indications we've got is things are very stable there and the people who have gone back have had absolutely no problems," he said. (Drogin 1994:A11)

The same news report stated that "a reporter who explained to several old women that it was safe to return" was shouted down by angry young refugee men. " 'You're telling lies!' they shouted angrily. 'It is not possible. Those who went back yesterday were all killed yesterday!' " (Drogin 1994:A11). On July 31, 1994, it was further reported that "U.S. Special Forces psychological warfare teams would bring in radio equipment to help the new government encourage more than a million refugees in neighboring Zaire to return home. The Tutsi-led government has assured Hutu refugees that there will be no reprisals for the massacres of Tutsis" (*Los Angeles Times* 1994:A7). Along the same lines, an August 6, 1994, report in the *Economist* states:

The U.N. hopes to persuade more to return by setting up counter-propaganda. It is establishing a "Blue Beret" radio station and is giving technical help to Radio Rwanda, now under RPF control, so that it can broadcast to the refugee camps. It also hopes to coax refugees back by deploying more peacekeepers in Rwanda and offering refugees food, water, and medical care at way-stations along the route home. (1994:35)

But how were these early assurances of safety to be reconciled with other, contradictory reports documenting the growing incidence of reprisals against returnees, seizures of land, disappearances, and other disturbing practices? *Le Monde*'s Langellier already reported on August 7, 1994, that "more and more people have been 'disappearing'" in Kigali, that homes and lands abandoned by the people fleeing into Zaire have been reallocated by the RPF, and that "arbitrary seizures, accompanied in rural areas by the large-scale displacement of communities, amounts to a de facto ban on their rightful occupants' return" (Langellier 1994:16). Some days later, on August 16, 1994, the *Los Angeles Times* quoted a "veteran relief agency leader," who declined to be identified, as saying that the RPF army in Rwanda "has never shown any interest in keeping this [Hutu] population. Rwanda was overpopulated. Now they have an abundance of fields" (Balzar 1994c:A4; compare Bonner 1994).

If reports of reprisals against the few Hutu returnees have convinced the refugees of the danger of repatriation, so, too, has the incarceration of some 58,000–60,000 people accused of participation in the genocide in Rwandan prisons. The criminal lawyer Adam Stapleton reports for the *Human Rights Tribune*:

The single most pressing concern was the arbitrary arrest and detention of hundreds of people each week. Suspects were detained on the say-so of anyone, particularly if the suspect was Hutu and the accuser Tutsi, and charged with genocide.... The army arrested and detained people unchecked (by March [1994] the average weekly rate was estimated to be 1,300) and the displaced persons and refugees refused to move out of their camps arguing... that it was not safe to return home. The appalling conditions and increasing daily death toll from dysentery and diseases associated with chronic overcrowding make the prisons a time-bomb. (1995:15)

The refugees' fears were further exacerbated in April 1995, when hundreds (by some accounts thousands)[22] of Hutu were killed by the RPF-led Rwandan forces in the displaced persons camp of Kibeho in southwestern Rwanda. Before people fled the camp in panic, 70,000–100,000 were living there. The government forces stated that the camp and others like it were "filled with armed militias" and had to be disbanded (Lorch 1995a:A1, A4).

It is plain to see that the repatriation question is very complex. It is problematic for many reasons to have hundreds of thousands of people living in exile outside of Rwanda; it is no less problematic to push them back into Rwanda. This essay does not presume to propose a solution to the crisis. So much said, it was a terrible responsibility that the international organizations assumed in urging the refugees to go back "home," for this has been the predominant argument throughout, despite the fact that the United Nations has more recently expressed concern over the dangers of repatriation, and has publicly objected to Zaire's recent announcements about closing the camps one by one.

How could anyone guarantee that no retaliatory violence would erupt, when anyone familiar with the region's history (and with the social struggles over history there) would be forced to recognize that such violence would be, at best, unsurprising? How could anyone think that in the wake of a genocide the political situation in Rwanda is "stable"? What questions, what considerations, override these in importance?

There is every reason to suppose that the violence that has so shocked the world has similarly shocked those who were its Rwandan victims and witnesses. This is a scale and kind of violence that is not often seen in the world. It is, literally, extraordinary. And because of this, it must have forced people in the region to rethink the universe of what is possible and thinkable – just as genocidal violence in recent European history has reconfigured social universes there. In the wake of the past two years, anything would seem to be possible. Politically, intellectually, conceptually, affectively – in all these ways it would seem wise and realistic to acknowledge the horror of what has happened by not forcing, cajoling, or tricking people to return to the still very dangerous sites of their shame and tragedy.

Time must be allowed to pass so that the refugees waiting and watching in Zaire can make a reasonable, well-founded assessment of their alternatives. Time is also required from the humanitarian agencies involved. Surely they would not wish to have to acknowledge that they have marched people to their deaths in their desire to do away with a refugee crisis.

Time must be given to the tasks of witnessing and testimony, on both sides of the Rwanda–Zaire border, among Tutsi and Hutu. Beresford has rightly observed that there is . . . a forgetfulness in the world's fixation with the relief disaster that is Goma. The story of Rwanda is not that of a cholera epidemic, terrible though it may be; cholera is the consequence of the central horror of the last few months – genocide. . . . Genocide invites a Nuremberg. (1994:6)

For any kind of accounting or public justice to become a real possibility, all the parties concerned (national, regional, and international) would have to consent to become an audience to the "involved" stories that the inhabitants of this terrorized region have to tell. The obstacles to such accounting at all levels have become very clear in the funding and other difficulties that the UN-organized war crimes tribunal has faced.

The genocide in Rwanda has already happened; it is not possible to go back and change interventions or omissions of the past. But the dangerous effects of silencing are still all too salient in currently unfolding events in the region. The Hutu refugees from Rwanda are still in Zaire, Tanzania, and elsewhere, and, as of this writing (February 1996), refusing repatriation, still the objects of concerted efforts from the Zairean government, the United Nations, and various other agencies to push them back where they "belong." The effects of such silencing are detectable in neighboring Burundi, also. By ignoring the continual political persecution, intimidation, and killings occurring in that country, the "international community" risks coming face to face with another Rwanda-like period of terror there and finding that nothing that could have been done has been done (Balzar 1994b).

But preventive measures do not come easily in the conventional logic of the "humanitarian operation." For humanitarian help to be mobilized, the disaster usually must have happened already. When refugees and orphans have been pro-duced, then the site for intervention is visible. Otherwise, the matter is "political" (or a "domestic" issue in a sovereign state) and thus beyond the realm of humanitarian intervention (De Waal 1994:10).

Conclusion

It is obviously neither logically nor practically necessary that humanitarian interven-tion in and of itself dehistoricize or depoliticize. And I would like to make perfectly clear that by studying certain of the transnationally shared aspects of humanitarian intervention in refugee issues, I am not thereby seeking to belittle the importance of the moral, ethical, and political motivations that are clearly at the core of humani-tarian interventions.[23] It *is* necessary to state that these forms and practices of humanitarianism do not represent the best of all possible worlds, and that it is politically and intellectually possible to try to come up with something better. Especially in the face of the political crisis in Rwanda, and the very real possibility that the political situation in Burundi will soon become much worse than it already is, it is necessary to do better. Perhaps a part (a crucial part) of the improvement is to be found in a radically "historicizing humanism" that insists on acknowledging not only human suffering but also narrative authority, historical agency, and political memory. Barthes' call for a progressive humanism (1980:101) addressed this very issue, as do Foucault's later writings; he suggested why it is more useful to seek to connect people through history and historicity than through a human essence (or "human nature"). This is not to make a simple, romantic argument about "giving the people a voice"; for one would find underneath the silence not a voice waiting to be liberated but ever-deeper historical layers of silencing and bitter, complicated regional struggles over history and truth.

It is a historicizing (and politicizing) humanism that would require us, politically and analytically, to examine our cherished notions of mankind and the human community, humanitarianism and humanitarian "crises," human rights and international justice. For if humanism can only constitute itself on the bodies of dehistoricized, archetypal refugees and other similarly styled victims – if clinical and philanthropic modes of humanitarianism are the only options – then citizenship in this human community itself remains curiously, indecently, outside of history.

NOTES

1   The term "selective genocide" is from Lemarchand and Martin (1974) and was widely used.
2   Compare Rée (1992) and Malkki (1994, 1995b).
3   I would like to thank Daniel Segal for pointing out the presence of the universal family in this imagery. The universal figures of man, woman, and child are, of course, often (but not always) constitutive of that other abstraction, "the family," as Barthes' classic essay, "The Great Family of Man," showed (1980:100–2; Segal, personal communication, March 8, 1996).
4   Humanitarian interventions take place largely within an internationalist institutional and conceptual framework; that is, they depend on the concept of an "international community" (compare Malkki 1994). Thus, the concept of internationalism is an integral part of any discussion of international community and international responsibility. In a longer essay it would be productive to combine the critical study of humanitarianism with longstanding debates about internationalism. For the present, this larger set of questions may be indicated by Craig Calhoun's particularly clearsighted discussion of internationalism in the context of Rwanda and Bosnia in his foreword to Micheline Ishay's *Internationalism and Its Betrayal*:

In both cases [Bosnia and Rwanda], the problem of internationalism does not just arise with questions about universal human rights and possible humanitarian interventions, but is constitutive of the very crises themselves in ways not unrelated to the blind spots of liberal individualism.

The problem is not just that international diplomats and multilateral agencies mishandled the two specific situations [Bosnia and Rwanda]: the entire international framework for understanding nationalism and related conflicts is deeply flawed. Among other things, it systematically obscures such international influences on the production of domestic, putatively entirely ethnic, struggles. It also leaves well-intentioned international actors with no good way of grasping their connection to the genocides and nationalist wars that have marred – but systematically marked – the twentieth century. Not only do these appear often as premodern inheritances, and therefore disconnected from genuinely modern and even contemporary sources, but they appear as fundamentally separate from the institutions and discourse of the respectable international community. Diplomats and analysts fail to see the connection between the structuring of the international community as a world system of putative nation-states, of making adaptation to the rhetoric of nationalism a condition for entrance into the United Nations, and the pernicious forms of nationalism they decry. Not only they but many of the rest of us fail to reflect on the ironic nationalism reproduced in asking whether intervention in genocidal wars is or is not a part of the compelling national interest of the United States or any other country. (Calhoun 1995:xiii)

5   The official designation of these camps by the Tanzanian Ministry for Home Affairs as well as TCRS and UNHCR was "refugee settlement"; however, the refugee residents of Mishamo always referred to it as a camp. Their reasons are discussed in Malkki (1995a).

6   It is not known how many people returned from the Hutu refugee camps in Tanzania to Burundi when the first democratic elections in that country brought a Hutu president, Melchior Ndadaye, to power in 1993 (compare Lemarchand 1994b).

7   This discussion also appears in Malkki (1995a).

8   I would like to thank Referee 1 for helping me to think further about this issue. Referee 1 remarks: "Antagonism against commercial classes is especially strong during periods of significant inflation as occurred with the economic policies of 'liberalization' followed by the Tanzanian [government] over these years. The idea that a 'fellow refugee' could raise prices and create hardship for those of his or her own group was a contradiction to the norm of refugee culture."

9   The officials of the Ministry of Home Affairs of the United Republic of Tanzania were also very generous in their assistance, but their relationship to the refugees was quite different from that of the non-governmental organizations, as I have shown elsewhere (Malkki 1995a).

10 I would like to thank Referee 1 for suggestions on this section.

11 Individual persons in UNHCR and TCRS have also engaged very seriously with my research in the Hutu refugee communities in Tanzania and have given me valuable critical feedback.

12 Referee 1 comments here: "From my experience, for example, in the Rwandan camps, it was astounding how the aid communities have selected texts that correspond with their image; having no other access to a wider range of discourse, and often dependent on their own interpreters for their impressions, they simply end up magnifying the very oppositions they claim to oppose – in a process that amount[s] to an excellent example of creating alterity."

13 Ortner's (1991) essay has helped me to think through issues of narrativity and historical agency.

14 Another news photograph of a tightly packed group of children with cups in their hands has the caption "A drop in the ocean of misery.... Rwandan children wait for water at Kibumba camp near Goma, Zaire" (Trequesser 1994:4).

15 Compare Debord: "The spectacle is not a collection of images, but a social relation among people, mediated by images" (1983:2).

16 Other pictures with short captions but without stories appeared in the *New York Times* (1995a:A5; 1995b:E2); compare *Life* (1994:74–80).

17 This should be seen in the more general context of the gross underreporting of the violence that started in Burundi in October 1993.

18 In a theme issue on Africa, *Granta*, a literary magazine, published twenty-two pages of black-and-white photographs of the dead and wounded in the Rwanda genocide. The photographs were taken by Gilles Press.

19 Estimates vary. The figure of 50,000 cholera victims is cited in Lorch (1995b:A1); compare Balzar (1994d:A23).

20 And, of course, "voluntary repatriation" is inscribed in the operating code of the UNHCR as the primary, and ideal, "durable solution" to displacement. See Warner's reflections on the implications of this ideal and its relation to the social imagination of "home" by refugee organizations (1994:1ff.).

21 Compare Balibar on citizenship: he contrasts "citizenship understood in its strict sense as the full exercise of political rights and in its broad sense as cultural initiative or effective presence in the public space (the capacity to be 'listened to' there)" (1988:724). It is in this broad sense that the international citizenship of the refugees from Burundi and Rwanda has been denied in the arena commonly named "the international community" (compare Foucault, as cited in Macey 1993:437–8).

22 Estimates vary. See, for example, Lorch (1995a:A1, A4).

23 I also do not wish to imply that all relief, aid, refugee, and humanitarian agencies espouse the same philosophy; I am only attempting to identify a dominant tendency. There are, happily, dissonant voices in the ranks of these agencies, as in the following case:

"If the U.N. doesn't learn from this, God help the next poor souls of the world who need help," said John O'Shea of the Irish relief agency GOAL, which has been active here [in Rwanda] since the beginning of the crisis. Using bitter profanities, O'Shea said the United Nations has failed to meet the refugees' needs and has made no serious effort to make them feel safe going home. (Cited in Balzar 1994a:A6)

REFERENCES

African Rights (1994). *Rwanda: Death, Despair and Defiance*. London: African Rights.

Amnesty International (1993). *Rwanda. Extrajudicial Execution/Fear of Extrajudicial Execution/Fear of Torture/Incommunicado Detention*. UA 41/93. AI Index AFR 47/03/93. February 18:1. Mimeograph marked for general distribution.

Balibar, Etienne (1988). "Propositions on Citizenship." *Ethics* 98:723–30.

Balibar, Etienne (1995). "Ambiguous Universality." *Differences: A Journal of Feminist Cultural Studies* 7(1):48–74.

Balzar, John (1994a). "UN Admits Its Efforts to Persuade Rwandans to Go Home Are Failing." *Los Angeles Times* (August 13):A6.

Balzar, John (1994b). "Burundi Battles Its Demons in Fight to Survive." *Los Angeles Times* (August 15):A3, A10.

Balzar, John (1994c). "Rwanda's New Leaders Accused of Harassing Refugees." *Los Angeles Times* (August 16):A4.

Balzar, John (1994d). "Plight of Sick and Dying Refugees Is Price Rwandans Pay for Hatred." *Los Angeles Times* (August 20):A23.

Barthes, Roland (1980). *Mythologies*. New York: Hill and Wang.

Beresford, David (1994). "Who Bears the Guilt of Africa's Horror?" *Manchester Guardian Weekly* (August 7):6.

Bonner, Raymond (1994). "Rwandan Refugees in Zaire Still Fear to Return." *New York Times* (November 10):A3.

Calhoun, Craig (1995). "Foreword." In M. Ishay, *Internationalism and Its Betrayal*. Minneapolis: University of Minnesota Press, pp. ix–xiv.

Clifford, James (1988). *The Predicament of Culture: Twentieth-Century Ethnography, Literature, and Art*. Cambridge, MA: Harvard University Press.

Debord, Guy (1983). *Society of the Spectacle*. Detroit: Black and Red.

Destexhe, Alain (1994). *Rwanda: Essai sur le génocide*. Brussels: Éditions Complexe.

De Waal, Alex (1994). "A Lesson to Learn from Rwanda." *Wider Angle*. Helsinki: United Nations University/World Institute for Development Economics Research 2/94 (December 28):9–10.

Drakulič, Slavenka (1993). *Balkan Express: Fragments from the Other Side of the War*. London: Hutchinson.

Drogin, Bob (1994). "Refugees Get Steady Diet of Propaganda." *Los Angeles Times* (July 27):A3, A11.

Economist (1994). "A Sort of Peace." August 6:34–5.

Feldman, Allen (1994). "On Cultural Anesthesia: From Desert Storm to Rodney King." *American Ethnologist* 21:404–18.

Ferguson, James (1994). *The Anti-Politics Machine: "Development," Depoliticization, and Bureaucratic Power in Lesotho*. Minneapolis: University of Minnesota Press.

Ferguson, James (1995). "From African Socialism to Scientific Capitalism: Reflections on the Legitimation Crisis in IMF-Ruled Africa." In D. B. Moore and G. J. Schmitz (eds.), *Debating Development Discourse: Institutional and Popular Perspectives*. New York: St. Martin's Press, pp. 129–48.

Ferguson, James (in press). "Paradoxes of Sovereignty and Independence: 'Real' and 'Pseudo' Nation-States and the Depoliticization of Poverty." In K. Hastrup and K. Fog Olwig (eds.), *Siting Culture*. New York: Routledge.

Forbes Martin, Susan (1992). *Refugee Women*. London: Zed.

Granta (1994). "Rwanda." Photographs by Gilles Peress. 48:104–25.

Guichaoua, André (1995). *Les Crises politiques au Burundi et au Rwanda (1993–1994)*. Paris: Karthala.

Ishay, Micheline (1995). *Internationalism and Its Betrayal*. Minneapolis: University of Minnesota Press.

Jefremovas, Villia (n.d.). "The Rwandan State and Local Level Response: Class and Region in the Rwandan Genocide, the Refugee Crisis, Repatriation and the 'New Rwanda.'" Unpublished manuscript.

Kismaric, Carole (1989). *Forced Out: The Agony of the Refugee in Our Time*. New York: Human Rights Watch and the J. M. Kaplan Fund in association with William Morrow, W. W. Norton, Penguin Books, and Random House.

Lamb, David (1994). "Threading through a Surreal World on the Way to Tragedy in Rwanda." *Los Angeles Times* (June 14):H1, H5.

Langellier, Jean-Pierre (1994). "Breaking through the Fear Barrier." *Manchester Guardian Weekly* (August 7):16.

Lemarchand, René (1994a). "The Apocalypse in Rwanda." *Cultural Survival Quarterly* (Summer/Fall):29–39.

Lemarchand, René (1994b). *Burundi: Ethnocide as Discourse and Practice*. New York: Cambridge University Press.

Lemarchand, René and Martin, David (1974). *Selective Genocide in Burundi*. Report No. 20. London: Minority Rights Group.

Life (1994). "Eyewitness Rwanda." *September*:74–80.

Loescher, Gilbert and Monahan, L. (eds.) (1989). *Refugees and International Relations*. Oxford: Oxford University Press.

Lorch, Donatella (1995a). "As Many as 2,000 Are Reported Dead in Rwanda." *New York Times* (April 24):A1, A4.

Lorch, Donatella (1995b). "A Year Later, Rwandans Stay and Chaos Looms." *New York Times* (July 15):A1, A5.

Los Angeles Times (1993). "Burundi Refugees Enter Rwanda." October 25:A3.

Los Angeles Times (1994). "First U.S. Troops Reach Rwandan Capital to Secure Airport." July 31:A7.

Macey, David (1993). *The Lives of Michel Foucault: A Biography.* New York: Pantheon.

Malkki, Liisa (1994). "Citizens of Humanity: Internationalism and the Imagined Community of Nations." *Diaspora* 3(1):41–68.

Malkki, Liisa (1995a). *Purity and Exile: Violence, Memory, and National Cosmology among Hutu Refugees in Tanzania.* Chicago: University of Chicago Press.

Malkki, Liisa (1995b). "Refugees and Exile: From 'Refugee Studies' to the National Order of Things." *Annual Review of Anthropology* 24:495–523.

Mbonimpa, Melchior (1993). *Hutu, Tutsi, Twa: Pour une société sans castes au Burundi.* Paris: L'Harmattan.

McClintock, Anne (1992). "The Angel of Progress: Pitfalls of the Term 'Post-Colonialism.'" *Social Text* 10(2–3):84–98.

McGreal, Chris (1994). "Chaos and Cholera Ravage Rwandans." *Manchester Guardian Weekly* (July 31):1.

New York Times (1995a). "Tanzania Closes Its Border to Rwandans Fleeing Burundi." April 1:A5.

New York Times (1995b). "Tired, Hungry, and Far from Home." April 2:E2.

Newbury, Catherine and Newbury, David (1994). "Rwanda: The Politics of Turmoil." *African Studies Association Newsletter* 27(3):9–11.

Newbury, Catherine and Newbury, David (1995). "Identity, Genocide, and Reconstruction in Rwanda." Unpublished manuscript.

Ortner, Sherry (1991). *Narrativity in History, Culture, and Lives.* Comparative Study in Social Transformations Working Paper, 66. Ann Arbor: University of Michigan.

Pottier, Johan (1994). "Representations of Ethnicity in Post-Genocide Writings in Rwanda." Unpublished manuscript.

Prunier, Gérard (1995). *The Rwanda Crisis: History of a Genocide.* New York: Columbia University Press.

Rée, Jonathan (1992). "Internationality." *Radical Philosophy* 60:3–11.

Reyntjens, Filip (1994). *L'Afrique des grands lacs en crise: Rwanda, Burundi: 1988–1994.* Paris: Karthala.

Rusciano, Frank and Fiske-Rusciano, Roberta (1990). "Towards a Notion of 'World Opinion.'" *International Journal of Public Opinion Research* 2(4):305–22.

Smith, Steven (1994). "A Butare." *Libération,* May 27.

Stapleton, Adam (1995). "Amateurs Posing as Professionals: The United Nations Human Rights Field Operation in Rwanda." *Human Rights Tribune* 3(2):13–15.

Stein, Barry (1981). "The Refugee Experience: Defining the Parameters of a Field of Study." *International Migration Review* 15(1):320–30.

Tambiah, Stanley (1985). *Culture, Thought, and Social Action: An Anthropological Perspective.* Cambridge, MA: Harvard University Press.

Trequesser, Gilles (1994). "UN Ready for New Refugee Exodus." *Manchester Guardian Weekly* (August 14):4.

Warner, Daniel (1994). "Voluntary Repatriation and the Meaning of Return to Home: A Critique of Liberal Mathematics." Paper prepared for the Fourth International Research and Advisory Panel Conference, Somerville College, University of Oxford, January 5–9.

Warrick, Pamela (1994). "Tipper Gore's Mission of Mercy." *Los Angeles Times* (August 15):E1, E2.

Zolberg, Aristide, Suhrke, Astri, and Aguayo Sergio, (1989). *Escape from Violence: Conflict and the Refugee Crisis in the Developing World.* Oxford: Oxford University Press.

Appendix:
Websites on Genocide

General genocide websites with key links (both to other general sites and to sites with information about specific genocides; some of these sites also include on-line bibliographies, news reports, data banks, survivor memoirs, documentation, syllabi, warning alerts, and general information about genocide).

- **The Genocide Research Project, University of Memphis and Penn State University**
  http://www.people.memphis.edu/~genocide/
- **Institute for the Study of Genocide**
  http://www.isg-ags.org
- **Montreal Institute for Genocide and Human Rights Studies**
  http://www.migs.org
- **Web Genocide Documentation Centre**
  http://www.ess.uwe.ac.uk/genocide.htm
- **The Center for Holocaust and Genocide Studies, University of Minnesota**
  http://chgs.hispeed.com/
- **Australian Institute for Holocaust and Genocide Studies, Shalom College**
  http://www.aihgs.com/
- **Yale Genocide Studies Program**
  http://www.yale.edu/gsp/
- **Danish Center for Holocaust and Genocide Studies**
  http://www.dchf.dk/
- **Center for the Study of the Holocaust, Genocide, and Human Rights**
  http://www.webster.edu/~woolflm/cshghr.html
- **United States Holocaust Memorial Museum**
  http://www.ushmm.org
- **The Genocide Factor**
  http://www.genocidefactor.com

- Center for Holocaust, Genocide, and Peace Studies, University of Nevada, Reno
  http://www.unr.edu/chgps/blank.htm
- Fortunoff Video Archive for Holocaust Testimonies
  http://www.library.yale.edu/testimonies/index.html
- Cultural Survival
  http://www.cs.org

EARLY WARNING, PREVENTION, AND CRIMINALIZATION

- Minorities at Risk Project, University of Maryland
  http://www.bsos.umd.edu:80/cidcm/mar/
- Genocide Watch
  http://www.genocidewatch.com
- Prevent Genocide
  http://www.preventgenocide.org
- Rome Statute of the International Criminal Court
  http://www.un.org/law/icc/index.html
- Campaign to End Genocide
  http://www.endgenocide.org/

Index

Abacha, General Sani 342
Abel, Theodore 195
Aché Indians, destruction of 4, 63, 68
Africa
    Belgian and German colonization 336,
        347
    Berlin Africa Conference (1884–5) 148–9
    emigrants to France 223
    see also individual countries
agriculture, and ecology 147
Aguayo, Sergio 329
Ahmed, Akbar S., overview of chapter 10
Akuriyo Indians 153–4
Alberti, Leon Battista 121
Albigensian Crusade 49–50
alcohol, WWII, German-occupied
        countries 35
Algeria, colonization of 51, 61–2, 223
Alsace-Lorraine *see* Lorraine
Amazon Indians 147, 156–7
American Association for the Advancement
        of Science 320
Amnesty International 356
Anderson, Benedict 237, 292, 297
anemia, rise of in WWII 34
anti-Semitism *see* Jews
Appadurai, Arjun, overview of chapter 11
Arabs, and Palestinians 224
Arana, Julio César 170, 173–4, 176
arap Moi, Daniel 342

Arendt, Hannah 48, 74, 114, 320
    overview of chapter 6
Arensberg, Conrad M. 148
Argentina
    indigenous peoples 154
    population 141
    terror 316, 318
Armenians 52, 54, 85
Arnold of Cîteaux 49
Assyrian empire 48
Asturias, Miguel Angel 166
aucas 178–9
Australia
    Aborigines 139, 150, 151, 157
    population 141
    tribal depopulation 158, 159
Ayodhya riots 217–18, 221–2, 223, 225

Badayuni, Shakeel 220
Bailey, Robert 152
Balibar, Etienne 365
Balkans *see* Bosnia-Hercegovina; Croatia;
        Serbia; Yugoslavia
Bangladesh *see* East Pakistan
banks, WWII, German-occupied
        countries 32
Barillas, Danilo 316
Barrès, Maurice 114
Barthes, Roland 362
Bartov, Omer 194

Bateson, Gregory 15
Baum, Rainer 195
Bauman, Zygmunt 194, 213, 286, 287, 293
    overview of chapter 6–7
Belgium
    Africa, colonization in 336, 347
    WWII, German occupation 33, 34
Benjamin, Walter 166, 185, 307
Beresford, David 361–2
Berlin Africa Conference (1884–5) 148–9
Bettelheim, Bruno 100
Béziers, storming of (1209) 49–50
Bhindranwale, Sant 293
Biafra 342
biological genocide 32–3, 60
Birnblat, Hirsch 100
birthrates, German manipulation of in
        WWII 32–3
BJP (political party) 221, 222
Black Death 50
Bloch, Ernst 351
Boas, Franz 10
Bodley, John H., overview of chapter 7–8
body, as site of violence 289–92, 294–9
Bohemia-Moravia, German occupation in
        WWII 34, 54, 62
Böhme, General Franz 92–3
Bonner, Raymond 358–9
Borges, Jorge 168
Bosnia-Hercegovina
    civil war 246
    civil war, road to 241–3
    demographics 235, 236, 237, 238, 239
    ethnic cleansing 212, 215, 217, 224, 225,
        226
    Republika Srpska 231, 241
Bowen, John R., overview of chapter 13
Brazil
    genocide (1970) 85
    indigenous peoples 63, 159, 160
    northeast 309
    rubber industry 156
    Xavante tribe 154–5
Brecht, Bertolt 315
Brussels Act (1892) 149
Buddhism 254, 255, 261, 275, 277
Bulger, James 222
bureaucracy
    and dehumanization 128–30
    and the Holocaust 95–6, 130–2, 194, 195,
        213

and personal responsibility 6–7, 104–9,
        111, 125–8
    and social engineering 7
Burke, William 307
Burundi
    genocide (1972) 59, 69, 85, 289–90
    genocide (1993) 354–5
    history 336–7, 347
    refugees from 13, 344–52

Calhoun, Craig 363–4
Cambodia
    genocide, reasons for 15–16, 254–75
    history 276
    Khmer Rouge regime 2, 11–12, 52, 80,
        254, 263, 267–75
    peasant disaffection 266–7
    Samlaut rebellion (1967) 265–6
    US bombing 267
    Vietnamese invasion 261, 262
Cameroon, witchcraft 291
Camus, Albert 308
Canada
    Cree Indians 157
    population 141
    see also North America
cannibalism
    Bosnian genocide 295
    Burundi genocide 290
    Cambodia 261–2
    Cameroon 291
    Central and South America 321
    China 294–5
    as genocide tool 295
    Putumayo Indians 176, 177, 178, 180–2,
        190–1
capital punishment, among Huitotos
        181–2
capitalism
    and Khmer Rouge 268
    and South American rubber
        industry 172–5, 184
    see also globalization
Carthage, destruction of 48
Casement, Roger
    background 168
    and the Congo 168–9
    Putumayo report 8, 157, 169–85
categorization, and genocide 9–10
    see also ethnicity
Cathars, suppression of 49–50

Catholics and Catholic Church
  Albigensian Crusade 49–50
  Guatemala 318, 319
  and the Holocaust 108, 227
  and Huguenots 50
  Inquisition 49, 50
  in Northern Ireland 68
Cavalli-Sforza, Luigi 152
Cerezo, Vinicio 316
Ceylon see Sri Lanka
Chakrabarty, Dipesh 301
Chalk, Frank 79, 80, 81, 85
change, attitudes to 155
Charny, Israel W. 79
Châteaubriant, martyrs of 54, 62
Chatterjee, Suhas 146
Chiapas 340
children, as refugees 349, 353, 354–5
China, Cultural Revolution 294–5
Chinese, in Malaysia 341
Chittagong Hills peoples 143–5
cholera 358
Christians
  and the Holocaust 108, 227
  Ottoman empire 53
  see also Catholics and Catholic Church;
    Crusades; Protestants and Protestant
    Church; Tanganyika Christian Refugee
    Service
chupe del tabaco 181
Churchill, Winston S. 54, 223
citizenship, in Yugoslav successor
    states 243–5
Clausewitz, Karl Marie von 317
Clinton, Bill 342
Cohn, Carol 312
Colombia, rubber industry and Putumayo
    Indians 8, 169–85
colonization
  colonial aftermath 223
  colonizer and colonized, relations
    between 165–85
  conquistadores 168, 315
  and genocide 50–1, 52, 68, 79, 194,336–7
  justifications for 148–9
commercialization 140, 147
communism, Khmer Rouge ideology 267–9
CONAVIGUA 329–30
Congo
  in Heart of Darkness 167–8, 175
  Pygmies 152

rubber industry 167, 168–9
tribal depopulation 158
see also Zaire
Congress Party 221
Connerton, Paul 328
Connor, Walker 215
conquistadores 168, 315
Conrad, Joseph 167–9, 175, 177
consumption 140, 141–5
counterinsurgency 309, 312
Croatia
  citizenship 244–5
  civil war 246, 248, 339
  Constitution 240
  demographics 236, 237, 238, 239
  Serbian Krajina, Constitution 241
  WWII 335
Croats outside Croatia 242, 246, 335
Crusades 49
culture
  cultural activities, WWII, German-
    occupied countries 31
  cultural genocide 4–5, 51, 60–1, 78
  cultural models 255, 277
  and power 204–6
Cunninghame Graham, R. B. 168
Czechoslovakia
  ethnic purity 248
  WWII, German occupation 33, 97

Dadrian, Vahakn 79–80, 85
Darwin, Charles 157
Das, Veena 292–3
Dawidowicz, Lucy S. 132
Dayton-Paris Treaty 242–3, 246–7
de Gaulle, Charles 223
deathrates, WWII, German-occupied
    countries 34
debt-peonage system, rubber industry 156,
    170, 174–5
dehumanization, and genocide 68, 128–30,
    195, 271
denationalization 28
development projects 318–19
Diamond, Stanley 150
Dominican friars 50
Doughty, Paul 309
Douglas, Mary 9, 290, 291
Drost, Pieter N. 78
Dutch East Indies 341
  see also Indonesia

East Pakistan
  Chittagong Hills peoples, treatment
    of 143–5
  ethnic conflict (1971) 211
East Timor 340
Eckart, Dietrich 114
ecology, and agriculture 147
economic deprivation, and ethnic
    confrontation 218
Ecuador, Zaparos 177–8
education
  inter-faith education 227–8
  refugees 349
  see also schools
Egypt, and UN Genocide Convention 60
Eichmann, Adolf
  as bureaucrat 7, 95–6
  death 99, 103
  guilt 6, 99–109
  personality 102–3
  trial 91–8
El Salvador, civil war 313
Elias, Norbert 110, 196, 206
emigration, mass 141
Endre, László 94
Enghien, Duc d' 105
environmental issues
  ecology and agriculture 147
  resource consumption 140, 141–5
  species depletion 147
ethnic cleansing 10
  Bosnia-Hercegovina 212, 215, 217, 224,
    225, 226
  prevention 227–8
  reasons for 211–27, 231–48
  Yugoslavia 10–11, 231–48, 335–6, 339,
    342
ethnicity 215–16
  and colonization 336–7
  establishing 289–97
  and genocide 13
  and globalization 11, 286–9, 297–9
  as modern phenomenon 334–6
  and political instability 340–2
ethnocentrism, and small-scale
    cultures 145–9, 154–5
ethnocide 5, 146
eugenics, and the Nazis 32–3, 120
euthanasia, and the Nazis 118
evangelists 259, 318
Evans, Mike 259

Falla, Ricardo 310
Fanon, Frantz 350
fear, effects of 307–28
Fein, Helen, overview of chapter 5
Feldman, Allen 297, 299–300, 301, 318,
    353
fieldwork, methods of 234–5
Fiji 214
films
  Indian 220
  influence of 222
Final Solution see Holocaust
Fitzpatrick, Sheila 300
Flores, Gilda 316
food, WWII, German-occupied
    countries 33–4
Foucault, Michel 166, 167–8, 362–3
Four-Power Agreement (1945) 54
Fox, Richard 201
France
  Albigensian Crusade 49–50
  Algeria, colonization of 51, 61–2, 223
  Constitution 223
  Huguenots, persecution of 50
  humanitarian interventions 53, 54
  racism 214, 223, 286
  in seventeenth and eighteenth
    centuries 197–8
  and UN Genocide Convention 58, 65
  WWII, German occupation 33
Fromm, Erich 67
fuel, WWII, German-occupied countries
    34
Fuentes, Carlos 175
funerals, Guatemala 324

GAM see Grupo de Apoyo Mutuo
gambling, WWII, German-occupied
    countries 35
Gandhi, Indira 220
Gandhi, Mohandas Karamchand
    (Mahatma) 223
Genghis Khan 48–9
genocide
  biological genocide 32–3, 60
  as bodily discovery 289–92, 294–9
  and colonization 50–1, 52, 68, 79, 194,
    336–7
  contexts 84
  cultural genocide 4–5, 51, 60–1, 78
  definitions 2, 3, 5–6, 27–8, 76–82, 276

genocide (*cont'd*)
and dehumanization 68, 128–30, 195, 271
difficulty of explaining 1–2
and ethnicity 13
etymology 3–4, 27, 55
first use in legal documents 55
and governments 69
historic examples of 48–50
Holocaust as 103
and ideology 68–9, 84
and jurisprudence 35–8, 102–9
as metaphor 74
and migrations 297
and modernity 6–11, 110–32, 213
myths of 13
non-genocidal societies 69–70, 340–2
preconditions 86
previous research 2–3
primes of 14–15, 338–40
quantification 5, 61–2
and religion 49–50, 52
as social construct 6
as social engineering 120–2
and social man 67–8
and sociology 74–88
and the state 79
techniques 4, 28–35, 60–1
and totalitarianism 52
typologies 85–6
Germany
Africa, colonization in 336
anti-Semitism 194–5, 199, 292
and colonization 194, 199
Constitution 223
pre-Third Reich history 197–9
racism 214
South West Africa, colonization of 51
Third Reich 192–206
Thirty Years' War (1618–48) 50
WWII, conduct of 200–1
WWII, domestic food rationing 33
WWII, treatment of occupied nations 28–35, 76–7, 92–3
see also Holocaust; Nazi Party
Geschiere, Peter 291
Ghurye, G. S. 146
Giddens, Anthony 110, 125, 214, 218–19
Glenny, Misha 335

globalization
and ethnic confrontation 11, 218–22, 286–9, 297–9
and indigenous peoples 7–8, 137–41, 149–56
and refugees 352–5
Gluckman, Max 215
Glücks, Richard 96
GOAL 365
Goebbels, Joseph 91–2, 114, 120
Goldhagen, Daniel J. 196, 300
Gordon, Sarah 122–3
Göring, Hermann 33
Goulet, Denis 143
Gowalkar, M. S. 222
Graham, A. C. 140
Gramajo, General Alejandro 317
gratitude, in Cambodian culture 258
Great Britain
Ayodhya riots, aftermath 221
in Ceylon 337
citizenship 243
ethnic minorities 211–12, 214, 214–15
humanitarian interventions 53, 54
in India 103
and Putumayo Indians 169, 170, 174–5
resource consumption 141
and UN Genocide Convention 62
Greece, German occupation in WWII 33
Greek Independence, War of (1821–32) 53
Green, Alice 169
Green, Linda, overview of chapter 12–13
Grey, Sir Edward 169
Gridilla, Father 174, 181
Gross, Dr. Walter 118
Grupo de Apoyo Mutuo (GAM) 319
Guatemala, effects of genocide 12–13, 307–28
Guayaki Indians *see* Aché Indians
guerrilla warfare 69, 145
Gujjula, Dr. Ravindra 227
Gulag Archipelago 52
Gulf War (1991) 222
Gurr, Ted 15, 80, 85, 340
Gutiérrez, Emilio 180
Gütt, Dr. Arthur 117–18
Gypsies
Romania 297
WWII 92, 97

Habyarimana, Juvenal 338, 356
Hague Regulations 28, 35, 37, 38
Haiti 59
Hames, Raymond B. 147
Hardenburg, Walter 170, 174, 176, 181
Hardin, Russell 343
Harding, Thomas G. 155
Harerimana, Alphonse 359
Harff, Barbara 15, 80, 85
Hayden, Robert M. 287, 298
  overview of chapter 10–11
health, WWII, German-occupied
    countries 34
Heart of Darkness (Conrad) 167–8, 175
Hebron massacre (1994) 217
Herero 51
Hernandez, Crisóstomo 180–1
Hertz, Robert 324
Herzfeld, Michael 233, 300–1
heterophobia 115–16, 194–5
Hilberg, Raul 92, 131, 195
Himmler, Heinrich 93, 94, 95, 96, 97, 119,
    195
Hindus
  India, Hindu–Muslim relations 52,
    217–18, 219–22, 223, 225, 292–3, 336,
    343
  Kashmir 214
  racism 214
Hinton, Alexander Laban, overview of
    chapter 11–12
Hippler, Arthur 145–6
history, use to justify ethnic cleansing 226–7
Hitler, Adolf
  and bureaucracy 104
  death 201
  and euthanasia 118
  and genocide 29, 76–7
  and the Holocaust 95, 130–1
  Mein Kampf 197
  power of 93
  and racism 119–20
  Volksgemeinschaft 199
  see also Nazi Party
Hobbes, Thomas 111
Hochhuth, Rolf 107, 108
Hoffman, Piotr 286
Holland, Dorothy 275
Holocaust
  administration of 95–6, 130–2
  and anti-Semitism 194

brutality of 196
classification as type of crime 103
designation of victims 81, 292
as genocide 85
international condemnation of 54
Jewish resistance 100–1
as modern phenomenon 6, 120–32, 194–5
reasons for 193–5, 213
research into 75
responsibility for 102–9
Serbia 93
statistics 34
see also Eichmann, Adolf
Horowitz, Donald 341
Horowitz, Irving Louis 75
Hudson, W. H. 168
Huguenots, persecution of 50
Huitotos 169–85
Hull, Rev. William 99
humanitarian interventions 345, 349–62
  historic 53–4
Hun Sen 263, 276
Hungary, ethnic purity 248
Hunter, Monica 309
Hussites 50
Hutus
  Burundi genocide (1972) 13, 59, 69,
    289–90, 293, 344–52
  Burundi genocide (1993) 354
  identification of 5, 290, 337
  Kibeho massacre (1995) 361
  refugees 344–52, 356–62
  Rwandan genocide (1994) 13, 14, 292,
    338, 356–62
  Tutsi view of 292
  view of Tutsis 347
hydroelectricity projects 144
hygiene, Hitler and 120

ideology
  and genocide 68–9, 84
  Khmer Rouge 11–12, 15, 16, 267–9
  and Nazi Germany 8–9, 192–3, 197–206,
    293
illegitimacy, WWII, German attitude to 33
illness, and political violence 12–13, 325–8
India
  British rule 103, 336
  Constitution 223
  hill tribes, treatment of 146
  Kashmir 214, 224, 225

India (cont'd)
　　Muslim–Hindu relations 52, 217–18,
　　　　219–22, 223, 225, 292–3, 336, 343
　　Pakistan, relations with 225
　　partition 52, 66, 211
indigenous peoples
　　depopulation 157–60
　　and ethnocentrism 145–9
　　global-scale culture, effects of 7–8,137–41
　　global-scale culture, reaction to 149–56
　　resource consumption 141–5
　　"savagery" 175–83
　　and working for others 173–5
Indonesia
　　colonial 341
　　East Timor 340
　　mass killings (1965–6) 338–9
Inglis, Brian 168
Inquisition 49, 50
intelligentsia
　　Cambodia 272
　　Rwanda 359
　　WWII, treatment by Germans 30, 34
intent, inclusion in UN Genocide
　　　　Convention 4, 62–4
intermarriage
　　and ethnicity 297
　　Yugoslavia 237–8, 335
International Congress of Anthropological
　　　　and Ethnological Sciences (1968) 150
international law
　　development of 35–6, 54–5
　　on piracy 64
　　on prisoners of war 38
　　see also UN Genocide Convention
international organizations 345, 349–62
　　see also UN; UN Human Rights
　　　　Commission
Internet, use in research 234–5
Iran, and UN Genocide Convention 58, 60
Iraq, use of rape as tool 225
Ireland
　　Casement on 169, 177
　　Easter Rising (1916) 168
　　Irish peoples 215
　　see also Northern Ireland
Israel
　　Eichmann, right to try 102
　　Hebron massacre (1994) 217
　　Kfar Kassem massacre 105, 106
　　and Palestinians 224, 225–6

Jews
　　book burnings by Nazis 31
　　and Britain 223
　　conversions to Christianity 113–14
　　dehumanization of 68
　　German identification of 81
　　German view of 194–5, 199, 292
　　Jewishness, nature of 114
　　medieval treatment of 49–50
　　Middle East 214
　　Nazis on 77, 117, 118–19, 119–20, 200
　　Ottoman empire 53
　　Romania 53, 297
　　Russia 53
　　and the Vatican 108, 227
　　WWII, livelihoods 32
　　WWII, living conditions 33, 34
　　see also Holocaust; Israel
Jonas, Susanne 330
Jonassohn, Kurt 79, 80, 81, 85
jurisprudence, and genocide 35–8, 102–9
Juruna, Mario 155

Kafka, Franz 323
Kaltenbrunner, Ernst 95
Kampuchea see Cambodia
Kaplan, David 143
Kaptai Dam 144
Kar, Parimal Chandra 146
Karadšić, Radovan 231
Karl, Frederick 167
Kashmir 214, 224, 225
Kelman, Herbert 195
Kfar Kassem massacre 105, 106
Khieu Samphan 266–7
Khmer Rouge
　　ideology 11–12, 15, 16, 267–9
　　regime 2, 52, 254, 263, 267–75
　　use as political agents 88
Kibeho massacre (1995) 361
Kikuyus 342
kinship system, Cambodia 278
Kohinoor (film) 220
Kosok, Paul 206
Kosovo 236, 237
Kreen-a-kore Indians 153, 159
Kren, George A. 127
Kristeva, Julia 286
Krom Khuon 263
Kumar, Dilip 220
Kuper, Hilda 309

Kuper, Leo 14, 85
  overview of chapter 4–5
Kwakiutl people 196–7, 201, 203, 204, 206

Lamb, Harold 48–9
language 268, 312
Lanz, Adolf (Jörg Lanz von Liebenfels) 195
leaders, current lack of 222–3
League of Nations Covenant (1919) 149
Lebanon
  genocidal conflict (1975–6) 52
  nineteenth century 53
LeBlanc, Lawrence J. 78
legal system, and genocide 102–9
Legters, Lyman H. 79
Lemkin, Raphaël 55, 56, 60, 76–7, 78–9
  overview of chapter 3–4
Lemus, Roberto 319
Léon Carpio, Ramiro de 320
Lesser, Alexander 309
Lévi-Strauss, Claude 143
Lidice massacre 97
Lithuania, WWII, German occupation 33
Loizos, Peter 227, 233
Lomnitz, Claudio 299
Lon Nol 267, 268, 276
Lorenz, Konrad 67
Lorraine, WWII, German occupation 29, 31, 32
Lovell, George 315
Lowie, Robert 205
Luther, Dr. Martin 93, 95
Lutheran World Federation 349
Luxemburg, WWII, German occupation 29, 30–1, 32, 33, 34

McCarthy, Mary 100
Macedonia 236, 237, 240
Mack, Myrna 316
magic, black
  aucas 178–9
  Cambodia 260, 263
  West Africa 290
  witchcraft 291
Maka people 291
Makija, Kanan 217, 225
Malaysia 341
Malkki, Liisa H. 289–90, 293, 297
  overview of chapter 13–14
Mann, Michael 110

marriages
  WWII, German control of 32
  see also intermarriage
Marroquin, General Juan Jose 329
Marsh, Peter 128
Martin-Baro, Ignacio 312, 313, 317, 320
Marx, Karl 110
mass media
  and ethnic confrontation 218–22, 226
  genocide reporting 297
  and group identity 10, 11, 13
  refugees, images of 352–5, 357
  and Rwandan genocide 338
Matteotti, Giacomo 105
Maunz, Theodor 93
Maurras, Charles 114
Mayas, and Guatemalan genocide 307–28
Mbembe, Achille 301
Meggers, Betty J. 155
Mein Kampf (Hitler) 197
Meinecke, Friedrich 192
Mersky, Marcie 330
Mestrovic, Stjepan G. 217
Mexico, Tepoztecos 308–9
Micronesia, tribal depopulation 158, 160
migrations, and genocide 297
Mildner, Dr. Rudolf 95
Milošević, Slobodan 339
missionaries 153–4, 175–6, 188
  see also evangelists
Moasosang, P. 146
modernity
  collapse of 213
  and genocide 6–11, 110–32, 213
  and the Holocaust 120–32, 194–5
  and racism 113–15
Molotov, V. M. 54
Montenegro 236, 237, 240
Morales, Colonel Mario Enrique 329
morals, WWII, German-occupied countries 35
Moravia see Bohemia-Moravia
Morel, Edmund 168–9
Morgan, Lewis Henry 235
mortality rates see deathrates
Moscow Declaration (1943) 54
Mosse, George L. 206
muchachos 172, 183
Mühlmann, Wilhelm E. 192
Mukamunana, Frediana 359
Mukandemzo, Primitiy 359

Muslims
  Bosnia-Hercegovina 215, 217, 224, 226,
    238, 242–3, 246
  Britain 211–12
  Dutch East Indies 341
  Hebron massacre (1994) 217
  India, Hindu–Muslim relations 52,
    217–18, 219–22, 223, 225, 292–3, 336,
    343
  Kashmir 214
  Lebanon 52
  racism 214
  West's hostility, belief in 224
  see also Crusades
Mussolini, Benito 105

Nag, Amit Kumar 146
Nandy, Ashis 232
Napoleon Bonaparte 105, 109
nation-state
  and categorization 9, 335–6
  failure of the 223–5
  in former Yugoslavia 236–7, 239–45
  and Nazis 28
nationalism 335–6
Native Americans 142–3, 309
Naushad 220
Nazi Party
  and genocide 4, 52, 54
  in German-occupied countries 30, 31
  on Jews 77, 117, 118–19, 119–20, 200
  ideology 8–9, 192–3, 197–206, 293
  method of government 199
  and modernity 6–7
  and the nation 28
  social engineering 28–35, 117–20
  violence, use of 202
  see also Hitler, Adolf; Holocaust;
    Nuremberg war crime trials
Nazis and Nazi Collaborators (Punishment)
  Law (1950) 91
Ndadaye, Melchior 354
Nehru, Jawaharlal 220
Netherlands, WWII, German occupation 30,
  33, 34
Newfoundland Indians 157
Ngor, Haing 254, 270
Nhek Bun Chhay 263
Niehoff, Arthur H. 148
Nigeria, political divisions 342
Nirankaris 293

non-governmental organizations 345,
  349–62
  see also UN; UN Human Rights
    Commission
North America
  tribal depopulation 158
  see also Canada; USA
Northern Ireland, conflict in 68, 69, 212,
  299–300, 301, 318
Norway, WWII, German occupation 30, 33
Ntanshuti, Faustin 359
nuclear weapons 225, 312
Nuremberg war crime trials 4, 53, 54, 55,
  91, 95, 97, 107

Oakes, Maude 328
Oqueli, Hector 316
O'Shea, John 365
Ottoman empire see Turkey

Padgaonkar, Dileep 217–18
Pakistan
  genocide (1971) 85
  India, relations with 225
  Kashmir 224
  and UN Genocide Convention 65–6
  see also East Pakistan
Palacios i Mendiburu, S. 156
Palestinians, and Israel 224
Paraguay, destruction of Aché Indians 4, 63,
  68, 85
Paredes, Rómulo 182–3
Parsons, Talcott 326
Pasqua, Charles 223
Paul, Benjamin 314
Paust, Jordan 78
PAVYH 330
Penados del Barrio, Archbishop
  Prospero 319
Peru
  Incas 178
  rubber industry and Putumayo Indians 8,
    156–7, 169–85
Peruvian Amazon Company, Ltd. 156
Peruvian Rubber Company 170–6, 183
Philippines
  political system 340
  tribal peoples 152–3
photography, and refugees 352–5, 357
Pinell, Father Gaspar de 175–6
piracy, international law of 64

Pitt-Rivers, George 159
Pius XII, pope, and the Holocaust 108
Pol Pot 2, 263, 266, 270, 275
    see also Khmer Rouge
Poland
    ethnic purity 247–8
    Poles, Hitler's view of 29
    and UN Genocide Convention 57, 58
    WWII, German occupation 30, 31, 32,
        33, 34, 35, 77
Polanyi, Karl 174
political parties, inclusion in UN Genocide
    Convention 57–60, 78–9
Polynesia, tribal depopulation 158
Popenoe, Paul 142–3
population
    indigenous peoples 158–60
    world 140–1
pornography, WWII, German-occupied
    countries 35
Porter, Jack Nusan 74
poverty, and ethnic confrontation 218
power
    and fear 309–10, 311
    sources of 201–6
prisoners of war, and international law
    38
Protestants and Protestant Church
    France 50
    and the Holocaust 108
    Northern Ireland 68
psychosomatic disorders 12–13, 325–8
purification, metaphors of 120, 292,
    293–4
Putumayo Indians 8, 157, 169–85
Pygmies 152

Quinn, John 168
Quinn, Naomi 275

race, as social construct 6
racism
    France 223
    Guatemala 315–16
    and modernity 113–17
    Nazi social engineering 28–35, 117–20
    postmodern rise in 214
    see also ethnocentrism
Rademacher, Franz 92, 93
Rafi, Mohammed 220
Raglan, Lord Fitzroy 145

raison d'état 104–5
Ranariddh, Prince 263, 276
Rao, P. V. Narasimha 223
rape
    as genocide tool 225–6, 295–6
    Guatemala 324
Rappoport, Roy A. 206
Rappoport, Leon 127
"The Red Flag" song 270
Redfield, Robert 308
refugees
    Burundi genocide (1972) 344–52
    Burundi genocide (1993) 354–5
    media representations 352–5, 357
    Rwandan genocide (1994) 356–62
    viewed by others 13–14, 345, 349–62
    viewed by selves 346–9
religion
    and genocide 52
    as identifier of victims 215
    religious conflicts 226–7
    wars of 49–50
    in the West 215
    WWII, German-occupied countries 34
    Yugoslavia 335
    see also individual religions; missionaries
resources
    developed countries 140, 141–2
    indigenous peoples 142–5
responsibility, personal, and bureaucracy 7,
    104–9
revenge, in Cambodian culture 254–75
Revenge by Marriage (film) 262
Reyes, Rafael 178
Ribbentrop, Joachim von 95, 117
Ricoeur, Paul 167
Rivera, José Eustacio 175
Rivers, W. H. 159, 160
Roberts, Stephen Henry 159
Robertson, Roland 219
Robuchon, Eugenio 181
Rocha, Joaquin 174, 178, 179–80, 180–2
Romania, treatment of Jews 53
Roosevelt, Franklin D. 54
Rosenberg, Alfred 114, 117, 119
Rousseau-Portalis Doctrine 28
RPF see Rwandan Patriotic Front
rubber industry
    Congo 167, 168–9
    Peru and Colombia 8, 156–7, 169–85
    West Africa 174

Russia
  humanitarian interventions 53, 54
  Jews, treatment of 53, 54
  racism 214
  see also Soviet Union
Rwanda
  colonial 336–7
  genocide (1994) 292, 338–9, 356–62
  International Criminal Tribunal 5
  Kibeho massacre (1995) 361
  priming of 13, 14
  refugees from 14, 356–62
Rwandan Patriotic Front (RPF) 356, 360,
    361

Said, Edward 217
sanitation, WWII, German-occupied
    countries 34
Sânthor Mok 256
Sartre, Jean-Paul 50–1, 63–4
Sassen documents 92
"savagery" 175–83
Scarry, Elaine 329
Scheper-Hughes, Nancy 309, 310, 311,
    312
Schoen, Ivan L. 153
schools, WWII, German-occupied
    countries 30–1
Scotland 212, 215
Segal, Daniel 363
Serbia
  Constitution 240
  demographics 235, 236, 237, 238, 239
  mass media, use of 219
  WWII, German occupation 33, 92–3
Serbs outside Serbia 245, 335, 339
  Bosnia-Hercegovina 231, 235, 238, 241,
    242, 246, 247
  Croatia 233, 238, 244, 246
Servatius, Dr. Robert 91, 92, 96, 98–9
sexual abuse 225–6, 295–6
  Guatemala 324
shamans 175, 179
Shawcross, Sir Hartley 53
Shiloh, Ailon 75
Sihanouk, Prince 15, 263, 267, 276
Sikhs
  Britain 214
  India 52, 292–3
Simson, Alfred 177–9
Sinhalese 337

slavery *see* debt-peonage system
Slovenia
  citizenship 243–4, 245
  Constitution 240
  demographics 236, 237, 238, 239
  WWII, German occupation 30, 32, 33, 34
Sluka, Jeffrey 308
Smith, Carol A. 317
Smith, Roger W. 85
Snata Bahini 145
Snow, Clyde 319–20
social engineering
  and bureaucracy 7
  genocide as 120–2
  Nazi 28–35, 117–20
sociology, and genocide 74–88
somatization of suffering 12–13, 325–8
Son Sen 263
sorcery
  Cambodia 260, 263
  West Africa 290
Soto, Hernando de 168
South America
  conquistadores 168, 315
  tribal depopulation 158, 159
  see also individual countries
South West Africa, colonization of 51
Soviet Union
  breakdown of 339–40
  genocide 297
  Gulag Archipelago 52
  Stalin's regime 300
  and UN Genocide Convention 4, 57, 58,
    61, 62, 78
  see also Russia
Spain, colonization of Americas 168, 315
Spengler, Oswald 198
Sri Lanka, ethnic divisions 337, 341–2
Stapleton, Adam 360–1
Stein, Barry 353
Stern, Fritz 206
Steward, Julian 142
Stöcker, Adolf 114
Stolcke, Verena 232
"Stone Age" peoples 153
Strasser, George 114
Suárez-Orozco, Marcelo 316, 318, 322, 325
Surinam, Akuriyo Indians 153–4
surveillance, effects of 311
susto 326–7
Sutton, Donald 294–5

Taguieff, Pierre-André 116
Tambiah, Stanley 337
Tamerlane 48, 49
Tamils 337
Tanganyika Christian Refugee Service
    (TCRS) 349–52
Tanzania, refugee camps 13–14, 345–52
Tasmanians, depopulation 157, 159
Taussig, Michael 309–10, 315, 320, 324,
    328–9
    overview of chapter 8
TCRS see Tanganyika Christian Refugee
    Service
technology
    as aid to genocide 7, 52, 111, 125
    technological ethnocentrism 146–8
    and WWI 194
television
    influence of 222
    South Asia 220–1
Tenochka people 197, 201, 203, 204, 206
Tepoztecos 308–9
terrorism 68
testimony
    and refugees 351, 352–5, 361–3
    value of 322–3
Thadden, Eberhard von 95
Thiek, Hrilrokhum 146
Thion, Serge 258
Thirty Years' War (1618–48) 50
Thomas, W. I. 80
Tierra del Fuego, tribal depopulation
    159
Timerman, Jacobo 164–5, 166, 167, 179,
    184
Timur Lenk 48, 49
Tito, Marshal 335–6
tobacco sucking 181
torture 80, 299, 300
    explaining 164–85
    Guatemala 316
    Putumayo rubber workers 157, 169,
    170–2
totalitarianism, and genocide 52
transport and transportation
    Guatemala 321–2
    Holocaust 96
Troy, destruction of 48
Tudjman, Franjo 339
Tum Teav (Sânthor Mok) 256–7, 263–4,
    264–5, 274

Turkey
    Christians, treatment of 53
    Greek Independence, War of
        (1821–32) 53
    Jews, treatment of 53
    WWI, genocide against Armenians 52, 54
Turnbull, Colin M. 152
Turner, Harald 92
Turton, Andrew 309
Tutsis
    Burundi genocide (1972) 69, 289
    Burundi genocide (1993) 354–5
    Hutu view of 13, 292, 347
    identification of 5, 290, 336–7
    refugees 356
    Rwandan genocide (1994) 292, 338, 356,
        358, 359
Twa 347

Uganda, and Tutsi refugees 356
UK see Great Britain
Ukraine, genocide in WWI 52
UN 216, 224, 227
    see also League of Nations
UN Charter (1945) 149
UN Genocide Convention 3, 4–5, 43–7, 48,
    53, 77–9, 81
    enforcement of 5, 64–6, 88
    genesis of 55–67
UN Human Rights Commission 78, 317,
    349, 350, 351
Unification of Penal Law, International
    Conference for the (1933) 4, 36, 55
Uruguay, and UN Genocide Convention 60
USA
    and Aché Indians 63
    American Association for the
        Advancement of Science 320
    in Cambodia 15, 267
    Constitution 241
    counterinsurgency 309, 312
    humanitarian interventions 53, 54
    population 141
    racial segregation 217
    resource consumption 141–2
    tribal depopulation 159
    and UN Genocide Convention 5, 59, 60,
        78
    in Vietnam 50–1, 52, 63–4
    see also Native Americans; North America
Ustashe 335, 339

Valcarcel, Carlos 157
Vallejo, Cesar 1
van der Bruck, Möller 198
van Gennep, Arnold 296
Veblen, Thorstein 128
Venezuela 60, 62
vengeance, in Cambodian culture
    254–75
Verne, Jules 213
Versailles, Treaty of (1919) 35
Vietnam
    Cambodia, invasion of 261, 262, 276
    Vietnam War (1954–75) 50–1, 52, 69,
    125
Vilanova, Father Francisco de 176
violence
    and bureaucracy 125–8
    and modernity 124–5
    and Nazi Party 202
    see also torture
Vojvodina 236, 237, 238

Wales 212, 215
Wallace, Anthony 192, 205
war, in Nazi ideology 200, 203
"wardship principle" 148
Warsaw, WWII, heath and mortality
    34
Watt, Ian 167
Webb, W. E. 144
Weber, Max 110, 112, 198, 213
Weiss, Gerald 145–6
Wells, H. G. 213
Weltsch, Robert 108
West Africa, rubber industry 174
witchcraft 291
    witch hunting 80
    see also magic, black; shamans; sorcery
Wolf, Eric R., overview of chapter
    8–9

women
    Guatemalan Mayas 307–28
    as refugees 353, 354–5
World War I (1914–18)
    genocide against Armenians and in
        Ukraine 52, 54
    and rise of Nazis 199
    and technology 194
World War II (1939–45)
    German conduct of 200–1
    German treatment of occupied
        nations 28–35, 76–7, 92–3
    see also Holocaust; Nuremberg war crime
        trials

Xavante tribe 154–5

Yugoslavia
    ethnic cleansing 10–11, 231–48, 335–6,
        339, 342
    ethnicity 335
    federation, demographics of 235–9
    successor states, citizenship in 243–5
    successor states, civil wars 245–7
    successor states, constitutions of 239–43
    and UN Genocide Convention 59, 66
    WWII, German occupation 30, 32, 33,
        34, 92–3
    see also Bosnia-Hercegovina; Croatia;
        Serbia
Yun Yat 263

Zaire
    refugee camps 356–62
    see also Congo
Zanzibar, genocidal conflict 53
Zaparos 177–8, 178–9
Zimbardo, Philip 196
Zimmerman, Warren 339
Zizek, Slavoj 300